International Human Resource Management

companion
website

International Human Resource Management

Third Edition

Anne-Wil Harzing and Ashly H. Pinnington

Los Angeles | London | New Delhi
Singapore | Washington DC

SAGE Publications Ltd
I Oliver's Yard
55 City Road
London ECIY ISP

SAGE Publications Inc.
2455 Teller Road
Thousand Oaks, California 91320

SAGE Publications India Pvt Ltd
B 1/1 I Mohan Cooperative Industrial Area
Mathura Road
New Delhi 110 044

SAGE Publications Asia-Pacific Pte Ltd
33 Pekin Street #02-0 I
Far East Square
Singapore 048763

Library of Congress Control Number: 2010920407

British Library Cataloguing in Publication data

A catalogue record for this book is available from the British Library

ISBN 978-1-84787-283-8
ISBN 978-1-84787-293-7 (pbk)

Typeset by C & M Digitals (p) Ltd, Chennai, India
Printed and bound in Great Britain by TJ International Ltd, Padstow, Cornwall

Summary of Contents

Contents

There is one omen & one ~~~~ only,
that a man shall fight for his
country

Part 2   International Assignments and Employment Practices   183

Part 3   IHRM Practices   343

List of Contributors

Ashly H. Pinnington is Dean Faculty of Business and Professor of Human Resource Management, The British University in Dubai, United Arab Emirates. He has published extensively on the management of professionals, chiefly institutionalist perspectives in HRM, IHRM and organisational change. His recent work concentrates on careers, ethics and social responsibility.

Chris Brewster is Professor of International Human Resource Management at Henley Business School, University of Reading. He has conducted extensive research in the field of international and comparative HRM; and published over twenty books and more than a hundred articles.

Wolfgang Mayrhofer is full Professor of management and organisational behaviour at WU Vienna, Austria. His research interests focus on international comparative research in human resource management, leadership and careers. He has co-edited, authored and co-authored 24 books and more than 150 book chapters and peer reviewed articles.

Laurence Romani is Assistant Professor affiliated to the Center of Advanced Studies in Leadership, at the Stockholm School of Economics, Sweden (www. casl.se). Her research centres on culture and management adopting a critical perspective, and her publications appear in *International Journal of Cross-Cultural Management*, *Organizational Research Methods* and several book chapters.

Vladimir Pucik is Professor of IHRM and Strategy at IMD and a founding partner of several IT start-ups. He received his Ph.D. from Columbia University in New York. His research focuses on international management and HR strategies in global firms. He has consulted and conducted workshops for major corporations worldwide.

Ingmar Björkman is Professor of Management and Organization at the Hanken School of Economics in Helsinki, Finland. His latest book is *Global Challenge:*

International Human Resource Management (2010, McGraw-Hill), co-authored with Paul Evans and Vladimir Pucik. A frequent contributor to leading international academic journals, he works regularly with multinational corporations on issues related to people management.

Paul A.L. Evans is Shell Professor of Human Resources and Organizational Development and Professor of Organizational Behavior at INSEAD. His research focuses on leadership development and international human resource management. His most recent book, with Vladimir Pucik and Ingmar Björkman, is *The Global Challenge: International Human Resource Management* (2010).

Günter K. Stahl is Professor of International Management at WU Vienna, Austria, and Adjunct Professor of Organizational Behavior at INSEAD, France and Singapore. His research and teaching interests include sociocultural processes in teams, alliances, mergers and acquisitions; and how to manage people and culture effectively in those contexts.

(Chris) Professor Rowley, BA, MA (Warwick), DPhil (Nuffield College, Oxford), Director, *Centre for Research on Asian Management* and Professor of Human Resource Management at City University. He is Editor of the *Asia Pacific Business Review* and Series Editor of *Working in Asia* and *Asian Studies.* He researches in a range of areas, including human resource management and Asian business and has published over 350 articles, books and chapters.

Irene Hon-fun Poon, PhD, MBA, has been a human capital consultant and HR practitioner for many years in Europe, China and Far East. Recent publications can be found in Human Resources Management Change, Changing Face of China, and 21st Century Management.

Ying Zhu is an Associate Professor in the Department of Management and Marketing, University of Melbourne, Australia. He graduated from International Economics Department at Peking University in 1984 and worked as economist in Shenzhen Special Economic Zone Development Company in China between 1984 and 1988. He has published on employment relations, human resource management, cross-cultural management, business and economic development in Asia.

Malcolm Warner is Professor and Fellow Emeritus, Wolfson College, Cambridge and Judge Business School, University of Cambridge. His most recent book is [ed.] *"Making Sense" of HRM in China*, London and New York: Routledge, 2010. He is currently Co-Editor of the *Asia Pacific Business Review.*

B. Sebastian Reiche (sreiche@iese.edu) is Assistant Professor in the Department of Managing People in Organizations at IESE Business School, Spain. He earned his Ph.D. from the University of Melbourne, Australia. His research focuses on antecedents and outcomes of social interaction and knowledge exchange among individual actors, mainly from a cross-cultural and multinational perspective.

Anne-Wil Harzing is Associate Dean Research and Professor of International Management, Faculty of Business & Economics, University of Melbourne, Australia. Anne-Wil's research interests include international HRM, HQ-subsidiary relationships, transfer of HRM practices, the role of language in international business, the international research process, and the quality and impact of academic research.

Jill Rubery is Professor of Comparative Employment Systems, Manchester Business School, University of Manchester. She has published widely on comparative employment systems including the future of the European social models. In 2009 she published (with Gerhard Bosch and Steffen Lehndorff) *European Employment Models in Flux* by Palgrave.

Damian Grimshaw is Professor of Employment Studies , Manchester Business School, University of Manchester. He has published widely on comparative employment systems, including on wage systems and IT outsourcing. He is joint author with Jill Rubery of *The Organisation of Employment: an International Perspective* by Palgrave.

Phil Almond is Reader in International and Comparative HRM Leicester Business School De Montfort University. Dr Almond has published widely on cross-national comparisons in employment relations and HRM in multinational corporations and is the editor, with Anthony Ferner, of American Multinationals in Europe. (2006) Oxford University Press

Tony Edwards is Professor of Comparative Management at Kings College London. His research focuses on the management of labour in multinational companies, including the diffusion of practices across countries, the influence of the domestic business system in international HR policies and the management of human resources during and after international mergers and acquisitions.

Margaret Heffernan is a lecturer in Dublin City University and doctoral candidate at National University of Ireland, Galway. Her research focuses on the links between HRM and performance, employee experiences of high performance work systems and organisational justice.

Patrick C. Flood (PhD, LSE) is Professor of Organizational Behaviour at Dublin City University, Honorary Professor of Management at NEU, China and Academic Fellow, Centre for International HRM, Judge Business School; University of Cambridge. His current books include Leadership in Ireland (Blackhall) and Persuasive Leadership: Lessons from the Arts (Wiley).

Wenchuan Liu is Associate Professor at the Capital University of Economics and Business, Beijing. He got his BE and MBS degrees from Northeastern University, China and PhD from the University of Limerick, Ireland. His research interests are HRM and Business Strategy. He has published in ILRR and Human Resource Management.

Yaw A. Debrah is Professor of Human Resource and International Management at the Swansea University (University of Wales, Swansea), UK. He has worked in Africa, Canada, the UK and USA. He has published numerous articles and edited books on HRM in Asia and HRM and International Business/Management in Africa.

Dr. Christopher J. Rees is a Senior Lecturer in Human Resources at the Institute for Development Policy and Management, University of Manchester, UK. He is a Chartered Psychologist and Chartered Fellow of the Chartered Institute for Personnel and Development. He holds an honorary Chair in International Human Resources at Beijing University of Technology and is Visiting Professor of Human Resource Development at the University Teknologi Malaysia. His teaching and research interests focus upon HR-related organizational change and development initiatives and he has published widely on this subject.

Arup Varma, (Ph.D., Rutgers University) is Professor of Human Resource Management at the Institute of Human Resources & Employment Relations at Loyola University Chicago. His research interests include performance appraisal, expatriate issues, and HRM in India.

Pawan Budhwar is a Professor of IHRM and Associate Dean Research at Aston Business School, UK. He received his doctorate from Manchester Business School. Pawan has published over 60 articles on People Management related topics for the Indian context in leading journals. He has also written and co-edited 9 books on HRM in different regions.

Meredith F. Burnett teaches Human Resource Management and Compensation and Benefits at Florida International University. She has published in the *Journal of Business and Psychology, Cross Cultural Management: An International*

Journal, and the *Journal of Career Assessment*. She is a member of the Academy of Management and the American Psychological Association.

Mary Ann Von Glinow is the Knight Ridder Eminent Scholar Chair in International Management and the CIBER Director at Florida International University. She is President of the Academy of International Business (2010-2010), and past President of the Academy of Management. She has authored 11 books and over 100 journal articles.

Nancy J. Adler, the S. Bronfman Chair in Management at McGill University, conducts research and consults worldwide on global leadership and cross-cultural management. She has authored 125 articles, produced 2 films, and published 10 books and edited volumes. She is a Fellow of the Academy of Management, the Academy of International Business, and the Royal Society of Canada. Nancy is also an artist.

Helen De Cieri (Ph.D.) is Director of the Australian Centre for Research in Employment and Work (ACREW) and a Professor in the Department of Management, Monash University, Australia. Her academic experience includes appointments in Australia, China, Hong Kong, Malaysia and the USA. Her published research spans strategic and international human resource management, including over 80 journal articles and monographs. Current research projects include: the changing roles of human resource professionals; employee well-being and organizational performance, and the management of work-life issues.

Anne Bardoel is an Associate Professor in Management at Monash University, Australia. Anne currently heads the Work Life Research Program which is part of the Australian Centre for Research in Employment and Work (ACREW). She has developed a national and international reputation as a researcher in the work and family area and has published a number of articles in academic journals in this area. She is a member of the Victorian Government's Working Families Council and President of the Work/Life Association (Victoria).

Miguel Martinez Lucio is a Professor at the Manchester Business School, University of Manchester. He has worked on various projects and published on issues related to regulation and employment. He is concerned with the question of how marketisation, privatisation and new forms of managerialism impact on employment relations and their regulation. In addition he has published on the impact of globalisation on Industrial Relations, migrant networks and social movements.

Robert MacKenzie is Senior Lecturer in Industrial Relations at Leeds University Business School. His research interests are restructuring, labour market change, contingent contracts and the regulation of the employment relationship. These issues have been studied in various national and sectoral contexts, including telecommunications and construction, and through the social and economic experiences of migrant workers.

Dr Fang Lee Cooke is Professor of Human Resource Management and Chinese Studies at RMIT University, Melbourne, Australia. She was previously a professor at University of Manchester. Fang's research interest is in the area of strategic HRM, outsourcing and shared services, diversity management, employment and labour market studies and employment relations.

Guided Tour

International Human Resource Management

Third Edition

Anne-Wil Harzing and Ashly H. Pinnington

SAGE

Los Angeles | London | New Delhi
Singapore | Washington DC

Learning Objectives

After reading this chapter you will be able to

- Understand the process of strategic management and appreciate its implementation from differing perspectives
- Know and distinguish between the various modes of entry for international strategy
- Identify ways that project management and organisational behaviour conceptualise the implementation of strategy
- Explain why IHRM and SHRM are an integral part of all stages of the process of strategic management
- Analyse the competitive position of an organisation, its resources and core competences
- Formulate IHRM strategies, policies and practices based on the corporate, international and business level strategies of the organisation
- Critically evaluate the success of IHRM from multiples perspectives (e.g. customers, owners, managers and employees)

Chapter Outline

The chapter reviews common approaches to strategy and strategic management and then discusses different perspectives on strategy and the central importance of IHRM and SHRM. It ends with three major IHRM challenges which will be of strategic significance for most organisations in the future.

1 Introduction: value creation
through strategic management

Whenever organisations operate in a competitive market then they will find themselves under pressure to formulate and implement *value-creating strategies*. The relevance of strategic management also applies to the public and not-for-profit sectors, when they find themselves competing for resources, collaborating with private sector organisations, operating in quasi-markets and evaluated according to corporate policies

Learning objectives – The key learning objectives to be addressed in each chapter.

Learning Objectives

After reading this chapter you will be able to

- Understand the process of strategic management and appreciate its implementation from differing perspectives
- Know and distinguish between the various modes of entry for international strategy
- Identify ways that project management and organisational behaviour conceptualise the implementation of strategy
- Explain why IHRM and SHRM are an integral part of all stages of the process of strategic management
- Analyse the competitive position of an organisation, its resources and core competences
- Formulate IHRM strategies, policies and practices based on the corporate, international and business level strategies of the organisation
- Critically evaluate the success of IHRM from multiples perspectives (e.g. customers, owners, managers and employees)

Chapter Outline

The chapter reviews common approaches to strategy and strategic management and then discusses different perspectives on strategy and the central importance of IHRM and SHRM. It ends with three major IHRM challenges which will be of strategic significance for most organisations in the future.

1 Introduction: value creation
through strategic management

Whenever organisations operate in a competitive market then they will find themselves under pressure to formulate and implement *value-creating strategies*. The relevance of strategic management also applies to the public and not-for-profit sectors, when they find themselves competing for resources, collaborating with private sector organisations, operating in quasi-markets and evaluated according to corporate policies

Chapter outline – The main topics and issues to be covered in each chapter

---

and external lawyers (Pinnington et al., 2009). One of the many problems facing IHRM practitioners is the need to get more involved in the development and maintenance of high standards of ethical management. Selecting one from many of the current examples of innovations significant for IHRM is the development of the ISO 26000 standard for Social Responsibility. Social Responsibility can be defined as the responsibility of an organisation for the impacts of its decisions and activities on society and the environment, through transparent and ethical behaviour that:

- Contributes to sustainable development, health and the welfare of society
- Takes into account the expectations of stakeholders
- Is in compliance with applicable law and consistent with international norms of behaviour
- Is integrated throughout the organisation and practiced in its relationships

The ISO 26000 standard for Social Responsibility is scheduled for publication in September 2010. It is been developed by experts and stakeholders from six categories (consumer, government, industry, labour, NGOs, SSRO–Service support research and others). The process has involved numerous conferences and workshops held worldwide (e.g. Vienna, Sydney, Paris, New York, Santiago, Bahrain, Cape Town, Berlin, Tokyo). It has involved over 406 experts and 135 observers from 80 member countries and 37 external liaison organisations. The principles of social responsibility are central to good governance of the corporation and effective and ethical IHRM. They include principles of: accountability, transparency, ethical behaviour, stakeholders' interests, respect of the rule of law, universality of human rights and respect of international norms of behaviour.

IHRM practitioners and researchers can play a major strategic role in assisting with social responsibility, which according to ISO 26000 means that the organisation should understand:

- how its decisions and activities impact on society and the environment
- how these impacts affect specific stakeholders
- what the expectations or best practices are with respect to responsible behaviour concerning these impacts

8 Summary and conclusions

This chapter has introduced the concepts of strategic management and IHRM. It has argued that people are central to the long-term success of all organisations and in all sectors of employment. We discussed the central importance of value creation through strategic management and reflected on how it will often be evaluated from

Summary and conclusions – An overview of the key points from each chapter.

Strategic Management and IHRM *A. H. Pinnington* 41

Further reading

- Barney, J. (1991) 'Firm resources and sustained competitive advantage', *Journal of Management*, 17(1): 99–120.
  A classic and top ranked cited academic paper which outlines comprehensively Jay Barney's resource-based view of the firm. This was one of the articles which marked a watershed point for HR researchers and practitioners. It acknowledges more openly and clearly the role of people than typically is found in strategic frameworks based on industry environment analysis.

- Schuler, R. S. and Jackson, S. E. (1987) 'Linking competitive strategies with human resource management practices', *Academy of Management Executive*, 1(3): 207–19.
  Randall Schuler and Susan Jackson were one of the first researchers to link psychological and organisational behaviour concepts with the strategies of cost leadership, differentiation and innovation. Although now something of an 'oldie but goldie', many cohorts of undergraduate and postgraduate students have found this paper by Schuler and Jackson to be really helpful for understanding exactly how the people issues can be linked with the strategic issues.

- Yetton, P., Craig, J., Davis J. and Hilmer, F. (1992) 'Are diamonds a country's best friend? A critique of Porter's theory of national competition as applied to Canada, New Zealand and Australia', *Australian Journal of Management*, June, 17(1): 89–119.
  This paper critiques Michael Porter's diamond and argues that as a matter of empirical fact a country may achieve a comparative advantage through possession of just one or two of the determinant factors. The authors conclude therefore that the theory is over-stated and potentially misleading for government policy makers and business leaders.

- Hoskisson, R., Hitt, M., Wan, W. and Yiu, D. (1999) 'Theory and research in strategic management: swings of a pendulum', *Journal of Management*, 25(3): 417–56.
  If you are interested in finding out more about strategic management and where it all comes from, in terms of research schools of thought and core disciplinary concepts, then this is a very readable and accessible review of developments in the research field.

- Johnson, G., Scholes, K. and Whittington, R. (2010) Exploring Corporate Strategy, 8th edn. Harlow: FT Prentice Hall.
  Alternatively, if you are looking for a book to learn more about strategy and strategic management as a practical tool and way of thinking, then this classic textbook is an excellent resource for answering almost any question that you have on strategy.

- Whittington, R. (2001) *What is Strategy – and Does it Matter?* 2nd edn. London: Thomson Learning.
  There again, if you in fact are looking for something more concise, then this book is an excellent read on four theories of strategy (classical, evolutionary, processual and systemic) and is generally very popular with postgraduate students.

Further reading – Academic books and journals specifically chosen to reinforce or develop the learning from each chapter.

- Pinnington, A.H. and Gray, J.T. (2007) 'The global restructuring of legal services work? A study of the internationalisation of Australian law firms', *International Journal of the Legal Profession*, July, 14(2): 147–72.
  The research discussed in this journal article addresses the internationalisation strategies of knowledge workers based in a country with a comparatively small population and economy. It examines the ways that an elite group of law firms in Australia are contributing to the globalisation of business and restructuring of legal services work. It seeks to understand Australian law firms' collective strategic intent, which at the time of the research was to develop a global competitive presence in markets in the Asia Pacific region. It is an interesting study of the little guys rather than the big guys trying to establish a global presence. It examines the distinctive commercial orientation and institutional corporate connections of this group, focusing on how their strategic practice in many ways actually favours the elite group US and UK firms. The data specifically on the recent phase of internationalisation of legal services show Australian lawyers to be of lower status when compared to elite US and European law firms.

- Adler, P.S., Kwon, S-W. and Heckscher, C. (2008) 'Professional work: the emergence of collaborative community', *Organization Science*, March–April, 19(2): 359–76.
  A multidisciplinary journal article related to strategic management, knowledge management and IHRM which examines the historical evolution of the organisation of professional work. It provides examples from medicine and hospitals and proposes that the nature of professional work and its communities have changed from craft guild forms to state-based hierarchical institutions with a societal orientation. Adler et al. propose that organisations are now moving more towards new collaborative forms of work and organising.

- Krogh, G.V., Nonaka, I. and Aben, M. (2001) 'Making the most of your company's knowledge: a strategic framework', *Long Range Planning*, 34: 421–439.
  If you want to really get to grips with the multitude of ways in practice that corporations can implement knowledge management, then this is one of the best starting points for ideas. The authors show how Unilever engaged in a set of concurrent strategies to manage knowledge in ways that create value and may lead towards attaining a competitive advantage.

Internet resources

1 The Strategic Planning Society (SPS) (http://sps.org.uk/): The Strategic Planning Society (SPS) fosters and promotes research and best practice in strategic thought and action. SPS aims to create a link between the academic and practitioner worlds of strategy. It has been in existence for 40 years and members receive *Long Range Planning and Strategy Magazine*. SPS' stated purpose is: 'We exist to provide a forum for the propagation, advancement and education in strategy and strategic thinking.' SPS strategic intention is:

Internet resources – Useful and relevant websites chosen to aid research and further reading.

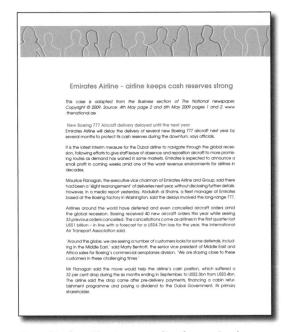

Emirates Airline – airline keeps cash reserves strong

This case is adapted from the Business section of The National newspaper. Copyright © 2009. Source: 4th May page 2 and 6th May 2009 pages 1 and 2. www.thenational.ae

New Boeing 777 Aircraft delivery delayed until the next year
Emirates Airline will delay the delivery of several new Boeing 777 aircraft next year by several months to protect its cash reserves during the downturn, says officials.

It is the latest interim measure for the Dubai airline to navigate through the global recession, following efforts to give staff leave of absence and reposition aircraft to more promising routes as demand has waned in some markets. Emirates is expected to announce a small profit in coming weeks amid one of the worst revenue environments for airlines in decades.

Maurice Flanagan, the executive vice chairman of Emirates Airline and Group, said there had been a 'slight rearrangement' of deliveries next year, without disclosing further details. However, in a media report yesterday, Abdullah al Sharra, a fleet manager at Emirates based at the Boeing factory in Washington, said the delays involved the long-range 777.

Airlines around the world have deferred and even cancelled aircraft orders amid the global recession. Boeing received 40 new aircraft orders this year while seeing 33 previous orders cancelled. The cancellations come as airlines in the first quarter lost US$1 billion – in line with a forecast for a US$4.7bn loss for the year, the International Air Transport Association said.

'Around the globe, we are seeing a number of customers looks for some deferrals, including in the Middle East,' said Marty Bentrott, the senior vice president of Middle East and Africa sales for Boeing's commercial aeroplanes division. 'We are staying close to these customers in these challenging times.'

Mr Flanagan said the move would help the airline's cash position, which suffered a 32 per cent drop during the six months ending in September to US$2.3bn from US$3.4bn. The airline said the drop came after pre-delivery payments, financing a cabin refurbishment programme and paying a dividend to the Dubai Government, its primary shareholder.

Case Study – Short case studies for use in class – relating to organisations in a variety of contexts – designed for use in a single teaching session to reinforce learning, as a prompt for discussion and for relating theory and concepts to IHRM practice.

3 *For M&A trends and list of deals:* Reuters (http://www.reuters.com/finance/deals/mergers): Product of a merger with Thompson Financials. This site is a great source for comprehensive and up-to-date information about latest M&As. It also includes feature articles and insights on key trends and issues and analysis of M&As by industry and regions.
CNN Money (http://money.cnn.com/data/markets/): CNN Money provides a listing of the most recent deals indicating the names of targets and acquirers, and the dollar value of the deal with a link to a report on each deal. See also a related Top 25 Deals year-to-date list, arranged by the dollar value of the deal.
M&A International (http://www.mergers.net/index.php?id=deal_of_the_month): Provides an informative section on 'Deal of the month'.

Self-assessment questions

Indicative answers to these questions can be found on the companion website at www.sagepub.co.uk/harzing3e.

1 Why is it that the role of cultural difference in influencing the success or failure of an M&A may be exaggerated?
2 A useful way of conceptualising M&As is to consider their desired end-state. What are the five end-states according to Marks and Mirvis (1998)? Briefly define each one.
3 What are the top ranked factors contributing to acquisition success according to well-known surveys and reports?
4 What do Evans and colleagues (2010) propose are the cultural and people issues in cross-border M&As?
5 Specify some of the questions that a cultural due diligence team should ask in order to understand the 'deep knowledge' of the culture.

References

A. T. Kearney, (1999) *Corporate Marriage: Blight or Bliss – A Monograph on Post-Merger Integration*. Chicago: A. T. Kearney.
Aguilera, R. V. and Dencker, J. (2004) 'The human resource management in cross-border mergers and acquisitions', *International Journal of Human Resource Management*, 15: 1357–72.
Angwin, D. and Savill, B. (1997) 'Strategic perspectives on European cross-border acquisitions: A view from top European executives', *European Management Journal*, 15: 423–35.

Self-assessment Questions – Brief questions for use by students to assess their understanding of key concepts and important points, either after each session or as end-of-course revision.

Companion Website

Be sure to visit the companion website at www.sagepub.co.uk/harzing3e to find a range of teaching and learning materials for both lecturers and students:

For lecturers, an **Instructor's manual** contains the following:

- **Learning objectives:** Clear objectives for each chapter help to focus each lecture and tutorial.
- **Chapter outlines:** Chapter outlines provide lecturers and tutors with the main points for each chapter.
- **Discussion questions:** Questions for seminars and tutorials are given, designed to provoke discussion and raise important issues.
- **Case study questions:** Case study questions provide tutors and seminar leaders with the key questions for each case study.

For students, the following resources are provided for each chapter:

- **Full-text journal articles:** Downloadable journal articles provide easy access to further reading, giving students a deeper understanding of each topic.
- **Self-Assessment Questions:** Questions for each chapter aid exam revision.
- **Self-Assessment Answers:** Answers to self-assessment questions allow students to check their answers to each question and find out what areas they need to revise.
- **Links to relevant websites:** Direct links to relevant websites for each chapter provided as appropriate.

Introduction

Ashly Pinnington and Anne-Wil Harzing

International Human Resource Management (IHRM) is a new and rapidly changing area of specialist and generalist practice. It is also a lively and growing academic subject having links with many different disciplines including economics, international business, strategy, communications, political science and public policy. Its origins can be traced back to the growth of international business operations and the development of multinational companies (MNCs) with their formal and informal approaches to staffing, personnel administration and personnel management. IHRM as a field of study has changed substantially over the years.

From the early beginnings to the present

Herbert Perlmutter (1969) is one of a small group of people who had a major influence on the early stages of development of IHRM (see Chapter 6). His three different approaches to MNC staffing (ethnocentric, polycentric and geocentric) are a mainstream method of conceptual analysis in much the same way that Michael Porter's generic strategies have profoundly shaped the field of strategy (see Chapter 1). The tendency of publications during the 1970s and 1980s was to concentrate on MNCs with headquarters based in a parent country in Europe, the US or Japan. This has created a substantial theoretical and empirical IHRM literature on parent country nationals (PCN), host country nationals (HCN) and third country nationals (TCN). One of the key research questions debated during those decades (e.g. Morgan, 1986) on topics such as staffing policies, differences between countries, types of employees, and the MNCs human resource management (HRM) activities was, 'What exactly are the best policies and practices when procuring, allocating and utilising international human resources?'

Since the 1980s the volume of material specifically produced addressing issues of IHRM has mushroomed and new journals such as the *International Journal of Human Resource Management* now have an established position alongside other business and management journals and in journal rankings. There is a lively community of academics specialising in areas of IHRM research employed in universities across many different countries. The subject is constantly changing in relation to new ideas and a variety of issues such as innovative approaches to high performance work systems (see Chapter 9) and work-life management (see Chapter 16) as well as changing ways of dealing with long-term areas of IHRM policy and practice such as recent concepts of global and local resourcing (see Chapter 12) and total rewards in the international context (see Chapter 14).

Interestingly, the opportunities and problems in IHRM since the 1990s have become on the one hand more straightforward and on the other hand more complex. Clearly, videoconference multimedia and simple e-mail facilities on desktop computers offer a wealth of opportunities for virtual working and rapid communication across massive distances. There again when we talk about MNCs, there are now a greater number of parent countries and their HRM policies and practices in host countries are more diverse (see Chapter 18). Their regulation has become more straightforward with the reduction of national barriers to trade, but has also at the same time become more complex with the growth of industry quality standards and different forms of global business regulation including the area of employment regulation (see Chapter 17). The characteristics of HRM in developed and developing countries often differ so that, for example, in developing countries there may be less comprehensive legislation and less effective enforcement than is practised in the developed countries. These and other political, economic, institutional and cultural differences between nations can all influence the local relevance and acceptability of HR practices. They are also likely to affect the extent of transfer of HR practices between the parent company and its various subsidiaries (see Chapter 8).

Intellectual roots

In addition to the early development of the field through Perlmutter's work, the intellectual roots of the field of IHRM can be traced back to three main strands of research.

Cross-cultural management

The first strand of this is the area of cross-cultural management. In this field, Geert Hofstede's work (1980, 2001) has had a tremendous influence on the development of IHRM. It is also highly cited in research studies on culture, cross-cultural communication, international and global management. Although his empirical survey study of many IBM subsidiaries has been criticised on various conceptual and methodological grounds, his ideas are now commonly understood jargon terms in academic and practitioner discourses on culture (see Chapter 3). Hofstede argues that there are substantial differences in national culture. He subdivided the major differences into: power distance, individualism versus collectivism, masculinity versus femininity, uncertainty avoidance, and long-term versus short-term orientation (see Chapters 3 and 13). Many other studies focusing on cross-cultural management (e.g. Hampden-Turner and Trompenaars, 1997; House et al., 2004; Kluckhohn and Strodtbeck, 1961) present very similar dimensions (see Chapter 3 for a summary and integration).

A striking example of differences in regional and national culture is related in one of the case studies found in this book on cross-cultural communication written by Nancy Adler and colleagues (see Chapter 15). The Women's Global Leadership Forum was a global women's conference organised by an MNC in the food industry specifically designed to motivate and develop women in the company. In several of the sessions during the conference the women experienced disagreement and some misunderstanding arising partly from national cultural differences in power distance and consequent general attitudes regarding the importance of status and hierarchy in decision making and communication.

Comparative management

Academic debate and modes of theorising in IHRM have also been very influenced by comparative approaches such as are adopted in research on comparative HRM and comparative employment relations. Studies set within these schools of thought concentrate on similarities and differences that exist between countries in policies and practices adopted by a wide range of stakeholders including the government, political and public sector institutions, professional groups, employers and employee associations, and private and non-profit sector organisations. Comparative IHRM researchers tend to be sensitive towards geographical and historical differences and often will pay attention to distinctions between regions and organisations within a country as well as between countries.

A large volume of theoretical critique and research studies have adopted institutional approaches when comparing and contrasting countries. One major strand of this work has been the neo-institutional theory (e.g. DiMaggio and Powell, 1983) which is based on the assumption that institutions and their structures, systems, policies and practices are subject to a range of general forces. Institutions may find themselves being pushed to follow a particular direction (coercive) or they may elect to copy others (mimetic) or they may simply feel the pressure to conform to what is socially accepted as the normal way of doing things (normative). One of the key distinguishing features of MNCs is that due to their size, scale, scope and reach, they have the capacity to implement expertise in their operations in one country that was developed in another. Exactly how individual MNCs proceed with the transfer of expertise depends on a range of political, economic, social and legal factors, for example, their actual transfer of employment practices depends on how they are embedded in distinctive national contexts (see Chapter 8).

International management and HQ subsidiary relationships

Another group of researchers concentrate less on the institutional and cultural contexts and adopt more of a specifically organisational focus, focusing primarily on its markets and the firm's strategy, structure and alignment of human resources. Major influences on this way of looking at things include Bartlett and Ghoshal's (1989) *Managing Across Borders*. These authors argue that MNCs are evolving towards a new form of management and organisational form typified in the concept of the 'transnational firm' which is understood to have global networks of managers, global projects and international mobility. In these transnational firms, competitiveness in global markets is argued to be based more on managers possessing a global mindset. Their organisations survive and grow by having the flexibility and capability to transfer knowledge and expertise across global networks (see Chapter 10).

One of the main problems executives must deal with when seeking to create a transnational management approach is how to integrate the organisation on a global scale and simultaneously, how to differentiate it to fit in with variations in the local conditions. The growth of global markets, reduction of trade barriers and increased activity across state boundaries have all had a major impact stimulating the long-term growth of international merger and acquisition (M&A) activity. A significant challenge for IHRM practitioners and researchers concerns dealing effectively with the integration processes in cross-border M&As. It requires understanding and managing cultural differences between organisations, successfully implementing the appropriate strategy and managing the process through its various stages of integration (see Chapter 4).

A brief overview of the chapter contents

This book is divided into four sections. The first section (Strategic, Comparative and Organisational Perspectives on IHRM) introduces some of the major ways of thinking about IHRM. The second section (International Assignments and Employment Practices) deals with the fundamental area of multinational companies and how they manage their workforce with specific reference to IHRM as well as national forms of HRM. The third section (IHRM Practices) focuses more on particular areas of policy and practice in IHRM commencing with contemporary advances in knowledge management and global leadership development, and then moving on to the topics of employee resourcing, performance management and employee rewards. The final section (Developments in IHRM Policy and Practice) concentrates on central strands of thought and innovation in IHRM commencing with the growing involvement of women across the world in all aspects of leadership, management and employment.

It then addresses the approaches to global work-life management in multinational enterprises and moves on to consider how IHRM is evolving in response to regulation and change in global employment relations. The final chapter considers a number of core areas of responsibility and accountability in IHRM that are likely to continue in significance as areas of innovation throughout future decades, notably matters of social responsibility, sustainability and diversity.

Part 1   Strategic, comparative and organisational perspectives on IHRM

This section presents various ways of thinking about IHRM theory and practice. Chapter 1 – Strategic Management and IHRM (Ashly Pinnington) – introduces some of the mainstream approaches to strategy and strategic management. It demonstrates the importance of strategy for IHRM and Strategic HRM (SHRM). Chapter 2 – Comparative HRM (Chris Brewster and Wolfgang Mayrhofer) – explores the differences between countries in their management of human resources. It presents a comparative perspective on HRM and within the context of MNCs considers the challenges of integration and differentiation. Chapter 3 – Culture in International Management (Laurence Romani) – offers a critique of several of the traditional approaches to culture and cultural difference and presents a new way of thinking more flexibly about culture and culture management as seen from distinct stakeholder perspectives. Chapter 4 – HRM in Cross-Border Mergers and Acquisitions (Vladimir Pucik, Ingmar Björkman, Paul Evans and Günter Stahl) – examines one of the most important contemporary organisational change phenomena in IHRM. It reviews the meaning and activities of integration in M&As, highlighting various challenges that may occur during different stages of the process. Chapter 5 – Approaches to IHRM (Chris Rowley, Irene Poon, Ying Zhu and Malcolm Warner) – charts the development of HRM as a background for IHRM. It considers five distinctive frameworks of HRM and IHRM: Matching model, Harvard model, Contextual model, 5-P model and European model. It then evaluates the extent that these models apply in theory and practice to different firms, country business systems, institutional contexts and cultural environments.

Part 2   International assignments and employment practices

This section concentrates on MNCs, IHRM and country approaches to HRM. Chapter 6 – International Assignments (Sebastian Reiche and Anne-Wil Harzing) – reviews the staffing options in MNCs and corporate motives for international transfers and then reviews the available forms of international assignment assessing the various processes and their success criteria. Chapter 7 – Multinational Companies and the Host Country Environment (Damian Grimshaw, Jill Rubery and Phil Almond) – explores the diverse environments for MNCs' overseas subsidiaries and appraises the extent that host countries will influence pay systems, work organisation and collective representation. In contrast with an emphasis placed on external (host country) environments, Chapter 8 – The Transfer of Employment Practices across Borders (Tony Edwards) – concentrates more directly on the internal context of MNCs. It explores MNCs' motivations for international transfer of expertise and presents a framework of four key influences. These are the country of origin effect, dominance effects, international integration and host country effects. Chapter 9 – High Performance Work Systems – International evidence of the impact on firms and employees (Margaret Heffernan, Patrick Flood and Wenchuan Liu) – reviews the literature and debates on high performance work systems (HPWS) examining organisational and employee outcomes.

Part 3 IHRM practices

This section reviews the traditional and newer approaches to IHRM policies and practices. Chapter 10 – Managing Knowledge in Multinational Firms (Ingmar Björkman, Paul Evans and Vladimir Pucik) – addresses issues of knowledge management in MNCs and contends that knowledge sharing is facilitated by such things as collaborative values and global mindsets. It assesses how MNCs can access and retain knowledge. Chapter 11 – The Development of Global Leaders and Expatriates (Yaw Debrah and Chris Rees) – explores the international Human Resource Development (HRD) of global leaders and expatriates. It discusses how competencies are developed through global leadership development programmes which include activities such as international assignments, participation in global teams, and cross-cultural sensitivity training. Chapter 12 – Global and Local Resourcing (Ying Zhu, Chris Rowley and Malcolm Warner) – considers IHRM recruitment and retention, discussing changes in labour market policy and regulations to assess their impacts. Four Asian economies (Japan, Taiwan, China and Vietnam) are examined for their degree of continuity and change in HRM policy and practice. Chapter 13 – Global Performance Management (Arup Varma and Pawan Budhwar) – discusses performance evaluation in IHRM and presents the key features of performance management systems in four major national economies (USA, UK, China and India). Chapter 14 – Total Rewards in the International Context (Meredith Burnett and Mary Ann Von Glinow) – provides comprehensive examples of rewards policies and practices for expatriates and short-term and long-term international assignments, drawing primarily on data from US MNCs. It provides a thorough account of the issues (including international taxation and cost-of-living), components (base salary, hardship premium, allowances and benefits) and available methods (going rate and balance sheet) for designing total rewards systems.

Part 4 Developments in IHRM policy and practice

This section concentrates on present and long-term issues of innovation in IHRM. Chapter 15 – Women Leading and Managing Worldwide (Nancy Adler) – reviews the increase of women expatriates and examines why in the past few women obtained international assignments. It discusses ways of critically evaluating the success of international assignments from the perspectives of the individual assignee and the company. A case study (Nancy Adler, Laura Brody and Joyce Osland) is presented that relates an organisation's approach to developing women for leadership and international management roles. The case emphasises the importance of continually improving employees' cross-cultural communication skills. Chapter 16 – Global Work-Life Management in Multinational Enterprises (Helen De Cieri and Anne Bardoel) – examines the management of work-life by MNCs. It considers work-life initiatives as those strategies, policies, programmes and practices maintained in workplaces to address flexibility, quality of work and life, and work–family conflict. The authors develop a framework to inform the allocation of responsibilities for work-life management. Chapter 17 – Regulation and Change in Global Employment Relations (Miguel Lucio and Robert MacKenzie) – studies the debate on the regulation of businesses and raises questions of power, control and democracy. The concepts of de-regulation and re-regulation are discussed in detail and in relation to ideas on human rights. Chapter 18 – Social Responsibility, Sustainability and Diversity of Human Resources (Fang Cooke) – makes an overview of the concepts of Corporate Social Responsibility (CSR), Equal Opportunities (EO) and Diversity Management. It analysis how they are understood in four different societal contexts (China, India, Japan and Korea) enabling an appreciation of the global challenges to MNCs in developing and implementing equality and diversity management strategies.

What makes this book different?

This book provides an *integrated* research-based perspective of the consequences of internationalisation for the management of people across borders. The book's comprehensiveness is evidenced by its broad and global coverage. We commence with a thorough overview of the main ways that IHRM has been conceptualised to date. IHRM has been linked to strategy, viewed through comparative HRM research, and seen from cultural, institutional, market and organisational perspectives. The second section of this book addresses expatriate management and employment practices seen from both their external environment and the internal environment of the MNC. It ends with a review of the state of the art of the literature on organisational and individual performance. In the third section we consider the current state of the field on IHRM practices, which attends to the role of globalisation and the extent to which HRM differs between countries, and the underlying reasons for these differences. In the fourth section we then turn to consider how IHRM appears to be developing and changing in relation to issues of gender, work-life, regulation of employment, social responsibility, sustainability and diversity.

A second distinctive feature of this book is its *solid research base*. All chapters have been specifically commissioned for this book and all authors are experts and active researchers in their respective fields. Rather than having a final chapter with 'recent developments and challenges in IHRM', we have given all authors the clear brief to supplement classic theories and models with cutting-edge research and developments.

A third and final distinctive characteristic of this book is that it is *truly international*, both in its outlook and in its author base. Authors use examples from all over the world and their research base extends beyond the traditional American research literature. Although many authors are currently working at American, European and Australian universities, virtually all have extensive international experience and their countries of origin are very varied.

Who is this book for?

As a textbook this book will appeal to advanced undergraduate students and Masters students wanting a comprehensive and integrated treatment of International HRM that includes the most recent theoretical developments. As a research book, it provides PhD students and other researchers with a very good introduction into the field and an extensive list of references that will allow them to get an up-to-date overview of the area. Finally, practitioners looking for solutions to their international HR problems might find some useful frameworks in Parts 1, 2 and 4, while the chapters in Part 3 will allow them to gain a better understanding of country differences in managing people.

In the following chapters of this book the authors contribute numerous worthwhile theoretical ideas and empirical observations on IHRM policy and practice. We hope that you will enjoy reading the third edition of *International Human Resource Management*. As we work and live in changing local and global contexts, inevitably there is much that we must learn from each other.

References

Bartlett, C.A. and Ghoshal, S. (1989) *Managing Across Borders: The Transnational Solution*. Boston, MA: Harvard Business School Press, Harvard Business Publishing.

DiMaggio, P.J. and Powell, W. (1983) '"The iron cage revisited" institutional isomorphism and collective rationality in organizational fields', *American Sociological Review*, 48: 147–60.

Hampden-Turner, C. and Trompenaars, F. (1997) *Riding the Waves of Culture: Understanding Diversity in Global Business*. Maidenhead: McGraw-Hill.

Hofstede, G. (1980) *Culture's Consequences: International Differences in Work Related Values*. Beverly Hills, CA: Sage Publications.

Hofstede, G. (2001) *Culture's Consequences: Comparing Values, Behaviors, Institutions and Organizations across Nations,* 2nd edn. London: Sage.

House, R.J., Hanges, P.J., Javidan, M., Dorfman, P.W. and Gupta, V. (eds) (2004) *Leadership, Culture, and Organizations: The GLOBE Study of 62 Societies.* Thousand Oaks, CA: Sage.

Kluckhohn, F.R. and Strodtbeck, F.L. (1961) *Variations in Value Orientations.* Evanston, IL: Row and Peterson & Co.

Morgan, P.V. (1986) 'International Human Resource Management: fact or fiction?', *Personnel Administrator*, 31(9): 43–47.

Perlmutter, H.V. (1969) 'The tortuous evolution of the multinational corporation', *Columbia Journal of World Business*, January-February, 4(1): 9–18.

Part 1

Strategic, Comparative and Organisational Perspectives on IHRM

1

Strategic Management and IHRM

Ashly H. Pinnington

Contents

Learning Objectives

After reading this chapter you will be able to

- Understand the process of strategic management and appreciate its implementation from differing perspectives

- Know and distinguish between the various modes of entry for international strategy

- Identify ways that project management and organisational behaviour conceptualise the implementation of strategy

- Explain why IHRM and SHRM are an integral part of all stages of the process of strategic management

- Analyse the competitive position of an organisation, its resources and core competences

- Formulate IHRM strategies, policies and practices based on the corporate, international and business level strategies of the organisation

- Critically evaluate the success of IHRM from multiples perspectives (e.g. customers, owners, managers and employees)

Chapter Outline

The chapter reviews common approaches to strategy and strategic management and then discusses different perspectives on strategy and the central importance of IHRM and SHRM. It ends with three major IHRM challenges which will be of strategic significance for most organisations in the future.

1 Introduction: value creation through strategic management

Whenever organisations operate in a competitive market then they will find themselves under pressure to formulate and implement *value-creating strategies.* The relevance of strategic management also applies to the public and not-for-profit sectors, when they find themselves competing for resources, collaborating with private sector organisations, operating in quasi-markets and evaluated according to corporate policies and management techniques. The success of these organisations' strategies often has a fundamental impact on their capacity to survive, grow and prosper.

Since Michael Porter's (1980, 1985, 1990) influential works on competitive strategy published three decades ago, executives and managers have been encouraged to identify ways that their organisations can gain a competitive advantage.

> A sustained or sustainable, competitive advantage occurs when a firm implements a value-creating strategy of which other companies are unable to duplicate the benefits or find it too costly to imitate. (Hanson et al., 2002)

Managing value means 'maximising the long-term cash-generating capability of an organisation' (Johnson et al., 2010: 490). The main ways of specifically increasing shareholder value are increasing revenue through sales volume and prices; disposal of unnecessary assets; efficient management of stock, debtors and creditors; and effective financing of the business through an appropriate mix of capital (debt and equity).

Porter (1985) specified the primary value-creating activities of an organisation when creating any product or service as inbound logistics, operations, outbound logistics, marketing and sales, and service. His basic idea of the value chain is that in each activity the organisation should add value or consider outsourcing it to another organisation which can do it either just as well or preferably can add more value. HRM is relegated to what Porter categorised as support value-creating activities along with firm infrastructure, technology development and procurement. His model is frequently criticised for having more relevance to the manufacturing sector and is seen as less applicable to the services and knowledge sectors of the economy. Nevertheless, in the context of competitive strategy, the value chain and value network (inter-organisational links to create products/services) remain prevalent concepts today.

HRM supports Value chain

In some contexts however, competitive strategy and competitive advantage are problematic concepts whenever organisations are not seeking to win necessarily at others' cost. This makes strategic management more complicated because the objectives of value-creation and excellent performance are salient, but gaining a unique advantage against peer organisations may not be a relevant goal. This ambivalent relation to competitive strategy is common in public-funded initiatives which usually serve multiple stakeholders as well as within collaborative partnerships and amongst partners in alliance networks (Skoufa, 2004).

2 Major stakeholders

Notwithstanding these complexities, whatever school of strategic management one subscribes to, ethically there is no doubt that people do matter and this is so even when managers behave as if employees and subcontractors are solely a cost

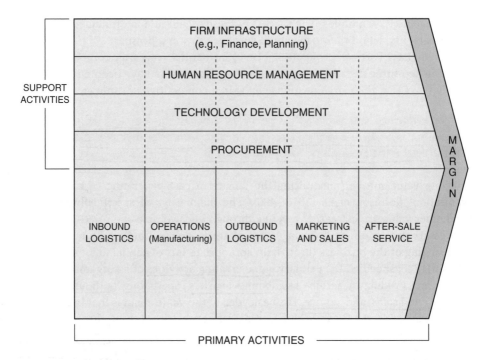

Figure 1.1 Porter's value chain

Source: Porter (1985): 37, Fig. 2.2 Reprinted with the permission of The Free Press, a Division of Simon and Schuster, Inc., from Competitive Advantage: Creating and Sustaining Superior Performance by Michael E. Porter. Copyright © 1985, 1998 by Michael E. Porter. All rights reserved.

to their business. The organisation and its employees are considered to be major stakeholders, although there is considerable debate on the extent that their interests should be acknowledged in relation to profits allocated to shareholders. They in effect underwrite much of the risk capital of the business through buying and selling company shares traded on the public stock markets.

The three major stakeholder groups are usually said to be the capital markets, product markets and organisations. Capital markets comprise shareholders and lenders such as banks. Product markets consist of primary customers, suppliers, host communities and unions. Organisational stakeholders include managers, employees and other members of the organisation. Stakeholder theory has its proponents and detractors. Its proponents can be subdivided broadly into those who concentrate on multiple economic claims and those who argue further in terms of diverse moral claims and expectations to have a voice in important decisions.

Stakeholder theory is based on two principles that balance the rights of the claimants on the corporation with the consequences of the corporate form. The first, the principle of corporate effects, states that 'the corporation and its managers are responsible for the effects of their actions on others' (Evan and Freeman, 2004: 79) … The second principle, namely the principle of corporate rights, states that 'the corporation and its managers may not violate the legitimate rights of others to determine their own future' (Evan and Freeman, 2004: 79). (Greenwood and De Cieri, 2007: 122–3)

Its detractors argue that the theory is problematic because it is often not clear exactly who are the valid stakeholders and some claim further that it draws attention away *must* from the major rights and responsibilities of shareholders and corporations. One way of *consider the* responding to this unitarist shareholder-dominated perspective is to argue that ethically *pluralities* its very exclusivity ignores the essentially pluralist nature of society and business, and furthermore that 'any intellectually and morally acceptable approach to HRM must take account of a pluralism of partially conflicting interests' (Campbell et al., 2007: 284).

3 Strategic management

Design School

The 'design school' (Ansoff, 1991) approach to strategy subdivides the process into an iterative cycle of stages which are also interactive and involve feedback loops. For the sake of ease of understanding, these stages can be considered to proceed *mission &* in a sequence which repeats itself. For example, the strategic management process *vision* commences with ideas on the mission, vision, intent, purpose, goals and objectives. These strategic intentions over time will become partially or totally changed through processes of reflection, analysis and debate and from direct experience in action and of course the results during implementation. These ideas go through refinement, revision, elaboration and change during the analysis stage.

The strategic analysis considers the external and internal environments of the *strategic* organisation (e.g. SWOT – Strengths, Weaknesses, Opportunities and Threats) and *analysis.* then moves on to the formulation of strategy (e.g. Corporate-level, International *strategy formation* Strategy, Business-level, Cooperative – alliances and partnerships, Acquisition and *strategy* Restructuring). Finally, there is the implementation of the strategy (e.g. Corporate *implementation* Governance, Organisational Structure, Coordination and Control, Leadership, Entrepreneurship, Innovation, Change and Sustainability).

In reality, the purposes and processes of strategic management are often complex and even confused and chaotic. These strategy processes are also interactive and *critique* simultaneously both reinforcing and contradictory. In all events nobody can predict the future exactly and in many situations people are actually unsure why they are doing things and unclear about unintended consequences which may occur. Henry Mintzberg's (1990) critique of the design school and his proposed theory of emergent strategy addresses the messiness and uncertainty of planning and action. Mintzberg notes the frequently ad hoc and even unanticipated nature of action and learning and provides a useful critique of the tendency for strategy teaching to be unrealistically

action is often ad hoc
→ can't really predict future.
Strategic Management is too "idealistic"

Difficulty in predicting future = Firms need to be flexible in strat. Man.

18 Strategic, Comparative and Organisational Perspectives

Need to engage in experimentation & improvisation.

rationalist in its assumptions and too idealistic in its core principles. So, the tools and techniques of strategic management must be applied flexibly and not become a substitute for learning by doing and learning from others. Organisations therefore must encourage experimentation and improvisation (Pinnington et al., 2003).

External analysis involves the scanning, assessment and evaluation of the environment for opportunities and threats often using tools that assist with understanding different levels of analysis. These may be subdivided into macro, mesa and micro levels. The macro environment is often surveyed using tools such as PESTEL (Political, Economic, Social, Technological, Environmental, Legislative). Then there are tools for the mesa level – typically the competition within the industry assessed through such frameworks as Porter's (1985) Five Forces analysis (Threat of New Entrants, Power of Buyers, Power of Suppliers, Threat of Substitutes, Competitive Rivalry within the Industry). Finally there are micro-level aspects to do with the immediate environment and on-going interactions with competitor firms (assessed through tools of competitor analysis).

An internal analysis also involves scanning, assessment and evaluation of the environment, and is concerned with identifying strengths and weaknesses of the organisation relative to its actual (current) and potential (future) competitors. During the 1980s and 1990s the concept of internal resources (Penrose, 1959) gained more attention and led to further elaboration and development of the Resource Based View of the Firm (Barney, 1991). Consequently, a wider range of tools and frameworks are now available to practitioners and researchers. A typical approach is to assess the internal environment of the organisation for its resources, capabilities and core competences (Kamoche, 1996; Hamel and Prahalad, 1994).

An audit of resources will include such aspects as financial, physical, human, organisational and reputational characteristics. In some industries, such as automotive assembly, the cost of human resources is a small percentage of total costs compared to physical plant, machinery and parts, whereas in knowledge intensive firms such as consultancies and law firms the major cost is human resources even when the information technology budget may run into many millions. The potential of the firm's resources for competitive advantage has become more recognised by strategy practitioners and researchers following the growth in significance of the services and knowledge sectors of the economy, in relation to the primary (e.g. agriculture, mining resources) and secondary (e.g. manufacturing) sectors.

Within business and management research, the fields of strategy and innovation were in fact the first to recognise the importance to organisations of strategies and tactics for managing knowledge. Academics interested in strategic management wrote about the importance of managing teams of resources so that they become productive, and capabilities of the firm (Grant, 1991: 118–19). They emphasised knowledge resources that deliver value as opposed to knowledge for its own sake (Wernerfelt, 1984). The resource-based view of the firm helped to focus interest on ways that resources can be managed strategically by attending to their capacity for creating uniqueness and competitive advantage through characteristics such as producing economic value,

Handwritten margin notes:
External analysis:
i) Macro: PESTEL
ii) Mesa: Five forces analysis
iii) Micro: competitor analysis

Their value depends on which industry firm is in.

Resources recognised as able to give competitive advantage with growth of service industry.

Resource view of an org; looks at how to manage resources strategically to create a competitive advantage.

possessing some rarity, being hard to copy and difficult to substitute (Barney, 1991). In summary, which ones out of the organisation's resources and capabilities are:

which of the resources is a competitive advantage.

- Valuable?
- Rare?
- Hard to copy?
- Difficult to substitute?

The knowledge-based theory of the firm developed by Spender (1996) emphasised the importance of managers getting involved in actively managing knowledge and learning from it through: (a) managing by thinking and interpreting multiple phenomena by exercising a high degree of flexibility, (b) managing the boundaries of the organisation such as its interfaces with customers and suppliers, (c) identifying institutional effects and influences on knowledge and its strategic management, and (d) distinguishing between the influence of wider systems as well as the elements and components of knowledge, systems and technologies.

Since the emergence of the resource-based view of the firm (Barney, 1991; Grant, 1991), there has been increased interest in strategic management based upon an internal analysis of the strengths and weaknesses of the organisation, the capabilities of its internal resources (physical, human and organisational), its management of the value chain (primary and support activities) and development of a sustained competitive advantage. The resource-based approach has encouraged more reflection on how HR practitioners can be better included in processes of strategic management (Grant, 1996a, b) and consequently become more proactive in incorporating ideas on ways that HRM can contribute by informing, designing and evaluating the organisation's strategy. Following the analysis of the strategy a choice has to be made regarding the available strategic options. A standard approach is to assess each anticipated and specified option for its suitability, acceptability and feasibility.

- *Suitability* – Does the strategy address the key issues relating to the competitive position of the organisation?
- *Acceptability* – Will the strategy achieve an acceptable return, is at reasonable levels of risk and likely to be acceptable to stakeholders?
- *Feasibility* – Can the strategy be pursued within the resources, capabilities and competences of the organisation?

The business-level strategy is still based on comparatively minor variations on Porter's three generic strategies. Hanson et al. (2002: 129) helpfully define it as: 'an integrated and coordinated set of commitments and actions designed to provide value to customers and gain a competitive advantage by exploiting core competencies in specific, individual product markets'. The firm has an opportunity to formulate and implement a business-level strategy with a specific competitive scope (broad, narrow)

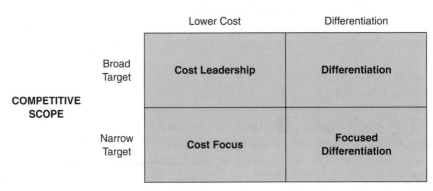

Figure 1.2   Business-level strategies

Source: Reprinted with the permission of The Free Press, a Division of Simon and Schuster, Inc., from Competitive Advantage: Creating and Sustaining Superior Performance by Michael E. Porter. Copyright © 1985, 1998 by Michael E. Porter. All rights reserved.

and approach to competitive advantage (cost, uniqueness). As Figure 1.2 below shows this creates four alternatives known as: cost leadership, differentiation, cost focus and differentiation focus.

While all firms are expected to have a business-level strategy only those that have several products and services and offer them in different markets and regions are likely to be of sufficient complexity to require a corporate strategy. A corporate-level strategy can be defined as: 'an action taken to gain a competitive advantage through the selection and management of a mix of businesses competing in several industries or product markets' (Hanson et al., 2002: 196). The corporate strategy concerns the nature and extent of diversification of the company. Through value-creating strategies the organisation has to make choices concerning the amount that it facilitates sharing between its different business units (known as operational relatedness) and the extent that the corporate headquarters leads through transferring knowledge and skills into businesses (known as corporate relatedness). The corporate strategy is significant for HRM because it creates organisational norms, systems and procedures for the amount that different business units are expected to share knowledge and skills with each other and the extent that the corporate headquarters is required to proactively manage and support the business units.

International corporate-level strategy is different in so far as it reflects specifically on the intended reach and scope of the organisation in terms of global integration and local responsiveness. Three alternative strategies are normally articulated:

- *Multi-domestic strategy* – Strategic and operating decisions are decentralised to the separate business units and management within individual countries. Philips was traditionally renowned for this approach.

- *Global strategy* – Corporate headquarters devises strategy and monitors and rewards standardisation and operational conformance to global specifications for products and services. Japanese corporations such as Sony and Komatsu have enjoyed strong reputation for success in this area. *[centralized]*
- *Transnational strategy* – Simultaneous implementation of strategies of global efficiency and local responsiveness. ABB is one of the most commonly cited MNCs advocating and implementing transnational strategies.

The field of strategic management contains a complex array of competing theories selecting the main unit of analysis as either the firm or the industry or the nation. There are a wide range of available approaches to the subject matter with strategy seen as evolutionary paths or as emergent change, and, its fundamental building blocks are very different so that it is conceptualised by some scholars as assets/resources while others see it as composed of processes of strategic management (Whittington, 2001). *[study of strategy]*

What is somewhat more surprising though is the nature of the specialist knowledge of the discipline of strategy. On the one hand strategy is very broad-based *[broad based]* including ideas from, for example, different branches of economics, evolutionary ecology, information sciences, and simulation and game theories (Hoskisson et al., 1999). Whittington (2001) subdivided the field into classical, evolutionary, processual and systemic schools of thought and identified a range of influential disciplines, in particular, military scholarship and economics (classical), economics and biology (evolutionary), psychology (processual) and sociology (systemic).

On the other hand, looking at how it is commonly taught in business schools and corporate training events the implementation issues connected with people seem almost to be sidelined and upstaged by a greater concentration on other functional areas of *[Yet, lack of focus to the implementation issues with people]* management such as: finance, accounting, sales, marketing, public relations, operations, logistics and information technology. The limited amount of attention given to the people issues is especially pertinent in the area of strategy implementation as it is presented in some of the popular texts widely used by training and education practitioners. For example, in a number of these textbooks and training guides, the human concerns of the organisation remain somewhat implicit rather than gain explicit mention.

4 Three perspectives on strategy implementation: strategic management, international strategy and national competitiveness

Strategic management

There are many different frameworks available on the implementation of strategy. Authors writing on the subject of strategy implementation attend to different issues concerning organisational action. Most of them make reference to issues of structure and control with some then focusing more on the topics of governance and leadership, or entrepreneurship and innovation or functional management (e.g. finance, accounting, public relations, sales and marketing, procurement, logistics, operations, human resource management, information technology, legal compliance, etc.) or the management of change.

Hanson et al. (2002) describe strategy implementation as involving four organisational processes of strategic management: Corporate Governance; Organisational Structure and Controls; Strategic Leadership; and Strategic Entrepreneurship.

- *Corporate governance* is the oversight of stakeholders in an organisation particularly the owners, managers and boards of directors. Effective governance is essential for ensuring ethical, transparent and fair practices in the implementation of the organisation's strategies.
- *Organisational structure and controls* need to be aligned with the strategy to maximise likelihood of achieving a competitive advantage. Organisational structure includes concerns such as the overall design of the organisation, its positions of authority, decision-making channels and networks of roles and jobs. Strategic competitiveness is said to be achieved when the firm's chosen structure and controls are aligned with the strategy.
- *Strategic leadership* is the ability of an individual or group to anticipate, envision, maintain flexibility and empower others to create strategic change. Grint (2005: 1–32) argues that leadership is an ambiguous concept related to many aspects including person-based leadership (groups acknowledge particular individuals as leaders), positional leadership (leaders occupy formal positions of power), result-based leadership (leadership only exists when it leads to effective results), process-based leadership (leaders are distinguished from non-leaders by what they do), and hybrid leadership (people and machines combined create leadership). In the context of implementation of strategy, leadership is complex, multi-functional, and requires the ability to manage and lead the organisation to achieve and sustain high performance.
- *Strategic entrepreneurship* is the ability to implement strategy, create innovations, achieve organisational renewal of mature and declining businesses, and develop new successful corporate ventures. Entrepreneurs are traditionally understood as the key individuals to stimulate new economic activity and as such as the primary agents responsible for growth and prosperity in the economy.

International strategy

An international strategy is one that sells products and services outside of the firm's domestic market. The most common reason given for an international business strategy is to extend the product lifecycle and gain new resources and markets from operating and selling outside of the domestic market (Vernon, 1996). Some of the main reasons for moving into international markets are given as the incentives: to increase *market size*; opportunity to make a greater *return on investments*; attainment of optimal *economics of scale and learning* through knowledge sharing and exploiting

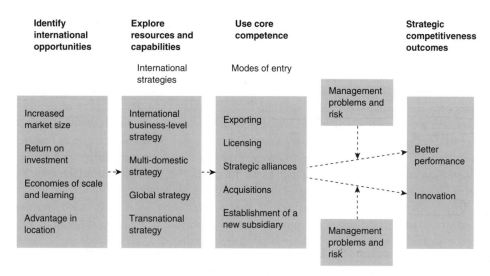

Figure 1.3   Opportunities and outcomes of international strategy

Source: Hanson et al., 2002: 274, Fig.8.1 Reprinted with the permission of Cengage Learning Australia Pty Ltd.

resources, capabilities and core competences; and achieving *advantages of location* such as reducing the cost of products and services combined with reaching superior networks of suppliers and customers.

International Business scholars often speak of the implementation of international strategy as involving distinct choices of organisational modes of entry into markets in other nations and regions. Once the choice has been made on the mode of entry, there has to be a successful implementation which takes account of the probable costs, risks, controls and likely returns associated with the entry mode (Kim and Hwang, 1992). The modes of entry into other countries and regions include: Exporting; Licensing; Strategic Alliances; Acquisitions; Establishment of a new Subsidiary.

In international strategy, the overall idea is that implementation involves different costs and varying degrees of risk and management control. With some simplification, the theory proposes that they can be seen as carrying different degrees of cost, risk and control. Exporting is characterised as high cost and low risk; licensing as low cost and low risk; strategic alliances as shared costs and shared risks but having problems of integration and therefore control; acquisitions are rapid, high cost and high risk; and whereas the establishment of a new subsidiary is also high cost and high risk, it offers greater opportunity for management control and achieving above-average returns in the market (based on Hanson et al., 2002).

National competitiveness

The Determinants of Competitive Advantage of Nations (Porter, 1990) operates at the country level rather than the organisational level as in the previous two examples. So the idea here is one of competitive advantage as seen from the perspective of nations of the world rather than from the position of one particular organisation in an industry.

The national determinants of competitive advantage are: Factor Conditions; Demand Conditions; Related and Supporting Industries; Firm Strategy, Structure and Rivalry; Role of Government; and Role of Chance. Porter called these determinants diamonds and proposed that nations with all four main determinants in the diamond are more likely to attain a competitive advantage. The theory has been criticised for over-emphasising the extent that all four are necessary and a number of theoretical and empirical research articles have demonstrated that a nation can exploit a comparative advantage and prosper possessing just one or two factors such as wealth generation through territorial ownership of valuable resources such as oil and copper (Yetton et al., 1992).

1. *Factor conditions* are the factors of production such as labour, land, natural resources, financial capital and physical infrastructure. They can be subdivided into basic and advanced factors. Labour is considered either as a basic or advanced factor

2. dependent on the education, skills and competences of the worker. *Demand conditions* are calculated on the basis of the amount of demand for basic and advanced goods and services in the home market. Economies of scale are achieved by organisations through efficient management and through competition winning a sizeable share of the market.

3. *Related and supported industries* are important networks of suppliers, buyers and services and are vital for the survival and growth of the business. Pools and clusters of expertise and experience emerge amongst the patterns of *firms' strategy, structure*

4. *and rivalry* such that some places in different countries are the location of choice for particular industries, products and services. Silicon Valley in California is one of the most commonly mentioned regions that is an incubator for innovation in new computer media, information and communication technologies. Porter (1990) argues that it is often easier to innovate and grow in these locations.

In addition to these four determinants, Porter identifies two further ones, fifth the

5. *role of government* in facilitating a supportive, or conversely creating a negative, environment and economy, and sixth the *role of chance* occurrences in making winners

6. and losers in the competition between nations.

The words 'human' or 'people' as in Human Resource Management or People Management do not gain specific mention and therefore are not given an obvious and sufficiently high profile. It can be counter-argued however that many of the above mentioned terms on strategy implementation actually do include these concepts, albeit implicitly. It is self-evident that in 'strategic management', strategic leadership has to involve leaders and followers, hence people. Similarly, in 'international business strategy' acquisitions are specified as one of the modes of entry to another country and are bound to involve the direct or indirect employment of people. Furthermore, in 'national competitiveness' phrases like factor conditions include advanced factors such as people with rare and specialised skills.

In fairness, some of the tools and techniques of strategy implementation do make more explicit mention of people. Where the significance of people is emphasised

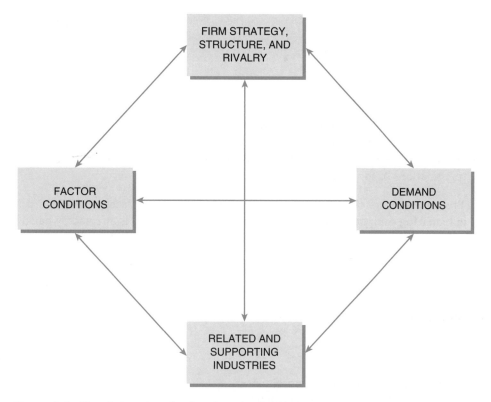

Figure 1.4   The determinants of national advantage

is in areas that have more of a concentrated focus on people working in teams and projects as in the disciplines of Project Management, Organisational Behaviour and Strategic (I)HRM.

5 Strategy viewed from two perspectives based on people: project management and organisational behaviour (OB)

Project management

Project management is the application of knowledge, skills, tools and techniques to project activities to meet project requirements. Project management is accomplished through the application and integration of the project management processes of initiating, planning, executing, monitoring and controlling, and closing. The project manager is the person responsible for accomplishing the project objectives.

Managing a project includes:

- Identifying requirements
- Establishing clear and achievable objectives
- Balancing the competing demands for quality, scope, time and cost
- Adapting the specifications, plans, and approach to the different concerns and expectations of the various stakeholders.

Project managers often talk of a 'triple constraint' - project scope, time and cost – in managing competing project requirements. Project quality is affected by balancing these factors ... (*A Guide to the Project Management Body of Knowledge*, Project Management Institute (PMI), 2004, p.8)

According to the PMI (2004: 11), the 'Project Knowledge Areas' are:

1 Project Integration Management
2 Project Scope Management
3 Project Time Management
4 Project Cost Management
5 Project Quality Management
6 Project Human Resource Management
7 Project Communications Management
8 Project Risk Management
9 Project Procurement Management

What is noticeable about the project management knowledge areas is that two of them concentrate primarily on people skills. Within the context of project management processes, 'Project Human Resource Management' is conceptualised in terms of a project and contains four processes: human resource planning, acquire project team, develop project team and manage project team. The following knowledge area in the sequence, 'Project Communications Management' also involves four processes: communications planning, information distribution, performance reporting and manage stakeholders.

At the centre of the concept of a project is the idea that it is temporary rather than like operations which are ongoing and repetitive. Projects and operations share in common many characteristics including that they are, 'performed by people, constrained by limited resources, and are planned, executed and controlled' (PMI, 2004: 6).

Organisational behaviour *deals with behaviour within an org.*

The knowledge domain of Organisational Behaviour (OB) has a strong focus on people commencing with an individual and largely psychological level of analysis and moving on to a broader organisational level. It specifically mentions the relevance of 'Human Resource Policies and Practice' within the organisation.

- *Individual Level* Attitudes, Job Satisfaction, Personality and Values, Perception and Individual Decision Making, Motivation, Emotions and Moods
- *Group Level* Understanding Work Teams, Communication, Leadership, Power and Politics, Conflict and Negotiation
- *Organisation Systems Level* Foundations of Organisation Structure, Organisational Culture, Human Resource Policies and Practices
- *Organisational Dynamics* Organisational Change and Stress Management (based on Robbins and Judge, 2009: xxiii)

It can be argued that OB attends more to people and their behaviour within organisations than it does specifically address strategy and strategic management. Where it is especially helpful is that it presents a number of reasons why strategies may fail and why they may not always be persuasive to managers and employees. In short, many other factors will interact with the best laid plans which are always subject to issues of culture, power, politics, conflict and negotiation. *& all could fail a plan*

OB can be distinguished from projects and project management in so far as both are concerned with individuals, teams, tasks and their available resources, but projects are temporary. In that way projects and OB are different because OB researchers and practitioners are interested in both the temporary and the more permanent aspects of organisations, including the on-going routine operations as well as the more unusual or one-off events. Therefore, OB tends to characterise HRM more broadly than project management, viewing it not so much as programmes of different projects, rather as a routine function and strategic element of the structure, systems, policies and practices of the organisation.

Robbins and Judge (2009) propose that the most important HRM considerations from the OB perspective are:

- selection practices
- training and development programmes
- performance evaluation
- managing diversity in organisations, and the
- global context and its implications for HRM

The last item in the above list effectively takes us on to International HRM (IHRM).

6 The rise of international HRM and strategic HRM

International Human Resource Management developed as a subject area a little after the massive wave of interest in HRM during the 1980s. It began as a cluster of teaching, training and research interests primarily around the opportunities and problems faced by MNCs and the success and failure of expatriates, the significance of cross-cultural communication skills in international business assignments, and international aspects of HRM policies and practices concerning policies and practices in employee resourcing, rewards, performance management (particularly appraisal), employee development and employee relations.

As well as practitioners and researchers diversifying from HRM into IHRM another group focused primarily on HRM and strategy. The idea of strategic HRM (SHRM) developed at the same time although it was initially less rooted than IHRM was on a body of literature and set of debates around international management and international business (Schuler et al., 1993). A primary motivation of the SHRM movement which grew in the late 1980s was to show that HRM was essential to strategic thinking and practice. Teaching and training in the area tended to be relatively a-theoretical and emphasised the importance of HRM policies and aligning them to the strategy of the business. Some early research studies and debates during the 1980s sought to apply basic concepts of strategy to the field of HRM.

One of the most well known pieces of work on the relationship between strategy and HRM is Schuler and Jackson's (1987) argument linking employee behaviours to organisation strategies for competitive advantage. They placed the employee behaviours within a standard set of HRM practices and demonstrated that different approaches will be required for effective strategic management of the workforce. Their main point was that employee behaviours should be selected, motivated, retained, developed and rewarded according to whether the strategy is one of cost leadership or differentiation (quality) or innovation. Their conceptualisation of strategy was based on Michael Porter's (1980, 1985) concept of competitive business strategy.

Schuler and Jackson (1987) summarised the role behaviours required of employees as follows:

- Innovation strategy — 'Work differently'
- Creative, long-term, independent, high concern for quality, high concern for quantity, high risk taking, high concern for results, high preference to assume responsibility, flexible to change, tolerant of ambiguity and unpredictability, broad skill application, high job (firm) involvement *everything, it sounds like.*
- Quality strategy — 'Commitment and utilisation'
- Repetitive, predictable, short-term, modest interdependence, modest cooperativeness, high concern for quality, modest concern for output, high concern for process, low risk-taking, commitment to goals of organisation
- Cost reduction strategy — 'Reduction in cost of work output per employee'
- Relatively repetitive and predictable behaviours, short-term focus, independent, modest concern for quality, high concern for output quantity, primary concern for results, low risk-taking, high comfort with stability.

Selected →
Strategy

– desired kind →
of employees

There is potential then for analysing links between the organisation's strategy and areas for individual learning. Schuler and Jackson's (1987) argument can be understood by analogy of the strategy with the appropriate role behaviours. Thus, if the strategy

[handwritten: Strategic Link between Individual & Organisation]

[handwritten top margin: Org' most critical Challenge = become & remain viable in their market. comes down to 3 stakes 1. set of goals 2. Resources 3. capable people]

is to be 'innovative' then entrepreneurial employee behaviours will be appropriate. Alternatively, if the strategy is one of 'quality' then role behaviours specifically connected with quality management processes of teamwork, continuous improvement, zero defects, role flexibility and systems thinking are more likely to be suitable.

Their overall line of argument of the strategic links between the individual and organisational levels is that:

1 *Individual characteristics* of top managers should MATCH with the *nature of the business*
2 Competitive *strategies* (innovation, quality, cost) should MATCH with needed *role behaviours* (creativity, time focus, autonomy, quality, quantity, risk, concern for results, responsibility, flexibility, tolerance of ambiguity, skill range, job involvement)
3 Competitive *strategies* (innovation, quality, cost) should MATCH with *HRM practices* (planning, staffing, appraising, compensating, training and development)
4 Firm's effectiveness will be increased when *HRM practices MATCH competitive strategies*
5 HRM is strategic only when *HRM practices MATCH each other in a consistent, reinforcing set of practices.*

In the 1990s a greater number of practitioners and researchers attended to the links between HRM and performance and several studies (see Chapter 9) showed there to be relationships between HRM and the success of the organisation's strategy. By the end of the decade several influential HRM and OB researchers (e.g. Purcell 1999; Wood, 1999) became disenchanted with broad-based studies using simple frameworks and typologies for strategy and urged improved constructs in survey research (e.g. Guest, 2001) as well as more case study and qualitative research analysis (Pinnington, 2005; Pinnington and Sandberg, 2009). Boxall and Purcell (2008) have consistently promoted the line of argument that HRM can be strategic and can create value through selecting capable people and motivating the workforce to achieve business goals. They claim that three fundamental goals specifically of HRM are to achieve labour productivity, organisational flexibility and social legitimacy. Their work on strategic human resource management has over the last decade been a source of inspiration for a number of (I)HRM researchers, practitioners and students. Boxall and Purcell argue that the most critical challenge faced by firms is to become and remain viable in their chosen markets. They suggest that this problem can be reduced to three major table stakes (a set of goals, resources and capable people). If the firm wants to survive over the long-term then its viability depends on recruiting and retaining capable people. It is only by getting this right and achieving and sustaining viability that attaining sustainable competitive advantage can become a realistic goal.

[handwritten right margin: HRM 3 fundamental Goals 1. labour productivity 2. org. flexibility 3. social legitimacy]

[handwritten right margin: Need capable people to survive & for strategic Management, because it is people that ask the questions and create strategy]

in making the answers a reality. This is desperately obvious but it has to be said because there are dozens of books on strategic management which assume that good strategy appear out of nowhere: human beings do not seem to be involved or only as an afterthought. (Boxall and Purcell, 2003: 31–32)

7 IHRM challenges

In a large number of ways HRM and IHRM are similar and often are treated synonymously. However, there are also some substantive differences between the two in terms of the theory and practice of strategic management. In IHRM it is impossible to consider the needs and assumptions of the organisation from the perspective of one country, national economy and single domestic market (e.g. Dowling et al., 2008; Evans et al., 2010). In this concluding section of the chapter, three major IHRM challenges are outlined: Cross-cultural Communication and Diversity, Global Knowledge Management, and Local and Global Sustainability.

Cross-cultural communication and diversity

As a starting point, the international and global diversity of IHRM makes it much more difficult to understand how one organisational culture can be achieved and furthermore whether its attainment is a desirable goal. It is worth remembering that

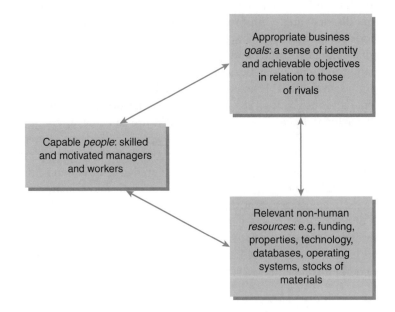

Figure 1.5   Three critical elements for the viability of the firm

Source: Peter Boxall and John Purcell, Strategy and Human Resource Management, published 2002, Palgrave Macmillan. Reproduced with permission of Palgrave Macmillan.

Hofstede's (1980) landmark research investigation of national culture and fundamental differences between country cultures was conducted all in one organisation – IBM – a company renowned for its corporate culture and uniformity of values symbolised by the organisation men in blue and grey suits and white shirts. Essentially, in HRM and especially in IHRM the cultural perspective should be a varied one that can accurately reflect the issues of homogeneity and heterogeneity.

In this regard Alvesson (1993) has offered a helpful framework for thinking flexibly about culture by viewing it in four distinct ways:

1 unitary and unique organizational culture
2 organizations as meeting points of 'fields' of culture , ~~after~~ *Societal level commonalities*
3 local subcultures *Variety of local contextual influences*
4 ambiguous cultural configurations. *plethora of Sources , complex & confused*

Understanding organizational culture as *unitary* and *unique* means making the assumption that the culture really is not like any other and thus is different from the rest. By contrast, understanding organizations as *meeting points of 'fields'* conceptualizes all organizational culture as being composed of societal-level commonalities and divisions. An individual organization culture following this way of thinking therefore can never be entirely distinctive or unique because it is entirely a manifestation of macro-social phenomena. The *local subcultures* approach plays down the macro-societal issues conceptualizing the organizational culture as constructed out of a variety of local, contextual influences. The fourth approach, understanding organizational culture as comprising *ambiguous cultural configurations,* assumes a plethora of sources of culture, simple and unique, macro and shared, local and others, complex and confused. Alvesson recommended using all four approaches to gain a more informed and comprehensive insight into organizational culture. (Pinnington, 2003: 216–17)

ambiguous cultural Configuration.

In the specific context of mergers and acquisitions the fourth of Alvesson's approaches *would explain a lot* 'ambiguous cultural configurations' probably best explains many of the IHRM issues faced by companies engaged in major strategic and organisational change such *over capacity* as merger and acquisition (M&A). When two industry giants are prompted by over-*Merger &* *(m&a)* capacity in the industry to engage in a merger or acquisition, these M&As are major *acquisition.* one-off events and are extremely hard to create and sustain value over time. This is *failures or* often due to the strategic problems with successfully integrating two assertive and *difficulties* independent organisational cultures, structures, systems, customers, suppliers and employees (Ashkenas et al., 1998). A number of past M&As have been problematic such as when Daimler-Benz acquired Chrysler Corporation in 1998 and when Tata Motors acquired the Jaguar Land Rover operations and the Rover Marque all bought from Ford in March 2008. In addition, in August 2007 the Chrysler group were sold to the private equity firm Cerberus Capital Management. Two years later, on 30 April 2009 Chrysler LLC filed for Chapter 11 bankruptcy and subsequently was

Mergers to extend Product line :
— more successful, can manage change incrementally
— less time pressure, longer time frame for implementation.

52 | Strategic, Comparative and Organisational Perspectives

rescued by US$6.6 billion financing from the federal US government; during the same year General Motors was reorganised following Chapter 11 bankruptcy. Tata Motors has experienced difficulties post-acquisition with financing its automotive assembly operations in the UK and during 2009 has been in conflict with the UK government over the relative financial responsibilities during the global economic recession. Mergers intended to extend the product line or international coverage often meet geographical and cultural differences but tend to be more frequently successful than M&As prompted by over-capacity in the industry (Bower, 2001). These mergers have more opportunity to manage change in a series of incremental steps and hence are more viable to manage with less time pressures and longer time frames to implement integration. Over-capacity and product or market extension are the two main strategic reasons for M&As and constitute over two thirds of the total. Other common reasons for M&As include: geographic expansion and roll-up, industry development and convergence in emergent industries, and R&D (Bower, 2001).

Geographic roll-up is more likely to be successful in win–win scenarios for the parties involved in M&A and industry convergence depends on M&As that maintain sufficient autonomy for key innovators to continue growing the organisation and entrepreneurially developing new products and services. M&As intended to gain access or acquire R&D expertise and intellectual property are an alternative to organic and in-house growth. They have been relatively common in MNCs, such as 3M and GE. Their competitive success depends on their capability to retain key talent during and post-acquisition.

R&D M&As depend on retaining key talent.

In M&As and other strategic changes IHRM practitioners clearly have a central role to play in the management of culture and cross-cultural communication. They need to remain current and up-to-date in their thinking and flexible in their approaches. Cultural differences should be considered from different perspectives. Theorists on culture argue that we should be sensitive in our cross-cultural communication to differences in national and organisation culture (Frost et al., 1991; Martin, 1992). They recommend that when working and collaborating in diverse cultural settings, people should seek to understand the extent of:

- *Integration* consistency and consensus
- *Differentiation* variation and sub-culture conflict
- *Fragmentation* ambiguity, inconsistency and fluctuation

Global knowledge management

Knowledge management faces both more opportunities and obstacles in the global environment. Some countries and cities hold a competitive advantage deriving from their historical development, established infrastructure, reputation and location advantages (Nachum, 2003; Nachum and Keeble, 2003; Sassen, 2001). As the following quotation from an Australian lawyer shows, from his experience as Partner-in-charge (Asia) for a top tier Australian law firm, the international commercial environment is not a level playing field in the high fee paying global legal services business:

International global environment is not a level playing field

ex:
people went to london for the legal work, when that could be done anywhere
↳ London has an advantage.

'I could never understand why in London to give you an example. You know, a Korean shipbuilder selling a new ship to a Norwegian ship owner or operator um with intending to use Greek crews with US dollar financing would come to London to have all the legal work done, but they did. Now they don't come to Australia for that! And that is. You just have to look at what work are we in and who do we meet as a result of that' (Partner-in-charge, Asia, top tier Australian law firm). (Pinnington and Gray, 2007: 163)

Unilever? Yes, ~~don't understand~~ But there are still large opportunities if they can exploit the scale & scope of knowledge sources.

There are though also massive opportunities for MNCs to exploit the scale and scope of their knowledge resources. Unilever, a multinational fast-moving consumer goods company, is one MNC that has been strategically managing its knowledge assets. A review of Unilever's knowledge management practices (Krogh et al., 2001) found knowledge creation and knowledge transfer were fundamental strategies and implemented simultaneously by the organisation. Unilever is just one example of the multitude of ways that MNCs can transfer, expand, appropriate and create new knowledge. Unilever worked across a broad range of fronts throughout the company using internal and external specialists for project advice, virtual teams, task teams, communities of practice (pools of people with practice-based expertise), world conferences (divided into various categories relevant to products and services), and partnerships and collaborations with customers, suppliers, professional associations and universities. Krogh et al (2001) identified four knowledge management strategies:

Knowledge Management Strategies

- *Leveraging strategy* – Communicate and transfer existing knowledge within your organisation
- *Expanding strategy* – Create and build on existing knowledge
- *Appropriating strategy* – Take new knowledge from external individuals and organisations and transfer it to your organisation
- *Probing strategy* – Create new, proprietory knowledge from your internal organisational resources

World in constant state of flux

Local and global sustainability

• demise of U.S. dollar
• Balance of power towards East, Shift

The global economy and local economies are in a constant state of change and flux. Even major policies, habitual practices and global patterns of trading activity are changing with the anticipated demise of the US dollar which was previously considered for over 50 years as the most reliable world currency. The world is undergoing a gradual change with the balance of power currently towards the East and away from the previous hegemony of Western advanced countries. Some financial markets, business practices, social customs and values are converging so that in some ways the world has become more uniform. In other ways, the environment is becoming more complex. As Reiche and Harzing (see Chapter 6) observe, MNRs are experimenting with many different forms of international assignment influenced by the advent of the dual career couple and greater political and cultural sensitivity around the traditional, standard concept of the 2–3 year long stay by a home country expatriate.

experimenting with making people more flexible.

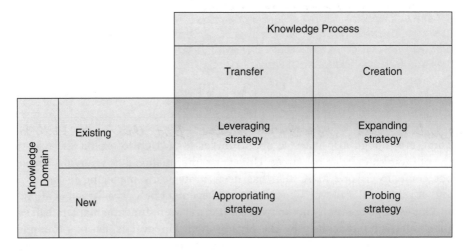

Figure 1.6 Four knowledge strategies

Source: Reprinted from *Long Range Planning*, 34, G.V. Krough, I. Nonaka and M. Aben, 'Making the most of your company's knowledge: a strategic framework', 421-439, 2000, with permission from Elsevier.

There are still state differences

There remain notable country differences. Reiche and Harzing note that Japan, Italy and Germany are more likely to have parent country expatriate foreign subsidiary managers than are Denmark, the UK and Norway. Further, some industries remain more Parent Country National (PCN) dominated such as Banking, Commodity Broking, Printing and Publishing. In contrast, Food, Computers and Electronics are comparatively less so (see Reich and Harzing, Chapter 6).

But now turning back on the globalisation

Unless the world sees a colossal wave of national isolation and re-introduction of trade tariffs and barriers, there are likely to remain a number of continuities in strategic management and IHRM. Amongst them is the fact that MNCs' overall motives for international transfer have not changed that significantly since their first theoretical formulation by Edström and Galbraith (1977) as: Position filling, Management Development, and Organisation Development (Coordination and Control). Moreover, senior executives formulating international corporate strategies will continue to make decisions on the extent that they want to achieve global integration (global strategy), local responsiveness (multi-domestic strategy) or some balanced articulation and combination by being both highly globally integrated and highly locally responsive (transnational strategy).

A major challenge for HR practitioners working in local and global contexts is to raise the professionalism of IHRM so that it can fulfil a more responsible contribution to organisations and society and consequently occupy and maintain higher status within the ranks of managers and executives (Macklin, 2007; Margolis et al., 2007). In effect, this means being able to act with similar authority and efficacy as do other in-house professionals such as in-house corporate and external lawyers (Pinnington et al., 2009). One of the many problems facing IHRM practitioners is the need to get more involved in the development and maintenance of high standards of ethical management. Selecting one from many of the current examples of innovations significant for IHRM is the development of the ISO 26000 standard for Social Responsibility. Social Responsibility can be defined as the responsibility of an organisation for the impacts of its decisions and activities on society and the environment, through transparent and ethical behaviour that:

essential for good governance, of the org.

- Contributes to sustainable development, health and the welfare of society
- Takes into account the expectations of stakeholders
- Is in compliance with applicable law and consistent with international norms of behaviour
- Is integrated throughout the organisation and practiced in its relationships

The ISO 26000 standard for Social Responsibility is scheduled for publication in September 2010. It is been developed by experts and stakeholders from six categories (consumer, government, industry, labour, NGOs, SSRO–Service support research and others). The process has involved numerous conferences and workshops held worldwide (e.g. Vienna, Sydney, Paris, New York, Santiago, Bahrain, Cape Town, Berlin, Tokyo). It has involved over 406 experts and 135 observers from 80 member countries and 37 external liaison organisations. The principles of social responsibility are central to good governance of the corporation and effective and ethical IHRM. They include principles of: accountability, transparency, ethical behaviour, stakeholders' interests, respect of the rule of law, universality of human rights and respect of international norms of behaviour.

IHRM practitioners and researchers can play a major strategic role in assisting with social responsibility, which according to ISO 26000 means that the organisation should understand: *Need to understand the org's impacts on everyone, & the expectations of those impacts.*

- how its decisions and activities impact on society and the environment
- how these impacts affect specific stakeholders
- what the expectations or best practices are with respect to responsible behaviour concerning these impacts

8 Summary and conclusions

This chapter has introduced the concepts of strategic management and IHRM. It has argued that people are central to the long-term success of all organisations and in all sectors of employment. We discussed the central importance of value creation through strategic management and reflected on how it will often be evaluated from different points of view by major stakeholders (e.g. customers, suppliers, management, employees, local community). We considered the major elements of the process of strategic management – analysis, choice, formulation, implementation – and identified different schools of thought such as the design and emergent approaches.

For IHRM to be aligned with the strategy of the organisation it must be clear on the way it links at corporate, international and business levels. We then turned to consider three perspectives on strategy implementation. First, strategic management, following Hanson et al.'s (2002) depiction of strategy implementation as involving four organisational processes of strategic management: corporate governance; organisational structure and controls; strategic leadership; and strategic entrepreneurship. Second, international business strategy, and its concept of modes of entry into other countries and regions include: exporting; licensing; strategic alliances; acquisitions; and establishment of a new subsidiary. Third, we changed from the organisation-level to the country-level of analysis and reviewed Porter's national determinants of competitive advantage which are: factor conditions; demand conditions; related and supporting industries; firm strategy, structure and rivalry; role of government; and role of chance. We then changed the focus from strategic management to address more specifically perspectives related to people and briefly overviewed two common frameworks respectively from project management and organisational behavior.

The next section related the rise of IHRM and strategic HRM, showing that both of these subjects emerged based on the forces of globalisation and changing interests of practitioners and researchers. We noted that IHRM and SHRM offer a wide variety of concepts, tools and techniques for managing people in circumstances of strong global and local competition. The final section selected three major IHRM challenges likely to be significant in the future – cross-cultural communication and diversity, global knowledge management, and local and global sustainability – and all three are major themes across the chapters in this book.

This first chapter has introduced some of the basic principles of strategy and strategic management that have had a substantial influence on IHRM practice and research thinking. IHRM practitioners are well advised to ensure their conversations and actions relate to line management and other employees' strategic discourses. In the following chapters of this first section of the book on Strategic, Comparative and Organisational Perspectives on IHRM, we move forward with these ideas and consider them more broadly from the viewpoint of comparative HRM and organisational perspectives in the contexts of two areas of innovation and change, cross–cultural Communication and M&As.

Discussion questions

1 'People are our greatest asset' – debate for and against this statement on the basis of strategic management.

2 What is the relevance of IHRM for international strategy? Identify different aspects of international strategy and discuss how IHRM can be linked to its successful implementation.

3 Imagine that you are responsible for reorganising IHRM policy for a major airline. What would you want to know about the industry and the company to be able to undertake this task?

4 What are the difficulties with conducting an internal analysis of the organisation?

5 Specify a country of your choice. What are its strengths and weaknesses in relation to the determinants of competitive advantage?

6 A successful strategy from the perspective of the company does not necessarily imply success from the individual employees' point of view. Find examples for this statement and discuss them in class.

Emirates Airline – airline keeps cash reserves strong

This case is adapted from the Business section of The National newspaper, Copyright © 2009. Source: 4th May page 2 and 6th May 2009 pages 1 and 2. www .thenational.ae

New Boeing 777 Aircraft delivery delayed until the next year
Emirates Airline will delay the delivery of several new Boeing 777 aircraft next year by several months to protect its cash reserves during the downturn, says officials.

It is the latest interim measure for the Dubai airline to navigate through the global recession, following efforts to give staff leave of absence and reposition aircraft to more promising routes as demand has waned in some markets. Emirates is expected to announce a small profit in coming weeks amid one of the worst revenue environments for airlines in decades.

Maurice Flanagan, the executive vice chairman of Emirates Airline and Group, said there had been a 'slight rearrangement' of deliveries next year, without disclosing further details. However, in a media report yesterday, Abdullah al Shams, a fleet manager at Emirates based at the Boeing factory in Washington, said the delays involved the long-range 777.

Airlines around the world have deferred and even cancelled aircraft orders amid the global recession. Boeing received 40 new aircraft orders this year while seeing 33 previous orders cancelled. The cancellations come as airlines in the first quarter lost US$1 billion – in line with a forecast for a US$4.7bn loss for the year, the International Air Transport Association said.

'Around the globe, we are seeing a number of customers looks for some deferrals, including in the Middle East,' said Marty Bentrott, the senior vice president of Middle East and Africa sales for Boeing's commercial aeroplanes division. 'We are staying close to these customers in these challenging times.'

Mr Flanagan said the move would help the airline's cash position, which suffered a 32 per cent drop during the six months ending in September, to US$2.3bn from US$3.4bn. The airline said the drop came after pre-delivery payments, financing a cabin refurbishment programme and paying a dividend to the Dubai Government, its primary shareholder.

'Re-arranging these orders means that forecast pre-delivery payments will not take place,' he said. 'The cash position is strengthened, and the market will come back in a year from now.' Deferring the deliveries would give it more time to arrange financing, Mr Flanagan added.

The long-range 777 is a major feature in Emirates's plans to expand its network to six continents. The 777 aircraft costs between US$205 million and US$286 million each, at list prices. Emirates will receive a total of 17 new aircraft this year, including wide-bodied planes from Airbus, and is expected to receive a similar number next year.

Airlines from the Gulf gear up for recovery

At a time when Singapore Airlines is reducing its fleet, Emirates Airline is increasing the number of its aircraft and Etihad is installing new first-class seats.

And Qatar Airways is putting the finishing touches to a US$1 billion programme of airport improvements. Many of the world's largest airlines may have cut capacity and even parked aeroplanes because of the economic downturn, but Gulf carriers are instead uniting under a strategy to build up their networks to prepare for the recovery.

Sheikh Ahmed bin Saeed, the chief executive and chairman of Emirates Airline, likened his company to a surfer waiting for the next big swell – even though the sea is flat. 'Still, we are receiving 17 aircraft, that's a big number. So at least we want to catch the wave when it picks up,' he said at the Arabian Travel Market trade show in Dubai yesterday. Sounding a cautious but upbeat note, the chief executive – who has overseen the evolution of the Dubai airline from a small regional carrier into the Arab world's largest and most profitable operator – said the business was still generating cash. 'We remain very positive,' he said. 'But sometimes you have to be cautious.'

James Hogan, the chief executive of Etihad, said the carrier had achieved its first-quarter targets of 75 per cent seat load factors, while acknowledging that the airline industry was suffering from price discounting to lure customers. 'We hit our numbers, but we're entering a difficult second quarter. It's a tough cycle, but you've got to be flexible enough to adjust to move forward,' he said. Other airlines are expressing their caution in more significant ways.

Singapore Airlines is preparing to reduce its fleet by 17 aircraft due to declining ticket sales. Cathay Pacific Airways, Hong Kong's largest carrier, is cutting flights to London, Paris, Frankfurt and Sydney and asking staff to take unpaid leave as it faces steep drops in demand. And Qantas, the Australian flag carrier, is reducing its workforce by about 5 per cent and delaying the delivery of new planes in response to the depressed travel market.

Moves by the Gulf airlines to protect cash and lower expenses have come in more incremental ways. Qatar Airways, the second-largest Gulf long-haul airline, will cut one route to India this year even as it expands into new destinations on the subcontinent. The airline will pull out of its unprofitable Nagpur service and will redirect the aircraft into new destinations at Amritsar and Goa.

Investments to build up world class airlines

While Emirates Airline has had to make slight adjustments to its delivery schedule in the coming years for Boeing 777 and the Airbus A380, and has also begun offering staff unpaid leave, these moves pale in comparison to the strategic investments taking place. Several airlines in the Gulf countries are building up world-class airlines and airports. Their global growth strategies and related domestic infrastructure developments are anticipated to have significant benefits for the GCC.

'While our competitors are parking planes, we are doing the opposite, said Akbar al Baker, the chief executive of Qatar Airways. 'We are launching seven destinations. I would reveal more, but some of you may have a tummy upset.' Etihad Airways is introducing its new first-class product as first and business-class travel demand has fallen significantly. Within the Middle East, premium tickets fell 10.6 per cent this year compared with the same period last year, according to the International Air Transport Association. Premium travel between the Middle East and the Far East fell 14.5 per cent, while first-class travel between the region and the south-west Pacific dropped even further, by 23.6 per cent.

The lavish first-class cabin includes an 80.5-inch (204 centimetres) lie-flat seat, a changing room with full-length mirror and a sliding door that creates a private suite. The new product will be unveiled on a new Airbus A340–600 being delivered in September, and will then be outfitted on Etihad's existing aircraft that carry a three-class configuration. The project cost Eithad US$70.36 million, the airline said. 'Demand will come back, and when it does, we will be well positioned,' Mr Hogan said.

Likewise, Sheikh Ahmed warned that pulling back now could be detrimental in the long term. 'In our business, whatever action you take today will affect you in the long term. We know that it will pick up.'

Case questions

1 Based on what you know and can find out about the global airlines industry in mid-2009, make an assessment of the risks and opportunities facing Emirates Airlines.
2 In what ways may a corporate and professional approach to SHRM and IHRM assist Emirates Airlines to achieve its short-term and long-term strategic goals?
3 What human resources and skills does Emirates Airlines need for participation in the industry (i.e. threshold competences) and to achieve a competitive advantage (i.e. core competences)?

Case questions for further study and reflection

1 Imagine you are offered the opportunity to change your current employer from Emirates Airlines to another Gulf Country airline company. What are the main factors you need to consider for deciding whether to accept the offer?
2 Imagine you are about to finish your studies and are looking for a job that provides the opportunity to work internationally in the Gulf region. In what ways would the company's IHRM be influential in your choice of company?

Further reading

- Barney, J. (1991) 'Firm resources and sustained competitive advantage', *Journal of Management*, 17(1): 99–120.
A classic and top ranked cited academic paper which outlines comprehensively Jay Barney's resource-based view of the firm. This was one of the articles which marked a watershed point for HR researchers and practitioners. It acknowledges much more openly and clearly the role of people than typically is found in strategic frameworks based on industry environment analysis.

- Schuler, R. S. and Jackson, S. E. (1987) 'Linking competitive strategies with human resource management practices', *Academy of Management Executive*, 1(3): 207–19.
Randall Schuler and Susan Jackson were one of the first researchers to link psychological and organisational behaviour concepts with the strategies of cost leadership, differentiation and innovation. Although now something of an 'oldie but goldie', many cohorts of undergraduate and postgraduate students have found this paper by Schuler and Jackson to be really helpful for understanding exactly how the people issues can be linked with the strategic issues.

- Yetton, P., Craig, J., Davis J. and Hilmer, F. (1992) 'Are diamonds a country's best friend? A critique of Porter's theory of national competition as applied to Canada, New Zealand and Australia', *Australian Journal of Management*, June, 17(1): 89–119.
This paper critiques Michael Porter's diamond and argues that as a matter of empirical fact a country may achieve a comparative advantage through possession of just one or two of the determinant factors. The authors conclude therefore that the theory is over-stated and potentially misleading for government policy makers and business leaders.

- Hoskisson, R., Hitt, M., Wan, W. and Yiu, D. (1999) 'Theory and research in strategic management: swings of a pendulum', *Journal of Management*, 25(3): 417–56.
If you are interested in finding out more about strategic management and where it all comes from, in terms of research schools of thought and core disciplinary concepts, then this is a very readable and accessible review of developments in the research field.

- Johnson, G., Scholes, K. and Whittington, R. (2010) Exploring Corporate Strategy, 8th edn. Harlow: FT Prentice Hall.
Alternatively, if you are looking for a book to learn more about strategy and strategic management as a practical tool and way of thinking, then this classic textbook is an excellent resource for answering almost any question that you have on strategy.

- Whittington, R. (2001) *What is Strategy – and Does it Matter?* 2nd edn. London: Thomson Learning.
There again, if you in fact are looking for something more concise, then this book is an excellent read on four theories of strategy (classical, evolutionary, processual and systemic) and is generally very popular with postgraduate students.

- Pinnington, A.H. and Gray, J.T. (2007) 'The global restructuring of legal services work? A study of the internationalisation of Australian law firms', *International Journal of the Legal Profession,* July, 14(2): 147–72.

The research discussed in this journal article addresses the internationalisation strategies of knowledge workers based in a country with a comparatively small population and economy. It examines the ways that an elite group of law firms in Australia are contributing to the globalisation of business and restructuring of legal services work. It seeks to understand Australian law firms' collective strategic intent, which at the time of the research was to develop a global competitive presence in markets in the Asia Pacific region. It is an interesting study of the little guys rather than the big guys trying to establish a global presence. It examines the distinctive commercial orientation and institutional corporate connections of this group, focusing on how their strategic practice in many ways actually favours the elite group US and UK firms. The data specifically on the recent phase of internationalisation of legal services show Australian lawyers to be of lower status when compared to elite US and European law firms.

- Adler, P.S., Kwon, S-W. and Heckscher, C. (2008) 'Professional work: the emergence of collaborative community', *Organization Science,* March–April, 19(2): 359–76.

A multidisciplinary journal article related to strategic management, knowledge management and IHRM which examines the historical evolution of the organisation of professional work. It provides examples from medicine and hospitals and proposes that the nature of professional work and its communities have changed from craft guild forms to state-based hierarchical institutions with a societal orientation. Adler et al. propose that organisations are now moving more towards new collaborative forms of work and organising.

- Krogh, G.V., Nonaka, I. and Aben, M. (2001) 'Making the most of your company's knowledge: a strategic framework', *Long Range Planning,* 34: 421–439.

If you want to really get to grips with the multitude of ways in practice that corporations can implement knowledge management, then this is one of the best starting points for ideas. The authors show how Unilever engaged in a set of concurrent strategies to manage knowledge in ways that create value and may lead towards attaining a competitive advantage.

Internet resources

1 The Strategic Planning Society (SPS) (http://sps.org.uk/): The Strategic Planning Society (SPS) fosters and promotes research and best practice in strategic thought and action. SPS aims to create a link between the academic and practitioner worlds of strategy. It has been in existence for 40 years and members receive *Long Range Planning and Strategy Magazine*. SPS' stated purpose is: 'We exist to provide a forum for the propagation, advancement and education in strategy and strategic thinking.' SPS strategic intention is:

- 'To be recognised as an expert voice on strategy and strategic thinking
- To promote the case for strategy as a professional discipline'

SPS values are:

- 'Reflect the diversity of the organisations and communities we service.
- Committed to excellence – initially internally by creating a sustainable organisation.
- Committed to being a creative, trusting, knowledge centred organisation.
- To be unselfishly committed to the development of individuals and organisations to the benefit of their spheres of activity.
- Participative
- Open'

Email membership@sps.org.uk if you would like further details, or wish to apply to be a Trustee (attaching your CV for consideration).

2   The Society for Human Resource Management (SHRM) (http://www.shrm.org/about/pages/default.aspx): This website has information about SHRM, HR disciplines, legal issues, publications, research, education, conferences, communities and advocacy. SHRM is the world's largest association for HRM with more than 250,000 members in 140 countries. The Society serves the needs of HR professionals and the HR profession. SHRM was established in 1948 and has subsidiary offices in China and India.

3   The Chartered Institute of Personnel and Development (CIPD) (http://www.cipd.co.uk/default.cipd): The CIPD is the professional body for those involved in the management and development of people. It has 135,000 members. The CIPD mission is: 'to lead in the development and promotion of good practice in the field of the management and development of people, for application both by professional members and by their organisational colleagues'. The CIPD aims to serve the professional interests of members and to uphold the highest ideals in the management and development of people, and the website covers a wide range of topics in IHRM, SHRM and HRM.

Self-assessment questions

Indicative answers to these questions can be found on the companion website at www.sagepub.co.uk/harzing3e.

1   **What are the employee role behaviours that Schuler and Jackson (1987) recommend for a strategy based on: (a) Innovation, (b) Quality, and (c) Cost reduction?**

2 **What do the following commonly used acronyms stand for – (a) SWOT, (b) PESTEL, and (c) Five Forces?**
3 **List and define the three corporate-level international strategies that have a profound influence on the culture, structure, policies and practices of IHRM.**
4 **Identify and define each of Krogh et al., (2001) four knowledge management strategies.**
5 **During strategic management of the corporate culture in what three different ways do Frost et al. (1991) recommend that the culture and sub-cultures of the organisation should be evaluated?**

References

Alvesson, M. (1993) *Cultural Perspectives on Organisations.* Cambridge: Cambridge University Press.

Ansoff, I. (1991) 'Critique of Henry Mintzberg's "The design school: reconsidering the basic premises of strategic management"', *Strategic Management Journal,* 12(6): 449–61.

Ashkenas, R.N., DeMonaco, L.J. and Francis, S.C. (1998) 'Making the deal real: How GE Capital integrates acquisitions', *Harvard Business Review,* January–February 165–78.

Barney, J. (1991) 'Firm resources and sustained competitive advantage', *Journal of Management,* 17(1): 99–120.

Bower, J. (2001) 'Not all M&As are alike – and that matters', *Harvard Business Review, March* 93–101.

Boxall, P. and Purcell, J. (2008) *Strategy and Human Resource Management,* 2nd edn, (1st edn, 2003), Basingstoke: Palgrave Macmillan.

Campbell, T., Pinnington, A.H., Macklin, R. and Smith, S. (2007) 'Conclusion', in A.H. Pinnington, R. Macklin and Tom Campbell (eds), *Human Resource Management: Ethics and Employment.* Oxford: Oxford University Press. pp. 282–291.

Dowling, P.J., Festing, M. and Engle, A.D. (2008) *International HRM,* 5th edn. Singapore: South-Western/Cengage Learning.

Edström, A. and Galbraith, J. R. (1977) 'Transfer of Managers as a Control and Coordination Strategy in Multinational Organizations', *Administrative Science Quarterly,* 22 (June): 11–22.

Evan, W.M. and Freeman, R.E. (2004) 'A stakeholder theory of the modern corporation: Kantian capitalism', in T.L. Beauchamp and N.E. Bowie (eds), *Ethical Theory and Business,* 7th edn. Englewood Cliffs, NJ: Prentice Hall, pp. 101–5.

Evans, P., Pucik, V. and Björkman, I. (2010) *The Global Challenge: Frameworks for International Human Resource Management,* 2nd edn. New York: McGraw-Hill.

Frost, P.J., Moore, L.F., Louis, M.R., Lundberg, C.C. and Martin, J. (eds) (1991) *Reframing Organizational Culture.* London: Sage Publications.

Grant, R.M. (1991) 'The resource-based theory of competitive advantage: implications for strategy formulation', *California Management Review,* 33(2): 114–35.

Grant, R.M. (1996a) 'Towards a knowledge-based theory of the firm', *Strategic Management Journal,* 17(2S): 109–23.

Grant, R.M. (1996b) 'Prospering in dynamically-competitive environments: organizational capability as knowledge integration', *Organization Science,* 7: 375–88.

Greenwood, M. and De Cieri, H. (2007) 'Stakeholder theory and the ethics of HRM', in A.H. Pinnington, R. Macklin and Tom Campbell (eds), *Human Resource Management: Ethics and Employment.* Oxford: Oxford University Press. pp. 119–36.

Grint, K. (2005) *Leadership: Limits and Possibilities.* Basingstoke: Palgrave Macmillan.

Guest, D.E. (2001) 'Human resource management: when research confronts theory', *International Journal of Human Resource Management,* November, 12(7): 1092–106.

Hamel, G. and Prahalad, C. (1994) *Competing for the Future.* Boston, MA: Harvard Business School Press.

Hanson, D., Dowling, P., Hitt, M.A., Ireland, R.D. and Hoskisson, R.E. (2002) *Strategic Management: Competitiveness and Globalisation.* Southbank, Victoria: Nelson/Thomson Learning.

Hofstede, G. (1980) *Culture's Consequences: International Differences in Work-Related Values.* Sage: Beverly Hills.

Hoskisson, R., Hitt, M., Wan, W. and Yiu, D. (1999) 'Theory and research in strategic management: swings of a pendulum', *Journal of Management,* 25(3): 417–56.

Johnson, G., Scholes, K. and Whittington, R. (2010) *Exploring Corporate Strategy,* 8th edn. Harlow: FT Prentice Hall.

Kamoche, K. (1996) 'Strategic human resource management within a resource-capability view of the firm', *Journal of Management Studies,* 33(2): 213–33.

Kim, W.C. and Hwang, P. (1992) 'Global strategy and multinationals' entry mode choice', *Journal of International Business Studies,* 23: 29–53.

Krogh, G.V., Nonaka, I. and Aben, M. (2001) 'Making the most of your company's knowledge: a strategic framework', *Long Range Planning,* 34: 421–39.

Macklin, R. (2007) 'The morally decent HR manager', in A. H. Pinnington, R. Macklin and Tom Campbell (eds), *Human Resource Management: Ethics and Employment.* Oxford: Oxford University Press. pp. 266–81.

Margolis, J.D., Grant, A.M. and Molinsky, A.L. (2007) 'Expanding ethical standards of HRM: necessary evils and the multiple dimensions of impact', in A. H. Pinnington, R. Macklin and Tom Campbell (eds), *Human Resource Management: Ethics and Employment.* Oxford: Oxford University Press. pp. 237–51.

Martin, J. (1992) *Cultures in Organizations: Three perspectives.* Oxford: Oxford University Press.

Mintzberg, H. (1990) 'The design school: Reconsidering the basic premises of strategic management', *Strategic Management Journal,* March-April, 11(3): 171–95.

Nachum, L. (2003) 'Liability of foreignness in global competition? Financial service affiliates in the City of London', *Strategic Management Journal,* 24: 1187–208.

Nachum, L. and Keeble, D. (2003) 'MNC linkages and localised clusters: foreign and indigenous firms in the media cluster of central London', *Journal of International Management,* 9: 171–92.

Penrose, E. (1959) *The Theory of the Growth of the Firm.* Oxford: Blackwell.

Pinnington, A.H. (2003) 'Organizational culture: Liberation or entrapment?', in Dennis Tourish and Owen Hargie (eds), *Key Issues in Organizational Communication.* London: Routledge. pp. 205–19.

Pinnington, A.H. (2005) 'Learning in a competitive field: MBA students' improvised case studies of IHRM', *International Journal of Human Resource Management,* April, 16(4): 619–35.

Pinnington, A.H. and Gray, J.T. (2007) 'The global restructuring of legal services work? A study of the internationalisation of Australian law firms', *International Journal of the Legal Profession,* July, 14(2): 147–72.

Pinnington, A.H. and Sandberg, J. (2009) 'Employee Perspectives on Organisational Professionalism: Participation in the Firm's Business Strategies and Transient Knowledge Communities', *25th EGOS Colloquium* "Barcelona 2009 Passion for creativity and innovation: Energizing the study of organizations and organizing", Sub-theme 46: Energizing the study of organizations and organizing II, ESADE Business School, Barcelona, Spain, 2–4 July.

Pinnington, A.H., Kamoche, K. and Suseno, Y. (2009) 'Property in knowledge work: An appropriation-learning perspective', *Employee Relations,* 31(1): 57–80.

Pinnington, A.H., Morris, T.J. and Pinnington, C.A. (2003) 'The relational structure of improvisation: A case illustration from corporate video production', *International Studies in Management and Organization,* Spring 33(1): 10–33.

Porter, M.E. (1980) *Competitive Strategy: Techniques for Analyzing Industries and Competitors.* New York: Free Press.

Porter, M.E. (1985) *Competitive Advantage: Creating and Sustaining Superior Performance.* New York: Free Press.

Porter, M.E. (1990) *The Competitive Advantage of Nations.* London: Macmillan (now Palgrave Macmillan).

Project Management Institute, Inc. (PMI) (2004) *A Guide to the Project Management Body of Knowledge,* (PMBOK Guide), an American National Standard ANSI/PMI 99-001-2004. Pennsylvania: Project Management Institute, Inc.

Purcell, J. (1999) 'Best practice and best fit: chimera or cul-de-sac?', *Human Resource Management Journal,* 9: 26–41.

Robbins, S.P. and Judge, T.A. (2009) *Organizational Behaviour,* 13th edn. London: Pearson Education, Prentice Hall.

Sassen, S. (2001) *The Global City: New York, London, Tokyo.* 2nd edn. Princeton, NJ: Princeton University Press.

Schuler, R.S. and Jackson, S.E. (1987) 'Linking competitive strategies with human resource management practices', *Academy of Management Executive,* 1(3): 207–19.

Schuler, R.S., Dowling, P.J. and De Cieri, H. (1993) 'An integrative framework of strategic international human resource management', *International Journal of Human Resource Management,* 4: 717–64.

Skoufa, L. (2004) 'Industry reform in Australia: Privatisation/Corporatisation of the electricity supply industry', *Philosophy of Management,* 4(3): 23–36.

Spender, J.-C. (1996) 'Making knowledge the basis of a dynamic theory of the firm', *Strategic Management Journal,* 17S1: 45–62.

Vernon, R. (1996) 'International investment and international trade in the product cycle', *Quarterly Journal of Economics,* 80: 190–207.

Wernerfelt, B. (1984) 'A resource-based view of the firm', *Strategic Management Journal,* 5(2): 171–80.

Whittington, R. (2001) *What is Strategy – and Does it Matter?* 2nd edn. London: Thomson Learning.

Wood, S. (1999) 'Human resource management and performance', *International Journal of Management Reviews,* 1(4): 367–413.

Yetton, P., Craig, J., Davis J. and Hilmer, F. (1992) 'Are diamonds a country's best friend? A critique of Porter's theory of national competition as applied to Canada, New Zealand and Australia', *Australian Journal of Management,* June, 17(1): 89–119.

2

Comparative Human Resource Management[1]

Chris Brewster and Wolfgang Mayrhofer

Contents

Learning Objectives

After reading this chapter you will be able to

- Appreciate the importance of comparative HRM for IHRM

- Understand the difference between best practice and best fit models of HRM

- Identify the reasons why countries remain different in the ways that they conceptualise and conduct HRM

- Discuss some of the ways in which HRM differs between countries

- Understand how MNCs have to balance between being globally effective and fair whilst appreciating and benefiting from national differences

Chapter Outline

This chapter explores the differences between countries in the ways that they manage their human resources. Within a context of increasing globalisation, the chapter argues that context is everything: what the term HRM means, how it is understood, what would be considered 'good' HRM and the way that people management is practised, all vary from country to country. As such, these differences form the backdrop against which MNCs must manage the integration/ differentiation paradox, and against which all international HRM must be measured. Comparative HRM is a challenge to the universalist paradigm of HRM, generally expressed in the notion of 'best practice'.

Fundamental to understanding these differences between countries are two concepts: the ideas of cultural and institutional differences; and the notions of convergence and divergence. The chapter argues that we need to gain a better understanding of both pairs of concepts. They constitute important means of understanding what is actually happening in HRM. On the first issue, we argue that both cultural and institutional explanations are valuable; on the second we argue that convergence of trends is apparent, but final convergence remains unrealistic.

We provide more detail, as examples, of differences between countries in the configuration of HRM, flexible working practices and communications and consultation. Finally, we outline some of the key theoretical, empirical and practical challenges posed by a comparative approach to HRM.

1 Introduction

A major problem for those who study and practise HRM is that much of our understanding and most of our knowledge about the topic comes from the USA and are assumed to apply universally. The version of HRM propounded in most books on HRM and published in most of the HRM journals, the lessons taught in most business schools around the world, the recommendations put forward by the major consultancy companies and the whole best practice movement in HRM are all based on the US model. This creates built-in cultural assumptions and contextual limitations for HRM specialists and for those working in internationally operating organisations. The fact that HRM differs from country to country should not be read as an indicator that some countries are just 'backward' or need to 'catch up' to more modern ways of doing things. The fact that some of the richest countries in the world manage their HRM in different ways, and that there are world-beating MNCs from an ever-increasing number of countries, warns us that 'different' does not mean 'worse'.

If we want to run effective HRM policies in an internationally operating organisation, we have to understand the different national cultures and institutional constraints – at least in terms of their importance for organisations, restrictions or limited room for manoeuvre in imposing organisation-wide policies and practices, and their opportunities and limitations when managing an international workforce (see Chapter 6). Organisations operating across national and cultural borders will need to bridge the divide between being globally coherent and consistent in their HRM policies and practices for reasons of cost-effectiveness and equity with the imperative of being sensitive to local variations in national, cultural and institutional requirements. Arguably, this dilemma is best summarised in an early statement by Laurent:

> The challenge faced by the infant field of international human resource management is to solve a multidimensional puzzle located at the crossroad of national and organisational culture. (Laurent, 1986: 101).

From its beginnings, International HRM (see Introduction and Chapter 1) was aware of these requirements. Dealing with an international workforce, especially expatriates, looking at HRM specifics of multinational companies (MNCs) and comparing HRM policies and practices constituted the fundamentals for International HRM in the early 1980s (Dowling, 1999). Various developments at the global level such as globalisation and the rising significance of MNCs have not only quickened the development of international HRM as an established part of HRM, but also paved the way for more detailed discussions on the topic. In this sense, comparative HRM has become an established part of International HRM, and a major perspective on how to look at HRM in an international setting (see, for example, contributions taking an explicitly comparative angle in HRM such as Brewster et al., 2007c; Harzing and van Ruysseveldt, 2004; or the global HRM series edited by Schuler, Jackson, Sparrow and Poole). European researchers in particular have made significant contributions to theoretical, empirical and methodological advances in the field of comparative HRM (e.g., Brewster et al., 2000, 2004; Brunstein, 1995; Gooderham et al., 1999; Poole, 1990). There have also been important contributions from other parts of the world such as Asia (e.g., Budhwar, 2004; Zanko, 2002; Zanko and Ngui, 2003), in Africa (Kamoche et al., 2003) and the developing countries (Budhwar and Debrah, 2001).

Box 2.1   Stop and reflect

Look up the table of contents of the following books and analyse:

(1) In which book does comparative HRM play a major role?
(2) Is comparative HRM a major angle around which the book is organised or is it just one element among many others?

- Briscoe, D. R., Schuler, R. S. and Claus, L. (2008) *International Human Resource Management: Policies and Practices for Multinational Enterprises.* London, New York: Routledge.
- Dickmann, M., Brewster, C. and Sparrow, P. R. (eds) (2008) *International HRM: A European Perspective.* London: Routledge.
- Dowling, P. J., Festing, M. and Engle, A. D. (2008) *International Human Resource Management: Managing People in a Multinational Context,* 5th edn. London: Thomson Learning.
- Larsen, H. H. and Mayrhofer, W. (eds) (2006) *Managing Human Resources in Europe. A Thematic Approach.* London: Routledge.
- Stahl, G. K. and Björkman, I. (eds) (2006) *Handbook of Research in International Human Resource Management.* Cheltenham: Edward Elgar.

The way that people think about HRM and the way it is practised vary from country to country. Managers have their own approaches to managing their people, each unit manages differently, as does each function within the company – and each organisation has its own unique form of HRM. There is commonality too in so far as organisations of a similar size or in a particular sector tend, other things being equal, to have similar forms of HRM. Both common and distinctive social institutions exist and are nested at a range of levels in societies (Hollingsworth and Boyer, 1997). Each country has its own generic recipes for HRM and there are general approaches to the subject that draw universal conclusions about HRM. The differences, often linked to a named country as the 'nutshell' for cultural, institutional or regional specifics, are one of the fundamental reasons why International HRM is more difficult than HRM in one country since, out of all of the aspects of management, HRM is the one most subject to local influences (Rosenzweig and Nohria, 1994).

Any discussion of International HRM, therefore, needs to include an understanding of Comparative HRM. Despite this, comparative research in HRM has been somewhat rare (comparative research in the fields of industrial and employment relations, rooted in institutional explanations, has been more common). The main reason for this is that comparative IHRM research work is difficult: there are, 'noble and not so noble' (Mayrhofer and Brewster, 2005) problems, including questions of conceptualisation such as finding an adequate theoretical frame, and practical difficulties such as bringing together international research teams and sustaining working relationships between researchers of different nationality, culture or scientific tradition.

Drawing the previous paragraphs together encapsulates a key issue: to understand and analyse the complexity of *International* HRM requires an understanding of *Comparative* HRM. This chapter concentrates on comparative HRM. We mention (briefly because it is also covered in Chapters 7, 8, 12 and 18) the issues of globalisation and MNCs as a major source for the importance of International HRM in general and comparative HRM in particular; we examine the importance of context and look at some of the different ways that it has been analysed, how it is changing and whether HRM is converging; we look at country–related differences of core HRM elements; and finally we comment on the drive to both standardise HRM practices and simultaneously to deal with the need to adapt these practices to the local environment.

2 Globalisation and HRM

IHRM continues to attract continuing interest, which is not surprising. At the time of writing, the effect of the global recession that began in 2008 is unclear. Figures from UNCTAD (various years), the United Nations' body measuring the extent of international trade and development, show that the growth of international trade had been patchy in the first years of the twenty–first century, after a long period of almost exponential growth towards the end of the twentieth century. The economic crisis of the end of the first decade of the new century could exacerbate that trend and governments may react to a severe economic downturn even with protectionist measures.

The term 'globalisation' is widely used but often harbours different meanings. Generally it refers to processes of unification that have taken place in markets and consumer tastes, an increasingly mobile investor capital, and the rapid spread of technology. Within and between firms, actions are increasingly grounded in an overall perspective that views the whole world as nationless and borderless (Ohmae, 1990, 1995). Globalisation theories hold that economies are becoming globally integrated, resulting in the proliferation of global management structures and the convergence of management techniques around shared notions of 'best practice' (Sera, 1992). MNCs are exposed to the forces of globalisation and, so, are most likely to comply with dominant worldwide practices aimed at enhancing competitiveness in world markets. Hence, they attempt to promote integrated international standards and resist pressures to be locally responsive (Ashkenas et al., 1995; Hamel and Prahalad, 1986; Kim and Gray, 2005; Yip, 1995). These global strategies encourage greater homogenisation to create greater efficiency (Kostova and Roth, 2002). Grounded in the rational choice tradition, this global perspective assumes that firms pursue economic advantage through choices 'guided by unambiguous preferences and bounded rationality' (Gooderham et al., 1999: 507). Whilst the diffusion process may be slow or uneven, it will eventually make for inter-industry and international practices that are to a large degree uniform. Firms will either attempt to enforce their own view of the most efficient ways of handling HRM in other countries; or they will all gradually drift towards HRM policies that mirror the most rational and efficient approach, as propounded in the US model of management (Jain et al., 1998; McDonough, 2003; Smith and Meiksins, 1995).

Global competition can encourage increasing levels of coordination of resources, equipment, finance and people (Sparrow et al., 2004). For example, it is important to coordinate pricing, service and product support worldwide since multinational customers can compare prices in different regions. Through global trade, traditional and domestic business boundaries become increasingly permeable, accelerating the rate of convergence of business practices and firms face more risk in becoming decoupled from familiar settings, thus challenging national mindsets and assumptions (Sparrow and Hiltrop, 1997).

Sceptics and critics of the globalisation thesis (see for example Dunning, 1997; Rugman, 2000; Whitley, 1999) have contested even the assumption that globalisation is new (Parker, 1998). Others have suggested on the contrary that even multinational firms are extremely local in terms of key areas such as employment practices: 85 per cent of multinationals produce more than two-thirds of their output in their home market, with two-thirds of their employees being nationals of their home country (*Economist*, 2000). Indeed, most MNCs cannot easily be defined as stateless (Hu, 1992); the United Nations Conference on Trade and Development (UNCTAD) index of transnationality lists only six organisations scoring above 90 out of 100.

For our purposes, it is worthwhile reminding ourselves that human resources are, in most organisations, the largest single element of operating costs. That is why MNCs locate many of their operations in low-wage economies. Although there is little thought, either in the literature or in practice, given to the idea that firms should equalise wages globally, there is a widespread assumption, as we shall see, that the rest of HRM can be standardised to match the global reach of MNCs (Brewster et al., 2008)

3 The importance of context

HRM viewed through a comparative lens is always contextualised, such that how HRM works, what is covered by HRM, what is regarded as good HRM etc., depends

Best Practice = firm applying a practice, in the hoped of improved performance, regardless of the location. Typically used by the MNC's Head Quarters.

benefits:
- mutual learning
- alignment of global systems

cons → does not consider local circumstances - where such practices could be seen as illegal.

Heavily on the respective context. Context in this sense includes the internal context (e.g., organisational size, structure and demography) as well as the external context, which covers national culture and values, as well as elements of the institutional environment such as legal regulations, the respective industry and the type of economy.

Contextualising HRM leads us on to asking at least three questions. First, can HRM in different contexts be conducted in a similar way or does it have to adapt to the respective circumstances? Behind this question lies the discussion on best practice vs. best fit, which asks whether there is one best model of HRM as is often assumed in US–based HRM concepts, alternatively is it necessary to take into account specific contextual issues in order to achieve the best outcome? Second, what are the crucial forces leading to relevant contextual differences in HRM? Two major factors often treated as mutually exclusive are culture and institutions. Third, how do similarities and differences between various contexts develop over time? Taking a temporal perspective, the issues of convergence, divergence or stasis arise, and so the question is will the different contexts – most often countries – become more alike, more different or stay relatively stable? This section explores all three questions consecutively.

Best practice vs. best fit

It can be argued that an organisation's HRM policies and practices should be tightly connected to the organisation's corporate strategy and should be coherent in all its operations. However, for companies operating in more than one country the question arises as to whether that is sensible or even possible.

There are some advantages for MNCs in adopting 'best practice' – that is, choosing to apply the practices with which they are most familiar, or those that appear to promise high returns in performance, regardless of the location of their subsidiary (Gooderham and Nordhaug, 2003). In most companies and in most circumstances, it appears that best practice is the one used in the headquarters country. It is common for a multinational based in the USA to insist that its policies are best practice and could and should be applied in Venezuela whereas it is very rare for such companies to find an example of excellent practice in Venezuela and insist that it is applied by managers in the USA.

The advantages of a best practice approach include mutual learning, so that an effective practice discovered in one location can be spread across the world, without the costly and often ineffective need for each subsidiary to 're–invent the wheel'. In addition, global alignment of systems will facilitate an internal labour market and make expatriation and other forms of cross–border movement of personnel easier (Almond et al., 2003). Common systems of HRM may then be easier to control and easier to monitor from headquarters. Alongside these benefits, there are ethical considerations of equity and fair treatment for all employees – why should the organisation treat people differently just because they come from or are located in different countries?

Besides these benefits there are disadvantages, too. Companies' policies and practices may not be seen as legitimate, or even be legal, in some countries and the approaches of companies from around the world in relation to issues of gender,

Best Fit = HRM policies Vary by country
Form of implementation of world practices is Varied at national levels.

54   Strategic, Comparative and Organisational Perspectives

ethnic or age discrimination will be very different. Some countries have legislation requiring companies to discriminate in favour of certain ethnic groups; equality legislation in the USA encourages positive discrimination but it is illegal in the European Union. Therefore, some degree of adaptation to local circumstances is inevitable.

As a result, researchers increasingly acknowledge that HRM is one of the management subjects in which organisations are most likely to maintain a national flavour and have a strong contextual interface. This switches the focus from best practice to best fit, especially related to different contexts. Many studies reveal substantive differences between various aspects of HRM in European countries (e.g. Brewster et al., 2004, 2008; Farndale et al., 2008; Scholz and Böhm, 2008; Johnson et al., 2009; Morley, 2009). A large survey of HR Directors of the biggest firms in Germany, the USA and Japan found that HRM practices differ widely (Pudelko, 2000, 2004). There is considerable evidence that, even in the most centralised MNCs, forms of control (Harzing and Sorge, 2003), work systems (Geppert et al., 2003) and team work (Woywode, 2002) vary by country and that, in practice, the form of implementation of 'worldwide' policies is negotiated or varied at the national level (Ferner, 1997; Wächter et al., 2003).

The background for these two views is the distinction between the universalist and the contextual paradigms in HRM research (Brewster, 1999). The universalist paradigm is dominant in the USA but also widely used elsewhere. It assumes that the purpose of the study of HRM is to improve the way that human resources are managed strategically within organisations. The ultimate aim of this work is to improve organisational performance, as judged by its impact on the organisation's declared corporate strategy (Huselid, 1995), the customers (Ulrich, 1989) or shareholders (Becker et al.,1997). It is implicit in these writings that this objective will apply in all cases: it is, in analogy with the physical sciences, to test 'yes/no' hypotheses with the objective of identifying universal rules.

In contrast, the contextual paradigm searches for an overall understanding of what is contextually unique and why it is different. It is focused on understanding what is distinctive between and within HRM in various contexts, and what the antecedents of those differences are. The policies and practices of 'leading-edge' companies, something of a value–laden term in itself, which are often the focus of universalist HRM research, are of less interest than identifying ways that labour markets work and examining what the more typical organisations are doing. For most researchers working within this paradigm, it is the explanations that matter and links to firm performance are secondary. It is assumed that HRM applies to societies, governments or regions as well as to firms. At the level of the organisation (and not just the 'firm' because public–sector and not–for–profit organisations should be included), even the organisation's objectives and strategy are not necessarily assumed to be 'good' either for the organisation or for society (Mayrhofer and Brewster, 2010 forthcoming).

Box 2.2   Best practices or best fit?

An MNC applied a diversity policy across its worldwide operations. It issued polices to enforce non–discrimination, changed its recruitment and promotion procedures and set up online support groups and meetings opportunities for disadvantaged workers. It found that its Japanese subsidiary (based in an ethnically remarkably homogenous country) was not interested in 'blacks and so on' but was enthusiastic about gender equality. Japan is a country in which people prefer to work for indigenous rather than foreign firms but in which those indigenous firms expect their female employees to give up work when they get married, as did many Western countries up until as late as the 1960s. This Japanese subsidiary of a foreign company thought that it would be able to recruit top quality female graduates who were looking for a lifetime career. But when they asked for financial support for crèche facilities and minders this proved too much for HQ, who had not intended to spend a lot of cash on these policies (Sparrow and Brewster, 2009).

It is not that either HRM paradigm is necessarily correct or more instructive than others, but that the level and focus needs to be specified to make the analysis meaningful (Brewster, 1999). Comparative HRM falls squarely within the contextual paradigm.

Culture vs. institutions

Comparative HRM should attempt explanation as well as description (Boxall, 1993). So what are the reasons for the differences in the way that countries conceive of and practise HRM? There are, broadly, two competing sets of theoretical explanation: the cultural and the institutional.

Cultural explanations One reason for the differences between countries in the way they think of and undertake HRM can be found in the concept of cultural differences (see Chapters 3 and 15 for a cultural view on differences in communication). Culture is, as one of the classic texts put it, 'one of those terms that defy a single all–purpose definition and there are almost as many meanings of culture as people using the term' (Ajiferuke and Boddewyn, 1970: 154). Related to management issues, three approaches to culture have become prominent over the past decades.

- Hofstede's view of culture as consisting of five cultural dimensions – power distance, individualism, masculinity, uncertainty avoidance, complemented by long-short-term orientation which was added later (Hofstede, 1980, 2001) – is widely known and dominated much of the discussion in the 1980s and 1990s. Its great success can be attributed to a very straightforward approach to culture, regarding it as 'the software of our minds'. Ready-made data that was conveniently applicable in econometric analyses proved particularly helpful for those who believe in the illusion of rigour in quasi-quantitative management research.

- Schwartz's concept of culture as value oriented and reducible to systemic cultural dimensions (Schwartz, 1992, 2010). Values are beliefs, refer to desirable goals, transcend specific actions and situations, serve as standards or criteria, and are ordered by importance. Schwartz's most recent model has three cultural dimensions: mastery vs. harmony (which addresses the issue of economic and social viability), hierarchy vs. egalitarianism, and embeddedness vs. autonomy (intellectual and affective autonomy).

- The Global Leadership and Organisational Behaviour Effectiveness (GLOBE) project (House et al., 2004) shares with Hofstede and Schwartz the perception of culture as something rather stable. It provides an integrated theory of the relationship between culture and societal, organisational and leadership effectiveness. Looking at modal practices ('how things are done in a culture') and modal values ('the way things should be done'), the study uses nine culture dimensions, partly overlapping with other models such as Hofstede: uncertainty avoidance, power distance, institutional collectivism, intra-group collectivism, gender egalitarianism, assertiveness, future orientation, performance orientation and social orientation. Against this backdrop, the GLOBE study focused on actual and ideal leadership.

National cultures will, typically, reflect national boundaries, but this is by no means always the case. Thus, countries like Belgium, Spain and Switzerland contain communities speaking different languages and following different religions and legislation: seeming, at least to the resident citizens, profoundly different in their approach to life. Cultural groups in the Middle East and Africa were divided by the colonial map-makers and in many instances may have more in common with groups in countries across the national border than they do with many citizens of their own country. In many countries, however, especially the longer established ones and those within coherent geographical boundaries, such as islands, culture in many spheres of social life equates to country – and that is certainly the conclusion of the research into workplace values (e.g. Spony, 2003) or the world-value studies (see, for example, Welzel and Inglehart, 2005).

The 'culturalist' school is an extremely broad one, it covers many different approaches and addresses the interaction between national culture and the behaviour of organisations and individuals. Cultural differences will inevitably be reflected in differences in the way people are managed and HRM is conducted.

Institutional explanations The institutional perspective sees the institutions of a society as environments that maintain their distinctiveness. All transactions are assumed to be embedded in specific social settings (Hollingsworth and Boyer, 1997) and organisations are understood to adhere to formal rules and unwritten social norms in the interests of efficiency and legitimacy (DiMaggio and Powell, 1983; Marsden, 1999). The institutional line of argument runs broadly as follows. There are a number of different and equally successful ways of organising economic activities (and management) in any capitalist economy (Amable, 2003; Hall and Soskice, 2001; Whitley, 1999). These different patterns of social and economic organisation tend to be a product of the particular institutional environments occurring within the various nation states.

Neo–institutional theory (Powell and DiMaggio, 1987) argues that organisations are subject to a range of forces – coercive, mimetic and normative – that require them to develop an HRM approach that is perceived to be legitimate to influential stakeholders within each context. According to Paauwe and Boselie (2003) coercive mechanisms include the influence of trade unions, works councils, employment legislation and the government; mimetic mechanisms refer to the benchmarking and imitation of strategies and practices of successful competitors; and normative mechanisms include the impact of professional bodies and employers associations, the impact of business schools, consultancies and pressure groups and the expectations of public opinion. Organisations need to achieve legitimacy within the environment in which they operate, since they have to work with other bodies – employees, trade unions, governments, shareholders, financial institutions and other influential stakeholders – who can refuse or restrict access to necessary resources (Deephouse, 1999). As these institutional bodies and their views of what is legitimate vary from country to country, so MNCs have to adapt their HRM policies in each location (Farndale et al., 2008).

From a pragmatic perspective, all this means is that the types of organisations that are dominant, the shape of customer–supplier relationships, and the work systems and employment practices differ significantly from society to society despite the pressures of globalisation. The institutions are likely to shape the social construction of any organisation within the society. Thus, the specific patterns of ownership within a society, general and vocational education systems, the way labour markets work, employment legislation and the industrial relations system will all impact on the way that HRM can be conducted in particular states (Brewster, 2004).

Box 2.3   Variety of contexts

> Clearly, for an internationally operating organisation, it does not make much sense
> to have the same HRM policies all over the world. In Uganda, where most of the
> working population is unemployed, and Denmark, where employers have a short-
> age of labour; in Japan, where women are generally expected to leave the work-
> force on marriage and Canada, where women expect a lifetime career; in Finland
> where everybody is well-educated, and Columbia, where only a minority are; and
> in the United States where a highly educated elite and functionally non-literate
> millions live side by side. Such organisations would, properly, not dream of pay-
> ing the same salaries in Germany and in Thailand; or to have the same number of
> working hours in France and in Korea.

Through increasingly reflecting on the importance of institutional differences in comparative HRM (Boxall, 1995) it becomes more evident that HRM is a function of the country's particular institutional arrangements – known as the 'societal effect' (Maurice et al., 1986). As with the culture effects, there seems to be a kind of societal recipe that it is possible to go against or even ignore, but only at some cost. Most people and the majority of organisations, in general, do not do so.

Combining the two Whilst proponents of these two streams of thought often give no more than a passing nod to the others' viewpoint, it seems that neither an exclusively culturalist nor an exclusively institutional approach are satisfactory accounts. Many of the 'culturalist' writers treat institutions as being key artefacts of culture reflecting deep underlying variations in the values that they see between societies and likewise many 'institutionalist' writers include culture as one of the institutional elements explaining differences. These two forms of theoretical explanation are not necessarily mutually exclusive. Organisations are not fully rational. Issues of history and personality play a great part. In addition, just as individual behaviour and social structure are reciprocally constituted, so too are cultures and institutions. Thus, institutions cannot survive without legitimacy, but individual perspectives are partially created and sustained by their institutional context. Arguably, the two schools of thought examine and explain the same factors from different points of view (Brewster, 2004; Sorge, 2004), encouraging one to draw the conclusion that 'both institutional and cultural dimensions ... have an important impact on HRM practices in different countries' (Romani, 2004: 163).

Static vs. dynamic

Comparing HRM in different contexts inevitably leads to questions about developments over time and changes in the actual similarities and differences. Given the underlying dynamic developments of the current political, economic and social systems across the globe, static 'snapshot' analyses using cross–sectional designs do have some value, but leave many questions unanswered. While it is important to analyse the status quo, it is of equal importance to be able to estimate future developments in the light of past events and processes. For example, comparing the relative size of HRM departments at the country level and at a given point in time provides valuable information about the relative position of each country. However, further information about the development path through observing changes over time would help answer questions such as: is this an increase compared to a decade ago? Do we see a pendulum swing in all countries? Do countries move in the same direction? Has there been a general increase or decrease of the relative size of HR departments over time?

From a comparative HRM angle, this raises the question of convergence and, by implication, divergence and stasis. The concept of convergence is worth examining. The meaning most commonly assumed in the literature (even if it is rarely stated explicitly) is movement towards greater similarity. At the comparative national level of HRM this would mean countries becoming more like each other in the way that they manage their human resources. Much of the evidence that is adduced for this, however (found in the literature cited above), comes from research conducted either at a single point in time, or from the identification of similar trends across countries. Logically, these research study assumptions and designs cannot prove movement towards greater similarity. An attempt has been made, therefore, to disaggregate the notion of convergence in comparative HRM so that we can consider three forms of convergence (Mayrhofer et al., 2002). These forms are:

- directional convergence, in which the trends go in the same direction but commence from different starting points and may mean that countries remain parallel, staying in the same relationship to each other, or even diverging somewhat;
- final convergence, where the practice of HRM in these countries becomes more similar even though that might, on occasion, mean that different countries are heading in different directions; and
- majority convergence where organisations within one country become more alike, again perhaps by some heading in opposite directions to others.

Box 2.4   Stop and reflect

In which areas of HRM would you expect final convergence, i.e. HRM practices moving toward a common ground? And where would you assume directional convergence, i.e. practices moving into the same direction without necessarily coming closer together or further apart? Why?

The convergence debate in HRM is dominated by two major issues: first, and linked with the best practice vs. best fit debate, there is the question of whether a more or less common global model of HRM is emerging; second, within global regions or selected groups of countries, do we see convergence, divergence or stasis when we follow the development of HRM in these countries over time.

Regarding the emergence of a global model of HRM, an assumption frequently made is that there is an optimal set of strategies, decisions and practices at any specific time (Kostova and Roth, 2002) and that global markets promote greater homogenisation as companies compete with similar products and under a similar rate of technological change (Duysters and Hagedoorn, 2001). Hence, it is argued, HRM practices, especially through MNCs and their global as well as local effects, are likely to converge towards an emerging global paradigm, or, perhaps, towards the US model that is often held up as an example of the success of lightly regulated markets (Smith and Meiksins, 1995). The best practice debate and thinking around high–performance work systems (US Department of Labor, 1993), follows this route and makes the built–in normative claim that these practices should be a universal benchmark.

The empirical evidence for a one–world model is certainly mixed. While undoubtedly MNCs have a strong influence on local HRM practices and policies with their sophisticated policies and practices rolled out internationally and policed by a central HRM function, it also is quite clear that there are no simple homogenising effects at work. Rather, HRM practices and policies are reshaped, resisted and redeployed by the socially embedded processes of the host locale, emphasising country–level distinctiveness (Comaroff and Comaroff, 2001; D'Aunno et al., 2000; Ferner, 1997; Ferner and Quintanilla, 1998). In this sense, national differences are strong, robust and deeply embedded and are unlikely to change significantly. Recent research on the role of MNCs, using the large–scale Cranet database rather than case studies, argues that MNCs do indeed manage their people differently from indigenous companies and that this applies to indigenous MNCs as well as foreign ones: but, overall, country of location rather than country of origin is still the most convincing explanation of differences in HRM (Farndale et al., 2008). The role of MNCs seems to be a mixture of bringing in new practices, adapting to local ones and developing hybrid forms.

In terms of converging or diverging developments over time within a group of countries or a region, the best evidence comes from the European section of the longitudinal set of Cranet studies. Cranet shows conclusively that there are significant differences between the countries in all major functional areas of HRM (Brewster et al., 2004). What is widespread or standard practice in one country plays much less of a role in others. More significantly in relation to the convergence/divergence debates, HRM in these countries tends not to change very much and countries tend to sustain their relative positions. For example, the presence of HRM at Board level (or equivalent) changes very little and the countries retain their positions, with the single exception of a clear trend in Germany towards more organisations having an HR Director appointed to the

Board. To take a completely different example; the number of companies with more than 10 per cent of their workforce on part–time contracts shows more fluctuation, but less sign of any overall pattern or trend (Tregaskis and Brewster, 2006).

These examples could be multiplied, but overall there are consistent developments towards directional convergence in Europe to be found in three areas of HRM configuration (the strategic potential of the HRM department; the assignment of HRM responsibilities to line managers; and HRM professionalisation) and four areas of HRM practices (the increasing use of more sophisticated practices in recruitment and selection; increased individualisation of employee relations; increased information to employees; and increased use of contingent compensation systems). These common trends are limited: the ratio of HRM specialists to the rest of the organisation, or the size of the HRM department, varies considerably and mainly with country, but it also differs according to the size of the organisation (Brewster et al., 2006) but overall it has no clearly discernible direction. Neither does training and development reveal much clarity regarding its pathway, so although it is given high priority in many countries it nonetheless seems to be the first area selected for cutbacks whenever finances become tight.

In terms of final convergence, however, the overall evidence, for all of the HRM practices analysed, is unequivocal: there is no trend towards final convergence. Countries continue to manage their people in markedly different ways. Despite the similarities in trends, there is very little evidence of globalisation of HRM. 'None of the HR practices converge' (Mayrhofer et al., 2004: 434).

It is clearly evident therefore that we need a more nuanced view and in–depth understanding of convergence in HRM policies and practices than has been apparent hitherto. Whilst, on the basis of the available evidence, things appear to change slowly in HRM, there does seem to be at least some clear indication of directional convergence in a few areas. However, the country recipes remain powerful. HRM varies by country, sector and size of organisation; by subjects within the generic topic of HRM; and by the nature of the organisation, for example, life–stage, governance or market. Further, we should distinguish the policy intentions of those at the top of organisations from practice on the ground. Overall, then, the evidence overwhelmingly supports the continuing importance of an internationally comparative dimension of HRM.

4 Differences in HRM practice

Context–related differences in HRM abound, as we have noted above. Reasons of space mean that it is impossible here to examine all the international variations in HRM so this section provides three typical examples, one of which relates to the more strategic aspects of HRM, the representation of HRM in formal top decision–making bodies and the role of line managers in HRM, and another two relating to HRM practices, flexible working patterns and communications.

HRM department and role of line managers

The role of the HRM function varies considerably across countries. Most commentators argue that HRM has become more important to organisations in the last two decades. Since human resources and the knowledge and skills they incorporate are difficult to replicate, they offer organisations the opportunity of obtaining a sustained competitive advantage, at a time when traditional ways of obtaining competitive advantage become ever easier to copy (Collins and Clark, 2003). Some experts have argued that we should expect to see the influence of the human resource function on corporate decision increasing over time (e.g. Pfeffer, 1998; Ulrich and Brockbank, 2005). Arguably, where the human resource function is represented at the key decision making forums of the organisation, and becomes closely involved in strategic decision-making, awareness of the problems or opportunities that effective HRM might provide will be raised and the decision making in increasingly knowledge-reliant organisations consequently will be improved.

One perceptive commentator on HRM made the point some time ago that the rhetoric of integration of the HR specialist function at Board level and its position of influence has outpaced the reality (Legge, 1995). In terms of membership of the Board, the Cranet research data show considerable stability over time set alongside large variation between countries (Brewster et al., 1997; Mayrhofer and Brewster, 2005; see also Cranet, 2006). France, Spain, Sweden and Japan, for example, consistently report seven or eight out of ten organisations having an HR director on the main decision–making body of the organisation (the Board in shareholder companies). In the Central and Eastern European countries and Israel the figures are much lower. Many other European countries, including the UK and Germany, and Australia, show a little less than half of the organisations with HRM departments being directly represented at the top decision–making level. In the Netherlands and Germany employees have rights to have representatives at the supervisory Board level: presumably the employee representatives ensure that the HRM implications of corporate strategy decisions are taken into account. Germany is a particularly interesting case, as it is one of the few countries where HRM representation on the Board has increased significantly over the rounds of the study, and at a time that human resources have become more critical for organisations and the function itself has become less administrative in focus. In terms of HRM influence on the corporate strategy, there is more uniformity: in most countries the personnel departments are involved from the outset in strategy formulation in approximately half of the organisations.

What about the size of the HRM department (or, more precisely, its ratio to the rest of the organisation)? Against the backdrop of organisations becoming smaller over a decade of downsizing, the introduction of new technology leading to Human Resource

Information Systems (HRIS) or electronically enabled HRM (e–HRM), the pressure on 'overhead' departments to prove themselves, and line management taking over some HRM tasks, one would expect HRM departments to have become smaller. However, its size relative to the total organisation hardly changed at all during 1990s and early 2000s (Brewster et al., 2006).

The role of line managers has been seen as a touchstone for HRM (Storey, 2001). The notion is that people can only be managed cost–effectively and well when their immediate superiors have a substantial responsibility for that management. In Europe the trend during the 1990s was to give line managers more responsibility for the management of their staff and to reduce the extent to which HRM departments control or restrict line management autonomy in this area (Brewster et al., 1997) but this trend has since reversed (Mayrhofer and Brewster, 2005). Seemingly regardless of the overall trend, countries tend to hold their positions relative to each other. On a range of personnel issues, it is the Italians who are most likely to lodge responsibility with the personnel department; the British come next. This stands in sharp contrast to the Danes, for example, who, on all issues, tend to give much greater responsibility to line managers. These country differences in responsibility for HRM persist over time.

Flexible working practices

Flexibility in labour patterns is now widely accepted as a critical issue in HRM, although it is bedevilled with problems of terminology: what is called 'flexibility' amongst European employers and academics is known as 'atypical working' by the European Commission, 'vulnerable work' amongst trade unionists and 'contingent working' in the USA. Research conducted by the Cranet network, comparing organisations at national level across Europe (Tregaskis and Brewster, 2006) is consistent with the national labour market statistics (European Commission Eurostat, 2008) and workplace level data (Kersley et al., 2006) in showing extensive use of flexible working across Europe. Furthermore, some of these forms of flexibility – temporary employment and self–employment – are more widespread in Europe than in the US. In part-time work the USA has fallen behind the European Union since the mid-1990s to about a median position on a ranking with the European countries. Japan has a different pattern of flexible working to these two continents, with considerable part–time and temporary working (Buddelmeyer et al., 2005).

The Cranet data shows that despite differences within countries and between sectors, particularly, flexible working practices are growing in both extent and coverage almost everywhere. This is so in nearly all countries in Europe, in Japan and Australasia, in all sectors, in organisations both large and small, and whatever the form or origin of ownership. 'Atypical' work patterns or contracts, such as temporary, casual, fixed–term, home–based and annual hours contracts, are spreading, despite differing legal, cultural and labour traditions.

However, organisations where these forms of flexibility cover the majority of their workers continue to be in a clear minority. Furthermore, the increase in the use of flexible contracts tends to be significantly higher among those organisations already making comparatively high use of such contracts. The result is to confirm patterns of difference: countries like the Netherlands and the UK with a substantial proportion of part–time contracts amongst their workforce (more than 25 per cent) tend to increase usage; countries with very few part–timers continue to have very few. And the same applies to the other forms of flexible working. Between countries, there are clear preferences for different kinds of flexibility. No country or organisation makes extensive use of the full range of flexible working patterns and contracts. Thus, in Spain there is a high level of short–term employment with low levels of part–time work. Countries such as Austria, the Netherlands, Sweden and the UK have a third or more of organisations with over 5 per cent of the workforce on temporary contracts. Most of the other countries in Europe have far fewer. By contrast, the Netherlands, Sweden and the UK all have more than a quarter of their working population employed in part–time jobs. These differences correlate with differences in the institutional environment of these countries. Similarly, analyses of the extent of flexible working in Japan need to take into account the Japanese practice of generally restricting employment to women after they are married. Overall, although the trends are similar, there are still varied situations, assumptions and practices occurring in the different countries. Flexibility is dependent upon a complex, interlocking web of national culture, history, institutions, trade union approaches and strength, governmental policies and practices (including legislation) and managerial tradition (Tregaskis and Brewster, 2006).

Communications

Effective communication is a requirement for all organisations and is vital to those looking for commitment from workers to the objectives of the enterprise. Yet there is less clarity about the most effective form and content of communication for these purposes and whether it varies by country. Much of the literature associates the concept of HRM with the individualisation of communication and a move away from, or even antagonism towards, communication and consultation which is collective and particularly that which is trade–union based. This non–union implication sits uneasily with the history and circumstances of not just Europe but of a number of other countries around the world. Trade unionism remains widespread and important in places like Japan and Korea for example which have extensive, legally backed, systems of employee communication. In Europe, consultation with employees is required by law. These arrangements give considerable (legally backed) power to the employee representatives and, unlike consultation in the USA for example, they tend to supplement rather than supplant the union position (Brewster et al., 2007a, 2007b). In relatively highly unionised countries it is unsurprising that many of the representatives of the workforce are, in practice, trade union officials (for example, four–fifths of them are in Germany). The balance between individual and collective communication is a matter for empirical investigation.

Research shows that there have been increases in all forms of communication: through representative bodies (trade unions or works councils), as well as through direct verbal and written communication (Brewster et al., 2004). The latter two channels have expanded considerably.

When upward communication is examined, the two most common means, by a considerable margin, are through immediate line management and through the trade union or works council channel. The evidence tends to support the analyses of those researchers (Hollingsworth and Boyer, 1997) who focus on the presence or absence within countries of communitarian infrastructures that manifest themselves in the form of strong social bonds, trust, reciprocity and cooperation among economic actors. There are clear differences between countries, with more communication being apparent in, broadly, the richer countries and less in, for example, the southern European countries. In addition, increases in communication, both up and down, appear to be larger in the countries where most communication goes on (Mayrhofer et al., 2000).

Furthermore, access to financial and strategic information is clearly hierarchical: if you are in a higher position in the organisation you are more likely to be briefed regularly about the strategy or the financial performance of the organisation. While the hierarchy still persists, the information gap appears to have narrowed during the 1990s as an increasing number of organisations make sure that their administrative employees are informed about the organisation's plans and performance. Unionised organisations are more likely than non–union ones to provide such information. There are noticeable differences in average 'slopes' in the distribution of this information: lower level employees in the Nordic countries, for example, receive considerably more information than those working elsewhere.

5 Conclusions: future issues in comparative HRM

Comparative HRM exposes significant differences in the way the concept of HRM is understood, managed and implemented in different countries. For researchers and commentators and for internationally operating organisations this raises crucial academic and practical issues.

Theoretical issues

In many areas of comparative HRM we lack adequate theory to explain the complexity of the differences between the meaning, policies and practices of HRM in different countries. For the future, three groups of theories seem especially fruitful for meaningful contributions to knowledge on IHRM.

First there is a group of theories focusing on differences. The theoretical arguments run along the broad line of identifying crucial differences occurring at the macro-level that lead to distinct differences at the level of organisations or individual behaviour. Examples include concepts such as varieties of capitalism (Hall and Soskice, 2001), national business systems (Whitley, 1999) or culture theories (House et al., 2004; Schwartz, 2004). Second, there is theoretical thinking that predicts that the strong logic of global capitalism is ultimately leading to similar approaches at the organisational level. Rational choice models (for their application to HRM see, for example, Matiaske, 2004) are a major example of this type of argument. Third, and in a somewhat middle-position, is the world polity approach (e.g. Meyer et al., 1997). It argues that there is an ongoing worldwide replacement of traditional particularistic schemes through *universal* standards associated with modernity. Global myths such as rationality or equality exist that exert considerable influence on all kinds of actors, be it individual or collective, economic or political. However, these global myths do not lead to uniformity. On the contrary, due to specific local conditions there is a great variety of difference in how these global myths are actually realised. All three groups of theories may contribute towards fruitful answers to core questions of comparative HRM such as reasons for contextual differences, mechanisms for translating contextual conditions into organisational and individual action or the long-term development of country differences and their effects on HRM.

Empirical issues

Empirically, a rich, if somewhat daunting, empirical research agenda exists since there are many countries in the world about which we still have little information; and in many cases the information we have is stereotyped, inadequate or non-comparable. At this point in our knowledge we still need the deep, but narrow, understanding of meaning and process that can be provided by detailed comparative case studies; the wide, but shallow, evidential base that large-scale surveys can bring; and the further exploration of secondary data provided by governments and international organisations. And if our evidence about and understanding of national differences remains a research gap, there is a research chasm in our knowledge of developments in HRM over time that can only be filled by longitudinal research. Comparative HRM research is both more complex and more difficult than research that is based in one country or focuses solely on the practices of MNCs. Both more complex and difficult but equally exciting and informative (Mayrhofer and Brewster, forthcoming); as the world becomes more global, so must our research.

Practical issues

For HRM practice, the task is daunting: if an organisation covers more than just a few countries even the experts at the centre cannot know the details of HRM expectations and common practice in each local context. They are at the mercy of the information they obtain from their expatriate managers and the (usually local) HRM practitioners in each country – and they may have different agendas and understandings. The fact that most companies manage to cope with this complexity at all is perhaps more noteworthy than are the times they may get it wrong. Comparative HRM can contribute to better HRM practice by providing and improving the information base HRM practitioners rely on when deciding on concrete HRM practices as well as strategic issues. Working together with practitioners in organisations operating across national and cultural borders as well as with international professional HRM organisations increases the potential impact of comparative HRM as it leads research and theory building towards practically relevant issues, especially when new phenomena come up that are first detected by people involved in HRM practice rather than by academia.

Concluding remark

As we pointed out at the beginning of this chapter, HRM differences between countries should not be read as implying that some countries have not yet 'caught up': 'different' does not mean 'worse'. That means that IHRM has an additional layer of complexity. The academic study may be just catching up but this has always been a problem for MNCs. But it also provides a rich opportunity to learn. The more we know about HRM in other countries, the way it is conceived, what good practice there implies, and how it is conducted, the more we can learn. That is one of the major challenges for students of HRM today and an increasingly pertinent issue for students of IHRM.

Discussion questions

1 Discuss the pros and cons of a 'best practice' type of HRM rolled out in a globally operating company. Focus specifically on the consequences for employees and organisational performance.

2 What do you regard as the most pressing practical questions comparative HRM should tackle? Why do you see them as the most urgent?

3 Give one example each for a cultural and an institutional determinant of HRM practice and discuss how HRM practitioners are restricted by these factors in their practical action.

4 Discuss potential tensions between taking into account cultural and institutional drivers supporting differentiation in HRM and standardisation tendencies leading to integration in the area of recruitment and of compensation. How would you handle these tensions?

5 What five core competencies do you see as essential for an HRM practitioner working in a globally operating company that is sensitive to various contexts? Why? How could you train and develop these competencies?

Flextronics University – qualifying line managers for leadership and HR tasks

Founded in 1969 and headquartered in Singapore, Flextronics is a leading Electronic Manufacturing Services (EMS) provider operating in 30 countries on three continents with a total workforce of about 162,000 employees and revenues of US$ 27.6 billion in 2008. The majority of its manufacturing capacity is located in low-cost regions such as Brazil, China, Hungary, India, Malaysia, Mexico, Poland and Ukraine. It offers the broadest worldwide EMS capabilities, from design resources to end-to-end vertically integrated global supply chain services. Flextronics operates in seven distinct markets: infrastructure, e.g. networking equipment; mobile communication devices; computing, e.g. handheld computers; consumer digital devices such as cameras; industrial, semiconductor and white goods, e.g. plastics injection moulding; automotive, aerospace and marine, e.g. bar code readers; and medical devices which includes, among others, telemedicine devices. Flextronics designs, builds and ships complete packaged products for its Original Equipment Manufacturing (OEM) customers such as Microsoft for consumer electronics products such as the X-box, Hewlett Packard for its inkjet printers and storage devices, or Sony–Ericsson for cellular phones, and provides after-market and field services to support customer end-to-end supply chain requirements.

In early 2000, Flextronics Central and Eastern European (CEE) operations were head-quartered in Vienna, Austria, and covered primarily Austria and Hungary, with plans to expand into the Ukraine. The Austrian sites consisted of an experienced workforce and had well-functioning work routines. The newly established Hungarian plants, by contrast, were characterised by typical start-up problems such as insufficiently experienced personnel, high fluctuation and, because of a highly volatile sales market, significant needs to adapt production capacity to consumer demand. As part of the response to this situation, Peter Baumgartner, then CEE Executive HR director, lobbied internally for a Flextronics Academy in the CEE region and finally implemented it. As an effort to increase qualifications of Flextronics CEE employees, it covered both technical qualifications as well as soft skills. Together with an external consultancy, Flextronics also developed a high-potential programme for a future cadre of line managers that specifically was designed to offer the individuals selected for the programme with a broad range of activities and equip them with leadership and HRM qualifications. In the mixed groups from different countries, cultural specifics soon turned out to be important elements for the long-term success of this programme. For example, Hungarian participants were much less likely to fully complete the programme or stay with Flextronics for some time after the end of the programme. Due to a greater readiness to 'jump ship' even in the light of only minimal pay increases, Flextronics often was faced with a higher rate of fluctuation compared to Austrian employees and sunk costs when individuals left the company and joined a competitor or changed industry. Likewise, learning and communication styles were quite different between Hungarian and Austrian participants. For example, in terms of directness and interpersonal distance, typical differences between Austria and Hungary occur with Austrians being more direct and more concerned with formal and distant behaviour.

At the overall Flextronics level, training of line managers was strongly influenced by the introduction of the corporate-wide Flextronics University. Originally, this programme started as a web-based learning platform and knowledge-management tool for the US and Mexican operations. As e-learning got more and more popular, the idea to use this platform throughout the corporation took hold. The goal was to use the 'collective intelligence' of a global corporation in the most effective way. However, in practice the realisation of this idea turned out to be much more time-consuming than anticipated. It took off only after it was integrated with a second initiative within Flextronics: the Flex Factory. After a decade of rapid growth in the 1990s with a substantial number of acquisitions, factories within Flextronics varied widely in terms of production processes, quality standards and service orientation. After increasing customer complaints about Flextronics being not reliable enough, an initiative to create 'ONE Flextronics' started. It was aiming at standardising production relevant processes to make the 'ONE Flextronics' idea effective in practice and visible to customers, suppliers and employees. Globally, various teams collected worldwide best practice ideas in the areas of SixSigma, quality and material management, production, programme management, engineering, finances and training. Soon it became obvious that for sharing these ideas and for training individuals along these lines, a common platform was needed.

This led to a new drive for the Flex University idea and to an integration of both Flex University and Flex Factory. Flex University offered the possibility to have immediate and global access to standardised training content, technical as well as leadership and HRM related, which can be tailored to the needs of employees in general and line managers in particular. It offered a tailored training administration which included supervisors as well as users and a learning management system that allowed the definition of specific training packages.

In the setting of a globally operating company with employees coming from 30 countries, a number of issues emerged due to cultural idiosyncrasies. For example, handing out certificates on the basis of a successfully accomplished training module led to quite different reactions. Whereas in Eastern European countries as well as in the US certificates are generally welcomed and regarded as a sign for one's achievement, many Western Europeans are more cautious. They see certificates not primarily as a positive feedback, but as an appraisal with the danger of being 'boxed in'. Employees from these countries prefer a sober, stripped down feedback without too many frills seen as artificial. Although Flex University worked with such certificates, the varying degree of acceptance of such certificates across employees from different countries illustrated the emerging difficulties. In a similar vein, controlling learning progress in such a system can be interpreted as being interested in a person's development and as a valuable source for feedback. At the same time, especially in Western Europe this was also regarded as a means of control, observation and surveillance that employees tend to see in a negative light.

Case questions

1. What challenges were faced by Flextronics University?
2. Assess the achievements and future development needs of Flextronics University.
3. In what other ways might global and local training and development programmes have been delivered by Flextronics?
4. Suggest three alternative training solutions for Flextronics situated in specific cultural contexts. These may be countries mentioned in the case study or others that you can assume have a Flextronics workforce.

Further reading

Basics of comparative management

Warner, M. (ed.) (2004) *Comparative Management*. London: Routledge.

An edited volume offering access to the material that has shaped this field to date. It includes articles on principles and methods of comparative management, and a wide range of country-based studies, covering North America, Europe, Asia and the developing world. The topics range from leadership to HRM and contributions written by scholars from a great number of countries discuss the impact of cultural, institutional and societal variables across countries.

Comparative HRM

- Boxall, P. (1995) 'Building the theory of comparative HRM', *Human Resource Management Journal*, 5(5): 5–17.

This article outlines the basic requirements for building a theory of comparative HRM. It also argues that it is important to identify dominant models of HRM in each country, recognising that there is significant variation both within and between nations. The article points towards the array of stakeholders that play a role when explaining HRM. While management in firms plays a critical role in shaping models of HRM, analyses must also take account of the impact of other actors such as state and labour.

- Brewster, C. (1995) 'Towards a "European" Model of Human Resource Management', *Journal of International Business Studies*, 26(1): 1–21.

This paper examines the concept of HRM from a European perspective and arguably is the starting point for an extensive discussion about regional models of HRM deviating from the 'generic' models provided by US authors. It builds on the criticism related to the US bias and goes beyond general critiques by addressing the core of the concept and suggesting a more internationally applicable model. Drawing on data collected in Europe, the paper analyses major characteristics of European HRM.

- Brewster, C., Mayrhofer, W. and Morley, M. (eds) (2004) *Human Resource Management in Europe. Evidence of convergence?* Oxford: Elsevier/Butterworth–Heinemann.

An edited book that enables readers to become 'fluent' in the many various environments, approaches and practices that exist across Europe for managing human resources. It employs comprehensive comparable representative data collected longitudinally during the last decade through Cranet. It deals with concepts and theoretical issues, trends in relation to these issues, makes comparisons between individual countries, and gives summaries and conclusions on the issue of convergence and divergence.

- Budhwar, P. S. (ed.) (2004) *Managing Human Resources in Asia–Pacific.* London: Routledge.

This edited volume presents an HRM scenario in a number of South–East Asian and Pacific Rim countries and highlights the growth of the personnel/HRM function in these countries, their dominant HRM system(s), along with the influence of different factors on their HRM and the challenges faced by HR functions in these nations.

- Budhwar, P. S. and Mellahi, K. (eds) (2006) *Managing Human Resources in the Middle–East.* London: Routledge.

The edited volume presents the HRM scenario in a number of countries in the Middle East, highlighting rapid developments in the fields of HRM and International HRM (IHRM) and giving the reader an understanding of the dynamics of HRM in the area. The text moves from a general overview of HRM in the Middle-East to an exploration of the current status, role and strategic importance of the HR function in a wide range of country-specific chapters, before highlighting the emerging HRM models and future challenges for research, policy and practice.

- Kamoche, K., Debrah, Y., Horwitz, F. and Muuka, G. N. (eds) (2003) *Managing Human Resources in Africa.* London: Routledge.

This edited volume looks at the HRM challenges in countries right across Africa, examining the impact of contextual factors on the development of HRM practices in Africa. Taking a regional approach to the subject, and featuring chapters on South Africa, Botswana, Zambia, Mauritius, Tanzania, Kenya, Ethiopia, Ghana, Ivory Coast, Tunisia and Libya, this comprehensive study offers a fresh perspective on a growing subject area that shows readers not only how to develop techniques and practices that reflect the real needs of workers in Africa, but also provides a more balanced analysis of the area than they might be used to.

- Mayrhofer, W. and Brewster, C. (2005) 'European human resource management: researching developments over time', *Management Revue*, 16(1): 36–62.
This paper uses insights and data gained from 15 years of studying HRM developments in Europe to explore the meanings of convergence and divergence in HRM. Conceptually, the paper puts forward a more nuanced view of the notions of convergence and divergence. Empirically, it gives evidence of directional convergence, but little evidence of final convergence: whilst there are trends which point in similar directions, national differences remain a key factor in HRM.

Internet resources

1 www.cranet.org: Cranet, a global academic network studying the development of HRM in more than 40 countries worldwide since 1990; contains information about the network as well as a list of publications.

2 www.epp.eurostat.ec.europa.eu: Eurostat, the statistical arm of the European Union (EU), offers a wealth of data about various aspects relevant for HRM such as labour market data, living conditions or population, information about economic data in general, e.g. gross domestic product (GDP) per capita or GDP growth as well as a number of EU policy indicators.

3 www.ilo.org: The International Labour Organisation (ILO), a tripartite UN agency that brings together governments, employers and workers of its member states in common action to promote decent work throughout the world. Provides a number of statistics, e.g. official core labour statistics and estimates for over 200 countries since 1969, and databases such as Labordoc which contains references to a wide range of print and electronic publications, including journal articles, from countries around the world, on all aspects of work.

4 www.worldvaluessurvey.com: World Values Survey investigating values and cultural changes in societies all over the world; allows access to the complete Values Studies results online and tailored analyses.

Self-assessment questions

Indicative answers to these questions can be found on the companion website at www.sagepub.co.uk/harzing3e.

1   A multinational corporation (MNC) is planning to implement a common set of performance management practices throughout its global subsidiaries. What advice would you offer to the HRM director of the firm in relation to this plan and why?

2   Show how the local environment influences a firm's approach to flexible working practices, taking the example of a country you know.

3   What would be the best way for multinational companies, operating across borders, to ensure that their Human Resource policies were applied equitably throughout the organisation in order to generate company–wide thinking?

4   Compare and contrast the role of HRM departments in your country and one other you know about, critically appraising the impact on firm competitiveness.

5   Evaluate whether cross–cultural differences in HR practices are increasing or decreasing and why. You may want to use examples to illustrate your argument.

Notes

Much of the evidence reported in this chapter is taken from Carnet. The authors acknowledge the work of colleagues in the network in collecting the data and discussing the issues and the role of the Cranfield School of Management in the UK in co-ordinating the network.

References

Ajiferuke, M. and Boddewyn, J. (1970) '"Culture" and other explanatory variables in comparative management studies', *Academy of Management Journal,* 13: 153–163.

Almond, P., Edwards, T. and Clark, I. (2003) 'Multinationals and changing national business systems in Europe: towards the 'shareholder value' model?', *Industrial Relations Journal,* 34(5): 430–445.

Amable, B. (2003) *The Diversity of Modern Capitalism.* Oxford: Oxford University Press.

Ashkenas, R., Ulrich, D., Jick, T. and Kerr, S. (1995) *The Boundaryless Organization. Breaking the Chains of Organizational Structure.* San Francisco: Jossey-Bass.

Becker, B., Huselid, M., Pickus, P. and Spratt, M. (1997) 'HR as a source of shareholder value: research and recommendations', *Human Resource Management Journal,* 36(1): 39–47.

Boxall, P. (1993) 'The significance of human resource management: a reconsideration of the evidence', *International Journal of Human Resource Management,* 4(3): 645–64.

Boxall, P. (1995) 'Building the theory of comparative HRM', *Human Resource Management Journal,* 5(5): 5–17.

Brewster, C. (1999) 'Strategic Human Resource Management: the value of different paradigms', *Management International Review,* 39(9): 45–64.

Brewster, C. (2004) 'European perspectives on human resource management', *Human Resource Management Review,* 14(4): 365–82.

Brewster, C., Brookes, M., Croucher, R. and Wood, G. (2007a)' 'Collective and individual voice: convergence in Europe?', *International Journal of Human Resource Management,* 18 (7): 1246–62.

Brewster, C., Larsen, H.H. and Mayrhofer, W. (1997) 'Integration and assignment: a paradox in Human Resource Management', *Journal of International Management,* 3(1): 1–23.

Brewster, C., Mayrhofer, W., and Morley, M. (eds) (2000) *New Challenges in European Human Resource Management.* London: Macmillan.

Brewster, C., Mayrhofer, W. and Morley, M. (eds) (2004) *Human Resource Management in Europe. Evidence of convergence?* Oxford: Elsevier/Butterworth-Heinemann.

Brewster, C., Sparrow, P. and Vernon, G. (2007c) *International Human Resource Management,* 2nd edn. London: Chartered Institute of Personnel and Development.

Brewster, C., Wood, G. and Brookes, M. (2008) Similarity, isomorphism or duality: recent survey evidence on the HRM policies of multinational corporations', *British Journal of Management,* 19 (4): 320–42.

Brewster, C., Wood, G., Brookes, M. and van Ommeren, J. (2006) 'What determines the size of the HR Function? A cross-national analysis', *Human Resource Management,* 45(1): 3–21.

Brewster, C., Wood., G., Croucher, R. and Brookes, M. (2007b) 'Are works councils and joint consultative committees a threat to trade unions? A comparative analysis', *Economic and Industrial Democracy,* 28 (1): 53–81.

Brunstein, I. (ed.) (1995) *Human Resource Management in Western Europe.* Berlin: de Gruyter.

Buddelmeyer, H., Mourre, G. and Ward-Warmedinger, M.E. (2005) 'Part–Time Work in EU Countries: Labour Market Mobility, Entry and Exit', *IZA Discussion Paper No. 1550.*

Budhwar, P. S. (ed.) (2004) *Managing Human Resources in Asia-Pacific.* London: Routledge.

Budhwar, P. S. and Debrah, Y. A. (eds) (2001) *Human Resource Management in Developing Countries.* London: Routledge.

Collins, C. J. and Clark, K.D. (2003) 'Strategic human resource practices, top management team social networkers, and firm performance: the role of human resource practices in creating organizational competitive advantage', *Academy of Management Journal,* 46(6): 740–51.

Comaroff, J. and Comaroff, J. (2001) 'Millenial capitalism: first thoughts on a second coming', in J. Comaroff and J. Comaroff (eds), *Millenial Capitalism and the Culture of Neoliberalism.* Durham: Duke University Press.

Cranet (2006) *Cranet Survey on Comparative Human Resource Management – International Executive Report 2005.* Cranfield, UK: Cranfield University.

D'Aunno, T., Succi, M. and Alexander, J. (2000) 'The role of institutional and market forces in divergent organisational change', *Administrative Science Quarterly,* 45: 679–703.

Deephouse, D. L. (1999) 'To be different, or to be the same? It's a question (and theory) of strategic balance', *Strategic Management Journal,* 20(2): 147–66.

DiMaggio, P. J. and Powell, W. W. (1983) 'The iron cage revisited: institutional isomorphism and collective rationality in organizational fields', *American Sociological Review,* 48: 147–60.

Dowling, P. J. (1999) 'Completing the puzzle: issues in the development of the field of international human resource management', *Management International Review,* 39(4): 27–43.

Dunning, J. H. (1997) *Alliance Capitalism and Global Business.* London: Routledge.

Duysters, G. and Hagedoorn, J. (2001) 'Do company strategies and structures converge in global markets? Evidence from the computer industry', *Journal of International Business Studies,* 32(2): 347–56.

Economist (2000) 'The world's view of multinationals', *The Economist,* 354 (29 January): 21–2.

European Commission Eurostat (2008) *Europe in Figures: Eurostat Yearbook 2008.* Luxembourg: Office for Official Publications of the European Communities.

Farndale, E., Brewster, C. and Poutsma, E. (2008) 'Co-ordinated vs liberal market HRM: the impact of institutionalisation on multinational firms', *International Journal of Human Resource Management,* 19 (11): 2004–23.

Ferner, A. (1997) 'Country of origin effects and HRM in multinational companies', *Human Resource Management Journal,* 7(1): 19–38.

Ferner, A. and Quintanilla, J. (1998) 'Multinationals, national business systems and HRM: the enduring influence of national identity or a process of "anglo-saxonisation"', *International Journal of Human Resource Management,* 9(4): 710–31.

Geppert, M., Williams, K. and Matten, D. (2003) 'The social construct of contextual rationalities in MNCs: and Anglo-German comparison of subsidiary choice', *Journal of Management Studies,* 40(3): 617–41.

Gooderham, P. N. and Nordhaug, O. (2003) *International Management. Cross-Boundary Challenges.* Oxford: Blackwell.

Gooderham, P. N., Nordhaug, O. and Ringdal, K. (1999) 'Institutional and rational determinants of organizational practices: human resource management in European firms', *Administrative Science Quaterly,* 44: 507–31.

Hall, P. A. and Soskice, D. (eds) (2001) *Varieties of Capitalism. The Institutional Foundations of Comparative Advantage.* Oxford: Oxford University Press.

Hamel, G. and Prahalad, C. K. (1986) 'Do you really have a global strategy?', *Harvard Business Review* (Jul): 139–48.

Harzing, A.-W. and Sorge, A. (2003) 'The relative impact of country of origin and universal contingencies on internationalization strategies and corporate control in multinational enterprises: worldwide and European perspectives', *Organization Studies,* 24(2): 187–214.

Harzing, A.-W. and van Ruysseveldt, J. (2004) *International Human Resource Management.* London: Sage.

Hofstede, G. (1980) *Culture's Consequences. International Differences in Work–Related Values.* Newbury Park: Sage Publications.

Hofstede, G. (2001) *Culture's Consequences: Comparing Values, Behaviors, Institutions and Organizations Across Nations.* London: Sage.

Hollingsworth, J. R. and Boyer, R. (1997) 'Coordination of economic actors and social systems of production', in J. R. Hollingsworth and R. Boyer (eds), *Contemporary Capitalism.* Cambridge: Cambridge University Press.

House, R. J., Hanges, P. J., Javidan, M., Dorfman, P. W. and Gupta, V. (eds) (2004) *Culture, Leadership, and Organizations: The GLOBE Study of 62 Societies.* Thousand Oaks, CA: Sage.

Hu, Y-S. (1992) 'Global or stateless corporations', *California Management Review,* 34(2): 107–126.

Huselid, M. A. (1995) 'The impact of human resource management practices on turnover, productivity, and corporate financial performance', *Academy of Management Journal,* 38(3): 635–72.

Jain, H., Lawler, J. and Morishima, M. (1998) 'Multinational corporations, human resource management and host-country nationals', *International Journal of Human Resource Management,* 9(4): 533–66.

Johnson, P., Wood, G. T., Brewster, C. and Brookes, M. (2009) 'The rise of post–bureaucracy: theorists' fancy or organizational praxis?', *International Sociology,* 24 (1): 37–61.

Kamoche, K., Debrah, Y., Horwitz, F. and Muuka, G. N. (eds) (2003) *Managing Human Resources in Africa.* London: Routledge.

Kersley, B., Alpin, C., Forth, J., Bryson, A., Bewley, H., Dix, G. and Oxenbridge, S. (2006) *Inside the Workplace: Findings from the 2004 Workplace Employment Relations Survey.* London: Routledge.

Kim, Y. and Gray, S. J. (2005) 'Strategic factors influencing international human resource management practices: an empirical study of Australian multinational corporations', *International Journal of Human Resource Management,* 16(5): 809–30.

Kostova, T. and Roth, K. (2002) 'Adoption of an organizational practice by subsidiaries of multinational cororations: institutional and relational effects', *Academy of Management Journal,* 45(1): 215–33.

Laurent, A. (1986) 'The cross-cultural puzzle of international human resource management', *Human Resource Management,* 25(1): 91–102.

Legge, K. (1995) 'HRM: rhetoric, reality and hidden agendas', in J. Storey (ed.), *Human Resource Management: A Critical Text.* pp. 33–59. London: Routledge.

Marsden, D. (1999) *A Theory of Employment Systems.* Oxford: Oxford University Press.

Matiaske, W. (2004) 'Pourquoi pas? Rational choice as a basic theory of HRM', *Management Revue,* 15(2): 249–63.

Maurice, M., Sellier, F. and Silvestre, J. (1986) *The Social Foundations of Industrial Power.* Cambridge, MA: MIT Press.

Mayrhofer, W. and Brewster, C. (2005) 'European human resource management: researching developments over time', *Management Revue,* 16(1): 36–62.

Mayrhofer, W. and Brewster, C. (forthcoming) 'Conducting international comparative research: managing international research networks', in C. Brewster and W. Mayrhofer (eds), *A Handbook of Research into Comparative Human Resource Management Practice.* Cheltenham: Edward Elgar.

Mayrhofer, W., Brewster, C. and Morley, M. (2000) 'Communication, consultation and the HRM debate', in C. Brewster, W. *Mayrhofer and M. Morley (eds), New Challenges for European Human Resource Management.* pp. 222–245. London: Macmillan.

Mayrhofer, W., Morley, M. and Brewster, C. (2004) 'Convergence, stasis, or divergence?', in C. Brewster, W. Mayrhofer and M. Morley (eds), *Human Resource Management in Europe. Evidence of Convergence?*pp. 417–36. London: Elsevier/Butterworth–Heinemann.

Mayrhofer, W., Müller–Camen, M., Ledolter, J., Strunk, G. and Erten, C. (2002) 'The diffusion of management concepts in Europe – conceptual considerations and longitudinal analysis', *Journal of Cross-Cultural Competence and Management,* 3: 315–49.

McDonough, T. (2003) 'What does long wave theory have to contribute to the debate on globalization', *Review of Radical Political Economics,* 35(3): 280–86.

Meyer, J. W., Boli, J., Thomas, G. M. and Ramirez, F. O. (1997) 'World society and the nation-state', *The American Journal of Sociology,* 103(1): 144–81.

Morley, M. (ed.) (2009) *Managing Human Resources in Central and Eastern Europe.* London: Routledge.

Ohmae, K. (1990) *The Borderless World.* New York: Harper Collins.

Ohmae, K. (1995) *The End of the Nation State: The Rise of Regional Economies.* New York: Free Press.

Paauwe, J. and Boselie, P. (2003) 'Challenging "strategic HRM" and the relevance of the institutional setting', *Human Resource Management Journal,* 13(3): 56–70.

Parker, B. (1998) *Globalization and Business Practice: Managing Across Boundaries.* London: Sage.

Pfeffer, J. (1998) *The Human Equation: Building Profits by Putting People First.* Harvard: Harvard Business School Press.

Poole, M. (1990) 'Human resource management in an international perspective', *International Journal of Human Resource Management,* 1(1): 1–15.

Powell, W. and DiMaggio, P. J. (eds) (1987) *The New Institutionalism in Organizational Analysis.* Chicago: University of Chicago Press.

Pudelko, M. (2000) *Das Personalmanagement in Deutschland, den USA und Japan.* Düsseldorf: Jörg Saborowski Verlag.

Pudelko, M. (2004) 'HRM in Japan and the West: what are the lessons to be learnt from each other?', *Asian Business and Management,* 3(3): 337–61.

Romani, L. (2004) 'Culture in management: the measurement of differences', in A.-W. Harzing and J. van Ruysseveldt (eds), *International Human Resource Management.* London: Sage.

Rosenzweig, P. M. and Nohria, N. (1994) 'Influences on human resource development practices in multinational corporations', *Journal of International Business Studies,* 25(1): 229–51.

Rugman, A. M. (2000) *The End of Globalisation: Why Global Strategy is a Myth and how to Profit from the Realities of Regional Markets.* London: Random House.

Scholz, C. and Böhm, H. (eds) (2008) *Human Resource Management in Europe: Comparative Analysis and Contextual Understanding.* London: Routledge.

Schuler, R., Jackson, S., Sparrow, P.S. and Poole, M. Series editors of a publication list *Global Human Resource Management,* published by Routledge (London).

Schwartz, S. H. (1992) 'Universals in the content and structure of values: theoretical advances and empirical tests in 20 countries', *Advances in Experimental Social Psychology,* 25: 1–65.

Schwartz, S. H. (2004) 'Mapping and interpreting cultural differences around the world', in H. Vinken, J. Soeters and P. Ester (eds), *Comparing Cultures, Dimensions of Culture in a Comparative Perspective.* pp. 43–73. Leiden: Brill.

Schwartz, S. H. (2010) 'Values: cultural and individual', in S. M. Breugelmans, A. Chasiotis and F. J. R. van de Vijver (eds), *Fundamental Questions in Cross-cultural Psychology.* Cambridge: Cambridge University Press.

Sera, K. (1992) 'Corporate globalization: a new trend'. *Academy of Management Executive,* 6(1): 89–96.

Smith, C. and Meiksins, P. (1995) 'System, societal and dominance effects in cross-national organisational analysis', *Work, Employment and Society,* 9(2): 241–68.

Sorge, A. (2004) 'Cross-national differences in human resources and organization', in A.-W. Harzing and J. van Ruysseveldt (eds), *International Human Resource Management.* pp. 117–140. London: Sage.

Sparrow, P. and Brewster, C. (2009) *Global HRM in Practice.* London: Chartered Institute of Personnel and Development.

Sparrow, P. R. and Hiltrop, J.-M. (1997) 'Redefining the field of European human resource management: a battle between national mindsets and forces of business transition?', *Human Resource Management,* 36(2): 201.

Sparrow, P. R., Brewster, C. and Harris, H. (2004) *Globalizing Human Resource Management.* London: Routledge.

Spony, G. (2003) 'The development of a work–value model assessing the cumulative impact of individual and cultural differences on managers' work–value systems: empirical evidence from French and British managers', *International Journal of Human Resource Management*, 14 (4): 658–79.

Storey, J. (ed.) (2001) *Human Resource Management. A Critical Text,* 2nd edn. London: Thomson Learning.

Tregaskis, O. and Brewster, C. (2006) 'Converging or diverging? A comparative analysis of trends in contingent employment practice in Europe over a decade', *Journal of International Business Studies,* 37(1): 111–26.

Ulrich, D. (1989) 'Tie the corporate knot: gaining complete customer commitment', *Sloan Management Review,* 30(4): 19–28.

Ulrich, D. and Brockbank, W. (2005) *The HR Value Proposition.* Cambridge, MA: Harvard Business School Press.

UNCTAD (various years *World Investment Report.* New York: United Nations.

US Department of Labor (1993) *High Performance Work Practices and Firm Performance.* Washington DC: US P.M. Wright, Government Printing Office.

Wächter, H., Peters, R., Tempel, A. and Müller-Camen, M. (2003) *The 'Country-of-Origin-Effect' in Cross-national Management of Human Resources.* München, Mering: Hampp.

Welzel, C. and Inglehart, R. (2005) *Modernization, Cultural Change, and Democracy.* New York: Cambridge University Press.

Whitley, R. (1999) *Divergent Capitalisms: The Social Structuring and Change of Business Systems.* Oxford: Oxford University Press.

Woywode, M. (2002) 'Global management concepts and local adaptations: working groups in the French and German manufacturing industry', *Organization Studies,* 23(4): 497–524.

Yip, G. S. (1995) *Total Global Strategy.* Englewood Cliffs, NJ: Prentice-Hall.

Zanko, M. (ed.) (2002) *The Handbook of Human Resource Management Policies and Practices in Asia-Pacific Economies – Volume 1.* Cheltenham: Edward Elgar.

Zanko, M. and Ngui, M. (eds) (2003) *The Handbook of Human Resource Management Policies and Practices in Asia-Pacific Economies – Volume 2.* Cheltenham: Edward Elgar.

3

Culture in International Human Resource Management[2]

Laurence Romani

Contents

Learning Objectives

After reading this chapter you will be able to

- Understand the origin and validity of three different views on culture: positivist, interpretive and critical

- Explain the major points of difference between these views. Present the different management knowledge developed by each view

- Analyse a situation using each of the three views

- Combine each mode of analysis to reach an enriched understanding of a situation

Chapter Outline

The chapter provides an analytical tool useful for dealing with situations involving culture in International Human Resource Management (IHRM). This analytical tool derives from the combination of three views on culture, and the resulting knowledge they bring. Together, these views provide a rich understanding and consequently, can be advantageous when dealing with cultural situations.

1 Introduction

What is culture? A set of norms, beliefs and values shared by a group? Rather is it how people make sense of the world around them? Or even a rhetorical device used by those in power to reproduce inequalities in organisations? In management research, views on what culture is, and its implications for IHRM, strongly differ. The aim of this chapter is to present an analytical tool for understanding IHRM situations involving culture. This tool is based on the combination of three major views on culture used in management research. Combining these three views, and their respective forms of knowledge, develops a rich analysis which can be to your advantage when dealing with IHRM.

Different scientific views

Research on culture is prolific, and contributes to developing our knowledge with an increasing number of books, journal articles and conferences in management and organisation studies. These studies can be considered as belonging to three or four major research paradigms (see, for example, Guba and Lincoln, 2005; Primecz et al., 2009). The term paradigm is used broadly here in the sense of very different views on what research, knowledge or science are (Burrell and Morgan, 1979; Deetz, 1996; Kuhn, 1970). It is not necessary though to go further into detail on what is meant by a paradigm. Simply, it is important for the purpose of this chapter to remember that paradigms can be seen as broad scientific world views which are defined by how researchers see the reality they are investigating (ontology), and by what they believe their role is, as researchers.

Different views bring different kinds of knowledge

Different views of reality (ontology) can lead to different ways of investigating it (epistemology), and consequently, create different knowledge. Combining these various forms of knowledge can lead us to an enriched understanding of a situation, and this is an advantage if we want to manage it. I present in this chapter three views, albeit somewhat briefly and consequently incompletely, and concentrate on providing you with the essential elements of each view.

Some researchers consider that their role is to explore reality, explain how this reality functions in order to reach informative knowledge, upon which one can plan actions. I call this view 'positivist'. For example, Chapter 6 investigates international assignments. It presents various possible forms of international assignments, the factors that influence their choice, describes the assignment process, and discusses assignment success. The knowledge gained from reading this chapter is helpful for making decisions on the selection, preparation and repatriation of staff.

Other researchers consider that their role is to show that our reality is partly constructed by ourselves. They believe that the goal of research is to understand reality's meaning; that is to say, what sense it makes to people dealing with it. I call this view 'interpretive'. This knowledge is helpful for handling a situation. For example, Chapter 2 presents how the role of line managers is understood differently across countries. This knowledge can help to clarify misunderstandings, or work towards the best fit between people's expectations and what the organisation is able to offer them.

Other researchers consider that their role is to reveal how reality is also the outcome of power struggles between various actors. Their research goal is to display these power struggles so that people can become more aware of them, and maybe even change them. I call this view 'critical'. In Chapter 8, for example, the 'political approach' to the transfer of employment practices attends to the stakes and interests involved, and their resulting struggles. Some actors, for example, may hinder the diffusion of best practices within their organisation in order to keep their operational advantage and related rewards. This view is helpful to change a situation and possibly work towards achieving more equality between different organisational members.

Table 3.1   Brief outline of the three views and related knowledge

Positivist view	Interpretive view	Critical view
Reality is external to researchers and its investigation is the search for laws and regularities	Reality is also partly defined by researchers investigating it. They search for meanings: how people make sense of their situation	Reality is the temporary outcome of social constructions and power struggles. Its investigation reveals silenced voices
Instrumental knowledge, predictions, development and test of models	Knowledge on sense making and cognitive processes, on social constructions	Knowledge that questions and challenges, that exposes power relationships and inequalities

Researchers adopting different views may even so all share a research topic in common, for example, the role played by culture in IHRM practices. Together, their different perspectives provide us with complementary knowledge for the analysis of complex phenomena such as IHRM and culture.

Structure of the chapter

With the aim of understanding the consequences of 'culture' for IHRM, this chapter explicates three major views. First, it explains their origin, in order to clarify their equally legitimate positions and scientific validity, and the kinds of knowledge that they contribute. It is important to understand the rationales behind each of these views on culture to later be able to recognise and reproduce them in real-life situations. Then, the chapter illustrates the implications of these views for management and identifies the knowledge they develop. It will be argued that considering them simultaneously, rather than adopting only one view, provides a richer understanding and can lead to more appropriate solutions for IHRM challenges linked to cultural diversity in organisations. This process is illustrated through a case study, which is briefly analysed using the three views presented in the chapter.

2 Studies on culture in management

Studies on culture and management are as prolific as diverse. It is a challenging task to gain a clear overview since one needs to take multiple research streams into consideration. On the basis of previous reviews in organisational culture studies (Alvesson, 2002a), comparative management (Child, 2000; Redding, 1994), cross-cultural management (e.g., Kirkman et al., 2006; Leung et al., 2005; Lowe et al., 2007; Søderberg and Holden, 2002; Tsui et al., 2007), international management (e.g., Boyacigiller et al., 2004; Sackmann and Phillips, 2004) and cross-cultural psychology of organisational behaviour (e.g., Gelfand et al., 2007), we may identify contributions to the investigation of culture and management, and examine their conceptualisation of culture.

Studies on culture and management can be classified according to how they address culture, either as a main effect or as a moderator (Kirkman et al., 2006; Leung et al., 2005), and further whether culture is seen as a variable or a root metaphor (Alvesson, 2002a). Søderberg and Holden (2002) separate the studies according to views of culture: a barrier or a resource, essentialist or relational. Redding (1994) organises them along the themes they address such as leadership or motivation across countries. Others classify culture by the methodology used in the investigation (Earley and Singh, 1995) or debates raised (Adler et al., 1986). Often, reviews employ several kinds of classification, providing a detailed if not complicated picture. In order to go beyond this very complex depiction, I choose to move up to the higher level of scientific paradigms, or scientific views of culture. The first two views of culture presented in this chapter, the 'positivist' and the 'interpretive' ones, have been established for a longer period of time; they are illustrated in the distinction between culture and Kultur, itself echoing the distinction between etic and emic studies.

The distinction between culture and Kultur

Probably the most striking distinction between studies of culture and management is whether culture is viewed according to the concept of 'culture', or as 'Kultur'. For centuries, a well-accepted explanation of the differences encountered between human populations was that they were at distinct stages of social and cultural evolution (see Herodotus' four stages of evolution, already expressed in the civilisation of Ancient Greece). More recently, the Enlightenment philosophers from the seventeenth century onwards claimed that there is a common human psyche, and interpreted human diversity as a hindrance created by environmental or societal conditions acting against 'the free unfolding of human reason' (Jahoda and Krewer, 1997: 9). Humanity it was assumed is universal (e.g., all humans have similar cognitive structures), and it is their culture that differentiates them. This concept of culture is the one most commonly adopted in management studies.

The Universalist approach of the Enlightenment stands in contrast to other beliefs in the uniqueness of peoples and their specific 'Kultur'. Herder's 'Volkgeist' proposes that history is the result of interaction between culturally contrasting entities, each of them being composed of a distinct community and people, often with their own language. Dumont (1991) explains that in the nineteenth century, in the German-speaking area of Europe, the values of 'Gemeinschaft' (community) and 'Volk' (people and/or nation) are associated in a way that 'makes a German feel German first of all and a human only through being German' (Gingrich, 1998: 568). Von Humboldt (1830) holds that people who share a language develop a similar subjectivity ('Weltanschauung'), that is, a similar way of perceiving and understanding the world. This foreshadows the 'Sapir-Worf hypothesis'.

The Sapir-Worf hypothesis seems intuitive enough and has enthused many researchers. It posits that man perceives and understands the world principally through language. A famous example is the one of the Inuit (also referred to as 'Eskimos') who know approximately 20 words for the semantic category that the Indo-European languages represent by the single word 'snow'. Do the Inuit perceive more varieties of snow than speakers of Indo-European languages? Similarly, do Hopi speakers (among Native American) have a very different perception of time (since they are said to have no word or grammatical constructions to refer to past/present/future)? Do differences in language lead to behavioural differences? Evidence supporting the Sapir-Worf hypothesis can be found, and although it is not extensive the debate continues amongst researchers (for a discussion, see, for example, Berry et al., 1992).

This distinction between 'culture' and 'Kultur' (or 'Volkgeist') is central to understanding the different conceptualisations of culture because it reflects a fundamental ontological opposition and therefore a fundamental difference in the ways that researchers understand reality. On the one hand, culture is approached as something universal to humankind, and therefore something that can be investigated with similar constructs across countries. This view is the one most commonly adopted by positivist researchers. On the other hand, culture is seen as local, emergent, specific and even unique to a particular environment or language. This view is adopted by interpretive researchers. The fundamental ontological opposition between positivist and interpretive perspectives lies at the core of the etic/emic debate which is discussed below. This dichotomy is useful for understanding the distinct conceptualisations of culture expressed in the management literature.

Etic and emic

Originally used in linguistics, the concepts etic and emic gradually reached anthropological and organisation studies. It developed a slightly different meaning in each discipline (see Headland et al., 1990 and Peterson and Pike, 2002 for a discussion). Etic and emic are used to distinguish primarily between the perceived nature of (scientific) knowledge and consequently the different epistemologies (the appropriate ways to reach this scientific knowledge).

From an etic position on reality, there is an external significance that is consistent and meaningful across various contexts. The etic approach is viewed as general, and it focuses often on previously developed constructs or concepts that are then investigated, for example, in a number of different countries. For instance, cultural dimension constructs such as 'Individualism-Collectivism' are argued to be etic: and the concept is understood to be valid and coherent across countries. This means that the influence of this dimension on IHRM practices can be compared across countries. Etic studies are commonly associated with positivist approaches to science aimed at developing generalisable knowledge.

From an emic position, meaning exists within the context of its experience. The emic approach is seen as situated and focused on the particular meanings given by a specific group of individuals, thus implying that there are implicit aspects to knowledge and understanding. For example, the idea of statistical theory that was applied to product quality control in the United States in the 1920s was further made sense of in a comprehensive way in post Second World War Japan. Quality was not interpreted as the feature of a finalised product, but rather as the outcome of a process. The focus expanded from quality of products to quality of numerous other aspects of organisations, leading to what became later internationally known as Total Quality Management. Similarly, the same IHRM tool can lead to distinct practices in the various (cultural) environments where it is implemented, since the local interpretations and the local views will vary. Emic studies are reflected in an interpretive approach to science that emphasises the interpretations of individuals and the significance of the local context in the development of these meanings.

Interpretive approach

The next three sections of this chapter briefly explain and discuss the positivist and then the interpretive and critical viewpoints on culture and IHRM.

3 Positivist views

Positivist views on science and knowledge are the ones traditionally associated with the natural sciences; they are dominant in management research and inspire the search for models and general theories. A more thorough presentation of these views can be found in Burrell and Morgan (1979), Chalmers (1999), Donaldson (2003) or Guba and Lincoln (2005). Management research adopting a positivist view has built on the foundation of previous research on culture, including psychological anthropology and functionalism. These approaches are succinctly presented below and have influenced the current way positivist researchers think about and investigate culture in IHRM.

Psychological anthropology

In North American anthropology, the concept of culture was developed as 'something carried around in people's heads' (Erickson, 1998: 76). Psychological anthropology (e.g., Benedict, 1934/1989; Mead, 1928/1990) influenced the investigation of the relationship between culture and individuals with its focus on personality. Today, this is expressed through the concept of a modal personality that implies a relative frequency of certain personality types within any country. The modal personality type is investigated mostly in cross-cultural psychology (see Church, 1998 for a review).

Functionalist anthropology (and sociology)

After the Second World War, Clyde Kluckhohn and Alfred Kroeber (both influential anthropologists in North America) argued in favour of a 'mentalistic' conception of culture (Kuper, 1999). In their opinion and consistent with the work of leading sociologist Parsons (e.g., 1951), values are claimed to be the core elements of culture and taken as the theoretical focus of cultural investigations. Subsequent studies investigated the importance of value orientations for making comparisons between different cultures, such as in empirical interview research on five communities in the Southwest of the United States (two American Indian, a Spanish American, a Mormon and a farming village community) by Florence Kluckhohn and Fred Strodtbeck (1961).

They adopt a functionalist argument: cultures are fulfilling functions; they provide answers to basic human needs. These basic human needs are the same across societies, and therefore can be seen as human universals. Human universals offer a conceptual framework for the comparison of cultures: cultures can be compared for how they fulfil these universal needs.

The influence of the North American functionalist approach to the study of culture is the most visible in cross-country comparative studies using cultural dimensions or similar etic constructs. It presents culture as composed of universal constructs that can be measured through, for example, individual values.

'Culture and values'

In the functionalist approach, culture is seen as providing answers to the basic needs that human beings have to fulfil and this is the foundation for what are known as cultural dimensions (Hofstede, 1980). The idea is that there are distinct ways in which culture can fulfil these human needs, thus creating variations in the cultural dimensions. These variations are linked to different values. For instance, human societies are compelled to deal with their environment (see Kluckhohn and Strodtbeck, 1961) and the different ways in which they can do this are claimed to be variations (e.g., harmony, mastery or subjugation) within the cultural dimension 'Relation to broad environment' (see, for example, Maznevski et al., 2002; Trompenaars, 1993). Each variation is embedded in a set of values, that 'people carry around in their heads', thus giving to positivist and functionalist researchers the possibility of investigating culture through values.

The functionalist approach to culture is recognisable in research on cross-national management such as the seminal contributions by Hofstede (see Hofstede, 2001) and by Schwartz (see below), the works by Maznevski et al. (2002), as well as by the GLOBE (Global Leadership and Organisational Behaviour Effectiveness) project (House et al., 2004). Likewise, the legitimacy of searching for social axioms (beliefs endorsed and used by people to guide their behaviour in different work situations) is also based on the functionalist argument: they are important for human survival and functioning (see Leung et al., 2002: 288). It is a similar foundation that supports the investigation of 'sources of guidance' (see Smith et al., 2002). In sum, culture is said to fulfil the function of meeting human needs. Since they are universal human needs, they are universal (etic) aspects to culture (the cultural dimensions) and to human behaviour. These dimensions can be investigated through the study of people's orientation to values.

An impressive amount of studies have used these dimensions to test the relationship between culture and various aspects of management, such as motivation, reward allocation, hierarchy, preferred forms of training, and leadership (see a review by Kirkman et al., 2006 on the studies using Hofstede's cultural framework). For example, in a cultural environment with high Power Distance, organisations are likely to have centralised decision-making structures, tall hierarchies, a large proportion of supervisory personnel, privileges and status symbols for managers that are both expected and accepted, and a wide salary range between employees at the top and the bottom of the organisation pyramid (Hofstede, 2001: 107–8).

In the GLOBE project (House et al., 2004), additional cultural dimensions are developed and existing dimensions are further refined. For example, GLOBE considers the dimension 'Humane Orientation' that encourages and rewards individuals for being fair, altruistic, generous, caring and kind to others (Kabasakal and Bodur, 2004). In an environment scoring low on Humane Orientation, there will tend to be greater control of organisations exerted through IHRM practices, than in an environment scoring high on Humane Orientation, where 'organisations are relatively autonomous in their employee relations' (Kabasakal and Bodur, 2004: 584).

Cross-cultural management research largely adopts a mainstream psychological approach (see Smith and Bond, 1998), that tends to define culture as an independent variable influencing human cognition or behaviour. Values, and consequently the study of values across countries, are a fundamental part of cross-cultural comparison studies. The Rokeach Value Survey (Rokeach, 1973) is the point of departure for the seven value-types (similar to cultural dimensions) devised by Schwartz and colleagues (see Schwartz and Bilsky, 1987). He distinguishes the same seven types of values in each country (see Smith and Schwartz, 1997, Schwartz, 2004) and assesses their implications for management. For example, role overload and role conflicts are more likely to be reported by managers working in a cultural environment where values of 'Mastery' and 'Hierarchy' are praised, and where values linked to 'Harmony' have a low priority (Sagiv and Schwartz, 2000: 427). In environments where values of 'Embeddedness' are important for individuals, it is less likely that managers will choose pay levels exclusively based on their employees' work productivity. They tend to also take employees' family situation into account (Sagiv and Schwartz, 2000: 432).

Another important contribution made by psychologists to cross-cultural management research is the work of Triandis (e.g., 1995) on Individualism and Collectivism. This dimension has been investigated regarding its direct or moderating impact on,

Table 3.2   Characteristics of the positivist views on selected items

Items	Positivist views 'Culture and values'
Basic goal	Identify law-like relations of the influence of culture on management. Explanation; prediction and control
Perceived reality	Real (in the sense of realism) and apprehendable
Perceived role of the researcher	'Disinterested' scientist: inform decision makers
Approach to culture	Culture is approached with constructs replicable and valid across countries (e.g., cultural dimensions)
Example of methodology	Large-scale studies, questionnaires and database analysis, etic constructs
Problems addressed	Inefficiency, disorder
Example of achieved knowledge	Models showing cultural factors' influence on management. Measurement of cultural differences between countries or organisations
Organisational benefits	Control, expertise
Example of influential research	Hofstede (1980); House et al. (2004); Schwartz (1994)

Source: inspired by similar tables made by Deetz (1996: 199) and Guba and Lincoln (2005: 193ff.).

for example, motivation, job attitudes and group processes (see reviews by Earley and Gibson, 1998; Gelfand et al., 2004). In sum, the positivist viewpoint on culture with its predilection for values and their influence on attitudes and behaviour is the basis of a large body of research that describes how culture influences management. Culture in summary is seen as an external variable that has an impact on both people and organisations.

4 Interpretive views

Interpretive views, in contrast to the positivist ones, pay a stronger attention to the way individuals make sense of their reality. For interpretive researchers, 'behaviour [cannot] be "observed"; rather, it has to be understood and experienced from within, and interpreted' (Chapman, 1997: 5). Briefly stated, the interpretive approach emphasises symbols and meanings, and is often associated with the work of Weber and Schutz (see Burrell and Morgan, 1979; Guba and Lincoln, 2005; Schwandt, 1994, 2000). For example, Weber (e.g., 1911/1978) argues for a distinct approach to social sciences, where 'verstehen' (understanding) is central, contrasting with the positivist approach where the aim is 'begreifen' (grasping). Meaning for actors is essential to understanding their actions. In interpretive studies, the researcher's attention is focused on local, specific and perhaps unique meanings. The interpretive view used in research on culture and management is highly influenced by the disciplines of cultural anthropology and interpretive sociology, which are very briefly introduced and explained below.

Cultural anthropology

In anthropology, the emphasis placed on meanings, and the symbols that support meanings becomes predominant with Geertz. Geertz (1973/1993) developed a semantic conceptualisation of culture as webs of significance spun by individuals. He asserts that the analysis of these webs is not an experimental science but an interpretive activity in search of meanings. Interpretive anthropologists abandon claims of explanation and comparison in order to focus on the frameworks of interpretations used by individuals from distinct groups. A culture is not described as a set of dimensions, with high or low scores, but rather as a system of sense-making. For example, Geertz (1973/1993) explains a range of socio-cultural interactions between Balinese people using a metaphor of a specific (emic) kind: Balinese cockfights.

Interpretive sociology

Sociological works, too, have influenced the conceptualisation of culture in management. In simplified terms, traditional Western sociology has explored culture through two principal traditions. In Durkheim's view, culture is engraved in society and within its structures. As culture is seen as pervasive, it does not however receive particular attention. In contrast, through the Weberian tradition culture is studied through investigation of the forces influencing individuals. For instance, Weber's work on the *Protestant Ethic and the Spirit of Capitalism* (1904/1996) provides an analysis of socio-economic transformations with a focus on material and ideational forces. Material forces are for example, technological innovations (in communication and transport) or the development of capitalist modes of production. The ideational forces are seen as the religious beliefs (such as those which hold ascetic behaviour to be desirable) or more broadly speaking, the meaning that people give to social institutions. Together, these forces shape socio-economic development along different paths, which contributes to explain differences between countries.

'Culture and meanings'

The influence of Geertz on research on culture and management is particularly noticeable in organisational culture and comparative management studies.

In studies of organisational culture, shared interpretations are frequently seen as the expression of a common (sub)culture in the organisation (Czarniawska-Joerges, 1992; Ybema, 1997). In these studies, meanings and especially shared meanings are at the core of the understanding and investigation of culture. For example, subgroups of employees of an organisation may have developed the same meanings linked to certain organisational practices, such as how the corporate code of conduct should be interpreted, but their subculture and views may differ from the one promulgated by the headquarters. Other interpretive contributions, inspired by anthropologists such as Goodenough, are adopted in the study of employees' cognition or collective mental frameworks (Shrivastava and Schneider, 1984; Sims and Gioia, 1986) or symbols and meanings (Czarniawska, 1986; Gagliardi, 1990; Pondy et al., 1983). In sum, interpretive studies of organisational culture(s) often tend to regard cultural groupings as composed of people sharing the same interpretations.

cultural
Metaphors

In comparative management, Gannon (2004, 2009) proposes 'cultural metaphors' to help understand the culture of a nation. When positivist studies offer scores on dimensions, Gannon sketches the cultural profile of a country by comparing it with one of its local features. For example, Nielsen et al. (2009) use the metaphor of the 'Fado' (a popular form of song) to describe the Portuguese culture. Using the rich metaphor of a social institution in a given country, cultural metaphors explain the complexity of a local culture in an intuitive way. Similarly, fine wine serves as a metaphor for French culture, American Football for the US culture and the summer cottage of the *stuga* helps people to understand the Swedish culture (see Gannon, 2004). Cultural metaphors can contribute to the preparation of employees for expatriation, as well as assist with making sense of the cultural differences between two partners in a merger.

The attention given to *structures of meanings* is also applied in comparative studies of management across countries, for instance in the works of d'Iribarne (1989, 2009). This approach interprets the ways that local structures of meanings (culture) are mobilised to make sense of a situation. For example, a French multinational had repeatedly tried to implement Total Quality Management (TQM) in its Moroccan subsidiary, without success, and then it suddenly worked. The origin of the success was attributed to a combination of elements that enabled employees to make sense of TQM, and thus to implement it. The new CEO adopted an 'exemplary' leadership attitude, combining it with a new form of TQM training that articulated parallels between the key principles of TQM and verses of the Qur'an. This ability to relate the values of TQM in a culturally meaningfully way meant that employees could make sense of the implementation of TQM with the emic concept of the *Zaouia*. They drew a semantic parallel between the community of the Zaouia, with its exemplary leader and its religious connotations, and their own organisation, now including an exemplary leader, a community of employees, and TQM principles associated with moral guidance (see d'Iribarne, 2002).

Resistances, failures or difficulties in the transfer of HRM practices have been linked to disparate understandings and cultural practices occurring between for example, the headquarters and foreign subsidiaries. Henry (2007) investigates the resistance of a French consulting firm to the implementation of detailed job descriptions in the Société d'Electricité du Cameroun, when these job descriptions were in fact explicitly requested and thus were part of the consultants' brief. After the analysis of the cultural meanings associated with job descriptions by the French consultants (e.g., lack of freedom, disempowerment) and the Cameroonian employees (e.g., protection against arbitrary and pervasive use of power, clarification and delimitation of tasks) both interlocutors were then able to come to an agreement and move forwards with the specification of acceptable job descriptions.

Interpretive views on culture are not solely linked to investigating shared meanings in organisations; they also include the study of meanings developed by institutions and their implications for organisations' practices. Child (2000: 40f.) shows the relationship between Weber's view and institutional theory. He explains that management and business have distinctive institutional foundations in different societies. These institutions (e.g., state, legal system, etc.) and the role they play shape different 'national business systems' (Redding, 2005; Whitley, 1992a, b). Local systems of ideas (political, religious etc.) influence the ideology, structure and culture of institutions, which themselves influence organisations, organisational behaviour and HRM. Budhwar and Sparrow (2002) report how different contextual variables (such as industrial relations, labour markets, business systems) in India and the United Kingdom shape different logics of actions for managers, even when they are aiming to achieve the same goal of improving integration between HRM and business strategy. Institutional influences are presented in this book (see Chapter 2) to explain differences across countries regarding HRM practices (see also Ferner et al., 2001).

Table 3.3   Characteristics of the interpretive views on selected items

Items	Interpretive views 'Culture and meanings'
Basic goal	Reveals shared meanings on how people make sense of their reality (e.g., the organisation/department they work in). Understanding ('verstehen')
Perceived reality	Local and specific realities
Perceived role of the researcher	Participant, facilitator
Approach to culture	Culture is approached as a combination of local components that make sense in their specific context (sense making)
Example of methodology	Qualitative interviews, ethnographic studies, emic constructs
Problems addressed	Meaninglessness, illegitimacy
Example of achieved knowledge	Sense-making processes and how culture (meanings, institutions, etc.) influences how people make sense of their environment
Organisational benefits	Commitment, quality of work life
Example of influential research	Frost et al. (1985, 1992); Geertz (1973/1993); Whitley (1992a, b)

Source: inspired by similar tables made by Deetz (1996: 199) and Guba and Lincoln (2005: 193ff.).

5 Critical views

In contrast to the interpretive and positivist views, the critical views aim to reveal how our reality is influenced by social and historical forces that are in tension with each other. What I call here the 'critical views' on culture and IHRM aim to show these tensions, power struggles, social constructions and extent of closure. Briefly stated, critical researchers contend that social situations are the temporary outcome of struggles between various views defended and perpetuated by actors engaged in power relationships. A situation can be seen as the status quo imposed by people occupying a powerful position, who have silenced the voice of others. Critical researchers investigate for example how the power of the dominant party in the relationship is exerted pervasively by influencing norms, habits, rules and 'discourses' (that is ways of talking about people and the content of the messages). Revealing these mechanisms may improve a situation, thus, critical studies can be constructive (see Carr, 2006). Critical views are pluralist in nature and a more thorough presentation of them are found in Alvesson and Deetz (2000) and Guba and Lincoln (2005). In research on culture and management, several streams of thought have been influential, and I present just two of them below: critical and post-colonial anthropology.

Critical anthropology

Due to the influence of predominantly French writers on structuralism (e.g. Lévi-Strauss, Barthes), semiotics (e.g., Pierce, de Saussure) and later post-structuralism (e.g., Derrida, Baudrillard), the considerations of discourses, texts, power and science have become more central. The activity of writing about culture, for example, is carefully examined in terms of power relations and its use of language. For example, Geertz (1988) advises that anthropologists' monographs are not neutral reports since they are constructed for particular purposes (e.g., gaining credibility within the academic discipline or satisfying an influential stakeholder or sponsor) and on closer inspection reveal the problematic relations existing between the ethnographer, reader and subject matter. In addition, the account being produced arises from a particular viewpoint: most often that of the white, middle class, educated Euro-American male, whose country of origin often politically or militarily dominates or previously dominated the one studied (Erickson, 1998: 135ff.). In critical anthropology, language and literary analysis become the centre of anthropological research endeavour (see Clifford and Marcus, 1986, and for example, Mutman, 2006). It is no longer the 'foreign' or 'exotic' culture itself that needs to be elucidated, but rather the anthropologist's explanation of that culture (in order to understand from which standpoint the description is made). In anthropology as a discipline, issues of power relationships and cultural hegemony animate research debates and are a major influence on the literature (D'Andrade, 2000; Harris, 1999).

Post-colonial perspectives

The very notion of culture is challenged by post-colonial studies (see Bhabha, 1994; Said, 1978; Spivak, 1987). They denounce the idea that talking about 'culture' implies one is addressing and dealing with simplifications, exclusions and power relationships. For example referring to the 'Hungarian culture' implies sameness, homogenisation and also positions certain features as representing 'Hungary' (and thus excludes – or silences – others). Those journalists, ethnologists or researchers using cultural dimensions, 'decide' what the Hungarian culture is, and from their relative position of power impose their views on others.

Guided by Foucault's ideas on power/knowledge, Said (1978) outlines that knowledge and political, military, or economic interests are connected. By making statements ('scientific' or not) about others, one gains a superior position, since one has a voice and is free to talk in the name of other. 'Western' academia, for example, with its way of talking about culture (definitions, measurements, ethnographies, etc.) creates a discourse that otherises and classifies non-Western peoples so that they often appear as very different (other) and even inferior (since they are not as 'individualist' or 'assertive' as the implicit Euro-American norm). Post-colonial views can help us to question the fact that cultural differences are presented as real, when they are also social constructions of researchers or politicians and serving various agendas such as increasing managerial influence on employees or justifying colonisation. Additional aspects on post-colonial perspectives in research can be found for example, in Young (2001), and in Özkazanç-Pan (2008) and Westwood (2006) regarding management.

'Culture and power'

The 'linguistic turn' has been influential on many subject disciplines including management and organisation studies (Alvesson, 2002b). Since the 1980s, there has been a greater focus on language itself, the study of metaphors being a notable example (see Morgan, 1980, 1986 or Alvesson, 2002a for the concept of organisational culture and its associated metaphors). Critical thinking influences the study of organisational culture through its rejection of what is argued is the illusion of achieving comprehensive knowledge with broad theories and meta-narratives (Kunda, 1992; Parker, 2000; Willmott, 1993). It searches for poly-vocality and thus 'several voices', for instance, the voices of managers together with the voices of blue-collar workers.

Critical thinking can help to reveal the multiplicity of cultures across and within organisations in regard to functions, tenure, hierarchy and gender, etc. Respecting cultural diversity for HR managers goes beyond the consideration of 'traditional' forms of diversity (such as gender, age, people with a disability) to include for example, religious belonging, professional training and sexual preferences. IBM and Volvo group for example, are actively managing this multi-faced diversity of their international workforce through programmes such as 'Diversity and inclusive leadership'. Critical perspectives can contribute to diversity management for HR managers by encouraging more questioning on their views on diversity. Zanoni and Janssens (2004) assert that HR managers' discourse on diversity may reflect dominant views and reaffirm management practices and underlying inequalities. Critical perspectives can thus help HR managers to realise that they may involuntarily be reproducing the inequalities they intend to address.

Organisational or national culture differences are shown, for example by Riad (2005) or Vaara (2002), as a narrative construction (in other words a story) to explain the success or the failure of mergers and acquisitions (see Chapter 4). Discourses on cultural differences between organisations present suitable narratives for explaining incompatibility between organisations and legitimising partial actions, or making sense of failures. They appear for example in conversations, company case studies, press releases or corporate internal communication. Using for example, cultural incompatibility to explain a merger's failure can be a convenient way to silence other analyses, for example, a poorly prepared merger, lack of managerial commitment, hostile attitude from one organisation and its consequence on workers' motivation, strategic misfit, underestimated costs, and structural incompatibility in operations.

Other studies show that discourses on culture are constructed and mobilised during power struggles. Ybema and Byun (2009) reveal that when Dutch and Japanese employees collaborate at work, in Japan or in The Netherlands, the cultural differences they report depict a negative picture of the other culture, and especially so whenever its representatives are in a superior position. For example, they show that Dutch interviewees, 'annoyed at being excluded by their Japanese bosses' tend to emphasise their 'Dutch' values of egalitarianism. This is done in opposition to the Japanese regime. They 'claim that Japanese management tries to preserve the status quo by emphasizing Japanese values of hierarchy and consensus'. However, interviewed Japanese employees working in The Netherlands mention that they 'are being encouraged by their "approachable" Dutch superiors to be more assertive'. Yet, when they talk about the Dutch way of decision-making, they refer to it 'as being "top-down", rather than egalitarian' (Ybema and Byun, 2009: 350). The authors reveal how employees use 'culture' to discursively erect symbolic boundaries between them (and their co-nationals) and others belonging to a foreign culture. In other words, the cultural differences are talked about in a way that creates two different groups: 'the Japanese' and 'the Dutch' who are essentialised as different, especially when they are connected to different hierarchical levels. These boundaries serve the reproduction of power and status inequalities in their organisations.

Critical views address the discourse about the other and about concepts of difference. They contribute to cross-cultural management knowledge that is used for expatriation training (e.g., Dahlén, 1997; Lowe, 2001, 2002). Pre-expatriation training may implicitly reproduce stereotypes about non-Western cultures, thereby justifying the transfer of HRM practices from the headquarters to subsidiaries in developing countries. For example, the use of discourse essentialising others and presenting them as culturally determined and 'backward' (Fougère, 2006; Fougère and Moulettes, 2007; Kwek, 2003) may lead to IHRM policies and practices in favour of bureaucratic

Table 3.4   Characteristics of the critical views on selected items

Items	Critical views 'Culture and power'
Basic goal	Unmask domination (e.g., of the acquiring company and its managers on the acquired staff). Critique and transformation
Perceived reality	The temporary outcome of power struggles, between e.g., political, social, gender, ethnical forces
Perceived role of the researcher	Transformative intellectual: advocate and activist
Approach to culture	Culture can be seen as a rhetorical device used in a power struggle. It essentialises, otherises, silences and establishes unspoken hierarchies
Example of methodology	Discourse analysis, language and literary analysis, ideology critique
Problems addressed	Domination, consent, status quo
Example of achieved knowledge	Unmasking of the reproduction of inequalities between various actors (e.g., between headquarters and subsidiaries, 'Western' management techniques and indigenous ones)
Organisational benefits	Participation, expanded knowledge
Example of influential research	Clifford and Marcus (1986); Prasad (2003); Said (1978)

Source: inspired by similar tables made by Deetz (1996: 199) and Guba and Lincoln (2005: 193ff.).

control mechanisms rather than cultural ones based on training – since the assumption is that 'they' are not going to change – or that any change will be difficult. Further contributions from critical views to IHRM are presented in Peltonen (2006).

6 Applying the three views to the case study (pp. 103–110)

This case presents a real situation that arose in a European multinational corporation. At first sight, the email exchange seems to be about technicalities, cultural differences and tense communication. To explain how to use the three approaches (positivist, interpretive and critical) I provide below three succinct analyses showing some of the cross-cultural dimensions involved in the exchange. Inevitably, multiple issues are present in this case, and additional questions are posed at the end of each analysis to assist further reflection.

A positivist analysis

Cross-cultural differences in the case are expressed very clearly in the emails sent by Per Jonson. He mentions cultural differences between Finland and Sweden regarding client relationships (email 1), leadership (email 3) and decision making (email 3 and 5).

Bengt supports Per's opinion regarding desired decision-making processes in Sweden (email 4). Tapio too uses cultural differences between Finland and Sweden in his analysis of the situation (footnote email 2).

Can positivist views on culture and its implications on management enlighten us about the differences between Finland and Sweden that appear in the emails? Finland scores significantly higher than Sweden on the cultural dimensions of Assertiveness (House et al., 2004) and Uncertainty Avoidance (Hofstede, 1980). Assertiveness is found to have a positive relationship with an 'autonomous' leader (independent and individualistic), and a negative relationship with a leader who is team-oriented and participative (Den Hartog, 2004). In an environment scoring higher on Uncertainty Avoidance (such as is Finland compared to Sweden), there is a tendency for more formal conceptions of management, hierarchical controls and roles. There is also a tendency for a stronger belief in specialists and in expertise (see Hofstede, 2001: 169–70). In brief, some reported cultural differences between Finland and Sweden posit that in Finland there is a tendency toward more autonomous leaders, formal conceptions of management, and hierarchical control and roles.

On the remaining dimensions, Sweden and Finland tend to have similar scores, such as for example a low score on Power Distance (Carl et al., 2004: 539; Hofstede, 2001: 87). Hofstede describes representative behaviour for low scores on Power Distance as 'decentralised decision structures; less concentration of authority. The ideal boss is a resourceful democrat and subordinates expect to be consulted' (Hofstede, 2001: 107–8). Sweden does score lower on Power Distance than Finland, but is this difference strong enough to explain the altercation?

Research on 'structures of values' (Schwartz, 1994) organises values into patterns of oppositions. For example, Egalitarianism is opposed to Hierarchy. In Sweden and Finland, high priority is given to items that comprise the value structure of Egalitarianism (Sagiv and Schwartz, 2000; Schwartz, 2004). In Egalitarianism, voluntary cooperation is emphasised, 'leaders motivate by enabling', and members 'flexibly enact their roles' (Sagiv and Schwartz, 2000: 420).

In sum, the information provided by the positivist view and its knowledge give us elements to support both the arguments that there are cultural differences involved in this altercation, as well as an inadequate leadership style enacted by Tapio.

Case questions

1 What other issues are reflected in the emails?
2 Continue the positivist analysis of the case by considering for example cultural differences in work/life balance, client relationships or communication styles. Can you now more strongly defend one argument?
3 In the light of your positivist analysis, how do you explain the situation?
4 What would you do as a HR manager receiving this case? What would you recommend Jaap van der Dorp to do?

An interpretive analysis

This heated email exchange, and especially the escalation that happened over just a few hours leads us to wonder: why does Per react so strongly to the email sent by Tapio and the communication mode he would like to implement? Why are Per and Bengt not accepting that Tapio is from Finland and that his style could simply be different? In other words, what does Tapio preferred leadership and communication style possibly mean to Per and Bengt?

Leadership studies inform us that an ideal of idea-oriented leadership tends to be shared between Swedish top and middle managers. 'Idea-oriented leadership means that leaders bring about involvement, commitment and motivation through skilfully communicating inspiring [ideas] (...). The relationship to the supervised is built on confidence and trust (rather than coercion) and openness' (Åkerblom, 1999: 48). Leaders are seen as visionary, team-oriented, and favouring collaboration and consultation, rather than supervision and instruction.

In addition, Abrahamsson (2007: 15–23) explains that in Sweden, hierarchy 'has been coupled to an authoritarian way to treat the subordinates', because it is associated with a social system that used to stratify Swedish society. Now, 'modern Swedish democracy' stands in contrast to this socially structured system, 'the old system', when formal terms of address were used. Leaders are seen as visionary and team-oriented, and supervision and instructions are placed in opposition to a desirable leadership style. An informal and frequent communication between superiors and subordinates is the preferred communication style. This portrait of Swedish leadership style resonates with positivist studies on Swedish and Scandinavian leadership (Holmberg and Åkerblom, 2006; Smith et al., 2003).

Images of democracy, consensus and frequent informal communication are thus associated with desirable superior–subordinate relationships in Sweden. This association of meanings explains why Per reacts so strongly to Tapio's email. First, he reacts to the hierarchical system that Tapio is following, imposing a decision from the top (email 1). Then, Per reacts against the communication style that Tapio would like to adopt with them (email 3). Per uses references to the old system (email 3: 'it was a long time ago that man stood with the hat in the hand...') to which current views on leadership in Sweden are opposed. Bengt brings his support to Per exactly on that point: decision-making should be participative rather than top-down.

In their view, employees should be able to freely communicate with their superiors (immediate or not) so that opinions can be shared and a properly collaborative decision-making process can take place. The importance of unhindered communication is critical to the decision-making process supported by Bengt and Per. This explains why Per quickly uses references to a dictatorial system (in the phone conversation with Robin and in email 5). The absence of references to a democratic management style, in accordance with the cultural way in which Per sees it, makes him associate Tapio with a dictator (the very opposite of a democrat). The radical as well as emotional reactions encompassed in the email exchange are explainable: Tapio's behaviour is associated by Per (and Bengt) with the 'old system', a background against which the Swedish modern society now defines itself. Accepting Tapio's way, somehow means reconsidering the societal fundamentals of equality and democracy, and they seem to be too deeply rooted in the Swedish culture to be reconsidered (see Schwartz's studies in the positivist analysis of the case).

In light of the previous (positivist) analysis, we know the importance of values of equality and democracy for the Swedish society. Now, the interpretive analysis enables us to understand Per's (and Bengt's) emotional emails, the references made to the way things used to be, and the seemingly out of place reference to dictatorship in reaction to Tapio's management style. This explains the intensity of the exchanges and why neither Per nor Bengt are ready to reconsider participative decision-making. Per and Bengt perceive Tapio's email as a potential threat to not only fundamental social values of equality and consensus, but also to the social progress achieved by the 'modern' Swedish society.

Case questions

5 Continue the interpretive analysis of the case by addressing the issues you identified previously.
6 In light of the positivist and the interpretive analyses, how do you now explain the situation?
7 What would you do now as a HR manager receiving this case? What would you recommend Jaap van der Dorp to do?

A critical analysis

Power struggles are also present in this case, using culture and cultural differences as an available discourse to support or challenge the situation (such as in Ybema and Byun, 2009).

In the first email, Per essentialises the Swedish customers and client relationships by using terms such as 'the Swedish customers'; and he does so in opposition to Finland, making it foreign and 'other' (see 'by acting like puppet dolls we have never reached any success in Sweden, but is it maybe different in Finland?'). These mechanisms of essentialisation in opposition to a norm (in this case, the Swedish one) are also shown in Zanoni and Janssens (2004). Cultural differences are used as a rhetorical device to introduce an opposition (Sweden versus Finland, see similar constructions in Vaara, 2002) and to present a situation as given and in this case, non-negotiable. The critical view investigates whether the use of this rhetorical tool serves a power struggle.

In the altercation, two different kinds of knowledge are in opposition: the client knowledge is represented by Tapio, and the technical knowledge is represented by Per. Per's first email is about technicalities, but also very much about the client relationship developed between Tapio and Bekvema. Per is thus attacking Tapio on his grounds, and, in Tapio's eyes, without legitimacy since Tapio argues about Per's lack of knowledge of the situation (email 2). In addition (in his footnote), Tapio also attempts to use the rhetorical device of cultural differences. He does so in order to undermine Per's opposition, trying to present it as irrelevant feelings. In Tapio's answer, Per is thus criticised in two ways: lack of client knowledge and expression of feelings related to Sweden versus Finland that are besides the point.

Per then focuses his reply (email 3) on cultural arguments, this time going further than essentialising the differences, which he does in his third point. Per presents the current situation in Sweden as being more advanced than the one in Finland ('we are not going back to that time'), thus implying that there is a (cultural) development that Finland has not reached yet. With this comment, Per positions Sweden in a superior position. Essentialisation and othering now lead to an unspoken hierarchy (see also Fougère and Moulettes, 2007; Westwood, 2006).

The Swedish position is not only maintained as superior, it is also a position that is difficult to argue against. Indeed, the interpretive analysis points to associations of leadership and participative decision-making with democracy, and it is difficult to argue against democracy in Western nations. Bengt too (email 4) positions the 'Swedish' way in a superior position ('we have it good in Sweden'), and the well-being of employees is a delicate point to argue against (especially in the 'Feminine' or 'Humane Oriented' Nordic countries – see the scores provided by the positivist studies such as Hofstede, 2001 or House et al., 2004).

The essentialisation and the othering of Tapio's management style occur in a power struggle between two legitimate forms of knowledge: the client relationship and technical knowledge. A central question remains however, why are the two forms of knowledge in opposition in this case? What are the risks? What is at stake? Per's technical explanations reveal that the process used in Bekvema is not only under-performing ('this brings no significant disinfection' – email 1) but also is against the company's policy ('according to the book not authorised by our company' – email 5). It becomes clear that what is at stake here is more than a power struggle between two individuals, two forms of knowledge or two cultural ways of managing. It is also between two persons' responsibility in relation to food poisoning occurring in Bekvema.

Case questions

8 Continue the critical analysis of the case by addressing the issues you identified previously.

9 In light of the three analyses, how do you now explain the situation?

10 What would you eventually recommend Jaap van der Dorp to do? And, with the little you know about him, how would you present the situation and your recommendations?

11 In the event of food poisoning occurring in Bekvema, who should bear the consequences in Finland and in Sweden? Why? What should be the consequences?

Discussion

The three views applied to the case and their three succinct analyses when combined contribute to a richer understanding of the situation. The positivist analysis introduces support for two different lines of argument: cultural differences or alternatively, an inappropriate leadership style are the primary causes of the conflict. The strength of the positivist analysis is its focus on values. It shows that differences exist in Swedish and Finnish preferences regarding autonomous (thus not participative) leaders and formal views on management and hierarchical control, at the same time as it reveals similarities in an orientation toward low Power Distance and Equalitarianism. Key elements are thus already introduced in the first analysis: non-participation, formality, control and equalitarianism. The discussion in the emails is influenced by these values.

Participative decision-making and information are requested from the Swedish sales-team, but it is the formal aspect that causes the situation to escalate. Why is formality problematic? What can it possibly mean to the Swedish sales-team? The interpretive analysis points to the meaning associated with directive leadership: the 'old system', when interactions between superior and subordinates were more formal. Thus, Tapio's email touches upon a key defining aspect of the (modern) Swedish society, where equalitarianism and limited formality are praised. Formal hierarchy and control, and autonomous leadership are thus elements that stand in semantic opposition to the ones praised by contemporary views on leadership in Sweden.

But what triggered this seemingly sudden conversation about cultural differences? The critical view complements our analysis. In this view, discourses about culture potentially serve power struggles: culture is used as a rhetorical device to establish unspoken hierarchies, thus giving the advantage to one party. But which are the struggles in this exchange? Client knowledge versus technical knowledge are clearly in opposition regarding one process: the disinfection system. With the critical view and resulting analysis, it becomes clearer that an ethical issue is at stake, and the way to solve it is at the core of the exchange.

In sum, provided with the three views on culture, it is possible to develop a richer understanding of the case which first appeared to be linked to cultural differences and leadership preferences. We realise that albeit diverging values and cultural meanings associated with leadership are part of the issue, they are also utilised by each side to polarise the two positions in the debate on an ethical problem.

7 Conclusion

IHRM is intrinsically international and multi-cultural, contributing to making culture a frequent component of issues IHR managers deal with in their work. The three views presented in this chapter are an analytical tool to better investigate, and then to understand more comprehensively, situations that are influenced by culture, or that employ culture as an argument in the pursuit of certain goals.

The positivist view considers cultural differences resulting from the external influence of culture on management. The positivist analysis is frequently employed in the management literature and provides an answer to a central question: What are the value discrepancies that can be identified in this situation? And consequently: What are the external influences of culture on what is happening? This investigation is especially useful for identifying culture as a central consideration in any analysis of IHRM.

The interpretive view regards management as cultural. In other words, culture is the way that people make sense of their situation, thus the meanings attached to it by actors are at the core of the investigation. In the case study, the investigation of the meanings associated with a formal leadership style enlightens the heated email exchange. A main question of the interpretive analysis is: What does the situation mean to each of the people involved? This investigation is especially useful for explicating how people experience the situation, why they react the way they do, and how new processes are adopted or rejected.

The critical view considers that culture can be a rhetorical device serving the stake of parties involved in power struggles. This device can essentialise (thus imprison in a state of affairs) and organise in an unspoken hierarchy, often to the primary advantage of one camp. A central question to what I call here the critical view is: What is at stake? It is especially useful to unmask the stakes at play in a situation and to expose it in a new light, leading to more possibility for change. Together, these three views compose a flexible tool for performing a complex analysis of a situation, and consequently, can lead to more effective IHRM.

Table 3.5   Sample questions to use in the analysis of a situation dealing with culture

Positivist views 'Culture and values'	Interpretive views 'Culture and meanings'	Critical views 'Culture and power'
How does culture influence this situation?	What does this situation mean to those involved?	Is there a struggle between two camps?
Which are the cultural dimensions that can explain people's behaviour?	What do they associate with the situation/elements of the situation?	Who is in a position of power? Who is silenced? What is at stake?
Which are the cultural dimensions' score differences between the two countries/organisations?	What does the situation remind them of?	What are the risks for each camp?
	Which terms, which metaphors do people use when talking about it? What are the arguments advanced, how do the arguments make sense?	What is said to be 'normal' (status quo or stated situation)? And by whom? Is culture talked about explicitly?
		Which stake/camp does it serve?

Discussion questions

1 'With globalisation, people's behaviour and values are increasingly becoming similar, and especially so in organisations. Therefore, in a near future, the IHRM of multinational organisations will be conducted globally.' Comment on this statement.

2 'Using multiple views on culture (functionalist, interpretive and critical) for the analysis of a situation is only making things more complicated. Models should simplify reality, so that we can act upon it.' Explain why this comment is partial to the functionalist view and discuss the difference between a rich and a complicated analysis.

3 Every researcher tends to do research in mainly one paradigm. Similarly, you, as a manager, will also tend to spontaneously do one type of analysis of the situations you will encounter. Which one is it? The functionalist, the interpretive or the critical one? Reflect on your view and its inherent limitations. Then, discuss which will be your strategy in order to bring in your analysis the other two views.

4 An etic view on culture reflects a functionalist position, whereas an emic view reflects an interpretive position. Which view on culture is reflected by the critical position?

'Not the way we do business around here'

This case is based on original email material in Swedish, from Nickell Sweden (Nickell is a pseudonym). The English translation reflects the original proficiency of Swedish and writing style of the authors of the emails.

Introduction

Robin hangs up the phone, it's almost 11 p.m. and tomorrow will be a long day. Today was spent visiting an important client and Robin was out of reach most of the time, while installing a new system. The phone call that just ended with Tapio Mäkelä, the managing director of the Nordic Area, is worrying. If Tapio does what he threatens to do, Robin will lose one of the most important members of the Swedish team: the technical specialist, Per Jonson. How can things go so wrong in just one afternoon? Robin decides that a good night of sleep is needed before writing – or not – a report to the European Human Resource manager.

Background

Robin works as the sales director of Sweden, for a European company called Nickell, specialising in the development, production and sales of cleaning chemicals and dosing systems for the food-processing industry (cleaning of pipes, tanks etc.). The Swedish operations of Nickell are a subsidiary of Nickell Nordic Area, located in Finland. The problem started last year, when Bekvema (a pseudonym), one of the most important international customers of Nickell established a subsidiary in Sweden. Bekvema is a centrally run corporation, with headquarters in Finland where its activities make about 70 per cent of the turnover of Nickell Finland. Tapio Mäkelä is personally in charge of the relationships with Bekvema and will not tolerate Per Jonson continuing with his attacks on his work.

Robin is sceptical. Is Per right in saying that the system used by Bekvema in all its subsidiaries is not appropriate, thereby criticising the solution developed together with Nickell Finland? On the other hand, Tapio often said that Bekvema does not always follow his recommendations and that they tend to do what they think is right, or enough. Bekvema wants now to have a new system installed for its Swedish subsidiary during the holiday weekend of Midsummer. This is the most important holiday here in Sweden! Robin understands the importance given to the midsummer celebrations. They mark the beginning of the summer break for very many people in the country. But what is the most upsetting for Per? Is it really that Tapio said yes to Bekvema, which means that they are going to have to work during Midsummer? But Per will not even be there! Robin scrolls down the email inbox searching for the first email sent by Per.

EMAIL 1

From: Per Jonson

Sent: Thursday, June 21, 2007 12:17 PM

To: Tapio Mäkelä

Cc: Robin; Bengt Karlson; Göran Söderberg

Subject: Bekvema Sundbyberg

Dear Tapio,

To my consternation I hear that we are going to install the system Propre at Bekvema in Sundbyberg. I must decisively protest against this coward attitude toward Bekvema and its demand to start up Propre in Sweden. To accept this was not good to any party involved, in view of the circumstances.

The success we have reached through the years in Sweden depends to a large extent to the fact that we have demands on our customers, as much as they have demands on us. Many times, a No from us was positively perceived by the Swedish customers. By acting like puppet dolls we have never reached any success in Sweden, but it is maybe different in Finland?

As you certainly remember, I was from the start of Bekvema Sweden in Sundbyberg strongly critical to the inferior (the least we can say) cleaning system they use. To dose 1,2g PXX at 60° is like doing nothing, because this brings no significant disinfection. Besides this remarkable recommendation, the cleaning process is performed without FGcs?? What is it for process??

Your answer was that it is Bekvema's decision and that we don't have anything to say as far as processes are concerned. In my eyes this sounds like a coward attitude to the client!!!! If the processes were right from the start we probably would not have ended in that situation. The fact that Bekvema Finland experiences an awesome good result with Propre does prove that the earlier processes were not good?

You also said that we, in Sweden, don't know anything since we don't have experience with PXX. Nothing can be more wrong!! Long before you started using PXX in Finland, we had an extensive international project where we investigated the PXX processes and disinfection in ClientX in Karlstad. The fact that it has never been a success in Sweden is linked to the too high costs it implies. Unfortunately, all the documentation was lost in the three moves. (Per refers to the recent changes that occurred in the company. Both Finnish and Swedish activities of Nickell were before part of a larger multinational corporation, itself the result of a merger between business units of other companies. Previously, another ownership change had taken place.)

Without doubts, the best in this case would have been to install instead of Propre **a real PXX process** during the month of July. (...)

If the client were Client Y, they had applauded such a clear decision, especially when one knows that the service resources are limited during the summer vacations. We did so with Client Z and they were thankful for it.

Someone must learn to say no now and then to Bekvema too, and maybe learn to motivate why one says no.

Next time we have a common meeting, I think that we must discuss in detail how we are going to do in the future, because we cannot successfully continue in this way.

Note that my critics are about actions, not persons.

Best regards and best wishes for a nice Midsummer.

Per Jonson

Technical Specialist

Robin remembers the criticisms that Per Jonson made loudly to the other members of the sales team during their last meeting. His convincing arguments had gained the agreement of the other sales technicians. It is true that Per is the only technical specialist in the Nordic area. His influence on the Swedish sales team is clear and Robin already wondered whether this could be a problem. Robin searches for Tapio's answer.

EMAIL 2

From: Tapio Mäkelä

Sent: Thursday, June 21, 2007 12:36 PM

To: Per Jonson

Cc: Robin; Bengt Karlson; Göran Söderberg

Subject: RE: Bekvema Sundbyberg

My dearest Per,

You think you can just like that criticise the case Bekvema although you don't even have taken part in the work for the last months. How can you think that you would know better?

Unfortunately, you don't have now enough information to judge the situation. For this reason I cannot either answer to your assertive email. In case you want to learn more about the situation, you are welcome to call me today or next week (although I don't understand why you are so interested in a client you did not even work with for the last months). If you call you'll get answers.

I wish you a nice holiday and hope at the same time that you can get some rest. In the future, please learn more about the background before you start sending emails that can be seen as written with a negative attitude. I rather have this kind of discussion on the phone since emails are a much too powerful media for sensitive matters and often opinions are polarised unnecessary. Same wishes to the other as well. I hope this will become a habit in the future.

Best wishes

Tapio

PS. I would love to know why you have so many feelings in regard to everything that has to do with Bekvema. I could almost believe that this has something to do with Sweden versus Finland… could that be the case? ;)

Robin wonders whether Tapio has a point. It seems that the feelings of competition between Sweden versus Finland are there. In Nordic sports, very often the finalists are Sweden and Finland, and both countries tend to see the other as the eternal adversary. It appears to Robin that whatever comes from Nickell Finland is received negatively. On the other hand, it seems that Tapio does not know much about the situation here, since he believes that Per does not work much with Bekvema. This is not the case. Per's response came two hours later.

EMAIL 3

From: Per Jonson

Sent: Thursday, June 21, 2007 14:33 PM

To: Tapio Mäkelä

Cc: Robin; Bengt Karlson; Göran Söderberg

Subject: RE: Bekvema Sundbyberg

Tapio,

1   If I was involved or not has nothing to do with the matter, and nothing to do with knowing better. You don't know much of my commitment to Bekvema. However, I know that it was a bad decision, at this point of time, to start the installation of a project like Propre.

2   I have enough information to see that this is a stupid decision, and furthermore, I know very well how the processes they use today (don't) work.

3   No one in Sweden is interested in working in a company where they cannot (or should not) write their true opinion in emails. The coming situation with Bekvema touches us all to a great deal. In this country, it is a habit to circulate one's opinion, via mail or phone. I assume this will continue in the future. To insinuate that we should not do so in the future is weak and pure dangerous leadership.

4   I don't understand what you mean with 'first learn about the background'. The background facts I have are more than enough to judge that starting up a Propre project at this point of time is risky.

5   It is not about feelings, don't you understand the problem? If not, I'd be happy to explain again.

6   The cleaning processes used so far are hardly professional and I suppose, this is why it is so urgent to start Propre.

I repeat point 3 in other words, just to be sure because this is important:

To suggest that we should go quiet and carefully with our opinions is not only stupid, it is also wrong. I cannot even see that this would polarise into something negative. In Sweden, it was a long time ago that man stood with the hat in the hand, and we are never going to go back to that time. Your wish that we should not write down our opinion in mail does not scare only me… I can also mention that most of the decisions that we make in Sweden are based on consensus.

This is not about Sweden versus Finland, it is just that business and management are fundamentally different in our countries, well, one could say incompatible. It would never occur to a Swede to implement a system that was wrongly developed by the client. In this case, you have to have good arguments to explain where the mistake lies. We are good at that. To say No, too.

Of course I will rest during the holiday, but this does not imply that I will tie me a muzzle. On the contrary. Tremble should the ones I'll meet.

Honestly, I was expecting a better, actually a much better answer from you Tapio. Your answer felt empty. A bit unpleasant.

Best regards, with the hope that you too will get the possibility to rest during the holiday, and maybe reflect about life.

Per Jonson

Technical specialist

Per called around the other sales technicians and even Robin during the afternoon. Robin remembers how upset Per was, saying that Tapio is some kind of Stalinist dictator, and that keeping one's head down in front of the hierarchy, or clients, is unacceptable. It may be the usual way in Finland, but 'this is not the way we do business around here!' Robin tried to calm him down. The afternoon was tense and Robin spent also some time with Tapio on the phone, trying to calm him down too. That afternoon, another sales technician reacted:

EMAIL 4

From: Bengt Karlson

Sent: Thursday, June 21, 2007 17:55 PM

To: Tapio Mäkelä; Per Jonson

Cc: Robin; Göran Söderberg

Subject: RE: Bekvema Sundbyberg

Tapio and Per!

Without going into detail in your exchange on whether things are done this way or that way, whether one does this or that in Sweden or Finland, I consider too that this is crazy to start a new project just before the holidays. This shows imprudence and a big faith that everything is going to happen the way we want. In my world there is a guy call Murphy (the devil's assistant) and we meet him quite often. Free translation: If something can go wrong, then it goes wrong. And especially because we purposefully did not take any safety measure. And then the fact that if something goes wrong, someone has to go to the client and fix the problem when we are on holiday. Is this going to give trust to the client?

If you see that as a critic from Per, you need to know that it was I who first was upset about all this. I am not as much in touch with all the technical details as Per, but it does not mean that I don't have an opinion.

Finally, I want to say that I agree with Per, we have it good in Sweden. We basically discuss everything. Even your behaviour in the Bekvema related matters. You have to understand that what you decide on the other side of the Baltic Sea, we have to implement it on this side. So I think this is more than right that we should be in the decision process too.

And yes, Bekvema touches us all in Sweden. Not just Göran who is responsible for the client. Everyone of us feels responsible, and will get mobilised if for some reason Göran is not available.

All in all, I want to calm down this storm a bit with wishing you a happy Midsummer. We'll sort things out in the future.

Best regards,

Bengt

The conversation Robin just ended with Tapio was mostly about Per's latest email (see below). Tapio found Per's attitude unacceptable and disrespectful. He said he could no longer tolerate such an attitude from one of his subordinates. And since whatever he says to Per is misinterpreted, he rather meet Per next time with a lawyer, to serve as a witness. Tapio wants Robin to translate the emails and to send them to Jaap van der Dorp, the European Human Resource Manager. He asked Robin to send along a note to Jaap van der Dorp, in order to give a third party's opinion on the matter. Tapio wants to use this note, together with the emails, as material in his case against Per. If Per continues like that, he wants him to go.

EMAIL 5

From: Per Jonson

Sent: Thursday, June 21, 2007 20:06 PM

To: Bengt Karlson; Tapio Mäkelä

Cc: Robin; Göran Söderberg

Subject: RE: Bekvema Sundbyberg

Unlike Bengt, I don't see all this as a storm, in fact just an illustration of how things go wrong when one tries processes with a quasi science and let the client take over knowledge*, and at the same time, a lack of ability to say No.

Tapio's nonanswer (!) to me gave no explanation as why it could not have worked with a normal PXX-process during the month of July (which would have been easier and more cost effective in time).

This would have been much safer, but instead Tapio came with an answer asking us to shut up with our cap in the hand and bow, which is never going to happen, this we have, in this country, left behind us for a long time (circa 1950s). I indicated this in my previous answer.

Now I don't only think that Tapio's answer was unpleasant, it was even alarming (I get vibes from the old East block).

In general, I agree with Bengt. Business and application decisions must, in the future, be made in consensus, this way is accepted with thankfulness.

The current decision measure with Bekvema is what we call in Sweden, in a modern language, something low, and even very low.

Regards

Per Jonson, who will be available most of the holidays

Technical specialist

*Like the 1,2g PXX/m which is according to the book <u>not authorised</u> by our company, Bekvema made it up!

Robin was out of email reach for the entire day and thought to react to this email exchange in writing now. What am I going to answer? Wonders Robin. What is the situation really about? Why are they so upset? How could the situation go so wrong within a few hours? Of course tensions have occurred before ... The communication between the Swedish sales team and Tapio usually goes all right; he makes the effort to speak Swedish although his mother tongue is Finnish. 'What am I going to write to Jaap van der Dorp?' wonders Robin. Robin has met Jaap only once, and he came across to him as being an old and conservative manager, clearly from another generation, and certainly not used to trying to understand that there are different ways of managing people in Sweden than in Belgium – where the General Head Quarters of Nickell are located.

Further reading

* Hofstede, G. (2001) Culture's Consequences: Comparing Values, Behaviors, Institutions, and Organisations Across Nations, 2nd edn. Thousand Oaks: Sage.
This volume is the second edition of the seminal work of Geert Hofstede. It presents five cultural dimensions (Power Distance, Individualism–Collectivism, Masculinity–Femininity, Uncertainty Avoidance and Long-term or Short-term Orientation). Each dimension is comprehensively introduced and discussed in its implications for, amongst others, work situations and HRM. This study is archetypical of the views on culture adopted in the positivist perspective.

* House, R. J., Hanges P. J., Javidan M., Dorfman, P. W. and Gupta, V. (eds) (2004) Culture, Leadership and Organisations: The GLOBE Study of 62 Societies. Thousand Oaks, CA: Sage.
This edited volume is the second major source of reference regarding cultural dimensions. It investigates how 62 societies compare on nine cultural dimensions, in practice and in value preferences. Each dimension is richly introduced and discussed in its implications for, amongst others, work situations, but especially leadership. The GLOBE database is more recent than the one used by Hofstede.

* D'Iribarne, P. (2002) 'Motivating workers in emerging countries: universal tools and local adaptations', Journal of Organisational Behavior, 23(3): 243–56.
This publication illustrates an interpretive analysis of radical changes in the Human Resource Management of the subsidiaries of two multinationals, Sgs-Thomson and Danone, in Morocco and in Mexico. The interpretive analysis shows how the same situation, which was workers' lack of motivation, had dissimilar origins, and thus had to be addressed differently.

It explains how motivation is introduced by changing the system of meanings that employees used to associate with their work, in other words, how they were accustomed to making sense of their work.

- Sackmann, S. A. (ed.) (1997) *Cultural Complexity in Organisations: Inherent Contrasts and Contradictions*. Newbury Park, CA: Sage.

This edited volume gathers interpretive works studying cultural influences on organisations in their various forms (e.g., national, organisational, sub-organisational). It illustrates the kind of knowledge achieved with the interpretive views and how this knowledge is useful to better understand some of the challenges faced by management. The edited volume starts with a broad review of various schools of thoughts in culture and management research.

- Zanoni, P. and Janssens, M. (2004) 'Deconstructing differences: the rhetoric of human resource managers' diversity discourses', *Organisation Studies*, 25(1): 55–74.

This article is an illustration of the type of knowledge and the mode of analysis performed by critical research using critical discourse analysis. Through critical examination of verbatim interviews with Human Resource managers of Flanders (Belgium), the authors show how discourses essentialise the others (those who are seen as 'different': persons with a disability, migrant workers, etc.), how their discourses devalue or value diversity, and also reaffirm management practices.

- Riad, S. (2005) 'The power of 'Organisational Culture' as a discursive formation in merger integration', *Organisation Studies*, 26(10):1529–1554.

This contribution illustrates the narrative construction of 'organisational culture' as something real, and which needs to be taken into account in for example, mergers and acquisitions. Adopting a Foucauldian perspective, the analysis is concerned with what discourses do: the way knowledge circulates and functions in relation to power. The report of two discourses on 'organisational culture' provides enlightening illustrations.

- Romani, L., Primecz, H. and Topçu, K. (forthcoming) 'Paradigm interplay for theory development: a methodological example with the *Kulturstandard* method', *Organisation Research Methods*.

This article details how to perform a positivist and an interpretive analysis of critical incidents occurring in cross-cultural work relations. The case of Swedish scientists involved in collaboration with Japanese researchers is used as an example. Data collection techniques but especially analytical steps are carefully detailed to help perform the two analyses. This article goes further than juxtaposing different views (as in this chapter), it places them in interaction (in interplay) to foster new theory development. Contributions are discussed for cross-cultural leadership. This article can help further your understanding of the positivist and the interpretive modes of analysis. It provides additional arguments on the benefit of applying several views for the analysis of a situation.

Internet resources

1 www.geert-hofstede.com: This site, developed by the International consulting organisation Itim (www.itim.org/) presents and utilises Geert Hofstede's research to provide visitors with comparative tools, country profiles and other valuable information to those who want to access Hofstede's research and outcomes (see also www.geerthofstede.nl)

2 www.sietar.org: The Society for Intercultural Education, Training and Research (SIETAR) is the world's largest interdisciplinary network for professionals working in the field of intercultural relations. SIETAR encourages the development and application of knowledge and skills that promote and reinforce intercultural relations at the individual, group, organisation and community levels. The society is represented in many countries around the world and organises frequent conferences and workshops.

3 www.intercultural.org: The Intercultural Communication Institute (ICI) is a private, non-profit foundation designed to foster an awareness and appreciation of cultural differences in both the international and domestic arenas. It provides for example, education and professional development in intercultural communication.

4 www.dialogin.com: The mission of the Delta Intercultural Academy is to act as a global knowledge and learning community on culture, communication and management in international business. The website provides information or reviews of a large range of books, articles and commentaries on cross-cultural activities. It advertises conferences, training and job offers and regularly organises e-conferences between Dialogin members (open membership) and influential researchers in the field of culture and management.

Self-assessment questions

Indicative answers to these questions can be found on the companion website at www.sagepub.co.uk/harzing3e.

1 **When facing a situation involving culture, you will need to ask yourself different kinds of questions to use the different views presented in this chapter. Can you name sample questions that are helpful to adopt positivist, interpretive and critical views?** pg 101

2 **Each view is best suited to develop a certain kind of knowledge. Can you provide an example of knowledge achieved by the positivist view?** 100

3 **Can you provide an example of knowledge achieved by the interpretive view?** See page 90.87 100

4 **Can you provide an example of knowledge achieved by the critical view?**
5 **Which are the characteristic elements of the positivist, interpretive and critical views on culture?**

Notes

This work was made possible thanks to the financial support of the Swedish Research Council (Vetenskapsrådet].

References

Abrahamsson, B. (2007) *Hierarki. Om ordning, makt och kristallisering*. Malmö: Liber.

Adler, N., Doktor, R. and Redding, G. (1986) 'From the Atlantic to the Pacific century: cross-cultural management reviewed', *Journal of Management*, 12(2): 295–318.

Åkerblom, S. (1999) *Delade meningar om ledarskap? En enkätstudie av mellanchefers föreställningar om framstående ledarskap*. Stockholm: EFI.

Alvesson, M. (2002a) *Understanding Organizational Culture*. London: Sage.

Alvesson, M. (2002b) *Postmodernism and Social Research*. Buckingham: Open University Press.

Alvesson, M. and Deetz, S. (2000) *Doing Critical Management Research*. London: Sage.

Benedict. R. (1934/1989) *Patterns of Culture*. Boston: Houghton Mifflin Company.

Berry, J.W., Poortinga, Y.H., Segall, M.H. and Dasen, P.R. (eds) (1992) *Cross-Cultural Psychology: Research and Applications*. Cambridge: Cambridge University Press.

Bhabha, H.K. (1994) *The Location of Culture*. New York, NY: Routledge.

Boyacigiller, N.A., Kleinberg, M.J., Phillips, M.E. and Sackmann, S.A. (2004) 'Conceptualizing culture: elucidating the streams of research in international cross-cultural management', in B. J. Punnett and O. Shenkar (eds), *Handbook for International Management Research*, 2nd edn. pp. 99–167. Ann Arbor: University of Michigan Press.

Budhwar, P.S. and Sparrow, P.R. (2002) 'Strategic HRM through the cultural looking glass: mapping the cognition of British and Indian managers', *Organization Studies*, 23(4): 599–638.

Burrell, G. and Morgan, G. (1979) *Sociological Paradigms and Organisational Analysis*. London: Heinemann Educational Books.

Carl, D., Gupta, V. and Javidan, M. (2004) 'Power distance', in R.J. House, P.J. Hanges, M. Javidan, P.W. Dorfman and V. Gupta (eds), *Culture, Leadership and Organizations: The GLOBE Study of 62 Societies*. pp. 513–63. Thousand Oaks, CA: Sage.

Carr, A. (2006) 'In the constructive tradition of being critical', *Critical Perspectives on International Bus iness*, 2(2): 79–90.

Chalmers, A.F. (1999) *What is This Thing Called Science?* 3rd edn. Buckingham: Open University Press.

Chapman, M. (1997) 'Social anthropology, business studies and cultural issues', *International Studies of Management and Organization*, 26(4): 3–29.

Child, J. (2000) 'Theorizing about organization cross-nationally', in L.C. Cheng Joseph and R. B. Peterson (eds), *Advances in International Comparative Management*, Vol. 13. pp. 27–75. Greenwich, CT: JAI Press.

Church, A.T. (1998) 'The cross-cultural perspective in the study of personality', *Journal of Cross-Cultural Psychology*, 29(1): 32–62.

Clifford, J. and Marcus, G.E. (eds) (1986) *Writing Culture. The Poetics and Politics of Ethnography.* Berkeley, CA: University of California Press.

Czarniawska, B. (1986) 'The management of meaning in the polish crisis', *Journal of Management Studies*, 23(3): 313–31.

Czarniawska-Joerges, B. (1992) *Exploring Complex Organizations.* Newbury Park, CA: Sage.

Dahlén, T. (1997) *Among the Interculturalists: An Emergent Profession and its Packaging of Knowledge.* Stockholm: Gotab-Almqvist and Wiksell International.

D'Andrade, R. (2000) 'The sad story of anthropology 1950–1999', *Cross-Cultural Research*, 34(3): 219–32.

Deetz, S. (1996) 'Describing differences in approaches to organization science: rethinking Burrell and Morgan and their legacy', *Organization Science*, 7(2): 191–207.

Den Hartog, D. (2004) 'Assertiveness', in R.J. House, P.J. Hanges, M. Javidan, P.W. Dorfman and V. Gupta (eds), *Culture, Leadership and Organizations: The GLOBE Study of 62 Societies.* pp. 395–436. Thousand Oaks, CA: Sage.

d'Iribarne, P. (1989) *La logique de l'honneur.* Paris: Le Seuil.

d'Iribarne, P. (2002) 'Motivating workers in emerging countries: universal tools and local adaptations', *Journal of Organizational Behavior*, 23(3): 243–56.

d'Iribarne, P. (2009) 'National cultures and organizations in search of a theory. An interpretative approach', *International Journal of Cross-Cultural Management*, 9(3): 309–21.

Donaldson, L. (2003) 'Organization theory as a positivist science', in H. Tsoukas and C. Knudsen (eds), *The Oxford Handbook of Organization Theory.* pp. 39–62. Oxford: Oxford University Press.

Dumont, L. (1991) *L'ideologie allemande.* Homo aequalis II. Paris: Gallimard.

Earley, P.C. and Gibson, C.B. (1998) 'Taking stock in our progress on Individualism-Collectivism: 100 years of solidarity and community', *Journal of Management*, 24(3): 265–304.

Earley, P.C. and Singh, H. (1995) 'International and intercultural management research: What's next?', *Academy of Management Journal*, 38(2): 327–40.

Erickson, P. with L. Murphy (1998) *A History of Anthropological Theory.* Peterborough: Broadview Press.

Ferner, A., Quintanilla, J. and Varul, M.Z. (2001) 'Country-of-origin effects, host-country effects, and the management of HR in multinationals: German companies in Britain and Spain', *Journal of World Business*, 36(2): 107–27.

Fougère, M. (2006) 'Cultural (In)Sensitivity in International Management Textbooks: A Postcolonial Reading. Paper presented at the Annual Meeting of the Academy of Management, Atlanta, Georgia, August 11–16.

Fougère, M. and Moulettes, A. (2007) 'The construction of the modern west and the backward rest: studying the discourse of Hofstede's culture's consequences', *Journal of Multicultural Discourses*, 2(1): 1–19.

Frost, P.J., Moore, L.F., Louis, M.R., Lundberg, C.C. and Martin, J. (eds) (1985) *Organizational Culture.* Beverly Hills, CA: Sage.

Frost, P.J., Moore, L.F., Louis, M.R., Lundberg, C.C. and Martin, J. (eds) (1992) *Reframing Culture.* Thousand Oaks, CA: Sage.

Gagliardi, P. (ed.) (1990) *Symbols and Artifacts: Views of the Corporate Landscape*. Berlin: de Gruyter.

Gannon, M.J. (2004) *Understanding Global Cultures: Metaphorical Journeys Through 28 Nations, Clusters of Nations, and Continents*, 3rd edn. Thousand Oaks, CA: Sage.

Gannon, M.J. (2009) 'The cultural metaphoric method. Description, analysis, and critique', *International Journal of Cross-Cultural Management*, 9(3): 275–87.

Geertz, C. (1973/1993) *The Interpretation of Cultures*. London: Fontana Press.

Geertz, C. (1988) *Works and Lives: The Anthropologist as Author*. Stanford, CA: Stanford University Press.

Gelfand, M.J., Bhawuk, D.P.S., Nishii, L.H. and Bechtold, D.J. (2004) 'Individualism and collectivism', in R.J. House, P.J. Hanges, M. Javidan, P.W. Dorfman and V. Gupta (eds), *Culture, Leadership and Organizations: The GLOBE Study of 62 Societies*. pp. 437–512. Thousand Oaks, CA: Sage.

Gelfand, M.J., Erez, M. and Aycan, Z. (2007) 'Cross-cultural organizational behaviour', *Annual Review of Psychology*, 58(1): 479–514.

Gingrich, A. (1998) 'Review essay: toward an anthropology of Germany: a culture of moralist self-education?', *Current Anthropology*, 39(4): 567–72.

Guba, E. and Lincoln, Y.S. (2005) 'Paradigmatic controversies, contradictions, and emerging confluences', in N.K. Denzin and Y.S. Lincoln (eds), *The Sage Handbook of Qualitative Research*, 3rd edn. pp. 191–215. Thousand Oaks, CA: Sage.

Harris, M. (1999) *Theories of Culture in Postmodern Times*. Walnut Creek: Altamira Press.

Headland, T., Pike, K. and Harris, M. (eds) (1990) *Emics and Etics: The Insider/Outsider Debate*. Newbury Park, CA: Sage.

Henry, A. (2007) 'Revolution by procedures in Cameroon', in P. d'Iribarne and A. Henry, *Successful Companies in the Developing World: Managing in Synergy with Cultures*. Paris: Agence Française de Développement.

Hofstede, G. (1980) *Cultures' Consequences*. Beverly Hills, CA: Sage.

Hofstede, G. (2001) *Culture's Consequences: Comparing Values, Behaviors, Institutions, and Organizations Across Nations*, 2nd edn. Thousand Oaks, CA: Sage.

Holmberg, I. and Åkerblom, S. (2006) 'Modelling leadership – implicit leadership theories in Sweden', *Scandinavian Journal of Management*, 22(4): 307–29.

House, R.J., Hanges, P.J., Javidan, M., Dorfman, P.W. and Gupta, V. (eds) (2004) *Culture, Leadership and Organizations: The GLOBE Study of 62 Societies*. Thousand Oaks, CA: Sage.

Jahoda, G. and Krewer, B. (1997) 'History of cross-cultural and cultural psychology', in J.W. Berry, Y.H. Poortinga and J. Pandey (eds), *Handbook of Cross-Cultural Psychology*, *Vol. 1 Theory and Methods*, 2nd edn. pp. 1–42. Boston: Allyn and Bacon.

Kabasakal, H. and Bodur, M. (2004) 'Humane orientation in societies, organizations, and leader attributes', in R.J. House, P.J. Hanges, M. Javidan, P.W. Dorfman and V. Gupta (eds), *Culture, Leadership and Organizations: The GLOBE Study of 62 Societies*. pp. 564–601. Thousand Oaks, CA: Sage.

Kirkman, B.L., Lowe, K.B. and Gibson, C.B. (2006) 'A quarter century of culture's consequences: a review of empirical research incorporating Hofstede's cultural values framework', *Journal of International Business Studies*, 37(3): 285–320.

Kluckhohn, F. and Strodtbeck, F. (eds) (1961) *Variations in Value Orientations*. New York, NY: Row, Peterson and Company.

Kuhn, T.S. (1970) *The Structure of Scientific Revolutions*, 2nd edn. Chicago: University of Chicago Press.

Kunda, G. (1992) *Engineering Culture: Control and Commitment in a High-tech Corporation*. Philadelphia: Temple University Press.

Kuper, A. (1999) *Culture: The Anthropologists' Account*. Cambridge: Harvard University Press.

Kwek, D. (2003) 'Decolonizing and *re*-presenting Culture's Consequences. A Postcolonial Critique of Cross-cultural Studies in Management', in A. Prasad (ed.), *Postcolonial Theory and Organizational Analysis: A Critical Engagement*. pp. 121–46. New York, NY: Palgrave Macmillan.

Leung, K., Bond, M.H., Reimel de Carrasquel, S., Muñoz, C., Hernández, M., Murakami, F., Yamaguchi, S., Bierbrauer, G. and Singelis, T.M. (2002) 'Social axioms. The search for universal dimensions of general beliefs about how the world functions', *Journal of Cross-Cultural Psychology*, 33(3): 286–302.

Leung, K., Bhagat, R.S., Buchan, N.R., Erez, M. and Gibson, C. (2005) 'Culture and international business: recent advances and their implications for future research', *Journal of International Business Studies*, 36(4): 357–78.

Lowe, S. (2001) 'In the kingdom of the blind, the one-eyed man is king', *International Journal of Cross-Cultural Management*, 1(3): 313–32.

Lowe, S. (2002) 'The cultural shadows of cross-cultural research: images of culture', *Culture and Organization*, 8(1): 21–34.

Lowe, S., Moore, F. and Carr, A. N. (2007) 'Paradigmapping studies of culture and organization', *International Journal of Cross-Cultural Management*, 7(2): 237–51.

Maznevski, L.M., DiStefano, J.J., Gomez, C.B., Noorderhaven, N.G. and Wu, P.-C. (2002) 'Cultural dimensions at the individual level of analysis', *International Journal of Cross-Cultural Management*, 2(3): 275–95.

Mead, M. (1928/1990) *Coming of Age in Samoa*. Magnolia: Peter Smith.

Morgan, G. (1980) 'Paradigms, metaphors, and puzzle solving in organization theory', *Administrative Science Quarterly*, 25: 605–22.

Morgan, G. (1986) *Images of Organization*. Thousand Oaks, CA: Sage.

Mutman, M. (2006) 'Writing culture: postmodernism and ethnography', *Anthropological Theory*, 6(2): 153–78.

Nielsen, C.S., Soares, A.M. and Páscoa Machado, C. (2009) 'The cultural metaphor revisited. Exploring dimensions, complexities and paradoxes through the Portuguese Fado', *International Journal of Cross-Cultural Management*, 9(3): 289–308.

Özkazanç-Pan, B. (2008) 'International management research meets 'the rest of the world'', *Academy of Management Review*, 33(4): 964–74.

Parker, M. (2000) *Organizational Culture and Identity: Unity and Division at Work*. London, Sage.

Parsons, T. (1951) *The Social System*. New York, NY: Free Press.

Peltonen, T. (2006) 'Critical theoretical perspectives on international human resource management', in G. Stahl and I. Björkman (eds), *Handbook of Research in International Human Resource Management*. pp. 523–35. Cheltenham: Edward Elgar.

Peterson, M.F. and Pike, K. (2002) 'Emics and etics for organizational studies. A lesson in contrast from linguistics', *International Journal of Cross-Cultural Management*, 2(1): 5–19.

Pondy, L.R., Frost, P., Morgan, G. and Dandridge, T. (eds) (1983) *Organizational Symbolism*. Greenwich: JAI.

Prasad, A. (ed.) (2003) *Postcolonial Theory and Organizational Analysis: a Critical Engagement*. New York, NY: Palgrave Macmillan.

Primecz, H., Romani, L. and Sackmann, S.A. (2009) 'Multiple perspectives in Cross-cultural management', *International Journal of Cross-Cultural Management*, 9(3): 267–74.

Redding, S.G. (1994) 'Comparative management theory: Jungle, zoo or fossil bed?', *Organization Studies*, 15(3): 323–60.

Redding, S.G. (2005) 'The thick description and comparison of societal systems of capitalism', *Journal of International Business Studies*, 36(2): 123–55.

Riad, S. (2005) 'The power of organizational culture as a discursive formation in merger integration', *Organization Studies*, 26(10): 1529–54.

Rokeach, M. (1973) *The Nature of Human Values*. New York, NY: Free Press.

Romani, L., Primecz, H. and Topçu, K. (Forthcoming) 'Paradigm interplay for theory development: a methodological example with the Kulturstandard method', *Organization Research Methods*.

Sackmann, S. (ed.) (1997) *Cultural Complexity in Organizations: Inherent Contrasts and Contradictions*. Newbury Park, CA: Sage.

Sackmann, S.A. and Phillips, M.E. (2004) 'Contextual influences on culture research: shifting assumptions for new workplace realities', *International Journal of Cross-Cultural Management*, 4(3): 370–90.

Sagiv, L. and Schwartz, S.H. (2000) 'A new look at national culture: illustrative applications to role stress and managerial behaviour', in N.M. Ashkanasy, C.P.M. Wilderom and M.F. Peterson (eds), *Handbook of Organizational Culture and Climate*. pp. 417–35. Thousand Oaks, CA: Sage.

Said, E. (1978) *Orientalism*. London: Routledge and Kegan Paul.

Schwandt, T. (1994) 'Constructivist, interpretivist approaches to human inquiry', in N.K. Denzin and Y.S. Lincoln (eds), *Handbook of Qualitative Research*. pp. 118–37. Thousand Oaks, CA: Sage.

Schwandt, T. (2000) 'Three epistemological stances for qualitative enquiry: Interpretivism, hermeneutics, and social constructivism', in N.K. Denzin, and Y.S. Lincoln (eds), *The Handbook of Qualitative Research*, 2nd edn. pp. 189–213. Thousand Oaks, CA: Sage.

Schwartz, S.H. (1994) 'Beyond individualism/collectivism: new cultural dimensions of values', in U. Kim (ed.), *Individualism and Collectivism: Theory, Method, and Applications*. pp. 85–119. London: Sage.

Schwartz, S.H. (2004) 'Mapping and interpreting cultural differences around the world', in E. Vinken, J. Soeters and P. Ester (eds), *Comparing Cultures. Dimensions of Culture in a Comparative Perspective*. Leiden: Brill.

Schwartz, S.H. and Bilsky, W. (1987) 'Towards a psychological structure of human values', *Journal of Personality and Social Psychology*, 53: 550–62.

Shrivastava, P. and Schneider, S. (1984) 'Organizational frames of references', *Human Relations* 37: 795–809.

Sims, H. and Gioia, D. (eds) (1986) *The Thinking Organization: Dynamics of Organizational Social Cognition*. San Francisco, CA: Jossey-Bass.

Smith, P.B. and Bond, M.H. (1998) *Social Psychology Across Cultures*, 2nd edn. Harlow: Prentice Hall, Pearson Education.

Smith, P.B. and Schwartz, S.H. (1997) 'Values', in J. Berry, M.H. Segall and C. Kagitcibasi (eds), *Handbook of Cross-Cultural Psychology, Vol. 3 Social Behavior and Applications*, 2nd edn. pp. 77–118. Boston: Allyn and Bacon.

Smith, P.B., Peterson, P.F. and Schwartz, S.H. (2002) 'Cultural values, sources of guidance, and their relevance to managerial behaviour. A 47-nation study', *Journal of Cross-Cultural Psychology*, 33(2): 188–208.

Smith, P.B., Andersen, J.A., Ekelund, B., Graversen, G. and Ropo, A. (2003) 'In search of Nordic management styles', *Scandinavian Journal of Management*, 19(4): 491–507.

Søderberg, A.-M. and Holden, N. (2002) 'Rethinking cross-cultural management in a globalizing business world', *International Journal of Cross-Cultural Management*, 2(1): 103–21.

Spivak, G.C. (1987) *In Other Worlds: Essays in cultural politics*. New York, NY: Routledge.

Triandis, H.C. (1995) *Individualism and Collectivism*. Boulder: Westview Press.

Trompenaars, F. (1993) *Riding the Waves of Culture: Understanding Cultural Diversity in Business*. London: Nicholas Brealey Publishing Limited.

Tsui, A.S., Nifadkar, S.S. and Yi Ou, A. (2007) 'Cross-national, cross-cultural organizational behavior research: advances, gaps, and recommendations', *Journal of Management*, 33(3): 426–78.

Vaara, E. (2002) 'On the discursive construction of success/failure in narratives of post-merger integration', *Organization Studies*, 23(2): 211–48.

Von Humboldt, A. (1830–1835/1985) 'Über die Verschiedenheit des menschlichen Sprachbaues und ihren Einfluß auf die geistige Entwicklung des Menschengeschlechts', in M. Riedel (ed.), *Geschichte der Philosophie in Text und Darstellung*, Vol. 7: pp. 66–100. Stuttgart: Reclam.

Weber, M. (1904/1996) *Die protestantische Ethik und der 'Geist' des Kapitalismus*, herausgegeben und eingeleitet von K. Lichtblau and J. Weiss. Weinheim: Beltz Athenäum.

Weber, M. (1911/1978) *Economy and Society: an outline of interpretive sociology*. Vol. 1. Edited by G. Roth and C. Wittich. Berkley, CA: University of California Press.

Westwood, R. (2006) 'International business and management studies as an orientalist discourse: a postcolonial critique', *Critical Perspectives on International Business*, 2(2): 91–113.

Whitley, R.D. (1992a) *Business Systems in East Asia*. London: Sage.

Whitley, R.D. (1992b) *European Business Systems: Firms and Markets in their National Contexts*. London: Sage.

Willmott, H. (1993) 'Strength is ignorance; slavery is freedom: managing culture in modern organizations', *Journal of Management Studies*, 30(4): 515–52.

Ybema, S.B. (1997) 'Telling tales: contrasts and commonalities within the organization of an amusement park. Confronting and combining different perspectives', in S.A. Sackmann (ed.), *Cultural Complexity in Organizations: Inherent Contrasts and Contradictions*. pp. 160–86. London: Sage.

Ybema, S.B. and Byun, H. (2009) 'Cultivating cultural differences in asymmetric power relations', *International Journal of Cross-Cultural Management*, 9(3): 339–58.

Young, R. (2001) *Postcolonialism: An Historical Introduction*. Oxford: Blackwell.

Zanoni, P. and Janssens, M. (2004) 'Deconstructing differences: the rhetoric of human resource managers' diversity discourses', *Organization Studies*, 25(1): 55–74.

4
Human Resource Management in Cross-Border Mergers and Acquisitions

**Vladimir Pucik, Ingmar Björkman,
Paul Evans and Günter K. Stahl**

Contents

Learning Objectives

After reading this chapter you will be able to

- Understand the impact of cultural differences on M&A performance

- Master the logic behind different approaches to cross-border post-merger integration

- Identify which cultural and people issues are particularly critical to the success or failure of mergers and acquisitions

- See the importance of HRM in executing international M&A strategies

Chapter Outline

The chapter reviews prior research dealing with integration processes in cross-border M&As and then considers the meaning and strategic logic of cultural integration. Major HRM challenges occurring at different stages of the M&A are discussed and conclusions made on the implications for research and practice.

1 Introduction

Mergers and acquisitions (M&As) have become an increasingly popular strategy for achieving corporate growth and diversification, and there has been a dramatic growth in M&As in the global marketplace during the last two decades. During this period the global profile of M&As has changed. One significant shift is that the proportion of cross-border M&As increased from less than 30 per cent in 2000 to almost half of the total value of M&As worldwide in 2007.

The ultimate driver of cross-border M&A activity is the increase in global competition and the corresponding erosion of national boundaries. Companies have followed their customers as they respond to the pressures of obtaining scale in a rapidly consolidating global economy. In combination with other trends, such as increased corporate restructuring, reduced trade barriers, easier access to global pools of capital, and access to new markets and specialised resources, globalisation has spurred an unprecedented surge in cross-border M&As (Finkelstein, 1999; Shimizu et al., 2004; Stahl and Javidan, 2009). Even if M&A fever subsides whenever the global economy cools off – such as after the dot.com-boom ended in 2000 and during the global financial crisis that began in 2008 – more M&A deals can be expected in the long

More M&As because of Globalization

run. Another change in the worldwide profile is that more M&As are now carried out within Asia and by Asian firms – in 2007, 18 per cent of the value of M&As was conducted by Asian firms (Evans et al., 2010).

Extensive research has been conducted on the performance of M&As. Much of the early research was conducted by consulting firms and investment banks but there is now also a large and rapidly growing body of academic research on the topic. Several early non-academic studies suggested that only a minority of the deals achieved the promised financial results (*The Economist*, 1997; A.T. Kearney, 1999; KPMG, 1999). However, recent academic research (Dobbs et al., 2006; King et al., 2004) and consulting reports are more positive – for example it was reported that 31 per cent of deals created value while 26 per cent reduced value (KPMG, 2006). In other words, some M&As are successful, some have little effect on the performance of the acquiring firm, and some are disasters for the buyer, and specifically its owners.

The sellers virtually always emerge as winners as the buyer typically pays a significant premium for the target. When the buyer does overpay, no amount of post-merger integration skill can bring back the value lost when the deal was signed. However, more companies, such as CEMEX, Cisco and GE, have become very experienced and effective in managing M&As. For every troubled mega-deal that attracts publicity, there will be many small acquisitions that are substantially more successful.

M&A failures are often due to problems of integrating the different cultures and workforces of the combined firms (Marks and Mirvis, 2001; Schweiger and Lippert, 2005; Shrivastava, 1986). Socio-cultural integration of different organisational cultures, human resource systems, managerial viewpoints, and other aspects of organisational life can lead to sharp inter-organisational conflict (Cartwright and Cooper, 1996; Stahl and Sitkin, 2005). In a survey of more than 200 chief executives of European companies conducted by Booz, Allen and Hamilton (cited in Cartwright and Cooper, 1996: 28), respondents ranked the ability to integrate culturally as more important than financial or strategic factors in M&As.

Problems are often exacerbated when M&As occur between companies based in different countries. Cross-border M&As involve unique challenges, as countries have different legal systems and regulatory requirements, accounting standards, employment systems, and so on (Aguilera and Dencker, 2004; Child et al., 2001; Shimizu et al., 2004). In addition to obstacles created by differences in the broader institutional environment, cultural differences in management styles and business norms as well as the often unanticipated challenges of communicating across long distances, can undermine the success of M&As that otherwise have a sound strategic and financial fit – along with problems arising from different communication styles, and, in some instances, cultural chauvinism and xenophobia (Goulet and Schweiger, 2006; Olie, 1990; Vaara, 2003).

Daimler Chrysler

For example, the poor performance of DaimlerChrysler, one of the most talked-about mergers of the past decade, is often attributed to a culture clash that resulted in major integration problems (Epstein, 2004; Kühlmann and Dowling, 2005; Vlasic and Stertz, 2000). Differences between Daimler and Chrysler in management philosophy, compensation systems, and decision-making processes caused friction between members of senior management, while lower level employees fought over issues such as dress code, working hours, and smoking on the job. Language also became an issue. While most managers on the Daimler side could speak some English, not all were able to do so with the ease and accuracy that is needed for effective working relationships. And among the Chrysler managers and employees, few had any knowledge of German. Cases like these highlight the need to understand more insightfully the cultural aspects of international M&As. We need better answers to questions such as how much of the tension and conflict that emerged in the Daimler–Chrysler merger was due to cultural differences and how much was caused by poor execution of post-merger integration and in particular the neglect of its people-related dimensions?

need to know how much of conflict was due to culture, and how much was due to poor integration.

This chapter begins with a review of prior research dealing with integration processes in cross-border M&As, examining the potentially critical role that cultural differences play in the M&A process. The second part of the chapter focuses on how the meaning of cultural integration depends on the strategic logic behind the merger or acquisition. The third part discusses the key HRM challenges at different stages of the M&A process. The chapter concludes with a discussion of the implications for M&A research and practice.

prior Research

meaning of cultural integration

challenges

implications

2 Cultural differences and cross-border M&A performance

It has often been argued that cross-border M&As are less successful than domestic transactions. For example, a survey of top managers in large European acquirers showed that 61 per cent of them believed that cross-border acquisitions are riskier than domestic ones (Angwin and Savill, 1997). As suggested above, the reasoning is that cultural and communication barriers can be a major obstacle to achieving integration benefits. The 'cultural distance hypothesis', in its most general form, states that the difficulties, costs and risks associated with cross-cultural contact increase with growing cultural differences between two individuals, groups or organisations (Hofstede, 2001; Kogut and Singh, 1988).

Consistent with the cultural distance hypothesis, post-merger integration problems have often been explained in terms of 'cultural distance' (Morosini et al., 1998), 'culture compatibility' (Cartwright and Cooper, 1996), 'cultural misfit' (Weber et al., 1996), 'management style dissimilarity' (Larsson and Finkelstein, 1999), 'acquisition cultural risk' (David and Singh, 1994), or similar concepts. Traditional theories of M&A integration suggest that the organisational and/or national cultures of merging firms should be similar, or at least complementary, in order to facilitate successful integration (see the models of Cartwright and Cooper, 1993; Nahavandi and Malekzadeh, 1988; Sales and Mirvis, 1984). For example, Cartwright and Cooper's cultural fit model proposes that, in mergers between equals, the corporate cultures of the two firms should be similar or adjoining types because both organisations have to adapt to the other culture while creating a kind of 'third culture'. Integration in international M&As seems to be particularly difficult because this requires 'double layered acculturation', whereby different national cultures as well as corporate cultures have to be combined (Barkema et al., 1996).

3 Research on culture in international M&A

The empirical evidence suggests that the fear of cultural differences may be exaggerated. Contrary to the propositions reviewed in the above section of this chapter, much of the recent research shows that cross-border M&As are not less successful than domestic transactions (for reviews, see Schoenberg, 2000; Schweiger and Goulet, 2000; Stahl and Voigt, 2008; Teerikangas and Very, 2006). In fact, there is some evidence that the success rate of cross-border deals may even be higher (Bertrand and Zitouna, 2008; Bleeke et al., 1993; Chakrabarti et al., 2009; KPMG, 1999; Larsson and Finkelstein, 1999). One source of evidence comes from studies that examined the impact of cultural distance on M&A performance. While some studies found that cultural differences had a negative effect on M&A performance (e.g. Chatterjee et al., 1992; Datta, 1991; Weber, 1996), others found a positive effect (e.g. Larsson and Risberg, 1998; Morosini et al., 1998; Very et al., 1996).

A number of reasons have been suggested for these contradictory findings. One explanation is that there tend to be greater complementarities between the parties in international acquisitions (Björkman et al., 2007; Morosini et al., 1998; Vermeulen and Barkema, 2001). Cross-border acquirers often buy companies in related industries – familiar businesses to which they can add value and, conversely, from which they can gain value. For instance, the acquisition of a foreign competitor can give the buyer access to local markets as well as to new products, technologies and local market knowledge. The target may benefit from similar resources and competences from the buyer, while the increased scale and international experience of the combined organisation are additional benefits of such mergers. Also, companies that acquire internationally often have prior M&A experience, learning from their mistakes and implementing processes that enable them to execute cross-border deals more and more effectively (Pucik and Evans, 2004).

Finally, it may be that the more overt cross-cultural dimensions of such deals lead buyers to pay more attention to the softer, less tangible, but critical human resource aspects of M&A management (Björkman et al., 2007; Morosini et al., 1998). Larsson and Risberg (1998) found higher degrees of acculturation (defined as the development of jointly shared meanings that foster cooperation between the merging firms), lower levels of employee resistance, and a higher extent of synergy realisation in cross-border M&As. Acculturation and synergy realisation were particularly high in cross-border acquisitions that were characterised by strong differences in organisational culture – culture clash – a finding that directly contradicts the cultural distance hypothesis. They argue that, in contrast to domestic M&As, where organisational culture differences tend to be neglected, the presence of more obvious national cultural differences may increase the awareness of the significance of such cultural factors in the integration process. They conclude that 'cross-border M&A may not only be "cursed" with additional culture clashes but also be "blessed" with a higher propensity for culturally aware selection and integration management' (1998: 40).

Other authors have offered additional explanations why cultural differences in M&As, under some circumstances, can be an asset rather than a liability. Morosini and colleagues (1998), in a study of cross-border acquisitions, found that national cultural distance enhanced post-acquisition performance by providing access to the target's and/or the acquirer's diverse set of routines and repertoires embedded in national culture. In a study of acculturative stress in European cross-border M&As, Very and colleagues (1996) found that cultural differences elicited perceptions of attraction rather than stress, depending on the nationalities of the buying and acquiring firms. Consistent with the findings of Morosini and colleagues (1998) and of Larsson and Risberg (1998), they concluded that the cultural problems associated with integrating acquisitions may be amplified in domestic rather than cross-national settings. 'Acculturative stress is a complex phenomenon, sometimes influenced by cultural differences, but not necessarily in the expected direction' (1996: 103).

4 Beyond cultural difference

In summary, there is evidence that cross-border M&As, under some circumstances at least, can be more successful than domestic deals, and that the inherent cultural differences can be as much as an asset as a liability. Indeed, results from a recent study of 800 cross-border acquisitions suggest that these may perform better in the long run if the acquirer and the target come from countries that are culturally more disparate (Chakrabarti et al., 2009), reinforcing the conclusion that the cultural distance hypothesis provides too simplified a view of the cultural processes involved in international M&As.

If handled properly,

cross-border M&As, with greater cultural distance can perform better.

Consistent with a 'process perspective' on acquisitions (Haspeslagh and Jemison, 1991; Jemison and Sitkin, 1986), research suggests that M&A outcomes depend heavily on the strategic logic behind the merger as well as the management of the integration process (Evans et al., 2010). Whether cultural differences have a positive or negative impact on M&A performance is likely to depend on the nature and extent of the cultural differences, the interventions chosen to manage these differences, and the integration approach that is adopted. Here, the research on the impact of culture in cross-border M&As offers two important conclusions.

First, it is important to distinguish between different levels of culture. For example, in a related acquisition that needs a higher degree of business integration, cultural differences can create tensions that make integration more difficult. However, these differences are more likely to be due to differences in organisational than national culture (Stahl and Voigt, 2008). Also, not all American firms are like GE and not all German firms are like Daimler. And in a recent acquisition of a French-owned global business by an American firm, what mattered for the integration in China to be successful was not the difference between the Americans and the French, but between the 'Beijing' and 'Shanghai' cultures of the two local affiliates to be merged.

Second, the nature of the deal matters (Chakrabarti et al., 2009). In addition, there is some evidence that a lower level of integration in international acquisitions may be associated with better performance (Slangen, 2006) and cultural differences were actually found to be positively associated with post-acquisition performance in M&As that required lower integration, probably due to increased opportunities for mutual learning (Stahl and Voigt, 2008).

In today's global business environment, where strategic imperatives drive many potential M&A deals forward, companies no longer have the luxury of avoiding potential deals on the grounds of cultural issues. The proper response to cultural differences between buyer and target is not to avoid deals where there is a risk of culture clash but to manage and mitigate the risks. This requires disaggregating imprecisely defined cultural issues into discrete, manageable elements. Most of these are connected to the management of people. In this context, Evans and colleagues (2010) observed that cross-border M&As promote some convergence in HRM policies and practices towards accepted 'best practice', such as performance-related compensation and team-based work organisation.

5 What does integration mean?

In a merger or acquisition, the concept of 'integration' has different meanings depending on the strategic logic behind the merger in question. Most companies use the term 'integration' to describe the post-merger activities designed to bind the two

[handwritten margin notes: assimilation VS true integration / choice between them depends on / Strategic intent & intended culture of the new org. / make it like the Buyer]

companies. But what happens in many integration processes is actually assimilation, a process that is fundamentally different from 'true' integration – indeed, the vast majority of so-called mergers are in fact acquisitions.

The logic of assimilation is simple: make the acquired company just like the purchaser. However, companies are sensitive to public perceptions and do not want to be seen as being a foreign bully, and so they are often hesitant to proclaim their objective of assimilating the acquired firm, fearing that it may compromise the deal. This frequently creates confusion and mistrust that makes the assimilation process more difficult. In contrast, GE Capital, the financial services arm of General Electric offers blunt advice to the management of firms that it acquires around the world: 'If you do not want to change, don't put yourself for sale'. GE makes it very clear to the acquired company that it now has to play by GE's rules, and provides a framework for guiding the process of integration and formation of new relationships.

[handwritten margin notes: firms try to sugar coat the process to outsiders / – But it's better to be blunt]

In the case of true integration, the emphasis is on capturing hidden synergies by sharing and leveraging capabilities. Sometimes companies may decide to establish a new identity as with Novartis, which was formed through the merger of Ciba-Geigy and Sandoz in 1996 to create a global life sciences giant. Both approaches to M&A implementation have their merits. The choice between assimilation or true integration depends on the strategic intent behind the acquisition and the desired cultural characteristics of the new organisation. Choosing an approach that does not match with the strategy or the desired cultural outcomes can significantly reduce the value created by the acquisition.

[handwritten margin note: capturing hidden synergies by sharing & leveraging capabilities.]

A useful way of formulating the acquisition logic, as shown in Figure 4.1, is to focus on the cultural 'end-state' and the path to reach this (Marks and Mirvis, 1998). What kind of culture is desired for the new entity, and how much change will be required within both acquiring and acquired companies in order to achieve the goal?

When no cultural change is desired in the acquired company, then it can be considered as a *preservation* acquisition. When a large amount of change in the acquired company is expected but with relatively little change for the acquirer, then *absorption* is the most likely path. When major cultural change is expected in both entities then the result is a *cultural transformation* while the selective combination of the most appealing features of the two cultures is often described as a *best-of-both' acquisition*. In rare cases, the culture of the acquirer is blended into that of the acquired firm in a *reverse merger*.

Preservation acquisitions

When a deal is announced, it often contains a reference saying that the acquired company will preserve its independence and cultural autonomy. This often occurs when one of the rationales behind the merger is to secure talented management or other soft skills (such as speed of product development) and to retain them; or when conformance to the rules and systems of the acquiring company could be detrimental to the acquired company's competitive advantage.

[handwritten margin note: purpose →]

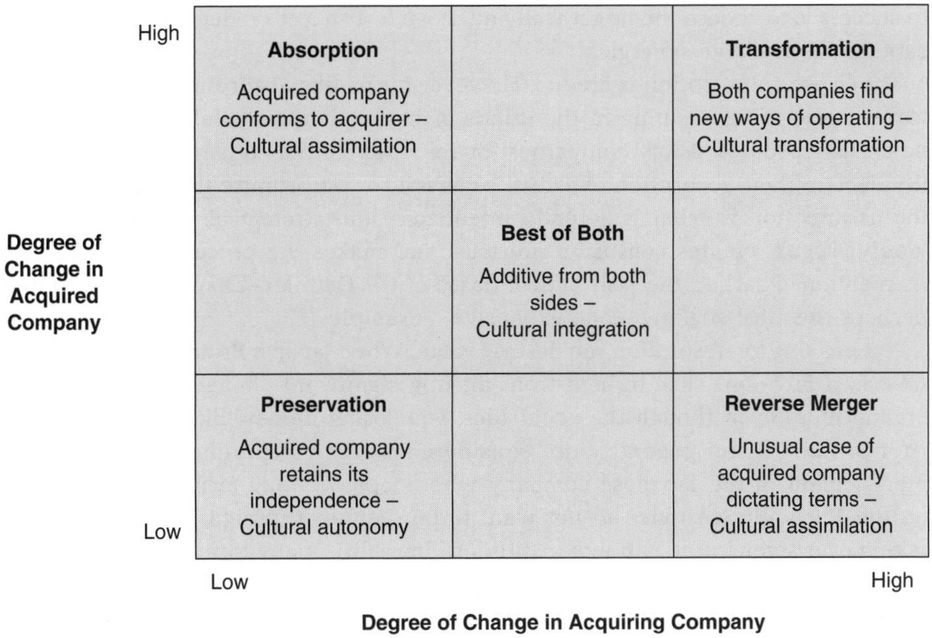

	Low		High
High	**Absorption** Acquired company conforms to acquirer – Cultural assimilation		**Transformation** Both companies find new ways of operating – Cultural transformation
Degree of Change in Acquired Company		**Best of Both** Additive from both sides – Cultural integration	
Low	**Preservation** Acquired company retains its independence – Cultural autonomy		**Reverse Merger** Unusual case of acquired company dictating terms – Cultural assimilation

Degree of Change in Acquiring Company

Figure 4.1 Strategies for post-merger outcomes

Source: Reprinted with kind permission from the author. Mirvis, P.M. and M.L.Marks (1994). *Managing the Merger: Making It Work*. Upper Saddle River, N.J.: Prentice Hall, 1994.

The key to success here is to protect the boundary of the new subsidiary from unwarranted and disruptive intrusions from the parent, though this can be hard to ensure. However, even with the best of intentions, there is a danger of creeping assimilation – while the buyer allows the new unit to work in its own way, there is encouragement to develop systems and processes that match those of the parent organisation. Due to operational pressures, most stand-alone acquisitions do not last (Killing, 2003). While the acquired company may appear independent to the outside world, some functions at least are merged with the rest of the organisation.

Absorption acquisitions

This kind of acquisition is fairly straightforward, and it is probably most common when there are differences in size and sophistication between the two partners involved in the deal. The acquired company conforms to the acquirer's way of working and the focus is on full cultural assimilation. Such deals are particularly common when the acquired company is performing poorly, or when the market conditions force consolidation. The majority of the synergies may be related to cost cutting, most likely on the side of the acquired company, although some may come from improvements in systems and processes introduced by the acquiring firm. The key

Key to success is to move fast to capture synergies

to success is to choose the target well and move fast so as to reduce uncertainty, and capture the available synergies.

The logic of absorption is simple. However terms like absorption or assimilation carry a pejorative meaning in the minds of many; and assimilation may at times be an ugly process. Many companies for reasons mentioned earlier do not explicitly declare their absorption objective so as not to compromise the deal. But when the assimilation is what is actually intended – and strategically desirable – this 'double-speak' creates confusion, mistrust and makes the process more difficult. As mentioned earlier, the well-known fiasco of the Daimler–Chrysler integration is perhaps the most striking – and expensive – example.

double-speak creates confusion

Not pushing for absorption can destroy value. When Japan's Bridgestone purchased US-based Firestone, it refrained from making significant changes in the acquired organisation, even though the acquisition was losing money. Firestone was bankrupt in the US and generally not considered worthy of purchase except by the management of the Japanese company who adopted a long term 20 year horizon on the M&A. Bridgestone did not want to be seen as a foreign Japanese intruder taking over a venerable national institution. In reality, many local middle managers were looking forward to the takeover, expecting that their new owners would tackle both the unions and the entrenched old-style of top management – so when nothing happened, they left in droves. Faced with growing losses, Tokyo finally moved in several years later to 'clean up the mess'. But it was too late, Firestone was by then too thin on local talent, drifting for years from crisis to crisis and at a heavy cost to the parent company.

employees can welcome the absorption

When managed well, absorption can be of benefit to the employees of the acquired firm. This is especially true when these employees are afraid of losing their jobs and see the new owner as helping them to remain competitive; or when they are unhappy with the management style of the old leaders and see the acquiring company as having a more progressive culture; or there again when employees see other positive outcomes associated with the acquisition (such as better benefits, better pay, or more prestige). Cisco, for example, is well known for buying companies to gain access to their technology and R&D talent, assimilating them into the Cisco culture. During the post-acquisition process of assimilation, it strives to retain most of the employees, including top management. Here, the emphasis is on finding targets that will match Cisco's way of managing the business, thus increasing the likelihood of cultural compatibility.

Reverse mergers

This is the mirror opposite of assimilation, although it does not happen that frequently. In a reverse merger, the organisation that makes the purchase usually hopes to gain capabilities from the acquired company. The acquired company is made into a business unit that then absorbs the parallel unit from the acquiring firm. When Nokia, for instance, bought a high tech firm in California for its R&D knowledge, it gave the new unit global responsibilities, which meant that part of the business in Finland now reports to California.

Sometimes, the reverse merger is unintended. A few years ago, a French metal products company acquired its smaller British competitor. Today, to the surprise of many, the management style and systems of the new company resemble the culture of the acquired firm. What happened? When the two companies merged, it was easier for everyone to adopt the explicit and transparent systems of the British firm, more suitable for cross-border business, than to emulate the ambiguous and subtle rules embedded in the French organisation. If the practices of the company that has been acquired are more clear and transparent, it is quite possible that they will prevail.

Best of both

This intriguing option is meant to be the 'best of both' worlds and is often described as a 'merger of equals'. This holds out the promise of no pain since in theory it adopts best practices from both sides and integrates them. There are, however, very few examples of such mergers that have succeeded since it is very difficult to undertake. The strength of a culture comes from the internal consistency of the practices, which may evaporate when the best parts from different organisations are put together (see Chapter 5).

Another danger in the 'best of both' situation is that the integration process may become too political and time consuming. Who decides what is 'best'? When the Swedish bank Nordbanken and the Finnish bank Merita were combined in a 'merger of equals' in the late 1990s, the Finnish employees coined and used the phrase 'Best practices are West practices' – 'West' meaning 'Swedish,' as Sweden is located west of Finland (Vaara et al., 2003).

The process of decision making can be excessively complex, plagued by inconsistencies. If both companies declare that the merger to be one of equals, does that mean that top management is split 50/50, even if the real split is 80/20 in terms of competences? The controversy surrounding the Daimler–Chrysler merger is a visible example of this dilemma. Without strong mutual respect for the knowledge and skills of each company, the 'best of both' strategy cannot work.

The key to success is the fairness of the process. The test of the 'best of both' approach may be the ability to retain the people who do not get the top jobs. Having similar cultures helps to keep everyone together. The AstraZeneca and Exxon/Mobil mergers have proceeded relatively smoothly because the similarities were more pronounced than the differences. The new groups have been relatively successful at identifying the best practices from each side, as well as having a balance of top management from the two firms.

Transformation

In contrast with 'best of both' acquisitions that take the existing cultures as they are, both companies in a transformation merger are hoping to use the merger to break sharply with the past. Merger or acquisition can be the catalyst for trying to do things differently, for reinventing oneself. This can focus on the way in which the company is run, what business it is in, or both. When Novartis was created by the merger of two Swiss-based pharmaceutical firms, the proposed management style for the new company reflected the desired transformation: 'We will listen more than Sandoz, but decide more than Ciba'.

For a long time, the creation of ABB through the merger of Asea and Brown Boveri, was considered an archetype of transformational merger, with its successes and failures (Barham and Heimer, 1998). More recently, the merger of the two pharmaceutical companies Astra and Zeneca into AstraZeneca could be described as a case of transformation through M&A (Killing, 2004), as was Lenovo's acquisition of IBM's PC business.

This kind of merger is complex and difficult to implement. It requires a full commitment to strong leadership at the top to avoid getting trapped in endless debates while the ongoing business suffers. Speed is essential, with top management in the merging companies using the time period immediately after the merger announcement to carry out major changes. Like the best-of-both strategy, the transformation strategy has a better chance of success if key people from both parties are excited by the vision of the merger leading to a new leading company with superior capabilities (Killing, 2003).

Finally, another complicating factor in international acquisitions is that there will often be parts of the organisation where a particular approach to the merger makes sense and others where it does not. There are few M&As that fit neatly into the assimilation, integration or other categories. For some countries or regions, or for some parts of the business, a full assimilation may be the best approach; in other parts of the firm, a reverse merger might be a more appropriate strategy.

6 Managing cross-border integration: the HRM implications

There is no shortage of evidence that attention to people and to cultural issues is one of the most critical elements in achieving the cross-border acquisition strategy. In an early McKinsey study of international M&A, the four top ranked factors identified by responding firms as contributing to acquisition success all related to people: retention of key talent (identified by 76 per cent of responding firms); effective communication (71 per cent); executive retention (67 per cent) and cultural integration (51 per cent) (Kay and Shelton, 2000). According to a subsequent consulting report, published nearly a decade later, the problems remained the same. Differences in organisational culture (50 per cent) and people integration (35 per cent) were top of the list of M&A challenges – in fact, four of the six top issues were people related (Marsh et al., 2008).

In fact, it is hard to find an acquisition where people issues do not matter (Schmidt, 2002). In particular, when the objective of the acquisition is to establish a new geographic presence, then managing people, communication and cross-cultural issues are top of the list of priorities. When the aim is to acquire new technology or to buy market share or competencies, retaining key technical employees or account managers is the principal challenge. When the objective of the deal is consolidation, dealing effectively with redundancies at all levels is the dominant concern.

Based on these observations, it may seem natural that the HR function should play a significant role in all phases of the acquisition. The acquisition process is typically divided into stages – the *initial planning stage*, including due diligence; the *closing of the deal*; and the *post-merger integration stage*. Yet while human resource management issues tend to receive attention during the last – implementation – phase, the overall influence that HR has during the whole acquisition process is patchy, even though many of the problems of merger integration stem from failure to consider these issues early on. In addition, many companies have neither the resources nor the know-how to give this HR area the priority it deserves (KPMG, 1999: 15).

As suggested earlier, one of the reasons why cross-border mergers may be successful, despite their complexity, is that the people, cultural and integration challenges are more obvious, leading management to pay close attention to them at all stages in the acquisition process. We focus here on those cultural and people issues that seem to be particularly critical to the success or failure of mergers and acquisitions (see Evans et al. (2010) for an extended discussion of the issues in this section):

- Assessing culture
- Undertaking a human capital audit and selecting the management team
- Effective communication
- Retaining talent
- Creating the new culture
- Managing the transition

[handwritten margin note: important, people things to remember in a M&A.]

Assessing culture in the due diligence phase

[handwritten margin note: Culture due Diligence]

The purpose of cultural assessment is to evaluate factors that may influence the organisational fit, to understand the future cultural dynamics as the two organisations merge, and to prepare a plan for how the cultural issues should be addressed if the deal goes forward. Before a valid cultural integration strategy can be developed on the part of the acquiring company, or between the two merger partners, differences and similarities of the cultures of both companies must be well understood. This crucial step is often neglected, sometimes even ignored, in most M&A planning processes.

Metaphorically, cultural understanding has often been likened to an iceberg (Black et al., 1999; Schein, 1987). The tip of the iceberg, visible to the observer, does not reflect the way in which it is connected to a much larger mass beneath the ocean's surface. Similarly, the external manifestation of cultural dynamics – artifacts and behaviours – do not reflect the dynamics behind the scenes that create and sustain them. One common mistake that is often made in the cultural due diligence process is that measures used to delineate the culture are superficial in nature (such as the number of levels in the organisational structure, the type of employee benefit programmes, level of detail in policy manuals) and do not adequately plumb its depths (Mendenhall et al., 2001).

Evans and colleagues (2010) suggest that cultural due diligence teams must focus their efforts on data collection to extract the 'deep knowledge' of the culture. Cultural due diligence teams need to ask questions and find answers to questions such as:

- What are their core beliefs about what it takes to win?
- What drives their business strategy? Tradition or innovation?
- Is the company short-term or long-term in its outlook and execution of initiatives?
- How much risk is the company used to accepting?
- Is the company results-oriented or process-oriented?
- How is power distributed throughout the company?
- How are decisions made: consultation, consensus or authority?
- How is information managed and shared?

Questions of this nature require the due diligence team to probe into the normative structure, core values and assumptions, and the core philosophy of the company itself in order to understand the company from a holistic cultural perspective.

In addition, the culture of a company does not exist in a vacuum. It is usually embedded in a specific industry; and it reflects as well the regional and national culture (Schneider and Barsoux, 1997). In order to comprehend a company culture, one must be able to understand the cultural strands that reach out and attach themselves to values, assumptions, norms and beliefs in the environment. Thus, the cultural due diligence team must assess not only the company itself but also the context in which the company exists.

Finally, the due diligence team must not only pay attention to the target's or potential partner's culture, but to its own culture as well. Cultural assessment is not just a question of assessing the other company's culture; it is also a matter both of having a clear culture oneself and understanding it. The criteria used in cultural assessment of the target will to a great extent reflect the cultural attributes of the buyer. The 'know thyself' adage applies equally well to companies as it does to people.

Undertaking a human capital audit and selecting the management team

There are two dimensions to the human capital audit (Pucik and Evans, 2004). One dimension is preventive, focused on liabilities such as pension plan obligations, outstanding grievances and employee litigation. It also includes comparing the compensation policies, benefits and labour contracts of both firms. The other dimension is focused on talent identification, and in the long run it is probably more critical to the success of the acquisition. A number of facets on this are important – ensuring that the target company has the talent necessary to execute the acquisition strategy, identifying which individuals are critical to sustaining the value of the deal, and assessing any potential weaknesses in the management cadre. It is also important to understand the motivation and incentive structure, and to highlight any differences that may impact retention. Finally, understanding the structure of the organisation means not just reporting lines but clarifying who is who.

Here are some examples of questions to consider (Chaudhuri and Tabrizi, 1999; Pucik and Evans, 2004):

- What kind of employees create most value for the organisation?
- What unique skills do the employees have?
- How does the target's talent compare to the quality of our own?
- What is the background of the management team?
- What are the reporting relationships?
- What will happen if some of the management team leave?
- What is the compensation philosophy?
- How much pay is at risk at various levels of the firm?

Getting access to talent data may take some effort, and many companies ignore the talent question in the early stages of the M&A process. They do not take the time to define the skills that are critical to the success of the deal, relying instead on financial performance data as a proxy. Early assessment helps to pinpoint the potential risk factors so the acquiring company can develop strategies to address them as early as possible. Moreover, this will speed up decisions about who should stay and who should leave (Harding and Rouse, 2007).

Without early assessment, companies may acquire targets with weaker than expected skills or talent that has a high likelihood of departure. The consequence will be delays after the merger announcement in deciding on the structure and management team in the acquired company, which fuels post-merger anxiety and confusion, often prompting the most valuable contributors to exit. At the same time, the audit may also uncover significant weaknesses that may call for recruiting replacement candidates (external local hires or expatriates) to be ready to commence work immediately after closing the deal.

Effective communication

Communication is always a vital part of any process of change, but it is critical in cross-border acquisitions where cultural differences may intensify tensions that stem from misunderstanding and distance. For example, the intention of top managers in an acquired company to stay rather than leave following an acquisition is associated with their positive perceptions of the merger announcement (Krug and Hegerty, 2001). Furthermore, in the design of the communication process there are two additional objectives that are particularly important in any acquisition. On the one hand, communication is intended to alleviate the anxiety and stress that accompany every acquisition, and on the other hand it provides feedback to top management about the progress of the integration process and any potential roadblocks.

Many M&As are shrouded in secrecy during their pre-merger phases, and the ensuing public announcement often triggers shock and anxiety in the workforce and local communities. Rumours of possible layoffs, reassignments and changes can drain employees' energy and productivity. Whereas the employees in the acquiring or dominant partner feel a sense of superiority, victory and power; conversely, feelings of fear, betrayal and anger are relatively common among employees in the acquired or less dominant company especially when the acquirer is a foreign rival.

In the first 100 days of a merger, Mirvis and Marks (1994) argue that certain actions must be taken in order to counter this 'merger syndrome' in employees. First, everyone should appreciate that it is a perfectly normal and human response to experience a wide variety of emotions regarding the merger or acquisition. Employees should be helped in developing the necessary coping skills to deal with stress created during major organisational change. Second, information must be transparent and freely communicated to employees. The merger syndrome with its stress and anxiety is exacerbated when executives guard and delay decisions announcing them often abruptly and only 'as needed'. This fuels an emerging distrust of management's motives, ethics and decision-making effectiveness on the part of employees (Stahl and Sitkin, 2005). Information can be shared in a wide variety of forums: lunch gatherings, company intranets, emails and so forth.

Third, senior management must communicate a positive vision throughout the company, pointing to a new and better future. Combined with symbolic acts that show positive regard for all employees, messages to create a positive image of the new company as it moves ahead are a critical aspect of initial post-merger management. Finally, it is important to involve people at all levels from both companies. Forming cross-border teams to share knowledge, pushing for direct contact to break down stereotypes, and extensive training workshops were some of the initiatives introduced by Carlos Ghosn when attempting to integrate the cultures of Nissan and Renault (Donnelly et al., 2005) in order to dissipate the destructive power of ethnocentric 'us versus them' factions.

Retaining talent

Many acquired businesses lose key employees soon after the acquisition, and this is a major contributing factor to the failure of acquisitions. Research evidence from US acquisitions indicates that the probability of executives leaving increases significantly when their firm is acquired by a foreign multinational (Krug and Hegerty,

1997). When insufficient attention is paid to retaining talent, and especially if staff cuts are expected, employees will leave. Headhunters inevitably move in, and the best will exit first since they have other choices. Given this context, it is not surprising that when the Chinese company Lenovo acquired IBM's PC division, the board of Lenovo's controlling shareholder allowed the company to proceed with the deal if, and only if, it could retain IBM's senior executives to manage the merged enterprise (Harding and Rouse, 2007). But the talent that Lenovo wanted was not limited to senior executives. When the deal closed, the company offered a job to every IBM employee worldwide, with no obligation to relocate or accept a pay-cut.

Retention of talent is particularly important for firms, such as Lenevo, where the value of the deal lies in the acquisition of intangible assets – the knowledge and skills of the people inside the acquired firm. This is the situation for many such deals in the high technology sector where companies use acquisitions to plug holes in their R&D portfolio or to rapidly build new capabilities (Chaudhuri and Tabrizi, 1999).

This means knowing exactly who the talented people are and why they are essential to the new organisation, including identification of valuable employees from the lower levels of the acquired firm. Obtaining this information as part of the human capital audit may not be a simple task; indeed one of the biggest obstacles in international acquisitions is the difference in performance measures and standards. Even if standards are comparable, many companies are not aware of where their talent is; in one study only 16 per cent of surveyed executives believed that their employers could identify their high performers (Michaels et al., 2001). Furthermore, local managers may be protective of their people and therefore be unwilling to provide information about poor performers.

Effective and open communication is the foundation for retaining talent. While financial incentives are also important (stock options, retention bonuses or other incentives given to employees who stay through the integration or until completion of a specific merger-related project), they cannot substitute for a one-on-one relationship with executives from the acquiring firm. Senior management involvement is critical to successful retention. High potential employees in most companies are used to receiving attention from senior management. Without the same treatment from the acquiring company, they question their future and will be more likely to depart. Distance may be an obstacle to be overcome, but it cannot be used as an excuse. When BP–Amoco acquired Arco, another international oil major, it quickly organised Key Talent Workshops – two-day events to network senior BP executives with Arco's high-potential employees.

Talent retention efforts should not stop after the completion of the first 100 days of integration. Junior employees may find the initial impact of the acquisition to be quite positive, offering them opportunities for responsibility and higher pay (especially when their seniors leave *en masse*). Even so, many of them will depart later if they do not become integrated into the leadership development of the new parent company (Krug and Hegerty, 2001).

Creating the new culture

Strong and committed leadership is the foundation for successful integration – and for successful change management. Lack of clear vision and the leadership style of top management have consistently topped lists of factors explaining why acquisitions failed to deliver their expected value. Three capabilities are seen as fundamental to the effectiveness of the top leadership: a credible new vision, a sense of urgency and effective communication (Fubini et al., 2006; Sitkin and Pablo, 2005). In a study of M&As in Japan, respondents indicated again and again that creating a sense of urgency around implementing the vision as well as maintaining momentum in driving change are the keys to success (Pucik, 2008).

The role of top management is especially important in large-scale mergers because creation of a new common culture is difficult unless there is some explicit leadership philosophy with values and norms that guide practice and behaviour. To create the new culture of ABB after the cross-border merger of Asea and Brown Boveri in the late 1980s, the CEO Percy Barnevik spent three months with the new senior management team defining a policy bible to guide the intended new organisation. This was a manual of 'soft' principles such as speed in decision making ('better to be quick and roughly right than slow and completely right') and for conflict management ('you can only kick a conflict upstairs once for arbitration'), as well as 'hard' practices such as the Abacus measurement system that would apply across all units of the newly merged enterprise.

Companies with strong and successful cultures usually impose their culture onto the acquired company. Indeed they typically perceive their success as originating from their own culture and the practices based on it. Therefore GE will impart to the acquired company GE's meaning of a performance commitment which is anchored to stretch goals, its underlying business planning process and the way it goes about managing people. However, as illustrated by Evans and colleagues (2010), acquiring a 'culture' may be part of the reason behind an acquisition. A case in point is the takeover of an Anglo-Saxon competitor by a French multinational that is the global leader in its industry. Top management in the French corporation had known for some time that their own culture had to change, but it was unable to do so organically. The most attractive feature of acquiring its competitor was not the expanded market share but the opportunity to accelerate change in its own company. Senior management recognised that the whole integration process would have to be managed with this aim in mind.

In the process of culture building or cultural assimilation after an acquisition, values and norms have to be translated into behaviours. One model of change implementation argues that it is a four-step process (Beer et al., 1990). It commences with establishing the new roles and responsibilities after the restructuring, ensuring that skilled champions of the desired culture are in place to drive the culture change process. The second step is coaching and training, helping people to develop the desired competences and behaviours. Then, the third step is being prepared and focusing on *recruitment, succession planning and rewards.* People who are not responding well to the coaching will be replaced, and those who respond ably may be given broader responsibilities. The fourth and final step in the implementation and culture change process is the *fine-tuning and formalisation of the new system* into a coherent, consistent and transparent whole.

The quality of coaching is particularly important for the effectiveness of culture change. Take AXA as an example, a French company that in a relatively short time has grown through acquisitions from being a local player in the French insurance industry to becoming a top global financial services institution. Just as BP, Cisco and GE all do, AXA makes no pretence that its acquisitions are mergers, moving quickly to AXA'ise the cultures of the firms it acquires. Managers from companies brought into AXA commented that one of the most helpful tools for them to assimilate quickly into the company is its 360° feedback process. The AXA values are encoded in this appraisal instrument, and to accelerate the process of cultural integration, all managers and professionals in the acquired company participate in feedback workshops. It helps to make the desired culture and values more concrete, identify personal needs for improvement and provide coaching implemented in the AXA way.

Managing the transition

As all acquisitions require some degree of integration (even preservation deals generally require the integration of financial reporting systems), it is important to tailor integration to the purpose of the acquisition and the characteristics of the companies involved. The integration process requires an engaged leadership and often a dedicated integration manager working with a transition team. In most cases, moving with speed is an advantage. A critical part of the process is focusing on those areas where the acquisition can create new value, while maintaining the ongoing business.

Integration manager and transition teams The post-merger integration is always a delicate and complicated process. Who should be responsible for making it happen? After closing, the due-diligence team with its deep knowledge of the acquired company disbands or goes on to another deal. Meanwhile, the new management team is not yet fully in place. To avoid the vacuum, companies are increasingly turning to dedicated integration managers supported by transition teams.

The role of the integration manager is to guide the integration process, making sure that timelines are followed and that key decisions are taken according to the agreed schedule. The first task is to spell out the logic of the new business model and translate this into operational targets. This is important in international acquisitions where 'big picture' statements from the corporate centre may not mean much in a different national and business context. Integration managers should also champion norms and behaviours consistent with new standards, communicate key messages across the new organisation, and identify new value-adding opportunities (Ashkenas and Francis, 1998; Ashkenas et al., 1998).

An important aspect of the job is helping the acquired company to understand how the new owner operates and what it can offer in terms of capabilities. The integration manager can help the new company take advantage of the owner's existing capabilities and resources, facilitate social connections, and assist with essential but intangible aspects such as interpreting a new language and way-of-doing-things. Acquired companies typically do not know how things work in the corporation that now owns them, moreover the integration manager can likewise help the parent to understand the acquired business and what it can contribute.

A major source of frustration in many deals is not so much what the parent wants the newly acquired unit to do, but what it wants to know. Therefore, another role for the integration manager is that of an information 'gatekeeper' between the two sides, protecting the acquired business from the eager embrace of an owner who unintentionally could undermine what makes the business work. When Nokia acquires small high-tech venture companies, one of the rules is that all requests for information from the parent go to the integration manager. He or she will decide if and how the unit should comply with the request.

In most acquisitions, the integration manager is supported by integration teams and task forces. These teams should have a clear mandate, with targets and accountability for a specific area where integration is required. Since many of these teams are expected to start work on the first day after the acquisition is completed, the identification of potential members should ideally be an outcome of the pre-acquisition due-diligence process. HR professionals are often key members of the team because many of the team's activities will have implications for human resource policies and practices.

Who else should be appointed to the transition team? It may be attractive to leverage functional and business unit managers by adding this transition project role to their responsibilities. However, the mixing of line responsibility with transition task-force roles often means that neither is done well. Customers do not like to wait until the transition team reaches agreement. On the other hand, integration teams should be staffed by people with leadership qualities and not by low priority managers or by laggards in the race for line business jobs – they simply will not have the credibility to get the job done successfully. So probably the best staffing approach is to appoint 'up-and-coming' managers, leaving the daily business under the original leadership until the new organisation can be created.

Transition teams are most effective when members come from both the acquired and acquiring companies. By facilitating personnel exchange, the transition team can help to develop a better understanding of each other's capabilities. People who are suited for a transition team usually have a mix of functional and interpersonal competencies (including cross-cultural skills), backed up by strong analytical skills. Having an ability to accept responsibility without full authority and being effective in mobilising resources across organisational boundaries are two competencies that are especially important, and consequently such roles are good development opportunities for those with high potential.

The effective transition team serves as a role model for how the new organisation should act. It disseminates the shared vision and makes sure that practices are appropriately aligned with the vision. However, too many task forces and teams will slow things down, creating coordination problems, conflict and confusion. The projects should focus on the integration tasks with high potential savings at low risk, leaving those with greater risk or lower benefits until later. In the process of transition, prioritisation is critical.

Moving with speed Evans and colleagues (2010) observe that most companies with experience in acquisitions recommend rapid implementation of the integration. Creeping changes, uncertainty and anxiety that last for months are debilitating and immediately start to drain value from an acquisition (Ashkenas et al., 1998). While this may seem counterintuitive to some, a problem jeopardising the success of many acquisitions has been a tendency to restructure too slowly. Even when such delays are motivated by the very best of intentions, while time and resources are spent on giving people time to adjust by not upsetting the old culture, competitors will seize the opportunity to take away the business. Such procrastination and indecision fails to make use of the window of opportunity that occurs for a short period of time immediately after acquisition when the organisation is in effect 'unfrozen' – employees expect change and are thus more open to new ways of doing things (Stahl, 2006). As one AstraZeneca executive noted: 'A merger is like an erupting volcano. Everything turns to lava, and lava is fluid. You can mould it and shape it and turn it into new things, but eventually it solidifies. In the period when the lava is molten you have an incredible opportunity to do things differently – take advantage of that situation' (Killing, 2004: 43).

Sometime, foreign acquirers' fear of cultural backlash slows down the process. At one foreign-owned financial company in Japan, the implementation of several elements of performance-based global HR policies was suspended for two years to give employees a chance to adapt. In retrospect, the company's Japanese CEO thinks this may have been overcautious. 'I think perhaps the grace period could have been a bit shorter. Some people got too comfortable for their own good. I think I may have been a bit too lenient because foreign companies are always criticised for being too harsh, for being vultures' (Pucik, 2008).

The desired speed of change may be influenced by norms in the business or regional culture of the acquiring firm. A survey of European acquisitions of US high-technology firms in the Silicon Valley reported that speed in integration was one of the key drivers of successful post-merger integration – but also one of the most problematic (Inkpen et al., 2000). The understanding of what is 'quick' or 'fast' among most of the European acquirers (usually large, established companies with entrenched routines and procedures) was very different from the norms of the Valley. This created confusion, frustration and ultimately the loss of market opportunities.

Research indeed shows differences in the speed of the integration process according to the national origins of the acquiring firm. Japanese and Northern European acquirers tend to move cautiously, conscious of potential cultural conflicts (Child et al., 2001). This works well if the approach involves preserving the culture and autonomy of the acquired organisation, but it may exacerbate the stress of the transition when expected decisions are not forthcoming, making subsequent changes more difficult to implement.

The other aspect of speed is a focus on delivering quick, visible wins, such as new sales through a joint effort, or improvements based on shared practices. It is important to take time to celebrate each success and to communicate the accomplishments to the whole organisation (Kotter, 1996; Kouzes and Posner, 1987). A quick win can motivate target employees because it offers tangible proof that the merger or acquisition was a step in the right direction, and shows that their efforts are appreciated.

Yet speed also has some unintended consequences. Bad decisions made under pressure can be avoided if time is spent on a judicious review of the issues. Conversely, good decisions meet resistance when no time is taken to explain the new business logic. Again, the optimal speed depends on the strategic intent of the acquisition and the desired end-state for the culture of the new organisation (Homburg and Bucerius, 2006).

An absorption strategy generally requires more urgency than a best-of-both approach. When the objective of the acquisition is to acquire knowledge and intellectual capital, the pace of change must be particularly carefully calibrated to minimise the risk of alienating talent. Also, it has been argued that successful cross-border acquirers from emerging economies whose aim is to obtain competencies, technology and knowledge essential to their global strategies do not see quick integration as a priority (Kumar, 2009).

In project management terms, the speed can be increased only to the degree to which a comprehensive integration plan has been formulated in the pre-merger phase. Indeed, 'speed kills' if decisions are taken without being guided by a carefully crafted plan. Alternatively, a slow pace due to the lack of a credible plan also has a negative impact, as it reinforces the impression in the minds of many subordinates that the executives do not know what they are doing, that no progress is being made, and that the entire merger or acquisition was a folly to begin with. If the post-merger phase is to be successful, then good preparation during the pre-merger/acquisition phase is essential.

7 Conclusions and implications for M&A practice

In mergers and acquisitions special emphasis is often focused on the strategic and financial goals of the transaction while the psychological, social and cultural implications do not receive sufficient attention (see Chapter 1). The purpose of this chapter has been to delineate the dynamics of people issues and cultural processes inherent to M&As, and to discuss their implications for management and in particular HRM.

What happens before a deal is signed is important. A well thought-out strategy and thorough due diligence are essential to success, as well as a negotiation team that does not succumb to escalation of commitment during the negotiation process that might lead to paying too much for the acquisition. However, even deals which are well structured and negotiated have to cope with the complexities of merging organisations across boundaries; inevitably the capacity to add value in the merged company depends mostly on what happens after the deal is done (Pucik and Evans, 2004). Not surprisingly, high returns are attained by organisations that execute post-merger integration well (A.T. Kearney, 1999). With this in mind, the research evidence discussed in this chapter indicates that when managed adequately, cultural differences inherent to cross-border M&As actually can be an asset rather than a liability. Cultural differences should not be confused therefore with ineffective communication and poor cross-cultural management (see Chapter 3).

The approach to the HRM challenges in a particular merger or acquisition depends on the strategic logic behind the deal and the integration approach that is adopted. Each of the integration approaches discussed in this chapter has different people and managerial implications. For example, in absorption acquisitions, one of the key managerial challenges is to ease the transition from separate to joint operations and to allay the fears of target firm employees through clear communication; whereas preservation acquisitions require arms-length status and a willingness on the part of managers to learn from the acquired firm. In general, attention to cultural and people issues is most critical to M&As that require a high degree of integration (Haspeslagh and Jemison, 1991; Stahl and Sitkin, 2005).

Although most M&A failures are linked to problems in post-merger integration, our discussion of the key HRM challenges suggests that cultural and people issues have to be considered at an early stage in the M&A process – as early as the phase of evaluation and selection of a suitable target as well as in planning the post-merger or post-acquisition integration. In the due-diligence process, the assessment of the organisation structure, corporate culture, and HR system in the company to be acquired is just as important as are the financial analysis and strategic fit considerations. Essential preconditions for the long-term success of the M&A are undertaking a human capital audit to ensure that the target company has the talent to execute the M&A strategy; identifying which individuals are important to sustain the value of the deal; and assessing any potential weaknesses in the management cadre.

No matter how well the M&A has been prepared, one can neither anticipate nor avoid all problems in the integration phase. In this chapter, we have identified various paths to follow to manage more effectively the challenges of post-merger integration. Most of the key management tasks are in the domain of HRM, such as open and timely communication, choosing the right management team, retaining key executives and leadership talent, facilitating the cultural integration process and managing the transition process. The research evidence shows that effective response to these HRM challenges can go a long way toward reducing dysfunctional culture clashes in cross-border M&As, and consequently increase the chances of successful integration.

The cultural and HRM implications of M&As discussed in this chapter also provide a rich field for further research. Although the psychological, social and cultural issues involved in integrating merging or acquired firms have received considerable research attention in recent years (for reviews see Evans et al., 2010; Schweiger and Goulet, 2000; Stahl and Sitkin, 2005), several important issues related to the post-merger integration process have been left unexplored. For example, few systematic attempts have been made to examine, either conceptually or empirically, the role that processes related to trust building, employee sense making and leadership may play in the M&A process. Other aspects of the post-combination integration process, such as the consequences of cultural fit or misfit, have received more research attention, but the empirical findings are mixed. Clearly, our current understanding of the socio-cultural dynamics in cross-border M&A is still limited.

One reason – and challenge – is that research in this complex area needs to be interdisciplinary or broad in its disciplinary orientation – linking strategic, cross-cultural and HRM perspectives. Each of these perspectives has something to contribute, but none can contribute significantly independently of the others (see Chapter 2). For example, as has been discussed earlier in this chapter, frameworks that focus exclusively on the cultural issues involved in integrating merging or acquired firms, such as the 'cultural distance' hypothesis, cannot explain why some cross-border M&A succeed and others fail. Whether cultural differences have a positive or negative impact on M&A performance will likely depend on a variety of factors, including the nature of the cultural differences, the interventions chosen to manage these differences and the strategic intent behind the M&A. Interdisciplinary research is needed to find out how these dimensions interactively influence M&A performance and to provide fresh insights into the socio-cultural processes and HRM issues involved in cross-border M&A.

Discussion questions

1 What are the various post-merger/-acquisition strategies that one can pursue and what are the factors to consider in determining the appropriate strategy? And what are the corresponding HRM implications?

2 What are the cultural and people issues that HR should focus on to ensure the success of a merger or an acquisition?

3 What is the role of the integration manager and the transition team? What professional and personal qualities should these incumbents possess?

Cemex

In September 2004, only a few months after defining its new global governance model and deciding to implement one global operating system, the Mexican building materials company CEMEX announced its intention of acquiring the UK-based Ready Mix Concrete (RMC) group for US$5.8 billion. With this acquisition CEMEX aimed to consolidate its position as one of the top three global players in the industry.

CEMEX was established in 1906 in Monterrey, Mexico. The current CEO, Lorenzo Zambrano, is the grandson of the company's founder and was appointed to his position in 1985 after working his way up through the organisation over 18 years. At that time, the company had five plants and 6,500 employees. Zambrano refused to diversify into other businesses, the route favoured by many other Latin American industrialists. Instead he focused on the cement and building materials business he knew well and built up his company through a series of carefully considered and implemented acquisitions, first in Mexico and then from 1992 in Spain, Latin America, Philippines and the US.

Top management quickly realised that the newly acquired companies were guided by different operating practices, structures and cultures than CEMEX. Most had been run quite ineffectively and CEMEX saw an opportunity to create value by implementing new processes and instilling new management behaviour. The backbone of this strategy was a global operating platform, labelled the CEMEX Way.

The aim of the CEMEX Way was to unify global operations, promote sharing of best practices, streamline and improve the value chain all the way down to the final customers, and allow rapid and simultaneous deployment of strategic initiatives. With the CEMEX Way in place, the company could move fast and confidently with the post-merger integration, largely because its own systems and practices were well developed and explicit.

To enable faster and smoother acquisitions, CEMEX put in place a systematic post-merger integration (PMI) process to promote best practices and learn from previous experiences. Overlapping teams of managers and functional specialists from different countries were sent to each newly acquired company so that knowledge and best practices would be passed on to the team responsible for each new acquisition.

The typical PMI had four stages. An initial integration and planning stage, during which pre-assessment teams were sent to the newly acquired company to analyse the situation and plan next steps, which was then followed by three execution phases. In phase one, also called 'the 100-day plan,' transition teams worked to identify further synergies through a gap analysis covering all business activities. Phase two focused on implementation, with the expectation that the CEMEX way would be fully operational by the end of this stage. Phase three was to return to business as usual – at a higher level of operational efficiency.

The RMC acquisition was bigger, covered more countries (22), and included more diverse cultures and languages than anything CEMEX had encountered previously. The PMI office divided the work between functional teams, like 'cement operations' and 'back-office'; each of these teams was replicated on a country by country basis. In total, 600 people from within CEMEX and over 400 RMC managers were involved in the RMC PMI. The HR integration was by far the most complex part of the process and CEMEX spent more than six months defining and building a framework that took staffing and country differences into consideration. At the kick-off of the execution phase Zambrano addressed RMC managers and executives:

YOU WILL QUICKLY DISCOVER THAT CEMEX TIME SEEMS TO HAVE FEWER MINUTES IN EVERY HOUR AND MORE HOURS IN EVERY DAY. WE ARE HIGHLY DISCIPLINED AND DEDICATED TO CONSISTENT, HIGH LEVEL PERFORMANCE. WE BELIEVE IN CONTINUOUS INNOVATION. ... OUR GOAL – AND OUR TRACK RECORD – IS TO OUT-PERFORM OUR COMPETITORS YEAR IN AND YEAR OUT.

The absorption of RMC did not result in large-scale firings and layoffs. In fact, 80 per cent of identified synergies were realised by changes in its processes, repositioning of business operations, and implementation of common management platforms. The results were impressive. Under its old owners, a large cement plant in Rugby, England often ran at only 70 per cent capacity. Two months after the takeover and the implementation of CEMEX Way it was increased to running at 93 per cent.

In October 2006, CEMEX announced an unsolicited offer to purchase Sydney-based Rinker group, with operations in Australia and the US. The target company was known to be very well managed. This acquisition was an opportunity to blend the best parts of CEMEX and Rinker to improve overall profitability, rather than to improve operating efficiency, the motive for previous acquisitions. The Rinker deal was sealed at the beginning of 2007. Instead of scrapping what Rinker had, the plan was to start with a thorough evaluation, identify the best of both parties, and determine which parts of Rinker's operating system should be incorporated in the CEMEX way – an obvious example was a waste burning initiative common to most Rinker plants.

CEMEX's integration of Rinker could be considered a best-of-both approach, as Rinker's production processes were very advanced in a number of technological areas and geographies. It would be to CEMEX's advantage to leverage this capability within the whole firm. However, without strong mutual respect for the knowledge and skills of each company, this kind of strategy will not work.

By December 2007, CEMEX had operations on four continents and in more than 50 countries – 85 cement plants, 2,365 ready-mix concrete facilities and 564 aggregates quarries. The only gaps in its global presence were China and India. CEMEX reported net sales of $21.7 billion and a net income of $2.6 billion. The company was also one of the world's leading traders of cement, as it maintained its own shipping fleet and trading relationships with customers in close to 100 nations.

Yet, by early 2009, because of the financial and economic crisis, the company global expansion was put on hold. A question which has to be asked is did the company's ability to grow through acquisitions lead it to underestimate the economic risks involved?

Case questions

1 Assess and discuss the extent that CEMEX may be in difficulty in 2010.
2 What do you think CEMEX should do in 2010 in relation to the four following HRM and operational issues: a) Multiskilling? b) Cost reduction? c) Talent management and retainment? and d) Process improvement?
3 What should CEMEX do regarding its global business operations and in relation to future expansion into China and India?

Case questions for further study and reflection

1 What during different stages of CEMEX's company history were the key success factors behind its growth and development through merger and acquisition?
2 What constitutes best practice in post-merger integration?

Further reading

Journal articles

- Ashkenas, A., DeMonaco, L. and Francis, S. (1998) 'Making the deal real: How GE capital integrates acquisitions', *Harvard Business Review*, Jan–Feb: 165–78.

This well-known article takes the reader through the GE approach to post-merger integration. It subdivides the process into four key stages and explains each. These stages are: 1) Preacquisition (due diligence, negotiation and announcement, close); 2) Foundation Building (launch, acquisition integration workout, strategy formulation); 3) Rapid integration (implementation, course assessment and adjustment); and 4) Assimilation (long-term plan evaluation and adjustment, capitalising on success).

- Bower, J. (2001) 'Not all M&As are alike – and that matters', *Harvard Business Review*, March: 93–101.

Joseph Bower begins his article by relating the collective wisdom on M&As. Acquirers usually pay too much; friendly deals done using stock often perform well; CEOs fall in love with deals and don't walk away when they should; integration is hard but a few companies do it well consistently. He then explains in depth the frequency, strengths and weaknesses of five reasons for M&As: 1) To deal with overcapacity through consolidation in mature industries; 2) Roll-up competitors in geographically fragmented industries; 3) Extend into new products or markets; 4) Substitute for R&D; and 5) Exploit eroding industry boundaries by inventing an industry.

- Henry Mintzberg (1990) 'The design school: Reconsidering the basic premises of strategic management', *Strategic Management Journal*, 11: 171–95.

A useful background article for thinking about M&As in the broader conceptual theoretical context of emergent strategy. It is helpful for drawing to the reader's attention the significance of learning from action and through reflection on action.

- Aguilera, R. V. and Dencker, J. C. (2004) 'The role of human resource management in cross-border mergers and acquisitions,' *International Journal of Human Resource Management*, December, 15(8): 1355–70.

This IJHRM article considers how cross-border mergers and acquisitions (M&As) have become the dominant mode of growth for firms seeking competitive advantage in the global business economy. The authors examine contingencies in national contexts that influence outcomes in the merger process. The empirical evidence is discussed to highlight HRM roles in terms of resources, processes and values that reflect the influence of both strategic fit and national context in the integration stage of cross-border M&A.

Books

- Child, J., Faulkner, D. and Pitkethly, R. (2001) *The Management of International Acquisitions*. Oxford: Oxford University Press.

Excellent summary of the M&A issues, targeted both for academics and managers based on research on acquisition by foreign companies in the UK. Three areas explored in detail are a review of key management challenges, which post-acquisition practices lead to better performance, and can national management style survive an international acquisition.

- Fubini, D., Price C. and Zollo, M. (2006) *Mergers: Leadership, Performance and Corporate Health*. New York: Palgrave Macmillan.

The book was written by a team of academics and McKinsey consultants based on survey data generated from company clients. It covers a wide range of M&A issues from M&A strategy and due dilligence to various approaches to managing integration and the role of senior leadership team in this process.

- Haspeslagh, P. C. and Jemison, D. B. (1991) *Managing Acquisitions: Creating Value through Corporate Renewal*. New York: The Free Press.

Written for academics as well as executives, this now classic text introduces a well-known model of the post-acquisition integration process. Although the primary focus is on the business aspects of determining M&A value drivers, the book is highly relevant to those interested in the human resource management aspects of M&A. Perhaps the most influential book on M&A management.

- Marks, M. L. and Mirvis, P. H. (1998) *Joining Forces: Making One Plus One Equal Three in Mergers, Acquisitions, and Alliances.* San Francisco: Jossey-Bass.

Popular and useful book on human resource management aspects of M&A. Targeted more towards practitioners than academics (both authors have extensive consulting experience), this book contains numerous mini-cases and best practice examples.

- Stahl, G. K. and Mendenhall, M. E. (2005) *Mergers and Acquisitions: Managing Culture and Human Resources.* Stanford: Stanford University Press.

This edited book provides a comprehensive research-based, yet practitioner-oriented, overview of a range of cultural and human resources issues in M&A. While the chapters are written by academics from Europe, North America, Asia and Australia, experienced corporate executives comment on each chapter.

Internet resources

A quick Internet search for merger and acquisition (M&A) yields nearly 2 million hits – considerably more information than most people will find helpful, especially when they are facing complex M&A transactions.

1 *For general reference*: Wikipedia (http://en.wikipedia.org/wiki/Mergers_and_acquisitions): This is a convenient reference site to look up definitions of principal terms, including historical overview and links for further reading.

2 *For library of articles on M&A issues*: Deloitte Merger & Acquisition Library (http://www.deloitte.com/view/en_US/us/Services/consulting/hot-topics/mergers-aquisitions/article/acb2d1800c0fb110VgnVCM100000ba42f00aRCRD.htm): The Deloitte M&A Library features a wide range of articles, points of view, discussion papers, research and industry reports. Topics drill deep into tough business issues, global strategies, investment and acquisition patterns, industry trends, management issues, private and public sector concerns, practical resources and more.

Institute of Mergers, Acquisitions and Alliances (http://www.imaa-institute.org/en/index.php): Based in Switzerland, IMAA provides information on the use and benefits of mergers, acquisitions (M&A) and strategic alliances. Among other services, it collects, maintains and provides specialised resources and information with respect to various aspects of M&A focusing on specific sectors and countries.

3 *For M&A trends and list of deals*: Reuters (http://www.reuters.com/finance/deals/mergers): Product of a merger with Thompson Financials. This site is a great source for comprehensive and up-to-date information about latest M&As. It also includes feature articles and insights on key trends and issues and analysis of M&As by industry and regions.

CNN Money (http://money.cnn.com/data/markets/): CNN Money provides a listing of the most recent deals indicating the names of targets and acquirers, and the dollar value of the deal with a link to a report on each deal. See also a related Top 25 Deals year-to-date list, arranged by the dollar value of the deal.

M&A International (http://www.mergers.net/index.php?id=deal_of_the_month): Provides an informative section on 'Deal of the month'.

Self-assessment questions

Indicative answers to these questions can be found on the companion website at www.sagepub.co.uk/harzing3e.

1 **Why is it that the role of cultural difference in influencing the success or failure of an M&A may be exaggerated?**
2 **A useful way of conceptualising M&As is to consider their desired end-state. What are the five end-states according to Marks and Mirvis (1998)? Briefly define each one.**
3 **What are the top ranked factors contributing to acquisition success according to well-known surveys and reports?**
4 **What do Evans and colleagues (2010) propose are the cultural and people issues in cross-border M&As?**
5 **Specify some of the questions that a cultural due diligence team should ask in order to understand the 'deep knowledge' of the culture.**

References

A. T. Kearney, (1999) *Corporate Marriage: Blight or Bliss – A Monograph on Post-Merger Integration*. Chicago: A. T. Kearney.

Aguilera, R. V. and Dencker, J. (2004) 'The role of human resource management in cross-border mergers and acquisitions', *International Journal of Human Resource Management*, 15: 1357–72.

Angwin, D. and Savill, B. (1997) 'Strategic perspectives on European cross-border acquisitions: A view from top European executives', *European Management Journal*, 15: 423–35.

Ashkenas, R. N. and Francis, S. C. (2000) 'Integration managers: special leaders for special times', *Harvard Business Review*, November–December: 108-16.

Ashkenas, R. N., DeMonaco, L. J. and Francis, S. C. (1998) 'Making the deal real: How GE Capital integrates acquisitions', *Harvard Business Review*, January–February: 165-78.

Barham, K. and Heimer, C. (1998) *ABB. The Dancian Giant*. London: Financial Times Management.

Barkema, H. G., Bell, J. H. and Pennings, J. M. (1996) 'Foreign entry, cultural barriers, and learning', *Strategic Management Journal*, 17: 151-66.

Beer, M., Eisenstat, R. and Spector, B. (1990) *The Critical Path to Corporate Renewal*. Boston, MA: Harvard Business School Press.

Bertrand, O. and Zitouna, H. (2008) 'Domestic versus cross-border acquisitions: which impact on the target firms' performance?', *Applied Economics*, 40(17): 2221-38.

Björkman, I., Stahl, G.K. and Vaara, E. (2007) 'Cultural differences and capability transfer in cross-border acquisitions: The mediating roles of capability complementarity, absorptive capacity, and social integration', *Journal of International Business Studies*, 38(4): 658-72.

Black, J. S., Gregersen, H. B., Mendenhall, M. E. and Stroh, L. K. (1999) *Globalizing People through International Assignments*. New York: Addison-Wesley Longman.

Bleeke, J., Ernst, D., Isono, J. and Weinberg, D. D. (1993) 'Succeeding at cross-border mergers and acquisitions', in J. Bleeke and D. Ernst (eds), *Collaborating to Compete: Using Strategic Alliances and Acquisitions in the Global Marketplace*. New York: John Wiley.

Cartwright, S. and Cooper, C. L. (1993) 'The role of culture compatibility in successful organisational marriage', *Academy of Management Executive*, 7: 57-70.

Cartwright, S. and Cooper, C. L. (1996) *Managing Mergers, Acquisitions, and Strategic Alliances: Integrating People and Cultures*, 2nd edn. Oxford: Butterworth & Heinemann.

Chakrabarti, R., Gupta-Mukherjee, S. and Jayaraman, N. (2009) 'Mars-Venus marriages: Culture and cross-border M&A', *Journal of International Business Studies*, 40(2): 216-35.

Chatterjee, S., Lubatkin, M. H., Schweiger, D. M. and Weber, Y. (1992) 'Cultural differences and shareholder value in related mergers: Linking equity and human capital', *Strategic Management Journal*, 13: 319-34.

Chaudhuri, S. and Tabrizi, B. (1999) 'Capturing the real value in high-tech acquisitions', *Harvard Business Review*, September–October: 123-30.

Child, J., Faulkner, D. and Pitkethly, R. (2001) *The Management of International acquisitions*. Oxford: Oxford University Press.

Datta, D. K. (1991) 'Organizational fit and acquisition performance: Effects of post-acquisition integration', *Strategic Management Journal*, 12: 281-97.

David, K. and Singh, H. (1994) 'Sources of acquisition cultural risk', in A. Sinatra and H. Singh (eds), *The Management of Corporate Acquisitions*. Macmillan: Houndmills.

Dobbs, R., Goedhart, M. and Suonio, H. (2006) 'Are companies getting better at M&A?', *McKinsey Quarterly (December)*; www.mckinseyquarterly.com (online only).

Donnelly, T., Morris, D. and Donnelly, T. (2005) 'Renault-Nissan: A marriage of necessity', *European Business Review*, 17(5): 428-40.

The Economist (1997) 'The Case against mergers,' January.

Epstein, M. J. (2004) 'The drivers of success in post-merger integration', *Organizational Dynamics*, 33(2): 174-89.

Evans, P., Pucik, V. and Björkman, I. (2010) *The Global Challenge: Frameworks for International Human Resource Management*, 2nd edn. New York: McGraw-Hill.

Finkelstein, S. (1999) *Safe Ways to Cross the Merger Minefield. Mastering Global Business.* London: Financial Times Pitman Publishing.

Fubini, D., Price C. and Zollo, M. (2006) *Mergers: Leadership, Performance and Corporate Health.* New York: Palgrave Macmillan.

Goulet, P. K. and Schweiger, D. M. (2006) 'Managing culture and human resources in mergers and acquisitions', in G. K. Stahl and I. Björkman (eds), *Handbook of Research in International Human Resource Management*, Edward Elgar, pp. 405–29. Cheltenham.

Harding, D. and Rouse, T. (2007) Human due diligence', *Harvard Business Review* (April): 124–131.

Haspeslagh, P. and Jemison, D. B. (1991) *Managing Acquisitions: Creating Value Through Corporate Renewal.* New York: The Free Press.

Hofstede, G. (2001). Culture's Consequences: International Differences in Work Related Values, 2nd edn. Beverly Hills: Sage.

Homburg, C. and Bucerius, M. (2006) 'Is speed of integration really a success factor of mergers and acquisitions? An analysis of the role of internal and external relatedness', *Strategic Management Journal*, 27(4): 347–67.

Inkpen, A., Sundaram, A. K. and Rockwood, K. (2000) 'Cross-border acquisitions of U.S. technology assets', *California Management Review*, 42: 50–71.

Jemison, D. B. and Sitkin, S. B. (1986) 'Corporate acquisitions: A process perspective', *Academy of Management Review*, 11: 145–63.

Kay, I. T. and Shelton, M. (2000) 'The people problems in mergers', *McKinsey Quarterly*, 4: 29–37.

Killing, P. (2003) 'Improving acquisition integration: Be clear on what you intend, and avoid "best of both" deals', *Perspectives for Managers*, no. 97. Lausanne: IMD.

Killing, P. (2004) 'Merger of equals: the case of AstraZeneca', in P. Morosini and U. Steger (eds), *Managing Complex Mergers.* London: Financial Times Prentice Hall.

King, D. R., Dalton, D. R., Daily, C. M., and Covin, J. G. (2004) 'Meta-analyses of post-acquisition performance: indications of unidentified moderators', *Strategic Management Journal*, 25(2): 187–200.

Kogut, B. and Singh, H. (1988) 'The effect of national culture on the choice of entry mode', *Journal of International Business Studies*, 19: 411–32.

Kotter, J. P. (1996) *Leading Change.* Boston: Harvard Business School Press.

Kouzes, J. M. and Posner, B. Z. (1987) *The Leadership Challenge: How to get Extraordinary Things Done in Organizations.* San Francisco: Jossey-Bass.

KPMG (1999) *Mergers and Acquisitions: A Global Research Report – Unlocking Shareholder Value.* New York: KPMG.

KPMG (2006) *The Morning After: Driving for Post Deal Success.* London: KPMG.

Krug, J. and Hegerty, W. H. (1997) 'Postacquisition turnover among U.S. top management teams: An analysis of the effect of foreign versus domestic acquisition of U.S. targets', *Strategic Management Journal*, 18: 667–75.

Krug, J. and Hegerty, W. H. (2001) 'Predicting who stays and leaves after an acquisition: A study of top managers in multinational firms', *Strategic Management Journal*, 22(2): 185–96.

Kühlmann, T. and Dowling, P. J. (2005) 'DaimlerChrysler: A case study of a cross-border merger', in G. K. Stahl and M. E. Mendenhall (eds), *Mergers and Acquisitions: Managing Culture and Human Resources.* Stanford, CA: Stanford University Press.

Kumar, N. (2009) 'How emerging giants are rewriting the rules of M&A', *Harvard Business Review* (May): 115–21.

Larsson, R. and Finkelstein, S. (1999) 'Integrating strategic, organizational, and human resource perspectives on mergers and acquisitions: A case survey of synergy realization', *Organization Science*, 10: 1–26.

Larsson, R. and Risberg, A. (1998) 'Cultural awareness and national versus corporate barriers to acculturation', in M. C. Gertsen, A.-M. Søderberg and J. E. Torp (eds), *Cultural Dimensions of International Mergers and Acquisitions*. Berlin: De Gruyter.

Marks, M. L. and Mirvis, P. H. (1998) *Joining Forces: Making One Plus One Equal Three in Mergers, Acquisitions, and Alliances*. San Francisco: Jossey-Bass.

Marsh, Mercer and Kroll (2008) *M&A Beyond Borders: Opportunities and Risks*. www.mercer.com.

Mendenhall, M., Caligiuri, P. and Tarique, I. (2001) 'Assessing and managing culture in mergers and acquisitions'. Presentation at the *Conference on Managing Culture and Human Resources in Mergers and Acquisitions*, Thurnau, Germany, 21 October.

Michaels, E. H., Handfield-Jones, H. and Axelrod, B. (2001) *The War for Talent*. Boston, MA: Harvard Business School Press.

Mirvis, P. H. and Marks, M. L. (1994) *Managing the Merger: Making it Work*. Upper Saddle River: Prentice Hall.

Morosini, P., Shane, S. and Singh, H. (1998) 'National cultural distance and cross-border acquisition performance', *Journal of International Business Studies*, 29: 137–58.

Nahavandi, A. and Malekzadeh, A. R. (1988) 'Acculturation in mergers and acquisitions', *Academy of Management Review*, 13: 79–90.

Olie, R. (1990) 'Culture and integration problems in international mergers and acquisitions', *European Management Journal*, 8: 206–15.

Pucik, V. (2008) 'Post-merger integration process in Japanese M&A: The voices from the frontline', in G. L. Cooper and S. Finkelstein (eds), *Advances in Mergers and Acquisitions*, Vol. 7. Bingley, UK: JAI Press.

Pucik, V. and Evans, P. (2004) 'The human factor in mergers and acquisitions', in P. Morosini and U. Steger (eds), *Managing Complex Mergers*. London: Financial Times Prentice Hall.

Sales, A. L. and Mirvis, P. H. (1984) 'When cultures collide: Issues of acquisition', in J. R. Kimberly and R. E. Quinn (eds), *Managing Organizational Transitions*. Homewood: Irwin.

Schein, E. H. (1987) *Organizational Culture and Leadership*. San Francisco: Jossey-Bass.

Schmidt, J. A. (ed.) (2002) *Making Mergers Work. The Strategic Importance of People*. Alexandria, VA: Towers Perrin and SHRM Foundation.

Schneider, S. C. and Barsoux, J. (1997) *Managing Across Cultures*. New York: Prentice Hall.

Schoenberg, R. (2000) 'The influence of cultural compatibility within cross-border acquisitions: A review', *Advances in Mergers and Acquisitions*, 1: 43–59.

Schweiger, D. M. and Goulet, P. K. (2000) 'Integrating mergers and acquisitions: An international research review', *Advances in Mergers and Acquisitions*, 1: 61–91.

Schweiger, D. M. and Lippert, R. L. (2005) 'Integration: The critical link in M&A value creation', in G. K. Stahl and M. E. Mendenhall (eds), *Mergers and Acquisitions: Managing Culture and Human Resources*. Stanford, CA: Stanford University Press.

Shimizu, K., Hitt, M.A., Vaidyanath, D. and Pisano, V. (2004) 'Theoretical foundations of cross-border mergers and acquisitions: A review of current research and recommendations for the future', *Journal of International Management*, 10(3): 307–53.

Shrivastava, P. (1986) 'Postmerger integration', *Journal of Business Strategy*, 7: 65–76.

Sitkin, S. B. and Pablo, A. L. (2005) 'The neglected importance of leadership in M&As', in G. K. Stahl and M. E. Mendenhall (eds), *Mergers and Acquisitions: Managing Culture and Human Resources*. Stanford, CA: Stanford University Press.

Slangen, A. H. L (2006) 'National cultural distance and initial foreign acquisition performance: The moderating effect of integration', *Journal of World Business*, 41(2): 161–70.

Stahl, G. K. (2006) 'Synergy springs from cultural revolution', *Financial Times*, 6 October.

Stahl, G. K. and Javidan, M. (2009) 'Comparative and cross-cultural perspectives on cross-border mergers and acquisitions', in R. S. Bhagat and R. M. Steers (eds), *Handbook of Culture, Organisation, and Work*. Cambridge, UK: Cambridge University Press.

Stahl, G. K. and Mendenhall, M. E. (2005) *Mergers and Acquisitions: Managing Culture and Human Resources*. Stanford: Stanford University Press.

Stahl, G. K. and Sitkin, S. B. (2005) 'Trust in mergers and acquisitions', in G.K. Stahl and M. E. Mendenhall (eds), *Mergers and Acquisitions: Managing Culture and Human Resources*. Stanford, CA: Stanford University Press.

Stahl, G. K. and Voigt, A. (2008) 'Do cultural differences matter in mergers and acquisitions? A tentative model and examination', *Organisation Science*, 19(1): 160–76.

Teerikangas, S. and Very, P. (2006) 'The culture-performance relationship in M&A: From yes/no to how', *British Journal of Management*, 17(1): 31–48.

Vaara, E. (2003) 'Post-acquisition integration as sense making: Glimpses of ambiguity, confusion, hypocrisy, and politicization', *Journal of Management Studies*, 40(4): 859–94.

Vaara, E., Tienari, J. and Björkman, I. (2003) 'Global capitalism meets national spirit', *Journal of Management Inquiry*, 12(4): 377–93.

Vermeulen, G. A. M. and Barkema, H. G. (2001) 'Learning through acquisitions', *Academy of Management Journal*, 44(3): 457–76.

Very, P., Lubatkin, M. and Calori, R. (1996) 'A cross-national assessment of acculturative stress in recent European mergers', *International Studies of Management & Organization*, 26: 59–86.

Vlasic, B. and Stertz, B. (2000) *How Daimler-Benz drove off with Chrysler*. New York: Morrow.

Weber, Y. (1996) 'Corporate cultural fit and performance in mergers and acquisitions', *Human Relations*, 49: 1181–202.

Weber, Y., Shenkar, O. and Raveh, A. (1996) 'National and corporate fit in mergers & acquisitions: An exploratory study', *Management Science*, 4(8): 1215–27.

5

Approaches to IHRM

Chris Rowley, Irene Hon-fun Poon, Ying Zhu and Malcolm Warner

Contents

Learning Objectives

After reading this chapter you will be able to

- Describe and analyse the characteristics, contributions and limitations of prominent models of human resource management (HRM)

- Explain the differences between contingency and divergence theories of HRM and different institutional and cultural factors

- Understand how and why HRM approaches in the Asian context are similar to, or different from, those in the West

- Evaluate the applicability of HRM approaches and discuss the implications of change for HRM

Chapter Outline

This chapter examines the varieties of International HRM (IHRM) approaches, identifies the development and transformation of HRM, and explores some basic questions on the universality of HRM. Contemporary research on IHRM has considerable variation in its theoretical perspectives, HRM approaches and types of organisation included. This chapter compares and contrasts the dominant IHRM approaches in the US and Europe, namely the 'Matching Model', the 'Harvard Model', the 'Contextual Model', the '5-P Model' and the 'European Model'. The outcome of the comparison is then reviewed in the light of their key aspects and current practices in different organisations and countries. The chapter evaluates whether various HRM approaches are applicable and can be transferred to different firms, business systems, institutional contexts and cultural environments. It shows that HRM practices developed in one context cannot simply be assumed to work in the same way in other countries. The chapter concludes that though differences in HRM approaches exist, they are often subject to dynamic change over time. The evolutionary nature of change in organisations and approaches to IHRM is illustrated using ideas and examples from Asia.

1 Introduction

Globalisation effects, such as the expansion of overseas markets, aided by information and communication technologies (ICT) and the growing importance of multinational companies (MNCs), has resulted in a proliferation of IHRM research. With the growth of new markets such as in China, India, South East Asia, and Eastern Europe and an increased level of competition among firms at both national and international levels, there is a clear need to develop an understanding of how to manage human resources working in different parts of the world (see Chapter 18).

Academics have responded positively to the challenges of internationalisation proposing different HRM approaches. The majority of IHRM scholars are concerned with the design of HRM processes in global organisations/MNCs, interactions between institutions, societal norms and government regulations and comparative analysis of HRM approaches across economies (Metcalfe and Rees, 2005). There is also substantial interest in issues of culture and acculturation. Yet, many of the prominent theoretical models and concepts of HRM were developed based on American or European countries. The relevance of such American or European ('Anglo-Saxon') experience to other institutional and cultural contexts, as well as the applicability of these approaches to dynamic, emerging economies, such as some Asian countries, is questionable. Some argue that IHRM is a recent subject discipline and that its roots are not explicitly accounted for nor fully explained (Rowley and Warner, 2007b). Besides, there are series of questions pursued by comparative HRM researchers that require further attention (See Box 5.1).

Box 5.1   Questions to be Considered by Comparative HRM Researchers

- How much are existing HRM approaches that are based on Western ways of thinking relevant and applicable to other parts of the world?
- What evidence is there for one model or set of 'best' HRM practices?
- What are the similarities and differences in HRM systems across different countries?
- What are the reasons for these similarities and differences in HRM?
- As business becomes more global, to what extent is HRM becoming more uniform?
- To what extent will different regions retain their own distinctive approaches to HRM?
- Is HRM converging or diverging at the cross-national level?
- What is the influence of institutional and cultural factors on the HRM approaches of global firms?
- What are the changes in HRM approaches over time?

A starting point for investigating such questions is to examine the key characteristics of different HRM approaches developed so far. This can assist with answering some of the basic questions about the universality of HRM. In the next section, five models of HRM are analysed. These models are well documented in the literature and have wide-ranging implications for contemporary research. Based on the comparison of key characteristics, contributions and limitations of these models, the second part of the chapter then evaluates whether various HRM approaches can be transferred to different business systems, institutional contexts and cultural environments. In the final section, some cases and examples of firms in Asia are used to show the dynamic changes in HRM approaches over time. The chapter then draws its conclusions and outlines some future directions for IHRM.

2 Review of IHRM approaches

This section compares and contrasts the dominant paradigm of HRM in North America and Western Europe. The literature contains many theoretical models of HRM. However, due to limitations of space, only five main models of HRM are addressed. These are the: 'Matching Model' (Tichy et al., 1982), 'Harvard model' (Beer et al., 1984), 'Contextual Model' (Hendry and Pettigrew, 1990), '5-P' Model (Schuler, 1992), and 'European Model' of HRM (Brewster, 1995). The reason for analysing these models is to identify their principal contributions to the development of HRM and their application in the international environment. In addition, many of these models exemplify particular cultural characteristics of their country of origin which can help readers to reflect on the transferability of Western-oriented models to other contexts and institutional environments (Hsu and Leat, 2000).

Matching model

Characteristics The main contributors to the Matching Model of HRM come from the Michigan and New York schools. Tichy and colleagues (1982) propose this model which highlights the 'resource' aspect of HRM and emphasises a 'tight fit' between organisational strategy, organisational structure and HRM system (see Box 5.2). On the surface the matching model bears a strong resemblance to earlier ideas, such as scientific management (Taylor, 1911) in so far as it promotes the idea of 'best fit' or 'best practice'. The model shares similarities with Galbraith and Nathanson (1978) who link different personnel functions to an organisation's strategy and structure, and emphasise the significance of the HR function for achieving an organisation's mission.

Contributions Despite the many criticisms, the matching model deserves credit for providing a framework for subsequent theory development in the field of HRM.

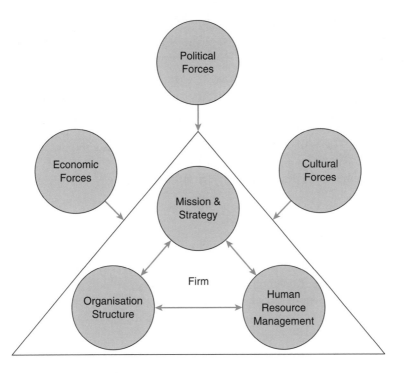

Figure 5.1   Matching model

Source: From MIT Sloan Management Review. © 1982 by Massachussetts Institute of Technology. All rights Distributed by Tribune Media Services.

When working within this model, a company is concerned with performance systems that exercise tight control over individual activities, with the ultimate goal of securing a competitive advantage (Guest, 1995).

Limitations The matching model is based on a classical view of strategy formulation which assumes that design and implementation are separate activities and that HR policies and practices can simply be 'matched' to business strategies at the formulation stage. It fails to acknowledge the complexities within and between concepts of strategy and HRM (Dyer, 1985) and underestimates the difficulties inherent to obtaining a reciprocal relationship between strategy and HRM (Boxall, 1992). The model also overlooks 'human' aspect of HRM and does not take account of significant variations in power, politics and culture (Purcell and Ahlstrand, 1994) and therefore has been categorised as a 'hard' model of HRM (Guest, 1997; Legge, 1995; Storey, 1995).

Box 5.2   Example 1: Theoretical perspectives on HRM fit

The SHRM literature distinguishes between what has been termed vertical or external fit and horizontal or internal fit. While external fit denotes the alignment between HRM practices and the specific organisational context (e.g. organisational strategy), internal fit refers to the coherent configuration of individual HRM practices that support each other (Becker et al., 1997; Delery, 1998) and the arrangement of HRM activities (e.g. HRM policies and practices) that work in concert.

Contingency perspective

This predicts that the relationship between HRM practices and organisational effectiveness is contingent upon an organisation's strategy (Delery and Doty, 1996). It proposes that organisations which have HR policies and practices that are more responsive to external factors will report superior performance.

Configurational Perspective

This takes a more holistic view that is aligned with the concept of equifinality and highlights the importance of fit and complementarity among HRM practices in predicting organisational effectiveness (Delery and Doty, 1996). According to the concept of equifinality, 'different HRM practices that fit together can yield identical outcomes' (1996: 386–7). Internal fit is usually referred to as an arrangement of HRM activities (e.g. HRM policies or practices) that work in concert. Some researchers may call these arrangements 'systems' (e.g. Delery and Doty, 1996), 'bundles' (e.g. MacDuffie, 1995), or 'clusters' (e.g. Arthur, 1992).

Harvard model

Characteristics During the same period that the 'hard' oriented 'Matching Model' was developed, the 'Harvard Model' (Beer et al., 1984) with more 'soft' characteristics was produced. It pays attention to the 'human' aspect of HRM and is more concerned with the employer–employee relationship (Zhu et al., 2007). This model highlights the interests of different stakeholders in the organisation and links their interests with the objectives of management. It regards people as the most important single asset of the organisation and emphasises employee's needs and societal well-being. In short, it comprises a broader area of focus than the 'hard model' and aims to increase the sum of human satisfaction at a variety of interrelated levels (ibid.). Some people have equated this model with the concept of a 'high commitment work system' (Walton, 1985). The Harvard model conceives HRM as a series of policy choices, comprising (a) HR flows (selection, appraisal, development and outflows), (b) reward systems, (c) work systems, and (d) employee influence (through trade unions and work councils). The outcomes of these four HR policies are commitment, competence, congruence and cost effectiveness.

Contributions This model provides a broad classification of the content of HRM and a range of outcomes at the individual, organisational and societal levels, and hence it can provide a useful basis for comparative analysis of HRM (Poole, 1990). It also encourages useful holistic thinking about the sources of skill supply and draws attention to skill as an important concept for HRM (Hendry and Pettigrew, 1990).

Limitations However, this model has been criticised for not explaining the complex relationships between strategic management and HRM (Guest, 1991). By outlining a range of policy choices and not recommending specific approaches, this model is descriptive rather than prescriptive and therefore does not predict the relationships between HRM policies and outcomes (Guest, 1997).

Contextual Model

Characteristics In reality, both hard and soft elements are present in organisations. The interactive process within the HRM system can be complex and is heavily influenced by a variety of contextual and historical factors. Hendry and Pettigrew (1990) argue that the existence of a number of linkages between the outer environmental context (socio-economic, technological, political-legal and competitive) and inner organisational context (culture, structure, leadership, task technology and business output) form the content of HRM. To analyse this 'Contextual model', past information related to the organisation's development and management of change is essential (Sparrow and Hiltrop, 1994). Organisations may follow different pathways to achieve positive results and there is no straightforward flow from business strategy to HRM (Budhwar and Debrah, 2001).

Contributions Under this model, changes in HR practices can be conceived as a response to business strategy and the scope of the HRM function to respond effectively depends on the contextual factors. This implies that two firms facing the same set of external circumstances may not respond in the same way or evolve in HRM to

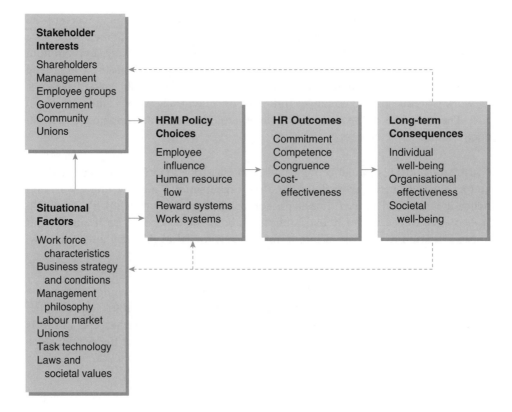

Figure 5.2 Harvard model

Source: Reprinted with kind permission from Michael Beer. Beer, M., Spector, B., Lawrence, P.R., Mills, D.O. and Walton. R.E. (1984), *Managing Human Assets,* New York: Free Press.

the same degree, and hence their HR practices will remain different. The model can be used for detailed contextual analysis and case study research.

Limitations A potential problem that can arise from this approach is that personnel policy and practice become the dependent variable of the analysis and outcomes such as company performance become the independent variable (Guest, 1991). Besides, different views and interests of management and employees (Purcell and Ahlstrand, 1994) can influence the interactive process. The issues of lagged response, emergent business strategy and limited resources (Brewster, 1993) can also complicate the relationship of HR practices and contextual factors.

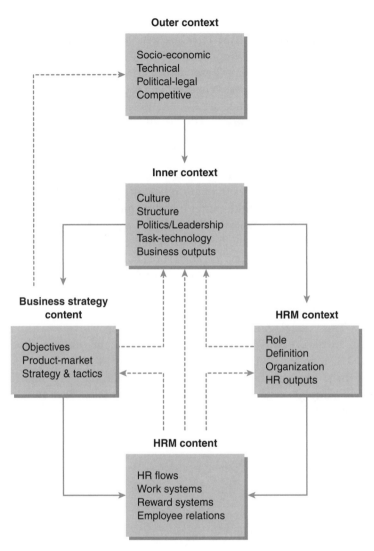

Figure 5.3   Contextual model

Source: From 'HRM: An agenda for the 1990s', Hendry, C., and Pettigrew, A. (1990) *International Journal of Human Resource Management* 1(1): 17-43. Reprinted by permission of the publisher (Taylor and Francis Group, http://www.informaworld.com).

5-P model

Characteristics The field of IHRM became substantially more important in the early 1990s due to globalisation and accelerated changes in economic, social, legal, technological and workforce conditions. One result was that MNCs became more concerned to integrate HRM into business strategy on an international or global platform. Schuler (1992) proposes a '5-P model' which combines various HR activities with strategic needs. These activities are philosophy, policies, programmes, practices and processes. Whether they are categorised as strategic or not depends on (1) if the HR activities are systematically linked to the strategic needs of the business or the operational needs, or (2) if they occur over the long term or in the short term, or (3) if they focus on senior managers or non-managerial employees (Schuler, 1992).

Contributions This model shows the inter-relatedness of activities (see Box 5.3) that were often treated separately in the earlier literature and provides an understanding of the complex interaction between organisational strategy and strategic HRM activities (Budhwar and Debrah, 2001). Another contribution is that it demonstrates the influence of both internal characteristics (organisational culture and nature of the business) and external characteristics (economy and industry) on the strategic business needs of an organisation.

Limitations This model, however, suffers from being over-prescriptive and too hypothetical in nature and is difficult to implement in practice (Budhwar and Debrah, 2001). It may be of interest to scholars, but it is limited in its applications for management practitioners. HR managers who have not had to align HR activities with strategic needs will find that the process takes time and developing a detailed understanding of the needs requires extra effort (Schuler, 1992).

Box 5.3   Example 2: Strategy and HR activities link

One benefit of the 5-P model is that it highlights the complex interaction of the strategy–HR activity link.

- Philosophy: Makes statements to define business values and culture
- Policies: Expresses as shared values and guidelines for action the people-related business issues and HR programmes
- Programmes: Articulates as HR strategies for coordinating effort and facilitating change to address major people-related business issues
- Practices: Motivates needed role behaviours, e.g. leadership, managerial and operational roles
- Processes: Defines how HR activities are carried out

Source: Schuler, 1992

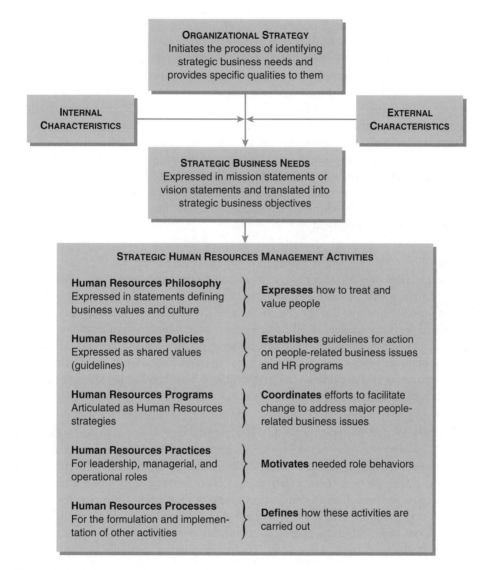

Figure 5.4   5-P model

Source: Reprinted from *Organization Dynamics*, 21(1), Schuler, R.S. 'Strategic HRM: Linking the people with the strategic needs of the business' pp18-32, 1992, with permission from Elsevier.

European model

Characteristics While various approaches to IHRM were proposed in the 1980s and 1990s, an international comparison of HR practices indicates that the basic functions of HRM are given different value in different countries and implemented differently

(Gaugler, 1988). Surveying European management, Pieper (1990: 11) concludes that 'a single universal model of HRM does not exist'. What is needed is a model of HRM that explains country differences in the context of national culture and its manifestations in history, law, institutions and organisation structures (Filella, 1991). Hence, Brewster (1993, 1995) proposes a 'European model' of HRM to reflect increasing European Union (EU) integration and the adoption of common EU labour legislation. His model assumes that European organisations operating with restricted autonomy are constrained (a) at the international and national level by national culture and legislation, (b) at the organisation level by patterns of ownership, and (c) at the HRM level by trade union involvement and consultative arrangements. In addition, Brewster (1995) emphasises the need for a more comprehensive understanding of the role of different players in developing the concept of HRM and testing its applications in the international environment.

Contributions The European model moves beyond countries' borders and enables analysis of HRM at a broader geographical and continental level. This places HRM concepts firmly within the cross-national border context and allows better understanding of situations in Europe (Budhwar and Debrah, 2001). Significantly, factors that in the previous models of HRM were seen as external to organisations become a part of the HRM model, rather than understood as a set of external influences. This can show differences in HRM practices between nations and across clusters of similar countries and provide an understanding of how MNCs may attempt to adopt or reject local practices (Brewster, 1995).

Limitations Within Europe, large differences exist between countries with more labour regulations in, for example, the Scandinavian and German countries than in comparatively less regulated countries, like Ireland or the UK (Mayrhofer and Brewster, 2005). Hence, there exists considerable variety across countries in the single European model and even within clusters of similar countries. Besides, a number of subsequent studies have argued that differences in HRM might be due to factors not included in the model, such as skill-level and available types of qualifications in the workforce, the role of HR and employees' participation in decision making.

Implications of HRM models

The above discussion presents an outline of theoretical developments in HRM and compares and contrasts the characteristics of five models of HRM. Whereas these five models in no way provide a complete picture of the field of HRM, the comparison reviews certain patterns of formation and development of the HRM paradigm in North America and Western Europe. This leads us to three conclusions and sets of questions.

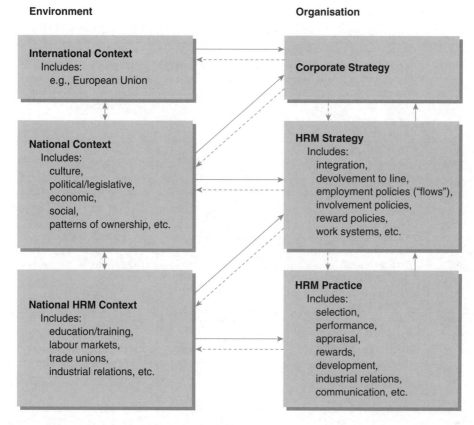

Figure 5.5   European model

Source: Reprinted by permission from Macmillan Publishers Ltd: *Journal of International Business Studies,* 26(1): 1-21. Brewster, C (1995) 'Towards a European Model of HRM', Copyright 1995.

First of all, HRM as a field of academic study is primarily of North American/Anglo-Saxon origin. Despite the fact that research into HRM is now taking place in many countries around the world, current IHRM research that is genuinely international in orientation remains limited. Among these five models, is there one (or a set of) best HRM approaches? And if so, what is the conceptualisation of HRM in the international context?

Second, as management and organisational writers have noted the field of HRM has expanded beyond the management of HR to include a strong connection with corporate strategy, regional integration, extension into cross-cultural management and transnational organisations. Consequently, scholars are steadily extending their knowledge of HRM beyond specific national boundaries with information about HRM in many other countries. Can any of these HRM approaches be applicable to other national contexts, such as the Asian economies?

Table 5.1   Comparison of five dominant HRM models

HRM model	Basic assumptions	Contributions	Limitations
Matching model (Tichy et al., 1982)	• Existence of best HRM practices • Does not consider synergies, interdependencies or integration mechanisms	• Demonstration of the importance of HRM in organisations	• Excessive emphasis on 'fit' issues • Does not take account of power, politics and culture aspects
Harvard model (Beer et al., 1984)	• No best HRM practices • Effects depend on variables such as internal and external environment	• Inclusion of other variables that mediate the relationship between HRM and performance	• Narrow objectives, non-prescriptive • Difficult to apply to complex relationships
Contextual model (Hendry and Pettigrew, 1990)	• Consideration of HRM as part of a bigger social macro system that both influence and is influenced by HRM strategy	• Introduction of social and processual dimensions of HRM	• Personnel policies and practices as dependent variables
5-P model (Schuler, 1992)	• Combination of various elements that create the HRM system and consideration of those elements that may be equally efficient	• Consideration of synergy and interdependence between different elements of the system	• Definition of management patterns is a simplification of reality • Difficult to implement in practice
European model (Brewster, 1995)	• Consideration of national culture and legislation, in addition to organisational characteristics	• Integration of the HRM system in a macro institutional context and revealing differences between nations	• Differences in HRM model may be due to factors other than national culture and external influences

Finally, a large number of factors may affect HRM approaches in an international environment. What might these be? What are the implications of change to IHRM approaches? The following sections will explore these questions in detail and concentrate on examples from Asia.

3 The concept of HRM

Despite an extensive and growing body of literature addressing the HRM paradigm in North America and Western Europe and the increasing importance of an international perspective, there remains limited consensus as to the substance, nature and implications of IHRM concepts. Firstly, of the five models reviewed, there is an identifiable difference between the way in which HRM is conducted and understood in North America and in Western Europe, and probably elsewhere too. This, in part, reflects theoretical developments in debates about how HRM should be conceived.

The word 'HRM' can simply be used as an updated word for personnel management (PM), and can also be used to cover other concepts, such as employee relations. In the international context, the notion of HRM can be extended to incorporate a business-integrated approach or can include MNCs' cross-cultural management of the global workforce and its fit with their organisations' international strategies.

Nevertheless, many researchers (e.g, Easterby-Smith et al., 1995) have criticised HRM for being a culturally bound and Anglo-American biased concept that cannot be divorced from its institutional context. To apply the HRM concept in other countries, it is important to understand its meanings. Western notions of HRM might not be present in organisations in Asia (Warner, 1995; 2009) because the roles of PM common in Asia can be far from the concept of HRM as understood in Western business management theory due in part to the cultural differences that exist between the East and the West. Traditional practices predominately used in Asia, for example lifetime employment, seniority-based pay, and organisational specific/technical skills training, can be very different from those practices used in the West.

4 Are IHRM models applicable to other contexts?

In understanding the concepts of HRM and IHRM, some key questions arise: Is HRM becoming more uniform as business becomes more global? Or will HRM remain distinct in different regions? If so, are the differences increasing or decreasing? This leads us to questions concerning possible divergence in HRM. To locate these questions within an international context, the analysis should include consideration of factors such as the differential impact of globalisation upon organisations operating within different geographical regions, the role of MNCs in promoting global HRM practices, and the variety and different forms of national business system.

Universalist view

On one side of the coin, globalisation, internationalisation, and technological advancement are some of the factors thought to push national systems towards uniformity (Kerr et al., 1960) such as when copying, benchmarking and transferring of practices are encouraged. Competition and market development may encourage international companies to adopt some 'best practices' in order to survive and compete. International 'best practice' research suggests that proactive management strategies significantly affect business outcomes and that the search for a 'transnational solution' (Bartlett and Ghoshal, 1992) will lead to the convergence of structural forms and processes.

The forces of globalisation and search for optimal management practices by MNCs have the potential to make a significant impact on the field of HRM. For example, firms tend to adopt broadly similar policies towards their staff and in their relations with other stakeholders within specific national contexts (Whitley, 1999). When universalist viewpoints that there is 'one best way' of managing, are influential on MNCs or when simplified ideas of strategic alignment and fit are prevalent such as in the matching model, then one might assume emulation of universally identified 'best practice' will lead to greater convergence in management approaches (Rowley et al., 2004).

Contingency vs. divergence

On the other side of the coin, the forces of globalisation and socio-economic integration imply increased cultural diversity in management composition as well as more varied influences on the contextual development of cross-national organisations. As proposed by the contextual model and the 5-P model, the right mix of HRM strategies depends on a complex variety of critical environmental and internal contingencies. Thus, under a contingency view, international organisations should constantly adjust and change their IHRM strategies to fit with the external environment (Heenan and Perlmutter, 1990; Jackson et al., 1989), or to correspond to firms' international corporate lifecycle (Adler and Ghadar, 1990), or to align with the business strategy (Becker and Gerhart, 1996; Delery and Doty, 1996). Hence, there is a need to develop an understanding of how to manage HR when working in different parts of the world.

Nevertheless, various IHRM models, regardless of whether a 'hard model' or 'soft model' is applied, can be constrained at international, national and organisational levels. Similar to the difficulty of applying the North American matching model to Europe, the degree to which IHRM approaches can be applicable elsewhere, may vary. Turbulent, competitive and changing environments can limit the case for one best way (Guest, 1991).

Besides, structural variations and interactions in terms of social, political, economic systems, culture and history, and the dominance of different economic sectors, produce distinctive forms of national business system, as claimed by the divergency view (Valiukonyte and Parkkonen, 2008). For instance, different varieties of capitalist economic organisations in North America, Western Europe and Asia have been developing over some time interdependently within dominant societal institutions. Their implications for existing forms of capitalism are by no means straightforward. The ways in which different types of internationalisation operate are path dependent and reflect their historical legacies as well as current institutional linkages (Whitley, 1998). Distinctive and homogenous cultures in Asia have developed their own integrated business systems. This in turn generates significant variations in how firms in Asia operate. Hence, the 'best' IHRM approach in one situation may not be the 'best' approach in another business system given that institutional forces and structural factors are very different between countries and organisations (Zhu et al., 2007).

Crossvergence and hybridisation ✳

The concept of crossvergence has been operationalised and studied among developing economies and newly industrialised economies (see Jackson, 2004; Priem et al., 2000). Zhu and colleagues (2007) commenting on the characteristics of HR practices in East Asia conclude that a hybridisation of the people management system has been developed in Asia. The hybrid system has the characteristics of maintaining indigenous management value and practices while being highly adaptive and flexible to utilising 'good' practices developed in other countries. This concept challenges the conventional wisdom of the contingency approach and helps to overcome the tension and contradiction created by Western HRM systems.

5 What factors affect HRM approaches internationally?

Developing management models that are universally applicable in all contexts presents a considerable challenge. Practice, norms and concepts from different countries, whatever their origin, tend to show some cultural specificity and contextual and institutional factors often vary from country to country.

Institutional theory

Institutional forces of coercion and imitation play an important role in IHRM. Norms and expectations shared by members of a society or a particular industry influence how organisations should be structured and the kinds of managerial behaviour that are considered legitimate (Meyer and Rowan, 1977). International organisations, as social entities, are affected by domestic, regional and global forces. They tend to seek approval for their behaviours in a socially constructed environment (Jackson and Schuler, 1995), constituted by a range of institutional forces including local governments (Walder, 1995), social networks (Child, 1994) and regional economic policy (Tse et al., 1997) (see Box 5.4). Hall and Soskice (2001) argue that societal institutions (such as market, culture and history), together with the complementarities among them, mould the specific institutions of corporate governance, management practice, inter-firm relations and labour markets. Thus there exist a large number of institutional ways of organising economic activity rather than a 'one-best-way' and they create many alternative, distinctive national business systems within the parameters of capitalism (Tempel and Walgenbach, 2007).

Social forces can act as constraints on the degree of international transfer of HRM when MNCs adopt local institutional norms and rules for structuring companies and managing activities. Summarising the institutional perspective, Hoffman (1999: 351) states that the HRM model an MNC adopts 'is seen not as a choice among an unlimited array of possibilities determined by purely internal arrangements, but rather as a choice among a narrowly defined set of legitimate options'.

Box 5.4   Example 3: What roles do institutional forces play in HRM change in Asia?

Institutionalists argue that assumptions, beliefs and expectations existing within society determine how firms should be organised and which functions they do and do not perform. In some Asian economies, the opening up of markets to MNCs in China and Vietnam as well as implementation of economic reforms in Malaysia and Korea to match the standards of global competition have created a new institutional environment and exerted pressure on indigenous Asian companies to adopt new ways of working. Joining the World Trade Organisation (WTO) accelerated economic development but at the same time pressurised China's state-owned enterprises (SOEs) to imitate the practices of Western MNCs to demonstrate that they are in step with international markets. The popularity of business schools in many Asian economies (such as Hong Kong, Singapore and Taiwan) also promotes the transfer of business ideas and managerial practices prevalent in the West.

Source: Poon, 2010; Rowley and Poon, 2008; Walsh and Zhu, 2007.

Cultural approach

Another factor affecting the approach to HRM in an international environment is national culture. Two paradoxical trends run through HRM in international businesses. First, there are clear cross-country differences which can be understood and explained in the context of each national culture and its manifestations in history, regulations (Florkowski and Nath, 1993), political systems (Carroll et al., 1998) or socialisation factors (Lockett, 1988; Rowley and Yukongdi, 2009).

Second, cultural distance from the home country can create problems for MNCs operating in, and adapting to, a host setting (Davidson, 1980) because change in decision making, communication and personnel practices are difficult (Child and Markoczy, 1993) and concepts of ideal management practice are different.

Furthermore, traditional philosophies embedded in Asian societies have an influence on the transfer and adoption of international managerial approaches (Child, 1994; Noronha, 2002). Evidence has shown that, for example, Japanese firms operating in the Asian context tend to adapt to local conditions (Rodgers and Wong, 1996; Wong, 1996) as a consequence of the similarity of cultural values between Japan and Asian countries (Ngo et al., 1998). It is, therefore, important to extend previous research by investigating whether practices brought by companies from different nationalities, and hence different cultural contexts, are likely to be compatible and hence adopted. It has been suggested (Braun and Warner, 2002) that some HRM approaches are more cross-cultural and hence transferable than others. For instance, many recruitment and training practices are less culture-bound because they are often characterised by the technical skills, roles and responsibilities attached to various positions (Anderson, 1992; Watson, 1994).

6 What are the implications of change for IHRM approaches?

The management approach in general, and HRM in particular, can be subject to systematic reform and change. Transfer and adoption of international practice demonstrates change in both directions towards greater similarity and difference. The degree of acceptance of change can vary, but there are a number of general implications change holds for IHRM approaches.

First, in Asia there is a strong foreign influence on the process of change, in particular the North American approach. The more dependent the economy on foreign capital and MNCs' activities (e.g. Taiwan, Malaysia and Thailand), the more Western HRM approaches may be adopted and greater change in management approach can be expected. For example, West European or North American-owned firms tend to have more individualist values and hence are more accustomed to individual based rewards schemes. These schemes are different from rewards practices prevalent among Asian firms, such as residual 'iron rice bowl' policies in China (Warner, 2009), seniority based wage in Japan, or 'collective equality' in South Korea (Zhu et al., 2007).

Economic restructuring in East Asia has led to relocation of some production processes from developed to developing countries, such as China, Cambodia, Malaysia, the Philippines, Thailand and Vietnam (Rowley and Abdul-Rahman, 2008; Rowley and Paik, 2009; Zhu and Warner, 2004). Such liberalisation of the economy has created more opportunity for domestic enterprises to adopt some of the widely used Western and Japanese HR practices (Benson and Zhu, 1999). Thus, key HRM practices, such as individual fixed term contracts, individual performance evaluation, individual career development and strategic roles for HRM have become more apparent in the East Asian approaches to HRM.

The state has played a major role during the change process. 'State-led development' has impacted not only on processes of modernisation but also on the role of active labour market practice in Asia (Lee and Warner, 2007). Among the Asian economies, China and Vietnam have undergone a period of state-led economic reform and change in their people management systems, transforming from the traditional PM model into a hybrid model combining PM and HRM (Zhu et al., 2007).

State can encourage change

However, other factors can generate some resistance towards change and certainly slow down the speed of diffusion of HRM approaches in Asia. The role of the state can hinder change in HRM as well. For instance, bureaucratic control and inertia in Japan means that change has been difficult. This, combined with the sophistication of sub-contractor networks, has meant that change can be resisted. In South Korea,

State can provide resistance.

direct government involvement has exemplified the business–government relationship while the network links of the *chaebol* have often made change more difficult to implement (Rowley et al., 2004).

Moreover, the HRM approach may be opposed by the country's specific culture and institutions. Some Asian values, such as emphasis on hard work, respect for elders, strong family ties and passion for learning, mean that any imported HRM approach will be subject to change and adaptation to these cultural preferences (Rowley et al., 2004). HRM approaches and ideas tend to be more readily assimilated in different cultures when developed and tested in culturally compatible settings. Likewise, history is an important factor requiring due consideration in the adoption and implementation of HRM policies and practices and success is related to the 'fit' of the historical path of change with general societal norms in a particular local setting.

In short, reform, evolution and transformation, each have different implications for HRM approaches since there is no homogeneous universal approach to IHRM. HRM practices and ideas from different countries tend to possess some cultural specificity whatever their origin and may run into difficulty when transplanted into other countries.

7 Conclusion

This chapter reviews some dominant IHRM approaches in North America and Western Europe and then explores the questions about the universality of HRM in other contexts. There are a number of factors affecting the applicability of HRM to different institutional contexts and international environments, particularly in the context of globalisation. HRM's transfer and application to the Asian economies can be affected by the traditional philosophies embedded in Asian societies, the role the State plays during the change process and the degree of Western influence (Warner, 2009). Hence, the degree of acceptance of change in any HRM approach can vary. This chapter has examined and focused on HRM with an international dimension, indicating scope for diversity in IHRM approaches, and argued in favour of making HRM more relevant and accessible to different economies.

First, IHRM is complex and multi-faceted and brings together a variety of approaches and factors. Practices developed in one context, for example in the West, cannot simply be assumed to work in the same way in other countries, such as Asian economies, which have substantially different value-sets. One of the future challenges for IHRM researchers is to synthesise national and comparative studies in developing economies and develop and clarify the field of IHRM (see Chapter 2). Future research should also integrate research across countries and regions, and access the complex interaction of culture, institutions, societal norms and values.

Second, MNCs are competing not only on a global level, but also on a regional or local level (Ghemawat, 2005). Local conditions relevant to HRM practices vary greatly. MNCs usually find themselves having different HRM practices across localities (Schuler and Tarique, 2007). In order to obtain consistency across all subsidiaries, some MNCs may develop common corporate values that guide the development of local HR policies while leaving the detailed plans to be designed by local branches or offices (see Case Study, pp. 174–176). This practice requires MNCs to have a good understanding of the issues in the global context and in turn, requires an understanding of their local environments.

Third, understanding the environment requires that MNCs adjust their IHRM approach continually towards the external and internal contextual factors. Even though differences in HRM approaches exist, they are often subject to dynamic change over time; and the direction of change is not necessarily towards some final destination or universal model of best practice. This chapter has illustrated the *evolutionary* nature of change in organisations' approaches to IHRM.

Above all, IHRM research should move beyond exploring practices and approaches that are exclusively organisation-bound, to examine the socio-cultural contexts, varieties of business systems and political and economic environments in which the global workforce is managed. The turbulence in the firms' environments due to downturns as well as upswings in the business cycle, given the current global crisis, should also be considered in IHRM research.

Discussion questions

1 Discuss the different IHRM approaches that have contributed to the development of HRM.

2 Universalistic and contingent theorists have differing views on how IHRM is used in the international context. Discuss the core arguments on both sides.

3 How do you think HRM practices might be transferred between countries?

4 What might be some of the constraints on the transfer of Western HRM approaches to Asian economies?

5 Choose a country and discuss the implications of the latest change in that country to the 'best practices' in HRM approach.

HSBC in East Asia (before the 2008 credit crunch)

Data are extracted from companies' websites, industry reports, and authors' long-term research and work experience in this region.

The forces in the world economy have necessitated that financial institutions become more international in outlook if they are to survive in the global arena. Noticeable changes, for example mergers, acquisitions, emergence of new players, deregulation, and application of modern technology, have been observed in the structure of the global financial industry (Qing, 2001). These changes have intensified competition among financial institutions in many countries, such as East Asian economies. Rapid changes in the industry can pose serious challenges even for the giant financial institutions and their approaches to HRM. Three areas of HRM that concern the banks most in their Asian operations are recruitment, rewards, training and development. The following case considers HSBC's HRM policies and practices in East Asia and discusses how relevant and applicable existing IHRM approaches are to other parts of the world, what institutional and cultural factors influence HRM approaches in global firms, and what the implications of change are for their HRM approaches.

Company background

HSBC Holdings plc, number one in the Fortune Global 500 in 2007, is the world's largest company and bank. The Holdings was established in 1991 to become the parent company to the Hong Kong and Shanghai Banking Corporation. It has a significant presence in the major financial markets. By 2008, HSBC operated a network of around 600 offices in 20 countries in the Asia Pacific region. Its long history in East Asia can be traced back to the nineteenth century. It has been the largest note-issuing bank in Hong Kong since the 1880s, handled the first public loan in China in 1874 and was the first bank to be established in Thailand in 1888.

Recruitment

When entering the Asian market, many MNCs have adopted an ethnocentric approach to their recruitment policies. Key top positions were often filled by expatriates from home countries although a number of MNCs have used a geocentric staffing policy to search for the best people. The key issue however for many Asian economies, such as China and Vietnam, which have had a large pool of unskilled and semi-skilled workers, combined with a shortage of sufficient numbers of well-trained managers and technical people. Furthermore, recruiting qualified bankers in the local markets can be very difficult.

Business expansion during recent years has fuelled the talent war in the labour market. For instance, HSBC had planned to double its number of branches in China over the next few years. According to its manpower planning policy, there has always been 'a need to recruit managers to oversee new branches and handle new services, but experienced and talented bankers are limited in the market'. Consequently, HSBC implemented a global talent management process to attract, motivate and retain its employees. HR professionals first visited all countries to describe key principles and nomination guidelines for talent assessment to ensure employees 'buy-in' to the recruitment process. Multiple sources of data, including interviews, panel interviews and 360 degree feedback, were then used to review capability ratings for all global talent nominees. A list of potential leaders and specialists were identified to fill future positions planned for the next 3–7 years (Gakovic and Yardley, 2007).

Nevertheless, cultural and social influences played a key role in talent decisions. The globally consistent talent nomination criteria and instructions were subject to local interpretations (Gakovic and Yardley, 2007). Cross-cultural differences further impacted on the consistency of the process. Besides, the panel members who reviewed nominations were not equally comfortable with challenging one another or voicing negative criticisms because such views often can mean that people 'lose face', which is not acceptable to East Asian cultures (McGreal, 1995).

Rewards

The intensified competition resulting from the enhanced globalisation of the Asian market created high demand for qualified bankers and professionals. In competing for human talent, compensation has been increasingly used as an effective means to recruit, motivate and retain much needed professionals. According to some salary surveys, financial institutions witnessed the biggest salary increases among all industries in most Asian economies during the period 2005 to 2007.

Interestingly, HSBC adopted an ethnocentric approach to its rewards practices. Its grading structure, salary adjustment and bonus scheme were inherited from its head offices. For example, to encourage employees to have a direct interest in the bank, an employee share option saving plan was offered to employees in most countries. Global bonus schemes designed to align employees more closely with the achievement of long-term strategic objectives were introduced in Asia.

The implementation of standardised rewards practice might imply that the head office was concerned with consistent HRM approaches across its overseas operations, and that it was interested in having the ability to compare performance across countries. However, the connection between global rewards schemes and local performance evaluation involved lengthy delays and consequently failed to keep employees highly motivated.

Training and development

Due to their large size and extensive networks, most MNCs can leverage their training resources across the Asian region. In HSBC, training programmes were organised by regional training teams and launched by local offices. Typically, managers with 1 to 2 years company service would attend fundamental management skills training and those with 3 to 5 years company service would attend advanced courses. Some managers might go through job shadowing of their counterparts in other Asian countries (Poon and Rowley, 2008). In addition, similar to other financial institutions, HSBC launched online training programmes and learning resource centres which enabled geographically dispersed staff to gain access to learning materials and packages. The use of more flexible training and development methods provided wider choice and better access to development opportunities for employees.

Nonetheless, the high level of training investment could at times generate negative returns whenever the trainees 'job-hopped', were 'poached' or became misaligned with organisational objectives. Moreover, these changes pressurised HR departments and practitioners to manage increased diversity and utilise different systems to cope with employees' increasingly diverse needs and demands (Rowley and Poon, 2008).

Discussion

Transferring the bank's global HRM approach without making any adaptation to the local market was not without pain. Past success or 'best practice' in the head office did not automatically guarantee its effective transfer and adoption in local subsidiaries. In summary, there is no single management model that can prescribe the way companies are organised and their people are managed, regardless of their Asian or Western origin (Warner, 2003). To make an HRM approach work, change in HRM practice often involves modifying global or international approaches and blending them with Asian characteristics. Consequently, the resultant characteristics of the IHRM approach may be difficult to predict and so there needs to be a greater appreciation of cultural and institutional contexts as well as more understanding of the dynamics of HRM change in international markets.

Case questions

1 Will HSBC's HRM policies and practices become more uniform as business expands in Asia? Or will HSBC adopt distinct HRM policies and practices in different Asian economies?
2 Discuss the advantages and disadvantages of the following HRM policies and practices: (a) global talent management process; (b) standardised rewards practice, and (c) high level of training investment.
3 What alternative HRM policies and practices would you recommend to HSBC for its operations in East Asia?

Case questions for further study and reflection

1 Imagine you are offered the opportunity to propose new HRM policies and practices for a multinational company starting in Asia. What are your suggested international HRM policies and practices?
2 Imagine you are given a task to harmonise HRM policies and practices among three operations in US, Europe and Asia. What would you propose? And why?

Further reading

- Budhwar, P.S. and Debrah, Y. (2001) 'Rethinking comparative and cross-national HRM research', *International Journal of HRM*, 12(3): 497–515.
  This article questions universal applicability of Anglo-Saxon models of HRM and critically analyses five main HRM models and their main research propositions. It provides the basis for a framework for HRM evaluations in different contexts and comparisons across nations.

- Rowley, C. and Benson, J. (2002) 'Convergence and divergence in Asian HRM', *California Management Review*, 44(2): 90–109.
  This article discusses how globalisation of HRM has led to some common changes in international HRM practices. It suggests that many differences in HRM remain due to a variety of limiting factors, ranging from economic stages of development to business strategies, national culture and fixed enterprise mindsets.

- Mayrhofer, W. and Brewster, C. (2005) 'European HRM: researching developments over time', *Management Revue*, 16(1): 36–62.
  The article studies HRM developments in Europe to explore the notion of 'European HRM' and the meanings of convergence and divergence in HRM. It presents a more nuanced view of the notions of convergence and divergence, finding evidence of directional convergence, but national differences remain a key factor in HRM.

- Rowley, C., Benson, J. and Warner, M. (2004) 'Towards an Asian model of HRM? A comparative analysis of China, Japan and South Korea', *International Journal of HRM*, 15(4/5): 917–33.
  This study examines China, Japan and South Korea to see if a degree of convergence is taking place and if it is towards an identifiable 'Asian' model of HRM. A model of change is presented that distinguishes between levels of occurrence and acceptance. The development and practice of HRM in each country is analysed.

- Zhu, Y., Warner, M. and Rowley, C. (2007) 'HRM with "Asian" characteristics: a hybrid people-management system in East Asia', *International Journal of HRM*, 18(5): 745–68.
  This study illustrates the similarity and difference of people management system among the key economies in East Asia. It concludes that HRM is in a process of reform moving towards hybrid forms of people management in East Asia. A large number of factors are shaping the outcome of the process of reform.

- Brewster, C., Morley, M. and Mayrhofer, W. (2004) *HRM in Europe: Evidence of Convergence*. Oxford: Butterworth-Heinemann.
  This book outlines the origins of HRM and reflects several European countries on the universalist model of strategic HRM.

- Hall, P.A. and Soskice, D. (2001) *Varieties of Capitalism: The Institutional Foundations of Comparative Advantage*. Oxford: University Press.

This book proposes comparative institutional advantage to explain differences among national political economies and distinguish between 'liberal' and 'coordinated' market economies.

- Rowley, C. and Warner, M. (eds) (2007) *Globalising International HRM*. London and New York: Routledge.

This book covers a wide range of regional and national cultures. It explores how cultures might shape both theory and practices in the field of international HRM.

- Rowley, C. and Warner, M. (eds) (2005) *Globalisation and Competitiveness*. London and New York: Routledge.

This book evaluates the evolution of 'Big Business in Asia'. It focuses on recent issues affecting large corporations, both indigenous and foreign owned, such as multinational companies and international joint venture, as well as key events such as the Asian crisis and its aftermath, China's entry into the World Trade Organisation, and the downturn in the world economy.

- Warner, M., Edwards, V., Polansky, G., Pucko, D. and Zhu, Y. (2005) *Management in Transitional Economies Central/Eastern Europe, Russia and China*. London: Taylor and Francis.

This book examines the past, present and future management in several transitional economies, discusses the nature of the transition process and outlines a number of theoretical approaches.

Internet resources

1 Chartered Institute of Personnel and Development (www.cipd.org.uk): A validating agency for HRM professionals.

2 Department for Business, Innovation and Skills (www.berr.gov.uk): UK government's department responsible for developing a remit for higher and professional/vocation education and training.

3 World at Work (www.worldatwork.org): US-based community specialising in research into compensation and rewards at work.

4 HRM The Journal (www.hrmthejournal.com): Association of discussion forum and publication networks for researchers and practitioners in HRM and international HRM.

Self-assessment questions

Indicative answers to these questions can be found on the companion website at www.sagepub.co.uk/harzing3e.

1 **What are some key questions to be considered when conducting a comparative HRM study?**
2 **What are the pros and cons of the Harvard model in explaining HRM approaches?** *158*
3 **What does 5-P stand for?** *161-2*
4 **What roles do institutional forces play in HRM change?**

168

References

Adler, N.J. and Ghadar, F. (1990) 'Strategic HRM: a global perspective', in R. Pieper (ed.), *HRM in International Comparison*, pp. 235–60. Berlin: Walter de Gruyter.

Anderson, G. (1992) 'Selection', in B. Towers (ed.), *Handbook of Human Resource Management*. Oxford: Blackwell.

Arthur, J.B. (1992) 'The link between business strategy and industrial relations systems in American steel minimills', *Industrial and Labour Relations Review*, 45(3): 488–506.

Bartlett, C. and Ghoshal, S. (1992) *Transnational Management*. Boston, MA: Irwin.

Becker, B. and Gerhart, B. (1996) 'The impact of HRM on organisational performance: progress and prospects', *Academy of Management Journal*, 39(4): 779–802.

Becker, B., Huselid, M., Pickus, P. and Spratt, M. (1997) 'HR as a source of shareholder value: research and recommendations', *Human Resources Management*, 36(1): 39–47.

Beer, M., Spector, B., Lawrence, P.R., Mills, D.O. and Walton. R.E. (1984) *Managing Human Assets*. New York: Free Press.

Benson, J. and Zhu, Y. (1999) 'Market, firms and workers: the transformation of HRM in Chinese manufacturing enterprises', *HRM Journal*, 9(4): 58–74.

Boxall, P.F. (1992) 'Strategic HRM: Beginning of a new theoretical sophistication?', *HRM Journal*, 2(2): 60–79.

Braun, W. and Warner, M. (2002) 'The "culture-free" versus "culture-specific" management debate', in M. Warner and P. Joynt (eds), *Managing across Cultures: Issues and Perspectives*, 2nd edn. London: Thomson Learning.

Brewster, C. (1993) 'Developing a "European" Model of HRM', *International Journal of HRM*, 4(4): 765–84.

Brewster, C. (1995) 'Towards a European Model of HRM', *Journal of International Business Studies*, 26(1): 1–21.

Brewster, C., Morley, M. and Mayrhofer, W. (2004) *HRM in Europe: Evidence of Convergence*. Oxford: Butterworth-Heinemann.

Budhwar, P.S. and Debrah, Y. (2001) 'Rethinking comparative and cross-national HRM research', *International Journal of HRM*, 12(3): 497–515.

Carroll, G.R., Delacroix, J. and Goodstein, J. (1988) 'The political environments of organisation: an ecological view', *Research in Organisation Behaviour*, 10(1): 359–92.

Child, J. (1994) *Management in China during the Age of Reform*. Cambridge: Cambridge University Press.

Child, J. and Markoczy, L. (1993) 'Host-country managerial behaviour and learning in Chinese and Hungarian joint ventures', *Journal of Management Studies*, 30(4): 611–31.

Davidson, W. (1980) 'The location of foreign direct investment activity: country characteristics and experience effects', *Journal of International Business Studies*, 11(2): 9–22.

Delery, J. (1998) 'Issues of fit in strategic HRM: implications for research', *Human Resource Management Review*, 8(3): 289–309.

Delery, J. and Doty, D. (1996) 'Modes of theorising in strategic HRM: tests of universalistic, contingency, and configurational performance predications', *Academy of Management Journal*, 39(4): 802–35.

Dyer, L. (1985) 'Strategic HRM and planning', in K.M. Rowland and G.R. Ferris (eds), *Research in Personnel and HRM*, pp. 1–30. Greenwich: JAI Press.

Easterby-Smith, M., Malina, D. and Lu, Y. (1995) 'How culture sensitive is HRM? A comparative analysis of practice in Chinese and UK companies', *International Journal of HRM*, 6(1): 31–59.

Filella, J. (1991) 'Is there a Latin Model in the management of HR?', *Personnel Review*, 20(6): 15–24.

Florkowski, G.W. and Nath, R. (1993) 'MNC responses to the legal environment of international HRM', *International Journal of HRM*, 4(2): 305–24.

Gakovic, A. and Yardley, K. (2007) 'Global talent management at HSBC', *Organisation Development Journal*, 25(2): 201–5.

Galbraith, J.R. and Nathanson, D.A. (1978) *Strategy Implementation: The Role of Structure and Process*. St Paul, MN: West Publishing.

Gaugler, E. (1988) 'HRM: an international comparison', *Personnel*, 65(8): 24–30.

Ghemawat, P. (2005) 'Regional strategies for global leadership', *Harvard Business Review*, 83(12): 98–108.

Guest, D.E. (1991) 'Personnel management: the end of orthodoxy?', *British Journal of Industrial Relations*, 29(2): 149–75.

Guest, D.E. (1995) 'HRM, trade unions and industrial relations', in J. Storey (ed.), *HRM: A Critical Text*. London: Routledge.

Guest, D.E. (1997) 'HRM and performance: a review and research agenda', *International Journal of HRM*, 8(3): 263–76.

Hall, P.A. and Soskice, D. (2001) *Varieties of Capitalism: The Institutional Foundations of Comparative Advantage*. Oxford: Oxford University Press.

Heenan, D.A. and Perlmutter, H.V. (1990) *Multinational Organisation Development*. Reading, MA: Addison-Wesley Longman.

Hendry, C. and Pettigrew, A. (1990) 'HRM: An agenda for the 1990s', *International Journal of HRM*, 1(1): 17–43.

Hoffman, A. (1999) 'Institutional evolution and change: environmentalism and the US chemical industry', *Academy of Management Journal*, 42(4): 351–71.

Hsu, Y.R. and Leat, M. (2000) 'A study of HRM and recruitment and selection policies and practices in Taiwan', *International Journal of HRM*, 11(2): 413–35.

Jackson, S.E. and Schuler, R.S. (1995) 'Understanding HRM in the context of organisation and their environment', *Annual Review of Psychology*, 46(1): 237–64.

Jackson, S.E., Schuler, R.S. and Rivero, J. (1989) 'Organisational characteristics as predictors of personnel practices', *Personnel Psychology*, 42(4): 727–86.

Jackson, T. (2004) 'HRM in developing countries', in A.W. Harzing and J.V. Ruysseveldt (eds), *International HRM*, 2nd edn. pp. 221–48. London: Sage.

Kerr, C., Dunlop, J., Harbison, F. and Myers, C. (1960) *Industrialism and Industrial Man*. London: Heinemann.

Lee, G.O.M. and Warner, M. (eds) (2007) *Unemployment in China*. London: RoutledgeCurzon.

Legge, K. (1995) *HRM: Rhetorics and Realities*. Chippenham: Macmillan Business.

Lockett, M. (1988) 'Culture and the problem of Chinese management', *Organisation Studies*, 9(4): 475–96.

MacDuffie, J.P. (1995) 'HR bundles and manufacturing performance: organisational logic and flexible production systems in the world auto industry', *Industrial and Labour Relations Review*, 48(2): 197–221.

Mayrhofer, W. and Brewster, C. (2005) 'European HRM: researching developments over time', *Management Revue*, 16(1): 36–62.

McGreal, I. (1995) *Great Thinkers of the Eastern World: The Major Thinkers and the Philosophical and Religious Classics of China, India, Japan, Korea and the World of Islam*. New York, NY: Harper Collins.

Metcalfe, B.D. and Rees, C.J. (2005) 'Theorising advances in international HR development', *HR Development International*, 8(4): 449–65.

Meyer, J. and Rowan, B. (1977) 'Institutionalised organisation, formal structure as myth and ceremony', *American Journal of Sociology*, 83(2): 340–60.

Ngo, H.Y., Turban, D., Lau, C.M. and Lui, S.Y. (1998) 'Human resource practice and firm performance of multinational corporations: influences of country origin', *International Journal of HRM*, 9(4): 632–51.

Noronha, C. (2002) *The Theory of Culture-Specific Total Quality Management: Quality Management in Chinese Regions*, London: Palgrave; New York: St Martin's Press.

Pieper, R. (ed.) (1990) *HRM: An International Comparison*. Berlin: Walter de Gruyter.

Poole, M. (1990) 'Editorial: HRM in an international perspective', *International Journal of HRM*, 1(1): 1–15.

Poon, H.F. and Rowley, C. (2008) 'Company profile: East Asia', in C. Wankel (ed.), *Encyclopaedia of Business in Today's World*. Thousand Oaks, CA: Sage Publications.

Poon, H. F. (2010) Human Resources Management Changes in China: A Case Study of the Banking Industry. Berlin: Lap Lambert Academic Publishing.

Priem, R.L., Love, L.G. and Shaffer, M. (2000) 'Industrialization and values evolution: the case of Hong Kong and Guangzhou, China', *Asia Pacific Journal of* Management, 17(3): 473–92.

Purcell, J. and Ahlstrand, B. (1994) *HRM in the Multi-divisional Company*. Oxford: OUP.

Qing, W. (2001) 'The challenges facing China: Financial Services industry?', In P. Nolan (ed.), Changing the Chinese Business Revolution. London: Palgrave. pp. 813–83.

Rodgers, R.A. and Wong, J. (1996) 'Human factors in the transfer of the "Japanese Best Practice" manufacturing system to Singapore', *International Journal of HRM*, 7(4): 455–88.

Rowley, C. and Abdul-Rahman, S. (2008) *The Changing Face of Management in South East Asia*. London: Routledge.

Rowley, C. and Paik, Y. (2009) *The Changing Face of Korean Management*. London: Routledge.

Rowley, C. and Poon, H.F. (2008) 'HRM best practices and transfers to the Asia Pacific region', in C. Wankel (ed.), *21st Century Management*. pp. 209–20. Thousand Oaks, CA: Sage Publications.

Rowley, C. and Warner, M. (2005) *Globalisation and Competitiveness*. London: Taylor and Francis.

Rowley, C. and Warner, M. (2007a) *Globalising International HRM*. London: Routledge.

Rowley, C. and Warner, M. (2007b) 'Introduction: Globalising IHRM', *International Journal of HRM*, 18(5): 703–16.

Rowley, C. and Yukongdi, V. (2009) *The Changing Face of Women Managers in Asia*. London: Routledge.

Rowley, C., Benson, J. and Warner, M. (2004) 'Towards an Asian Model of HRM? A comparative analysis of China, Japan and South Korea', *International Journal of HRM*, 15(4/5): 917–33.

Schuler, R.S. (1992) 'Strategic HRM: Linking the people with the strategic needs of the business', *Organisation Dynamics*, 21(1): 18–32.

Schuler, R.S. and Tarique, I. (2007) 'IHRM: A North American perspective, a thematic update and suggestions for future research', *International Journal of HRM*, 18(5): 717–44.

Sparrow, P.R. and Hiltrop, J.M. (1994) *European HRM in Transition*. London: Prentice Hall.

Storey, J. (ed.) (1995) *HRM: A Critical Text*. London: Routledge.

Taylor, F. (1911) *Scientific Management*. New York: Harper and Row.

Tempel, A. and Walgenbach, P. (2007) 'Global standardisation of organisational forms and management practices? What new institutionalism and the business-systems approach can learn from each other', *Journal of Management Studies*, 44(1): 1–24.

Tichy, N.M., Fombrun, C.J. and Devanna, M.A. (1982) 'Strategic HRM', *Sloan Management Review*, 23(2): 47–61.

Tse, D.K., Pan, Y. and Au, K.Y. (1997) 'How MNCs choose entry modes and form alliances: the China experience', *Journal of International Business Studies*, 28(3): 779–805.

Valiukonyte, D. and Parkkonen, V. (2008) 'Conceptual framework for the analysis of business systems: national perspective', *Economics and Management*, 13(1): 729–38.

Walder, A.G. (1995) 'Local governments as industrial firms: an organisational analysis of China's transition economy', *American Journal of Sociology*, 101(2): 263–301.

Walsh, J. and Zhu, Y. (2007) 'Local complexities and global uncertainties: a study of foreign ownership and HRM in China', *International Journal of HRM*, 18(2): 249–67.

Walton, R.E. (1985) 'From control to commitment in the workplace', *Harvard Business Review*, 63(2): 77–84.

Warner, M. (1995) *The Management of HR in Chinese Industry*. London: Macmillan; New York: St Martin's Press.

Warner, M. (2003) 'China's HRM revisited: a step-wise path to convergence?', *Asia Pacific Business Review*, 19(4): 15–31.

Warner, M. (ed.) (2009) *Human Resource Management with Chinese Characteristics: Facing the Challenges of Globalisation*. London and New York, NY: Routledge.

Warner, M., Edwards, V., Polansky, G., Pucko, D. and Zhu, Y. (2005) *Management in Transitional Economies Central/Eastern Europe, Russia and China*. London: Taylor and Francis.

Watson, T. (1994) 'Recruitment and selection', in K. Sisson (ed.), *Personnel Management*. Oxford: Blackwell.

Whitley, R. (1998) 'Internationalisation and varieties of capitalism: the limited effects of cross – national coordination of economic activities on the nature of business systems', *Review of International Political Economy*, 5 (3): 445–481.

Whitley, R. (1999) *Divergent Capitalisms: The Social Structuring and Change of Business Systems*. Oxford: University Press.

Wong, M. (1996) 'Shadow management in Japanese companies in Hong Kong', *Asia Pacific Journal of HR*, 34(1): 95–110.

Zhu, Y. and Warner, M. (2004) 'HRM in East Asia', in A.W. Harzing and J.V. Ruysseveldt (eds), *International HRM*, 2nd edn, pp. 195–220. London: Sage.

Zhu, Y., Warner, M. and Rowley, C. (2007) 'HRM with "Asian" characteristics: a hybrid people-management system in East Asia', *International Journal of HRM*, 18(5): 745–68.

Part 2
International Assignments and Employment Practices

6
International Assignments

B. Sebastian Reiche and Anne-Wil Harzing

Contents

Learning Objectives

After reading this chapter you will be able to

- Understand and evaluate different staffing options that are available to MNCs

- Differentiate between the main motives for using international assignments in MNCs

- Identify different forms of international assignments and assess their distinct advantages and disadvantages

- Explain why the selection, preparation and repatriation form an integral part of the international assignment process

- Critically evaluate the success of an international transfer, both from the perspective of the individual assignee and the company

Chapter Outline

The chapter reviews the various staffing options in MNCs in general and then discusses different corporate motives for using international transfers as well as the different forms of international assignments available to MNCs. It also gives a detailed overview of the assignment process and presents a set of criteria for assessing assignment success.

1 Introduction

This chapter deals with several aspects of international assignments. Section 2 reviews different staffing policies and looks in some detail at the factors influencing the choice between host country and parent country nationals. Subsequently, Section 3 takes a strategic perspective on international transfers and looks at the underlying motives that MNCs have to transfer international assignees between MNC units. We review two of the motives for international transfers – control and coordination, and knowledge transfer – in detail. Section 4 then deals with alternatives to expatriation, including the use of inpatriate, short-term, self-initiated and virtual assignments. In Section 5, we examine the international assignment process which consists of the pre-assignment phase, the actual assignment and repatriation. Here, we review recruitment and selection issues associated with international assignments, discussing both the prescriptive models found in the expatriate literature and the circumstances that seem to persist in practice. We also

Table 6.1   MNC staffing policies

Parent country national (PCN)	Nationality of employee is the same as that of the headquarters of the multinational firm	e.g. a German employee working at the Chinese subsidiary of Volkswagen
Host country national (HCN)	Nationality of employee is the same as that of the local subsidiary	e.g. a Chinese employee working at the Chinese subsidiary of Volkswagen
Third country national (TCN)	Nationality of employee is neither that of the headquarters nor the local subsidiary	e.g. an Indian employee working at the Chinese subsidiary of Volkswagen

consider expatriate adjustment during the assignment and describe organisational support upon repatriation. The final section critically reflects on the concept of expatriate failure and outlines a multidimensional perspective on assignment success.

2 Staffing policies

In his seminal work, Perlmutter (1969) identified three different international orientations (ethnocentric, polycentric and geocentric) that have become the standard way to describe MNC staffing policies. MNCs following an *ethnocentric* staffing policy would appoint mostly parent country nationals (PCNs) to top positions at their subsidiaries, while MNCs following a *polycentric* staffing policy would prefer to appoint host country nationals (HCNs). Firms with a *geocentric* staffing policy would simply appoint the best person, regardless of his/her nationality and that could include third country nationals (TCNs), nationals of a country other than the MNC's home country and the country of the subsidiary (see Table 6.1). In a later publication, Heenan and Perlmutter (1979) defined a fourth approach, which they called *regiocentric*. In this approach, managers are transferred on a regional basis, such as Europe, and it often forms a midway station between a pure polycentric/ethnocentric approach and a truly geocentric approach. It is important to note that these staffing policies apply to key positions in MNC subsidiaries only. Although some PCNs or TCNs might still be found at middle management, MNCs normally appoint host country managers at this and lower levels.

Recent research has criticised the HQ-centric nature of these orientations. Indeed, irrespective of the specific approach chosen in a given MNC the staffing decisions are usually initiated centrally and then imposed on the foreign units by the HQ. In this regard, Novicevic and Harvey (2001) call for a pluralistic orientation in which subsidiaries are given more autonomy and flexibility in the staffing process. This pluralistic orientation would consist of multiple, diverse and possibly competing orientations of subsidiary staffing that operate independently within the MNC context and requires coordinating mechanisms such as the socialisation of key MNC staff. Inpatriates (see Section 4) may take on such an integrative role by serving as link pins between the various subsidiaries and the HQ.

The term expatriation is often used to describe the process of international transfer of managers. Although the term expatriate could literally be taken to mean any employee that is working outside his or her home country, it is normally reserved for PCNs (and sometimes TCNs) working in foreign subsidiaries of the MNC for a pre-defined period, usually 2–5 years. Given the range of alternative forms of international transfers which we will discuss in Section 4, it is common to use the generic term 'international assignee' to refer to any person that is relocated internationally.

In this section, we offer a more detailed discussion of the advantages and disadvantages of using PCNs, HCNs or TCNs as well as some recent statistics on the use of PCNs and HCNs in different countries and industries. We also present a conceptual model that summarises the factors influencing the choice between PCNs and HCNs.

PCNs, HCNs or TCNs: (Dis)advantages and statistics

A review of the advantages and disadvantages of employing these different groups of employees will clarify the applicability of the different staffing policies identified above. Some of the most frequently mentioned advantages and disadvantages (Dowling et al., 2008; Negandhi, 1987; Phatak, 1989) are summarised in Table 6.2.

It will be clear that none of the options is without its disadvantages. In the next subsection, we will discuss several factors that might influence the choice between these different types of managers, but first we will provide some recent statistics on the relative use of these groups. Given the fact that staffing policies might have an important impact on the functioning of the subsidiary, it is surprising that there is such a paucity of research on the relative use of PCNs, HCNs and TCNs. In fact until recently, only two studies had been conducted which provide any details on this issue (Kopp, 1994; Tung, 1982). Kopp's results were limited to the use of PCNs in MNCs from various home countries only and neither Tung nor Kopp discussed the use of PCNs in different industries. Moreover, both studies conceptualised Europe as one supposedly homogeneous group, both in terms of home and host country.

A recent study (Harzing, 2001a) – based on archival data for 2,689 subsidiaries of nearly 250 different MNCs – provides us with detailed information on the relative use of PCNs for the managing director position in foreign subsidiaries. Overall, 40.8 per cent of the subsidiaries had a PCN as managing director, but as Table 6.3 shows this percentage differed substantially by home country, host country cluster and industry. With regard to home countries, subsidiaries of Japanese MNCs are much more likely to have a PCN as managing director than are subsidiaries of European MNCs. The exact percentage of PCNs in subsidiaries of European MNCs differed considerably across the various countries ranging from a low of 18.2 per cent for Denmark to a high of 48.1 per cent for Italy. At subsidiary level, the highest

Table 6.2 Advantages and disadvantages of using PCNs, HCNs or TCNs

	Advantages	Disadvantages
PCNs Parent country nationals	• familiarity with the home office's goals, objectives, policies and practices • technical and managerial competence • effective liaison and communication with home-office personnel • easier exercise of control over the subsidiary's operations	• difficulties in adapting to the foreign language and the socio-economic, political, cultural and legal environment • excessive cost of selecting, training and maintaining expatriate managers and their families abroad • the host countries' insistence on localising operations and on promoting local nationals in top positions at foreign subsidiaries • family adjustment problems, especially concerning the unemployed partners of managers
HCNs Host country nationals	• familiarity with the socio-economic, political and legal environment and with business practices in the host country • lower cost incurred in hiring them as compared to PCN and TCN • provides opportunities for advancement and promotion to local nationals and, consequently, increases their commitment and motivation • responds effectively to the host country's demands for localisation of the subsidiary's operation	• difficulties in exercising effective control over the subsidiary's operation • communication difficulties in dealing with home-office personnel • lack of opportunities for the home country's nationals to gain international and cross-cultural experience
TCNs Third country nationals	• perhaps the best compromise between securing needed technical and managerial expertise and adapting to a foreign socio-economic and cultural environment • TCNs are usually career international business managers • TCNs are usually less expensive to maintain than PCNs • TCNs may be better informed about the host environment than PCNs	• host country's sensitivity with respect to nationals of specific countries • local nationals are impeded in their efforts to upgrade their own ranks and assume responsible positions in the multinational subsidiaries

percentage of PCNs can be found in Latin America, Africa, Asia and the Middle East, while expatriate presence is much lower in Canada and Western Europe and is particularly low in Scandinavia. In general, MNCs operating in the financial sector and the automobile industry show the highest percentage of PCNs as managing directors. A low expatriate presence is found in some service industries and in

Table 6.3 Sample size and percentage of PCN subsidiary managing directors in different HQ countries, subsidiary country clusters and industries

Country of origin of HQ	N	% of PCNs	Industry	N	% of PCNs
Denmark	88	18.2%	Business & management services	71	12.7%
UK	381	23.1%	Rubber & miscellaneous plastics	30	20.0%
Norway	49	24.5%	Stone, glass & clay products	72	23.6%
Switzerland	207	25.6%	Pharmaceutical	156	25.0%
France	247	30.0%	Food & related products	132	25.8%
Finland	200	30.0%	Advertising agencies	109	26.6%
Netherlands	196	32.7%	Electronic & electric equipment	160	30.6%
Sweden	389	34.2%	Industrial equipment	282	32.6%
Germany	279	40.9%	Instruments	70	32.9%
Italy	52	48.1%	Paper	101	33.7%
Japan	601	76.5%	Computers & office machines	128	34.4%
			Industrial Chemicals	175	37.7%
Total	2,689	40.8%	Engineering services	41	39.0%
Subsidiary country cluster	**N**	**% of PCNs**	Insurance carriers & agents	139	39.6%
Scandinavia	164	14.6%	Household appliances	84	40.5%
Western Europe	1351	33.3%	Metal products	83	42.2%
Eastern Europe	81	39.5%	Printing & publishing	80	45.0%
Canada	94	41.5%	Oil & Gas	25	48.0%
Australia/ New Zealand	135	41.5%	Non depository financial institutions	46	52.2%
Latin America	254	50.8%	Telecommunications equipment	62	53.2%
Africa	53	58.5%	Motor vehicles and parts	82	62.2%
Asia	515	60.2%	Banks & banking services	481	76.1%
Middle East	42	66.7%	Security & commodity brokers	80	84.8%
Total	2,689	40.8%	Total	2,689	40.8%

'multidomestic' industries such as food. As the sample size for some of the categories is relatively small, results for these categories should be treated with caution. It must be noted though that the overall sample size is *much* higher than that of either Tung's or Kopp's study.

The results in Table 6.3 describe the percentage of PCNs in the managing director function only. Although much less information was available for the other functions, the level of expatriate presence was generally found to be lower in these functions. Only 17.2 per cent of the subsidiary finance directors (N = 358) were PCNs, while this was the case for 10.1 per cent of the marketing directors (N = 218). The lowest percentage of PCNs, however, was found in the personnel director's function (2.2 per cent, N = 92). In general, MNCs tended to have more PCNs for the managing director function than for any of the other functions. For both German and Italian MNCs, however, the percentage of PCNs for the financial director function comes close to the percentage of PCNs for the managing director function, while for British MNCs the financial director in subsidiaries is even more likely to be a PCN than is the managing director.

As less than 5 per cent of the positions in this study were taken up by TCNs we have not discussed this category in any detail. However, we can say that, similar to Tung's study, the highest percentage of TCNs in our sample can be found in African subsidiaries. Confirming the results of both Tung's and Kopp's study, European MNCs tend to employ more TCNs than Japanese MNCs. This might be a reflection of the availability of near-nationals in European countries (e.g. Denmark–Sweden, Spain–Portugal).

Our study also shows that a differentiated approach to subsidiary management, as advocated by many scholars in the field of international management (Bartlett and Ghoshal, 1989; Ghoshal and Nohria, 1993; Paterson and Brock, 2002), is important for staffing practices as well. Fewer than 10 per cent of the companies in this study had a uniform staffing policy (only HCNs or only PCNs). These companies were mostly Japanese MNCs in the financial sector, a sector that on average had a very high percentage of PCNs as managing directors. Other companies differentiated their approach according to host country and subsidiary characteristics. We will look into the factors that influence the choice between HCNs and PCNs in more detail in the next section.

Factors influencing the choice between HCNs and PCNs

The same study we referred to above (Harzing, 2001a) also gives us some insight into the factors that influence the choice between HCNs and PCNs for the managing director position in foreign subsidiaries. Figure 6.1 summarises the factors that had a significant impact on this choice. It is important to realise that this model was constructed based on multivariate statistical analysis (logistic regression). This means that although some of the factors might be intercorrelated, they all have a significant and independent impact on the choice between HCNs and PCNs.

With regard to parent country/company characteristics, MNCs from countries with a national culture that scores high on uncertainty avoidance (Hofstede, 1980, 2001) have a higher tendency to employ PCNs as managing directors for their subsidiaries. There is often suspicion towards foreigners as managers and a view that initiative arising from subordinates should be kept under control. Managers are expected to be experts in their fields and generally are selected based on seniority (Hofstede, 1980, 2001). These

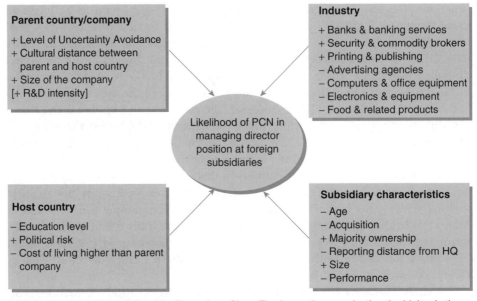

Parent country/company

+ Level of Uncertainty Avoidance
+ Cultural distance between
   parent and host country
+ Size of the company
[+ R&D intensity]

Industry

+ Banks & banking services
+ Security & commodity brokers
+ Printing & publishing
− Advertising agencies
− Computers & office equipment
− Electronics & equipment
− Food & related products

Likelihood of PCN in managing director position at foreign subsidiaries

Host country

− Education level
+ Political risk
− Cost of living higher than parent
   company

Subsidiary characteristics

− Age
− Acquisition
+ Majority ownership
− Reporting distance from HQ
+ Size
− Performance

* (+) denotes a positive relationship. Example: + Size= The larger the organisation the higher is the likelihood that a PCN holds the managing director position in its foreign subsidiaries.

Figure 6.1 Factors influencing the choice between HCN and PCN

characteristics usually point to a trusted PCN as the preferred alternative for senior positions in subsidiaries. Direct control of subsidiary operations will also be more important if the level of cultural distance, or institutional distance (Gaur et al., 2007) between home and host country is high. In this case, HQ managers might not trust the information they receive from local managers. Additionally, HQ managers might fear that local managers are less committed to the company. However, Gong (2003a) found that the reliance on PCNs in cases of high cultural distance weakens over time, suggesting that MNCs' longer presence in a host country may lead to the development of trust relationships with HCNs and thus a reduced need to deploy PCNs. Furthermore, communication between people from different cultural backgrounds can be very difficult (even if they speak the same language) and the opportunity for misunderstanding is usually high (Marschan-Piekkari et al., 1999). Therefore, HQ managers will prefer to have at least some home country managers in important positions to facilitate the information flow.

Larger MNCs have more PCNs as managing directors since they have more managerial resources and are more likely to have a formal management development programme in operation that involves the transfer of managers around the world. MNCs with a research intensive product are more likely to feel the need to transfer at least some of this knowledge to their subsidiaries and to train local managers (Hamill, 1989). Whereas Harzing did not find support for this relationship, Tan and Mahoney

(2002) showed that R&D intensity did increase the number of PCNs for Japanese firms, although not the likelihood of a PCN as managing director. This is probably due to the fact that R&D knowledge is transferred mainly by technical specialists rather than by the managing director.

More recent research has highlighted the role of MNC competitive strategy for subsidiary staffing (Tarique et al., 2006). Whereas MNCs with a global strategy are more likely to staff their subsidiaries with a focus on PCNs or HCNs/TCNs that have been socialised at the HQ, MNCs with a multidomestic strategy will concentrate on HCNs who have been socialised at the host-country subsidiary. This influence is likely to be moderated by parent-country cultural dimensions, the cultural similarity between parent and subsidiary country, and the managerial orientation at the HQ. For example, MNCs with a multidomestic strategy will more likely staff their culturally dissimilar subsidiaries with HCNs that have been socialised at the HQ. Similarly, MNCs with a global strategy and a polycentric managerial orientation will more likely staff their subsidiaries with HCNs that have been socialised at the HQ.

With regard to the influence of the industry, only those with a significantly higher or lower level of PCNs as managing director are included in this model. A high percentage of PCNs as managing director is found in the financial services and printing and publishing, while a low percentage of expatriates is found in the advertising industry, the computers and office equipment industry, the electronic and electric equipment industry, and the food industry. Some of the industry effects are easily explained. The control aspect will lead companies to employ a large percentage of PCNs in financial services, while the importance of knowledge of the local market will lead companies to employ a large percentage of HCNs in advertising and the food industry. The results for the other industries are less straightforward and would merit further investigation in a more controlled sample.

With regard to host-country characteristics, MNCs are more likely to employ PCNs when the level of education in the host country is low, since in that case qualified local personnel will be scarce. Further, a high level of political risk in the host country is likely to make direct control through expatriates more important because the risks of loss of income or assets might be substantial. It also makes the speed and clarity of communication facilitated by the use of PCNs crucial (Boyacigiller, 1990). As we have seen above, one of the advantages of having HCNs in top management positions is that they are less expensive to employ than PCNs. This motive is more important when the cost of living in the host country is higher than in the home country. In this case, an expatriate will expect to get additional compensation to maintain his/her previous lifestyle. Local managers have probably adjusted better to the high cost of living and would not require additional compensation.

Finally there are several subsidiary characteristics that impact on the choice between HCNs and PCNs as managing director. Subsidiary age will be negatively related to the likelihood of using PCNs as managing directors. When a subsidiary has just been established, HQ will feel a higher need to ensure its operations are in accordance with HQ policies and will hence use trusted PCNs. Furthermore, MNCs might have difficulty in attracting high-calibre locals for employment in recently established subsidiaries. When subsidiaries become more established, local recruitment may be easier and some transfer of knowledge and training of local managers will already have been effected (Boyacigiller, 1990; Gong, 2003b). In this regard, Hébert and colleagues (2005) even point to negative implications of using PCNs for a MNC's operational efficiency once the company has developed detailed host-country expertise because PCNs entail substantial costs and resource commitments. Furthermore, the parent company's lack of knowledge of the local labour market and a lack of recruitment potential will also be major reasons for greenfield establishments to appoint PCNs to top management positions. In contrast, acquired subsidiaries often already have an established local managerial cadre. When a subsidiary is very important to HQ, keeping its operations under control through PCNs will be felt to be more necessary (Belderbos and Heijltjes, 2005). Large, majority-owned subsidiaries that report directly to the HQ or subsidiaries that possess resources necessary for the parent to execute its strategy successfully are more important to the HQ. Finally, control of the subsidiary will also be more important when a subsidiary is under-performing, and direct HQ intervention by means of a PCN is necessary.

3 Motives for international transfers

Now that we have established the advantages and disadvantages of using different groups of managers and have reviewed the factors influencing the choice between HCNs and PCNs, we will take a closer look at the motives that MNCs have to send their staff abroad. In this section, we will first discuss the classification by Edström and Galbraith (1977) and will show that the results of German studies largely confirm this classification. We will then review two of the motives for international transfers – control and coordination, and knowledge transfer – in more detail.

Why do companies assign employees abroad? Edström and Galbraith's typology

There are few theoretical means of clarification or concepts regarding the motives for international transfers. At first sight, the study by Edström and Galbraith (1977) is the only one that theoretically explains why international transfer of managers occurs. They propose three general company motives for making this type of transfer. The first was to *fill positions*, which concerns the transfer of technical and managerial knowledge. This motive is quite important for developing countries, where qualified local nationals might not be available, but specific knowledge transfer might be necessary to MNC units in developed countries as well. Expatriates can be seen as the key bearers of tacit knowledge. The second major motive is *management development*. The transfer gives the manager international experience and develops him/her for future important tasks in subsidiaries abroad or with the parent company. This kind of transfer would be carried out even if qualified HCNs were available. For the third motive for international transfers, the final goal is not individual development but *organisation development*. This motive consists of two elements: socialisation of both expatriate and local managers into the corporate culture and the creation of a verbal information network that provides links between subsidiaries and HQ.

The classification of Edström and Galbraith is well accepted in the literature on international transfers. Virtually every publication that deals with this topic refers to Edström and Galbraith's now classic 1977 *Administrative Science Quarterly* article. A further investigation, however, revealed a substantial number of German studies, both conceptual and empirical, on this topic. The fact that they appeared in the German language only seems to have blocked their dissemination within the Anglophone research community. A summary of these studies and a comparison of their classifications to the one by Edström and Galbraith can be found in Table 6.4.

Table 6.4   Motives for international transfers according to various authors

Edström and Galbraith (1977)	Position filling	Management development	Organisation development/ Coordination and control*
Pausenberger and Noelle (1977) *(our translation)*	To ensure transfer of know-how; To compensate for a lack of local managers; Training and development of local managers.	To develop the expatriate's management capabilities; To develop managers' global awareness.	To ensure homogeneous practices in the company; To ensure a common reporting system in the company; Presence of different viewpoints in decision-making bodies.
Welge (1980) *(our translation)*	Position filling; Transfer of know-how.	International experience; Use management potential.	Coordination; Change management.
Kenter (1985) *(our translation)*	Lack of qualified local managers available; Transfer of know-how; Training of local managers.	Development of parent country nationals.	Control and coordination; Increase loyalty and trustworthiness of expatriates.
Kumar and Steinmann (1986) *(our translation)*	Transfer of know-how; The necessity to train German managers.	HQ wants Japanese managers to gain international experience.	To ensure coordination with HQ corporate policies and philosophies; To facilitate communication; Desired loyalty with HQ goals.
Pausenberger (1987) *(our translation)*	Transfer of know-how.	Management development.	To ensure a uniform company policy.

(Continued)

Table 6.4   *(Continued)*

Edström and Galbraith (1977)	Position filling	Management development	Organisation development/ Coordination and control*
Roessel (1988) *(our translation)*	Transfer of management know-how; Lack of qualified local personnel.	Managerial development of expatriates and local managers.	Coordination, control and steering; Reciprocal information flows; Internationalisation of the company as a whole.
Groenewald and Sapozhnikov (1990) *(our translation)*	Transfer of technological, administrative or sales know-how; Lack of qualified local personnel.	Management development; Better career opportunities for employees.	Steering and coordination.
Kumar and Karlhaus (1992) *(our translation)*	Transfer of know-how; Limited availability of local managers; The necessity to train foreign managers.	HQ wants German managers to gain international experience.	To ensure coordination and communication with HQ; Desired loyalty with HQ goals.
Macharzina (1992) *(our translation)*	Filling vacant positions.	Management development.	Coordination.
Wolf (1994) *(our translation)*	Filling vacant positions.	Personal or managerial development.	Coordination.

* Coordination and control is an alternative term to Edström and Galbraith's organisation development motive.

There seems to be a considerable consensus on the principal functions of international transfers, well represented by the original classification of Edström and Galbraith. In many of the German studies, though, the focus is more on a direct type of expatriate control than on the informal type of control or coordination identified by Edström and Galbraith. At the same time, the ultimate goal is similar in both cases: making sure that the various organisational units strive towards common organisational goals. It is interesting to note, however, that although Edström and Galbraith termed their third motive 'organisation development', their description of this organisational motive for international transfers focuses exclusively on control aspects. This is also the way in which this motive for international transfers has been interpreted in most of the English articles that refer to the Edström and Galbraith classification and the German studies. Pausenberger (1987), however, indicates that all three functions of international transfer can in fact lead to organisation development defined as the increase of the company's potential to succeed and compete in the international market. Roessel (1988) advances a similar view when he discusses how the various functions of international transfers can lead to the further internationalisation of the MNC, which would make it more effective in international markets. Maybe we should conclude that organisation development is not a goal of international transfers as such, but is rather the result of knowledge transfer, management development and the creation of a common organisational culture and effective informal information network? It might then be more appropriate to call the third category coordination and control rather than organisation development.

As Edström and Galbraith (1977) have argued, these three motives for international transfers are not mutually exclusive. The key point that companies should realise is the fact that expatriation is a strategic tool to achieve specific organisational goals and needs to be used as such. More recent research has highlighted the link between the reason for the international assignment and different dimensions of success (see Bolino, 2007). In this regard, Shay and Baack (2004) show that the management development motive positively relates to an assignee's personal change whereas the control motive is directly related to organisational change. In Section 6, we will look at assignment success in more detail.

Coordination through international assignees: Of bears, bumble-bees and spiders

In this section we will take a closer look at one of the motives for international transfers: coordination and control, based on a study by Harzing (2001b). Data were analysed by correlating the level of expatriate presence with the coordination mechanisms in question (direct expatriate control, socialisation/shared values and informal communication). The fact that there was a significantly positive relationship between expatriate presence and these three coordination mechanisms, while no such relationship was present for the other coordination mechanisms (e.g. bureaucratic control, output control) included in this study, independently confirms the importance of this function of expatriation.

As we have seen above the coordination and control function of international transfers has three distinct elements. Expatriates are employed to provide personal/cultural control in both a direct and an indirect way. They can serve to replace or complement HQ centralisation of decision-making and direct surveillance of subsidiaries by HQ managers. This is the kind of control that is alluded to in many of the German studies discussed above. We call this the *'bear'* role of expatriates. The bear is chosen as an analogy, because it reflects a level of dominance (and threat that might be perceived in the extreme case) associated with this type of expatriate control. Expatriates can also be used to realise control based on socialisation and the creation of informal communication networks, which is the kind of control described by Edström and Galbraith and some of the German studies. The role of expatriates in socialisation we refer to as *'bumble-bees'*. Organisational bumble-bees fly 'from plant to plant' and create cross-pollination between the various off-shoots. Weaving an informal communication network is of course the role of expatriates as *'spiders'*.

While expatriates seem to perform their roles as bears in any situation, an exploratory analysis showed that their roles as bumble-bees and spiders are more important in some situations than in others. They are more important in subsidiaries that were established more than 50 years ago than in younger subsidiaries, although the bumble-bee role is important in very young subsidiaries as well. Both the bumble-bee and the spider roles are particularly important in subsidiaries that show a high level of local responsiveness, and that are not at all or hardly dependent on the HQ for their sales and purchases. Finally, the bumble-bee and spider roles are more important in acquisitions than in greenfields. What these situations have in common is that they all represent situations in which subsidiaries operate quite independently from HQ. Apparently, expatriate presence is most effective in facilitating informal control in subsidiaries that are otherwise relatively independent from the HQ, whereas in subsidiaries that are quite dependent on the HQ, expatriate presence serves mostly to facilitate direct expatriate control. Since absolute expatriate presence is generally lower in subsidiaries that are relatively independent from the HQ (Harzing, 1999), we might also conclude that the 'marginal effectiveness' of expatriates in facilitating informal control decreases if expatriate presence increases In other words: if there are no or only a few expatriates employed in a particular subsidiary, 'adding' expatriates might have a strong positive effect on shared values and informal communication, while the effect of adding another expatriate is much weaker in a subsidiary that already employs a large number of expatriates.

International assignees as knowledge agents

Recently, research has increasingly highlighted the role of international assignees as carriers of knowledge between their home and host units. This is mainly due to MNCs' growing attempts to capitalise on business opportunities in developing and emerging economies. To offset their lack of experience in these culturally and institutionally more distant environments, MNCs face the challenge of accessing and applying local knowledge (Harvey et al., 2000). While the transfer of people is only one of many mechanisms to initiate knowledge flows in organisations, a large part of the knowledge transferred across MNC units is highly context-specific and tacit in nature (Riusala and Suutari, 2004). Contextual and tacit knowledge cannot be codified in written documents but requires the knowledge sender and recipient to interact directly in order to adapt the knowledge to the recipient's context and clarify the meaning.

Researchers have considered different directions in which assignees can transfer knowledge. One group of studies cover aspects of learning and knowledge creation from an individual point of view (e.g., Berthoin Antal, 2000; Hocking et al., 2007) and thus primarily focus on assignees as knowledge recipients. The knowledge assignees may acquire during their assignment is thought to help them in their future positions and includes

- an understanding of the company's global organisation and the corporate culture at the HQ
- factual knowledge about the assignment culture
- the acquisition of culture-specific repertoires

Implicit to this perspective is the idea that assignees acquire knowledge at the host unit and then may apply it back at their home unit at a later stage. This type of knowledge transfer thus represents a knowledge outflow from the host unit. In contrast, a second group of studies concentrate on the knowledge that assignees share during their assignment to the host unit (e.g., Bonache and Brewster, 2001; Hébert et al., 2005), conceptualising assignees as senders of knowledge. This type of knowledge transfer represents a knowledge inflow to the host unit. Relevant knowledge that assignees can share

- helps to streamline cross-unit processes
- creates common corporate practices and routines
- increases the chances of subsidiary survival, for example through the provision of local acquisition experience or product development know-how.

Scholars have also pointed out that the success of knowledge sharing through international transfers is not automatic but rather depends on social processes. Indeed, if we view individuals as carriers of knowledge we need to consider that this knowledge can only be shared through social interaction. In this regard, Reiche et al. (2009) argue that assignees need to establish social relationships, interpersonal trust and shared values with host-unit staff in order to share and acquire knowledge. In addition, assignees may act as boundary spanners that link the social networks at the home and host units. In doing so, assignees help to establish social interactions between MNC units and thus facilitate cross-unit knowledge exchange. Investigating the development of social relationships between people from different cultures and their effects on knowledge flows in MNCs has therefore become a key area of interest in current research on international assignments (Au and Fukuda, 2002; Mäkelä, 2007).

4 Alternative forms of international assignments

We have seen that international transfers can fulfil a number of very important functions in MNCs. Unfortunately, there are increasing signs that barriers to mobility – especially the issue of dual-career couples – are becoming more and more important, leading to a decline in the willingness to accept an assignment abroad (Forster, 2000; Harvey, 1998). In addition, sending out expatriates

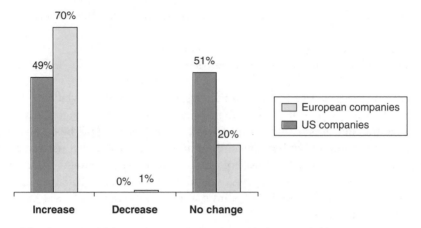

Figure 6.2   Expected future change in the inpatriate population

can be very costly. Increasingly, companies are therefore looking for alternatives to expatriation. In this section, we will discuss a range of other types of international assignments that include inpatriate, short-term, self-initiated and virtual transfers.

Inpatriate assignments

One alternative to expatriation is *inpatriation*, which involves the transfer of subsidiary managers to the HQ for a specific period of time (Harvey et al., 2000). This would allow key subsidiary managers to get to know the workings of the parent company and build up informal communication networks. It also allows the HQ to inculcate the subsidiary managers into the corporate culture in a more direct way than would be possible by the transfer of expatriates. Inpatriation is also a useful option if tacit knowledge needs to be transferred from subsidiaries to the HQ and it has the added advantage of exposing parent company managers to an international perspective. It is to be expected that the use of inpatriates, especially in European and US multinationals, will increase in the future (see Figure 6.2).

At first sight, expatriate and inpatriate assignments only constitute alternative forms of establishing HQ-subsidiary linkages. Indeed, both groups of assignees may act as boundary spanners or may help to reduce existing information asymmetries between the HQ and its subsidiaries. However, despite their similarities expatriates and inpatriates differ along several dimensions:

- *Status differences*   Expatriates possess the status and influence related to their role as HQ representatives. Coming from the MNC's periphery, inpatriates are, on the contrary, unlikely to receive the same level of respect (Harvey et al., 2005; Reiche, 2006).

- *Cultural adjustment challenges*   Barnett and Toyne (1991) delineate increased adjustment challenges for inpatriates in comparison to expatriates. They argue that inpatriates not only need to adjust to the national culture (see Section 5) but also need to be socialised into the MNC's HQ corporate culture. Indeed, learning the HQ corporate culture is considered an important motive for inpatriating foreign nationals. Expatriates, in contrast, often impose elements of the HQ corporate culture upon the subsidiary they are sent to.
- *Differences in the underlying MNC staffing policies*   The use of inpatriates also increases the cultural diversity and multicultural staff composition at the HQ, thereby fostering a geocentric approach to the allocation of human resources in MNCs. In particular, a higher share of employees with diverse cultural backgrounds will be collaborating directly as inpatriates are, for instance, temporarily integrated into the HQ's management teams. In contrast, the use of expatriates reflects an ethnocentric view towards international staffing and expatriates generally continue to coordinate with their own HQ management team.

Inpatriation seems to be an important addition to the company repertoire and can help to transfer knowledge, improve HQ-subsidiary relationships and develop managers. However, inpatriates have to cope with many of the same problems as expatriates, such as repatriation, and, as described above, in other cases even encounter additional problems such as increased adjustment pressures. It is therefore unlikely that they will ever completely replace expatriates.

Short-term assignments

Another alternative to expatriation that has received growing attention by practitioners and researchers alike and helps MNCs to contain their costs is short-term assignments. The literature commonly refers to short-term assignments as postings between 1 to 12 months in length (Collings et al., 2007). In contrast to traditional expatriate or inpatriate assignments, the assigned manager is usually unaccompanied by his/her family, thereby avoiding the disruption of relocating entire families. Moreover, selection and preparation procedures (see Section 5) for short-term assignments tend to be more informal and *ad hoc*. Short-term assignments are particularly useful when specific skills need to be transferred, for example in the scope of multinational project work, or particular problem-solving needs arise. Apart from the increased cost effectiveness, short-term assignments also require less bureaucratic effort and can be executed in a more flexible and timely manner. At the same time, research has highlighted that short-term assignees may fail to develop effective relationships with local colleagues and customers while also facing increased risks of marital problems (Tahvanainen et al., 2005).

A related but even more temporary staffing option is the use of business trips that may last from a few days to several weeks. These transfers are also frequently referred to in the literature as international business travel or frequent flyers assignments (Welch et al., 2007), thereby characterising work arrangements in which international travel forms an integral part. Frequent flyer trips are useful for conducting irregular specialised tasks such as annual budgeting meetings or for maintaining personal relationships with key colleagues and customers in the host country. Finally, companies make increased use of commuter and rotational assignments. Whereas the former refers to a work arrangement in which the individual commutes from his/her home unit to a foreign unit on a weekly or bi-weekly basis, the latter concerns alternations of intensive work postings abroad and prolonged periods of leave, as common on oil rigs. Given the increased levels of stress associated with these assignment types, they are unlikely to be maintained over an extended period of time (Collings et al., 2007).

Self-initiated assignments

While the traditional view of international assignments has been to focus on the employing organisation to initiate the transfer, a growing number of assignees make their own arrangements to find work abroad, facilitated by the introduction of free movement of labour in the European Union and other economic regions. In contrast to the aforementioned types of assignments, these so-called self-initiated assignees are employed on local work contracts. In their study of graduate engineers from Finland, Suutari and Brewster (2000) identified a series of distinct characteristics of self-initiated assignments compared to traditional expatriation. For example, self-initiated assignees tend to

- be slightly younger, single and female
- work for organisations with a lower focus on international business activities, at lower hierarchical levels and on more temporary contracts than expatriates
- be motivated to move abroad due to an interest in internationalism and poor employment situations at home
- receive no repatriation promises and see their relocation as a more permanent move

Overall, given the increased need for international and cross-culturally experienced personnel, self-initiated assignments serve as an important complementary staffing option for both domestic and international organisations.

Virtual assignments

Finally, companies have begun to make use of virtual assignments in order to address the competing needs for decentralisation and global interrelation of work processes, in a more flexible way. A virtual assignment does not require the individual to physically relocate to a foreign organisational unit but rather distributes international responsibilities as managed from the individual's home base (Welch et al., 2003). The growth of virtual assignments has been facilitated by improvements in information technology over the last decade to the extent that whole teams now regularly collaborate and communicate via email, telephone and videoconferencing. Despite the many advantages of virtual assignments that often exceed those of short-term assignments, face-to-face communication remains crucial in many circumstances, thus limiting the use of virtual work arrangements.

Since expatriation fulfils many roles, these four alternatives are unlikely to completely replace expatriates. However, they are often a cheaper alternative to expatriation, especially in the case of virtual transfers, and it is much easier to involve a large number of managers through short-term postings or virtual assignments than it is through expatriation. Moreover, each alternative form of transfer may also serve distinct purposes that are directly related to the successful operation of the company, which is why they are instruments that should form part of the repertoire of any MNC.

5 The international assignment process

The international assignment process is commonly considered to encompass three distinct phases (see Figure 6.3): the pre-assignment stage (selection and preparation), the actual assignment and the post-assignment stage referred to as repatriation (Bonache et al., 2001).

The following sections will discuss these key elements in more detail. Although the literature has dealt with all three phases, the majority of studies have centred on cultural adjustment during the actual assignment (Harrison et al., 2004).

Selection and preparation

In this section, we will discuss two popular studies concerning the recruitment and selection of international assignees and then evaluate the situation that seems to persist in practice. Then, we briefly review research dealing with the preparation of individuals for an international transfer.

Selection criteria: Prescriptions for good practice The first major study in this area was carried out by Tung (1981). Based on a review of the literature on the selection of personnel for assignments abroad, she identified four groups of variables that contribute to success or failure on the job and hence should be used to guide selection:

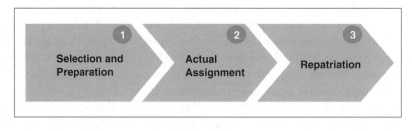

Figure 6.3   The international assignment cycle

- *Technical competence on the job*   As in the selection and placement of personnel in domestic operations, this factor is one of the primary determinants of success. It may be even more important for assignments abroad because the individual is located at some distance from the HQ, often the hub of technical expertise, and cannot consult as readily with his/her peers and superiors on matters related to the job.
- *Personal traits or relational abilities*   This refers to the ability of the individual to deal effectively with his/her superiors, peers, subordinates, business associates and clients. In assignments abroad, this variable greatly influences the probability of successful performance. This factor is not limited to simple knowledge of another culture. The crucial element is the ability to live and work with people whose value systems, beliefs, customs, manners and ways of conducting business may greatly differ from one's own.
- *Ability to cope with environmental variables*   In domestic operations the ability to identify and cope with environmental constraints, such as governments, unions, competitors and customers, is crucial to effective performance. This same requirement is no less valid in assignments abroad, but the political, legal and socio-economic structures which constitute the macro-environment in the host country may be very different from the systems with which the assignee is familiar. This poses problems of adjustment. The assignee has to understand these systems and operate within them.
- *Family situation*   This refers to the ability of the assignee's family (the partner in particular) to adjust to living in a foreign environment. Researchers and practitioners are becoming increasingly cognisant of the importance of this factor to effective performance abroad. The situation often becomes even more complex if the partner (male or female) has had to give up a job or even a career to accompany his or her partner abroad.

A second important contribution is the study by Mendenhall and Oddou (1985). According to them, there is insufficient knowledge about the relevant dimensions in expatriate acculturation, leading to the use of inappropriate selection procedures. They distinguish four dimensions as components of the expatriate adjustment process:

- The *self-orientation dimension*   Activities and attributes that serve to strengthen the assignee's self-esteem, self-confidence and mental hygiene.
- The *other's orientation dimension*   Activities and attributes that enhance the assignee's ability to interact effectively with host nationals.
- The *perceptual dimension*   The ability to understand why foreigners behave the way they do, the ability to make correct attributions about the reasons or causes of host nationals' behaviour.
- The *cultural toughness dimension*   This dimension can modify the importance of the first three dimensions. In culturally tough countries (countries that are culturally very different from the home country), the first three dimensions become even more important than in culturally similar countries.

The expatriate selection process should focus explicitly on the strengths and weaknesses of the applicant on the above-mentioned dimensions.

Expatriate selection in practice Recent studies have empirically confirmed that expatriate selection is a multi-faceted subject and that personality characteristics as well as interpersonal skills are very important (Caligiuri, 2000; Spreitzer et al., 1997). In practice, however, most companies still use technical competence and knowledge of company systems as selection criteria (Harris and Brewster, 1999a; Morley and Flynn, 2003; Sparrow et al., 2004). There are several reasons for this practice (see Bonache et al., 2001). First, it is difficult to identify and measure the relevant interpersonal and cross-cultural competences. Even in a domestic context there is still debate over the criteria that make good managers. Second, selection decisions are often made by line managers who circumvent selection criteria set out by the HR department, increasing the incoherence of the selection process. Third, there is also the self-interest of the selectors, who will try to minimise the personal risk involved in selecting a candidate who might fail on the job. Technical competence will almost always prevent immediate failure on the job.

Brewster (1991) notes that selection decisions for expatriate postings frequently rely on personal recommendations from either specialist personnel staff or line managers. The result is that the outcome of selection interviews is more or less pre-determined and negotiating the terms of the offer takes precedence over determining the suitability of the candidate. In a provocatively titled article: 'The coffee-machine system: how international selection really works' Harris and Brewster (1999a) develop this idea further and provide a typology of international manager selection systems based on the distinction between open and closed systems and formal and informal systems. The closed/informal system was most frequent among the organisations that Harris and Brewster studied. The researchers adopted the term 'the coffee-machine system', as a catchy summary for this type of selection system. The process starts with a senior line manager (usually male) who is joined by a colleague while waiting for his coffee at the coffee machine.

How's it going?

Oh, you know, overworked and underpaid.

Tell me about it. As well as all the usual stuff, Jimmy in Mumbai has just fallen ill and is being flown home. I've got no idea who we can get over there to pick up the pieces at such short notice. It's driving me crazy.

Have you met that Simon on the fifth floor? He's in the same line of work. Very bright and looks like going a long way. He was telling me that he and his wife had a great holiday in Goa a couple of years ago. He seems to like India. Could be worth a chat.

Hey thanks. I'll check him out.

No problem. They don't seem to be able to improve this coffee though, do they?

Excerpt from "The coffee-machine system: how international selection really works" Harris, H., & Brewster, C. in *International Journal of Human Resource Management* (1999); Taylor & Francis. Reprinted by permission of the publisher (Taylor & Francis Group, http://www.informaworld.com)

As Harris and Brewster indicate, the decision, that in effect has already been taken, is subsequently legitimised by organisational processes. The international HRM department will usually only become involved to deal with the financial aspects and practical arrangement related to the transfer. The disadvantages of this type of selection system are obvious. Candidates are not formally evaluated against ideal-type criteria, the pool of candidates is very much restricted and the organisation takes a reactive rather than strategic approach to expatriation.

Preparation In order to prepare individuals who have been selected for an international posting, and facilitate their adjustment to the foreign culture, diverse cross-cultural training programmes have been developed (Harris and Brewster, 1999b; Harvey and Miceli, 1999; Tung, 1981; see also Parkinson and Morley, 2006). The content and focus of these programmes are contingent upon factors such as

- the individual's cultural background
- culture-specific features of the host-country environment
- the individual's degree of contact with the host environment
- the assignment length
- the individual's family situation
- the individual's language skills

The effectiveness of cross-cultural training has been examined by Deshpande and Viswesvaran (1992) who undertook a meta-analysis to demonstrate a positive effect of training on a number of assignment-related outcome variables. Others have argued that pre-departure training assists transferees in developing accurate expectations towards the assignment which enhances their effectiveness abroad (Black et al., 1991). More recently, Mendenhall and Stahl (2000) have called for additional training measures, specifically highlighting the importance of in-country, real time training, global mindset training and CD-ROM/internet-based training. However, research also suggests that a gap remains between individual training needs and the actual training offered by MNCs (Harris and Brewster, 1999b), with the provision of language courses and general information on the host-country context often remaining the only instruments. All too often assignees are also expected to take responsibility for their own training and preparation.

Expatriate adjustment during the assignment

Despite the undoubtedly positive nature of certain aspects of the international assignment experience, the exposure to a foreign culture will involve high levels of stress and uncertainty. It has been common to describe this phenomenon as 'culture shock' (Oberg, 1960). Accordingly, much research has centred on analysing the process of adjustment to a new environment during the assignment. Black and colleagues (1991) provided a comprehensive model of expatriate adjustment that integrates perspectives from theoretical and empirical work in both the domestic and international adjustment literature. They argue that expatriate adjustment includes two components: anticipatory adjustment and in-country adjustment. Anticipatory adjustment can have an important positive impact on in-country adjustment. It is positively influenced by cross-cultural training and previous international experience, although it is reasonable to expect that the latter will only result if the earlier experience abroad was a positive one. Both help to build up realistic expectations and the more accurate the expatriate's expectations, the lower the level of uncertainty, the fewer the surprises and the lower the level of culture shock. The MNC can help anticipatory adjustment by providing cross-cultural training and using comprehensive selection criteria.

The in-country adjustment part of their model, which is reproduced in Figure 6.4, was tested by Shaffer et al., (1999) who introduced two moderating variables: previous assignments and language fluency. We have underlined the relationships that were confirmed in the empirical study in Figure 6.4. The model identifies three dimensions of adjustment: adjustment to work, adjustment to interacting with HCNs and general adjustment to the living conditions abroad. As expected, both role clarity (the extent to which what is expected from the assignee is clear and unambiguous) and role discretion (flexibility in the execution of the job) were positively related to work adjustment. Role conflict (conflicting signals about what is expected in the new work setting) and role novelty (the extent to which the current role is different from past roles) did not show the expected negative relationship to work adjustment, although role novelty was negatively related to general adjustment.

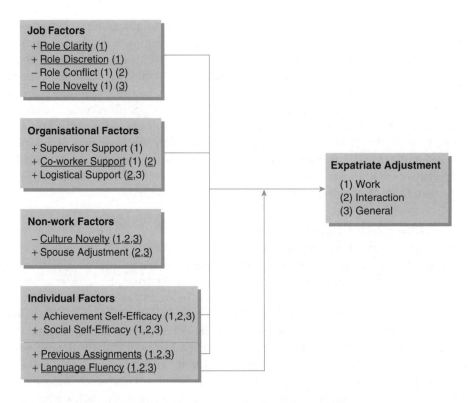

* Numbers in parentheses indicate the corresponding dependent variables

Figure 6.4   Determinants of expatriate adjustment*
Source: Adapted from Black et al. (1991) and Shaffer et al. (1999).

Support from co-workers and logistical support were positively related to interaction adjustment, although the expected impact of logistical support on general adjustment was not confirmed. Supervisor support did not have any significant influence on adjustment. Cultural novelty and spousal adjustment had a very strong impact on general adjustment and a weaker, yet still very significant, impact on interaction adjustment. Spousal adjustment did not influence work adjustment. The two self-efficacy variables seemed completely unrelated to adjustment, but contrary to the authors' expectations both the number of previous assignments and language fluency have a significant positive *direct* effect on interaction adjustment.

As expected, both previous experience and language fluency had important moderating effects as well. Previous experience moderated the relationship between supervisor and co-worker support. For individuals on their first assignments, supervisor support was negatively related to all aspects of adjustments, while for more experienced assignees this relationship was reversed. The same was true for co-worker support: experienced assignees relied more on their support for their adjustment. Shaffer et al. conclude that experienced assignees have learned to rely more on host-country management than on home-country management. Language fluency moderated the relationship between role conflict and all three dimensions of adjustment, which was more strongly negative for those assignees fluent in the host-country language. Shaffer et al. reason that the conflicting demands from host-country management and home-country management might go unnoticed for assignees with fewer language skills. Shaffer et al. also found distinct differences between the PCNs, TCNs and inpatriates in the sample. Whereas role clarity and co-worker support influenced all three dimensions of adjustment for inpatriates, they only affected one adjustment dimension for the other two groups of assignees. Consequently, we can assume that the adjustment process involved in moving to a firm's HQ differs considerably from the process of relocating to or between subsidiaries.

Overall, Shaffer et al.'s results provide general confirmation of Black et al.'s conceptual model and clearly point to the importance of job design, organisational support systems, the inclusion of the spouse in any training and support programmes, and the importance of language fluency as a selection criterion. Extending these findings, Kraimer et al. (2001) found that assignees' perceptions of overall support provided by both the home and host unit will positively influence different dimensions of adjustment. More recently, researchers have begun to examine the role of social networks that international assignees develop with local nationals and their positive effects on adjustment (Liu and Shaffer, 2005; Wang and Kanungo, 2004). In this regard, host-unit employees are increasingly viewed as important socialising agents (Toh and DeNisi, 2007) or host-country mentors (Mezias and Scandura, 2005) for assignees and therefore have to be explicitly considered in any meaningful assessment of expatriate adjustment.

Repatriation

Increased academic interest has also been placed on repatriation as the final phase of the assignment cycle. It has long been recognised that the return to one's home country after a prolonged stay abroad is subject to adjustment challenges similar to those of the initial transfer (Gullahorn and Gullahorn, 1963). However, despite the obvious importance of reintegration planning, this domain has only started to receive attention as an independent research area and is still judged to lack coherence and systematic consideration both in the academic and managerial context (Bolino, 2007; Lazarova and Cerdin, 2007). Given the trend towards using international transfers for knowledge transfer and management development purposes, the retention of repatriates is now even more crucial for MNCs to benefit from international staff transfers in the long run. Against this background, it is surprising that academic studies continue to find assignees to be largely unsatisfied with MNCs' repatriation support and to perceive their positions upon repatriation to be inadequate, leading to repatriate turnover intentions (Stahl et al., 2002; Tung, 1998; see also Box 6.1), a phenomenon we will look at in more detail in Section 6.

Box 6.1   Assignment in Saudi Arabia

[A senior engineer from a European electronics company] was sent to Saudi Arabia on a four-year assignment, at a cost to his employer of about $4 million. During those four years, he learnt fluent Arabic, gained new technical skills, and made friends with important businesspeople in the Saudi community. But upon returning home, the man was shocked to find himself frequently scolded that 'the way things were done in Saudi Arabia has nothing to do with the way we do things at headquarters'. Worse, he was kept waiting almost nine months for a permanent assignment which, when it came, gave him less authority than he had had abroad. Not surprisingly, the engineer left to join a direct competitor a few months later and ended up using the knowledge and skills he had acquired in Saudi Arabia against his former employer.

Source: Black and Gregersen (1999: 60).

In one study, Lazarova and Caligiuri (2001) examined 11 repatriation support practices which were considered important by repatriates but were shown to be available in only 10–50 per cent of the MNCs under study. Among others, these practices included

- pre-departure briefings on what to expect during repatriation
- career planning sessions
- an agreement outlining the type of position assignees will be offered upon repatriation
- mentoring programmes while on assignment
- reorientation programmes about the changes in the company
- repatriation training seminars on emotional responses following repatriation
- financial counselling and financial/tax assistance
- on-going communication with the home office

It is important to note here that repatriate turnover not only results in a loss of human capital investment for the MNC in general but also risks the possibility of losing this investment to a direct competitor. Furthermore, repatriate turnover is likely to have negative implications for the willingness of colleague workers within the organisation to accept an international transfer (Kamoche, 1997). To reduce the risk of repatriate turnover, MNCs will need to combine short-term oriented HR practices with longer-term instruments such as integrating international assignments into individual career paths. However, this requires treating the actual transfer and repatriation not as isolated incidents but rather linking the assignment experience to the expatriate's overall career.

6 Dimensions of international assignment success

Considering the complex challenges that emerge within the scope of international transfers, the analysis of assignment success is of crucial value for organisations with a high share of internationally mobile personnel. Consequently, the investigation into factors that influence assignment success has been a major research focus in the field of international transfers (e.g., Clarke and Hammer, 1995; Harrison et al., 2004; Kraimer and Wayne, 2004). Past research has identified numerous operational measures. The most prominent operational measure of assignment success is the intention or motivation to remain on the job, i.e. to complete the assignment (Feldman and Thomas, 1992; Thomas, 1998). However, empirical evidence on the magnitude of expatriate premature returns is ambiguous. In this section, we will therefore critically evaluate the issue of expatriate failure and introduce a multidimensional categorisation of assignment success.

Expatriate failure: is it just a myth?

If there is one thing that most publications in the area of expatriate management – and in particular those dealing with either cross-cultural training or adjustment – have in common is that they all refer to the 'fact' that expatriate failure rates – measured as premature return of the expatriate – are very high, with commonly cited figures in the region of 16–50 per cent for developed countries. Harzing (1995, 2002) has argued that there is no empirical foundation for these claims and that the myth of high expatriate failure rates has been perpetuated by careless and inappropriate referencing. She also argues that this myth may have had a negative impact on the effectiveness of expatriate management. When reading the academic and practitioner literature on expatriate management, practitioners cannot help but draw the false conclusion that expatriate premature return is one of the most important problems in sending employees abroad. This might lead companies to focus their attention and resources on avoiding assignees' premature return, while failing to notice or manage other issues that are, in fact, far more important for assuring the individuals' and the company's success. Forster and Johnsen (1996) suggest another practitioner reaction to the myth of high expatriate failure rates that might be equally detrimental to both expatriate and company success. They propose that this myth might well explain why the training and selection procedures of companies in their study diverge substantially from the ideal policies recommended in the literature. In reconciling the high expatriate failure rate figures with the actual practice in their company, each individual firm may believe that it is other firms who have a problem with high failure – not themselves. These companies would therefore see no reason to change training and selection policies and might lose out on the benefits of improved selection and training methods.

So should we conclude we can disregard expatriate failure? On the contrary! Further and more sophisticated research into expatriate failure is long overdue. Such research would first of all involve using a much broader definition of failure. The current definition used by the overwhelming majority of studies is the expatriate returning before his/her assignment contract expires. However, as Harzing and Christensen (2004) argue in some circumstances a premature return might actually indicate a success – a job accomplished in less time than originally anticipated – while in others an expatriate that stays on, but is under-performing, might in fact do much more damage than one who returns early. And what about the assignee who returns home, but finds that his/her skills developed during the assignment are not really valued in the home company and is so frustrated that he/she leaves the company soon after returning? Any definition of expatriate failure should therefore include under-performance and repatriate failure. Companies should also acknowledge that the costs of expatriate failure might go well beyond a simple calculation including the assignee's salary, relocation costs and training costs. They might include indirect costs such as damage to customer relationships and contacts with host government officials and a negative impact on the morale of local staff. Expatriate failure will also be very traumatic for the assignee and his/her family and might impact his/her future performance.

Multidimensional nature of assignment success

Given the evident problems arising from a narrow definition of expatriate failure, it is fruitful to view success as a multi-faceted construct. In developing a multidimensional categorisation of success, we can differentiate between two key dimensions: the level at which assignment success is assessed and the time frame (Yan et al., 2002). First, a range of studies has demonstrated a relatively high willingness among repatriates to leave their current organisation and look for employment opportunities elsewhere despite their generally positive assessment of the assignment, for example in terms of personal growth and new skill development (Stahl et al., 2002; Tung, 1998). A central problem in research on assignment success thus concerns the notion that a failure from the corporate perspective is not always a failure in terms of the individual assignee. Therefore, a meaningful assessment of assignment success must link both the individual and organisational perspectives. Second, the discussion in Section 5 has highlighted the importance of long-term assignment outcomes. From the point of view of the individual assignee, career advancement in terms of attractive subsequent postings and continuous development opportunities play a crucial role. For the organisation, learning is the most prominent aspect and refers to the transfer and application of acquired expertise within the firm. In this regard, Kamoche (1997) argues that any type of expatriate failure can be regarded as a waste of opportunities to learn and diffuse this newly acquired expertise within the organisation. Building on the distinction between individual and organisational success criteria on the one hand and short-term and long-term assignment outcomes on the other, we can develop a more comprehensive categorisation of assignment success criteria (see Table 6.5).

However, it has to be acknowledged that a precise and applicable conceptualisation of assignment success is still lacking in the corporate world (Thomas, 1998). In this vein, Gregersen et al. (1996) empirically demonstrate that systematic performance appraisal of international assignees in MNCs is far from being universally applied which may entail negative consequences for assignees' careers within the organisation.

7 Summary and conclusions

This chapter has given an overview of various dimensions and issues related to international assignments. We provided an analysis of the different transfer policies, looked at the specific motives for international transfers, reviewed alternative forms of international transfers, examined the key elements of the assignment process and discussed dimensions of assignment success. We have seen that the group of what constitutes international assignees is in fact very diverse and includes different transfer directions, different assignment lengths and different levels at which the assignment is initiated. From this perspective, the various assignment forms provide MNCs with a detailed toolbox to address the challenges of globalisation and tailor these staffing options to their individual needs. As a result, international assignments

Table 6.5   Success criteria for international transfers

	Individual benefits	**Organisational benefits**
During the assignment (short-term)	Task performance Skill building, learning, growth Adjustment Job satisfaction	Accomplishment of organisational tasks Achievement of key organisational objectives (such as control and coordination, knowledge transfer)
After the assignment (long-term)	Continued development Attractive future assignments Development of contacts with key people Promotion Enlargement of responsibility	Retention of repatriated employee Utilisation of new expertise Transfer of expertise Encouragement of international mobility among colleagues Willingness to accept future international transfers

Source: Reproduced with permission of the Academy of Management Review, from International assignments for career building: A model of agency relationships and psychological contracts, A. Yan, G. Zhu & D.T. Hall, 27 (3), 2002; permission conveyed through Copyright Clearance Center, Inc.

are increasingly becoming a strategic instrument for MNCs to successfully compete internationally. The key challenge for MNCs will then be to link international assignments more directly to their organisational career paths in order to be able to capitalise upon the experiences and skills that assignees develop during their transfers in the long run. Changes in the way careers are perceived among the younger generations suggest that individuals are less willing to focus their professional lives on a single employer. Companies therefore have a lot to lose if they do not manage international assignments well.

Discussion questions

1 With the growth in modern communication technologies, such as email and video conferencing, and the declining costs of international travel, expatriates will become an extinct species. Comment on this statement.

2 Imagine a European MNC having to staff one of its subsidiaries that acts as a regional HQ for the Asian market. Which staffing strategy would you choose? Explain why.

3 With regard to recruitment and selection, actual practice in MNCs seems to be quite different from recommendations for good practice. Why do you think this is the case?

4 Section 4 discusses alternative forms of international assignments. How will these types of assignee differ with regard to their role as knowledge agents between MNC units?

5 A successful international transfer from the perspective of the individual assignee does not necessarily imply success from the company's point of view. Find examples for this statement and discuss them in class.

Richard Debenham in Vienna:
Between Velvet Divorce and the Sydney Olympics

This case is an abridged version of IESE Business School Case DPO-121-E 'Richard Debenham in Vienna (A) – Between Velvet Divorce and the Sydney Olympics', prepared by Sebastian Reiche, Copyright © 2008, IESE.

It was a day in late November 1995 as Richard Debenham was sitting in the famous Café Sacher in Vienna's city centre reflecting about the offer he had received that morning. After 6 exciting years in which he had played a major role in driving Softdrinks Australia's expansion into the Central and Eastern European market, he considered the opportunity to return to Sydney together with his family.

Company background

Softdrinks Australia, headquartered in Sydney, was the main Australian licensee of Softdrinks US, one of the leading soft drink brands worldwide. Starting as a British subsidiary in the tobacco industry, Softdrinks Australia had entered the Australian beverage industry in 1964. In the early 1980s, Ken Grant, Softdrinks Australia's managing director, was looking to further expand the existing franchise operations to become Australia's sole licensee. Softdrinks US, initially keen on avoiding single franchisees to become too influential domestically, opposed this move. Instead, Softdrinks Australia was offered to expand the Australian franchise abroad. Incidentally, at this time local franchises in Graz and Vienna were for sale. Given Grant's personal attachments to Austria, Softdrinks Australia took advantage of the opportunity and acquired the two franchises in 1982. In the following years, Softdrinks Australia slowly expanded its operations throughout Austria.

The situation changed dramatically in 1989. With the fall of the Iron Curtain that had divided the whole of Europe, Softdrinks US suddenly found itself in an intense race with its major competitor to establish franchises in Central and Eastern Europe. Given that other Western European franchise owners seemed uninterested in expanding east, Softdrinks Australia's office in Vienna and its newly acquired franchises in Austria were seen as the perfect base to actively drive the expansion into Central and Eastern Europe. Philip Cameron, Softdrinks Australia's new managing director knew that it would be a dramatic international venture with an uncertain future but he also felt that his company's domestic success would give it the necessary resilience to shoulder the new challenge. Consequently, Cameron approached Werner Stegl, the local managing director in Vienna, to investigate the Central and Eastern European markets and compile a business plan for expansion. However, Stegl didn't believe that an eastward expansion would provide any opportunity for the current operations and opposed the plans. Given the local resistance, Cameron convinced the Sydney executive board to overrule Stegl's decision and go ahead with his strategy.

The decision to relocate

Knowing that he needed people from the headquarters to be positioned in Vienna for pursuing his plans in Europe, Cameron approached Richard Debenham in December 1989. The two had maintained a close relationship for a long time and Cameron was confident that Richard would be the right person to drive the new business. Richard had been involved with Softdrinks Australia for 16 years and knew the operations part of the business very well.

When receiving the offer to move to Vienna, Richard was 44 years of age. He felt it was a good time for a change. However, he was also conscious about the many personal challenges involved in such a move. It was clear to him that he would only embark on this move together with his wife and his three children. Were there any potential disruptions to the children's education and lives? How would his wife enjoy the new life? Professionally, Richard was also concerned whether the transfer would be a positive move for his career. How would the transfer fit into his career path at Softdrinks Australia? He felt that he would be somehow following the company into an uncertain future.

Without much time on his hands, Richard decided to accept the relocation for a period of three years. He was certain that, being a Western city, Vienna would be a comfortable place for him and his family to base themselves compared to the uncertainty that would await them in Eastern Europe. In January 1990, Richard and his family relocated to Austria. Richard was accompanied by a colleague from the finance department and a newly recruited expert on Central and Eastern Europe.

Amidst the Velvet Divorce

The move to Vienna was quite rushed and although the company offered to pay for various relocation expenses, Richard and his family had to organise everything themselves. However, despite the many difficulties in their new surroundings, they adapted well. While Richard's wife was not allowed to work, she was able to get involved with other spouses through their children's school and the children quickly built new friendships. Soon, Richard felt that the real challenges he was facing existed in his day-to-day professional life. The local staff in the Vienna office, having resisted the initial decision to expand Softdrinks Australia's operations eastwards, turned out to be of little help. At times, Richard even felt that local staff tried to complicate his already challenging assignments even further. For example, instead of being able to use office space at the local office, Richard had to go and find separate premises upon arrival.

A significant issue also arose over the allocation of human resources. Given their relative proximity, Softdrinks Australia would have liked to transfer more Austrians to the different Eastern European countries to run the daily business there. With Prague being three and a half hours by car from Vienna, it would have been a fairly undisruptive assignment even without moving one's whole life there. However, local staff was disinclined to relocate so in the end the company had to bring in more Australians over the years.

Another difficulty that Richard was facing when he started to negotiate acquisition agreements with local owners in Czechoslovakia was to find a suitable counterpart to negotiate with. During the transition from a socialist to a free-enterprise system it was difficult for Richard and his colleagues to understand who owned the factory they wanted to purchase or create a joint-venture with. In addition, when Softdrinks Australia finally began its own production in Prague in 1992, the country's 'velvet divorce' – a term referring to the dissolution of Czechoslovakia – meant that Richard and his team needed to treat Slovakia as a separate country and hence search for a suitable production site.

Richard saw an important part of his role not only in serving as the local representative of the Sydney office in Europe but also in actively supporting the shift from a socialist to a free-enterprise system. In his many interactions with locals, he sensed a deep-seated central planning and command orientation and constantly struggled to change this mindset among his local colleagues.

The Decision to Prolong the Stay

While Richard's transfer was initially intended to last only three years, in 1992 Softdrinks Australia was only at the beginning of a promising expansion path and was planning to further grow its ownership of local franchises. With the formal dissolution of Czechoslovakia and the completion of the separation of the Czech and Slovakian franchises in view, Softdrinks Australia felt that it could now move its expansion further eastwards. Without any clear prospect for a subsequent position in Sydney, Richard and his family decided to stay another few years in Vienna.

The following years saw a rapid expansion into other countries throughout Central and Eastern Europe, such as Slovenia, Ukraine, Belarus and Poland. In addition, driven by the early successes abroad the Sydney office also began to systematically explore different markets in Asia that were developing more rapidly and promised to offer substantial growth opportunities in a geographically less distant region.

Richard felt that he was able to build on his earlier experiences and his increasingly detailed understanding of the Eastern European cultures to further drive the company's efforts. He was becoming more effective in negotiating with local parties and instilling a customer-oriented mindset among the various franchisees. At the same time, with every year that passed in Europe he sensed an increasing difficulty to return to Sydney. In the meantime, Cameron, who had initially offered the relocation to Richard, had left the company due to personal differences at the headquarters and Richard's contacts to his home office became less frequent. What was more significant, his two Australian colleagues who had started the move with him had both encountered difficulties in finding appropriate positions back at the headquarters, ultimately leaving Softdrinks Australia in disappointment.

The offer

One morning in late November 1995, Richard received a call from the headquarters. The Sydney office was looking for someone to manage the Sydney Olympic programme that was to be launched in January 1996. Softdrinks US had traditionally been an important sponsor of the Olympic Games and, with the next games to be staged Down Under, Softdrinks Australia was selected as one of the Team Millennium Olympic Partners. Aware of Richard's interest in returning to Australia, Sydney management offered him a position to manage this programme and gave him a week to decide.

Hanging up the phone, Richard felt a strong sense of joy. He was about to call his wife to share the excellent news when he had second thoughts. He left the office and took a walk through the city centre until the cold November air forced him into one of the many Viennese café houses. He had always decided against pursuing an international career and knew that this would mean a return to the domestic market he had come to know during his first 16 years at Softdrinks Australia. However, he felt that he had invested much time and effort in building new skills that he was not sure he could use back home. Wouldn't it be more sensible to stay in Europe, even if this might ultimately mean to change employers? Of course, his family had signalled a desire to return to Sydney but they were also hesitant to leave behind the rich social relationships they had developed in Vienna. Moreover, with many of his former colleagues having left the company, Richard felt slightly detached from the Sydney office. How would he fit back into a company that had changed a lot during his absence? And what were his prospects after managing the Olympic programme? As he drank the last sip of his coffee, he realised the decision would be more difficult than he had initially thought.

Case questions

1 Should Richard accept the offer to return to Sydney or not? Why/why not? What are the implications of his decision?
2 How would you evaluate the decision of Softdrinks Australia to expand to Europe?
3 Which skills has Richard developed during his assignment? How valuable are they?

Case questions for further study and reflection

1 Imagine you are offered the opportunity to temporarily move overseas with your current employer. What are the main factors you need to consider for deciding whether to accept the transfer?
2 Imagine you are about to finish your studies and are looking for a job that provides the opportunity to work internationally. Would you work for Softdrinks Australia?

Further reading

- Harzing, A.W.K. (2001a) 'Who's in charge? An empirical study of executive staffing practices in foreign subsidiaries', *Human Resource Management*, 40(2): 139–58.
- Harzing, A.W.K. (2001b) 'Of bears, bumble-bees and spiders: The role of expatriates in controlling foreign subsidiaries', *Journal of World Business*, 36(4): 366–79.

The main conclusions of these two articles are summarised in this chapter, but the original articles provide much more detail on recent empirical studies dealing with staffing policies and the functions of international transfers.

- Collings, D.G., Scullion, H. and Morley, M.J. (2007) 'Changing patterns of global staffing in the multinational enterprise: Challenges to the conventional expatriate assignment and emerging alternatives', *Journal of World Business*, 42(2): 198–213.

This article provides a more detailed account of recent changes in the management of international assignments due to supply side issues, cost issues, demand side issues and career issues. It also reviews alternative forms of international assignments that have recently emerged and discusses the implications for the design of international HR policies and practices.

- Shaffer, M.A., Harrison, D.A. and Gilley, K.M. (1999) 'Dimensions, determinants and differences in the expatriate adjustment process', *Journal of International Business Studies*, 30(3): 557–81.

This study provides the most comprehensive and up-to-date empirical test of the expatriate adjustment model by Black, Mendenhall and Oddou. It introduces two new variables in the model – international experience and language fluency - and shows that both variables have an important direct effect as well as a moderating effect on some of the other variables related to adjustment.

- Reiche, B.S., Harzing, A.-W. and Kraimer, M.L. (2009) 'The role of international assignees' social capital in creating inter-unit intellectual capital: A cross-level model', *Journal of International Business Studies*, 40 (3): 509–526

This article offers a more complete picture of how international assignees initiate and contribute to knowledge flows in MNCs. It introduces two distinct roles that assignees possess as knowledge agents. First, assignees serve as knowledge brokers by linking their social networks at the home and the host unit, thereby generating access between previously unconnected knowledge resources. Second, assignees also act as knowledge transmitters, both by sharing their home-unit knowledge with host-unit staff and by transferring the knowledge they have acquired during the assignment to their home unit.

- Bonache, J. (2006) 'The compensation of expatriates: A review and a future research agenda', in G.K. Stahl and I. Björkman (eds), *Handbook of Research in International Human Resource Management*. pp. 158–175. Cheltenham: Edward Elgar.

This book chapter gives a good overview of issues related to the compensation of international assignees.

* Caligiuri, P.M. (2006) 'Performance measurement in a cross-national context', in W. Bennet, C.E. Lance and D.J. Woehr (eds), *Performance Measurement: Current Perspectives and Future Challenges*. pp. 227–43. Mahwah, NJ: Lawrence Erlbaum.
This book chapter discusses performance measurement strategies in MNCs and differentiates performance evaluation instruments with regard to different forms of international assignments.

* Black, J.S., Gregersen, H.B. and Mendenhall, M.E. (1992) *Global Assignments: Successfully Expatriating and Repatriating International Managers*. San Francisco: Jossey-Bass.
This book is a good source of reference on issues related to the management of the various phases of the international assignment process, with a particular focus on the balancing of family concerns and the repatriation of assignees.

* Scullion, H. and Collings, D.G. (eds) (2006) *Global Staffing*. Milton Park: Routledge.
This is an edited book that provides a wide range of topics on the strategic and operational aspects of staffing in MNCs, including international staff composition, international recruitment, talent management, cross-cultural management, and the management of international assignments.

Internet resources

1 Brookfield Global Relocation Services (www.brookfieldgrs.com): A US-based provider of relocation services and consulting that publishes an annual global relocation trends survey.

2 Delta Intercultural Academy (www.dialogin.com): A knowledge community on culture and communication in international business that maintains online forums on different topic areas, advertises job postings, publishes online articles and book reviews, organises e-conferences etc.

3 Living Abroad (www.livingabroad.com): An online provider of general information, country reports and tools for international assignees.

4 Relocation Journal (www.relojournal.com): An online provider of news and information on global relocation that includes a library of topical articles, informative white papers, a newsletter and general relocation service information.

5   Expatriate Exchange (www.expatexchange.com): An online community for meeting other expatriates, finding international jobs, getting expert advice on living abroad, international schools, taxes, relocation, etc.

Self-assessment questions

Indicative answers to these questions can be found on the companion website at www.sagepub.co.uk/harzing3e.

1   **Why is it more appropriate to call Edström and Galbraith's third motive for using international transfers 'Coordination and Control' rather than 'Organisation Development'?**   pg 196
2   **What type of staff do MNCs with an <u>ethnocentric</u> staffing policy appoint to top management positions in their foreign subsidiaries?**
3   **Why are MNCs increasingly looking for alternative forms of international assignments?**
4   **What are the advantages and disadvantages of using short-term international assignments?**
5   **On what criteria should assignment success be evaluated?**

References

Au, K.Y. and Fukuda, J. (2002) 'Boundary spanning behaviors of expatriates', *Journal of World Business*, 37(4): 285–97.

Barnett, S.T. and Toyne, B. (1991) 'The socialization, acculturation, and career progression of headquartered foreign nationals', in S.B. Prasad (ed.), *Advances in International Comparative Management*, Vol. 6. pp. 3–34. Greenwich, CT: JAI Press.

Bartlett, C.A. and Ghoshal, S. (1989) *Managing Across Borders. The Transnational Solution*. Boston, MA: Harvard Business School Press.

Belderbos, R.A. and Heijltjes, M.G. (2005) 'The determinants of expatriate staffing by Japanese multinationals in Asia: Control, learning, and vertical integration', *Journal of International Business Studies*, 36(3): 341–54.

Berthoin Antal, A. (2000) 'Types of knowledge gained by expatriate managers', *Journal of General Management*, 26(2): 32–51.

Black, J.S. and Gregersen, H.B. (1999) 'The right way to manage expats', *Harvard Business Review*, 77(2): 52–62.

Black, J.S., Mendenhall, M. and Oddou, G. (1991) 'Toward a comprehensive model of international adjustment: An integration of multiple theoretical perspectives', *Academy of Management Review*, 16(2): 291–317.

Bolino, M.C. (2007) 'Expatriate assignments and intra-organizational career success: Implications for individuals and organizations', *Journal of International Business Studies*, 38(5): 819–35.

Bonache, J. and Brewster, C. (2001) 'Knowledge transfer and the management of expatriation', *Thunderbird International Business Review*, 43(1): 145–68.

Bonache, J., Brewster, C. and Suutari, V. (2001) 'Expatriation: A developing research agenda', *Thunderbird International Business Review*, 43(1): 3–20.

Boyacigiller, N. (1990) 'The role of expatriates in the management of interdependence, complexity and risk in multinational corporations', *Journal of International Business Studies*, 21(3): 357–81.

Brewster, C. (1991) *The Management of Expatriates*. London: Kogan Page.

Caligiuri, P. (2000) 'Selecting expatriates for personality characteristics: A moderating effect of personality on the relationship between host national contact and cross-cultural adjustment', *Management International Review*, 40(1): 61–80.

Clarke, C. and Hammer, M.R. (1995) 'Predictors of Japanese and American managers job success, personal adjustment, and intercultural interaction effectiveness', *Management International Review*, 35(2): 153–70.

Collings, D.G., Scullion, H. and Morley, M.J. (2007) 'Changing patterns of global staffing in the multinational enterprise: Challenges to the conventional expatriate assignment and emerging alternatives', *Journal of World Business*, 42(2): 198–213.

Deshpande, S.P. and Viswesvaran, C. (1992) 'Is cross-cultural training of expatriate managers effective? A meta-analysis', *International Journal of Intercultural Relations*, 16(3): 295–310.

Dowling P.J., Festing, M. and Engle, A.D. (2008) *International Human Resource Management: Managing People in a Multinational Context*, 5th edn. London: Cengage Learning.

Edström, A. and Galbraith, J.R. (1977) 'Transfer of managers as a co-ordination and control strategy in multinational organizations', *Administrative Science Quarterly*, 22(2): 248–63.

Feldman, D.C. and Thomas, D.C. (1992) 'Career management issues facing expatriates', *Journal of International Business Studies*, 23(2): 271–93.

Forster, N. (2000) 'The myth of the international manager', *International Journal of Human Resource Management*, 11(1): 126–42.

Forster, N. and Johnsen, M. (1996) 'Expatriate management policies in UK companies new to the international scene', *International Journal of Human Resource Management*, 7(1): 177–205.

Gaur, A.S., Delios, A. and Singh, K. (2007) 'Institutional environments, staffing strategies, and subsidiary performance', *Journal of Management*, 33(4): 611–36.

Ghoshal, S. and Nohria, N. (1993) 'Horses for courses: Organizational forms for multinational corporations', *Sloan Management Review*, 34(2): 23–35.

Gong, Y. (2003a) 'Subsidiary staffing in multinational enterprises: Agency, resources, and performance', *Academy of Management Journal*, 46(6): 728–39.

Gong, Y. (2003b) 'Toward a dynamic process model of staffing composition and subsidiary outcomes in multinational enterprises', *Journal of Management*, 29(2): 259–80.

Gregersen, H.B., Hite, J.M. and Black, J.S. (1996) 'Expatriate performance appraisal in U.S. multinational firms', *Journal of International Business Studies*, 27(4): 711–38.

Groenewald, H. and Sapozhnikov, A. (1990) 'Auslandentsendungen von Führungskräften. Vorgehensweisen internationaler Fluggesellschaften', *Die Unternehmung*, 44(1): 28–42.

Gullahorn, J.T. and Gullahorn, J.E. (1963) 'An extension of the U-curve hypothesis', *Journal of Social Issues*, 19(3): 33–47.

Hamill, J. (1989) 'Expatriate policies in British multinationals', *Journal of General Management*, 14(4): 18–33.

Harris, H. and Brewster, C. (1999a) 'The coffee-machine system: how international selection really works', *International Journal of Human Resource Management*, 10(3): 488–500.

Harris, H. and Brewster, C. (1999b) 'An integrative framework for pre-departure preparation', in C. Brewster and H. Harris (eds), *International HRM: Contemporary Issues in Europe*. pp. 223–40. London: Routledge.

Harrison, D.A., Shaffer, M.A. and Bhaskar-Shrinivas, P. (2004) 'Going places: Roads more and less traveled in research on expatriate experiences', in J.J. Martocchio (ed.), *Research in Personnel and Human Resources Management*, Vol. 23. pp. 199–247. Oxford: Elsevier.

Harvey, M. (1998) 'Dual-career couples during international relocation: The trailing spouse', *International Journal of Human Resource Management*, 9(2): 309–31.

Harvey, M. and Miceli, N. (1999) 'Exploring inpatriate manager issues: An exploratory empirical study', *International Journal of Intercultural Relations*, 23(3): 339–71.

Harvey, M., Novicevic, M.M., Buckley, M.R. and Fung, H. (2005) 'Reducing inpatriate managers' "liability of foreignness" by addressing stigmatization and stereotype threats', *Journal of World Business*, 40(3): 267–80.

Harvey, M., Novicevic, M.M. and Speier, C. (2000) 'Strategic global human resource management: The role of inpatriate managers', *Human Resource Management Review*, 10(2): 153–75.

Harzing, A.W.K. (1995) 'The persistent myth of high expatriate failure rates', *International Journal of Human Resource Management*, 6(2): 457–75.

Harzing, A.W.K. (1999) 'MNC staffing policies for the CEO-position in foreign subsidiaries: The results of an innovative research method', In C. Brewster and H. Harris (eds), *International HRM: Contemporary Issues in Europe*. pp. 67–88. London: Routledge.

Harzing, A.W.K. (2001a) 'Who's in charge? An empirical study of executive staffing practices in foreign subsidiaries', *Human Resource Management*, 40(2): 139–58.

Harzing, A.W.K. (2001b) 'Of bears, bumble-bees and spiders: The role of expatriates in controlling foreign subsidiaries', *Journal of World Business*, 36(4): 366–79.

Harzing, A.W.K. (2002) 'Are our referencing errors undermining our scholarship and credibility? The case of expatriate failure rates', *Journal of Organizational Behavior*, 23(1): 127–48.

Harzing, A.W.K. and Christensen, C. (2004) 'Expatriate failure: time to abandon the concept?', *Career Development International*, 9(6–7): 616–26.

Hébert, L., Very, P. and Beamish, P.W. (2005) 'Expatriation as a bridge over troubled water: A knowledge-based perspective applied to cross-border acquisitions', *Organization Studies*, 26(10): 1455–76.

Heenan, D.A. and Perlmutter, H.V. (1979) *Multinational Organization Development*. Reading, MA: Addison-Wesley.

Hocking, J.B., Brown, M.E. and Harzing, A.-W. (2007) 'Balancing global and local strategic contexts: Expatriate knowledge transfer, applications and learning within a transnational organization', *Human Resource Management*, 46(4): 513–33.

Hofstede, G. (1980) *Culture's Consequences: International Differences in Work-related Values*. Beverly Hills, CA: Sage.

Hofstede, G. (2001) *Culture's Consequences: Comparing Values, Behaviors, Institutions, and Organizations across Nations*, 2nd edn. Thousand Oaks, CA: Sage.

Kamoche, K. (1997) 'Knowledge creation and learning in international HRM', *International Journal of Human Resource Management*, 8(3): 213–25.

Kenter, M.E. (1985) *Die Steuerung ausländischer Tochtergesellschaften. Instrumente und Effizienz.* Frankfurt am Main: P. Lang.

Kopp, R. (1994) 'International human resource policies and practices in Japanese, European and United States multinationals', *Human Resource Management*, 33(4): 581–99.

Kraimer, M.L. and Wayne, S.J. (2004) 'An examination of perceived organizational support as a multidimensional construct in the context of an expatriate assignment', *Journal of Management*, 30(2): 209–37.

Kraimer, M.L., Wayne, S.J. and Jaworski, R.A. (2001) 'Sources of support and expatriate performance: The mediating role of expatriate adjustment', *Personnel Psychology*, 54(1): 71–99.

Kumar, B.N. and Karlshaus, M. (1992) 'Auslandseinsatz und Personalentwicklung. Ergebnisse einer empirischen Studie über den Beitrag der Auslandsentsendung', *Zeitschrift für Personalforschung*, 6(1): 59–74.

Kumar, B.N. and Steinmann, H. (1986) 'Japanische Führungskrafte zwischen ensandten und lokalen Führungskräften in Deutschland', *Zeitschrift für betriebswirtschaftliche Forschung*, 38(6): 493–516.

Lazarova, M. and Caligiuri, P. (2001) 'Retaining repatriates: The role of organizational support practices', *Journal of World Business*, 36(4): 389–401.

Lazarova, M.B. and Cerdin, J.-L. (2007) 'Revisiting repatriation concerns: organizational support versus career and contextual influences', *Journal of International Business Studies*, 38(3): 404–29.

Liu, X. and Shaffer, M.A. (2005) 'An investigation of expatriate adjustment and perform-ance: A social capital perspective', *International Journal of Cross Cultural Management*, 5(3): 235–54.

Macharzina, K. (1992) 'Internationaler Transfer von Führungskraften', *Zeitschrift für Personalforschung*, 6(3): 366–84.

Mäkelä, K. (2007) 'Knowledge sharing through expatriate relationships: A social capital perspective', *International Studies of Management and Organization*, 37(3): 108–25.

Marschan-Piekkari, R., Welch, D. and Welch, L. (1999) 'In the shadow: The impact of language on structure, power and communication in the multinational', *International Business Review*, 8(4): 421–40.

Mendenhall, M. and Oddou, G. (1985) 'The dimensions of expatriate acculturation: A review', *Academy of Management Review*, 10(1): 39–47.

Mendenhall, M.E. and Stahl, G.K. (2000) 'Expatriate training and development: Where do we go from here?', *Human Resource Management*, 39(2–3): 251–65.

Mezias, J.M. and Scandura, T.A. (2005) 'A needs-driven approach to expatriate adjustment and career development: A multiple mentoring perspective', *Journal of International Business Studies*, 36(5): 519–38.

Morley, M. and Flynn, M. (2003) 'Personal characteristics and competencies as corre-lates of intercultural transitional adjustment among U.S. and Canadian sojourners in Ireland', *International Management*, 7(2): 31–46.

Negandhi, A.R. (1987) *International Management*. Newton, MA: Allyn and Bacon.

Novicevic, M.M. and Harvey, M.G. (2001) 'The emergence of the pluralism construct and the inpatriation process', *International Journal of Human Resource Management*, 12(3): 333–56.

Oberg, K. (1960) 'Cultural shock: Adjustment to new cultural environments', *Practical Anthropology*, 7: 177–82.

Oddou, G., Gregersen, H.B., Black, J.S. and Derr, C.B. (2001) 'Building global leaders: Strategy similarities and differences among European, US, and Japanese multinationals', in M.E. Mendenhall, T.M. Kühlmann and G.K. Stahl (eds), *Developing Global Business Leaders: Policies, Processes, and Innovations*. pp. 99–116. Westport, CT: Quorum Books.

Parkinson, E. and Morley, M. (2006) 'Cross cultural training', in H. Scullion and D. G. Collings (eds), *Global Staffing*. pp. 117–138. London: Routledge.

Paterson, S.L. and Brock, D.M. (2002) 'The development of subsidiary-management research: Review and theoretical analysis', *International Business Review*, 11(2): 139–63.

Pausenberger, E. (1987) 'Unternehmens- und Personalentwicklung durch Entsendung', *Personalführung*, 20(11–12): 852–6.

Pausenberger, E. and Noelle, G.F. (1977) 'Entsendung von Führungskraften in ausländische Niederlassungen', *Zeitschrift für betriebswirtschaftliche Forschung*, 29(6): 346–66.

Perlmutter, H.V. (1969) 'The tortuous evolution of the multinational corporation', *Columbia Journal of World Business*, 4(1): 9–18.

Phatak, A.V. (1989) *International Management*. Boston, MA: PWS-Kent Publishing Company.

Reiche, B.S. (2006) 'The inpatriate experience in multinational corporations: An exploratory case study in Germany', *International Journal of Human Resource Management*, 17(9): 1572–90.

Reiche, B.S., Harzing, A.-W. and Kraimer, M.L. (2009) 'The role of international assignees' social capital in creating inter-unit intellectual capital: A cross-level model', *Journal of International Business Studies*, 40 (3): 509–526

Riusala, K. and Suutari, V. (2004) 'International knowledge transfers through expatriates', *Thunderbird International Business Review*, 46(6): 743–70.

Roessel, R.V. (1988) *Führungskräfte-Transfer in internationalen Unternehmungen*. Köln: Wirtschaftsverlag Bachem.

Shaffer, M.A., Harrison, D.A. and Gilley, K.M. (1999) 'Dimensions, determinants and differences in the expatriate adjustment process', *Journal of International Business Studies*, 30(3): 557–81.

Shay, J.P. and Baack, S.A. (2004) 'Expatriate assignment, adjustment and effectiveness: An empirical examination of the big picture', *Journal of International Business Studies*, 35(3): 216–32.

Sparrow, P., Brewster, C. and Harris, H. (2004) *Globalizing Human Resource Management*. London: Routledge.

Spreitzer, G.M., McCall, M.W. and Mahoney, J.D. (1997) 'Early identification of international executive potential', *Journal of Applied Psychology,* 82(1): 6–29.

Stahl, G.K., Miller, E.L. and Tung, R.L. (2002) 'Toward the boundaryless career: A closer look at the expatriate career concept and the perceived implications of an international assignment', *Journal of World Business*, 37(3): 216–27.

Suutari, V. and Brewster, C. (2000) 'Making their own way: International experience through self-initiated foreign assignments', *Journal of World Business*, 35(4): 417–36.

Tahvanainen, M., Worm, V. and Welch, D. (2005) 'Implications of short-term international assignments', *European Management Journal*, 23(6): 663–73.

Tan, D. and Mahoney, J.T. (2002) 'An empirical investigation of expatriate utilization: Resource-based, agency, and transaction costs perspectives', *Office of Research Working Paper Number 02–0129*, University of Illinois at Urbana-Champaign.

Tarique, I. Schuler, R. and Gong, Y. (2006) 'A model of multinational enterprise subsidiary staffing composition', *International Journal of Human Resource Management*, 17(2): 207–24.

Thomas, D.C. (1998) 'The expatriate experience: A critical review and synthesis', in J.L. Cheng and R.B. Peterson (eds), *Advances in International Comparative Management*, Vol. 12. pp. 237–73. Greenwich, CT: JAI Press.

Toh, S.M. and DeNisi, A.S. (2007) 'Host country nationals as socializing agents: A social identity approach', *Journal of Organizational Behavior*, 28(3): 281–301.

Tung, R.L. (1981) 'Selection and training of personnel for overseas assignments', *Columbia Journal of World Business*, 16(2): 68–78.

Tung, R.L. (1982) 'Selection and training procedures of U.S., European, and Japanese multinationals', *California Management Review*, 25(1): 57–71.

Tung, R.L. (1998) 'American expatriates abroad: From neophytes to cosmopolitans', *Journal of World Business*, 33(2): 125–44.

Wang, X. and Kanungo, R.N. (2004) 'Nationality, social network and psychological well-being: expatriates in China', *International Journal of Human Resource Management*, 15(4–5): 775–93.

Welch, D.E., Welch, L.S. and Worm, V. (2007) 'The international business traveller: A neglected but strategic human resource', *International Journal of Human Resource Management*, 18(2): 173–83.

Welch, D.E., Worm, V. and Fenwick, M. (2003) 'Are virtual assignments feasible?', *Management International Review*, 43(Special Issue 1): 95–114.

Welge, M.K. (1980) *Management in deutschen multinationalen Unternehmungen. Ergebnisse einer empirischen Untersuchung.* Stuttgart: Poeschel Verlag.

Wolf, J. (1994) *Internationales Personalmanagement: Kontext – Koordination – Erfolg*, Wiesbaden: Gabler, MIR Edition.

Yan, A., Zhu, G. and Hall, D.T. (2002) 'International assignments for career building: A model of agency relationships and psychological contracts', *Academy of Management Review*, 27(3): 373–91.

7 Multinational Companies and the Host Country Environment

Damian Grimshaw, Jill Rubery and Phil Almond

Contents

Learning Objectives

After reading this chapter you will be able to

- Appreciate some of the main features that distinguish host country business and employment environments

- Identify the key issues for multinational companies in developing their HRM policies and practices in different host country environments

- Critically assess the evidence for and against trends towards convergence of country employment systems

- Explain how HRM practices of pay, work organisation and collective representation are shaped by host country factors

Chapter Outline

This chapter explores the diversity of host country environments that MNCs must engage with when managing overseas subsidiaries and analyses the extent to which these environments influence subsidiaries' HRM practices, particularly pay systems, work organisation and collective representation. Evidence of trends towards cross-national convergence in employment arrangements is also explored.

1 Introduction

When multinational companies (MNCs) set up subsidiaries in foreign countries they have to manage their operations in line with the rules prevailing in those national environments. At a minimum this can be expected to require compliance with legal regulations, but in practice MNCs will also need to take into account customary practices prevailing in the host environment, particularly if they wish to hire staff from the local labour market. It is therefore essential for MNCs to understand the local labour market environment and identify the kinds of factors that may affect both the attributes and the expectations of their employees drawn from the host community. Where the MNC takes over a brownfield site, there will be more pressure to accommodate to local custom and practices than when establishing a greenfield site; with a brownfield site the MNC inherits a whole history of employment relationships shaped by the past policies of previous owners, whether domestic owners or another MNC. Under a greenfield operation the MNC has more choice over how far to implement employment policies and practices in line with those prevailing within the host environment or to adopt practices consistent with the company's operations in other subsidiaries and indeed in line with those prevailing in the home country environment. The outcome is shaped by two institutional environments (Kostova and Zaheer, 1999), the *internal* environment of the multinational (including the strategic importance of the subsidiary, its position in the value chain and subsidiary managers' local sources of power) and the *external* environment described by the home and host country institutions. The focus of this chapter is on the nature of the host country environment – how it shapes and constrains diffusion of HRM practices within the multinational company and the degree of differentiation among host countries. Our concern is thus with the variety of different environments that MNCs may encounter in their subsidiary host environments and also with the importance of adjusting to host country economic conditions, institutional rules and social and cultural norms and expectations, according to both the type of HR policy and the type or group of staff under consideration.

While this chapter mainly discusses the influence of host country environments on MNCs it is worth noting that the influence likewise works in the other direction. MNCs' investment decisions may in fact be influenced by the nature of the host country environment so that the conditions that prevail are taken into account in the decision on where to locate subsidiaries. Many developing countries in particular have been willing to alter their environments in order to attract inwards Foreign Direct Investment; this has led in some cases to government deregulation of both product and labour markets – or to a tendency not to regulate on issues such as pollution levels. Alternatively some developing countries have set up specific enclaves within their countries – export processing zones – where MNCs are allowed to set up subsidiaries that are not subject to the normal regulations prevailing in the country. In other situations, special exemptions from regulations may be negotiated as part of the package to attract the FDI investment. MNCs may affect the host country environment in more positive ways – through establishing higher standards of HR practices, both within the subsidiaries and also possibly in local supplier organisations if the MNCs set up local supply chains with better HR activities than had previously prevailed. High levels of FDI may also change the labour market systems, particularly if MNCs tend to pay higher wages than domestic companies (Nichols and Cam, 2005). The result may be to increase the pressure on domestic companies to compete with MNCs or to reduce the capability of domestic companies to compete if they lack access to talented labour. While these effects may be more marked in developing economies, MNCs may also influence changes in more developed economies. They may be active in lobbying for changes to regulations and practices they find onerous or which restrict their access to parts of the markets. Furthermore, to the extent that they opt out of national institutional arrangements such as national or sectoral level collective bargaining or training arrangements, they may by so doing weaken those institutions by raising the possibility of opt out even for domestic employers.

The overall message here is that MNCs are powerful organisational actors. While our focus is on how they may adjust their practices to meet host country environments, it is important to recognise that over time MNCs are influential in shaping those same environments. This occurs either through their bargaining over the conditions under which the investment takes place (or is retained within a country) or through their actions at international and national levels in lobbying for regulatory and institutional changes in directions which they perceive to be in their interests as MNCs. For example, MNCs are known to be very active in lobbying at the European Union level so that changes in host environments linked to changes in EU regulations may, in part, be the outcome of MNCs lobbying for change (Coen, 1997).

This chapter is organised as follows. Section 2 outlines some of the main differences in host country environments that may impact on the international HRM policies of MNCs. Section 3 considers the impact of increasing globalisation on the sustainability of different employment systems and arrangements. Section 4 then addresses the more specific issue of the responses of MNCs to host country environments drawing on a selection of contemporary empirical research on transfer of HRM practices.

2 Varieties of host country environments

The vast majority of MNCs when choosing to set up wholly owned subsidiaries or joint ventures in foreign environments will employ staff under an internal employment relationship. This is a relatively ubiquitous institutional arrangement in advanced countries, as well as in the formal sectors of developing countries. It is sometimes referred to as a contract of service, to distinguish it from a contract for services. The former involves a commitment to work under the direction of an employer, often for a specified period of time, in return for a wage while the latter refers to a contract to provide certain goods or services for a price and pertains primarily to either sole account self-employment or to a business-to-business contract. MNCs also engage in subcontracting to local firms and implement it either through international subcontracting or through subcontracting that is entered into by their own subsidiaries in the host economy. It is through this more arms length involvement in host economy labour markets that MNCs are most likely to become involved in the informal sectors of host countries, as they may subcontract to local firms that use informal employment practices. Here however we focus on MNC's role as a direct employer; issues of social responsibility and the role of MNCs in informal and poor employment practices are discussed elsewhere (see Chapters 17 and 18).

The internal employment contract is a social institution which is shaped both by legal (or contractual) conditions and by social arrangements including custom and practice. Countries or nation states vary in their legal traditions and arrangements (Botero et al., 2004; Deakin, 2009), as well as in their customs and social institutions.

As a consequence employment arrangements are highly likely to take on diverse forms in different societies. These differences arise in part because although employment is a means to produce goods and services, its significance extends to a whole set of other institutional arrangements in society. The organisation of employment is shaped not only by labour market regulations and industrial relations systems (see Chapter 17), but also by production systems, education and training arrangements and their associated career structures, social stratification and standards of living, welfare arrangements and household, family and gender systems. Given this wide range of employment interfaces with areas of social organisation, there is considerable scope for variation in employment arrangements between national environments. Below we identify some of the most important differences along these institutional and social dimensions and how they may impact on MNCs to provide a flavour of the potential distinctions between host country environments.

Labour market regulations

One of the most visible differences between countries is the extent of protection afforded by the employment contract. The US is found at one end of the spectrum with its renowned 'employment at will' systems where employers face few legal constraints and requirements when stating their reasons, giving notice or making compensatory payments before terminating an employee's contract. According to the OECD's index of employment protection, the US scores just 0.2 for protection against individual dismissals, while the index rises to 4.2 for Portugal and 3.1 for the Netherlands (see Table 7.1). It is notable that Japan has a score in the mid range at 2.4 even though it has a tradition of providing 'jobs for life', these lifelong employment contracts exist primarily in the large firm sector and apply to around one third of the country's total workforce. In general, custom and practice is more influential in shaping employment protection than actual legal provisions. Table 7.1 also provides information on variations between countries in relation to collective dismissals and to temporary contracts. Again wide variation is found between countries although there has been a general liberalisation of restrictions on temporary contracts over recent years.

Another important form of labour market regulation is the presence or otherwise of a legal minimum wage (see Table 7.2). The impact of legal minimum wages on the employment system will depend in part on the level at which it is set, but also on whether there are higher minimum wages set through collective bargaining and the extent that these rates of pay cover most of the workforce; in many developing countries much of the available employment is in the informal sector where the minimum wage is not applied.

A third area that may be covered by legal regulation is working time, particularly maximum working hours and minimum paid holiday entitlements. These minimum regulations are often improved upon by collective bargaining where more detailed

Table 7.1   Trends and levels of employment protection in OECD countries

1 Overall strictness of protection against (individual) dismissals				2 Overall strictness of regulation on temporary employment			3 Overall strictness of regulation on collective dismissals	
	1990	1998	2003	1990	1998	2003	1998	2003
Australia	1.0	1.5	1.5	0.9	0.9	0.9	2.9	2.9
Austria	2.9	2.9	2.4	1.5	1.5	1.5	3.3	3.3
Belgium	1.7	1.7	1.7	4.6	2.6	2.6	4.1	4.1
Canada	1.3	1.3	1.3	0.3	0.3	0.3	2.9	2.9
Czech Republic	..	3.3	3.3	..	0.5	0.5	2.1	2.1
Denmark	1.5	1.5	1.5	3.1	1.4	1.4	3.9	3.9
Finland	2.8	2.3	2.2	1.9	1.9	1.9	2.6	2.6
France	2.3	2.3	2.5	3.1	3.6	3.6	2.1	2.1
Germany	2.6	2.7	2.7	3.8	2.3	1.8	3.5	3.8
Greece	2.5	2.3	2.4	4.8	4.8	3.3	3.3	3.3
Hungary	..	1.9	1.9	..	0.6	1.1	2.9	2.9
Ireland	1.6	1.6	1.6	0.3	0.3	0.6	2.4	2.4
Italy	1.8	1.8	1.8	5.4	3.6	2.1	4.9	4.9
Japan	2.4	2.4	2.4	1.8	1.6	1.3	1.5	1.5
Korea	..	2.4	2.4	..	1.7	1.7	1.9	1.9
Mexico	..	2.3	2.3	..	4.0	4.0	3.8	3.8
Netherlands	3.1	3.1	3.1	2.4	1.2	1.2	3.0	3.0
New Zealand	..	1.4	1.7	..	0.4	1.3	0.4	0.4
Norway	2.3	2.3	2.3	3.5	3.1	2.9	2.9	2.9
Poland	..	2.2	2.2	..	0.8	1.3	4.1	4.1
Portugal	4.8	4.3	4.2	3.4	3.0	2.8	3.6	3.6
Slovak Republic	..	2.5	2.3	..	1.1	0.4	4.0	3.8
Spain	3.9	2.6	2.6	3.8	3.3	3.5	3.1	3.1
Sweden	2.9	2.9	2.9	4.1	1.6	1.6	4.5	4.5
Switzerland	1.2	1.2	1.2	1.1	1.1	1.1	3.9	3.9
Turkey	..	2.6	2.6	..	4.9	4.9	1.6	2.4
United Kingdom	0.9	0.9	1.1	0.3	0.3	0.4	2.9	2.9
United States	0.2	0.2	0.2	0.3	0.3	0.3	2.9	2.9

Source: OECD Employment Outlook 2004. Data for Slovak Republic have been revised since the publication.

Table 7.2   Level of minimum wages and method of uprating

	Adult minimum wage relative to adult full-time median earnings mid-2006	Method of setting minimum wage	Additional notes
Belgium	51.6	Set by fixed rule (index-based) after negotiations with social partners	
Canada	40.5	Set by government	Weighted average of provincial/ territorial rates
France	61.4	Set by government after non binding tripartite negotiations	
Greece	52.7	Set by collective agreement but extended to all by law	For blue collar workers
Ireland	48.0	Set by tripartite negotiations	
Japan	33.3	Set by government	
Netherlands	44.6	Set by tripartite negotiations	52.1 if include 8 per cent holiday pay supplement
New Zealand	58.9	Set by expert committee	
Portugal	38.7	Set by tripartite negotiations	45.1 if include annual supplementary pay of two additional months
Spain	33.6	Set by government after non binding tripartite negotiations	39.2 if include annual supplementary pay of two additional months
UK	45.0	Set by expert committee, subject to government agreement	
US	30.7	Set by government	

Source: Low Pay Commission, 2008 and ICTWSS database.

regulations on, for example, premium rates for overtime and weekend work are determined. The approach to minimum regulations can vary widely from one country to another. For example, in relation to the EU working time directive, France is renowned as a country where national state legislation has had a major impact on actual working time practices. In 1998 a standard 35 hour week was introduced,

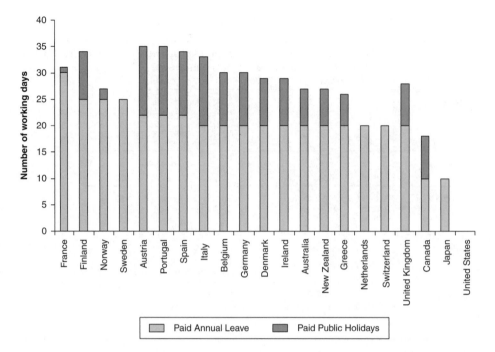

Figure 7.1 Paid annual leave and paid public holidays, OECD countries

Source: Reprinted with permission from the authors. Ray, R. and Schmitt, J. (2007) No vacation nation USA-a comparison of leave and holiday in OECD countries *European Economic and Employment Policy* Brief No.3 - 2007 ETUI-REHS Brussels.

although the mandatory regulations have since been loosened following the change of government in 2005. This contrasts with the UK which in principle is bound by the maximum 48 hour week in the EU's working time directive for all EU member states, although UK employers are legally permitted to ask employees to voluntarily opt out from this provision. One area of major variation between societies is the extent of paid holiday that is both provided for and taken. The US and Japan are known as societies where employees have limited entitlements to paid holidays and often fail to take up their full entitlement due to the pressures of work. There is, however, a much stronger development of rights to paid holidays in Europe and other developed countries (see Figure 7.1).

MNCs thus face considerable variations in host country environments with respect to legal regulations. The impact of working time regulations will depend upon how stringently they are stipulated, but the combination of legal and collectively agreed regulations may well have effects on both the opportunities for particular operating hours and their attendant costs. Minimum wage laws may have only a limited impact as MNCs tend to pay above average wages in many labour markets, although the minimum wages will have a more direct influence on the costs of subcontracting in the host environment particularly when suppliers are encouraged to adhere to them. Restrictions on dismissing employees or using temporary contracts are likely to have more impact. Where these regulations are further bolstered by customary expectations of job security, an MNC's recruitment decisions will take on even greater importance especially in countries with comparatively low rates of job mobility between organisations. A corollary of this long-term employment is that MNCs in this context may need to engage with the host country education and training systems and other indicators of employee quality to ensure that they make appropriate decisions at the point of hiring.

Industrial relations systems

The density of trade union membership and the coverage of collective bargaining perhaps constitute the second most frequently referred to set of indicators of employment differences across countries. As Table 7.3a demonstrates, there are very different levels of trade union membership and collective bargaining coverage across countries and even among developed countries (Visser, 2006). Moreover there is no simple correlation between trade union density and collective bargaining coverage; for example trade union membership is low in France but collective bargaining coverage is high. Table 7.3b indicates that there are differences in the form of collective bargaining across countries; in some cases the most common form of bargaining is at national level covering multiple sectors, while in others it is either primarily national single sector bargaining or primarily enterprise-level bargaining. National level bargaining is often associated with what is termed inclusive labour markets where most employees are covered by similar forms of protection and wages are set at similar levels for all employers. Enterprise level bargaining is associated with more exclusive labour markets; in these labour markets how much one is paid also depends on where one is employed. Australia, for example, is a country which for most of the last century was dominated by national and state level bargaining, but after 1996 started to make some moves towards more enterprise level bargaining alongside the more inclusive bargaining forms.

There are national variations in the legal arrangements for trade union recognition and collective bargaining coverage that are likely to impact on MNCs, irrespective of the MNCs' own orientations towards recognising unions or participating in collective bargaining. In some countries, employers may be required to recognise trade unions where the workforce votes in favour of recognition. Furthermore some countries make collective agreements binding on all employers in the sector whether or not the individual employer is party to the negotiations. In others engagement in collective bargaining is more voluntary but where it is customary to follow collective agreements, not to do so may lead to poor employment relations or motivate the MNC to pay higher wages to persuade the workforce that unions would not be beneficial (Bennett and Kaufman, 2007). The types of workforce groups organised by trade unions or covered by collective bargaining may also differ. In some societies white collar as well as blue collar workers may be members of trade unions, but in others

Table 7.3(a)   Union density and coverage of collective bargaining

Country	Union density 1995	Union density 2006/7	Coverage of collective bargaining 1995	Coverage of collective bargaining 2006/7
Australia	32.4	19.8	80	60
Austria	41.4	31.7	99	99
Belgium	55.7	54.1	96	96
Canada	33.7	29.4	36.7	31.5
Czech	60.2	21.0	60	44
Germany	29.2	20.1	68	63
Denmark	77	68	69	82
Estonia	30.1[b]	13.2	31[b]	22
Greece	33.6	23[f]	80	85[f]
Spain	16.3	14.6	78.4	80
Finland	80.4	71	81.6	90
France	9.1	8	95	95
Hungary	28.2[c]	17.8[f]	52[c]	35[d]
Republic of Ireland	52.3	35.1	N/A	N/A
Italy	38.1	33.2	82	80
Japan	24.4	18.2	21.5	16.1
Lithuania	39.9	14.4	16	12
Latvia	29.8	16.1	N/A	20
Netherlands	25.2	21.2	86	82
Norway	57.3	55	72	72
New Zealand	27.1	22.9	43.3	30[e]
Poland	28.6[c]	14.4	43[c]	35
Portugal	23.5	18.1	71[a]	62
Romania	46.1[c]	33.7	N/A	N/A
Sweden	86.6	73.8	90	92
Slovenia	42.8[c]	41.3[d]	100	100
Slovakia	49.8	23.6	55	35
Switzerland	22.8	19	46.5	48
United Kingdom	33.1	28.7	36	34.8
United States	14.3	12.0	16.6	13.5

Table 7.3(b)   Most common form of collective bargaining

Country	Codes	Level of bargaining 1995	Level of bargaining 2006/2007
Australia	AS	Central/industry/company	Industry/company
Austria	AU	Industry	Industry/company
Belgium	BE	Industry	Central/industry/company
Canada	CA	Company	Company
Czech	CZ	Industry/company	Industry/company
Germany	DE	Industry	Industry/company
Denmark	DK	Industry	Industry/company
Estonia	EE	Company	Company
Greece	EL	Industry	Industry
Spain	ES	Industry	Industry
Finland	FI	Industry	Industry
France	FR	Industry/company	Industry/company
Hungary	HU	Industry/company	Industry/company
Republic of Ireland	IE	Central/industry/company	Central/industry/company
Italy	IT	Industry	Industry
Japan	JA	Company	Company
Lithuania	LT	Company	Company
Latvia	LV	Company	Company
Netherlands	NL	Industry	Industry
Norway	NO	Central	Industry
New Zealand	NZ	Company	Company
Poland	PL	Company	Company
Portugal	PT	Industry/company	Industry/company
Romania	RO	Industry/company	Industry/company
Sweden	SE	Industry	Industry
Slovenia	SI	Central/industry/company	Central/industry/company
Slovakia	SK	Industry	Industry
Switzerland	SZ	Industry/company	Industry/company
United Kingdom	UK	Company	Company
United States	US	Company	Company

[a]1994; [b]1996; [c]1998; [d]2000; [e]2003; [f]2005

Source: ICTWSS database (http://www.uva-aias.net/208).

the role of trade unions may in practice be restricted primarily to the protection of manual workers.

Production systems and work organisation

There are different ways that industries can produce the same kinds of goods and services. Perhaps the most quoted example is the distinction made between Fordism and Toyotism in the production of automobiles. Although the differences between them can be over-emphasised, Fordism is characterised by reducing the scope for human error through minimising employee discretion and Toyotism is known for harnessing human knowledge, particularly tacit knowledge, utilised for the purpose of improving production processes (Appelbaum and Batt, 1994; Best, 1990). These differences in production methods are in part related to the epochs when Ford and Toyota developed into major car producers but also to the labour market systems operating in the US and Japan, respectively. The low discretion system may be more compatible with the short term, less stable employment relationships found in the US, while the development of employee commitment implied by the Toyotism model has been regarded as more compatible with lifelong contracts of employment in Japanese corporations.

Marsden (1999) has developed a fourfold typology of production systems, reflecting different ways of skilling the national workforce and specific systems of production organisation (see Table 7.4). Work organisation differs between societies and can be understood according to two different logics – the production approach focused on tasks to be done and the training approach focused on the capabilities of the job holder. Marsden subdivides these two systems into, what is in effect, high and low skill or high and low discretion systems. The US is characterised as having a production approach based on a simple task-centred, low discretion work system, whereas Japan's system is likewise a production approach focused not on discrete tasks but procedures or functions requiring higher levels of skill and discretion. The UK, Marsden defines as classified under the training approach, having traditionally organised work according to the training or trade of the employee; this is called a job territory or tools of the trade approach and is also task centred although the allocation of tasks relates to the trade of the job holder and is defined by materials or tools used. By contrast, Germany is considered as a training orientated system like the UK, but based on higher skill and discretion; here the focus is again on a function and not an individual task with the work assigned to workers according to their qualifications. Marsden argues that these distinctive approaches are underpinned by a range of different institutional arrangements and support systems. These various ways of organising work also have implications for supervision systems. In those where the work is task centred, managers are primarily coordinators and are not expected to have high technical competence or maintain an overview of the production systems; in contrast the function-centred systems rely on 'player managers',

Table 7.4 Marsden's varieties of employment systems: different logics
to work organisation

	Production approach	Training approach
Task-centred rules	Work post e.g. France, US	Job territory e.g. Britain
Function-centred rules	Competence rank e.g. Japan	Qualification rule e.g. Germany

Source: Based on Marsden (1999).

who are supervisors of the skilled workers and are themselves technically skilled
and able to understand and perform the work.

The significance for MNCs of these different approaches and arrangements lies in
the expectations and competences of the staff hired from the local labour market. For
example, an MNC may have adopted a task-oriented approach to production organisation, but whenever it locates within a host country that has a strong tradition of
high discretion systems of work organisation, then it may find that employees become
dissatisfied with its attempts to limit the scope they have in influencing how work is
to be undertaken (Geppert and Matten, 2006). Alternatively, an MNC may have difficulties recruiting employees with sufficient skill and problem-solving abilities in host
countries where work is organised according to a low skills paradigm. In some host
country environments the MNC may also aim to develop higher trust employment
relations than those normally prevailing in domestic firms if they are to implement
work systems that are reliant on worker commitment and involvement. The research
evidence suggests that such problems were encountered by, for example, Japanese
MNCs when they located in the UK and the US (Elger and Smith, 2005; MacDuffie,
1995) and German MNCs operating in the UK and Spain (Ferner et al., 2001).

Education, training and careers

Education and training systems provide the basis for developing the skills required
by organisations and often shape the career opportunities of individuals in the labour
market. This has not always been the case although even in societies more dominated by elite groups there is an increasing need for them to engage in education if
they are to retain their high status positions in the economic and social system. All
societies have hierarchical systems of education, but the gaps between, for example,
elite and non-elite higher educational establishments are greater in some societies
than others. There are also differences accorded to the status of particular types of
degrees; for example, many more students study engineering in Germany than in the
UK in part because engineering occupations hold higher status in Germany (Lee and

Smith, 1992). Understanding the finer points of educational institutions and qualification systems will be of greater concern to MNCs in host countries where internal labour market systems are strong – that is, where large firms tend to recruit employees at the bottom of a job ladder, provide structured training, and encourage an internal career within the firm rather than mobility across firms. In such a context, MNCs may need to recruit staff immediately out of the education system, rather than seek to recruit staff with more experience since if job mobility is generally low it may be more difficult to recruit higher level staff at mid-points in their careers.

The extent and value of workplace-based training also varies between societies. Where access to stable or quality employment is dependent upon having completed a workplace-based qualification, MNCs may feel obliged to provide such training for their staff even if they might expect normally to provide less intensive training in the initial phases of employment. The extent of workplace training may vary across the different subsidiaries of an MNC such that similar occupations may be staffed by people who are educated/trained primarily within the education systems in some host countries, while in others they may be primarily trained within the workplace. For example IT staff in the UK are mainly graduates recruited from a wide range of subject areas, whereas in Germany there was a major expansion of apprenticeships specifically within the IT area to meet this labour market need (Steedman et al., 2003).

While for the most part MNCs may be free to determine the extent to which they conform to host country systems of education and training, in some societies they are required to participate in the system or be subject to training levies/fines if they do not achieve the required training expenditure and standards. Among developed countries, training levy systems are in operation in France and Singapore (Billet and Smith, 2005). Many other countries set specific training and qualifications standards for professional and technical occupations to which MNCs have to conform or face difficulties in the local labour market.

Social stratification and living standards

Employment is often the main source of income for an individual and/or a household and thus employment rewards are a part of systems of social stratification and income inequality. Wage differentials between occupational groups may thus vary between societies, and will often reflect differences that persist in their social hierarchies (see Figure 7.2 for illustrations of wide variations in the ratios of CEO to average worker pay). There may also be some direct linkages between employment rewards and household income needs; for example, in some societies – for example Greece (see the European Job Mobility Portal at http://ec.europa.eu/eures/) – collective agreements may typically provide married or children allowances or provide additional support for the costs of children's education. Another variation between societies may be the extent to which wages are expected to rise in line with the cost of living – that is, whether there is a general institutionalised system of wage adjustments which are

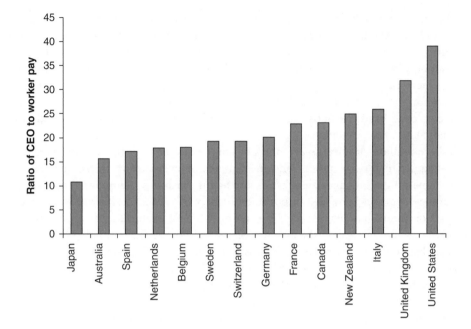

Figure 7.2   International comparison of CEO to worker pay

Source: Mishel, L., Bernstein, J. and Allegretto, S. (2005) *The State of Working America 2004/05*, Ithaca, NY: Economic Policy Institute and Cornell University Press. Reprinted with permission from Cornell University Press.

made independently of any adjustments linked to individual or group performance within the firm. These rewards and benefits are more likely to be the case in host country environments where there is extensive collective bargaining.

Welfare systems

Employment systems are often closely tied in to welfare arrangements – that is, systems of protection for employees and citizens during periods when they are not able to work. This is the case in countries where welfare is primarily provided through universal, state-financed schemes, but may also apply where state provision is limited and 'good employers' are expected to fund the gap.

Entitlements to statutory unemployment benefits, paid maternity or parental leave, sick pay and pensions are often linked directly to length of employment and/ or contributions to social protection made from wage income and/or by employers. In some countries, for example the UK (Deakin and Wilkinson, 2005), it was the development of the welfare system that was associated with the institutionalisation of the internal employment relationship. Moreover, eligibility may depend on records of continuous and full-time employment which might exclude from state social protection schemes part-time workers, giving some employers an incentive to utilise non-standard contracts to avoid social insurance costs. Likewise the costs of hiring the self-employed for specific tasks may be higher in countries where the self-employed have to pay high social protection insurance costs and lower in countries where they are largely excluded from the state system. On the other hand, in this context it may be more difficult to find staff willing to work part-time or on a self-employed basis, perhaps thereby reinforcing standard full-time and continuous employment arrangements.

Where welfare provisions are limited, employers may fill the gap by providing, for example, company-based pension schemes or even health insurance. The US is notable among advanced countries for having primarily employer-based health insurance schemes, and the importance of access to this healthcare has a major impact on the US labour market. One reason why, for example, many women work full-time in the US despite the absence of state childcare support is that part-timers can be legally excluded from health insurance benefits (Buchmueller and Valletta, 1999) while in the EU exclusion of part-timers is treated as indirect sex discrimination and thus illegal. Employer-based welfare policies tend to reduce the mobility of workers from one employer to another since there may be a risk of loss of benefits. Thus although Anglo-Saxon countries are regarded as having the most flexible labour markets, the greater importance of employer-based benefits in these societies introduces a form of rigidity that is not captured when only issues such as employment protection legislation are considered.

MNCs will be expected to conform to regulations regarding state level welfare systems, in addition, they may have to decide whether or not to offer company-level benefits, according to established norms in the host economy.

Household, family and gender systems

There remain major variations between societies in the access accorded to women to employment and in the provisions made to facilitate reconciliation of wage work with family life (Anxo et al., 2007), although there has been a widespread move towards more involvement of women in wage employment. The growth of dual earner households could be expected to lead to employers having to take more account of their employees' household and family obligations in scheduling working time. However even in societies where women stay at home, employers may have to organise working time taking into account expectations of shared family leisure time. Strong customary norms with respect to working hours, limiting for example work on Sundays or Saturdays or Fridays and other religious and state holidays, may be even stronger in more traditional societies.

Differences in gender and family regimes will affect arrangements at the workplace. In some societies it may not be regarded as appropriate for men and women to work in close proximity, while in others employers may need to be aware of strong societal norms and regulations promoting gender equality. There are also differences – and rapidly changing practices – with respect to employment patterns for women at the point of childbirth and afterwards. In some societies women may quit the labour market at the point of childbirth – or indeed marriage – and may not have the right to return to work. Up until 1945, in Britain female teachers and civil servants had to resign on marriage and this expectation was still the case for semi-professional or technical occupations in some Western countries during the 1950s–1960s. Increasingly, though, women are likely to return to employment after taking a period of leave. Length of leaves varies greatly (Moss and Korintus, 2008). In post-transition economies women have entitlement to paid leave for three years and when they return to work it is normally on a full-time basis, while in other European countries leave periods are shorter and the majority of women are more likely to return to part-time work. However in some societies – for example Sweden or France with good childcare provision – this may be only for a transitional period and in Sweden both mothers and fathers are able to reduce their hours of work while receiving some compensation for the lost hours. In other countries – for example the UK or the Netherlands – women often work part-time but receive no compensation for not working full-time.

MNCs will need to be aware of national norms with respect to equal opportunities as well as with respect to other areas of employment discrimination. Within MNCs, there may well be clashes in both directions between the equality policies adopted at headquarters and those prevailing in the local environment (Ferner et al., 2006). These clashes may have consequences for staff transferred within the MNC to the subsidiary as well as for locally hired employees. MNCs also should be aware of different societal expectations with respect to arrangements for leave and return to work for women when they have children. Nordic countries in particular are encouraging fathers to take a minimum of a few months of paternity leave, a parental leave practice that may be surprising to some MNC managers coming from societies where only women take responsibility for children.

This section has outlined the potential differences in employment arrangements that MNCs are likely to encounter when establishing subsidiaries in different host country environments. Variations in employment policies and practices arise influenced by differences in the institutional and social structures that shape employment practices. The pivotal role that employment plays in both the economic system and the social system means that there are a wide range of different institutions that impinge on human resource practices and employment arrangements. However, while these variations have been substantial in the second half of the twentieth century – particularly among developed countries – the increasing globalisation of economies is often argued to be leading to an erosion of differences through a process of convergence. The following section examines the arguments for convergence and divergence of employment systems. A process of convergence, with employment systems becoming more similar across the globe would facilitate perhaps the development of standard employment arrangements for MNCs across all of their subsidiaries.

3 Sustainability of divergent employment arrangements

While all developed countries now subscribe to the generalised systemic principles of capitalism (as opposed to some other form of economic system such as communism or feudalism), significant differences in the particular model, or brand, of capitalism have been identified that are also associated with distinctive forms of employment system. Two schools of thought have dominated explanations for the development and persistence of these divergent employment forms, the institutionalist approach and the culturalist approach (Rubery and Grimshaw, 2003; Sorge, 2004).

Institutionalist and culturalist approaches

The institutionalist approach has focused on complementarities between institutions, giving rise to both 'varieties of capitalism' (VoC) and 'worlds of welfare capitalism', popularised by Hall and Soskice (2001) and Esping-Anderson (1990), respectively. Here, the argument is that countries cluster around two or three ideal types – liberal and coordinated market economies in the VoC approach and liberal, social demo-cratic and conservative welfare systems in Esping-Anderson's approach. Each ideal type is characterised by a distinctive constellation of institutional arrangements – spanning education, R&D, welfare, industrial relations, inter-firm relations, corpo-rate governance, and so on. In particular, it is the complementarity or coherence of institutions across these areas that leads to the development of distinctive models of capitalism, associated with particular forms of comparative advantage. So, for instance, in Hall and Soskice's approach, the coordinated market economy is based on both stronger employment protection and stronger coordination among employ-ers. Together, these arrangements encourage long-term investment planning, which further generates positive incentives for skill development, incremental innovation and stable economic growth. In the liberal market economy model, labour markets are flexible and general education and short-term profit targets dominate. When combined, these arrangements encourage market growth in fast-changing sectors, radical forms of innovation and high job mobility. The argument is that the more a country's institutional arrangements cohere around one of these ideal types, the greater is the likelihood that it will achieve superior economic performance and be sustainable when faced with external shocks.

There is now widespread use of these typologies by government planners, con-sultants and academic researchers to understand country differences. Used as heuristic devices, ideal – type models can certainly assist our understanding and ability to organise the complex cross-country patterns of employment models, at least within developed countries. Considerable empirical evidence has also been assembled to support and to refine the notions of distinctive models and ideal types (Hall and Gingerich, 2004). However, there is no reason to suppose that countries neatly form clusters around two or three ideal types and as institutional arrangements and practices change there may be a need to pay more attention to hybrid forms (Bosch et al., 2009; Whitley, 1999).

The second approach to understanding country divergence draws on observations based on national cultural differences. This approach argues that a range of cultural factors help to explain differences in employment policy and practice, across society and within organisations. Citizens of different countries display cultural variety in their approach, for example, to authority relations, to a collective or individualist approach to decision making, to gender relations, to leadership behaviour and to many other aspects of organisational life, including day-to-day operational issues such as the significance of face-to-face contact or the meaning of a handshake. The most influential study is that of Hofstede (1980, 2001) who has developed four abstract dimensions of a national culture – power distance, individualism, masculinity and uncertainty avoidance – to which a fifth, long-term orientation is often added. A number of consulting organisations also utilise Hofstede's concepts (e.g., Itim International). Comparing France with the US and China, for example, France is categorised as distinctive for its high power distance, low masculinity and high uncertainty avoidance; the US ostensibly has a low power distance, very high individualism, low uncertainty avoidance and low long-term orientation; and China has a very high power distance, an extraordinarily low individualism, low uncertainty avoidance and a near maximum measure of long-term orientation (sourced from the website, http://www.geert-hofstede.com/hofstede_dimensions.php, accessed January 2009). The implications of a cultural approach to understanding country differences is that application of similar HRM policies in host country environments would be expected to have different effects due to differences in cultural attitudes and social norms.

Many studies have sought to replicate Hofstede's findings for a specific country but there are still relatively few studies that have collected robust cross-national empirical data (e.g., Jackson, 2001; Ronen and Shenkar, 1985; Schwartz, 1992; Van Oudenhoven, 2001). Moreover, several widely acknowledged critiques have been levelled at the analytical devices and empirical evidence used in the Hofstede-led cultural approach to country diversity. McSweeney (2002), for example, identifies problems with the data used in Hofstede's work. The data derive from a study of one company, IBM, so it is not clear whether the primary object of study is IBM's employee culture or national cultures. McSweeney calls this, 'the huge and unbridged conceptual chasm between the micro-local (IBM) and the national' (2002: 100). McSweeney also argues that only a narrow range of cultural variables are used to represent the dominant dimensions of a national culture. Finally he suggests that Hofstede's cultural approach does not allow for cultural values to be influenced by diverse and changing institutions (e.g., that US accountants' attitudes may reflect the short-termism of the American finance system rather than US culture *per se*, and moreover that time orientation may change with the onset of new accounting regulations). These limitations makes the cultural approach rather static and unresponsive to changing economic and social conditions.

In practice the major issue for the both approaches is that they predict the persistence of variety in employment systems yet the pressures of globalisation and new international governance systems may be pushing all country models in a similar direction towards greater market orientation. These pressures include the longstanding trends towards free trade (governed through the GATT and the IMF) and fewer restrictions on foreign direct investment (FDI) but also more recent phenomena, such as the massive expansion of financial markets, the increased power of institutional investors, and the pervasiveness of information and communication technologies. In addition, cultural ideas about lifestyle, gender relations and other norms are diffused worldwide far more rapidly in an age of fast-speed, broadband communications. The argument is that such pressures undermine the basis for varieties of capitalism by challenging those institutions associated with a coordinated market economy, for example, or a social democratic model welfare regime, leading to the emergence of a dominant US-type, market oriented model.

Towards convergence of country systems?

Many of these developments are potentially reducing the degree to which the nation state can exercise autonomy in the face of globalisation. In a new high-tech environment, internationalisation of financial markets, massive increases in capital movements and expansion of offshore financial markets combine to diminish governments' capacity to pursue autonomous fiscal policy, especially related to public expenditures and management of the public debt. Inside the euro-zone, pressures are arguably strengthened by governments' *greater concern with* inflation *even at the expense* of growth, *than has been time for* the US Federal Reserve (Bush, 2003). These trends have placed greater pressure on all countries for the wholesale deregulation of markets for products and services, including national utilities in the 1980s and 1990s and all services in the 2000s, and further restrict governments' role in managing a mixed economy. Policy changes have thus been oriented to benefit the internationalisation of business while traditional protective barriers around domestic economies have been weakened. The dominant economic approach for at least two decades was to foster growth through free market reform rather than other measures such as expansionary fiscal and industrial policies. Attempts by national governments to make their own countries more attractive to FDI, such as by reducing tax on business or removing restrictions on how to do business, have in turn diminished their distinctiveness and imposed restrictions on policy choice. An important representation of this tendency can be found on the World Bank's website, entitled 'doing business' (see http://www.doingbusiness.org/). This website ranks all countries in the world against 10 variables to demonstrate the relative ease of doing business; variables include 'getting credit', 'protecting investors' and 'employing workers'. The implication of the trends within this data is that countries must conform to a 'single peak' view of the world, where only one model of economic organisation is conducive to competitive success.

Against this background, several pieces of empirical evidence do indeed suggest that a process of convergence among developed countries is taking place, across a wide range of activities and policies. There is evidence of a good deal of convergence in the direction of policy reform to welfare state systems, with trends towards reduced or frozen public expenditures and a lowering of welfare benefits. Further, in the sphere of education and training, many countries appear to have followed the advice of Reich (1992) and switched investments from the specific, technical skills typically associated with vocational training to the 'symbolic analytical' skills acquired through higher education. For all OECD countries, the share of people graduating from higher education (for the relevant age group) increased from 20 per cent to 34 per cent between 1995 and 2006 (OECD, 2008 Table A3.2; figures refer to graduation from what the OECD defines as 'type A' tertiary education and only include those countries for which both 1995 and 2006 data are available). Germany and Austria, for example, have witnessed increases from 14 to 21 per cent and 10 to 21 per cent, respectively, over this time period. Scandinavian countries have seen a doubling from a relatively high level – from 25 to 45 per cent in Denmark and from 20 to 48 per cent in Finland (OECD, 2007).

National systems of wage-setting have also been changing. During the 1980s and 1990s centralised bargaining systems in many countries became more decentralised and unions lost strength in most countries. Countries as diverse as Sweden, Australia, the UK, Germany and Italy moved to greater intensity of local bargaining over payment systems, workplace restructuring or some form of concession bargaining in an overall context of weakened unions. As Katz (2004: 6) states, 'In nearly all countries, the per cent of the workforce covered by collective contracts declined and non-union employment became the ultimate decentralised way to set employment terms'. As shown in Table 7.3a, the declining trend has continued in several countries since the late 1990s; union density has fallen by around one third in Australia, Germany, Greece, Hungary and Ireland, and by approximately one quarter in Austria, Portugal and Japan. Moreover, in Estonia, Lithuania, Latvia and Slovakia union density has more than halved.

Yet there is still a good deal of detailed cross-national comparative research evidence that reveals continued and distinctive national systems of employment, welfare and production. For example, governments still enjoy considerable choice over the degree to which they promote public sector employment, as a means of creating market shelters to offset exposed sectors of the economy (Schmidt, 2002: 23–4). Moreover, governments still spend money in different ways – conforming more to Esping-Andersen's 'multi-peak' view of alternative welfare state regimes, than to the vision of a 'single-peak' form of Anglo-Saxon capitalism (see Freeman, 2002). Scandinavian countries and continental European countries have remained true to the principles of their social democratic and conservative models, respectively, even while introducing benefit cuts or new user fees. Glyn (2006) in fact shows a clear divergence between liberal economies and Europe in a key indicator of welfare regimes – the ratio of unemployment benefits to average earnings. Unemployment benefits were held steady at a much higher level during the 1990s in Europe, but allowed to fall from an already lower level in liberal economies such as the US and the UK (Glyn, 2006: Figure 5.5).

Further, while a common trend towards decentralised wage setting has been observed, it is also now accepted that the specific country models of decentralised wage-setting take many different forms, especially in the way local bargaining interacts with national level tripartite activities (Katz et al., 2004). Local bargaining in the UK occurred at the expense of multi-employer agreements (Brown, 1993) but in Germany, even though the influence of works councils has increased, the national and *state* sectoral agreements have *been retained* (Mückenberger, 2003) *even if more companies now opt out of the agreements in full or in part.* In Italy, social pacts agreed at a national level continue to provide framework agreements for local collective bargaining (Baccaro, 2000).

A nuanced pattern of change also characterises the arena of employment protection. OECD data on the strictness of employment protection against individual dismissals for regular workers (Table 7.1 above) suggest that out of the 20 countries for which data are available for the period 1990–2003, 4 saw an increase in strictness, 5 a decrease and 11 no significant change. More significantly, new research on country models of employment protection show quite clearly that countries can not be categorised along a simple one-dimensional continuum running from weak to strong employment protection, but instead may combine institutional arrangements for both weak and strong forms of employment protection (Auer and Cazes, 2003). For example, the Danish model scores low on the OECD index of protection against layoffs but provides very strong income protection through a generous system of unemployment benefits and high spending on active labour market policies (Madsen, 2003). Also, the Dutch model grants a great deal of flexibility to the employer in the use of temporary agency workers and at the same time establishes key principles of security for the worker relating to the phase of transition to a permanent employment contract (Van Oorschot, 2004). The range and distinctiveness of such models of 'flexicurity' suggest that the evidence in favour of convergence around one deregulated model of employment protection is weak.

4 Understanding how MNCs act in diverse host country environments

Given the context of diverse country environments for doing business and organising employment, much of the research to date on MNCs seeks to understand how MNCs implement and adapt their HRM practices in response to the 'receptiveness' or 'openness' of local institutional environments. Importantly, the research tends to be inter-disciplinary, bringing together scholars from four key management disciplines – organisation studies, international business, human resource management and industrial relations, and comparative business and employment systems. Some of the research contributions focus on MNCs as powerful and complex organisational actors; others are more concerned with the dynamic interactions of MNCs with institutions at national and international levels. These twin perspectives are only rarely articulated in a single research paper or project, but nevertheless represent an important contribution to knowledge arising from the overall collection of empirical and theoretical work.

MNCs as complex organisational actors

The focus on MNCs as complex organisational actors illuminates the fragmented set of interests among managers, investors and employees that generate internal conflict. Such conflict and tensions are found in a standard firm but in an MNC these are supplemented by diverse and conflicting interests among subsidiary managers and between subsidiary and head office managers (Ferner and Tempel, 2006). Subsidiary managers may resist or subvert head office orders to implement new HRM practices – for many different reasons – or may simply comply with what they are told, perhaps to meet performance targets required for additional investment in the subsidiary or to secure their own promotion (Morgan and Kristensen, 2006). The empirical evidence suggests certain factors can bolster the local power base of subsidiary managers, including where:

- the subsidiary is of high strategic importance (in terms of contribution to the global success of the multinational company);
- there is limited dependence on head office technology;
- the legacy is as a brownfield rather than a greenfield acquisition;
- it holds a key position in the global value chain;
- the scope of the subsidiary market is large; and
- the share of expatriate managers from the head office home country is low (e.g., Bjorkman and Lervik, 2007; Ferner and Edwards, 1995; Harzing, 2000; Martin and Beaumont, 1999).

Conversely, managers in the head office can deploy 'direct' and 'indirect' control strategies to harmonise practices across subsidiaries; direct control involves the issuing of formal policies and guidelines while indirect control involves such things as linking the implementation of practices with new investment or with pay and career prospects, or deploying a network of international managers to diffuse and implement new practices (Edwards et al., 1999; Fenton-O'Creevy et al., 2008).

So transferring HRM practices is a political and negotiated process (Geppert and Williams, 2006). The need to improve efficiency or to maximise cost savings may be an important factor driving the design of new practices. However, the research demonstrates many reasons internal to the MNC that facilitate transfer and conversely present obstacles to its realisation (Edwards et al., 2006). Bélanger et al. (2003: 483) refer to a 'two-way political process underpinned by creative tensions' between subsidiary and head office managers.

More detail on these political processes is provided in Chapter 8 (Edwards) of this edited collection. Here the key point is to emphasise the agency of subsidiary managers and other employees when acting in a particular local country context. Subsidiaries are neither passive recipients of head office orders, nor static respondents to local institutional rules and norms, but involved in 'a complex and dynamic interaction' (Morgan and Kristensen, 2006: 1472). Kostova and Zaheer (1999) argue subsidiaries are in fact engaged in a struggle for legitimacy in two institutional environments – the external (home and host country) and the internal (MNC).

MNCs in diverse host country environments

A second important insight to be drawn from recent research is that each host country environment is distinctive, not simply in terms of structural factors – that is, types of markets, economic conditions and access to basic infrastructure and technologies – but with respect to the complex web of institutional rules, cultural norms and traditions. Here we find a strong overlap between the study of HRM practices of MNCs and the literature on varieties of employment systems reviewed above in sections 2 and 3. Informed by this comparative employment systems literature, the research questions are often framed around identifying how 'open' or 'receptive' host country institutions are to novel practices introduced by MNCs (e.g., Ferner and Tempel, 2006). Other studies suggest it is the 'institutional distance' between home and host country that matters, defined using regulative, normative and cognitive dimensions drawn from the employment systems literature (e.g., Kostova and Roth, 2002).

There is therefore a strong connection between understanding the variety of country employment systems and identifying those factors that enable or hinder a MNC to transfer its HRM practices. The growing trend towards a 'high context' research approach on MNCs and their subsidiaries, as called for by Child (2000), is to be encouraged (see also Edwards and Kuruvilla, 2005). The challenge is to inform empirical research with both insights identified here – *that is that* multinationals *need to be considered* as complex organisational actors and *that they interact through* their subsidiaries with the diverse national institutional contexts of home and host countries (see Figure 7.3).

5 Host country effects on HRM practices of MNC subsidiaries

Table 7.5 summarises the way in which conditions in the host country environment potentially impinge upon key areas of HRM. Influences include socio-economic conditions (especially labour market conditions and the general economic climate

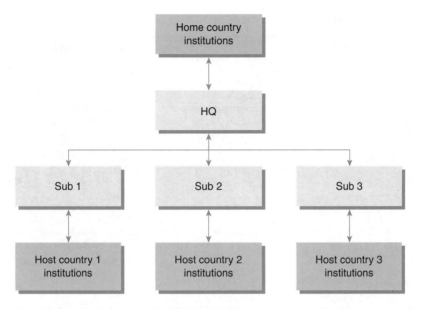

Figure 7.3 Organisational and institutional influences on multinational companies and their subsidiaries

Source: Geppert, M., Matten, D. and Walgenbach, P. (2006) 'Transnational building and the multinational corporations: An emerging field of research', *Human Relations*, 59 (11): 1451 - 1465. Reprinted with permission from SAGE Publications Limited.

for business), institutions (including legal rules as well as formal and informal rules set by employers and unions) and norms (associated with cultural and social traditions and routines). These influences vary by country and potentially constrain the capacity of an MNC to harmonise HRM practices across its global operations. Research does suggest, however, that some HRM practices are more sensitive to local environmental influence than others. In their widely cited study of HRM practices in 249 subsidiaries of foreign MNCs operating in the US, Rosenzweig and Nohria (1994) find that practices associated with executive bonus pay and participation in senior management decision making are very unlikely to be adapted to local conditions. In contrast, other HRM practices do display relatively close similarity with local practices, especially working time, benefits and gender composition of the employees. In the following discussion, we review the evidence for a selection of HRM practices, namely pay practices, work organisation and collective representation.

Pay practices

Research on US MNCs operating in European countries anticipates strong pressures for a common pay policy across subsidiaries but in fact reveals variation that reflects, in part, the local environmental influences. For example, in their detailed case studies

Table 7.5   Host country environment influences on HRM practices

HRM practices	Socio-economic influences	Institutional influences	Normative (social and cultural) influences
Recruitment	Availability of suitably trained labour	Legal requirement to recruit local labour Equal opportunity laws Restrictions on use of temporary agency workers	Ethics regarding meritocratic/ formal principles or informal customs based on personal recommendations Tradition of offering a job-for-life
Pay	Tightness of labour market Inflation rate Dispersion of wages	Minimum wage system Equal pay legislation	Collective or individualised approach to rewarding effort Norms of fair pay
Training and careers	Education and training levels of available workers Strength of occupational labour markets	Legal requirements to train System of vocational training	Expectations of skill development as a career route
Work organisation	Gender division of labour	Rules governing job classification and allocation Regulation of working hours Health and safety laws	Attitudes towards teamwork Norms of hierarchy
Job security	Labour market conditions Availability of temporary labour supply	Legal rules on individual and collective dismissals	Social perceptions of fairness
Collective representation	Membership of trade unions Coverage of collective bargaining agreements	Role of employer associations and trade unions in economy and society Use of legal mechanisms to extend collective agreements to non-union firms Union recognition requirements Employee representation laws	Attitudes towards trade unions Tradition of employee democracy and representation in the workplace

Source: development of Rubery and Grimshaw (2003: Table 8.2) based on Grønhaug and Nordhaug (1992).

of European subsidiaries of US MNCs, Almond et al. (2006: 126–8) report several examples of deviation from a centralised, harmonised pay policy. For example, Irish subsidiaries posted higher wage settlements than the company norm, reflecting the booming economic conditions at the time. They also negotiated a flexible benefits package that was more attractive to the mainly young and transient foreign workforce.

PRP

Several studies explore the variation in implementing performance-related pay (PRP) practices. Again drawing on data on US MNCs, with the expectation of strong corporate (and home country) pressures to diffuse performance-related pay, research on European subsidiaries finds variation. In their study of four European subsidiaries of a UK–US owned multinational company, Edwards et al. (2006: 78–9) identify significant pressure on managers from head office to implement PRP. However, managers in the German subsidiary were blocked by the works council which argued successfully that PRP conflicted with the tradition of group work and used its legal powers to restrict it solely to senior managerial grades. The study by Gooderham et al. (2006) also tests the implementation of individualised pay practices in subsidiaries of US MNCs, in this case drawing on the large scale Euronet–Cranfield (Cranet) survey of HRM in European and some non-European countries. Their data for six countries suggest that individualised pay practices, bundled with performance appraisals and formal training evaluation, are most likely to be implemented in Australia, followed by the UK and Ireland and lastly in Germany and Denmark/Norway (2006: Figure 1). The variation, they argue, is explained by the degree of institutional embeddedness of subsidiaries such that legal frameworks and industrial relations systems constrain them from applying new management practices, particularly in regard to pay policy (2006: 1496).

Work organisation practices

Turning to work organisation practices, we find special consideration of this area of HRM given strong interest among management practitioners and policymakers in transferring innovative practices that improve the learning and organisational capabilities of foreign-owned subsidiaries. During the 1990s, a good deal of research focused on the degree to which different host country environments were receptive to the work organisation practices of Japanese MNCs – reflecting the international interest at the time in diffusing what were assumed by some researchers and practitioners to be the superior management techniques of Japanese business. One early study of ten Japanese subsidiaries in the US identified an interesting divergence of host country effects in shaping practices of job rotation and training (Beechler and Yang, 1993). Among the banking subsidiaries in New York there was a strong Americanisation of all HRM practices, including the hiring of specialists, limited training provision and the adoption of employment-at-will. In strong contrast to banking among the manufacturing subsidiaries based in Tennessee, Japanese management practices were adopted with very limited adaptation to the host environment. Nevertheless, the local socio-economic conditions assisted Japanisation among these plants, especially the slack labour market conditions and low turnover rates. Also, some variation was observed with limited adoption of teamworking at the Tennessee tyre manufacturer owing to trade union resistance.

Host country environments play an important role in shaping the degree to which MNCs can export 'high road' models of work organisation – that is, models defined by investment in a high skill/high productivity approach – due to national and regional differences in the availability of skilled workers and systems of vocational training that support continued investment in workers' skills. In her study of Japanese companies in the UK during the 1990s, Lam (1997) argued that the UK environment was insufficiently receptive to novel practices in Japanese MNCs due to the poor skill profile among the pool of available workers. Other studies identify significant variety of implementation and effectiveness of work organisation practices among subsidiaries. For example, Woywode's (2002) study of German and French subsidiaries of MNC automobile companies finds higher training qualifications among German employees compared with their French counterparts (cited in Geppert and Williams, 2006). And Haipeter (2002) shows that German workers enjoy higher levels of autonomy in teams compared to French workers in comparable subsidiaries with similar HRM practices.

Collective representation

Perhaps the largest area of research on the influence of host country environments on MNC policy is in the area of collective representation. This was a key area of concern in research on global Japanisation in the 1980s and 1990s with the aim of understanding the extent to which subsidiaries followed the Japanese practice of enterprise unions. And the focus has intensified in research on US MNCs in Europe given the expectation that US firms will seek to adopt a strongly unitarist management style even in countries with a tradition of inclusive industrial relations (e.g., Muller, 1998; Royle, 1998).

The most recent evidence suggests a mix of centralised head office control and subsidiary pragmatism in response to local pressures to recognise trade unions. For example, Colling et al. (2006) show that US multinationals practised what they refer to as 'double breasting' in their Irish and UK subsidiaries, characterised by union recognition in the older sites and non-recognition in the newer sites. While acceptance by US subsidiaries of collective channels of decision-making seemed at first sight a surprising finding, the generally weak environment for trade unions in Ireland and the UK meant that 'the consequences of conceding unionised relations were not as far-reaching' (2006: 117–8). By contrast, US subsidiaries in Germany and Spain exhibited stronger resistance to collective channels because of an identifiable risk that co-determination might delay decision making and conflict with US MNCs' preference for standardised practices. A similar observation is made in the valuable study by Fenton-O'Creevy et al. (2008). Comparing country clusters of coordinated market economies and liberal market economies (following the Hall and Soskice typology – see section 3 above), the study hypothesises (and demonstrates) that US MNCs are least likely to adapt HRM policies to the host country environment in subsidiaries in more coordinated economies. However they also find that the greater the level of unionisation in a subsidiary the more likely the parent will delegate control (2008: 157, Table 7). These two findings considered together mean that it is non-union subsidiaries in coordinated market economies which show the weakest responsiveness to the local environment. This finding is consistent with the 'institutional distance' argument of Kostova and Roth (2002). Fenton-O'Creevy et al. offer the following explanation – 'US multinational companies clearly resist conceding HRM decision making to subsidiaries located in coordinated market economies. It is after all in coordinated market economies that there will be a particularly pronounced degree of inconsistency between institutional norms and the HRM concerns of US multinational companies' (2008: 162).

So, we observe strategies of resistance and avoidance among US subsidiaries. In Germany, Colling et al. (2006: 109) describe how managers were sometimes able to resist collective bargaining by paying above agreed rates or by switching from one collective agreement to another with a less militant trade union. Occasionally, trade unions make inroads in influencing MNCs and employment policies. In Italy, Pulignano (2006) demonstrates how local unions at three subsidiaries of a US MNC coordinated a national level campaign in an effort to counter the company's anti-union strategy. In an institutional context of centrally regulated company bargaining in Italy, the local unions were able to win a role in the joint regulation of pay and working conditions across all three plants – a practice that ran counter to the MNC's policy of individualisation of its employment relations. Likewise Meardi's (2006) comparative research on US and German MNCs in post-Communist Central and East European countries demonstrates numerous ways in which unions exercise formal and informal influence over subsidiaries' HRM practices. Examples include unions exercising veto power over the appointment of team leaders in a Polish subsidiary and local union adaptation of formalised employment relations in Slovenian subsidiaries.

6 Conclusion

Overall, MNCs are found to be responsive to their local host country environments but the degree and nature of responsiveness varies not only according to the characteristics of MNCs (see Chapter 8) but also from country to country, reflecting the diversity of country systems. It is difficult to be precise about the degree of adaptation of MNCs to their host country environment for two main reasons.

First, the host country environment is always changing, making it difficult to specify the goal posts, especially if managers are making decisions based on a projection of what the environment will look like in five years time. Moreover, as we argued in the introduction, the direction of change may in part reflect the powerful actions of MNCs – through their economic, political and normative influence on national and international decision makers; as Ferner and Tempel (2006: 21) put it, 'in the case of multinationals there is much evidence of the way in which they make the institutional weather'.

Second, it is difficult to disentangle what fraction of subsidiary actions are shaped by local institutions and conditions and what part results from what Morgan and

Kristensen (2006) call 'micro-politics'. Our interpretation of some of the recent carefully conducted case studies of subsidiary practices is that we ought to reject explanations that point simply towards the strength of institutions and instead recognise that organisational actors may be able to affect change even in tightly regulated environments. In her conclusion to a comparative case study of American subsidiaries in Italy and the UK, Pulignano argues, 'there is a space opened up by company specific organisational features of various groups of MNC actors to establish and pursue their group interests but this is mediated by the institutional effects of the host country environments' (2006: 513). More research is needed, therefore, that applies a combined organisation-centred and comparative systems approach to the diffusion and adaptation of HRM practices in MNCs.

Discussion questions

1 For any two countries, compare and contrast the different features that shape the way employment is organised in each country. Is there evidence of convergence of country systems of employment?

2 Why is it important to understand the character of a country's welfare system, including its family, household and gender system, for analysing HRM practices?

3 Compare the relative merits of an institutionalist approach and a culturalist approach for assessing changing cross-country differences in employment.

4 Section 4 describes two key insights that inform research on MNCs acting in host country environments. What are these insights? How do they help us understand the way MNCs diffuse HRM practices among their overseas subsidiaries?

5 Much of the evidence in section 5 refers to US-owned MNCs operating in Europe. Do the findings to date suggest an Americanisation of HRM practices in European subsidiaries? In making your assessment, consider carefully the particular socio-economic, institutional and normative features of a host country environment that influence diffusion of HRM practices.

CMM Industries

CMM Industries is a US-owned MNC in the engineering sector. It is a diversified company, but its main European activities are in the manufacture and sale of engines and related products. Its major European operations are in the United Kingdom, France, Germany and Hungary. The company was historically family-owned and controlled, and generally allowed the managers of foreign subsidiaries a fairly large degree of autonomy in setting human resource management and industrial relations policies which fitted with the host country context. Consequently, there were substantial differences in policies in different European countries, particularly in the areas of industrial relations and the management of pay and performance, with practices broadly conforming to national norms in the engineering sector.

The founding family relinquished control of the corporation in the 1990s, following years of disappointing business performance, and a new senior management team was put in place, largely recruited from outside the organisation. A new emphasis was placed on shareholder value, performance management and on subsidiary accountability. In the human resource management arena, there was a new focus on more coherent, centrally driven policies in the areas of industrial relations and the management of pay and performance.

The American operations of CMM had long resisted independent union organisation, but this had not been part of a strategic international HR philosophy. Now, though, foreign subsidiaries were expected to avoid trade union influence 'wherever possible', and subsidiary HR managers monitored on their 'achievements' in union avoidance.

This posed difficulties to the major European operations. Outside the Hungarian operations, which had been established relatively recently on a greenfield site and had always been non-union, there was substantial union influence, at least for some groups of workers, in all of the European facilities. The German operations had long based the management of workplace industrial relations on the works council system, and German managers felt that challenging these arrangements would be counter-productive, not least in reducing workforce cooperation. Under pressure from an expatriate manager assigned to the German operations, the subsidiary left the metalworking sector collective agreement. This had little direct impact on pay and conditions, however, and most German managers saw the move as 'pointless symbolism'.

Union avoidance was not an option in France. Although very few CMM employees were union members, the subsidiary was legally obliged to negotiate with representatives of the five nationally representative unions. There was a long history of overtly conflictual industrial relations in the main French plant, but no path available to a non-union model even if this were deemed desirable at the local level. As one senior French union official reflected, 'The managers here need no encouragement to be against unions, but they cannot just hope that we will disappear. They can never satisfy (the corporate managers of CMM)'.

The UK managers perhaps came under the most serious challenge here. This was because corporate managers could point to a number of successful large non-union establishments, often American-owned. The UK subsidiary had in fact derecognised unions for clerical workers and junior managers during the 1980s, at the height of Thatcherism, but even then it had stopped short of challenging the manual workforce over union recognition. Although the union was not particularly active in the workplace, its high membership meant that under the current British industrial relations settlement, 'successful' derecognition would be highly unlikely. The feeling among UK managers tended to be that union relations were 'simply not a big issue' in the UK operations, and that it would be counter-productive to launch a frontal attack against a trade union which showed little militancy outside pay rounds, and had some value to the firm in dealing with discipline and related issues.

European managers were able largely to convince their American counterparts that strong challenges to the status quo with regard to industrial relations were either not possible or unwise. Like other large firms, though, where new workplaces have been established on greenfield sites these have often been non-union from the outset.

A bigger challenge, which caused much greater disquiet within the company, was the new performance management regime. Performance-related pay had long been a feature of the employment relationship for managerial workers in all the European countries – and, in somewhat different form, for all the company's employees in France – but this was essentially treated by most workers as an annual bonus, as there was relatively little variation between 'high' and 'low' performers. The new corporate management team, however, had been inspired by the 'General Electric' model of performance management. This uses a forced distribution: that is, each unit is asked to identify a given percentage of 'high' performers and a given percentage of 'low' performers. In CMM, the top ten per cent, as well as being financially rewarded, would be seen as candidates for promotion, but the bottom ten per cent would be seen as candidates for dismissal.

This caused problems in all the European operations. Although managers in all countries can 'find ways of getting rid of bad performers', formalising a system in which a given percentage were to be seen as candidates for dismissal was felt to be very unhelpful. As one British line manager argued, 'OK, I have twenty staff. How come two of them are automatically not up to the job, ready for the sack? This isn't football, I can't have people looking over their shoulder all the time. How are people supposed to think long term about anything?'.

Several methods were used by European managers to try to move away from this policy. Representations were made to corporate managers, both by individual subsidiary managers and through the European headquarters function. For one international meeting of the international human resource function, British managers recruited an academic consultant on the 'psychological contract' to try to persuade their American counterparts of the potential effects on motivation and performance of the threat of dismissal under forced distributions.

These challenges were unsuccessful. The corporate HR function were adamant that it was important for the firm to have one system for performance management, not one for every country in which the company operated. Using a centralised system was both cheaper, and allowed an easier identification of high potential candidates for entry into the international internal labour market of the firm. 'What I don't get', argued the international HR Director, 'is why you are all so concerned with poor performers. I'm interested in good performers'.

The system is therefore in operation worldwide, although how closely it is, or can be, followed in spirit is open to question. In Britain, for example, the typical practice, according to a senior HR manager, was to give poor performance rankings to those 'who were leaving anyway', either to the external labour market or to retirement. The system was also finessed by altering the definitions of 'units', to try to avoid situations in which one manager would have to choose 'poor performers' from among small groups.

In France, where forced ranking, often covering manual workers and usually working in a fairly informal way, is not unusual, managers used the new system to identify candidates for redundancy after a series of job cutbacks. This led to a successful legal challenge, as it is not legitimate in French law to select candidates for redundancy on the grounds of competence (as this conflates two potentially valid reasons for dismissal). Although major corporations falling foul of employment law is not uncommon in France, this nevertheless led to unwelcome publicity for the company within France. Outside this, however, the longer tradition of performance bonuses being allocated to a given percentage of workers meant that the system caused, on the whole, fewer problems in France.

In Germany, the subsidiary was able to argue that the need to work with the works council meant that the immediate threat of dismissal for a poor position on a forced distribution was not practical. Instead, poorer performers are placed into training and developmental measures. A more prominent problem in Germany was that the performance management system also specified the pay gaps that should exist between different groups on the forced ranking. By German standards, these were very large. This not only upset nationally derived ideas about equity within organisations; according to one manager, it also challenged ideas around collective performance within the German work ethic. The German subsidiary in fact has gradually moved away from the pay gaps indicated in the 'global' system on a unilateral basis.

In summary, HR policies in CMM have become more uniform internationally. This has posed problems in European subsidiaries, whose managers have sought to mitigate some 'undesirable' effects, and to highlight to corporate managers constraints on policy-setting in European countries in other areas.

Case questions

1 From CMM's point of view, what arguments can be made in favour of standardised policies regarding union relations and performance management across the European subsidiaries? Do these outweigh the disadvantages?
2 In what ways, if any, would you expect HR policies in a newly established greenfield site in the UK to be different from those of the rest of the UK subsidiary?
3 What would be the obstacles involved in creating a performance management system similar to the one outlined here in your own country?

Questions for further reflection

1 In what ways could an overseas company operating in Britain, France and Germany make use of the national differences between these countries' employment systems, rather than seeing them as a barrier to having common policies?

2 What would be the advantages and disadvantages for CMM if it decided to give more control over its subsidiary HRM policies to American expatriate managers, rather than domestic subsidiary managers?

Further reading

- Freeman, R. B. (2002) 'The US economic model at Y2K: Lodestar for advanced capitalism?' *NBER Working Paper*, No. 7757 (available at http://www.nber.org/).
In this article, Richard Freeman asks whether we ought to think of the world as following the logic of a 'single peak' economy or a 'multi-peak' economy. The answer helps clarify our understanding of debates on convergence/divergence of employment systems, as well as the influences of dominant economies.

- Katz, H. C., Lee, W. and Lee, J. (eds) (2004) *The New Structure of Labor Relations: Tripartism and Decentralisation*. Ithaca: Cornell University Press.
An excellent collection of readings on the changing nature of industrial relations and collective bargaining in a selection of countries, including the US, Germany, Japan and Italy. Each country chapter provides a detailed account of labour, management and government interactions and considers trends of coordination and decentralisation of collective bargaining.

- Esping-Andersen, G. (2002) *Why We Need a New Welfare State*: Oxford: OUP.
Lewis, J. and Surender, R. (eds) (2004) *Welfare State Change: a Third Way?* Oxford: OUP.
Both books provide the student with an overview of the diverse models of welfare state regimes in developed countries. Issues considered include the interaction of welfare regimes with labour market policy, changing conceptions of family and gender relations and differences in policy approaches towards inequality and social cohesion.

- Vaughan-Whitehead, D. (ed.) (2009) *The Minimum Wage Revisited in the Enlarged EU*. Geneva: International Labour Organisation.
Auer, P. and Cazes, S. (eds) (2003) *Employment Stability in an Age of Flexibility*. Geneva: International Labour Organisation.
For a critical understanding of diverse country models of labour market regulation, these edited collections provide useful detailed accounts of the diverse policies shaping minimum wages and employment protection. Each book also considers the labour market consequences of these features of regulation. Minimum wage regulation is shown to have diverse effects on job growth and wage inequality contingent upon its relative level and system of uprating. And the twin policies of employment protection and social protection are shown to have diverse effects on employment stability and perceptions of job security.

- Rubery, J. and Grimshaw, D. (2003) *The Organisation of Employment: an International Perspective.* Basingstoke: Palgrave. Chapter 5, 'Skilling the labour force'.

This chapter provides a state-of-the-art review of the diverse characteristics of country systems of schooling, vocational training and higher education. It introduces the student to models of 'internal labour markets' and 'occupational labour markets' to understand the key differences in country models. It reviews the main pressures for change on each country system of training and asks whether or not countries are equipped to sustain, or develop, a highly skilled workforce.

- Rosenzweig, P. M. and Nohria, N. (1994) 'Influences on HRM practices in multinational corporations', *Journal of International Business Studies*, 25 (2): 229–51.

One of the earliest tests of the host country effect on HRM practices in MNC subsidiaries, this study makes an important distinction between different types of HRM practices. Drawing on data of 249 US subsidiaries of multinationals from a range of countries, it explores the reasons why some HRM practices are more likely to be adapted to the local environment than others.

- Almond, P. and Ferner, A. (eds) (2006) *American Multinationals in Europe.* Oxford: OUP.

This edited collection draws together the findings of a 5-country research project designed to explore the HRM practices of US-owned MNC subsidiaries in Europe. It explores on the one hand the US approach to employment relations and HRM and, on the other hand, the influence of different host country environments on the diffusion of these practices. With evidence from detailed case studies of US MNCs operating in a mix of sectors (e.g., engineering, chemicals, IT services, logistics) the book assesses the impact of host countries on selected HRM practices, with separate chapters on collective representation, pay, diversity and careers.

- Fenton-O'Creevy, M., Gooderham, P. and Nordhaug, O. (2008) 'Human resource management in US subsidiaries in Europe and Australia: centralisation or autonomy?', *Journal of International Business Studies*, 39: 151–66.

The main conclusions of this article are summarised in our chapter. It deserves a detailed read because it makes a valuable contribution to the field of study by applying a well-known institutional typology of country employment systems to a test of diffusion of HRM practices among MNC subsidiaries. It offers particularly interesting evidence on the degree of adaptation of HRM practices in coordinated as opposed to liberal market host country environments and in unionised as opposed to non-unionised subsidiaries.

- Bjorkman, I. and Lervik, J. E. (2007) 'Transfering HRM practices within multinational companies', *Human Resource Management Journal*, 17 (4): 320–35.

This article sets out a useful conceptual approach for interpreting the degree to which a multinational company has transferred a particular HR policy to one of its subsidiary units. Three dimensions of transfer are proposed – implementation, internalisation and integration – and considered in the context of a broader framework of the social and organisational factors that shape the transfer process.

- Ferner, A., Quintanilla, J. and Varul, M.Z. (2001) 'Country-of-origin effects, host country effects and the management of HR in multinationals: German companies in Britain and Spain', *Journal of World Business*, 36(2): 107–28.

This paper presents valuable empirical evidence on the pressures facing German companies in Britain and Spain to adopt 'Anglo-Saxon' HR practices in their subsidiaries. Drawing on rich interview data (more than 90 interviews), the authors illuminate the subtle interplay between national employment systems (host and home countries) and adoption of international HRM practices. Processes by which managers adapt international practices to a changing German model differ by host country environment – emphasising both the importance of management choice and the factors driving change in national business and employment environments.

- Meardi, G. (2006) 'Multinationals' heaven? Uncovering and understanding worker responses to multinational companies in post-communist Central Europe', *International Journal of HRM*, 17 (8): 1366–78.

Central European countries are often said to be characterised by low labour costs and a relatively quiescent workforce, therefore offering a favourable environment for multinational company operations. This article critically examines this contention by drawing on empirical evidence from three countries – Hungary, Poland and Slovenia. It shows that while formal labour conflict is rare, a number of otherwise 'hidden' forms of worker resistance do impinge upon the management practices of multinational companies.

Internet resources

1 www.eiro.eurofound.eu.int: Good, up-to-date reviews of country systems of industrial relations, EU member states only.

2 www.ilo.org: Data on international developments in work and employment, with a focus on labour market policy and labour standards.

3 www.oecd.org: Follow the links for detailed reports on employment trends in OECD economies, as well as excellent harmonised data.

Self-assessment questions

employment protection
– Terminating

Indicative answers to these questions can be found on the companion website at www.sagepub.co.uk/harzing3e.

1 **Identify three types of legal regulation that shape the type of labour market in a host country environment and provide one example of country differences for each type.** 2 31-234

2 **What are the major pressures encouraging a convergence of country employment systems and what pieces of evidence suggest change has in practice been mixed in recent years?** 246

3 **Describe the employment characteristics associated with Hall and Soskice's two types of market capitalism.**

4 What factors in host country environments have been found to constrain the diffusion of PRP and individualised payment practices in MNC subsidiaries?

5 What features of a host country environment can facilitate an MNC's attempt to diffuse a 'high road' (that is, high skill, high value-added) model of work organisation?

References

Almond, P., Muller-Camen, M., Collings, D. G. and Quintanilla, J. (2006) 'Pay and performance', in P. Almond and A. Ferner (eds), *American Multinationals in Europe*. Oxford: OUP.

Anxo, D., Fagan, C., Cebrian, I. and Moreno, G. (2007) 'Patterns of labour market integration in Europe – a life course perspective on time policies', *Socio-Economic Review*, 5(2): 233–60.

Appelbaum, E. and Batt, R. (1994) *The New American Workplace*. Ithaca: ILR Press, Cornell University Press.

Auer, P. and Cazes, S. (eds) (2003) *Employment Stability in an Age of Flexibility*. Geneva: International Labour Office.

Baccaro, L. (2000) 'Centralised collective bargaining and the problem of "compliance": lessons from the Italian experience', *Industrial and Labour Relations Review*, 53(4): 579–601.

Beechler, S. and Yang, J.Z. (1993) 'The transfer of Japanese-style management to American subsidiaries: contingencies, constraints, and competence', *Journal of International Business Studies*, 25.

Bélanger, J., Giles, A. and Grenier, J-N. (2003) 'Patterns of corporate influence in the host country: a study of ABB in Canada', *International Journal of HRM*, 14 (3): 469–85.

Bennett, J. and Kaufman, B. (2007) *What Do Unions Do?: A Twenty-year Perspective*. Edison: Transaction Publishers.

Best, M. (1990) *The New Competition*. Cambridge: Harvard University Press.

Billet, S. and Smith, A. (2005) 'Enhancing enterprise expenditure on VET: policy goals and mechanisms', *Journal of Vocational Education and Training*, 57 (1): 5–23.

Bjorkman, I. and Lervik, J.E. (2007) 'Transfering HRM practices within multinational companies', *Human Resource Management Journal*, 17 (4): 320–35.

Bosch, G., Lehndorff, S. and Rubery, J. (2009) *European Employment Models in Flux: A Comparison of. Institutional Change in Nine European Countries*. Basingstoke: Palgrave.

Botero, J., Djankov, S., La Porta, R., Lopez-de-Silanes, F. and Shleifer, A. (2004) 'The regulation of labor', *Quarterly Journal of Economics*, 119: 1339–84.

Brown, W. (1993) 'The contribution of collective bargaining in Britain', *British Journal of Industrial Relations*, 31(2): 189–200.

Buchmueller, T. and Valletta, R. (1999) 'The effect of health insurance on married female labor supply', *The Journal of Human Resources*, 34(1): 42–70.

Bush, J. (2003) 'Outlook for Europe: the neoliberal stranglehold on growth', in A. Pettifor (ed.), *Real World Economic Outlook: the Legacy of Globalization – Debt and Deflation*. London: Palgrave.

Child, J. (2000) Theorizing about organizations cross-nationally. In R.B. Peterson (Ed.), *Advances in international comparative management* (Vol. 13). Stamford, CT: JAI Press, 2000, pp. 27-75.

Coen, D. (1997) 'The Evolution of Large Firm Political Action In The European Union' *Journal of European Public Policy* 4(1):91–108.

Colling, T., Gunnigle, P., Quintanilla, J. and Tempel, A. (2006) 'Collective representation and participation', in P. Almond and A. Ferner (eds), *American Multinationals in Europe*. Oxford: OUP.

Deakin, S. (2009) 'Legal origin, juridical form and industrialization in historical perspective: the case of the employment contract and the joint-stock company', *Socio-Economic Review*, 7(1): 35–65.

Deakin, S. and Wilkinson, F. (2005) *The Law of the Labour Market*. Oxford: OUP.

Edwards, T. and Kuruvilla, S. (2005). International HRM: National Business Systems, Organisational Politics and the International Division of Labour in Global Value Chains, *Internatianal Journal of Human Resource Management*, 16 (1): 1–21.

Edwards, T., Rees, C. and Coller, X. (1999) 'Structure, politics and the diffusion of employment practices in multinationals', *European Journal of Industrial Relations*, 5(3): 286–306.

Edwards, T., Coller, X., Ortiz, L., Rees, C. and Wortmann, M. (2006) 'National industrial relations systems and cross-border restructuring: evidence from a merger in the pharmaceuticals sector', *European Journal of Industrial Relations*, 12 (1): 69–87.

Elger, T and Smith, C. (2005) *Assembling Work: Remaking Factory Regimes in Japanese Multinationals in Britain* Oxford: Oxford University Press

Esping-Andersen, G. (1990) *The Three Worlds of Welfare Capitalism*. Princeton: Princeton University Press.

Fenton-O'Creevy, M., Gooderham, P. and Nordhaug, O. (2008) 'Human resource management in US subsidiaries in Europe and Australia: centralisation or autonomy?', *Journal of International Business Studies*, 39: 151–66.

Ferner, A. and Edwards, P. (1995) 'Power and the diffusion of organisational change within multinational companies', *European Journal of Industrial Relations*, 1 (2): 229–57.

Ferner, A. and Tempel, A. (2006) 'Multinationals and national business systems: a 'power and institutions' perspective', in P. Almond and A. Ferner (eds), *American Multinationals in Europe*. Oxford: OUP.

Ferner, A., Morley, M., Muller-Camen, M. and Susaeta, L. (2006) 'Workforce diversity policies', in P. Almond and A. Ferner (eds.).

Ferner, A., Quintanilla, J. and Varul, M.Z. (2001) 'Country-of-origin effects, host country effects and the management of HR in multinationals: German companies in Britain and Spain', *Journal of World Business*, 36(1): 107–28.

Freeman, R.B. (2002) 'The US economic model at Y2K: Lodestar for advanced capitalism?', NBER Working Paper, and reprinted in D. Coates (ed.), *Models of Capitalism*. Cheltenham: Edward Elgar.

Geppert, M. and Matten, D. (2006) 'Institutional influences on manufacturing organisation in multinational corporations: The 'cherrypicking' approach', *Organisation Studies*, 27(4): 491–515.

Geppert, M. and Williams, K. (2006) 'Global, national and local practices in multinational corporations: towards a sociopolitical framework', *International Journal of HRM*, 17(1): 49–69.

Geppert, M., Matten, D. and Walgenbach, P. (2006) 'Transnational building and the multinational corporations: An emerging field of research', *Human Relations*, 59(11): 1451–65.

Glyn, A. (2006) *Capitalism Unleashed: Finance, Globalization and Welfare*. Oxford: OUP.

Gooderham, P., Nordhaug, O. and Ringdal, K. (2006) 'National embeddedness and calculative human resource management in US subsidiaries in Europe and Australia', *Human Relations*, 59(11): 1491–513.

Grønhaug, K. and Nordhaug, O. (1992) 'International human resource management: an environmental perspective', *International Journal of Human Resource Management*, 3: 1–14.

Haipeter, T. (2002) 'Banking and finance in France and Germany, new regulations of work and working time: A challenge for the trade unions? *Transfer*, 3 (2): 493-503.

Hall, P. A. and Gingerich, D. W. (2004) 'Varieties of Capitalism and Institutional Complementarities in the Macroeconomy: An Empirical Analysis', Discussion Paper 04/5, Cologne, Germany, Max Planck Institute for the Study of Societies. Available at *www.mpi-fg-koeln.mpg.de*

Hall, P. and Soskice, D. (eds) (2001) *Varieties of Capitalism: the Institutional Foundations of Comparative Advantage*. Oxford: OUP.

Harzing, A-W. (2000) 'An empirical analysis and extension of the Bartlett and Ghoshal typology of multinational companies', *Journal of International Business Studies*, 31 (1): 101–20.

Hofstede, G. (1980) *Culture's Consequences: International Differences in Work-related Values*. Beverly Hills, CA: Sage.

Hofstede, G. (2001) *Culture's Consequences*. Thousand Oaks, CA: Sage.

Jackson, T. (2001) 'Cultural values and management ethics: a 10-nation study', *Human Relations*, 54(10): 1267–302.

Katz, H. (2004) 'Introduction: the changing nature of labour, management and government interactions', in H. C. Katz, W. Lee and J. Lee (eds), *The New Structure of Labour Relations: Tripartism and Decentralization*, Ithaca NY: Cornell University Press.

Katz, H. C., Lee, W. and Lee, J. (eds) (2004) *The New Structure of Labor Relations: Tripartism and Decentralization*. Ithaca, NY: Cornell University Press.

Kostova, T. and Roth, K. (2002) 'Adoption of an organizational practice by subsidiaries of multinational corporations: institutional and relational effects', *Academy of Management Journal*, 45 (1): 215–33.

Kostova, T. and Zaheer, S. (1999) 'Organisational legitimacy under conditions of complexity: The case of the multinational enterprise', *Academy of Management Review*, 24 (1): 64–81.

Lam, A. (1997) 'Embedded Firms, Embedded Knowledge: Problems of Collaboration and Knowledge Transfer in Global Cooperative Ventures' *Organizatian Studies* 18 (6) : 973-996.

Lee, G. and Smith, C. (1992) *Engineers and Management: International Comparisons*. London: Taylor & Francis.

Low Pay Commission (2008) *National Minimum Wage: Low Pay Commission Report 2008* CM 7333.

MacDuffie, J.P. (1995) 'International trends in work organisation in the auto industry: national-level versus company-level perspectives' in K. Wever and L. Turner (eds), *The Comparative Political Economy of Industrial Relations*. Ithaca: Cornell University Press.

Madsen, P. K. (2003) 'Flexicurity through labour market policies and institutions in Denmark', in P. Auer and S. Cazes (eds), *Employment Stability in an Age of Flexibility*. Geneva: International Labour Office.

Marsden, D. (1999) *A Theory of Employment Systems*. Oxford: Oxford University Press.

Martin, G. and Beaumont, P. (1999) 'Co-ordination and control of human resource management in multinational firms: the case of CASHCO', *International Journal of HRM*, 10 (1): 21–42.

McSweeney, B. (2002) 'Hofstede's model of national cultural differences and their consequences: a triumph of faith – a failure of analysis', *Human Relations*, 55 (1): 89–118.

Meardi, G. (2006) 'Multinationals' heaven? Uncovering and understanding worker responses to multinational companies in post-communist Central Europe', *International Journal of HRM*, 17 (8): 1366–78.

Mishel, L., Bernstein, J. and Allegretto, S. (2005) *The State of Working America 2004/05*. Ithaca, NY: Economic Policy Institute and Cornell University Press.

Morgan, G. and Kristensen, G. H. (2006) 'The contested space of multinationals: Varieties of institutionalism, varieties of capitalism', *Human Relations*, 59 (11): 1467–90.

Moss, P. and Korintus, M. (2008) *International Review of Leave Policies and Related Research 2008*. Employment Relations Research Series No. 100. London: Department for Business, Enterprise and Regulatory Reform.

Mückenberger, U. (2003) 'German industrial relations in a period of transition', in B. Burchell, S. Deakin, J. Michie and J. Rubery (eds), *Systems of Production: Markets, Organisations and Performance*. London: Routledge.

Muller, M. (1998) 'Human resource and industrial relations practices of UK and US multinationals in Germany', *International Journal of HRM*, 9(4): 732–49.

Nichols, T. and Cam, S. (2005) *Labour in a Global World: Case Studies from the Shite Goods Industry in Africa, South America, East Asia and Europe*. London: Palgrave.

OECD (2004) *Employment Outlook*. Paris: OECD.

OECD (2008) *Educatian at a Glance*. Paris: OECD

Pulignano, V. (2006) 'The diffusion of employment practices of US-based multinationals in Europe: a case study comparison of British- and Italian-based subsidiaries between two sectors', *British Journal of Industrial Relations*, 44 (3): 497–518.

Ray, R. and Schmitt, J. (2007) 'No vacation nation USA – a comparison of leave and holiday in OECD countries', *European Economic and Employment Policy* Brief No. 3 – 2007 ETUI-REHS Brussels.

Reich, R. (1992) *The Work of Nations: Preparing Ourselves for 21st Century Capitalism*. New York: Knopf Doubleday.

Ronen, S. and Shenkar, O. (1985) 'Clustering countries on attitudinal dimensions: a review and synthesis', *Academy of Management Review*, 10: 435–54.

Rosenzweig, P.M. and Nohria, N. (1994) 'Influences on HRM practices in multinational corporations', *Journal of International Business Studies*, 25 (2): 229–51.

Royle, T. (1998) 'Avoidance strategies and the German system of co-determination', *International Journal of HRM*, 9 (6): 1026–47.

Rubery, J. and Grimshaw, D. (2003) *The Organisation of Employment: An International Perspective*. Basingstoke: Palgrave.

Schmidt, V. (2002) *The Futures of European Capitalism*. Oxford: OUP.

Schwartz, S.H. (1992) 'Universals in the content and structure of values: theoretical advances and empirical tests in 20 countries', *Advances in Experimental Social Psychology*, 25: 1–65.

Sorge, A. (2004) 'Cross-national differences in human resources and organisation', in A. Harzing, and J. Van Ruysseveldt, (eds), *International Human Resource Management*. London: Sage.

Steedman, H., Wagner, K. Foreman, J. (2003) The impact on firms of ICT skill-supply strategies: an Anglo-German comparison. Discussion Paper. Centre for Economic Performance, London School of Economics and Political Science, London, UK.

Van Oorschot, W. (2004) 'Flexible work and flexicurity policies in the Netherlands: trends and experiences', *Transfer*, 10 (2): 208–225.

Van Oudenhoven, J.P. (2001) 'Do organisations reflect national cultures? A ten nation study', *International Journal of Intercultural Relations*, 25: 89–107.

Visser, J. (2006) 'Union membership statistics in 24 countries', *Monthly Labor Review*, January: 38–49.

Whitley, R. (1999) Divergent Capitalisms: *The Social Structuring and Change of Business Systems*. Oxford: OUP.

Woywode, M. (2002) 'Global management concepts and local adaptations: working groups in the French and German car manufacturing industry', *Organisation Studies*, 23 (4): 497–524.

8

The Transfer of Employment Practices Across Borders in Multinational Companies

Tony Edwards

Contents

Learning Objectives

After reading this chapter you will be able to

- Appreciate how employment practices are embedded in distinctive national contexts

- Understand the different theoretical perspectives concerning why multinationals transfer practices across borders

- Evaluate the competing influences on the inclination and ability of multinationals to engage in transfer

- Explore the process of transfer in practice through studying case studies

Chapter Outline

This chapter addresses the issue of how multinational companies transfer expertise that was developed in one country to their international operations. It explores why multinationals seek to do this and develops a framework of four key influences that can help to analyse transfer practices.

1 Introduction

[handwritten margin note: Transfer of practices — improves efficiency — make host employees feel uncomfortable]

One of the key distinguishing features of multinational companies (MNCs) is that they have the capacity to implement expertise in their operations in one country that was developed in another. One element of this is the transfer of employment practices across borders. This capacity can be seen as a potential source of higher efficiency in MNCs compared with firms based solely at the national level. However, many of those who work for MNCs, including some managers, may see the transfer of practices as a challenge since the process can cause a shift away from practices that have become accepted in the country. Employee representatives, in particular, might see their interests as being threatened and attempt to block the introduction of practices that originated from elsewhere. Thus the process of transfer can be contested, even subverted in some cases, and may also create fraught relations between different organisational groups.

The problematic nature of transfer of employment practices arises in part from the way in which they are 'embedded' in distinctive national contexts. Employment practices, like any other social custom, are strongly influenced by the context in which they operate. The political system and the dominant political traditions within it shape several key aspects of the employment relation, notably the strength of organised labour and the nature of employment regulations (see Chapter 17). The legal system itself partly the product of the political system, not only constrains the range of courses open to management in devising procedures in areas such as employee representation, but also plays a part in conditioning the expectations of organisational actors. Related to this, the nature of key institutions in the labour market also limit the options available to management in employment relations and further contributes towards the creation of a set of norms and values. The existence of a set of values concerning work and organisations – often referred to as culture – is the most commonly cited source of national distinctiveness in employment relations (e.g. Tayeb, 1996). The dominant values in societies emerge from specific political, legal and institutional contexts and these contexts and values are central to the character of the employment relationship (see Chapter 7). Since context and the values differ markedly from country to country, transferring practices across diverse social systems is bound to be complicated.

In this chapter we tackle several of the key aspects of the transfer of employment practices within MNCs. An initial question is that given that such practices are embedded in particular national contexts, why do many MNCs seek to transfer practices to quite different national contexts? Three broad explanations of MNCs' motives to transfer employment practice are reviewed and the strengths and weaknesses of each are assessed. Identification of the weaknesses implies the need for a more integrated approach which can explain a number of aspects of the transfer of employment practices, such as the likely geographical origins of the practices that are transferred, how we can explain variations between MNCs in the extent of transfer, and the likely nature of the relations between different groups within MNCs in the transfer process. To this end, the fourth approach elaborated here consists of an integrative framework of four key influences. The chapter ends by examining the consequences of the transfer of practices for national systems, addressing in particular whether it contributes to the convergence of these systems.

2 Why transfer practices?

The complications involved in the transfer of employment practices raises a key management question: why do many senior managers seek to engage in such transfer at all? Why do they not simply take a highly decentralised approach, allowing actors in the various countries in which the firm has subsidiaries to determine the type of employment practices that are compatible with the particular national context? Some do, of course, seeing the pressures of multi-culturalism (Ghoshal and Bartlett, 1998) as significant enough to warrant a hands-off approach to employment practice from senior management. This nationally responsive style was termed 'polycentric' by Perlmutter (1969) more than 30 years ago. Perlmutter (1969: 13) argued that the polycentric style recognises that 'since people are different in each country, standards for performance, incentives and training methods must be different'. Indeed, some writers have argued that these pressures to adapt, often referred to as 'host country effects', are significant and arise from the necessity of going with the grain of the rules and norms in the various host countries in which the firm operates. Over-riding local norms entails significant costs, even for large internationalised firms. These costs can be tangible in the form of penalties for contravening laws and regulations, but more commonly they are intangible in the form of losing the goodwill of local actors, for example, a widely cited survey study (Rosenzweig and Nohria, 1994) on foreign-owned affiliates in the US, found that HR practices in these workplaces 'tend to resemble local practices' (1994: 248) in the US and that 'adherence to local practices is the dominant influence' (1994: 250). This is also in evidence in Gamble's (2003) study of a British retail firm in China in which he argued that local institutions and cultural features of the host environment offered a better explanation of the nature of employment practices than did a focus on the country of origin. A further example is Lunnan et al.'s (2005) study of a Norwegian MNC in which they revealed the range of ways in which local factors inform the operation of a global policy.

There are three broad categories of explanation – *market, cultural and political* – that have been used to explain the attractiveness of transfer (Edwards et al., 2007). The first term, the 'market-based' approach, sees the transfer of employment practices as a potential source of enhanced efficiency. For many writers on HRM in MNCs, the strength of competition in the global product markets that multinationals often inhabit means that a firm is missing an opportunity to enhance its own efficiency if it does not engage in the sharing of 'best practice'. One particularly influential book about the multinational company that emphasises the power of market forces is Ghoshal and Bartlett's (1998) *Managing Across Borders*. In this work, the authors argue that the mature stage of evolution for a firm which spans many different countries is the 'transnational' form, which is based on an 'integrated network' of plants sharing expertise and knowledge with each other. The transfer of employment practices is a central part of such a firm. The authors go so far as to claim that 'in the future, a company's ability to develop a transnational organisational capability will be the key factor that separates the winners from the mere survivors in the international competitive environment' (1998: 299). Some models of IHRM exhibit a strong element conceptualising how MNCs respond to market pressures. For example, a key element of the 'resource-based' model of IHRM developed by Taylor et al. (1996) is the idea of 'organisational competencies' and how MNCs can enhance their competitive position by transferring these competencies across their operations. Some empirical studies of MNCs also exhibit assumptions based on the market-based approach. Schmitt and Sadowski's (2003) study of MNCs in Germany, for instance, emphasised the influence of commercial imperatives on transfer arguing that a 'rationalistic cost-minimisation' approach is well equipped to explain the transfer of practices across borders.

The contribution of this approach stems from the recognition of the potential advantages that can arise from transferring employment practices, and especially its benefits for senior management, owners and shareholders. However, the market-based approach risks downplaying the contested nature of transfer. The balance between adopting policies that are both globally integrated and locally sensitive tends to be portrayed as a technical matter, on which senior managers simply need to make a reasoned decision. Where some recognition is given to the possibility that there will be differences of view on the desirability of transferring practices, as in Ghoshal and Bartlett's (1998) work, senior managers are seen as having the ability to resolve any problems through communication, persuasion and creating an appropriate 'management mentality'. However, as a range of studies of MNCs has revealed, the process of transfer across borders is an intensely political process, in which a number of organisational actors have some influence. Belanger et al.'s (1999) study of ABB, a company cited by Ghoshal and Bartlett themselves as a 'classic transnational organisation', emphasises the political nature of transfer. Belanger and his colleagues argued that Ghoshal and Bartlett's account of ABB downplays the tensions between groups that are a key feature of organisational life in MNCs, and demonstrated in their research that international coordination is strongly contested within the firm. A further illustration of the potential for conflict is evident in Kristensen and Zeitlin's (2005) longitudinal study of the British multinational APV in which they likened the firm to a 'battleground' between different factions.

cultural approach

The cultural approach is the second form of explanation for why MNCs transfer practices across their sites in different countries. Many argue that the transfer of practices is not so much a process governed by the forces of competition as one shaped by the legacy of national and corporate cultures. That is, the incentives that MNCs have to develop a global approach must be balanced against the need to be sensitive to local conditions. This is evident in some of the research concerned with the transfer of Japanese employment practices in MNCs from Japan as they expanded into Europe and North America in the 1980s and 1990s. Abo (1994), for example, saw the dilemma facing senior managers in Japanese firms concerning the management of employment relations in their foreign subsidiaries as essentially a trade-off between the competitive pressure to utilise those practices that formed a part of successful production at home on the one hand, and the need to adapt to the exigencies of local conditions on the other.

Writers adopting the cultural approach commonly draw on Hofstede's (2001) much cited work, originally published in 1980 with updated versions, in which he distinguished a number of dimensions along which national cultures differ. The culturalist approach raises two important points concerning the transfer of practices. First, it provides an explanation, albeit partial, for why MNCs must adapt their desired practices to local conditions rather than implement common practices across their operations. Hofstede's own study of IBM showed that even in a company with a strong company culture, there were marked variations in employee values at the local level. Second, an extension of this idea is that national cultures influence MNCs' behaviour by encouraging them to take aspects of national culture with them when they go abroad. In other words, their corporate culture is informed by the national culture in the original country. Thus some researchers have sought to explain the transfer of home country practices to foreign subsidiaries through this cultural lens (e.g. Ngo et al., 1998).

The value of this approach is in recognising that transfer is more than just a question of competition and rationality. Rather, national cultures differ and their distinguishing characteristics endure. This argument though has a number of problems. The key shortcoming arises from heavy reliance on the small number of available typologies in the literature on culture – primarily Hofstede's but also Trompenaars and Hampden-Turner (1994) – means these studies are open to the same criticisms as the original works themselves. In particular, these typologies tend to fail to locate cultural values in a convincing social context. As noted above, dominant values and attitudes in a society emerge in a specific political, legal and institutional environment, yet the culturalist approach fails to acknowledge the full force of these contextual and institutional influences. Moreover, while the culturalist approach says something about how tensions can arise during the process of transfer, it says little about how political activity is played out within organisations and this is worthy of consideration in its own right.

The third approach, which can be termed the 'political' approach, is one that looks at the way that actors in organisations can be willing to engage in the process of transfer as a means of obtaining legitimacy and to advance their own interests. A range of actors can seek to protect or advance their own positions by initiating or engaging in the transfer of practices. For example, those at the HQ may look to raise their status within the organisation by portraying themselves as key agents in controlling the transfer of practices. For those in senior positions in firms producing a component or providing a service to other firms, ensuring that their operational units are sharing practices with one another may also assist senior managers in their quest to obtain legitimacy – and consequently orders – from potential customers since creating an image of a networked 'transnational' is likely to be viewed favourably by potential customers. Those in key managerial positions in the subsidiaries may be keen to engage in sharing practices with their counterparts in order to portray themselves as key contributors to the network. Acting as 'good corporate citizens' in this way may be a way of advancing an individual's claims for promotion or for a pay rise (Edwards, 1998). Others who work in the subsidiaries of MNCs, particularly employees and their representatives may be willing to go along with transferring practices if they fear that failing to cooperate will result in their unit being less likely to receive future investment from the HQ. In contrast, as we noted at the outset, some actors may seek to block diffusion if they perceive it as challenging their interests (see Broad, 1994, for a case study of a Japanese transplant in the UK). Hence, diffusion is a contested and political process.

A key contribution of this approach is to recognise that the motivation that organisational actors have to engage in the transfer of practices is more than just a rational assessment of the potential gains to the organisation as a whole. However, the focus on the micro-politics of the organisation on its own does not tell us much about the wider 'national business systems' which influence MNCs and, consequently, is not particularly revealing in generating an understanding of where the imperative to transfer practices comes from, nor does it tell us much about constraints on transfer that are external to the firm.

These three approaches each make a contribution to understanding the transfer of practices across borders, but on their own each of these offers only a partial understanding. What is required is an integrated approach which does three things: first, it should recognise the competitive pressures on firms in international markets and the commercial interests in transferring practices (the market-based approach); second, it should analyse the influence of contexts and institutions as well as cultures in shaping the behaviour of MNCs (an amended version of the cultural approach); and, third, it should examine the role of organisational actors in initiating, engaging in, or obstructing, the transfer of practices (the political approach). This integrated approach, which is based on four sets of influences, is explained in the next section.

3 The four influences framework

The framework outlined here consists of four key influences – *country of origin, dominance, international integration and host country* – on the nature and form of the transfer of practices across borders. The influences arise from the combination of, first, the differences between national business systems and, second, the growing internationalisation of economic activity. In some cases the impact of the particular influences is contrary to those of others, creating a tension; in others, however, the impact is for one influence to reinforce another. Each of the four influences is now considered in turn.

Country of origin effect

The first influence is an enduring 'country of origin' effect in MNCs. This is where the country from which the multinational originates creates a distinctive national effect on management style in general and on the nature of employment practice in particular. A range of sources indicates that even the largest MNCs retain strong roots in their home country. Ruigrok and van Tulder (1995: 168), for instance, examined the geographical distribution of the operations of the biggest 100 MNCs in the world (ranked by foreign assets) and concluded that 'not one of these can be dubbed truly global, footloose or borderless'. Analysis of data from the UN's World Investment Report (2009) suggests that there have been some changes in this respect since Ruigrok and van Tulder's study was published but that the links with the home country remain strong. The Transnationality Index, which condenses the ratios of foreign assets to total assets, foreign sales to total sales and foreign employment to total employment into one ratio, shows that on average close to 40 per cent of the operations of the largest 100 MNCs are located in the home base. While there are some MNCs which have a high degree of global spread – mainly those originally based in small countries such as Nestlé and those formed through a string of mergers and acquisitions such as Vodafone – there are also many of the largest MNCs that have well over half of their operations in their home country. This is true for some of the largest firms by employment, such as Wal-Mart and Hitachi.

The influence of the home country over a multinational stems not just from the concentration of assets, sales and employment but also from other ways in which MNCs are 'embedded' in the country of origin. One such source of a country of origin effect is the dominance of home country nationals in senior managerial positions. The CEO of the vast majority of MNCs is a citizen of the original country of the firm, while the management boards are disproportionately filled by home country nationals. The significance of the effect of country of origin lies in the way that the managerial traditions of the country of origin shape the nature of key decisions. Another source of the country of origin effect relates to the way that firms are financed and governed. We know that financial systems differ markedly and that MNCs retain close links with banks, stock markets and other financial institutions at home (Doremus et al., 1998). For example, the fluid and arms-length relationship between shareholders and management in Britain and the USA contrasts with the stable and close relationship between the two groups in Germany (O'Sullivan, 2000). The consequence of this is the differing pressures on firms that the divergent financial systems create are carried over to the international level in MNCs. A further source of the country of origin effect is the concentration of key activities in the home base. In particular, R&D activities tend to be very home country focused and since national innovation systems differ this can lead to differences by nationality in the nature of innovations found in MNCs.

There is considerable evidence of the way in which the 'institutional configurations' (Hall and Soskice, 2001) in the country of origin of MNCs influence the style the firm adopts in managing its international workforce. For instance, the primacy of the rights of shareholders in the financial system in the USA and the hostility of management to trade unions have created among American MNCs a clear orientation at the international level towards shareholder interests and a related hostility to unions (Almond and Ferner, 2006). In contrast, other evidence testifies to the link between the way that the German system of corporate governance accords rights to a range of 'stakeholders' and facilitates a more consultative management style and pragmatic approach to dealing with unions in German MNCs (Ferner and Varul, 1999). Crucially, the influence of the country of origin also is revealed in the preferences of MNCs of different nationalities for particular practices. Many Japanese MNCs in the 1980s and

1990s, for example, made strenuous attempts to transfer the practices associated with 'lean production', such as team-working, functional flexibility and 'single status' (e.g. Oliver and Wilkinson, 1992). American MNCs, on the other hand, appear to have transferred 'human resource management' practices, such as performance-related pay and forms of direct communication, to their foreign subsidiaries (Muller, 1998). In the conclusion to a major survey of employment practice in Britain, Edwards et al. noted the 'persistent influence of nationality' and argued that the data confirm 'that national ways of doing things continue to inform the behaviour of multinationals in the world economy' (2007:100).

In terms of relations between different groups of organisational actors, the logic of the strength of the country of origin effect is that it is actors in the home country that are likely to be the key players in the transfer of practices. Thus transfer is characterised by a strong authority flow from the centre to the subsidiaries in different countries. Actors in the subsidiaries may adopt a variety of approaches in responding to this central influence: some may be very willing to learn from the parent company and implement the practices enthusiastically; others may question the appropriateness of 'foreign' practices that are being transferred but grudgingly accept that they should go along with the demands of the HQ; while others may seek to resist the transfer altogether or insist on these practices being adapted. Thus the focus on the role of the country of origin is also revealing in understanding the political nature of transfer.

The nature of the country of origin effect evolves over time. It tends to reduce in significance as a firm engages in international expansion, such as in the case of a cross-border merger which significantly extends the global reach of a firm. Moreover, many actors in MNCs, including some at the HQ, will not see a strong influence from the home country as necessarily advantageous for the firm and, consequently, may look outside the country of origin for 'best practice'. In other words, MNCs do not possess a fixed and rigid national identity which imposes a straightjacket on organisational actors; rather, national origin shapes and constrains the actions of these actors but leaves scope for them to draw on practices occurring in other countries.

Dominance effects

Given that actors have some scope to observe and implement practices from countries other than the country of origin, what influences how they go about this process? A key factor in this respect is their perceptions of the strengths and weaknesses of economic performance across countries. Strong performance in one country gives rise to interest from firms in other countries in 'borrowing' elements of that business system. Smith and Meiskins (1995: 255–6) argue that the hierarchy of economies within the international system gives rise to 'dominance effects'; at any one time, they argue, countries 'in dominant positions have frequently evolved methods of organising production or the division of labour which have invited emulation and interest'. In terms of the impact on the transfer of employment practices, the logic of the dominance effects argument is that such transfer is not solely created by the legacy and force of institutions, but is also shaped by competitive pressures at the international level.

For much of the post-war period it was the American economy which appeared to be the most influential. In a context of US political hegemony and industry in the USA emerging from the war relatively unscathed compared with its counterparts elsewhere, the American business system exerted a significant, albeit contested, influence over the forms of restructuring in Europe and Japan (Djelic, 1998). During the 1980s and early 1990s, however, the Japanese economy was widely perceived to be the dominant power, and writers and practitioners alike referred to the Japanese model in general, and lean production in particular, as providing the best solutions to common organisational problems. Towards the end of the twentieth century and into the twenty-first, however, the prolonged stagnation in Japan and the resurgence of the US economy have arguably led to a renewal of the influence of the American business system.

In its simplest form the concept of dominance is open to a number of lines of criticism. First, it rests on an assumption that there exist marked differences in rates of economic growth between the major developed economies; in fact, these differences are not as great as is often assumed. For instance, while the 1970s and 1980s was seen as a period of economic decline by many in the US, the growth rate of the American economy was actually higher than that in Germany, Sweden and the UK. Only compared with the Japanese economy was there a marked difference and even this was less significant than is often supposed (see, for example, Hall and Soskice, 2001). Second, even where there are significant differences in economic performance between countries, only a part of this can be explained by divergences in forms of economic organisation. Some of the explanation lies in the process of 'convergence and catch-up'. Very rapid economic growth in an economy is often due in large part to recovery from an adverse shock or the more intensive use of existing resources rather than the result of key features of the national business system. It is widely accepted that this factor explains part of the rapid rates of economic growth found in the so-called 'Asian Tiger' economies prior to 1997. Third, the notion of dominance might imply that a national business system is characterised by a homogeneous set of structures and practices that operate across firms, and that companies in other countries can identify and seek to emulate them. This is, of course, not the case; all national business systems are characterised by a degree of intra-national variety.

Despite these criticisms, the concept of dominance retains some utility. When thought of as an approximate measure of management ideology and way of explaining how the perceptions of actors create a dynamic for change and diffusion, it adds to the understanding of the process of transfer. Indeed, Pudelko and Harzing (2007) demonstrate that dominance effects are of great significance for how MNCs manage their international workforces. As they put it, they came to 'the surprising conclusion that a function (HR) generally considered to be the most local of business functions shows very strong signs of converging to a dominant model, regardless of the home or host countries involved' (2007: 536).

Actors within MNCs can perceive the diversity of employment practices that they experience across national systems as an opportunity for advancing the competitive position either of the firm as a whole in relation to other firms, or of the unit in which they work in relation to other units within the firm. There are traces here of the rational approach, moreover actors can utilise the notion of dominance to advance their own positions within a firm. For instance, managers in the American operations of European MNCs may use their knowledge and familiarity with the current dominant business system to develop an international role within the firm. In other words, dominance effects also shape the politics of transfer.

Part of the idea of 'dominance effects' is that the flow of practices can arise from different places and it is not solely from the home country to the firm's operations in other countries. As we saw in the previous sub-section, there certainly is evidence of the country of origin effect leading to transfer occurring in this direction, and we might expect this to be most common in MNCs from a dominant country since the two effects reinforce one another. However, in the case of MNCs from a developing economy, or a developed economy which has been performing poorly, dominance effects will challenge the country of origin effect. The possible result is that practices that are transferred across a multinational may originate in the foreign subsidiaries. Indeed, there is a growing body of evidence that such 'reverse' transfer does occur and that it is shaped by the notion of dominance (Edwards and Ferner, 2004). The case study of Swedco (see pp. 283–285) illustrates this process, and demonstrates the dynamic and competing influence of the country of origin effect and dominance effects.

International integration

The third element to the framework concerns the extent to which MNCs are internationally integrated, defined as the generation of inter-unit linkages across borders. A number of recent developments have created scope for MNCs to build stronger linkages between their international operations. In relation to product markets, differences in consumer tastes appear to have narrowed – a process in which the advertising and marketing strategies of MNCs themselves have contributed – while there has simultaneously been a trend toward deregulation of many markets, making it easier for firms to realise synergistic linkages between their subsidiaries.

Coupled with these changes improvements in communications and transportation have facilitated international coordination and many MNCs have strengthened inter-unit linkages by developing new structures for their international operations. Typically, they have moved away from country-based structures towards organising themselves around global divisions or regional blocks, so that comparable operations are linked together. The survey of MNCs in Britain by Edwards et al. (2007) found that 'relatively few are characterised by a straightforward hierarchical relationship between HQ and operating units. Instead, in most MNCs there are intermediate levels within complex, multi-layered corporate structures' (2007: vi). Indeed, amongst those MNCs that had multiple dimensions to how they were organised, only 4 per cent identified the 'national subsidiary' as the most important aspect of the structure. For example, IBM's operations are not structured along the lines of the various countries in which the firm operates, such as IBM China or IBM Canada; rather they are organised into both global divisions, such as software and services, and regional blocks, such as Europe, Middle East and Africa (EMEA) and North America.

The replacement of country-based structures with these types of international management structures appears to have been most developed within Europe. The process of European integration has created a product market which is largely free from formal barriers to trade, while aspects of the regulation of other issues, such as competition, industrial and social policies, have also become harmonised. Perhaps most significantly, the single currency has increased the transparency of costs and prices across Europe and created a large Euro capital market. Thus Marginson (2000: 11) has argued that Europe is 'an economic, political and regulatory space whose character and dynamic is distinctive when set against wider, global, developments or those in the other two "triad" regions'. Consequently, many MNCs have created an influential European aspect to the structure, with the potential to develop Europe-wide policies in HRM.

The developments described above in relation to the markets are uneven, however, and many sectors remain localised in that they are strongly influenced by nationally distinctive tastes or regulations. Commonly, these sectors are ones in which MNCs are generally absent, such as the provision of personal care and hairdressing. In some other sectors that are still influenced by national tastes or regulations, MNCs are present but tend to adopt management structures based on the countries in which they operate, and there are few inter-linkages between their operations. Examples are electricity provision, auditing and retail banking. In contrast, the scope for achieving a high degree of international integration are much stronger in sectors like textiles, automotive, IT services and investment banking, where units are strongly integrated with their counterparts in other countries.

This integration can take two forms, each of which has important implications for employment relations. International integration can take the form of the outsourcing of operations across countries, with those in one country providing components or services to those in another. Examples of this outsourcing and its integration are the producers of branded sports and fashion wear which subcontract production to nominally independent, but in fact closely controlled, firms mainly in south-east Asia. These arrangements, through which production is both internationalised and externalised, are often referred to as 'global value chains' (Gereffi et al., 2005).

A different form of integration is for MNCs to keep production or service provision in-house but to use segmentation in which the roles of operations in different countries are quite distinct from one another. For instance, Wilkinson et al. (2001) showed how

Japanese electronics manufacturers use segmentation as a production strategy within Asia, retaining high value-added functions such as design and testing in Japan and locating low value-added functions such as assembly in countries such as Malaysia. In this scenario, the various units across the world are performing quite distinct functions, leading to variations in the type of HRM practices that the firm deploys and there is little incentive for such firms to transfer practices across their sites.

International integration can also take the form of the standardisation of operations, with the units in different countries carrying out very similar activities. Examples of sectors in which this is the case are heavy engineering, pharmaceuticals production, some food manufacturing, auditing and fast-food, which have developed increasingly standardised products and, relatedly, similar production or service provision techniques but where there are technical or market factors that prevent the firms from servicing standard markets through exporting. Given that the operations in different countries have important similarities, there is considerable scope for such firms to transfer practices across borders (Edwards and Zhang, 2008).

In sum, the pressures to achieve international integration reflect the nature of competition and structure of operations in particular sectors. We have seen that the scope for transfer is constrained in MNCs which operate in sectors that are characterised by nationally specific tastes or regulations. Moreover, in MNCs which have outsourced or segmented their international operations, there will be little incentive to transfer practices across borders. In contrast, in those sectors in which MNCs have developed standardised operations the transfer of employment practices is likely to be more feasible and thus attractive to management. It is in such 'standardised' MNCs that the forces of the country of origin and of dominance will be felt most acutely, whereas sectors constrained by national differences and those in which MNCs have developed 'segmented' international operations, the influence of the country of origin and of dominance is likely to be more muted. The strength of these forces though is not determined exclusively by the extent and form of international integration, but also by the characteristics of the various host country employment systems in which MNCs operate.

Host country effects

There are a number of aspects of a national business system which can limit the scope a multinational has to transfer practices. The system of employment law to a greater or lesser degree poses constraints on employers implementing practices in the workplace. Moreover, the nature of key labour market institutions such as unions and works councils, presents similar limitations, both directly through affecting the form of employee representation, and indirectly through the impact these institutions are able to exert on other areas of employment relations. There are also cultural barriers to transferring practices to host environments. Broad's (1994) study of a Japanese transplant in the UK, for instance, found that the parent company's insistence that the plant operate the system termed 'High Involvement Management' clashed with the expectations of British managers who were not used to devolving responsibility for operating decisions to shopfloor workers. Similarly, the policy in many US MNCs of insisting that managers across countries adopt a 'forced distribution' in appraisals and ensure that negative consequences, such as a pay freeze or even dismissal, follow for those in the bottom category has been subjected to resistance by some managers who feel that such an approach clashes with the expectations of local workforces (Edwards et al., 2007). This illustrates the way in which the institutional and cultural features of national business systems constrain the scope for transfer, and the way in which actors in host countries may be able to block transfer when they see it as challenging their interests.

Transmutation – practice is adapted to fit the new national business system.

In other cases, however, the constraints may be only partial. A practice may be adapted to fit the new national business system as it is transferred. In this way, a particular practice 'may not operate in the same fashion in the recipient as in the donor unit but, rather, may undergo *transmutation* as actors in the recipient seek to adapt it to pre-existing models of behaviour, assumptions and power relations' (Edwards and Ferner, 2004: 64). One example is the adoption by many US MNCs of Japanese-style lean production. These practices have been implemented in a distinctive system of employment relations, involving a reliance on the external labour market and a pronounced hierarchy within work organisation. Maccoby (1997: 165) argues that US companies have concentrated on the use of lean production to eliminate waste and defects, and downplayed the Toyota-style emphasis on the creation of 'trust' and facilitating 'learning'.

interesting

While the peculiarities of the host business systems may exercise constraints on transfer, be they absolute or partial, these constraints will often be malleable to the influence of large MNCs. By appearing to be mobile rather than dependent on a particular set of operations, senior managers in large MNCs can pressurise governments to relax regulations and pressurise unions into making concessions during collective bargaining. Accordingly, Muller's (1998) study of American and British MNCs in Germany found that a significant number had opted out of the systems of sector-wide collective bargaining and vocational training. In this way, actors in the HQ may be able to break down resistance to transfer from those at the national or plant levels. Indeed, some writers have argued that local constraints are weaker than is commonly perceived, with MNCs in a strong position to over-ride them where they endeavour to do so (Kostova et al., 2008).

MNCs can at times override local constraints

However, the role of host country effects in the transfer of practices is not simply a matter of managers at HQ trying to break down resistance. To operate effectively, a particular practice may be dependent on workers possessing a high level of skills and knowledge. In the absence of these, organisational actors may lack the ability to operate the practice in question. In this case, the host country is not 'receptive' to transfer, but this lack of receptiveness is not due to any opposition. An example of this is the implementation by Japanese MNCs of amended versions of lean production in Brazil; the amendments reduced the requirements for workers to rotate across a range of tasks since the Brazilian workers tended to lack the breadth of skills necessary for this form of flexible working (Humphrey, 1995).

When resistance to transfer occurs it will not necessarily be confined to the implementation of practices. Resistance can also appear at an earlier stage, namely during the search for practices that have the potential to be diffused. Where those at the HQ set up mechanisms designed to identify practices in one part of the firm that can be implemented in another, and combine this with establishing competitive relations between different units, actors at plant level may be reluctant to share their expertise with their counterparts for fear of undermining their performance within the group. Instead of letting other plants with whom they are in competition use the practices developed in their own plant, some may prefer to keep to themselvesthe ones that they perceive give them an advantage. In doing so, they may draw on the peculiarities of the national business system concerned to obfuscate the nature of employment practice in their plant.

Thus since the transfer of practices entails the crossing of 'institutional divides' (Morgan et al., 2001), the process of transfer is evidently a highly political one. Actors at the centre of MNCs may find that the distinctiveness of host country systems of employment relations present constraints to the transfer of practices, although these will sometimes be malleable. Actors at subsidiary level, on the other hand, may be able to use host country distinctiveness to block either the implementation of practices or the initial search for them. The way in which the features of host countries complicate MNCs' initiatives to achieve international integration is clearly demonstrated in the case study regarding General Motors in Spain (see pp. 286–287).

4 Conclusion

The framework advanced in this chapter provides a method of analysing the transfer of employment practices across borders within MNCs. This approach, based on the framework of 'four key influences', has sought to integrate elements of the three categories of explanation (market-based, cultural and political) outlined at the beginning of the chapter. It recognises the strength of the competitive pressures on MNCs to engage in transferring practices across their operations. In particular, the notion of 'dominance' and the extent of the pressures for firms to achieve international integration capture this dynamic.

The 'four influences' framework attaches great significance to the institutional and cultural aspects of national business systems in shaping and constraining the nature of transfer. The legacy of institutions shows up most clearly in the concepts of country of origin and host country effects. Moreover, the framework accords importance to the political nature of transfer by recognising the way in which organisational actors can use a range of resources – relating for example to 'dominant' ideas in the international economy or to characteristics of the particular systems in which they are located – to initiate, engage in or obstruct the process of transfer. Thus this fourth, integrated approach has sought to use elements of the market-based, cultural and political approaches.

By way of conclusion, what do the arguments presented in this chapter tell us about the consequences for national systems of employment relations? One clear consequence is the way in which the transfer of practices within MNCs will lead to change within national systems as the practices introduced are spread throughout an economy. Some argue that the development of standardised policies on employment practice within many MNCs is a key factor influencing the convergence of national systems. Cases such as the move by General Motors towards establishing teamworking as the norm throughout their international operations appears to lend some weight to this argument. Yet the logic of this chapter has been that while transfer will lead to change, it will not necessarily lead to convergence because transferred practices often go through a process of transmutation, in that they will operate differently in the recipient unit from the way they operate in the donor unit. While it may be possible to execute some practices in a more or less identical way in different countries, many others will be adapted by management to 'fit' the new environment or will be interpreted in a different way by actors in the recipient country. Indeed, in this respect, the effects of the transfer of practices within MNCs is similar to the more general impact of the internationalisation of economic activity; national systems of employment relations evolve in response to these pressures, but do not necessarily converge.

Globalization is forcing systems of employment relations to evolve in response, yet not really converge.

Discussion questions

1 Which of the three perspectives on why MNCs engage in transfer – market-based, cultural and political – is in your opinion the most convincing?

2 Do you think that some of the four influences in the framework are becoming more influential while others are becoming less so?

3 You have been hired as a consultant to three firms: a British retail bank setting up in Spain; a German textiles firm relocating its production to Vietnam; and an American high-tech electronics firm opening a new site in Britain. You have been asked by all three firms to advise them on the desirability and feasibility of transferring practices to their new locations. How would your advice differ?

4 You have been appointed as an adviser to an international federation of national unions in the oil industry. The member unions are concerned at the growing tendency on the part of the major companies in the sector to transfer practices across their operations. You have been asked to advise them on how they might seek to block or amend those practices they see as challenging their interests. What would you tell them?

5 Does the transfer of practices result in MNCs from various countries becoming more like one another?

Swedco

The issue of the direction in which practices are diffused across a multinational's operations is particularly interesting in the case of Swedish MNCs. The small size of the domestic economy has meant that in order to grow, many firms became multinational at a relatively early stage in their development and subsequently became highly internationalised. Thus, compared to MNCs of most other nationalities, the domestic operations of Swedish MNCs comprise a small proportion of their total sales, assets and employment. Moreover, the nature of the Swedish system of employment relations – the historically highly centralised system of bargaining; the strength of union organisation and high level of density; the structures promoting codetermination and tradition of cooperation between management and labour – raises the issue of how such a distinctive system influences a firm's approach at the international level where the structural supports for such practices are much weaker.

The issue of the transfer of employment practices is at the heart of a case study of a Swedish multinational. Swedco is a highly internationalised firm providing IT and communications services and equipment for other firms. It employs tens of thousands of employees, with approximately 50 per cent based outside Sweden, while 95 per cent of the firm's sales are abroad. The case study involved research into the Swedish, Belgian and British units of the firm and sought to address the influence of the Swedish business system over employment relations in the firm and the role of the transfer of practices in reinforcing or eroding the effect of the home country.

There was evidence of a distinctively Swedish element to the management of the firm's international workforce, something which was evident in a number of respects. First, in the international context, Swedish workers operate with relatively little direct supervision; indeed, there is no direct translation in Swedish for the word 'supervisor' (Anderson, 1995: 72). Managers at the HQ of Swedco described attempts to spread a 'democratic' approach to decision making throughout the organisation. As one put it: 'I want to let my guys loose. I don't want to control them and stand behind their backs. This is typically Swedish, to be a coach'. Second, Hedlund (1981) has argued that in Swedish firms it is acceptable to 'bypass the hierarchy' in that organisational actors do not feel constrained by formal authority relationships. Accordingly, one of the British managers claimed that: 'the company encourages a Nordic approach to openness. Swedes think nothing of jumping the hierarchy to put forward their ideas'.

Third, the tradition of seeking agreement through compromise and negotiation – what Anderson (1995: 76) refers to as the 'quest for accord' – was also evident at the international level in Swedco. One of the Belgian managers argued that this style clashed with what he was used to: 'You cannot always agree or compromise. Sometimes you have to say no. In Belgium, we raise our voices, we explode sometimes. But Sweden says this is something you must not do'.

Fourth, the Swedishness of the firm shows up in the stability of ownership. Unlike most big American and British firms which have fluid ownership structures involving a large number of shareholders each holding a small proportion of the total stock, Swedco has three large shareholders who control nearly three-quarters of the voting shares and have done so for decades. Consequently, in an industry characterised by significant restructuring in recent years, involving a number of 'hostile' take-overs, Swedco has expanded internationally by 'greenfield' investments and through a series of collaborative joint ventures and 'friendly' acquisitions.

This evidence of a 'country of origin effect' is very significant; even in a highly internationalised MNC the nature of the domestic business system shapes the management of the international workforce. However, the evidence also indicated that the country of origin effect is being eroded as senior management seek to draw more actively on practices originating from other business systems. This process was most apparent in compensation and management development practices. The first of these is the development of 'flexible' or 'variable' compensation systems. An international policy-working group involving HR managers from across Swedco has recently introduced bonus systems that are linked to individual and company performance. In addition, for very senior managers, there is a 'Short Term Incentive Plan' which rewards the achievement of immediate goals. Moreover, four years ago all employees were given the right to subscribe to a convertible share debenture scheme, something that about 40 per cent of staff worldwide have joined. Perhaps most significantly, an individual performance-related pay scheme, in which an employee's performance is assessed against specified targets, affects all employees across the group worldwide. These variable forms of compensation appear to have much in common with practices which have become popular in America and Britain during the last two decades.

A similar process of adopting 'Anglo-American' style practices was evident in relation to management development. In recent years the HQ has made a concerted effort to develop a cadre of managers from across the multinational. Subsidiaries have been encouraged to submit nominations for individuals who should be considered for promotion to positions elsewhere in the firm, a group known as 'high potentials'. The identification of such 'high potentials' as part of an international cadre of managers is, according to Ferner and Varul (1999), a common trait of British and American MNCs. More generally, in Swedco the British operations appear to have been particularly influential in the formation of policy on management development. The manager of the firm's 'Management Institute' indicated that the UK subsidiary and UK universities have been influential in developing policy on training programmes and management development:

When I am developing a training programme for managers, I always include the UK. Firstly, it ensures I get the language right but, secondly, there are a lot of good training and management development ideas in the UK that I would like to benefit from. I always bring someone in from the UK site onto the team. We are also developing links with the UK universities such as Cranfield and LSE.

In sum, while there is evidence of the country of origin being influential over the way Swedco manages its international workforce, there is also evidence that senior managers in the firm perceive the USA and the UK as providing practices in the area of performance management and management development that are seen as desirable. This process of reverse transfer – arguably reflecting the perceptions of key actors of dominant systems – can be seen as contributing to the erosion of the country of origin effect.

For more detail, see Hayden, A. and Edwards, T. (2001) 'The erosion of the country of origin effect: a case study of a Swedish multinational', *Relations Industrielles*, 56(1): 116–40.

Case questions:
1   What is distinctively Swedish about this company?
2   Why was the firm keen to depart from traditional Swedish practice in some areas of HR?
3   Why did senior management look to the British and American subsidiaries for new practices?

General Motors in Spain

During the 1980s and 1990s many large American firms experimented with the practices that appeared to exist at the heart of the strong performance of their Japanese counterparts. In the case of General Motors, a principal way in which the firm learned about these practices was through the collaboration with Toyota which began in the early 1980s. The joint venture between the two firms, termed NUMMI, was significant because it was seen by the management of GM as a way of facilitating learning about Japanese management practices, and through joint venture a means of moving away from those practices which had characterised the company's North American plants. One important aspect of this cooperation was the emphasis on teamwork, involving groups of operators working flexibly within teams and taking on shared responsibility for the quality of their work (see O'Sullivan, 2000). Apparently persuaded by the idea that teamwork had potential benefits across its operations, senior managers sought to transfer it to other locations across the world as part of a standardised production system within the company.

In its Spanish subsidiary, as in many others, GM was faced with overcoming the potential resistance of its trade unions. There are two main union confederations in Spain: the UGT, which has enjoyed close links with the Socialist Party (PSOE), and is considered to be moderate; and the communist-oriented CCOO which has its roots in workplace resistance to Franco's dictatorship (Martinez Lucio, 1998). In addition to union representation, there exists another channel of worker representation known as the *comité de empresas,* or works committees. While formally separate from unions, in many cases the delegates elected by workers to these committees are also union representatives. The dual system of unions and works committees had to be confronted by GM's managers in attempting to implement teamwork.

The form of teamwork favoured by management for its Spanish plant had many elements in common with its other plants. The key aspects included: work being organised into teams of between 8 and 15 people; operators rotating across jobs within a team; members of a team meeting regularly to discuss possible improvements to their work; and 'the usual rhetoric about fostering a "team spirit" between workers and the company' (Ortiz, 1998: 46). The initial proposals envisaged maintenance workers being required to engage in 'mixed teams' with production workers. Moreover, the appointment of a team leader by the company was significant since he or she was to have a role in the appraisal and promotion of members of the team. Managers and unions began the process of negotiations concerning the introduction of teamwork. The unions were initially sceptical, expressing concerns about potential job losses, the prospect of work becoming intensified, the danger of unions being marginalised by the identification of workers with their teams, and the possibility that workers would not share in the benefits of the resulting higher productivity.

Despite these concerns, and a history of division between the UGT and the CCOO, the two main union groups did cooperate with management and managed to negotiate a number of concessions. For instance, teamworking was to be piloted for a year at first and workers would only join the experiment voluntarily, and maintenance workers were excluded from teamwork. While these concessions ameliorated the concerns of many union representatives, they also saw some possible advantages to the scheme: job rotation could help relieve monotony and avoid the danger of repetitive strains; many workers (particularly those in low grades) could be promoted; teamwork could increase the autonomy that workers enjoyed from supervisors; and it could also result in more information being provided to workers and unions. Potential opposition from unionists was further eroded by pressure from the company, since managers stressed the multinational character of the company and the competitive position of the plant within it. Many union leaders had been taken to visit other plants operating teamwork, creating a sense of it being an inevitable development in Spain too. For the leaders of the CCOO, now controlled by more 'moderates', opposing teamwork seemed futile and risked marginalising the union since the UGT would probably go along with management. In this context, agreement was reached at the works committee.

This shows the way that a powerful company can exert influence over the constraints of national business systems. By instilling competitive relations between plants, and by making concessions on some aspects of their plans, managers were able to break down resistance from unions, resulting in the constraints becoming partial rather than absolute. However, this was not the end of the story. At the end of the pilot scheme there was a call from the minority union, the USO, for a workforce ballot to decide on whether to stick with teamwork. Despite a campaign for ratification from all of the unions, the workers voted narrowly to reject the proposal. There appeared to be a number of reasons why employees were more hostile to teamwork than were their unions. Some workers, particularly those with scarce skills, were reluctant to engage in job rotation if this meant moving to less desirable jobs, and related to this was a concern over loss of status for these workers. More generally, the adversarial industrial relations traditions of the plant meant that many workers were sceptical about management's motives. While it is likely that many workers in GM's plants in other countries shared such concerns, the Spanish system of employment law presented a distinctive constraint.

Ortiz concludes that many characteristics of national systems of industrial relations shape the attitudes of unions and workers to teamwork, such as the organisational strength of unions and the legal support that they enjoy. He argues, for example, that the British unions were more opposed to teamwork than their Spanish counterparts because it endangered the important role of the shop steward. The peculiarities of these aspects of national systems of industrial relations are key forces on the nature of transfer of practices across borders, particularly for those MNCs seeking to use this as a way of developing internationally integrated operations. Yet, these dynamics of national industrial relations systems are not set in stone; in subsequent research in VW in Spain, Ortiz argues that after two unsuccessful attempts to introduce teamwork the multinational was eventually successful in implementing the practice. His interpretation of this is that host country constraints had become less influential and that management had found ways round what has appeared at first sight to be tight constraints.

For more details, see Ortiz, L. (1998) and Ortiz, L. and Llorente-Galera, F. (2008).

Case questions

1 Why did the Spanish context appear to set constraints for the introduction of teamwork?
2 How did senior management look to overcome these constraints?
3 Who benefitted from the introduction of teamwork? And who lost?

Further reading

- Almond, P. and Ferner, A. (2006) *American Multinationals in Europe: Managing Employment Relations across National Borders.* Oxford: Oxford University Press.
The book is a summary of the findings of a large project looking at US MNCs in four European countries.

- Becker-Ritterspach, F. (2009) *Hybridization of MNC Subsidiaries: The Automotive Sector in India.* London: Palgrave Macmillan.
This summarises the findings of a detailed examination of four MNCs in India, arguing that practices are amended when located in a new national context.

- Kristensen, P. and Zeitlin, J. (2005) *Local Players in Global Games: The Strategic Constitution of a Multinational Company.* Oxford: Oxford University Press.

The book is an extremely detailed account of the inner workings of a multinational company, showing how actors in different parts of the company use resources from their local context to advance or protect their own interests.

Internet resources

1   www.unctad.org/WIR

2   www.cipd.co.uk/subjects/intlhr

3   www.ilo.org/global/lang-en/index.htm

Self-assessment questions

Indicative answers to these questions can be found on the companion website at www.sagepub.co.uk/harzing3e.

1   **How would you assess the contribution of each of the three perspectives on transfer that are outlined in this chapter? Can elements of the three be combined into one 'eclectic' perspective?**
2   **What are the origins of the 'four influences' framework?**
3   **How useful is the concept of 'dominance' effects?**
4   **What is the range of ways in which a global HRM policy may be adapted to national contexts?**
5   **If MNCs engage in the transfer of employment practices to an increasing extent does this mean that national business systems will converge?**

Not really, →
pg 282

References

Abo, T. (1994) *Hybrid Factory: The Japanese Production System in the United States.* Oxford: Oxford University Press.

Almond, P. and Ferner, A. (2006) (eds) *American Multinationals in Europe: Managing Employment Relations Across Borders.* Oxford: Oxford University Press.

Anderson, B. (1995) *Swedishness.* Stockholm: Positiva Sverige.

Belanger, J., Berggren, C., Bjorkman, T. and Kohler, C. (1999) *Being Local Worldwide: ABB and the Challenge of Global Management.* Ithaca: Cornell University Press.

Broad, G. (1994) 'The managerial limits to Japanization: a manufacturing case study', *Human Resource Management Journal*, 4(3): 52–69.

Djelic, M. (1998) *Exporting the American Model: The Post-War Transformation of European Business.* Oxford: Oxford University Press.

Doremus, P., Keller, W., Pauly, L. and Reich, S (1998) *The Myth of the Global Corporation.* Princeton, NJ: Princeton University Press.

Edwards, P., Edwards, T., Ferner, A., Marginson, P. and Tregaskis, O. (2007) 'Employment practices of MNCs in organisational context: a large scale survey', Survey Report at http://www2.warwick.ac.uk/fac/soc/wbs/projects/mncemployment/conference_papers/full_report_july.pdf.

Edwards, T. (1998) 'Multinationals, work organisation and the process of diffusion: a case study', *International Journal of Human Resource Management*, 9(4): 696–709.

Edwards, T. and Ferner, A. (2002) 'The renewed "American Challenge": a review of employment practice in US multinationals', *Industrial Relations Journal*, 33(2).

Edwards, T. and Ferner, A. (2004) 'Multinationals, national business systems and reverse diffusion', *Management International Review*, 24(1): 49–79.

Edwards, T. and Zhang, M. (2008) 'Multinationals and national systems of employment relations: innovators or adapters?', *Advances in International Management*, 21: 33–58.

Edwards, T., Colling, T. and Ferner, A. (2007) 'Conceptual approaches to the transfer of employment practices in multinational companies: an integrated approach', *Human Resource Management Journal*, 17(3): 201–17.

Ferner, A. and Varul, M. (1999) *The German Way? German Multinationals and the Management of Human Resources in their UK Subsidiaries.* London: Anglo-German Foundation for the Study of Industrial Society.

Gamble, J. (2003) 'Transferring human resource practices from the United Kingdom to China: the limits and potential for convergence', *International Journal of Human Resource Management*, 14(3): 369–87.

Gereffi, G., Humphrey, J. and Sturgeon, T. (2005) 'The governance of global value chains: an analytical framework', *Review of International Political Economy*, 12(1): 78–104.

Ghoshal, S. and Bartlett, C. (1998) *Managing Across Borders: The Transnational Solution.* London: Random House.

Hall, P. and Soskice, D. (2001) *Varieties of Capitalism: The Institutional Foundations of Comparative Advantage.* Oxford: Oxford University Press.

Hayden, A. and Edwards, T. (2001) 'The erosion of the country of origin effect: a case study of a Swedish multinational company', *Relations Industrielles*, 56(1): 116–40.

Hedlund, G. (1981) 'Autonomy of subsidiaries and formalization of headquarters-subsidiary relationships in Swedish MNCs' in L. Otterbeck (ed.), *The Management of Headquarters-Subsidiary Relationships in Multinational Corporations.* Aldershot: Gower.

Hofstede, G. (2001) *Culture's Consequences: Comparing Values, Behaviors, Institutions and Organizations.* London: Sage.

Humphrey, J. (1995) 'The adoption of Japanese management techniques in Brazilian industry', *Journal of Management Studies*, 32(6): 767–87.

Kostova, T., Roth, K. and Dacin, M. (2008) 'Institutional theory in the study of MNCs: a critique and new directions', *Academy of Management Review*, 33(4): 994–1007.

Kristensen, P. and Zeitlin, J. (2005) *Local Players in Global Games: The Strategic Constitution of a Multinational Company.* Oxford: Oxford University Press.

Lunnan, R., Lervik, J., Traavik, L., Nilson, S., Amdam, R. and Hennestad, B. (2005) 'Global transfer of management practices across nations and MNC subcultures', *Academy of Management Executive*, 19(2): 77–80.

Maccoby (1997) 'Just another car factory? Lean production and its discontents', *Harvard Business Review*, November-December, 75(6): 161–8.

Marginson, P. (2000) 'The Eurocompany and Euro industrial relations', *European Journal of Industrial Relations*, 6(1): 9–34.

Martinez Lucio, M. (1998) 'Spain: regulating employment and social fragmentation', in A. Ferner and R. Hyman (eds), *Changing Industrial Relations in Europe*. Oxford: Blackwell.

Morgan, G., Kristensen, P. and Whitley, R. (2001) *The Multinational Firm: Organizing Across Institutional and National Divides*. Oxford: Oxford University Press.

Muller, M. (1998) 'Human resource and industrial relations practices of UK and US multinationals in Germany', *International Journal of Human Resource Management*, 9(4): 732–49.

Ngo, H., Turban, D., Lau, C. and Lui, S. (1998) 'Human resource practices and firm performance of multinational corporations: influences of country origin', *International Journal of Human Resource Management*, 9(4): 632–52.

Oliver, N. and Wilkinson, B. (1992) *The Japanization of British Industry: New Developments in the 1990s*. Oxford: Blackwell.

Ortiz, L. (1998) 'Unions' response to teamwork: the case of Opel Spain', *Industrial Relations Journal*, 29(1): 42–57.

Ortiz, L. and Llorente-Galera, F. (2008) 'Two failed attempts and one success: the introduction of teamwork at Seat-Volkswagen; *Advances in International Management*, 21: 59–88.

O'Sullivan, M. (2000) *Contests for Corporate Control: Corporate Governance and Economic Performance in the United States and Germany*. Oxford: Oxford University Press.

Perlmutter, H. (1969) 'The tortuous evolution of the multinational corporation', *Columbia Journal of World Business*, Jan–Feb: 9–18.

Pudelko, M. and Harzing, A. (2007) 'Country-of-origin, localization or dominance effect? An empirical investigation of HRM practices in foreign subsidiaries', *Human Resource Management*, 46(4): 535–59.

Rosenzweig, P. and Nohria, N. (1994) 'Influences on human resource management practices in multinational corporations', *Journal of International Business Studies*, Second Quarter: 229–51.

Ruigrok, W. and van Tulder, R. (1995) *The Logic of International Restructuring*. London: Routledge.

Schmitt, M. and Sadowski, D. (2003) A cost-minimisation approach to the international transfer of HRM / IR practices: Anglo-saxon multinationals in the Federal Republic of Germany', *International Journal of Human Resource Management*, 14(3): 409–30.

Smith, C. and Meiskins, P. (1995) 'System, society and dominance effects in cross-national organisational analysis', *Work, Employment and Society*, 9(2): 241–67.

Tayeb, M. (1996) *The Management of a Multicultural Workforce*. Chichester: Wiley.

Taylor, S., Beechler, S. and Napier, N. (1996) 'Toward an integrative model of strategic international human resource management', *Academy of Management Review*, 21(4): 959–85.

Trompenaars, F. and Hampden-Turner, C. (1994) *The Seven Cultures of Capitalism*. London: Piatkus.

United Nations (2009) *World Investment Report*. New York: UN.

Wilkinson, B., Gamble, J., Humphrey, J., Morris, J. and Anthony, D. (2001) 'The new international division of labour in Asian electronics: work organization and human resources in Japan and Malaysia', *Journal of Management Studies*, 38(5): 675–95.

9

High Performance Work Systems – International Evidence of the Impact on Firms and Employees

Margaret Heffernan, Patrick C. Flood and Wenchuan Liu

Contents

Learning Objectives

After reading this chapter you will be able to

- Understand the role of high performance work systems (HPWS) and identify its components

- Assess different theoretical frameworks within the HPWS literature

- Identify the international evidence empirically linking HRM to firm performance

- Review the international evidence linking HRM to employee outcomes

- Critically evaluate the HPWS-firm performance research through an understanding of recent critical debates

- Articulate the role of the line manager in HPWS-performance research.

Chapter Outline

This chapter reviews the burgeoning literature on high performance work systems (HPWS) which has emerged over the past decade. It gives a detailed overview of international empirically based research on HPWS and assesses the impact on both organisational and employee outcomes. In evaluating these studies, a number of HPWS debates are examined.

1 Introduction

This chapter aims to evaluate the international evidence on the HRM-performance link from a multiple stakeholder perspective and identify a number of tensions that exist in previous research. We commence with a definition of HPWS and a discussion of its origins in the SHRM literature. The HPWS-performance link is analysed incorporating the universalist, configurational and contingency arguments promulgated in the literature. Section 3 reviews the link between HPWS and firm level performance. Both financial and operational outcomes are examined along with an overview of international empirical studies. Section 4 critically evaluates these studies and discusses a number of criticisms that have been directed at previous HPWS-performance research. These include methodological problems, theoretical weaknesses and questions of causality that are raised in the 'HR black box' debates. Section 5 highlights the need to explore the employees' perspective of HPWS and critically examines research studies published on HPWS and employee outcomes. The chapter concludes with an examination of possible line manager actions which can be taken to ensure consistency in HPWS and suggestions for future research.

2 Evolution of High Performance Work Systems (HPWS)

There was much debate on the 'transformed workplace' in the 1980s which focused on the need for a greater commitment on the part of workers, to be achieved by expanding their jobs and involving them in problem-solving methods (e.g. (Kochan et al., 1989). These debates traversed a wide range of management subjects including scientific management, human relations, quality of work life and labour process theories that explored issues pertaining to work reform, control and employee participation. This new research on the organisation of work encompassed organisational functioning, worker motivation, work systems, control, autonomy and managerial styles and involved different ways of understanding and 'transforming' the organisation (Appelbaum and Batt, 1994). Human resource management (HRM) was one of the concepts arising from the 'transformation' literature, which received support and criticism as an approach for managing employees. HRM is concerned with overall work organisation and seeks to incorporate work relations, employment relations and industrial relations. How HRM practices affect organisation-wide outcomes is a key debate (Combs et al., 2006; MacMillan and Schuler, 1985).

Belanger et al. (2002) argue that the emergence of HPWS reflects the crisis in Fordist production and the need to develop new approaches to production. Changes in the economic environment and the emergence of new technologies have been seen as key drivers for workplace change (Appelbaum and Batt, 1994; Piore and Sabel, 1984). It was suggested that organisations can achieve competitive advantage through harnessing hitherto under-exploited financial, physical, human and organisational resources. When managed effectively, it was argued, human resources are more capable of increasing organisational effectiveness (Beaumont, 1993). This shift in attitude on the part of management broadened the focus of HRM research from micro analytic studies which had previously dominated the field to more macro and strategic perspectives.

The desire to demonstrate the importance of HRM practices for organisational performance (Delery and Doty, 1996) contributed to the development of more strategic perspectives on HRM. Seminal writings on SHRM (e.g. Miles and Snow, 1984; Schuler and Jackson, 1987) have argued that HR policies consistent with strategy will be more effective and contribute to the viability of the firm including its productivity, flexibility and legitimacy (Boxall and Purcell, 2003). Human resource practices proposed by SHRM theorists as performance enhancing are known as high-performance work practices (Huselid, 1995). The application of this term has evolved to cover a multitude of attempts by employers to improve the effectiveness of their organisations and its response to a range of pressures emanating from product, external market, internal labour market and financial markets (Whitfield and Poole, 1997).

The resource-based view (RBV) of the firm, advanced originally by economists such as Edith Penrose and later adapted to strategic management by such writers as Jay Barney (1991), attends to the competitive implications of differences in resource endowment. From the resource-based perspective, HRM systems are one form of resource endowment which differs between firms that might lead to a competitive advantage. In any firm, idiosyncratic patterns of human resource practices may be created which evolve over time in a path dependent manner and are difficult to imitate by competitors (Barney, 1991; Wright et al., 2001). As long as these resources are heterogeneous and difficult to transfer from one firm to another (resource immobility) they have potential for achieving a sustained competitive advantage. Wright et al. (2001) point out that the RBV plays an important role in establishing the relevance of HRM for theory and practice in strategic management.

Defining HPWS

There is no single agreed upon definition of a HPWS and there are a number of theoretical, empirical and practical dimensions on which they differ. The existing approaches do, however, share some common ideas on HPWS that include a focus on skill formation, work structuring, performance management, pay satisfaction, job flexibility and minimal status differentials that are assumed to reverse past Taylorist methods (Appelbaum et al., 2000; Osterman, 1994; Wood, 1999).

Appelbaum and Batt (1994) categorise the elements of HPWS along four dimensions – management methods, work organisation, human resource management practices and industrial relations. 'Management methods' include employee involvement in quality improvement; 'work organisation' includes autonomous work teams and vertical task work; 'human resource management practices' includes cross training, employment security and compensation contingent on performance; and finally 'industrial relations' focuses on the unitary perspective that there is no conflict of interest between management and workers.

Most writers on HPWS emphasise the active participation of employees in the work process, combining it with the organisational arrangements for information sharing, employee training and skill development. Pfeffer (1998), for example, considered components of 'high performance work systems' to include employment security and internal labour markets, selective hiring and sophisticated selection, extensive training, learning and development, employee involvement, teamworking, high compensation contingent on performance and reduction in status differentials. It has been argued that these high commitment practices should form a coherent, integrated 'bundle' or system of complementarities whose effect is greater than the sum of its parts (e.g., Appelbaum et al., 2000; Guest, 2002).

Recent practice has been to use the terms 'high commitment management' and 'high performance work systems' synonymously (Legge, 2005). In this chapter, we use the term high performance work system (HPWS) as an umbrella term encompassing all of the following phrases. Walton (1985) and Wood and Albanese (1995) used the term 'high commitment management' whereas Appelbaum and Batt (1994) preferred 'high performance work systems/practices'. Other labels include: high involvement management (Lawler, 1986), flexible work practices (Osterman, 1994) and flexible production systems (MacDuffie, 1995). Other researchers have published research in the HRM-performance area without specifically using any of the above terms (e.g., Guest, 1997). According to Wood (1999) these are all terms used to describe the organisational form held to be most appropriate for modern competitive conditions.

The central argument made in previous HPWS literature is that there is a positive relationship between integrating a HRM system and performance (see Box 9.1). This suggests that there are synergies among the work organisation and human resource practices that lead to positive interaction effects on performance when they are adopted together (Delery and Doty, 1996).

Box 9.1   HPWS research in Ireland and the business performance impact

> This research helps us to understand more fully the nature of the differences between high-performing and average-performing companies. The report reveals that high-performing companies in Ireland are concerned with managing a range of issues that include the management of employee involvement and participation, and of diversity and equality systems. The research establishes the quantifiable and positive impact of equality and diversity strategies and of employee involvement and participation on labour productivity, workforce innovation and employee turnover. These findings clearly reinforce the business imperative for managing employee involvement and participation, and implementing diversity and equality strategies, as legitimate concerns for organisational strategy in their own right.
>
> *Source*: Foreword by L. Fallon-Byrne and N. Crowley in Flood et al., 2008

In trying to understand how this positive interaction effect occurs, Boxall and Purcell (2003) adapt the work of Bailey (1993) and put forward the following formula:

$$P = f \, (A,M,O)$$

where P = Performance; A = Ability; M = Motivation and O = Opportunity. Accordingly, people perform well when:

- they are able to do so (they *can do* the job because they possess the necessary knowledge and skills). Policies to guarantee adequate skills include staffing practices and rigorous selection and recruitment procedures that enable a firm to obtain employees with the appropriate knowledge, skills and abilities; training which focuses on technical, problem solving and team building skills and an emphasis on multi-skilling.

- they have the motivation to do so (they *will do* the job because they are adequately incentivised). This introduces the need for incentive pay practices that align the interests of workers with those of the company such as in pay that is contingent on work group or company performance. Policies that provide employees with challenging work and a reasonable expectation of employment security can also help to release employees' discretionary effort (Doty and Delery, 1997).
- their work environment provides the necessary support and opportunities for expression, for example, participatory forms of work organisation that allow for greater autonomy and control over decisions that affect their job and the opportunity to be heard when problems occur (Boxall and Purcell, 2003: 20).

Taking the AMO equation into account, Figure 9.1 shows how the components of HPWS impact on firms' performance through the discretionary effort of its employees.

Figure 9.1   Components of high performance work systems

Source: Reprinted from *Manufacturing Advantage: Why High-Performance Work Systems Pay Off*, edited by Eileen Appelbaum, Thomas Bailey, Peter Berg and Arne L. Kalleberg. Copyright © 2000 by Cornell University. Used by permission of publisher, Cornell University Press.

Appelbaum et al. (2000) and Boxall and Purcell (2003) see this as a basic theory of performance which offers a structure for identifying the desirable components of HPWS. If practices fostering these variables are enhanced, better use will be made of employee potential and discretionary judgment. Konrad (2006) suggests that HPWS are employed by many organisations in order to develop positive beliefs and attitudes that are associated with employee engagement and commitment. The practices and the beliefs in turn generate discretionary behaviours that are necessary in enhancing firm performance. Some have also recently argued that diversity management practices should be included in an expanded definition of HPWS due to the fact that these practices impact on opportunity in the AMO framework (Flood et al. 2008).

This section of the chapter has examined the central argument of HPWS research and defined what the components of a HPWS system involve. The AMO performance rubric highlighted the importance of the concept of discretionary effort as a useful explanatory mechanism. However, as previously mentioned, much debate exists over the particular mix of HPWS (see Table 9.1 below for a summary of HR practices used in key HPWS research). Table 9.1 emphasises that many empirical studies have found significant firm performance effects using different combinations

Table 9.1 Summary results of HPWS studies on firm performance, by HRM practice

HRM practice	Results	Researcher (s)	Country
Recruitment & selection	HRM activities that lead to the right person being in the right place (employee skill and organisational structures) contribute to higher productivity and increased market value of the company. Moreover, they have a slight negative impact on turnover.	*Huselid (1995)*	USA
	Staffing selectivity is positively related to perceived market performance.	*Delaney and Huselid (1996)*	USA
	Evaluation and investment in recruitment and selection are positively related to labour productivity.	*Koch and McGrath (1996)*	USA
	Selective selection is positively related with perceived profit, market share, and investments in the near future.	*Verburg (1998)*	Netherlands
	Selective selection is negatively related to employee turnover.		
HR planning	Sophisticated human resource planning activities are positively related to labour productivity.	*Koch and McGrath (1996)*	USA
Rewards	Reward is positively correlated to the different dimensions of the performance of the firm: product quality, product development, profit, market share, customer satisfaction, and growth in sales.	*Kalleberg and Moody (1994)*	USA
	Higher rewards contribute to a better social climate between management and the other employees.	*Koch and McGrath (1996)*	USA
	Higher rewards contribute to a decrease in turnover.	*Arthur (1994)*	USA
	Incentive compensation has a positive impact on perceived organisational performance.	*Delaney and Huselid (1996)*	USA
	Outcome-based incentives on sales, customer satisfaction, and profit increases with the intensity of competition and the proportion of upscale customers and decreases with the level of supervisory monitoring.	*Banker et al. (1996)*	USA
	Flexible reward is positively related to profit.	*Leget (1997)*	Netherlands

Table 9.1 (Continued)

HRM practice	Results	Researcher (s)	Country
	Excellent reward systems are positively related to perceived profit, market share, and investments in the immediate future.	Verburg (1998)	Netherlands
	Employee share ownership schemes, profit-related pay, and performance related pay are positively related to financial performance.	McNabb and Whitfield (1997)	UK
	Pay for performance is positively related to employee trust and organisational commitment.	Appelbaum et al. (2000)	USA
	Perceived high wages are positively related to trust in decision making and perceived employee job security.	Boselie et al. (2001)	Netherlands
	Perceived excellent secondary work conditions are positively related to employee satisfaction and negatively related to intention to leave the organisation.	Boselie and van der Wiele (2001)	Netherlands
	Perceived high wages are positively related to employee satisfaction and negatively related to intention to leave the organisation.		
Participation	Employee involvement practices aimed at generating commitment have a positive influence on productivity and product quality.	Fernie et al. (1995)	UK
	Employee involvement results in better social climate.		
	Commitment (vs. control-) oriented HR systems have a positive impact on productivity and result in a lower degree of turnover.	Arthur (1994)	USA
	Quality and labour productivity improve over time after the formation of teams.	Banker et al. (1996)	USA
	Employee participation is positively related to trust in decision making and perceived employee job security.	Boselie et al. (2001)	Netherlands
Internally consistent HR bundles	Stimulating personnel management has a positive impact on employee commitment, organisational support, training and education facilities, level of education, and expectations with respect to wage increases.	Leijten (1992)	Netherlands
	Stimulating personnel management has a negative effect on illness.		

(Continued)

Table 9.1 (Continued)

HRM practice	Results	Researcher (s)	Country
	Bundles of internally consistent HRM practices are associated with higher productivity and quality.	MacDuffie (1995)	USA
	High-performance work systems are positively related to productivity.	Appelbaum et al. (2000)	USA
	High-involvement work practices are positively related to employee retention and firm productivity.	Guthrie (2001)	New Zealand
	High-performance work practices are positively related to employee retention, firm productivity and sales growth.	Flood et al. (2005)	Ireland
Decentralisation	Decentralisation of authority will result in a lower degree of turnover.	Arthur (1994)	USA
Training	Training has a positive impact on the different dimensions of the performance of the firm: product quality, product development, market share, and growth of sales.	Kalleberg and Moody (1994)	USA
	More investment in training results in higher profit.	Arthur (1994)	USA
	More investment in training results in a lower degree of turnover.	Kalleberg and Moody (1994)	USA
	Training has a positive impact on the relationship between management and the other employees.		
	Training has an impact on perceived organisational performance.	Delaney and Huselid (1996)	USA
	Management development is positively related to profit.	Leget (1997)	Netherlands
	Focus on training is positively related to perceived profit, market share, and investment in the immediate future.	Verburg (1998)	Netherlands
	Formal and informal training are positively related to employee trust and intrinsic motivation.	Appelbaum et al. (2000)	USA
	Training and development are positively related to employee trust in decision making and perceived employee job security.	Boselie et al. (2001)	Netherlands

Table 9.1 (Continued)

HRM practice	Results	Researcher (s)	Country
Opportunities for internal promotion	Internal promotion opportunities are positively related to perceived profit, market share, and investment in the immediate future.	*Verburg (1998)*	Netherlands
	Promotion opportunities are positively related to organisational commitment and job satisfaction.	*Appelbaum et al. (2000)*	USA
More autonomy	Autonomy is positively related to employee trust and intrinsic motivation.	*Appelbaum et al. (2000)*	USA
Formal procedures	Formal procedures (with respect to downsizing) are positively related to the number of dismissals/lay offs.	*Fernie et al. (1995)*	UK
Coaching	Coaching is positively related to profit.	*Leget (1997)*	Netherlands
	Support of direct supervisor is positively related to trust in decision making and perceived employee job security.	*Boselie et al. (2001)*	Netherlands
	Support of direct supervisor is positively related to employee satisfaction and negatively related to intention to leave the organisation.	*Boselie and van de Wiele (2001)*	Netherlands
Information sharing	Information sharing is positively related to trust in decision making and perceived employee job security.	*Boselie et al. (2001)*	Netherlands
	Information sharing is positively related to employee satisfaction and negatively related to intention to leave the organisation.	*Boselie and van de Wiele (2001)*	Netherlands
Employment security	Employment security is positively related to productivity, employee trust, and organisational commitment.	*Appelbaum et al. (2000)*	USA

Source: Summary Results of HPWS studies on Firm Performance. Abridged and updated from Paauwe (2004) Reprinted with kind permission from Paul Boselie.

of HR practices (Becker and Gerhart, 1996). Despite this debate, the HPWS literature advocates that the relevant HR practices will work much better when 'bundled' together (MacDuffie, 1995) to operate as a 'system' (Ichniowski et al., 1996). The justification for bundles (or systems of HRM) is based on the argument that while individual HR practices might be beneficial in their own right, "suites of practices that are mutually consistent will deliver performance outcomes greater than the sum of the outcomes of the individual practices used" (Purcell, 1999: 27).

Theoretical perspectives in HPWS research

HPWS research pays considerable attention to the role of HRM systems as solutions to business problems rather than treating *individual* HR management practices in isolation (Becker and Huselid, 2006). Similarly, the literature on SHRM stresses the importance of systems when analysing the integration of HR strategy with business strategy. Ulrich (1997), for example, called for rich integrated theoretical frameworks that focus research efforts and enable the practice of HR management to become a truly strategic discipline. However, theories of SHRM and HPWS advocate several way of linking HRM to strategy and three theoretical perspectives dominate the HPWS literature. These are universalist (also known as the 'best practice' approach), contingency (also known as 'best fit') and configurational (which focus on additive architecture of HRM) perspectives.

The universalist perspective is the simplest view and argues that practices are additive and enhance performance regardless of the circumstances. The work of Pfeffer (1995) is the best known study highlighting the universalist perspective. Pfeffer concluded that certain practices should be more universally effective than others, including employment security, selectivity in recruiting, high wages, incentive pay, employee ownership, information sharing, participation and empowerment, self-managed teams, training and skill development, cross-training and promotion from within. This perspective does not study either the synergistic interdependence or the integration of HR practices and implicitly denies that the different elements that build the system could be combined in different patterns of practices that may be equally efficient for the organisation (Martín-Alcázar et al., 2005). As a result, this perspective has been criticised for failing to consider: a) what other practices are in place; and b) the context in which these practices are used (Lepak and Shaw, 2008).

The contingency perspective meanwhile is consistent with the RBV work mentioned earlier in the chapter. This perspective goes beyond the simple linear causal relationships explored in best practice research and allows for interaction effects and varying relationships depending on the presence of contingency variables (Wood, 1999). Therefore while universalist writers might claim the benefits of best practice HRM, contingency writers recognise that sustained competitive advantage rests, not on best practice, but on developing unique, non-inimitable competencies (Barney, 1991). The effectiveness of HRM systems is therefore contingent on how well they connect with other idiosyncratic aspects or variables of the organisation, namely contingency variables (Boxall, 1996). Those variables moderate the link between HRM and performance and, therefore, deny the existence of best practices that could lead to superior performance under any circumstance (see Delery and Doty, 1996).

Within the contingency perspective, there are two types of relationship. The first concerns the influence of various contingencies on single HRM practices. Thus strategy becomes an important moderator in the SHRM–performance causal chain. The strategic direction of the firm can dictate what HRM practices are used. For example, Jackson et al. (1989) found that organisations pursuing an innovative strategy (rather than one based on cost reduction) tended to provide less incentive compensation and more job security and training in order to foster innovation. The second relationship focuses on whether the use and/or effectiveness of HRM systems depend on some contingency (i.e. a contingent configurational perspective). According to this argument, internally consistent HRM systems must also achieve external alignment with contingencies.

Finally the configurational perspective presents the HRM system as a multidimensional set of elements that can be combined in different ways to obtain an infinite number of possible configurations (Lepak et al., 2006). This school of thought follows a holistic principle of inquiry and is concerned with how patterns of multiple interdependent variables interact with the dependent variable (Delery and Doty, 1996; Miller and Friesen, 1984). The configurations of HRM acknowledge system interaction effects and take account of strategy, structure, culture and processes. The perspective also highlights the importance of HR systems developing both horizontal and vertical fit for organisational effectiveness. Any configuration of a set of internally aligned HRM practices will therefore have much greater capacity to explain variation in organisational performance than will analysis of single HRM practices taken in isolation (Delery, 1998). See Figure 9.2 below for an illustration of these theoretical perspectives.

The above perspectives raise questions as to whether HPWS is linked to performance through a universalist (additive), contingency (idiosyncratic) or configurational (patterned) perspective. Most empirical research appears to fall under the universalist umbrella in trying to establish that the greater the extent of HPWS the greater the impact on organisational performance irrespective of any contextual factors (see for example, Delery and Doty, 1996; Guest, 1997; Huselid, 1995). Conversely, there are some empirical studies which support the contingency position (see Hoque, 1999; Michie and Sheehan, 2005; Youndt et al., 1996) as well as some more speculative results that support the configurational perspective (Delery and Doty, 1996; Gooderham et al., 2008).

A number of problems are associated with the universal or best practice model of HRM. Purcell has argued that it leads research into a 'utopian cul-de-sac and ignores

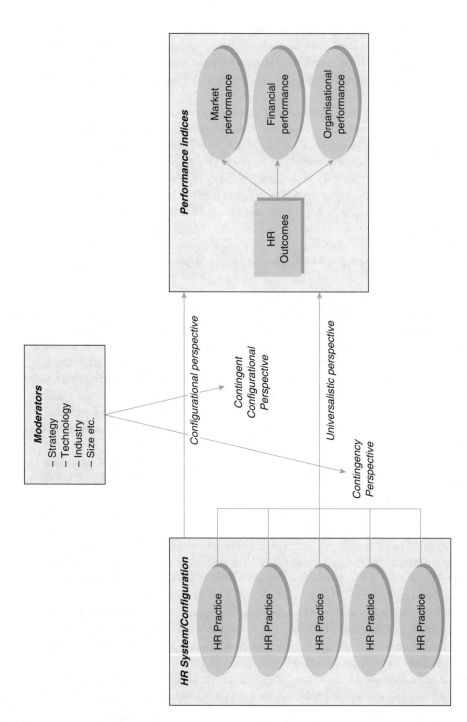

Figure 9.2 Universalist, contingency, configurational and contingent-configurational perspectives for HRM-performance relationship

Source: Lepak et al. (2006: 34) HRM activities in relation to HRM outcomes and firm performance, pp. 60, fig. 4.4, from "HRM and Performance: Achieving Long Term Viability" by Paauwe, J. (2004). By permission of Oxford University Press.

the powerful and highly significant changes in work employment and society visible inside organisations and in the wider community' (1999: 36). However, difficulties also persist within contingency perspectives such that the search for best fit might be a 'chimera.' This approach is limited by the impossibility of modelling all the contingent variables, the difficulty of showing their multiple interconnections, and the way changes in one variable impacts on others, let alone the need to model idiosyncratic and path dependent contingencies. Whilst these HPWS and methodological debates continue to abound the dominant stream of research explores the link between HRM and organisational performance.

The HPWS performance link

The body of research examining the relationship between HR practices and performance has grown exponentially over the past few years. This section examines SHRM research on how we evaluate the effectiveness of HR initiatives. In general, in assessing effectiveness of HPWS, research has predominantly used measures of financial or market based organisational performance as the dependent variable. Boselie et al. (2005), drew a distinction between different types of outcomes used in measuring effectiveness: (1) financial outcomes (profit, sales); (2) organisational outcomes (productivity, quality); and (3) HR-related outcomes (employee commitment, job satisfaction). Legge (2005) also notes such outcomes can be found at many different levels of analysis. Some researchers have examined the HPWS relationship at plant level (MacDuffie, 1995; Youndt et al., 1996); the business unit level (Wright and Gardner, 2003); and corporate level (Rogers and Wright, 1998).

In terms of specific expectations from the HPWS initiatives, improved efficiency and reduced costs are the primary financial outcomes. In addition, several operational outcomes are necessary to achieve the financial outcomes, including customer success/satisfaction, improved speed, improved quality and improved productivity.

In order to achieve these operational outcomes, Varma et al. (1999) found that an increase in a number of workforce initiatives was essential. These initiatives included empowerment, job security, risk-taking, innovation and teamwork. It is clear from his study that HR practices have a major impact on operational outcomes. The following section examines a number of studies linking HPWS and performance across a number of countries.

The benefits of HPWS are numerous. Organisation culture and value systems can be changed for the better by creating higher levels of cooperation and improved communication. In addition, substantial positive improvements in financial and operational outcomes can be achieved. HPWS have also been found to influence organisational performance indirectly, through lower employee quit rates (Batt, 2002). Low quit rates not only decrease the costs of recruitment and selection, but positively affect sales growth because new employees face a learning curve and retained, long-term employees develop tacit firm-specific skills and knowledge.

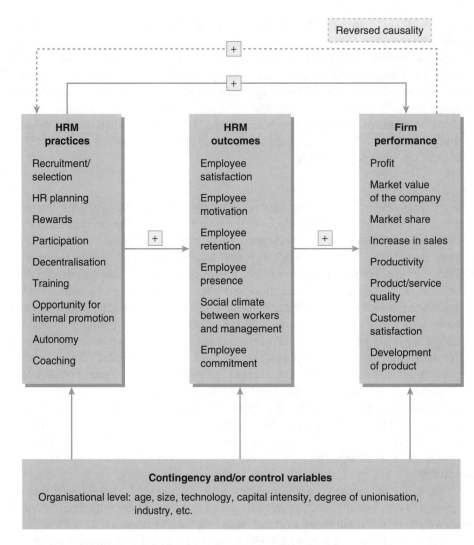

Figure 9.3   HRM practices, HRM outcomes and Firm performance
Source: Paauwe (2004).

The general framework presented in Figure 9.3 summarises previous research on HRM practices, HRM outcomes and firm performance (Paauwe, 2004). It lists HRM practices that give rise to HRM outcomes, which influence firm performance. The dashed reverse arrow indicates the possibility of reverse causality when the firm's performance influences a change in HRM practices that is often perceived as an improvement. Control variables could include factors both at the organisational level such as firm age, firm size, capital intensity, degree of unionisation, industry etc., and at the individual level such as gender, age, education level and job experience.

3 HPWS and firm outcomes – international evidence

This section reviews literature examining the impact of HPWS on firm level outcomes. Tables 9.2 and 9.3 identify countries where research has been conducted to-date. Most of the studies have been carried out in developed countries. Huselid (1995), Osterman (1994) and Pfeffer (1994) used universalist theories as their underlying framework for investigating linear relationships between HRM practices and organisational performance.

Huselid's (1995) seminal study adopted a systems-based view of HPWS, arguing that organisations implementing HPWS in conjunction with one another would perform better than organisations adopting individual practices. He surveyed nearly 1,000 firms nationally in the USA and found significant support for his hypothesis. Specifically, he found that the use of HPWS could lead to a significant decrease in employee turnover, increase in productivity (measured as sales per employee), and improved corporate performance (measured in profits and market value). Huselid's empirical study of the complementary nature of high performance practices supports the idea that HPWS design features should be understood from a holistic perspective rather than seen as a number of individual design features (Farias and Varma, 1998). Lawler's (1994) US study distinguished between the Fortune 1000 companies that make limited use of HPWS and those that make extensive use of these practices. This research found that organisations making extensive use of employee involvement practices reported significantly higher financial success than organisations making limited use of the high performance practices.

Holistic approaches to HPWS argue that to achieve high organisation performance it is important to utilise a set of mutually supporting practices. Macy and Izumi (1993) found that the organisations that recorded changes over 30 years including a combination of structural, human resource, and technological actions reported significant improvement in financial performance. A key finding of their survey is that start-up firms using high performance practices (greenfield sites) tend to perform better than redesigned brownfield sites (sites that had traditional designs to begin with that later transformed to HPWS designs) or traditional designs. Overall, work sites designed around HPWS principles reported financial performance 3 to 7 per cent higher than traditionally designed organisations. Those organisations reported improved financial performance, improved workplace behaviour (e.g., absences, employee turnover and safety) and improved quality of work-life for employees. However, nearly half of the organisations or units participating in a US survey (Macy et al., 1995) reported using relatively traditional designs, while the rest reported using HPWS designs. Results indicated that organisations using the high performance design tended to adopt design features from four categories, i.e., structural, human resources, technology and TQM. This finding reiterates the fact that many organisations have not yet fully implemented HPWS.

Research by Arthur (1994) further supports the positive HRM system-performance link in a US context. In his study, 'control' systems of HRM were compared with 'commitment' systems of HRM policies and practices. Control systems were defined as those seeking to improve efficiency by enforcing employee compliance with specified rules and procedures and basing employee rewards on some measurable output criteria. In contrast, commitment systems focused on empowering employees to make decisions to reach specific organisational goals. These systems were characterised by employee involvement and participation practices. Results of the study revealed that commitment-based systems were significantly related to shorter labour time/output and lower scrap rates. Turnover was found to be twice as high in control type systems.

Gooderham et al. (2008) used a similar framework in investigating HPWS and performance in a European context. Their study used CRANET data across 16 EU countries to investigate the relationship between 'calculative', 'collaborative' and 'intermediary' HR models on firm performance. Similar to Arthur (1994), they identify two generic HRM categories. Calculative HRM borrows from Walton's (1985) category of control HRM but is not entirely interchangeable. Calculative HRM is defined by Gooderham et al. (1999) as being designed to promote the efficient use of HRM in general rather than just encourage employee compliance (efficient use of human resources). Collaborative HRM aims to promote the goals of both employees and employers where employees are seen as significant stakeholders. This study makes significant contributions to the literature in that it examines HPWS across a variety of industries in the context of a variety of countries. We can see from Table 9.2 that the overall effect of HRM on performance was relatively modest (5 per cent significance level) with collaborative HRM having no significant impact on firm performance.

In a study of employee involvement in the US auto industry, MacDuffie (1995) found that bundling human resource practices and integrating them with the production system and business strategy led to higher levels of performance. An important feature of such organisations is that they are more flexible and able to adapt to change. This finding offers further support for Huselid's (1995) concept of a holistic and integrated HPWS design.

From a survey of 39 organisations in the service sector, Beatty and Varma, (1997); examined the antecedents, the design, and overall effectiveness of specific HPWS initiatives. Their results indicate that HPWS that create a change in the organisation's cultural behaviour (e.g., cooperation and innovation) and people management practices (e.g., reward and selection systems) can positively impact the financial and operational performance of these organisations. However, they found that the implementation of teams toward the HPWS effort had no significant impact on outcomes.

As for specific sectors of employment, empirical studies have shown that HPWS are associated with better performance in manufacturing plants in the US (Appelbaum et al., 2000; Arthur, 1992, 1994) and in services (Bailey, 1993; Batt, 2002). Combs et al., (2006) tested whether the benefits of HPWS in impacting organisational performance is larger for manufacturing than for service industries. This meta-analysis examined 92 published and unpublished studies totalling 19,319 organisations. They argued that HPWS practices align better with the nature of manufacturing work and allow manufacturers to benefit more from the flexibility created by HPWS. Following meta-analysis, manufacturing was found to have much stronger affects among manufacturing than service organisations due to industry context factors.

Some researchers have studied the moderating effects of some indicators on the relationship between high performance work systems and firm performance (e.g., (Batt, 2002; Guthrie, 2001). Many of these studies provide support for the view that external factors such as business strategy should moderate the HRM-performance link. Arthur (1994) distinguished between low cost and innovation strategies in his US study. He reports that mills with low-cost business strategies were more likely to have control-type human resource systems, and mills with differentiation strategies were more likely to have commitment-oriented human resource systems. Findings indicated that commitment-oriented HRM was significantly related to both fewer labour hours per ton and lower scrap rates. Control HRM was significantly higher in minimills with control systems than in those with commitment systems. Datta et al. (2005) found that industry specific variables such as capital intensity, growth rate and the level of product differentiation affected HPWS effectiveness. Michie and Sheehan's (2005) UK-based study found that a positive relationship exists between HR policies, practices and performance but that this relationship is dependent on business strategy. Further they found that companies pursuing an integrated approach to HR coupled with an innovator/quality enhancer focus within their business strategy perform best across all performance variables measured (sales growth, labour productivity and profitability). Heffernan et al.'s (2009) study of HPWS in Ireland found organisations identified as pursuing a differentiation strategy displayed greater investment in HPWS and had a significant positive correlation with two organisational performance outcomes – innovation and employee outcomes. However, further regression analysis showed no significant relationship. These associations between HRM and strategy, whilst not supported in regression analysis, are consistent with recent recommendations that strategic orientation should be re-introduced as a key variable in research studies (Becker and Huselid, 2006; Gerhart, 2005). Becker and Huselid (2006) suggest that organisations following a differentiation strategy concentrate on the processes of strategic value creation.

Nicholson and colleagues (1990) reported that HPWS have an important role to play in facilitating innovation through focusing upon objectives such as enabling people to think for themselves and to manage their own work. HPWS can increase innovation by: decentralising management in order to allow employees to discover and use knowledge; encouraging team practices that allow learning to grow through increased multidisciplinary knowledge; and putting that knowledge to good use (Laursen, 2002) (see Chapter 10). Richard and Johnson's study (2004) reveals that the use of HPWS affects innovation. An overview of the studies categorised by different authors is presented in Table 9.2. Overall it appears that the impact on performance of systems of interrelated HPWS practices appears from these studies to be greater than the sum of independent impacts when each component is implemented in isolation. By using meta-analysis to reduce the effects of sample and measurement error associated with some of these studies, Combs et al. (2006) estimated that organisations can increase their performance by .20 of a standardised unit for each unit increase in HPWS in use. Therefore, 20 per cent of the utility available from predicting performance differences among organisations is caused by HPWS.

Table 9.2   Summary results of HPWS studies on firm performance by country

Country	Study	Performance indicators	Results
USA	(United States Department of Labor, 1993) Survey of innovative practices	• Rate of return on capital • Quality	• Higher • Improved
USA	(Arthur, 1994) In a sample of steel minimills; compare between 'control' and 'commitment' systems	• Labour efficiency • Employee retention	• Higher • Improved
USA	(Huselid, 1995) Combination of HPWS practices vs. individual HR practices	• Employee retention • Productivity • Corporate performance	• Improved • Improved • Improved
USA	(Delery and Doty, 1996) Study on bank loan officers	• Financial performance	• Higher
New Zealand	(Guthrie, 2001) A multi-industry sample of 164 New Zealand firms	• Firm productivity • Employee retention	• Higher • Better
USA	(Batt, 2002) A nationally representative sample of the US telecommunications services industry	• Sales growth • Quit rates (the mediated effects of quit rate between HR practices and sales growth)	• Higher • Lower
UK	(Thompson, 2003) The UK Aerospace industry	• Innovation • Productivity • Psychological contract	• Higher • More • More positive
USA	Richard and Johnson (2004) 80 banking companies	• Marketing performance • Growth in sales • Profitability • Market share • Organisational innovation	• Better • Increased • Increased • Increased • Improved

Table 9.2   *(Continued)*

Country	Study	Performance indicators	Results
Ireland	Flood Guthrie, MarcCurtain and Liu (2005)	• Labour productivity • Employee retention • Sales growth • New product innovation	• Improved • Better • Improved • Increased
UK	Michie and Sheehan (2005) Study of stratified survey sample of publicly quoted UK manufacturing and service sector firms with 50 employees or more	Business strategy and HPWS • Sales growth • Labour productivity • Profitability	 • Increased • Increased • Increased
China	Ngo et al. (2008) Study of 600 enterprises across 4 Chinese regions. Majority of respondents were in the manufacturing sector	• Financial performance • Operational performance • Employee relations climate Moderating variable: ownership type • Financial performance • Operational performance • Employee relations climate	• Increased • Increased • Increased • Increased • No change • No change
European Union	Gooderham et al. (2008) Data derived from 1999 CRANET survey across 16 countries (n = 3281 firms). Countries are UK, France, Germany, Sweden, Spain, Denmark, The Netherlands, Italy, Ireland, Portugal, Finland, Former GDR, Greece, Austria, Belgium, Northern Ireland	Calculative HRM model • Firm performance Collaborative HRM model • Firm performance Intermediary HRM model • Firm performance	 • Increased • No change • Increased

Source: Summary results of HPWS studies on firm performance abridged and updated from Boselie (2002) Reprinted with kind permission from Paul Boselie.

Given the extent of variety and change in organisational context, it is important to know what HR metrics are appropriate to different situations (Colakoghu et al., 2006). Corporate level performance metrics are important although it cannot be assumed that outcomes at this level are definitely more important than others. As Table 9.2 shows, the majority of US-based academics explicitly base their analysis of the use of HR bundles on SHRM principles. They adopt a shareholder perspective, paying little attention to other stakeholders such as employees, trade unions and society at large and have a clear orientation towards financial based metrics (Paauwe, 2004). They, therefore, focus on firm level outcomes related to labour productivity (Huselid, 1995; MacDuffie, 1995), scrap rate (Arthur, 1994), sales growth (Batt, 2002; Guthrie, 2001), return on assets and return on investment (Delery and Doty, 1996) and market based performance (Huselid, 1995).

In contrast, UK research projects more often adopt a stakeholder perspective or apply a pluralist framework, and include such outcomes as absenteeism, employee turnover, commitment, motivation, satisfaction, trust, conflict and social climate (e.g. Guest, 1999). Also, the majority of UK academics are sceptical of what Guest (1990) called the 'American Dream' in HRM, which maintains that best practice will emerge from universal or normative modelling. Hitt and colleagues (2005) suggest that three primary groups of stakeholders exist and need to be considered in future research. These are capital market stakeholders (e.g., shareholders and banks), product market stakeholders (e.g., primary customers and suppliers) and organisational stakeholders (managers and employees). By focusing solely on financial metrics driven by capital market stakeholders, we ignore the importance of other potential stakeholder groups as well as other important performance measures.

Many of the studies also adhere to the complementary proposition of HPWS – that is, the interaction effects among HPWS practices explain some of the variation in firm performance in addition to the main effects of individual practices (Guest et al., 2004). However, few studies have really tested for these interaction effects directly. Datta et al. (2005) observe that those who have examined HPWS in a single sector, for example automobile assembly (MacDuffie, 1995) and steel industry minimills (Arthur, 1992), are therefore limited to one industry and its context specific characteristics. Godard (2001) meanwhile found a 'plateau effect' in HPWS adoption thus questioning the extent of the complementarities argument. He found from a study of 508 Canadian firms that firms with low to moderate HPWS adoption gained the most compared to firms with high adoption levels. Moderate levels of HPWS adoption were associated with 'increased belongingness, empowerment, task involvement, and ultimately job satisfaction, esteem, commitment, and citizenship behaviour' (Godard, 2001: 776). Whereas in firms with higher levels of HPWS adoption these positive associations were found to decline in magnitude and even were negative in some cases (e.g., empowerment and job satisfaction). This may be interpreted as supporting the line of argument that there are 'diminishing returns at higher levels of adoption, rather than the increasing returns predicted by the complementarities thesis' (Godard, 2004: 354).

Are HPWS globally applicable?

Quantitative research on the links between HRM and performance has been carried out in many countries worldwide (see Tables 9.1, 9.2 and 9.3). They draw on a variety of theories such as systems theory, best practice, contingency theory, socio-technical systems, and the resource-based view. Most studies are based in the USA and the UK, followed closely by Europe and East Asia.

Studies on the impact of HPWS on firm performance have been conducted in Asian companies and the results are mixed (Chow, 2005). More research is needed to test the transferability of the fundamental premises of HPWS into other parts of the world thus exploring the question of whether HRM can improve competitive advantage in an international context. Work is now being undertaken to explore these concepts in countries such as India, Finland (see Fey et al., 2008) and China (Ngo et al., 2008). Country of origin and the influence of type of economy are two

Table 9.3   Overview of studies of HRM and performance in different countries

Country	Studies
Australia	Gollan and Davis (1999)
Canada	Godard (1998, 2001)
China	Mitsuhashi et al. (2000)
Finland	Lähteenmäki et al. (1998)
France	d'Arcimoles (1997); Laroche (2001); Guerrero and Barraud-Didier, 2004
Germany	Backes-Gellner et al. (1997)
Greece	Panayopoulou (2001)
Ireland	Flood et al. (2005); Heffernan et al. (2009)
Japan	Ichniowski and Shaw (1999); Kato and Morishima (2002)
Korea, Taiwan (China), Singapore and Thailand	Bae and Lawler (2000); Bae et al. (2001)
Netherlands	Paauwe (2004)
New Zealand	Guthrie (2001)
Pakistan	Khilji and Wang (2006)
Russia	Fey et al. (2000)
Spain	de Saa Perez and Garcia Falcon (2001)
UK	Guest and Peccei (1994); Michie and Sheehan (2005)
USA	Huselid (1995); MacDuffie (1995); Arthur (1994)

Source: Overview of Studies of HRM and Performance in Different Countries abridged and updated from Paauwe (2004, p. 61).

issues highlighted which can advance a more contextual understanding of HPWS globally (see Box 9.2). This is particularly important for multinational organisations operating globally.

Box 9.2   International context and HPWS – the case between US and the Netherlands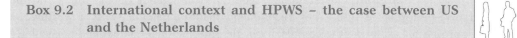

It is argued that the prevalence of managerial prerogatives is a dominant feature of the US work-related culture. In contrast the lack of authoritarian power of the manager is characteristic of the Dutch work-related culture. ... The US system of

(Continued)

(Continued)

industrial relations is characterised by the weak role of the state and a decentralised system of collective bargaining. In the United States the role of the state is restricted to ensuring that the bargaining process between management and unions is not obstructed by the abuse of power by either of them. ... In contrast to the US system of industrial relations, state involvement characterises the Dutch system of industrial relations. The Dutch government has issued numerous laws regulating employment relationships in many areas, including aspects such as dismissal protection, collective bargaining, co-determination and working hours and conditions. ... A further feature of Dutch industrial relations is its centralised nature ... At the plant level the Works Council Act regulates the relationship between management and workers. ... Finally one should note that the attitude of industrial players is characterised by an emphasis on 'consultation' and 'striving for consensus'. This attitude is in contrast with the principle of bargaining that underpins the interaction in the US industrial relations system (i.e. competitive through pressure/power).

The management-work relationship in the US is characterised by distance between supervisor and his immediate subordinates in terms of power. In contrast absence of authoritarian power in work relations is viewed as typical of the Dutch workplace. A Dutch supervisor cannot make use of their hierarchical position by giving orders or applying sanctions. The only means at their disposal is the power of persuasion. Employee participation is considered by US management as a tool to enhance performance rather than as a means to improve relations and the quality of working life. In contrast Dutch managers appear to be sceptical about certain US initiatives. They view participation as societal obligation to workers. Societal expectations in the Netherlands force managers to operate on an informal basis.

On the basis of these findings the widespread belief that global trends will lead to the homogenisation of employment relationship can be challenged. It can be claimed that a divergence in employment relations will continue.

Source: From "HRM and Performance: Achieving Long Term Viability" by Paauwe, J. (2004). By permission of Oxford University Press.

Boselie et al. (2001), for example, argue that contingency factors impact on the HPWS-performance link. They recommend institutional theory as a worthwhile approach for exploring the complexity of the international context and particularly for understanding the effective operation of MNCs. There are 'powerful, non-market institutional factors' (Gooderham et al., 2004: 20) at play in Europe; many of which make the central features of some US HPWS unworkable in European organisations. These factors include national culture, legislation, state intervention, organisational level union involvement and participation and requirement for consultation, dialogue and communication between social partners (Morley et al., 2000). Fey and Björkman (2001) investigated this issue when looking at the effect of HRM practices on MNC subsidiary operations in Russia. Their findings highlighted the importance of national culture as a key factor in effective HRM and performance. This included stronger hierarchy in Russia, less willingness to share information and higher levels of employee-management mistrust. Paauwe (2004) also rejects the universalist application of HRM best practices across firms regardless of country locations. He argues that we must look to find a clearer understanding of the reasons why firms adopt particular HRM practices beyond considerations of financial performance. Paauwe (2004) contrasts HRM in the USA and Netherlands to explore these reasons and concludes that the belief that global trends will lead to the homogenisation of employment relationships is incorrect. Instead, due to contextually bound decisions, institutional settings and corporate strategic choice, divergence in employment relations will persist. The results from other studies of HRM abroad differ widely. Bird et al. (1998) showed that Japanese MNCs have been successful in replicating Japanese style management techniques and HRM in their foreign subsidiaries. Royle and Towers' (2003) study of McDonalds in Germany also show how a company can introduce their uniform world policies in a country characterised by high levels of union regulation and institutionalised forms of employee representation (e.g., works councils). Royle and Towers (2003) reported that McDonalds achieved uniformity through strategies of avoiding compliance with collective bargaining agreements and aggressively deterring employee interest in union representation.

Much of the HPWS research to-date uses data obtained from the US, UK, Canada and Australia. These countries all operate in an institutional background focused on liberal economies. Godard (2004) proposes that the potential pay-offs from introducing HPWS may increase in more coordinated market economies such as Finland and Germany where firms are managed as stakeholder institutions and where workers have strong representation and rights of co-determination. This contrasts with the US or UK where employee representation is weaker and as a result net benefits from the work intensification approach to HPWS dominate (Godard, 2004) as there is the view that these initiatives are management-driven and used solely for performance improvements and not employee well-being (Harley, 2001). Guerrero and Barraud-Didier (2004) examined HPWS in 180 large French companies. Whilst their research showed there was a significant and positive relationship between HPWS and organisational performance, they also highlighted some country specific differences. Whilst compensation policy seems to be of prime importance in many countries (UK, USA, Asiatic countries and Russia), empowerment and communication was identified as more important in France. Kalmi and Kauhanen (2008) describe the Finnish labour market as characterised by strong unions and statutory employee representation and job protection with a strong collectivist culture and low power distance. Their research supports Godard's (2004) argument that institutional settings can shape employee outcomes of HPWS and in a country that has a more coordinated market economy, the complementarity argument was confirmed. In their study of 493 full-time employees Kalmi and Kauhanen (2008) found that there are increasing returns from HPWS within Finland.

4 HPWS debates internationally

The above section reviewed the international evidence supporting the argument that investment in HPWS impacts on bottom line organisational outcomes. However Ichniowski et al. (1996) claim that there are a number of problems which seriously weaken the utility of these studies. This section will identify some of the major problems identified in the research.

The most fundamental difficulty surrounding HPWS research is related to theoretical and methodological issues. Some authors have referred to this as the 'black box' problem, noting that the conceptual development of the mediating mechanisms through which HRM has an impact on profitability has thus far eluded empirical testing (Boxall and Purcell, 2003; Hutchinson and Purcell, 2003). Hesketh and Fleetwood (2006) claim that whilst empirical research might be a useful starting point for understanding the HPWS-performance link and demonstrating the potential value created through HPWS, it should be treated as providing findings that are open to interpretation rather than treated as conclusive evidence. A great deal of HPWS empirical research, including many of those examined in this chapter, does not proceed beyond attempts to find an empirical association between HPWS and organisational performance. These studies have revealed very little regarding the processes through which this valuable association is created (Wright and Gardner, 2003). Becker and Huselid (2006) claim that a clearer articulation of the 'black box' between HRM and firm performance is the most pressing theoretical and empirical challenge in the HPWS literature.

Debates also exist on the efficacy of methodological choices that have been made in previous HPWS research. The predominant methodological problems relate to the difficulty of establishing causality, measurement issues, the use of single respondents in questionnaires, the definition of performance and the time period, or lag, between HR activities and performance outcomes (Purcell, 1999; Purcell and Kinnie, 2007).

Low agreement exists among the proponents of this approach about what practices should be included within the scope of the term HPWS. Legge (2001) observes that of 15 high-commitment practices identified in the UK WERS 98 study, only 7 appear in US studies. While Pfeffer (1998) stressed the importance of job security, it was not included in other lists (Delaney and Huselid, 1996; Patterson et al., 1997). This lack of a consensus among HPWS researchers is a problem and provides insufficient justification for why certain practices have been included. The challenge surrounding measurement of HPWS practices has also been subjected to scrutiny by critical scholars. Legge (2001) argues that studies of HPWS reveal confusion in their approach, in that individual practices such as contingent pay are measured in different ways by different researchers. These issues need to be resolved before any confidence can be shown in the magnitude or causality of such relationships (Gerhart, 1999).

Whose perspective?

The HPWS-performance literature reviewed so far has focused on firm level outcomes. However, there is also the assumption that a causal link flowing from

HPWS to organisational outcomes occurs via the responses of employees (e.g., see the AMO theory on page 296). This places the employee as a central mediator in explaining the impact HPWS has on performance. The issue of taking the worker's view of HRM into account however has only recently emerged in the HPWS debate. Clark and colleagues (1998) have argued that while workers are the primary recipients and consumers of HRM, their voice has been muted. They recommend that 'the inside view' should become more prominent if we are to gain a fuller understanding of HRM. This includes examining the role employee perceptions play in translating HR practices into desired organisational outcomes. The effect of HPWS may reside in the meanings that employees attach to those practices. People have different perceptions of reality (Fiske and Taylor, 1991) and therefore not all employees will interpret HR practices in the same way or attach the same meanings to these practices. Also it is important to be aware that HR activities can also have very different effects on different categories of employees (Benschop, 2001).

Only 3 out of 25 studies examined by Wall and Wood (2005) included employee surveys. Boselie et al. (2005) found only 11 of 104 studies examined used employee survey data. Empirical research that begins to explore the role of employees' perceptions of HR practices in the practice-performance causal chain is sorely needed (Nishii et al., 2008). Section 5 below examines international research on HPWS and employee outcomes.

5 HPWS and the employee outcomes – international evidence

As we can see from section 2, literature on the impact of HPWS on organisational performance is abundant. However, there is a much smaller body of literature on what HPWS can do to or for employees, who are equally important stakeholders in the employment relationship. There are ample studies of micro HR research addressing the relationship between individual HR practices and employee level outcomes (e.g., Wright and Boswell, 2002), however there is little research evidence investigating bundles of HRM practices and employee outcomes (Macky and Boxall, 2007). Boxall and Purcell (2003) argue that all studies of HPWS should include data on costs and benefits for *both* companies *and* workers because 'worker motivation and broader legitimacy are unlikely to improve if only management gains' (2003: 20). Where research has been carried out, the evidence has been partly contradictory. Some authors argue that HPWS leads to mutually beneficial, win–win outcomes where both employers and employees end up being better off (Appelbaum et al., 2000; Huselid, 1995; Pfeffer, 1994). In contrast, other authors argue that owners' gain at the expense of more stressed employees (Harley, 2005; Ramsay et al., 2000). An overview of studies incorporating international research on HPWS and employee outcomes is detailed in Table 9.4.

Table 9.4   Summary results of HPWS studies on employee outcomes

Country	Study	Employee outcomes	Results
USA	Nishii et al. (2008) 362 departments across 95 stores of a US supermarket chain Data on HPWS collected from 4,500 employees and 1,100 department managers	• HR attributions impact on employee attitudes (affective commitment and satisfaction combined) i Quality and employee enhancement ii Cost and employee exploitation iii Union compliance • Impact of employee attitudes on organisational citizenship behaviours	 • Improved • Decreased • No change • Improved
USA	Appelbaum et al. (2000) Study of companies in steel, apparel and medical electronics manufacturing	• Job satisfaction • Commitment • Stress • Wages	• Improved • Improved • No change • Improved
UK	Guest (1999) UK study cross-sectional telephone interview examining HPWS n = 1,000	• Psychological contract • Job satisfaction • Job satisfaction (mediated model) • Pressure at work • Employment security • Motivation • Motivation (mediated model)	• Increased 50 per cent • No change • Increased • Slight increase • Increased • No change • Increased
UK	Ramsay et al. (2000) WERS98 data from both management and employees HPWS scores broken down into SWP1, SWP2 and HPWP. Findings are reported for HPWP only	*HCM and HIM models* • Extrinsic satisfaction • Management relations • Job discretion • Commitment *Labour process model* • Work intensification • Job insecurity • Discretion • Job strain	 • Increased • Increased • Increased • Increased • Increased • Decreased • Increased • Increased
New Zealand	Macky and Boxall (2008) Representative national survey Computer assisted telephone interview with 775 randomly selected NZ employees	• Job satisfaction • Stress • Fatigue • Work-life imbalance	• Increased • Slight decrease • No change • No change

Table 9.4   *(Continued)*

Country	Study	Employee outcomes	Results
UK	White et al. (2003) National Survey 'Working in Britain 1992' and 'Working in Britain 2000'	• Negative job to home spillover	• Increased
Canada	Godard (2001) Telephone survey of 508 employed Canadians investigating alternative work practices	• Belongingness • Stressfulness • Commitment • Job satisfaction • Empowerment • Workload • Fatigue • Citizenship • Task involvement	• Increased • Increased (for linear model only) • Increased • Increased • Increased • No change • No change • Increased • Increased
Finland	Kalmi and Kauhanen (2008) Quality of Work national survey 4,104 surveyed; focus of study on 493 full-time employees	• Job intensity • Job influence • Job security • Wage • Stress • Job satisfaction	• No change • Increased • Increased • Increased • Decreased • Increased
UK	Danford et al. (2004) In-depth case study in multinational 'blue chip' aerospace manu-facturing plant (high skill, high technology) Qualitative interviews with 72 staff 604 questionnaires and company responses to WERS98 data	• Stress • Work place decision making • Quality of working life	• Increased • Decreased • Decreased
Australia	Harley (2002) 1995 Australian Workplace Industrial Relations Survey (AWIRS95)	• Discretion • Job satisfaction • Attitude to management • Insecurity • Effort • Stress • Composite discretion	• No change • No change • No change • No change • No change • No change • No change
Australia	Harley et al. (2007) Survey of two occupational groups – registered nurses and aged-care/personal care workers in Victoria Survey administered to 3,136 members of Australia Nursing Federation (Victoria), 1,318 usable responses	• Autonomy • Affective commitment • Job satisfaction • Psychological strain • Turnover intention • Work effort	• Positive increase • Positive increase • Positive increase • Positive decrease • Positive decrease • Positive decrease

Two primary approaches to examining the impact of HPWS on employees exist. The first way is what Harley et al. (2007) term the 'mainstream' approach which follows the argument that HPWS leads to mutually beneficial, win–win outcomes for both employees and organisations through increased commitment, autonomy and satisfaction. A number of studies adhere to the mainstream account of HPWS. Appelbaum et al. (2000) conducted research on three manufacturing sectors in the US – 15 steel mills, 17 apparel manufacturers and 10 electronic and imaging equipment producers. Their study showed positive employees attitudes to HPWS, including increased trust in management, intrinsic rewards and enjoyment of the work. Table 9.4 reports similar positive findings for studies conducted in the UK (Guest, 2002; Patterson et al., 1997), New Zealand (Macky and Boxall, 2007) and Australia (Harley et al., 2007). For example, Guest (1999) found the employees who reported experiencing higher numbers of these HR practices reported high job satisfaction and higher motivation. Vandenburg et al. (1999) found that HPWS influence organisational effectiveness (turnover and return on equity) via improved employee job satisfaction and organisational commitment.

Macky and Boxall's (2007, 2008) study of 775 New Zealand employees adds strength to the mutual gains argument. They report a clear relationship between HPWS and employee job satisfaction. They also report no significant relationship between autonomy, training and performance related reward and negative employee outcomes in the form of increased stress or fatigue or poorer work-life balance. These positive findings for HPWS are in contrast to the work of White et al. (2003) and Danford et al. (2004) in the UK. White et al. (2003) reported a significant negative relationship between HPWS and spill-over from work to home. Macky and Boxall (2007) tested the complementarity thesis of HPWS that argues that each HR practice has interactive, additive effects (similar to Godard, 2004) on predicting employee attitudinal variables. For three of their four variables (job satisfaction, trust in management and behavioural commitment) significant interaction terms were found among HR practices. However the effect sizes were weak and the directions of these influences on work attitudes were negative. The authors suggest that there are limits to the positive effects of HPWS for employees.

White et al. (2003) can be categorised as following the second way of examining HPWS which focuses on labour process theory and argues that the positive outcomes for organisations is not through commitment or discretionary effort but through work intensification, increased stress and heightened workload. Labour process theorists argue that there has been no systematic research on whether the gains are shared and present counter-arguments demonstrating why they might not be (Ramsey et al., 2000; Wood, 1999; Wood and de Menezes, 1998). These counter-arguments include work intensification through involving employees in decisions previously made by managers and team work (e.g., Barker, 1993, refers to 'concertive control' through peer pressure driven by team-based pay for performance).

Ramsay et al.'s (2000) UK study used WERS98 data and sought to challenge the conventional accounts of HPWS as a 'win–win' approach. They presented three models constructed on high commitment, high involvement and labour process models. Overall, their findings supported the HPWS rhetoric in that HPWS practices were positively associated with employees' self-reported levels of discretion, relations with management, satisfaction with pay, organisational commitment and work effort. However, they found weak effects for employee outcome mediator variables in their three models of HPWS-performance. Their work highlighted that 'the widely held assumption that positive performance outcomes from HPWS flow via positive employee outcomes has been shown to be questionable, (Ramsay et al., 2000: 521). They concluded that the impacts of HPWS are neither simplistically exploitative or straightforwardly win–win. Godard (2001) too found notable associations for negative outcomes and HPWS. He reported a positive association between HPWS and stressfulness. Whilst he found no statistically significant associations between HPWS and workload and fatigue, there are signs that HPWS are associated with decreases in workload and fatigue at low to moderate levels only, and are followed by possible increases at higher levels of adoption. He concluded that 'none of these benefits is realized, because workers are in effect overwhelmed by higher stress levels. Thus, any initially positive implications ... diminish' (2001: 797).

Others also urge caution in accepting that HPWS is universally positive for employees and suggest that the promise of 'mutual gains' is often not fulfilled. Harley's (1999) study in Australia found no links between employee involvement practices (e.g., TQM, semi autonomous teams and quality circles) and self-reported employee discretion. Osterman (2000) examined lay offs and pay outcomes and concluded that organisations with HPWS in place were more likely than other firms to lay staff off, and no more likely to have higher rates of pay. Harley et al.'s (2007) more recent study of HPWS and employee experience of work in the service sector however reports more positive outcomes. In a survey of registered nurses and aged-care/personal care workers in the aged-care sector, Harley et al. (2007) found overwhelmingly positive outcomes. They also found that HPWS practices are no less applicable to low skilled workers than high skilled workers. This refutes the belief that HPWS are only implemented and effective when applied to high skilled categories of workers.

Researchers in the UK and US who have refuted the work intensification argument focus on the evident gains to workers of HPWS practices: job satisfaction (Patterson et al., 1997), the intrinsic value of having a degree of job autonomy (Appelbaum et al., 2000), organisational commitment (Ashton and Sung, 2002) and 'new' skills acquisition that result from employees' use of information technology and problem-solving methods (Appelbaum, 2002). Guest (1999) reported that overall the verdict is positive for HPWS with employees reporting a more positive psychological contract, greater satisfaction, job security and motivation as well as lower levels of work.

Taking context into account the majority of studies examining HPWS and employee outcomes have done so in manufacturing settings (e.g. Appelbaum et al. 2000). Harley and colleagues (2007) argue that the generally positive outcomes reported may reflect the relatively high levels of unionisation in the manufacturing settings where these studies were conducted. Eaton and Voos (1992) argued that unionised companies make more extensive use of workplace innovations than non-union companies, and are likely to be more effective in improving economic performance due to the union's role in designing and overseeing the new work structures. Recent research by Liu et al. (2009) in an Irish context is at odds with these findings. Their study of 165 firms operating in Ireland indicates that as union representation increases, there is a significant decrease in the use of HPWS. They also found that the mediating effect of providing employment security significantly reduced any negative impacts.

6 The critical role of the line manager

So far this chapter has examined the impact of HPWS on organisational outcomes with employee outcomes often being seen as the critical linking mechanism in the HR-performance causal chain (e.g., see Figures 9.1 and 9.3 above where the HR policies influence employees' ability, motivation and opportunity to perform). Wright and Snell (1998) made a distinction between intended and actual HR practices. Wright and Nishii (2004) elaborate further by proposing a model that they believe provides a framework that allows researchers to identify some of the sub-processes through which HR practices impact on organisational performance. In this model they differentiate between *intended* HR practices, *actual* HR practices and *perceived* HR practices. Wright and Nishii's model highlights the gap that can exist between espoused and enacted HR policies. *Intended* HR practices refers to the practices developed by policy makers and reflects the outcome of the development of an HR strategy that seeks to elicit desired employee behaviours. *Actual* HR practices refer to practices operationalised in organisations. There is recognition that not all intended HR practices are successfully implemented. *Perceived* HR practices are actual HR practices as perceived and interpreted subjectively by each employee in the focal group. The perceived HR practices then impact on employee reactions and consequently on performance.

From this model we can see that HR policies are often converted into practice by front line managers who conduct performance reviews, make promotion choices and communicate employment termination decisions (see Box 9.3). Wright and Nishii (2007) explain that variance exists from the fact that the practices are often implemented by multiple individuals (line managers, interviewers, trainers, etc.) who will not be uniform in their implementation efforts. This raises two important concerns with regard to the study of HPWS. This first centres on the challenge, institutionally, to implement a consistent set of processes in a consistent manner across large and diverse organisations with multiple individuals. The second concern occurs at the individual level where the implementation of HPWS is made difficult by the fact that those charged with the actual execution of practices (i.e. line managers) develop a comfort that comes with familiarity of behaviour and results (Wright and Nishii, 2007). The framework proposed by Wright and Nishii suggests that for HRM to have an impact on organisational performance it is crucial that HR departments and line managers be committed and supportive to the development of effective HRM systems by focusing upon actual 'implementation' within organisations.

Box 9.3   The role of the line manager

Store managers have to interpret what Head Office wants. Effectively, store management is the interface between Head Office and those who work in the store. The key is how you apply the Head Office policies – that's the difference! (Hutchinson and Purcell, 2003)

There has been a growing trend towards devolving more and more HR responsibility to the line manager. This devolution of human resource responsibilities from what were previously the primary domain of personnel and human resource managers is a growing and global trend with both positive and negative consequences reported (Perry and Kulik, 2008). Whittaker and Marchington (2003) for example suggest that by devolving HR decision making down the line, managers should be better able to make faster decisions that are more tailored to individual circumstances. The negatives of devolvement included HRM being seen as a 'poor second' to immediate business goals (McGovern et al., 1997), inconsistency in applying HR practices, insufficient attention being given to HRM issues (Bond and Wise, 2003) and failure to treat employees fairly and consistently (Renwick, 2003). Questions regarding the utility of full devolvement of HRM down to the line still exist. Dany et al. (2008) maintain that the role of qualified HRM specialists is too critical to be given away to front line managers and they continue to have an important role to play in devising HR policy. This raises debates on how much influence on HRM is distributed between HRM specialists and line managers. Forbringer and Oeth (1998) contend that HRM specialists who are too powerful may be tempted to make the sophistication of tools and development of HR practices ends-in-themselves which will lead to its development as a 'bureaucratic bastion'. Legge (1989) concludes that HRM is 'vested in line management as business managers responsible for coordinating and directing all resources in the business unit in pursuit of bottom line profits' (1989: 27).

Using recent CRANET data, Dany et al. (2008) found that countries such as Denmark, New Zealand, Bulgaria and Slovenia tended to have organisations where major HRM decisions were mostly undertaken by line managers alone. In contrast, they report that companies from UK, France, Spain, Germany and the USA were characterised by high levels of HRM assignment to HRM specialists. Further analysis showed that too much or too little influence of HRM specialists in decisions regarding major HRM policies nullified the HRM integration-organisational performance link. Instead, HRM organisation (i.e. its level of integration and influence distribution between HRM specialists and line managers), had positive performance implications only in particular settings where the HRM function is shared between HRM specialists and line managers and HRM decision-making happens with HRM specialists in consultation with line managers. Boxall and Purcell (2008) point out that line manager action or inaction is often responsible for the difference between espoused HR policies and enactment. As a result their role and their behaviour in enacting HR policies are extremely important in HPWS-organisational performance research (Purcell and Hutchinson, 2007) as they exert greater influence over employee behaviour (Redman and Snape, 2005). According to McGovern et al., (1997) line management involvement is problematic because it requires both institutional reinforcement and personal motivation (see Box 9.4). Their research showed that personal motivation of managers was of much greater importance in explaining the successful involvement of line managers with HRM than formal institutional incentives and pressures.

Box 9.4   Line manager skills

A major block is the people management skills of our line managers. It's to do with software and hardware. You can put the courses out there and the development plans and processes etc and that can all be incredibly practical. But unless you get the software right – the way they do it – it will fail. A lot of managers still feel that managing people is what personnel do. (Personnel manager, Lloyds Bank)

In other words, while the institutional recognition of the role of line managers is a necessary condition in placing personnel activities firmly among line managers, it is not sufficient without the goodwill of the managers themselves. (McGovern et al., 1997)

Purcell and Hutchinson (2007) also reported that employees respond to both the HRM practices and their line managers' leadership behaviour. Employees' judgment of their line managers' leadership behaviour was directly related to higher levels of affective commitment and to better aspects of job experience. According to Purcell and Hutchinson (2007), an effective line manager helps to create, or transmit, impressions of the organisation as a whole (commitment) and make jobs satisfying by influencing how demanding the job is, how much autonomy the employee has in the job and the sense of achievement that comes from doing the job.

This section has demonstrated that one cannot consider how HPWS and performance are linked without understanding *how* HR policies are translated into practice. In understanding how HRM policies are implemented in practice the role of the line manager comes to the fore. Research has shown that when preferences of HRM choices by employees are similar to actual HR practices currently used by the company, satisfaction and competitive advantage are achieved (Sparrow and Wu, 1998). Khilji and Wang (2006) similarly found that when intended and implemented HRM are congruent, employee satisfaction and organisational performance are higher. Therefore line managers must establish consistency between intended and implemented practices if investment in HPWS is to have beneficial organisational performance outcomes.

7 Summary and conclusions

This chapter shows that, whilst there is considerable evidence of a link between investment in HRM and performance, the link is still not absolutely established methodologically or theoretically thus undermining definitive conclusions (Boselie et al., 2005; Fleetwood and Hesketh, 2007; Truss, 2001; Wall and Wood, 2005). At best, there is a degree of convergence in the studies supporting the belief that HRM has an effect on organisational performance. Many different models have been proposed to explain the contribution of HRM to organisational performance, drawing on diverse theoretical frameworks and using many different methodologies. These include the AMO framework and the resource-based view of the firm. Three theoretical perspectives of HPWS were discussed in this chapter. These are the universalist, contingency and configurational perspectives. We have seen the international evidence that shows a strong link between investment in HPWS and performance. However, evidence suggests that there are still some omitted variables in the HPWS-performance linkage that reduce the explanatory power of these models (Beltrán-Martín et al., 2008).

A number of debates in HPWS literature were discussed. The main concern was with the explanatory void that is said to exist – what is often called the 'black box'. One suggestion was that employee perspectives on how these HPWS policies are enacted in practice should be introduced into the HPWS research. Two perspectives exist in the literature on employee experiences of HPWS. One is based on the 'mutually beneficial' argument that HPWS increases employee autonomy and skill and allows them greater say in how they do their jobs. The second perspective incorporates labour process theory and suggests that these HPWS practices lead to work intensification, with any gains in employee discretion being marginal (Ramsey et al., 2000). This chapter shows that there has not yet been a resolution of this debate with some scholars finding benefits for workers (e.g. Appelbaum et al., 2000; Guest, 1999) while others report negative effects (e.g. White et al., 2003). However, the majority of studies report positive outcomes.

Future research needs to address the wider question of what success and performance is from a variety of stakeholder standpoints, including societal or ethical dimensions, and not just discuss it solely from a financial perspective (Delbridge and Lowe, 1997). Lepak and Shaw (2008) more recently suggest that a variety of contingencies may also affect the nature of the relationship between HRM systems and measures of organisational performance. These include the role of technology, work force trends, and changing worker values.

The chapter concluded with an analysis of the role of the line manager as an agent in HPWS implementation. Recent research has shown that 'the immediate supervisor plays a critical role as a key agent of the organisation through which members form their perceptions of the organisation' (Liden et al., 2004: 228). However decision makers must include consideration of how line managers can apply HRM. As McGovern et al. (1997) showed, the short-term nature of managerial activity means that line managers often place a greater priority on the achievement of numbers (e.g. sales targets) rather than the achievement of numbers through people (i.e. softer issues such as development). Purcell and Hutchinson (2007) suggest that greater emphasis on improving front-line managers' skills in people management is needed. For HPWS to have performance effects, organisations should invest in their front line managers as enactors and leaders of HRM. In doing so they should introduce better selection with greater emphasis given to leadership behaviours as well as technical skills and knowledge, access to further development, coaching and guidance and career management (see Chapter 11).

Discussion questions

1 Which theoretical perspective are you most convinced by: 'best practice', 'best fit', or the configurational perspective, or are you not convinced by any of these? Why?

2 How should the success of HPWS be evaluated in your opinion?

3 Do you agree with the argument that HPWS lead to mutually beneficial win–win outcomes for both organisations and employees? Why/why not?

4 What can organisations do to support front line managers in implementing intended HR practices?

5 Why is there a difference between the intended and realised practices of HRM?

The high performance work system in an Irish manufacturing company: mechanisms between HR practices and organisational performance

This case is based on 'Principal and Agent in the 'Black Box': The Influence of Line Managers on the Effectiveness of High Performance Work Systems', Masters in Business Studies (HRM) Dissertation by Annika Huelsen, 2008, Dublin City University. (The company and all individuals' names are changed.)

Medical Ltd Ireland operates a sophisticated system of HR practices that depend, to a large extent, on implementation by its line managers. There is a divergence of opinion amongst line managers however on their role within the HRM system. The line managers who are in daily contact with the production employees have differing opinions about the HRM function and their own role in enacting HR practices. This has had a significant impact on the quantity and quality of HR practices that each employee experiences.

Company background

Medical Ltd Ireland is a manufacturer of medical devices. Its production plant in western Ireland employs over 500 employees who are primarily organised across 11 production teams. All production employees are unionised, while management and technical employees are not. Medical Ltd operates according to the principles of lean manufacturing. Following the principle of producing to markets' demands, the primary goal of lean manufacturing is to eliminate waste, such as over-production, waiting time, transportation costs, unnecessary stock, unnecessary movement and the production of defective goods. HR practices have been introduced to support the principles of lean manufacturing.

HR practices at Medical Ltd

Mary, the senior HR manager at Medical Ltd invested substantial effort and resources in the development of a sophisticated system of HR practices. The HRM system encompasses three key areas. These are a careful and rigorous selection process, an integrated performance management system and practices encouraging employee engagement. These areas are linked horizontally to ensure cohesion within the system, in particular through the central performance management system. A 'staffing review' is carried out several times a year, which informs staffing and training and development needs and assesses employee engagement levels. At Medical Ltd, employee engagement means that line managers actively seek employees' ideas and value their input. The ability to involve employees is a selection criterion for managers. Employee engagement is an important means of deploying the organisational operating system of lean manufacturing.

Deriving the system of HR practices, the senior HR manager carefully considered the metrics-driven lean manufacturing environment. For, Michael, the HR director, 'HR is a critical piece. These (lean manufacturing principles) are only philosophies ... without people actually performing within the system with the rules that are governing those systems. So without the people piece it's only a dream.' Indeed, at Medical Ltd new hires are familiarised with the lean systems and processes right from induction. The central performance management system is predominantly metrics-driven and previous experience with lean manufacturing is an advantage when applying for a job. Furthermore, employee engagement is central for the lean manufacturing belief that continuous improvement can only happen from the bottom-up. Continuous improvement also requires constant increases in individual ability and performance as well as workers with multiple skills in order to operate a system of job rotation and allow for flexibility on the production site. At Medical Ltd, each key production process or piece of equipment can be operated by a minimum of two primary operators and a backup operator per shift.

The responsibility for implementation

The effectiveness of this HR system depends to a great extent on its implementation by line managers. In particular, production team leaders play a crucial rule in enacting HR practices as they are in daily contact with production staff. In general, HR enables the process by establishing systems and procedures and facilitating implementation, and the production team leaders deploy the policies developed by the HRM function. Therefore, the HR team assumes responsibility for only about one third of all HR practices. Another third is sole line responsibility. The final third is shared between HR and the line.

Bearing responsibility for their team and at the same time being accountable for production metrics exerts great pressure on line managers at Medical Ltd. One experienced production team leader, Bill, admits sacrificing the HR responsibilities which can deliver long-term benefits for short-term production needs. Though he acknowledges this dilemma, he finds that 'the major part of the role of a production team leader is to manage the people on the shop floor'.

Like Bill, many line managers exercise considerable discretion on the amount of practices enacted when implementing HR practices. Therefore, the percentage of employees that the HR function initially intended to cover by the different HR practices is higher than the percentage of employees towards whom line managers actually enact the HR system. In addition, there are remarkable differences between the teams, which depend on the attitude as well as experience of the respective team leader. Nevertheless, production team leaders are conscious of the consequences of their HR actions. Bill's colleague Paul summarises this fact: 'If you don't get on with your team, every metric will suffer'. Indeed, Bill, the line manager who shows the least passion for HR topics leads the lowest performing team.

The relationship between HR and line managers

Given the shared responsibility for the HR system at Medical Ltd, the relationship between the HR function and each production team leader is vital for the success of the company. At Medical Ltd, most staff describe this relationship as one of partnership, mutual respect, trust and honesty. Mary emphasises that 'we are not (…) slapping them for being bad production team leaders. We say, 'Can we help there?'' First and foremost, she runs the weekly HR forum, a 'doctor's visit' where she discusses HR issues with the production team leaders. Besides this formal meeting, problems may be entrusted informally to her or one of her colleagues. Training and development opportunities are not only provided to solve problems reactively, but also to proactively foster competences. For example, Mary developed a leadership programme that enables production team leaders to follow a continuous career path. Moreover, Mary wrote the 'Production Team Leader Manual' that provides an initial level of guidance on all aspects of line managers' HR tasks.

In general, production team leaders greatly appreciate the support provided by HRM. In particular, they value the training and development opportunities and are thus comfortable with their HR responsibilities. Similarly, line managers praise HR's advice on vital people issues. Nonetheless, with his long experience Bill perceives HR 'details drilling down (…) what has to be (done)' as controlling. He feels impaired in his freedom to undertake his HR responsibilities. By contrast, Bill's younger colleague Paul finds that HR 'don't get involved with issues unless we bring the issues to them'. Not surprisingly, Bill implements much less of the HR practices intended by his HRM department than Paul.

Case questions

1 Analyse the HPWS at Medical Ltd. Consider the organisational context and the different mechanisms through which HRM provides value for the organisation.
2 What consequences may the different levels of implementation of HR practices have on team and organisational performance?
3 Critically discuss the attitudes of HR and the different line managers towards each other. What are the advantages and downsides of their positions?

Case questions for further study and reflection

1 Imagine you are the HR director at corporate headquarters of a company such as Medical Ltd in the USA with a number of international divisions across the world including Europe, Asia and South America. What issues would you need to consider in implementing a coherent global HR strategy across all divisions worldwide? What unique HR challenges might you encounter?
2 Imagine you are the local HR manager of Medical Ltd Ireland and you are trying to implement the newly developed global HR strategy whilst dealing with major country level constraints at the local level. How would you persuade corporate headquarters that local conditions need to be accommodated if they are to be successful?

Further reading

- Combs, J., Liu, Y., Hall, A. and Ketchen, D. (2006) 'How much do high-performance work practices matter? A meta-analysis of their effects on organizational performance', *Personnel Psychology*, 59: 501–28.
Meta-analysis review of 92 previous HPWS studies and their impact on performance. It reviews key arguments in previous studies and provides suggestions for future research.

- Becker, B.E. and Huselid, M.A. (2006) 'Strategic human resource management: Where do we go from here?', *Journal of Management*, 32(6): 898–925.
This theoretical article examines the future direction of SHRM research. They examine the notion of the 'black box' and suggest strategy implementation as the focal mediating construct in SHRM. They also examine challenges facing future empirical work and highlight new directions in SHRM research.

- Ramsay, H., Scholarios, D. and Harley, B. (2000) 'Employees and high performance work systems: Testing inside the black box', *British Journal of Industrial Relations*, 38: 501–31.
Using UK WERS data, the authors set about testing three models of HPWS. This paper was one of the first to analyse the impact of HPWS on employee outcomes (both negative and positive outcomes) and assesses the plausibility and adequacy of the mutually beneficial claims made in previous studies. The authors choose three models – a high commitment model, a high involvement model and a labour process model. Amongst their findings was a higher association between HRM and stress levels. The authors also found positive associations between HRM and employee outcomes.

- Godard, J. (2004) 'A critical assessment of the high performance paradigm', *British Journal of Industrial Relations*, 42(2): 349–78.
This paper takes a more critical view of the high performance paradigm. The author makes a distinction between 'involving' and 'intensifying' cultures which suggests there are differences in how HPWS are applied by employers and how they are perceived by employees. Godard also argues that firms need to be sceptical about the economics of HPWS. Whilst they may offer benefits they will not be costless and we need to take into account context and views of capitalism when investigating the high performance paradigm.

- Boxall, P. and Purcell, J. (2008) *Strategy and Human Resource Management*, 2nd edn. Hampshire: Palgrave MacMillan.
This textbook introduces the reader to the topic of SHRM. The authors discuss the origins of SHRM and examine how strategy connects to SHRM. Chapter 8 provides a useful examination of the 'black box' issues and introduces the role of the line manager in the HRM-performance chain. They also include discussions of work systems and production, managing individual performance and also the complexities in managing HRM in a global economy.

- Boxall, P., Purcell, J. and Wright, P. (2007) *The Oxford Handbook of Human Resource Management.* Oxford: Oxford University Press.

This edited book brings together the writings of some of the leading international scholars in HPWS research. Chapter 5 by Allen and Wright goes into more detail on strategic HRM and the resource-based view of the firm. Part IV discusses issues of measurement and outcome in HPWS research and gives further details on some of the key issues explored in this chapter including problems of method, measurement and theory and scope.

- Paauwe, J. (2004) *HRM and Performance: Achieving Long-term Viability.* Oxford: Oxford University Press.

This book provides an overview of HRM and strategy and then introduces the reader to the institutional perspective on HRM, strategy and performance bringing in professional and societal dimensions. Case studies are presented to apply the theory to US and European firms.

Internet resources

1 NCPP (http://www.ncpp.ie/): Conducts research on high performing organisations in Ireland – both domestic and multinational. You can find useful case studies examining HPWS in a number of multinational companies operating in Ireland across many sectors.

2 The Chartered Institute of Personnel and Development (http://www.cipd.co.uk/subjects/corpstrtgy/busiperfm/dtihpwprac.htm): The CIPD presents results of research examing high performance working in organisations' in the UK. The report includes a survey of CIPD members and case studies from a sample of companies.

3 Eurofound (http://www.eurofound.europa.eu/): The European Foundation for the Improvement of Living and Working Conditions, is a European Union body. This website provides up-to-date information on employment issues across the EU.

4 The Society for Human Resource Management (http://www.shrm.org/): US based group with international linkages. This website provides up-to-date information on key SHRM issues and research topics whilst also providing useful templates and tools.

5 The IIRA HRM study group working paper series (http://www.zagelmeyer.com/pageID_3782043.html): Provides full text access to a number of papers examining SHRM across a number of countries such as Ireland, UK, Canada and the US.

Self-assessment questions

Indicative answers to these questions can be found on the companion website at www.sagepub.co.uk/harzing3e.

1 **What makes up a high performance work system (HPWS)?**
2 **Explain the universalist theory of HRM.**
3 **Explain the contingency theory of HRM.**
4 **How does HPWS impact on employee behaviour and firm performance?**
5 **What are the main debates within HPWS research?**

References

Appelbaum, E. (2002) 'The impact of new forms of work organization on workers', in G. Murray, J. Belanger, A. Giles and P.A. Lapointe (eds), *Work and Employment Relations in the High Performance Workplace.* pp. 120–49. London: Continuum.

Appelbaum, E. and Batt, R. (1994) *The New American Workplace: Transforming Work Systems in the United States.* Ithaca, NY: Cornell University Press.

Appelbaum, E., Bailey, T., Berg, P. and Kalleberg, A. (2000) *Manufacturing Advantage: Why High-Performance Work Systems Pay Off.* Ithaca London: ILR Press.

Arthur, J.B. (1992) 'The link between business strategy and industrial relations systems in American steel mini mills', *Industrial and Labor Relations Review,* 45: 488–505.

Arthur, J.B. (1994) 'Effects of human resource systems on manufacturing performance and turnover', *Academy of Management Journal,* 37: 670–87.

Ashton, D. and Sung, J. (2002) *High Performance Work Practices: a Comparative Analysis on Issues and Systems.* Geneva: ILP.

Backes-Gellner, U., Frick, B. and Sadowski, D. (1997) 'Codetermination and personnel policies of German firms: The influence of works councils on turnover and further training', *International Journal of Human Resource Management,* (8): 328–74.

Bae, J. and Lawler, J.J. (2000) 'Organizational performance and HRM in Korea: Impact on firm performance in an emerging economy', *Academy of Management Journal,* 43: 502–17.

Bae, J., Lawler, J.J., Chen, T.W., Wan, J.J. and Roh, H. (2001) Human resource strategy and firm performance in pacific countries: A comparative study of Korea, Taiwan, Singapore and Thailand. Paper presented at the Global HRM Conference, Barcelona.

Bailey, T. (1993) Discretionary effort and the organization of work: Employee participation and work reform since Hawthorne. Unpublished work. Teachers College and Conservation of Human Resources, Columbia University.

Banker, R.D., Field, J., Schroeder, R. and Sinha, K. (1996) 'Impact of work teams on manufacturing performance: A longitudinal field study', *Academy of Management Journal,* 39: 920–49.

Barker, J.R. (1993) 'Tightening the Iron Cage: concertive control in self-managing teams', *Administrative Science Quarterly,* 38: 408–37.

Barney, J.B. (1991) 'Firm resources and sustained competitive advantage', *Journal of Management,* 17(1): 99–120.

Batt, R. (2002) 'Managing customer services: human resource practices, quit rates and sales growth', *Academy of Management Journal,* 45(3): 587–97.

Beatty, R.W. and Varma, A. (1997) 'An empirical study of high performance work systems: Implications for Practitioners', in *Human Resource Planning Society Research Symposium.* Ithaca, NY.

Beaumont, P.B.(1993) *Human Resource Management.* London: Sage.

Becker, B., and Gerhart, B. (1996) 'The impact of human resource management on organizational performance: Progress and prospects', *Academy of Management Journal*, 39(4): 779–801.

Becker, B.E. and Huselid, M.A. (2006) 'Strategic human resources management: Where do we go from here?', *Journal of Management,* 32(6): 898–925.

Belanger, J., Giles, A. and Murray, G. (2002) 'Towards a new production model: potentialities, tensions and contradictions', in G. Murray, G.A. Belanger and P. Lapointe (eds), *Work and Employment Relations in the High Performance Workplace.* London and New York: Continuum.

Beltrán-Martín, I., Roca-Puig, V., Escrig-Tena, A. and Bou-Llusar, J.C. (2008) 'Human resource flexibility as a mediating variable between high performance work systems and performance', *Journal of Management*, 34(5): 1009–44.

Benschop, Y. (2001) 'Pride, prejudice and performance. Relations between diversity, HRM and performance', *The International Journal of Human Resource Management*, 12: 1166–81.

Bird, A., Taylor, S. and Beechler, S. (1998) 'A typology of international human resource management in Japanese multinational corporations', *Human Resource Management*, 37: 173.

Bond, S. and Wise, S. (2003) 'Family leave policies and devolution to the line', *Personnel Review*, 32: 58–72.

Boselie, J.P. and van der Wiele, A. (2001), 'Employee perceptions of HRM and TQM and the effects on satisfaction and intention to leave', *Managing Service Quality*, 12: 165–72.

Boselie, J.P., Paauwe, J. and Jansen, P.J. (2001), 'Human resource management and performance: Lessons from the Netherlands', *International Journal of Human Resource Management*, 12: 1107–25.

Boselie, P., Dietz, G. and Boon, C. (2005) 'Commonalities and contradictions in research on human resource management and performance', *Human Resource Management Journal*, 15(3): 67–94.

Boxall, P. (1996) 'The strategic HRM debate and the resource-based view of the firm', *Human Resource Management Journal*, 6.

Boxall, P. and Purcell, J. (2003) *Strategy and Human Resource Management.* Basingstoke: Palgrave MacMillan.

Boxall, P. and Purcell, J. (2008) *Strategy and Human Resource Management*, 2nd edn. Basingstoke: Palgrave MacMillan.

Chow, Irene Hau-siu (2005) 'The impact of institutional context on human resource management in three Chinese societies', *Employee Relations*, 26: 626–42.

Clark, T., Mabey, C. and Skinner, D. (1998) 'Experiencing HRM: The importance of the inside story', in C. Mabey, D. Skinner and T. Clark(eds), *Experiencing Human Resource Management.* pp. 1–13. London: Sage Publications.

Colakoglu, S., Lepak, D.P. and Hong, Y. (2006) 'Measuring human resource management effectiveness: Considering multiple stakeholders in a global context', *Human Resource Management Review*, 16: 209–18.

Combs, J.G., Ketchen, D., Hall, A. and Liu, Y. (2006) 'Do high performance work practices matter? A meta-analysis of their effects on organizational performance', *Personnel Psychology*, 59: 501–28.

d'Arcimoles, C.H. (1997) 'Human resource policies and company performance: a quantitative approach using longitudinal data', *Organization Studies*, 18(5): 857–74.

Danford, A., Richardson, M., Stewart, P., Tailby, S. and Upchurch, M. (2004) 'High performance work systems and workplace partnership: a case study of aerospace workers', *New Technology, Work and Employment*, 19: 14–29.

Dany, F., Guedri, Z. and Hatt, F. (2008) 'New insights into the link between HRM integration and organizational performance: the moderating role of influence distribution between HRM specialists and line managers', *International Journal of Human Resource Management*, 19: 2095–112.

Datta, D., Guthrie, J. and Wright, P. (2005) 'Human Resource Management and labor productivity: does industry matter?', *Academy of Management Journal*, 48(1): 135–45.

de Saa Perez, P. and Garcia Falcon, J.M. (2001) Human resource management and organizational performance from a resource-based view. Paper presented at the Global HRMM Conference, Barcelona.

Delaney, J. and Huselid, M.A. (1996) 'The impact of human resource management practices on perceptions of organizational performance', *Academy of Management Journal*, 39(4): 949–69.

Delbridge, R. and Lowe, J. (1997) 'Introduction: workplace change and HRM', *International Journal of Human Resource Management*, 8: 759–63.

Delery, J.E. (1998) 'Issues of fit in strategic human resource management: Implications for research', *Human Resource Management Review*, 8: 289–309.

Delery, J.E. and Doty, D.H. (1996) 'Modes of theorizing in strategic human resource management: tests of universalistic, contingency, and configurational performance predictions', *Academy of Management Journal*, 39: 802–35.

Doty, D.H. and Delery, J.R. (1997) The Importance of holism, interdependence and equifinality assumptions in high performance work systems: Toward theories of the high performance work force. Paper presented at *Academy of Management Conference*, Boston, MA.

Eaton, A.E. and Voos, P. (1992) 'Unions and contemporary innovations in work organization, compensation, and employee participation', in L.M.P. Voos (ed.), *Unions and Economic Competitiveness*. New York, NY: M.E. Sharpe.

Farias, Gerard F. and Varma, A. (1998) 'High Performance Work Systems: What we know and what we need to know', *Human Resource Planning*, 21(2): 50–55.

Fernie, S., Metcalf, D. and Woodland, S. (1995) *What has Human Resource Management Achieved in the Workplace?* London: McGraw Hill.

Fey, C.E. and Björkman, I. (2001) 'The effect of human resource management practices on MNC subsidiary performance in Russia', *Journal of International Business Studies*, 32: 59–76.

Fey, C.E., Bjorkman, I. and Pavlovskaya, A. (2000) 'The effect of human resource management practices on MNC subsidiary performance in Russia', *International Journal of Human Resource Management*, 11(1): 1–18.

Fey, C., Morgoulis-Jakoushev, S., Park, H.J. and Björkman, I. (2008) 'Opening up the black box of the relationship between HRM practices and firm performance: A comparison of USA, Finland and Russia', *Journal of International Business Studies*, 40: 690–712.

Fiske, S.T. and Taylor, S.E. (1991) *Social Cognition*, 2nd edn. New York: McGraw Hill.

Fleetwood, S. and Hesketh, A. (2007) 'HRM-performance research: Under-theorised and lacking explanatory power', *International Journal of Human Resource Management*, 17(2): 1977–93.

Flood, P., Guthrie, J., Liu, W. and MacCurtain, S. (2005) 'High Performance Work Systems in Ireland – The economic case', *Forum on the Workplace of the Future Research Series Number 4*: National Centre for Partnership and Performance.

Forbringer, L. and Oeth, C. (1998) 'Human resources at Mercantile Bank Corporation Inc.: A critical analysis', *Human Resource Management*, 37(2): 177–89.

Gerhart, B. (1999) 'Human Resource Management and firm performance: measurement issues and their effect on causal and policy inferences', in G. Ferris (ed.), *Research in Personnel and Human Resources – supplement 4*. Connecticut: JAI Press.

Gerhart, B. (2005) 'Human resources and business performance: findings, unanswered questions, and an alternative approach', *Management Revue*, 16: 174–85.

Godard, J. (1998) 'Workplace reforms, managerial objectives and managerial outcomes and perceptions of Canadian HRM/IR managers', *International Journal of Human Resource Management*, 9(1): 18–40.

Godard, J. (2001) 'High performance and the transformation of work? The implications of alternative work practices for the experience and outcomes of work', *Industrial and Labor Relations Review*, 54(4): 776–805.

Godard, J. (2004) 'A critical assessment of the high performance paradigm', *British Journal of Industrial Relations*, 42(2): 349–78.

Gooderham, P., Nordhaug, O. and Ringdal, K. (1999) 'Institutional and rational determinants of organisational practices: Human resource management in European firms', *Administrative Science Quarterly*, 44: 507–53.

Gooderham, P., Parry, E. and Ringdal, K. (2008) 'The impact of bundles of strategic human resource management practices on the performance of European firms', *International Journal of Human Resource Management*, 19(11): 2041–56.

Gollan, P. and Davis, E. (1999) The Australian experience of high involvement management and organizational change. Paper presented at the Dutch HRM Network Conference, Rotterdam.

Guerrero, S. and Barraud-Didier, V. (2004) 'High-involvement practices and performance of French firms', *International Journal of Human Resource Management*, 15: 1408–23.

Guest, D.E. (1990) 'Human resource management and the American dream', *Journal of Management Studies*, 27: 377–97.

Guest, D.E. (1997) 'Human Resource Management and performance: a review and research agenda', *International Journal of Human Resource Management*, 8(3): 263–76.

Guest, D. (1999) 'Human Resource Management – the workers verdict', *Human Resource Management Journal*, 9: 5–25.

Guest, D. (2002) 'Human Resource Management, corporate performance and employee wellbeing: building the worker into HRM', *Journal of Industrial Relations*, 44: 335–58.

Guest, D. and Peccei, R. (1994) 'The nature and causes of effective human resource management', *British Journal of Industrial Relations*, 32: 219–40.

Guest, D., Conway, N. and Dewe, P. (2004) 'Using sequential tree analysis to search for "bundles" of HR practices', *Human Resource Management Journal*, 14: 79–96.

Guthrie, James P. (2001) 'High-involvement work practices, turnover, and productivity: evidence from New Zealand', *Academy of Management Journal*, 44: 180–90.

Harley, B. (1999) 'The myth of empowerment: work organisation, hierarchy and employee autonomy in contemporary Australian workplaces', *Work Employment and Society*, 13: 41–66.

Harley, B. (2001) 'Team membership and the experience of work in Britain: an analysis of the WERS98 data', *Work, Employment and Society*, 15: 721–42.

Harley, B. (2002) 'Employee responses to high performance work systems: an analysis of the AWIRS95 data', *Journal of Industrial Relations*, 44: 418–34.

Harley, B. (2005) 'Hope or hype? High performance work systems', in B. Harley, J. Hyman and P. Thompson (eds), *Participation and Democracy at Work: Essays in Honour of Harvie Ramsay*. pp. 38–54. Houndmills: Palgrave Macmillan.

Harley, B., Allen, B.C. and Sargent, L.D. (2007) 'High performance work systems and employee experience of work in the service sector: The case of aged care', *British Journal of Industrial Relations*, 45: 607–33.

Heffernan, M., Harney, B., Cafferkey, K. and Dundon, T. (2009) 'Exploring linkages between HRM, creatitivy and organisational performance: Evidence from Ireland', in *Academy of Management Conference Proceedings*. Chicago, Illinois.

Hesketh, A. and Fleetwood, S. (2006) 'Beyond measuring the human resources management-organizational performance link: applying critical realist meta-theory', *Organization*, 13: 677–99.

Hitt, M.A., Ireland, R.E. and Hoskisson, R.D. (2005) *Strategic Management: Competitiveness and Globalisation*. US: South-Western Publishing.

Hoque, K. (1999) 'Human resource management and performance in the UK hotel industry', *British Journal of Industrial Relations*, 37: 419–43.

Huselid, M. (1995) 'The impact of human resource management practices on turnover, productivity, and corporate financial performance', *Academy of Management Journal*, 38: 635–72.

Hutchinson, S. and Purcell, J. (2003) *Bringing Policies to Life: The Vital Role of Front Line Managers in People Management*. London: Chartered Institute of Personnel and Development.

Ichniowski, C. and Shaw, K. (1999) 'The effects of human resource management systems on economic performance: An international comparison of US and Japanese plants', *Management Science*, 45: 704–21.

Ichniowski, C., Kochan, T.A., Levine, D., Olson, C. and Strauss, G. (1996) 'What works at work: overview and assessment', *Industrial Relations*, 35: 299–333.

Jackson, S.E., Schuler, R.S. and Carlos Rivero, J. (1989) 'Organizational characteristics as predictors of personnel practices', *Personnel Psychology*, 42: 727–86.

Kalleberg, A. and Moody, J.W. (1994) 'Human resource management and organizational performance', *American Behavioural Scientist*, 7: 948–62.

Kalmi, P. and Kauhanen, A. (2008) 'Workplace innovations and employee outcomes: evidence from Finland', *Industrial Relations*, 47: 430–59.

Kato, T. and Morishima, M. (2002) 'The productivity effects of participatory employment practices: evidence from new Japanese panel data', *Industrial Relations*, 41: 487–520.

Khilji, Shaista E. and Wang, Xiaoyun (2006) '"Intended" and "implemented" HRM: the missing linchpin in strategic human resource management research', *International Journal of Human Resource Management*, 17: 1171–89.

Koch, M.J. and McGrath, R.G. (1996) Improving labour productivity: Human resource management policies do matter', *Strategic Management Journal*, 17: 335–54.

Kochan, T.A., Katz, H. and McKersie, R.B. (1989) *The Transformation of American Industrial Relations*. New York, NY: Basic Books.

Konrad, A.M. (2006) 'Engaging employees through high-involvement work practices', *Ivey Business Journal*, March/April: 1–6.

Lähteenmäki, S., Storey, J. and Vanhala, S. (1998) 'HRM and company performance: the use of measurement and influence of economic cycles', *Human Resource Management Journal*, 8: 51–65.

Laroche, P. (2001) The impact of human resource management practices and industrial relations on the performance: An empirical study in the French context. Paper presented at the Global HRM Conference, Barcelona.

Laursen, K. (2002) 'The importance of sectoral differences in the application of complementary HRM practices for innovation performance', *International Journal of the Economics of Business*, 9: 139–56.

Lawler, E. (1986) *High-involvement Management*. San Francisco: Jossey-Bass.

Lawler, E.E. (1994) 'Creating the high-performance organization', in J.R.Galbraith and E.E. Lawler (eds), *Organising the Future: The New Logic for Managing Complex Organizations*. San Francisco, CA: Jossey-Bass.

Leget, J. (1997) *Human Resource Management in Netherlands*. Deventer: Kluwer.

Legge, K. (2001) 'Silver bullet or spent round? Assessing the meaning of the "high commitment management"/performance relationship', in J. Storey (ed.), *Human Resource Management: A Critical Text*. London: Thomson Learning.

Legge, K. (2005) *Human Resource Management: Rhetoric and Realities*. Basingstoke: Palgrave.

Leijten, A. (1992) 'Stimulerend personeelsmanagement: een effectiviteitsdiagnose', Thela Thesis, Amsterdam.

Lepak, D. and Shaw, J. (2008) 'Strategic HRM in North America: looking to the future', *International Journal of Human Resource Management*, 19: 1486–99.

Lepak, D.P., Takeuchi, R., Erhardt, N.L. and Colakoglu, S. (2006) 'Emerging perspectives on the relationship between human resource management and performance' in R. Burke and C. Cooke (eds), *The Human Resources Revolution: Research and Practice*. pp. 31–54. Oxford: Elsevier.

Liden, R.C., Bauer, T.N. and Erdogan, B. (2004) 'The role of leader–member exchange in the dynamic relationship between employer and employee: Implications for employee socialization, leaders and organizations,' in L. M. S. J.A.-M. Coyle-Shapiro, Susan M. Taylor and L.E. Tetrick (eds), *The Employment Relationship, Examining Psychological and Contextual Perspectives*. Oxford: Oxford University Press.

Liu, W., Guthrie, J., Flood, P. and MacCurtain, S. (2009) 'Unions and the adoption of high performance work systems: does employment security play a role?', *Industrial Labor Relation and Review*, 69: 108–126.

MacDuffie, J.P. (1995) 'Human resource bundles and manufacturing performance: Organizational logic and flexible production systems in the world auto industry', *Industrial and Labor Relations*, 48: 197–221.

Macky, K. and Boxall, P. (2007) 'The relationship between "high-performance work practices" and employee attitudes: an investigation of additive and interaction effects', *International Journal of Human Resource Management*, 18: 537–67.

Macky, K. and Boxall, P. (2008) 'High-involvement work processes, work intensification and employee well-being: A study of New Zealand worker experiences', *Asia Pacific Journal of Human Resources*, 46: 38–55.

MacMillan, I.C. and Schuler, R.S (1985) 'Gaining a competitive edge through human resources', *Personnel*, 62: 24–9.

Macy, B.A. and Izumi, H. (1993) 'Organizational change, design, and work innovation: A meta-analysis of 131 North American field studies – 1961–1991', in R. Woodman and W. Pasmore (eds), *Research in Organizational Change and Development*. Greenwich, CT: JAI Press.

Macy, B.A., Thompson, R. and Farias, G.F. (1995) 'Describing and assessing high performance work practices in innovative organisations: A benchmarking study of 82 North American organisations', in *National Academy of Management Meetings*. Vancouver, Canada.

Martin-Alcazar, F., Romero-Fernandes, P.M. and Sanchez-Gardey, G. (2005) 'Strategic human resource management: integrating the universalistic, contingent, configurational and contextual perspectives', *International Journal of Human Resource Management*, 16: 633–59.

McGovern, P., Gratton, L., Hope-Hailey, V., Stiles, P. and Truss, C. (1997) 'Human resource management on the line?', *Human Resource Management Journal*, 7: 12–29.

McNabb, R. and Whitfield, K. (1997) 'Unions, flexibility, team working and financial performance', *Organization Studies*, 18: 821–38.

Michie, J. and Sheehan, M. (2005) 'Business strategy, human resources, labour market flexibility and competitive advantage', *International Journal of Human Resource Management*, 16: 445–64.

Miles, R. and Snow, C. (1984) 'Designing strategic human resource systems', *Organization Dynamics*, Summer: 36–52.

Miller, M. and Friesen, P. (1984) *Organizations: A Quantum View*. Englewood Cliffs, NJ: Prentice-Hall.

Mitsuhashi, H., Park, H.J., Wright, P.M. and Chua, R.S. (2000) 'Line and HR executives' perceptions of HR effectiveness in firms in People's Republic of China', *International Journal of Human Resource Management*, 11: 197–216.

Morley, M., Brewster, C., Gunnigle, P. and Mayrhofer, W. (2000) 'Evaluating change in European industrial relations' in C. Brewster, W. Mayrhofer, and M. Morley (eds), *New Challenges for European Human Resource Management*. pp. 1999–222. London: Macmillan.

Ngo, H.Y., Lau, C.M. and Foley, S. (2008) 'Strategic human resource management, firm performance, and employee relations climate in China', *Human Resource Management*, 47: 73–90.

Nicholson, N., Rees, A. and Brooks Rooney, A. (1990) 'Strategy, innovation and performance', *Journal of Management Studies*, 27: 511–34.

Nishii, L.H., Lepak, D.P. and Schneider, B. (2008) 'Employee attributions of the "why" of HR practices: Their effects on employee attitudes and behaviors, and customer satisfaction', *Personnel Psychology*, 61: 503–45.

Osterman, P. (1994) 'How common is workplace transformation and who adopts it?', *Industrial and Labour Relations Review*, 47(2): 173–88.

Osterman, P. (2000) 'Work reorganization in an era of restructuring: Trends in diffusion and effects on employee welfare', *Industrial and Labor Relations Review*, 53: 176–96.

Paauwe, J. (2004) *HRM and Performance: Achieving Long Term Viability*. New York: Oxford University Press.

Panayotopoulou, L. (2001) Strategic human resource management and its link to form performance: An implementation of the competing values framework. Paper presented at the Global HRM Conference, Barcelona.

Patterson, M., West, M., Lawthom, R. and Nickell, S. (1997) *Impact of People Management Practices on Business Performance*. London: Institute of Personnel Development.

Perry, E. and Kulik, C.T. (2008) 'The devolution of HR to the line: Implications for perceptions of people management effectiveness', *International Journal of Human Resource Management*, 19(2): 262–73.

Pfeffer, J. (1994) *Competitive Advantages Through People*. Boston, MA: Harvard Business School Press.

Pfeffer, J. (1995) 'Producing sustainable competitive advantage through the effective management of people', *Academy of Management Executive*, 9(1): 55–69.

Pfeffer, J. (1998) *The Human Equation: Building Profits by Putting People First*. Boston, MA: Harvard Business School Press.

Piore, M. and Sabel, C. (1984) *The Second Industrial Divide: Prospects for Prosperity*. New York: Basic Books.

Purcell, J. (1999) 'Best practice and best fit: chimera or cul-de-sac?', *Human Resource Management Journal*, 9: 26–41.

Purcell, J. and Hutchinson, S. (2007) 'Front-Line managers as agents in the HRM-performance causal chain: Theory, analysis and evidence', *Human Resource Management Journal*, 17(1): 3–20.

Purcell, J. and Kinnie, N. (2007) 'HRM and business performance', in P. Boxhall, J. Purcell and M. Wright (eds), *The Oxford Handbook of Human Resource Management*. pp. 533–51. Oxford: Oxford University Press.

Ramsay, H., Scholarios, D. and Harley, B. (2000) 'Employees and high performance work systems: Testing inside the black box', *British Journal of Industrial Relations*, 38: 501–31.

Redman, T. and Snape, E. (2005) 'Unpacking commitment: multiple loyalties and employee behavior', *Journal of Management Studies*, 42(2): 301–28.

Renwick, D. (2003) 'Line manager involvement in HRM: An inside view', *Employee Relations*, 25: 262–80.

Richard, O. and Johnson, N.B. (2004) 'High performance work practices and human resource management effectiveness: Substitutes or complements?', *Journal of Business Strategies*. 21(2): 133–48.

Rogers, E.W. and Wright, P.M. (1998) 'Measuring organizational performance in strategic human resource management: Problems, prospects, and performance information markets', *Human Resource Management Review*, 8: 311–31.

Royle, T. and Towers, B. (2003) 'Regulating employee interest representation: The case of McDonalds in the European Union', in W. Cooke(ed.), *Multinational Companies and Global Human Resource Strategies*. Westport, CN.: Quorom Books.

Schuler, R.S. and Jackson, S.E. (1987) 'Linking competitive strategies and human resource management practices', *Academy of Management Executive*, 1(3): 207–219.

Sparrow, P. and Pei-Chuan, W. (1998) 'Does national culture really matter? Predicting HRM preferences of Taiwanese employees', *Employee Relations*, 20: 26–56.

Thompson, M. (2003) *High Performance Work Organisation in UK Aerospace*. London: DTI/ Society of British Aerospace Companies.

Truss, C. (2001) 'Complexities and controversies in linking HRM to organizational outcomes', *Journal of Management Studies*, 38(8): 1121–49.

Ulrich, D. (1997) *Human Resource Champions: The Next Agenda for Adding Value and Delivering Results*. Boston: Harvard Business School Press.

United States Department of Labor (1993) *High Performance Work Practices and Firm Performance*. Washington, D.C.

Vandenberg, R.J., Richardson, H.A. and Eastman, L.J. (1999) 'The impact of high involvement work processes on organisational effectiveness: A second-order latent variable approach', *Group and Organization Management*, 24(3): 300–39.

Varma, A., Beatty, R.W., Schneier, C.E. and Ulrich, D.O. (1999) 'High performance work systems: exciting discovery of passing fad?', *Human Resource Planning*, 22(1): 26–38.

Verburg, R. (1998) *Human Resource Management: Optimal HRM-Practice*. Amsterdam: Vrije University.

Wall, T.D. and Wood, S.J. (2005) 'The romance of human resource management and business performance and the case for big science', *Human Relations*, 58(4): 429–62.

Walton, R.E. (1985) 'From control to commitment in the workplace', *Harvard Business Review*, March-April: 25–32.

Whitfield, K. and Poole, M. (1997) 'Organizing employment for high performance: theories, evidence and policy', *Organization Studies*, 18: 745–64.

Whittaker, S. and Marchington, M. (2003) 'Devolving HR responsibility to the line: Threat, opportunity or partnership?', *Employee Relations*, 25(3): 245–61.

Wood, S. (1999) 'Human resource management and performance', *International Journal of Management Review*, 1: 367–413.

Wood, S. and Albanesse, M.T. (1995) 'Can we speak of high commitment management on the shop floor?', *Journal of Management Studies*, 32: 215–47.

Wood, S. and de Menezes, L. (1998) 'High commitment management in the UK: Evidence from the workplaces industrial relations survey and employer: manpower and skills practices survey', *Human Relations*, 51: 485–515.

Wright, P.M. and Snell, S.A. (1998) 'Toward a unifying framework for exploring fit and flexibility in strategic human resource management', *Academy of Management Review*, 23: 756–72.

Wright, P.M. and Boswell, W.R. (2002) 'Desegregating HRM: A review and synthesis of micro and macro human resource management research', *Journal of Management*, 28: 247–76.

Wright, P. and Gardner, T. (2003) 'Theoretical and empirical challenges in studying the HR practice – firm performance relationship', in T.D.W.D. Holman, C. Clegg, P. Sparrow and A. Howard (eds), *The New Workplace: People Technology, and Organisation*. Sussex, UK: John Wiley and Sons.

Wright, P. and Nishii, L. (2004) Strategic HRM and organizational behavior: integrating multiple level analysis. Paper presented at the 'What Next for HRM?' conference, Rotterdam, June.

Wright, P.M. and Nishi, L. (2007) 'Strategic HRM and organizational behavior: integrating multiple levels of analysis' in *CAHRS Working Paper Series*, vol. 07–03.

Wright, P.M., Dunford, B.B. and Snell, S.A. (2001) 'Human resources and the resource based view of the firm', *Journal of Management*, 27(6): 701–20.

Youndt, M.A., Snell, S.A. Dean, J.E. and Lepak, D.P. (1996) 'Human resource management, manufacturing strategy, and firm performance', *Academy of Management Journal*, 39: 836–66.

Part 3
IHRM Practices

10

Managing Knowledge in Multinational Firms

Ingmar Björkman, Paul Evans and Vladimir Pucik

Contents

Learning Objectives

After reading this chapter you will be able to

- Explain the importance of knowledge sharing for the competitiveness of the multinational

- Distinguish the range of mechanisms that multinationals have at their disposal to enhance knowledge sharing

- Discuss how multinationals can access and retain external knowledge

- Understand dualities involved in exploring existing knowledge and exploiting new areas

Chapter Outline

In this chapter we discuss knowledge sharing in multinationals, arguing that it is facilitated by cross-unit social capital, organisational values of collaboration and sharing, and global mindsets. We also examine structural mechanisms and a range of HR practices that enhance knowledge sharing. We then assess how multinationals can access and retain external knowledge. In the final section we discuss the dualities involved in exploring existing knowledge and exploiting new knowledge.

1 Introduction

The argument was made more than 15 years ago, in the early days of scholarly and practitioner interest in knowledge management, that a primary rationale for the existence of multinational firms is their ability to transfer knowledge more effectively and efficiently than through market mechanisms (Kogut and Zander, 1992, 1993). The competitive advantage of a multinational corporation stems in part from its ability to replicate operational principles that have proved to be effective elsewhere in the corporation, and in part from its ability to access and recombine new knowledge from different parts of the world into innovations. This is a perspective on multinational organisations that today seems very significant. Certainly, the way in which the multinational firm manages knowledge is important for its competitiveness.

In this chapter we will lead the reader through the challenges of how to manage knowledge in the multinational enterprise. After first having defined different types of knowledge, we discuss knowledge sharing across geographically dispersed units. We

Information = Statement of facts, such as data

Knowledge = a justified true belief.

argue that within multinationals, knowledge sharing is facilitated by cross-unit social capital, organisational values of collaboration and sharing, and global mindsets among employees, among other factors. We also discuss structural mechanisms and a range of human resource management (HRM) practices that enhance knowledge sharing.

We then assess how multinationals can access and retain external knowledge from different parts of the world. Knowledge acquisition requires investment in external scanning on a global scale; the development of partnerships with customers, research labs and other organisations; and an ability to use the open market to identify complementary knowledge and interesting ideas. Again, people management and social capital play an important role in this endeavour.

In the final section we discuss the dualities involved in both exploring existing knowledge and exploiting new knowledge. Throughout the chapter the focus is on HRM aspects of how to manage knowledge in multinationals.

2 Different types of knowledge

A natural point of departure is to ask what we mean by the term 'knowledge'. Knowledge can be distinguished from information which is a statement of facts such as numerical data about the size of a geographical market or the number of employees of the corporation. Knowledge can be defined as justified true belief (Nonaka, 1994). In this chapter we will focus on knowledge as the (justified true) beliefs that organisational members hold about what constitutes effective organisational actions and practices. However, we will also discuss the organisational practices that knowledge is both embedded in and reflects (Kostova, 1999).

Two basic categories of knowledge processes can be identified, one concerned with *exploiting existing knowledge* and the other concerned with *generating (or exploring) new knowledge* (March, 1991). Although organisations and their units learn and thus generate new knowledge through their individual members, we focus in this chapter on how units can generate new knowledge either through deliberate efforts at learning or as a byproduct of activities that may have other objectives (Chakavarthy et al., 2003). In this context, we highlight the issues concerning knowledge sharing which refers to the process of exchange of knowledge among individuals, teams and units.

Two types of knowledge are important to multinational firms. The distinction between explicit and tacit knowledge was first made by Polanyi (1967) and developed by Nonaka (1994; Nonaka and Takeuchi, 1995). Explicit or codified knowledge is knowledge that individuals and organisations know that they have – objective, formal, systematic, incorporated in texts and manuals, and relatively easy to pass on to others at a low marginal cost. Virtually all knowledge stored in IT-based databases and systems is explicit. In contrast tacit knowledge is personal, context specific, and

explicit knowledge = knowledge that people know they have objective, formal; catalogued-

Tacit Knowledge: knowledge that a person may not know they have – harder to pin down.

hard or perhaps even impossible to formalise and communicate. Individuals may not even be conscious of the tacit knowledge they possess. Tacit knowledge often underlies complex skills and is built on the intuitive feel acquired through years of experience.

In the past, the success of internationalisation was typically dependent on the ability of the firm to transfer the superior tacit knowledge residing in the home country organisation to its overseas affiliates. When multinational firms established new units abroad, this knowledge allowed them to compete successfully against local enterprises that enjoyed the advantage of superior local knowledge. Expatriates played key roles in the transfer of tacit knowledge from headquarters to foreign subsidiaries. In spite of technological advances over the last few decades, the transfer of personnel and person-to-person interaction are still the main ways in which tacit knowledge can be shared across boundaries. However, the development of information technology (IT) has had a big impact on the ability to store and transfer explicit knowledge. While written manuals and blueprints have always been important in the transfer of knowledge across units, the development of advanced IT-based systems played a central role in fueling interest in knowledge management during the 1990s. So tacit and codified knowledge are shared through different mechanisms.

Indeed, from an HRM standpoint, the development and sharing of different types of knowledge should be managed in different ways. Another important issue is the value of knowledge. Some knowledge is unique to the enterprise, and this should be managed differently from knowledge that is generic and freely available to all competitors. Knowledge also varies according to its strategic importance for the enterprise. Lepak and Snell (1999) developed a framework that emphasises the need for a differentiated approach to knowledge management and HRM depending on the strategic value and firm specificity of the knowledge. Core knowledge is both unique to the firm and high in strategic value, such as Wal-Mart's expertise in logistics and inventory control, or Toyota's manufacturing capabilities. It is crucial to retain and develop such knowledge within the corporation, which implies a focus on retaining and developing the talent of people in whom this core know-how resides. Compulsory knowledge is of high strategic importance but is generally available. It is akin to the notion of 'table stakes' in card games, essential for an opportunity to compete, but offering no distinctive competitive advantage. Consequently it is more likely to be managed through close attention to performance management. Idiosyncratic knowledge refers to know-how that is unique to the firm but does not have clear current strategic value at the present time, though it may represent the core knowledge of the future. The risks with idiosyncratic knowledge mean that it may be best managed through partnerships such as R&D alliances. Ancillary knowledge, which is low on both strategic value and uniqueness, may be outsourced or automated. Different types of knowledge thus imply different strategies in the employment relationship.

The capability of the firm to develop, retain and exploit core knowledge through internal sharing across geographically dispersed units is an important source of

[Margin handwritten note: Core knowledge: - competitive advantage - HR concern: - must retain & develop talent!]

competitiveness. In today's world of sophisticated worldwide markets and increasingly competent affiliates, the focus has increasingly shifted from the home country organisation (transferring knowledge and new products from the parent organisation abroad) to the ability to generate and transfer knowledge from local units to the parent and other parts of the corporation. The ability of the firm to access and recombine new knowledge from different parts of the world into innovations is becoming increasing important. This involves the exploration of new knowledge more so than the exploitation of existing know-how from the home country.

3 Factors influencing knowledge sharing

Multinational organisations have the potential to access knowledge across a variety of different geographic, cultural, institutional and social contexts (see Chapter 2). Units located in different environments are likely to develop different types of knowledge. For the multinational, the diversity of knowledge residing throughout the organisation can be a great asset if it can be shared effectively across these boundaries.

Knowledge sharing however is not easy and is often a complex task. Knowledge is 'sticky' in the sense that there are costs associated with knowledge sharing (Szulanski, 1996), and the sharing of tacit ambiguous knowledge is particularly difficult (Simonin, 1999; van Wijk et al., 2008). To overcome the challenges involved in inter-unit knowledge sharing, firms will need to pay attention to a range of technological, organisational and people-related issues. Our focus here is on HR aspects of knowledge sharing but we also address a number of organisational issues.

Consider the following example from a firm with which one of the authors has been working. This multinational corporation has six factories around the world, manufacturing almost identical products using the same equipment, the same tools and roughly the same work processes. The subsidiaries' yields vary from 77 to 98 per cent but they neither knew the productivity of the other units nor shared information about the production process. The obvious question to ask in this situation is how to make sure that the units share knowledge with each other, improving the productivity of the laggards and perhaps also that of the top performers. We suggest that the following factors should be analysed when attempting to answer this question:

1 the ability and willingness of the sending unit or source to share knowledge,
2 the motivation and ability of the receiving unit, and
3 the suitability of the mechanisms (channels) used to share the knowledge.

Sender unit ability and willingness

Pedagogical ability

ability & willingness to share knowledge

The measure of a unit's ability to share knowledge with others can be labelled its pedagogical ability (Minbaeva and Michailova [2004] use a different term 'disseminative capacity' to refer to the ability and willingness of organisational members to share knowledge). For sharing explicit knowledge, pedagogical ability is partly shown by the source unit's proficiency in codifying knowledge in manuals, reports and physical systems that are available to other parts of the corporation. However, sharing tacit knowledge is more difficult. It almost always requires interpersonal and often face-to-face interaction. Good language and communication skills and a good understanding of cross-cultural factors are some of the ingredients of the pedagogical ability needed to share knowledge across borders. One of the many paradoxes that we meet in the knowledge management arena, is that much of the most valuable knowledge, typically firm specific and tacit in nature, is hard to share and transfer.

For knowledge sharing to take place, the source of the knowledge must be willing to share it (Szulanski, 1996). In the example presented at the beginning of this section, the manufacturing units were unwilling to share information about their productivity with others, and they perceived no interest in teaching others how to improve their operations. The strong competition that existed between plants helps to explain their attitudes. These units were competing for resources, even for survival, since the head-quarter's executives were critically reviewing the structure of the company's international network of manufacturing units. Why then help others to learn something that is a key advantage for one's own unit? The subsidiary managers were mostly evaluated on their own unit's performance, strengthening their internal focus and reinforcing the political atmosphere of the firm. Thus, the example shows how inter-unit knowledge sharing is influenced by the firm's performance management system and its compensation and rewards (Hansen et al., 2005).

Social status and reputation play important roles in shaping the context for knowledge sharing. People gain status when they are perceived as knowledgeable, and sharing knowledge with others is a good way for them to enhance their reputation. People who are given credit for having shared knowledge are more likely to do so again in the future (Cross and Prusak, 2003). This mechanism operates both at the inter-unit level (does the other unit acknowledge the knowledge source?) and the corporate level (does top management recognise those who share knowledge?). Knowledge sharing requires strong social networks within the multinational organisation where reputations are built and where people learn not only what the useful sources of knowledge are but also who is willing to engage in joint problem solving.

Norms of reciprocity are also important. Units and individuals are more willing to invest in sharing their knowledge with others if they trust them to reciprocate these favours in the future. Teaching others requires considerable effort, and in the absence of strong social relationships between the parties, the decision to engage in knowledge sharing is usually based on some instrumental calculation of whether or not it is worth the time and money (Cross and Prusak, 2003). A higher level of trust is therefore associated with more knowledge sharing, as is the existence of a strong organisational culture, where knowledge sharing is an important shared value.

Receiver unit ability and willingness

Not surprisingly, research has shown that the ability of the receiver to absorb new knowledge is a strong predictor of the extent to which the unit receives knowledge (Szulanski, 1996). The term *absorptive capacity* (Cohen and Levinthal, 1990) is commonly used in the scholarly literature to describe the ability of the receiving unit to evaluate, assimilates and exploit new knowledge from the environment (see Zahra and Georg [2002], and Lane et al. [2006] for discussions of the concept of absorptive capacity). A meta-analysis of 75 studies revealed a significant relationship (r = 0.19) between receiver absorptive capacity and knowledge transfer (van Wijk et al., 2008). Naturally, a subsidiary may have a higher level of absorptive capacity in some areas than in others and the ability to receive knowledge successfully will therefore vary from case to case. Knowledge changes when it is introduced into or absorbed by a new context. Consequently a certain level of existing knowledge and experience with knowledge transfer is necessary for a firm to be able to absorb new knowledge.

Successful implementation of traditional HR practices can enhance a unit's absorptive capacity (Minbaeva et al., 2003), for example by recruiting people with required skills and knowledge. Investments in the training and development of existing employees can also contribute to the unit's capability to absorb new knowledge. In addition, performance management systems provide employees with feedback on their performance and offer them more direction on how they can enhance their competencies to benefit the firm. An integral part of most performance management systems is the establishment of objectives and targets for self-development and employee training (see Chapter 11).

Furthermore, those involved must speak a common language well enough to share tacit knowledge. Fluency in a common language has also been found to be positively associated with inter-unit trust and shared cognition (Barner-Rasmussen and Björkman, 2006), which in turn are important drivers of knowledge sharing. While multinationals from many different countries have adopted English as their corporate language, this has not eliminated the language-related problems in knowledge sharing among geographically dispersed units. A Swedish multinational provides an illustration. Headquarters managers noticed that there was a lack of knowledge sharing between the German subsidiary and its Scandinavian sister units. On investigation, it turned out that the general manager of the German subsidiary was not a confident English speaker and therefore did not participate in the informal discussions with his Scandinavian peers that were intended to lead to exchange of know-how. The appointment of an English-speaking deputy to the German subsidiary solved this problem (Monteiro et al., 2008).

However, although the unit's general absorptive capacity undoubtedly is important, much of the knowledge transfer that occurs within multinational firms takes place in dyadic relationships between two units. Therefore, in many instances it makes more sense to examine absorptive capacity at the level of two units interacting and sharing knowledge. The term *relative absorptive capacity* (Lane and Lubatkin, 1998) has been coined to refer to the unit-specific ability to absorb knowledge from another party. While it would seem natural for units with similar levels of relative absorptive capacity to seek each other out, there are knowledge management paradoxes associated with relative absorptive capacity. When two units are similar, it is much easier for them to understand and absorb knowledge from the other. But on the other hand, similar units usually have less to learn from each other. In other words, the more their knowledge overlaps, the less there is to be gained from investment in knowledge sharing.

Absorptive capacity is more than just the ability of a unit to recognise the value of new information, to assimilate and apply it to commercial ends (Lane et al., 2006; Zahra and George, 2002). It also includes the capacity to unlearn, to challenge existing ways of doing things. Generally speaking, the more satisfied people are with current practices and results, the less willing they are to seek out and absorb new knowledge. And even if people realise that they are facing a problem that needs to be tackled, inward-looking units with strong internal social networks may not actively search for relevant knowledge held by other parts of the multinational.

Lack of motivation to learn from other units, even within the same enterprise, is well documented. There is a natural psychological tendency to inflate the perceived quality of one's own knowledge while deflating that of others. The Not-Invented-Here (NIH) syndrome has been described in a number of case studies, and it can be particularly strong if a unit is financially successful and has a long proud history.

Also, for the receiving unit the value of the knowledge held by another unit is rarely clear. When the source unit is perceived as knowledgeable, others will be more interested in learning from it (Szulanski, 1996). In the absence of reliable information about the quality of other units' knowledge, people tend to rely more on the knowledge residing in well performing subsidiaries and those located in the most advanced markets, discounting the potential value of low performers – the term 'halo effect' is used to describe this tendency (Gupta et al., 2008). There is also an understandable tendency to prefer similar units – those that follow a similar strategy and share common organisational characteristics – as those one can learn most from (Darr and Kurtzberg, 2000). Moreover, it is not only the potential usefulness of the knowledge that is difficult to assess; the efforts and costs associated with accessing and assimilating this knowledge into the receiver units are also unclear. Therefore, the likely return on investment associated with knowledge acquisition and sharing are extremely difficult to estimate (Cross and Prusak, 2003).

In our view, too much emphasis has been placed on the *push* of knowledge transfer and sharing, and too little on the *pull* from the receiving unit (see Szulanski, 1996). As the old saying goes, you can lead a horse to water but you cannot make it drink – unless it wants to. We therefore recommend that multinationals focus more on stimulating units to seek and adopt knowledge and practices from other parts of the corporation.

The mechanisms to share knowledge

Explicit and tacit knowledge need to be shared in different ways. Explicit knowledge is the easiest to access and acquire, and also to share within global firms. To the extent that tacit knowledge can be codified, it can be shared through databases, manuals and blueprints. The consultancy firm Accenture made big investments in the development of a global knowledge management system consisting of several thousand databases. The system is managed and promoted by 500 knowledge managers around the globe. Consultants are expected to enter knowledge about their projects into the system, where it can be accessed by other members of the organisation. One study reported that it was common for an Accenture consultant to access more than 10 different databases daily (Paik and Choi, 2005). However, most organisational members are notoriously bad at entering useful knowledge into databases and not all tacit knowledge can be made explicit. And even though some knowledge is codified, there is usually a need to combine it with the sharing of tacit knowledge that can take place through interactions between persons from different parts of the multinational (Noorderhaven and Harzing, 2009).

International transfers of personnel is one of the most important levers of knowledge sharing that multinationals have at their disposal. Typically, the transfer and assimilation of complex tacit knowledge into a new context requires the physical relocation of someone with experience – often an expatriate from headquarters. The motives for why multinationals choose to staff foreign units with expatriates have been extensively discussed in the literature, and they are also discussed elsewhere in this book (see Chapter 6). The close interactions of experienced expatriates with employees in their units offer many opportunities for sharing tacit knowledge (Lazarova and Tarique, 2005). Impatriates may be expected to play similar knowledge-sharing roles during assignments at headquarters and on their return to foreign units. Short-term personal interactions during visits, international conferences and meetings, and corporate training sessions, may fulfil the same function but they are likely to be most successful for knowledge that is explicit and/or relatively narrow in scope (Bonache and Zárraga-Oberty, 2008).

In spite of the importance of international assignments for knowledge sharing, expatriation has its limitations. Consider the example of Toyota. Over the last three decades the company's global strategy has been to gain market share by adding new manufacturing capacity in all its major markets (Takeuchi et al., 2008). To ensure Toyota's flawless quality and performance, the company taught local employees in every new location the Toyota Way – its production and management philosophy of continuous improvement. This essentially tacit knowledge was transferred through extensive use of expatriates. However, as effective as Toyota was in deploying expatriates to diffuse tacit knowledge, it simply did not have enough of them to support the company's rapid global expansion (Watanabe, 2007). The company had to become even better and faster in building its operating capabilities abroad.

Therefore, in order to speed up the learning process and to reinforce the knowledge transfer mechanism, Toyota created a Global Production Center in Toyota City. Its goal was to accelerate the development of local employees with deep knowledge of the Toyota production system (TPS) so the company would not have to rely solely on its experienced – and increasingly expensive – expatriates.

4 How to stimulate knowledge sharing

Multinational firms can use various levers to make knowledge sharing effective, efficient, and fast:

- Improving information about superior performance and knowledge
- Designing appropriate structural mechanisms
- Selecting expatriates who possess skills in sharing their knowledge
- Building a conducive social architecture
- Developing supportive performance management and incentive systems.

Improving information about superior performance and knowledge

One of the most basic reasons for not using knowledge residing in other parts of the multinational is that people are unaware of its existence. For instance, several units may have encountered similar problems in the manufacturing process but be unaware that one has already found a viable solution. An often-heard expression illustrates this common problem: 'If we only knew what we know.' In fact, much of the interest in knowledge management stems from the problem of locating potentially valuable knowledge in large corporations.

As we pointed out earlier, units perceived by others to be highly capable are more likely to be sought out as sources of knowledge (Monteiro et al., 2008). However, the evaluation of a subsidiary's capabilities contains a significant subjective element. Studies have revealed that there are only modest correlations between how managers from headquarters and foreign subsidiaries view the capabilities of overseas units (Dentrell et al., 2004). Therefore, it is important to identify superior practices by measuring relevant dimensions of unit performance. By making performance data widely available – turning the multinational into a fishbowl where strong performance is showcased – the units can themselves uncover examples of unique and valuable knowledge. For instance, Alfa Laval Agri from Sweden held quarterly meetings for all its subsidiary managers where they were required to present performance data along multiple dimensions. This approach helped to reduce the bias and ambiguity present in internal assessments of capabilities, and stimulated knowledge sharing among the units (Monteiro et al., 2008).

Structural mechanisms

Various lateral structural mechanisms are used in part or even primarily to stimulate knowledge sharing. For instance *product development committees* with members representing different geographic units and functional areas (e.g., R&D, manufacturing and marketing) are established with the aim of tapping into the different perspectives and pools of experience that the members bring to the committee. Temporary *international task forces* can serve the same purpose. Multinationals may also appoint *individuals* with the specific task of liaising between units, for example within a specific functional area.

The Knowledge Management Programme (KMP) at the world's largest steel manufacturer ArcelorMittal (formed in 2006 through Mittal Steel's acquisition of Arcelor) illustrates how multinationals may create horizontal teams or committees to enhance inter-unit knowledge sharing. Mittal Steel developed the programme during the 1990s when it expanded into Eastern Europe. KMP continues to play an important role in the new ArcelorMittal group, where the KMP process helps build peer networks and facilitates the integration process. Mittal Steel chose 25 activities, including manufacturing, finance, maintenance, purchasing, legal work and information technology, for their Knowledge Management Programme. Each of these had groups of approximately 20 members from different plants. They would meet regularly to benchmark the activities undertaken in the different units and to discuss common problems. For specific problems, the groups would use conference calls and smaller specialised *ad hoc* meetings. The diversity of the groups was viewed as a particular strength – according to Mittal Steel's chief operating officer: 'These countries have some very good technology. The Poles, for instance, have always been good in coke-making, and we have recently had a Romanian manager who was very helpful in sorting out a blast furnace problem in Chicago' (ICFAI, 2005).

Working in project or so called *'split egg' roles* (Evans et al., 2010) where managers and professionals have vertical and horizontal responsibilities, is at the heart of BP's focus on global knowledge management in its oil exploration and production business (Hansen and von Oetinger, 2001). Peer groups of business unit heads meet regularly. They are given joint responsibility for capital allocation and for setting unit performance goals, complemented by a host of cross-unit networks on shared areas of interest. These 'top of the egg' knowledge sharing activities take up to 20 per cent of the manager's time. 'The model here is an open market of ideas,' says one business unit head. 'People develop a sense of where the real expertise lies. Rather than having to deal with the bureaucracy of going through the centre, you can just cut across to somebody in Stavanger or Aberdeen or Houston and say, "I need some help. Can you give me a couple of hours?" And that is expected and encouraged' (Hansen and von Oetinger, 2001).

The knowledge management groups at ArcelorMittal and BP have many of the features associated with open *communities of practice*. These communities are characterised by some form of collaboration around a common set of interests. They differ from project teams and committees in that the participants' roles are not defined by the firm. Although the focus of these communities is on internal company issues, they may also broker relationships with outside experts. Communities of practice cannot and should not be fully controlled by the firm, building instead on voluntary participation, although support and guidance is essential (Probst and Borzillo, 2008; Wenger and Snyder, 2000). BT Global even provides a corporate version of Facebook, allowing people to mix professional and private networking, so that staff can tap into the experience of others around the world.

Research on communities of practice offers some guidelines on how to make them successful. First, it is important to have clear, shared objectives and a leader tasked with making sure that knowledge and best practices are shared and developed further. Second, the quality of interactions can be reinforced with workshops, training, exchange of staff, and an appropriate reward structure, with part-time coordination funded by the corporate budget. A study of unsuccessful communities of practice revealed that they lacked a core group of members; there was little one-to-one interaction between members; members did not identify with the community; participants had a strong belief in their own competence; and the issues discussed were not illustrated concretely enough for others to understand and visualise them (Probst and Borzillo, 2008).

Mittal refrained from appointing a 'best plant' for others to emulate, believing that all units had something to teach others. Some multinationals have appointed geographically dispersed centres of excellence that, among other things, are in charge of knowledge sharing. Such centres can for instance be formed in various locations around a small group of individuals recognised for their leading-edge, strategically valuable knowledge. These centres of excellence are mandated to make their knowledge available throughout the global firm and enhance it so that it remains at the cutting edge. Three types of centre have been identified in global service firms – charismatic (formed around an individual), focused (a small group of experts in a single location), and virtual (a larger group of specialists in multiple locations, linked by a database and proprietary tools). The charismatic and focused centres are well equipped to handle tacit knowledge, while the focused and virtual centres can process more firm-specific knowledge than a single individual (Moore and Birkinshaw, 1998). In contrast to parent-driven knowledge development, these centres tend to rely more on informal networks, often acting as a hub for knowledge sharing activities.

Selecting expatriates with knowledge sharing in mind

When selecting people for international assignments, some of the general characteristics that one looks for in expatriates are relevant here:

- professional and technical competence
- relationship and communication abilities
- cultural sensitivity and flexibility.

Whenever you go abroad, you must be non-evaluative when interpreting local behavior.

Appropriate professional and technical competence is a pre-requisite for most international assignments. The person must have the relevant training and experience not only to teach and coach others but also to learn him/herself on the job. Relationship and communication abilities help the expatriate build close interpersonal contacts that improve collaboration and facilitate knowledge transfer to the local unit, also giving the person access to local knowledge. Cultural sensitivity and flexibility improves the ability to adapt knowledge to the different local context. Expatriates who are non-evaluative when interpreting the behaviour of local employees are more likely to be effective in sharing and acquiring knowledge.

Pre-departure *training* as well as training, *coaching* and *mentoring* during the assignment abroad can assist the expatriate in the knowledge sharing role. More important, however, may be the objectives that are set for expatriates within the *performance management system*. If transfer of knowledge or organisational practices to the local unit is defined as a key performance indicator (KPI) for the expatriate, it provides a clear motivation to focus on achieving this target. An explicit localisation strategy for which the expatriate is held responsible may also further enhance the transfer of knowledge.

Social capital, social norms and global mindsets

The social relationship between the source and the receiver is another strong determinant of knowledge sharing within multinationals (Hansen et al., 2005). These relationships constitute the *social capital* of the firm. They comprise an intangible resource – a form of capital in the same way that human skills represent human capital – since the firm derives benefits from the connections and interpersonal relationships of people within the organisation and outside it. All three dimensions of social capital – structural, relational and cognitive (Nahapiet and Ghoshal, 1998) – are important.

The *structural* dimension of social capital refers to the pattern of relationships between people and units in the multinational. Without possessing a connection of some kind between two units or individuals, it is close to impossible to share tacit knowledge. Two units that already have a history of interaction are more likely to be aware of potentially useful knowledge residing in the other unit. Through relationships people may also gain important and fortuitous insights even when they are not searching for ideas on immediate problems. A large number of studies have confirmed that the degree of inter-unit communication is positively associated with knowledge sharing and innovation (Nahapiet and Ghoshal, 1998).

The *cognitive* dimension reflects the extent to which two parties are capable of sharing their understanding. A shared language and specialised vocabulary facilitate the interaction of organisational units and greatly enhance their ability to learn from each other. It has been suggested that the construction and recounting of shared narratives – collective stories and myths – in a community can aid the sharing of tacit knowledge. The use of metaphors may fulfil the same purpose.

Trust is at the core of the *relational* dimension of social capital. When two parties trust each other, they are more likely to share knowledge, in part because they are confident that the other party will reciprocate tomorrow for help they receive today. Units or individuals that are perceived as trustworthy are likely to be sought out by others to share their know-how and experience. Therefore, the reputation of an organisational unit, team or individual will influence whether or not others initiate processes of knowledge sharing with them. Trust was found to be the strongest predictor of inter-unit knowledge transfer in a recent meta-analysis of research on knowledge transfer (van Wijk et al., 2008).

Social networks naturally emerge in all social settings, although corporations can work with the explicit aim of strengthening social capital across units. The establishment of committees, projects and centres of excellence lead to the emergence and development of social relationships among the participants. A range of HR practices have the increase of social capital as one of their aims – from corporate training programmes with participants from different parts of the corporation to regional induction programmes for new recruits to transfers of personnel. However, it is also important to build a context which makes it more likely that people from different units around the world will engage in collaborative efforts. Therefore, two other aspects of the social architecture of the multinational – social norms and global mindset – are also crucial for knowledge sharing.

Social norms should support knowledge sharing. A social structure where hoarding knowledge is seen as violating the company's values and where those who transfer know-how to other units are presented as heroes will obviously encourage knowledge sharing. In such firms, knowledge is more likely to be viewed as a corporate resource to be exploited throughout the organisation (Gupta et al., 2008). An organisational culture where sharing and reciprocity are the norm will encourage people to share insights and ideas with others, and to volunteer to find solutions to problems encountered in other parts of the multinational.

More knowledge sharing can be expected in organisations where employees are encouraged to identify areas where improvements are necessary, and in firms where nobody fears that saying something negative about their own unit or organisation will be detrimental to their career (Currie and Kerrin, 2003). During one stage in GE's globalisation, the company set up a series of workshops where executives shared their 'global battlefield' experiences – with an explicit focus on where and why they failed. The message was loud and clear. It is OK to try something new and fail, but you had better learn from the experience and make sure that others do not repeat your mistake.

Knowledge sharing is also influenced by peoples' state of mind, and the term *global mindset* has recently gained prominence in the international management and HRM literatures. There are two different and complementary perspectives on global mindset, both relevant to knowledge management. One is rooted in a psychological focus on the development of managers in multinational firms, and the other coming from scholars and practitioners with a strategic viewpoint on the transnational enterprise. The first views global mindset as *the ability to accept and work with cultural diversity*, reflected in research that tries to map the skill or competency sets associated with management of diversity. Cultural self-awareness, openness to and understanding of other cultures are the core elements of the psychological or, as some scholars prefer to label it, the cultural perspective on global mindsets (Levy et al., 2007). This dimension of global mindset is concerned with why some persons are better in sharing – and especially receiving – knowledge across cultures. For instance, a paint technician with a global mindset in a car plant in China would seek knowledge from colleagues in the US or India.

The second complementary perspective on global mindset focuses on a way of thinking (or cognition) that reflects conflicting strategic orientations; it can therefore be labelled a strategic perspective. Since most multinational firms face strategic contradictions (the determining feature of the transnational enterprise), scholars have emphasised the need for 'balanced perspectives', arguing that a critical determinant of success in multinationals lies in the cognitive orientations of senior managers – their ability to cope with complexity embedded in the business (Levy et al., 2007). Knowledge embedded in diverse roles and dispersed operations is easier to harness when managers understand the need for multiple strategic capabilities, and view problems and opportunities from both local and global perspectives.

The task for the multinational firm is not to build a sophisticated structure, but to create a matrix in managers' minds (Bartlett and Ghoshal, 1989). International mobility and project work, international training programmes, and performance objectives that go beyond their own local unit, and top managers who 'walk the talk' are some of the ways in which multinationals can build global mindsets (Evans et al., 2010).

Performance management and incentives

The performance management and compensation systems of the firm play key roles in creating a knowledge-sharing context. Compensation strategies can be a significant obstacle to knowledge sharing. When individuals perceive that they are rewarded for their unique and individual expertise, sharing knowledge with others will naturally be seen as contrary to their interest.

At Schlumberger, GE and many other firms, knowledge sharing is part of managers' and engineers' formal performance reviews. Most Schlumberger field engineers have objectives relating to best practices, lessons learned, and other aspects of knowledge sharing (Åbø et al., 2001). Not surprisingly, an incentive system that encourages collaboration and knowledge sharing is more likely to produce this than a performance evaluation system where the hoarding of knowledge and destructive internal competition are tolerated or even encouraged (Björkman et al., 2004; Gupta et al., 2008). The logic of systems in place in many multinationals is that managers and executives should be motivated to contribute to company performance at least one level above the unit for which they are responsible. A foreign subsidiary manager may receive a bonus based on the regional or even global performance of the division or the corporation as a whole. This can encourage knowledge sharing and more general collaboration between organisational units.

Conversely, tying incentives to the performance of a subsidiary relative to its sister companies will create a strong disincentive to share information and knowledge. A retail company where the heads of neighbouring areas were married to each other constitutes an amusing example of the perverse effects that such reward systems may have. The general managers – husband and wife – failed to share knowledge with each other because their bonuses were tied to the relative performance of the two units!

In addition to financial rewards, the career implications of knowledge sharing send strong signals about the kind of behaviour that is valued and rewarded in the corporation.

5 Gaining access to external knowledge

Historically, firms have paid little attention to ways in which they might get access to new external knowledge through their international operations. Today, put simply, innovations are more likely to come from the field than from the headquarters. Academics and practitioners agree that the successful multinational corporations are increasingly those that are better at exploiting the possibilities offered by their worldwide networks to gain access to new knowledge and ideas from foreign locations. These opportunities can then be shared and combined with knowledge residing in the parent company with the aim of producing new innovations. This was the objective of the Connect + Develop model championed by P&G, the aim of which was to find external ideas that could be further developed within the corporation, often in collaboration with external partners (Huston and Sakkab, 2006). Many other firms are now trying to emulate P&G's model. In this section we discuss different strategies for gaining access to external knowledge as well as how to ensure that valuable knowledge is retained.

Turning new knowledge that has been acquired from outside the corporation into a commercially viable innovation involves capabilities in assimilating and recombining that new knowledge. So the acquisition of new knowledge also requires internal knowledge sharing, as discussed earlier. The levers that multinationals have at their disposal to enhance cross-border knowledge sharing are also relevant for external knowledge acquisition. Indeed the meta-analysis conducted by van Wijk and colleagues (2008) found that both external and internal knowledge sharing/transfers were largely influenced by the same mechanisms. However, firms may use additional approaches to access knowledge from the outside: scanning or tapping into the local knowledge base; partnering or merging with other firms; and what might be called playing the virtual market. Each of these has its own set of HRM implications.

Scanning global learning opportunities

Scanning involves gaining access to external knowledge from what people read, hear or experience at first hand. Important observations and innovative ideas can emerge from anywhere in the multinational. Although new insights often come as a by-product of ongoing operations and especially when lateral thinking is encouraged and rewarded in the organisation, specific investments in scanning may also enhance the external acquisition of new knowledge.

The establishment of a 'listening post' is a fairly inexpensive way to begin. P&G appointed 70 technology entrepreneurs to work in the company's regional hubs to scan their environments for ideas that might be useful for the corporation world-wide. The Taiwanese PC-manufacturer Acer established a small design shop in the US, through which it acquired skills in ergonomic design that were fed back to the parent organisation (Doz et al., 2001). Ericsson, the Swedish telecommunications firm, created 'cyberlabs' in New York and Palo Alto (next to Stanford University in Silicon Valley) whose task was to monitor developments in these markets and to build relationships with local companies (Birkinshaw, 2004).

While listening posts can be a useful way to access codified knowledge and facilitate the firm's identification of potential partners, they are less effective when the objective is to acquire tacit knowledge. Small units and individual scanners may lack the influence that is necessary to get the attention of corporate headquarters for new ideas. Many multinationals therefore establish fully fledged units in business centres at the forefront of the development of their respective industries, such as Silicon Valley (high technology), North Italy (fashion), and the City of London (financial services) (Inkpen and Tsang, 2005). These districts contain networks of producers, advanced users, supporting industries, universities, and research labs, and have fluid labour markets with highly competent individuals. Scanning in centres like these takes place through formal collaboration among organisations, formalised networks like trade associations and professional organisations, and more informal social networks.

From an HRM perspective, there are pros and cons associated with establishing a unit in locations such as Silicon Valley. On the one hand, there is an ample supply of people with relevant experience and the opportunity for social contacts can be invaluable. However, at the same time there is often fierce competition for talent, escalating salaries and the attendant risk of losing people to competitors. The winners are firms that are better than others at retaining their star performers, the losers tend to be those firms that suffer from high rates of attrition. Tight social networks not only help a firm tap into external knowledge but also serve as a conduit for its proprietary knowledge. Research has shown that firms that try to constrain their employees, in terms of what they are allowed to talk about with others, are likely to lose. They tend to get a bad reputation, which impairs their ability to hire the best people (Fleming and Marx, 2006).

In the past, it may have been obvious where the Hollywood or Silicon Valley of a certain industry was located. However, the situation today has become more complex; in many industries valuable knowledge can be found in several pockets around the world.

In 1998, an industry magazine listed ten world hot spots in the information technology industries, among them Austin, Texas; Bangalore, India; Cambridge, England; Sophia Antipolis, France; and Tel Aviv, Israel (Doz et al., 2001). Consequently, Cisco decided to split its corporate headquarters into two locations – the western-facing headquarters in Silicon Valley and the eastern-facing headquarters in Bangalore, India.

Accessing and assimilating complex tacit knowledge requires considerable investment in time and resources. Shiseido from Japan learnt this when establishing itself in France to learn about designing, manufacturing and selling scent. After attempting an unsuccessful joint venture with a French company, it formed a wholly owned subsidiary, Beauté Prestige International, to develop and produce fragrances. It also established a high-end beauty parlour in Paris and bought two functioning beauty salons. After a prolonged process, Shiseido learnt to let host country people with long-term industry experience take charge of its operations in France. In the end, Shiseido succeeded in acquiring capabilities in product development, manufacturing and marketing that the company was able to transfer back to Japan, through close observation and interaction between Japanese expatriates and French employees (Doz et al., 2001).

A crucial HRM issue when establishing a unit abroad is the company's ability to attract competent personnel at competitive costs. Experienced multinationals like Nokia always carry out in-depth HR analyses before they set up new units. Questions they typically ask include: Do the local universities produce engineering graduates with the required competence level for an R&D centre? Will the influx of other corporations to hotspots like Bangalore or Beijing lead to salary escalation that undermines current cost advantages?

Partnering or merging

A significant proportion of knowledge acquisition comes about through partnering, that is, deep relationships with other organisations. Partners include suppliers, distributers, competitors and research organisations. Some alliances and joint ventures with partner organisations are established with the explicit objective of co-creating new knowledge; but much knowledge acquisition takes place in partnerships where the focus is on on-going manufacturing or distribution of products. P&G quickly realised the potential of the 50,000 R&D staff in their 15 top suppliers. Several measures were taken to increase the number of joint R&D projects with suppliers, including the development of a secure IT platform used to communicate technology briefs (descriptions of what P&G is looking for) with suppliers, and face-to-face meetings to improve relationships and strengthen the understanding of the other's capabilities. The effect was a clear increase in the number of jointly staffed projects (Huston and Sakkab, 2006).

One of the challenges in learning alliances and joint ventures is that they may involve firms with competing interests, where parties strive to learn from each other to improve their individual position. The Nummi joint venture formed between Toyota and GM in California more than two decades ago is a classic example. GM's aim was to learn about lean manufacturing from Toyota, whereas the Japanese firm wanted to learn about the US market and gain experience in establishing and operating a local production unit. Most observers agree that Toyota was the more successful of the two in this 'race to learn', and it has been argued that to a large extent this was because its HR strategy and learning objectives were fully aligned (Tapscott and Williams, 2007).

The use of outsourcing has become widespread in virtually all industries. However, while most attention has been given to the outsourcing of support activities, like accounting and customer service, to India, companies also use contractors for more advanced activities. For instance, over the last few years, original equipment manufacturers (OEMs) in the mobile phone industry have invested in building their own product development capabilities, which they offer to companies like Nokia and Motorola. The development of a new mobile phone can be a highly complex process, involving an OEM, a specialised R&D company, and several units from the mobile phone company. There are significant challenges in developing appropriate structures for such projects and considerable attention must be paid to developing the social relationships needed for the collaboration to run smoothly. A major challenge for firms is to capture the individual learning of the key people involved in such partnerships, translating it into organisational know-how that can be conveyed to others.

Mergers and acquisitions (M&As) are the ultimate form of partnering. Not all M&As focus on knowledge acquisition, but a key objective in cross-border M&As is usually the acquisition and retention of local knowledge. The mechanisms for encouraging knowledge sharing that were discussed earlier in this chapter (such as creating social capital and social norms, developing structural mechanisms, and specifying supportive performance management and incentive systems) are relevant also in M&As.

Playing the virtual market

In the last decade we have seen a tremendous increase in the variety of mechanisms used to access company-external knowledge. One of the effects of the digital revolution described by Friedman (2005) in *The World is Flat* is the use of new technologies to link individuals and organisations in all parts of the world. For example, firms can post a specification of what they are looking for on the Internet, together with information about the reward that will be given to anyone who comes up with a solution. In 1999, the CEO of a troubled Canadian goldmine (an intensely secretive industry) decided to post all the geological data about the mine on the web, offering half a million dollars in prize money to virtual inspectors. The resulting ideas and gold discoveries catapulted Goldcorp from a $100 million underperformer into a $9 billion juggernaut that is one of the most innovative and profitable mining firms in the industry today. Companies can also issue more general calls for research projects. In 2008, HP's open innovation office announced a call for research proposals. It received more than 450 submissions from 200 universities in 22 countries. Forty-one of those proposals were funded (Jaruzelski and Dehoff, 2008).

P&G has paid considerable attention to the question of how best to use the 'market' for knowledge acquisition. Together with other large corporations, P&G has helped create firms specialising in connecting companies with technology problems with other companies, universities, labs and individuals who may be able to offer solutions. These market brokers can help write technology briefs and facilitate the interaction between the corporation with the problem and the organisation or individual with the potential solution. Market brokers often have a relatively well-specified scope of activities. P&G works with NineSigma which connects companies and organisations, InnoCentive which brokers solutions to more narrowly defined technical problems, and with YourEncore, a business that connects retired scientists and engineers with client corporations (Huston and Sakkab, 2006).

The challenges involved in the use of virtual cross-border teams and international alliances are amplified when playing the virtual market. The professional competences and interpersonal skills of the people managing these relationships are particularly important – they must be able to develop trust-based relationships swiftly with new partners. They also need to reach a shared understanding of performance expectations and decide how they will work together to achieve their objectives. Aligning the reward structure is critical. Without incentives, knowledge will not flow in. But with too many incentives, some talented individuals may decide that playing the market is more rewarding than staying with the firm – which brings us to the problem of retention.

6 Knowledge retention

While codified knowledge can be physically stored in databases and reports, tacit knowledge resides in people. When individuals with unique and valuable knowledge walk out of the door, the company might be losing part of its competitive advantage. What can the firm do to dissuade core tacit knowledge from making that exit?

There are three basic knowledge retention strategies. The first, which we have already discussed, is to stimulate knowledge sharing among individuals and units, so that the company is less dependent on a small number of people. An obvious illustration of this is when people with unique knowledge are approaching retirement – but with increasing professional employee turnover in most countries and corporations, knowledge sharing has to be encouraged on a continuous basis.

A second strategy is to try to reduce employee turnover, reducing in turn the leaking of proprietary knowledge to competitors. This means, among others, trying to make sure that employees believe that they have good development opportunities in the firm and paying attention to the individual interests of the person (for a more extensive discussion see Evans et al., 2010). However, knowledge retention should also be a factor when considering involuntary turnover, during periods of recession, or when companies are considering relocating operations.

When the price of oil reached its nadir in the late 1990s, many energy firms responded by curtailing exploration activities and laying off experienced staff. Less than five years later, when prices moved in the opposite direction, they had to buy back the same skills from outside at a much higher cost. In some cases they even had to forgo pursuing major opportunities as they simply did not have a sufficiently experienced workforce to manage the projects.

The third strategy is to invest in making tacit knowledge explicit. The Japanese knowledge management scholar Ikujiro Nonaka (1994) calls this 'externalisation.' He suggests that metaphors can help individuals to explain tacit concepts that are otherwise difficult to articulate by conveying intuitive images that people can understand. The explicit knowledge can then be codified and saved in databases and the like, where they can be accessed after the people with the embedded knowledge have left the firm. For this strategy to work, the firm must be clear about the type of knowledge that is accorded high value and how it will be made accessible (see Chapter 1).

The example of how to manage repatriates illustrates all three strategies. Multinationals typically pay too little attention to how the organisation can benefit from the knowledge that repatriates have gained abroad. Many returnees are dissatisfied with the career opportunities they are offered and begin looking for jobs elsewhere. Numerous studies and anecdotes have shown that a large percentage of international assignees resign shortly after returning home. Successful retention management is therefore part of a successful approach to repatriate knowledge sharing. The receiving organisation must make sure that repatriates have opportunities to share their knowledge by appointing them to positions where they can work with others on issues related to their experience, and by assigning them to relevant projects and committees (Oddou et al., 2009). In some situations, reports and presentations can be appropriate tools for capturing and sharing insights gained during overseas assignments (Lazarova and Tarique, 2005).

7 From the management of knowledge to innovation

So far we have discussed knowledge transfer within the multinational and acquisition of new knowledge from outside the company. Both activities are crucial for nurturing innovation in the multinational. The fact is that big, complex global organisations have difficulty with innovation. As Kanter (1989) notes, it is like teaching elephants how to dance. The biggest problem may not be that multinationals do not know how to be innovative – it is that the properties needed to be innovative are different from those needed to be successful in exploiting what they are doing well today. This is just one of the many paradoxes in the domain of global knowledge management.

Effective knowledge management is important both to exploit existing capabilities on a global scale and to explore new ideas that can be developed into new product and service offerings. While both exploration and exploitation are needed, finding a balance between the two is challenging (March, 1991). Companies easily fall into the trap of focusing too much on one at the expense of the other; one of the many dualities that multinationals are facing (see Evans et al., 2010). We have considered other dualities in this chapter – combining network modes of operating with structural modes of organisation, and inside versus outside orientations on how a unit can gain access to new knowledge.

Let us take another paradox that we have not yet explicitly mentioned – the transfer paradox and the evaluation paradox. The transfer paradox argues that the most valuable knowledge – complex and contextual tacit knowledge – is also the most sticky. It is expensive and difficult to transfer within the multinational, requiring linking mechanisms that build on face-to-face relationships. The evaluation paradox holds that this same tacit know-how is also the most difficult and expensive to evaluate and assess. Organising for innovation means managing the tensions that underlie such dualities.

The management of knowledge and innovation on a global scale is clearly a challenge, with numerous HRM implications, although nothing that confers sustainable competitive advantage comes easily. Performance management systems and compensation schemes have to encourage both exploration and exploitation. Multinationals need to recruit and select employees bearing in mind the acquisition of valuable external knowledge, but they also need to socialise new employees to make sure that this knowledge is shared across units. And a key decision-making criterion for staffing decisions should increasingly be the innovative ability of the firm. Multinationals which handle such HRM issues well can achieve a competitive advantage that will be difficult for their competitors to match.

8 Summary and conclusions

In this chapter we have reviewed knowledge management in multinational firms and conclude that HRM is central to firms' knowledge sharing and strategic capabilities. The achievement of sustainable competitive advantage will depend substantially on the ability of the firm to explore new and exploit existing knowledge.

In the second section we distinguished explicit and tacit knowledge noting that these different types of knowledge are often shared through different mechanisms. Knowledge varies according to its strategic significance and may therefore be subdivided into core, compulsory, idiosyncratic and ancillary knowledge. Then, in section 3, we considered the different factors that influence knowledge sharing between units including the ability and willingness of senders, the motivation and ability of receivers and the suitability of channels used to share knowledge.

We reviewed in section 4 various ways of stimulating knowledge sharing and considered information on performance and knowledge, structure, expatriation, social architecture, performance management and supportive incentive systems. Ways of exploiting and sharing knowledge were discussed such as showcasing performance data in review and conference meetings, product development committees, international task forces, knowledge management programmes, communities of practice, centres of excellence (charismatic, focused and virtual), and informal networks. In relation to expatriation, we noted the wide range of competences required if the expatriate is to be successful, and then discussed key factors which characterise units engaging in effective knowledge sharing. The research on these units reveals that they have relatively high levels of inter-unit trust and collaborate through deploying their social capital resources (structural, relational and cognitive). Social norms across these units encourage knowledge sharing and promote a global mindset involving coping productively with cultural diversity and being open to different cultural perspectives and ways of working. At all levels in the organisation (corporate, unit, group and individual) the performance management and incentive systems will influence employees' motivation and commitment to knowledge sharing. In firms such as Schlumberger and GE, knowledge sharing is part of managers' and engineers' formal performance reviews.

Access to internal and external knowledge is often influenced by similar mechanisms. However, firms can develop specific initiatives to identify and appropriate external knowledge. This requires a culture of openness and activities of scanning the environment and may lead to structural reorientation such as when Cisco decided to divide its corporate headquarters into two locations (Silicon Valley and Bangalore). Partnering (M&As) and virtual surveys and competitions are three major ways used by companies to capture and utilise external knowledge. In addition to identifying and capitalising on new knowledge, companies continuously face the threat of losing valuable knowledge and skills and so many ensure a number of strategic and HRM initiatives to promote the appropriate level of employee retention. As the final section demonstrates, as well as retaining valuable knowledge and expertise, companies must retain their competence in innovation which means dealing with complexity and its many contradictions and uncertainties such as the transfer and evaluation paradoxes.

Discussion questions

1 With so much information available through the internet and so much data stored in company-internal databases, social interaction will gradually become less important for knowledge sharing. Comment on this statement.

2   For a foreign subsidiary that controls unique and valuable knowledge, it does not make much sense to share such knowledge with other units of the corporation because it will lose an important source of power. Discuss arguments for and against this statement.

3   What advice would you give a multinational corporation that plans to change its global performance and incentive system in order to increase knowledge sharing across its international units?

4   Discuss the pros and cons of different approaches to retaining knowledge in the corporation.

Spurring innovation through global knowledge management at Procter & Gamble

Procter & Gamble (P&G) was founded in Cincinnati in 1837. Initially, the company produced soap and candles, but the firm eventually diversified into a range of consumer goods. An important reason behind P&G's growth and success in the decades after the Second World War was its ability to create innovations, like the industry's first cavity-prevention toothpaste Crest, the heavy-duty synthetic detergent Tide, and the two-in-one shampoo product Pert Plus.

P&G had established its first overseas marketing and manufacturing unit through an acquisition in the UK in 1930, and it proceeded to expand abroad rapidly after 1946. The company originally based its R&D activities in the US, but since the mid-1980s, P&G established a worldwide R&D network, with research hubs in the US, Europe, Japan and Latin America (see www.pg.com/tranlations/history_pdf/english_history.pdf). However, while the company continued to develop innovative new products in the 1990s, by 2000 profits were lacklustre, the stock was underperforming (*New York Times*, 2008), and P&G was facing decreasing returns on its investments in R&D (Huston and Sakkab, 2006). In fact, from all of its new product introductions, only a minority were returning their development costs (*New York Times*, 2008).

At the beginning of this century, the US operations were still dominant, with the flow of knowledge and innovations mostly flowing from the centre to its foreign subsidiaries. P&G had some positive experiences of leveraging knowledge from foreign subsidiaries (see Bartlett, 2003) and also with acquiring new products from outside the firm. The problem was that such successes occurred all too infrequently. While the company knew that many of its best innovations came when combining ideas from different parts of the corporation, the inflow of knowledge from the overseas units was limited as was lateral knowledge transfer among the foreign subsidiaries. The foreign units were fairly autonomous and had limited experience in sharing knowledge across borders. For instance, it took P&G five years after the successful launch of the Pampers diapers in Germany to introduce the product in France, allowing Colgate-Palmolive to enter the market with a similar product that gained a dominant market share (Hansen and Birkinshaw, 2007).

While P&G had some positive experiences acquiring new products from outside the firm, these innovations and their connections were too seldom. Consequently, in 2000, the new CEO, A.G. Lafley, set out to change radically the way the company went about innovation. He set a challenging strategic goal that 50 per cent of new products should stem from ideas acquired from outside the company. Lafley believed that this would require a change in the company's attitude from its resistance to innovation and a 'not invented here' syndrome to an enthusiasm for those ideas and products 'proudly found elsewhere'. Reflecting on this need for fundamental change, Lafley further observed, 'And we needed to change how we defined, and perceived, our R&D organisation – from 7,500 people inside to 7,500 plus 1.5 million outside, with a permeable boundary between them' (Huston and Sakkab, 2006: 61).

Clearly, enhancing how P&G captured and shared knowledge across borders would not be an easy undertaking. The functional silos between R&D, marketing research, manufacturing, and other functions would have to be eliminated, as well as reducing the barriers that existed between the different business units. There was also a need to improve the linkage between problem identification, external knowledge acquisition, internal knowledge sharing across units, and global exploitation of innovations (in terms of products but also in terms of internal ways of working).

The new model that P&G developed was called 'Connect + Develop' (Laffley and Charam, 2008). The goal was to tap into knowledge and ideas outside the company, from small and medium-sized companies, university labs, individual researchers, its business partners and even from its competitors. An additional aim was to improve the sharing of knowledge and ideas within the company. P&G appointed 70 senior technology entrepreneurs to work in six regional Connect + Develop hubs, focusing on finding products and technologies that were specialties within their regions. P&G established 21 global communities of practice – networks of experts working in the different business areas (*Business Week*, 2004). The company also helped to create several firms that operated open networks, typically web-based, connecting scientists, companies, universities and government labs (Huston and Sakkab, 2006).

A number of additional organisational changes were also implemented. The country organisations lost much of their previous independence. New regional organisations were introduced – for instance, a new European regional headquarters was established in Geneva, which was mostly staffed by expatriates from different parts of Europe. While P&G had always used expatriation as a management development tool, the new structure led to increased interaction and knowledge sharing among people with diverse experiences and personal networks and ties to different parts of the corporation. The co-location of the different business unit management teams also led to stronger connections and relationships across the units. Finally, P&G established regional service centres responsible for a range of functional activities.

The Connect + Develop model has led to significant changes in how P&G approaches its innovation projects. A case in point was the development of a new Pringle potato chip printed with words and pictures. Somebody had come up with the idea in a brainstorming session but it was not clear how it could be done technically. In the past, P&G would have launched an internal R&D project, but for the printed Pringle it developed a technology brief that was communicated throughout the corporation and its external networks (when a new opportunity is spotted, such briefs are developed and circulated throughout the corporation). This led to the identification of a small bakery in Bologna, run by a university professor who had invented a method for printing on food products that could be adapted to fit the purpose. The new product, Pringles Prints, was launched in 2004. In less than a year and at fraction of what it otherwise would have cost, P&G had developed a double digit growth business. P&G's innovation success rate (the percentage of new products that return the investments made on them) has more than doubled since 2000. The number of new products originating from outside the firm has risen to 35 per cent, while R&D spending has been reduced from 4.5 per cent of sales in the late 1990s to 2.8 per cent in 2007 (see www.strategy-business.com/press/freearticle/08304).

Case questions

1 Evaluate P&G's approach to managing knowledge and innovation.
2 What are the barriers that a multinational organisation has to overcome so as to harness the potential of a 'Connect+Develop' model? What are the implications for HR?

Case question for further reflection

1 What are the lessons of P&G's success in enhancing innovation through global knowledge management, and how does this apply to another organisation that you know well – perhaps in a different industry?

Further reading

* Van Wijk, R., Jansen, J.J.P. and Lyles, M.A. (2008) 'Inter- and intra-organisational knowledge transfer: a meta-analytic review and assessment of its antecedents and consequences', *Journal of Management Studies*, 45: 830–53.
Recent meta-analysis of factors associated with knowledge sharing.

* Kamoche, K. (1997) 'Knowledge creation and learning in international HRM', *The International Journal of Human Resource Management*, 8(3): 213–25.
As this chapter has argued the issues of knowledge creation and learning are central to successful knowledge management. This article examines how IHRM specifically can contribute to improving the performance and achievements of international assignments.

* Doz, Y., Santos J. and Williamson, P. (2001) *From Global to Metanational.* Boston, MA: Havard Business School press.
Doz, Santos and Williamson's highly influential book discusses the 'metanational' corporation that excels in managing knowledge and innovation on a global scale.

- Furuya, N., M. J. Stevens, A. Bird, G. Oddou and M. Mendenhall (2009) 'Managing the learning and transfer of global management competence: Antecedents and outcomes of Japanese repatriation effectiveness', *Journal of International Business Studies*, 40: 200–15.

Furuya, et al. (2009) provide a comprehensive analysis of factors affecting individual learning during expatriate assignments and the application of their competences in new assignments following repatriation.

- Easterby-Smith, M. and Lyles, M.A. (eds) (2003) *The Blackwell Handbook of Organisational Learning and Knowledge Management.* Malden, MA: Blackwell.

Excellent overview of a range of issues related to management of knowledge and organisational learning.

- Evans, P., Pucik, V. and Björkman, I. (2010) *The Global Challenge: International Human Resource Management*, 2nd edn. New York: McGraw-Hill.

Takes a general management perspective on people management issues in the multinational, including the role of HRM for the management of knowledge and innovation.

Internet resources

1 *Journal of Knowledge Management* (http://info.emeraldinsight.com/products/journals/journals.htm?PHPSESSID = u6odfe9017skkoegsq42cakua7&id = jkm): This is a peer-reviewed publication dedicated to the exchange of the latest academic research and practical information on all aspects of managing knowledge in organisations.

2 CIO (http://www.cio.com/article/40343/Knowledge_Management_Definition_and _Solutions): CIO magazine and its portfolio of properties offer technology and business leaders articles on information technology trends and a keen understanding of IT's role in achieving business goals.

3 Knowledge Management (http://www.bing.com/images/search?q = Knowledge+Management&form = QB&qs = n#): A *bing* website offering access to many images relating to the topic of knowledge management. Very useful content materials, for example, to illustrate PowerPoint presentations on the topic.

4 World Bank Institute's Knowledge Management Initiative (http://web.worldbank.org/WBSITE/EXTERNAL/WBI/WBIPROGRAMS/KFDLP/0,,contentMDK:20934415 ~ menuPK:2882148 ~ pagePK:64156158 ~ piPK:64152884 ~ theSitePK:461198,00.html): Aims to enhance the capacity of development-oriented organisations in the client countries to achieve greater impact through the application of knowledge management tools and practices.

Self-assessment questions

Indicative answers to these questions can be found on the companion website at www. sagepub.co.uk/harzing3e.

1 **List three ways of assessing the capacity of an organisation to stimulate knowledge sharing.**
2 **Define tacit and explicit knowledge. In what ways are they different and also how are they the same?**
3 **List the nine ways of gaining access to external knowledge that are discussed in Section 5 of this chapter.**
4 **What aspects of the Knowledge Management Groups and centres of excellence at ArcelorMittal and the unit heads networks and meetings at BP are associated with typical features of open communities of practice?**
5 **Give two examples of 'listening posts' established to scan the environment and diffuse innovation from one geographical location to other parts of the company.**

References

Åbø, E., Chipperfield, L. Mottershead, C. Old, J. Prieto, R. Stemke, J. and Smith, R.G. (2001) 'Managing knowledge management', *Oilfield Review*, 13(1): 66–83.

Barner-Rasmussen, W. and Björkman, I. (2006) 'Language fluency, socialization and inter-unit relationships in Chinese and Finnish subsidiaries', *Management and Organization Review*, 3(1): 105–28.

Bartlett, C.A. (2003) *P & G Japan. The SK-II Globalization Project* (case 303003). Boston: Harvard Business School.

Bartlett, C.A. and S. Ghoshal (1989) *Managing Across Borders : The Transnational Solution.* Cambridge, MA: Harvard Business School Press.

Birkinshaw, J. (2004) *'External sourcing of knowledge in the international firm'*, in H. Lane, M. J. Maznevski, M.E. Mendenhall and J. McNett (eds), *Handbook of Global Management.* pp. 289–300. Oxford: Blackwell.

Björkman, I., W. Barner-Rasmussen. and Li, L. (2004) 'Managing knowledge transfer in MNCs: The impact of headquarter control mechanisms', *Journal of International Business Studies*, 35(5): 443–55.

Bonache, J. and Zárraga-Oberty, C. (2008) 'Determinants of the success of international assignees as knowledge tranferors: A theoretical framework', *International Journal of Human Resource Management*, 19(1): 1–18.

Chakravarthy, B., McEvily, S., Doz, Y. and Rau, D. (2003) 'Knowledge management and competitive advantage' in M. Lyles and M. Easterby-Smith, (eds), *Handbook of Organizational Learning and Knowledge Management.* Oxford: Blackwell. pp. 305–23.

Cohen W.M. and Levinthal, D.A. (1990) 'Absorptive capacity: a new perspective on learning and innovation', *Administrative Science Quarterly*, 35(1): 128–52.

Cross, R. and Prusak, L. (2003) 'The political economy of knowledge markets in organizations', in M. Lyles and M. Easterby-Smith (eds), *Handbook of Organisational Learning.* Oxford: Blackwell.

Currie, G. and Kerrin, M. (2003) 'Human resource management and knowledge management: enhancing knowledge sharing in a pharmaceutical company', *International Journal of Human Resource Management*, 14(6): 1027–45.

Darr, E.D. and Kurtzberg, T.R. (2000) 'An investigation of partner similarity dimensions on knowledge transfer', *Organizational Behavior and Human Decision Processes*, 82(1): 28–44.

Dentrell, J., Arvidsson, N. and Zander, U. (2004) 'Managing knowledge in the dark: an empirical study of the reliability of capability evaluation', *Management Science*, 50(11): 1491–503.

Doz, Y., Santos, J. and Williamson, P. (2001) *From Global to Metanational: How Companies Win in the Knowledge Economy*. Boston: Harvard Business School Press.

Evans, P., Pucik, V. and Björkman, I. (2010) *The Global Challenge: International Human Resource Management*, 2nd edn. New York: McGraw-Hill.

Fleming, M. and Marx, M. (2006) 'Managing creativity in small worlds', *California Management Review*, 48(4): 6–27.

Friedman, T.L. (2005) *The World is Flat: A brief history of the twenty-first century*. New York: Farrar, Straus and Giroux.

Gupta, A.K., Govindarajan, V. and Wang, H. (2008) *The Quest for Global Dominance*. San Francisco: Jossey-Bass.

Hansen, M.T. and Birkinshaw, J. (2007) 'The innovation value chain', *Harvard Business Review*, 85 June (6): 121–30.

Hansen, M.T. and von Oetinger, B. (2001) 'Introducing T-shaped managers: Knowledge management's next generation', *Harvard Business Review* (March): 107–16.

Hansen, M.T., Mors, M.L. and Løvås, B. (2005) 'Knowledge sharing in organizations: multiple networks, multiple phases', *Academy of Management Journal*, 48(5): 776–93.

Huston L. and Sakkab, N. (2006) 'Connect and develop: inside Procter & Gamble's new model for innovation', *Harvard Business Review*, 84 March (3): 58–66.

ICFAI (2005) *Mittal Steel's Knowledge Management Strategy*, ICFAI Case Study, no. 305-543-1.

Inkpen, A.C. and Tsang, E.W.K. (2005) 'Social capital, networks, and knowledge transfer', *The Academy of Management Review*, 30(1): 146–65.

Jaruzelski, B. and Dehoff, K. (2008) *Beyond Borders: The Global Innovation 1000*. Available at www.booz.com.

Kanter, R.M. (1989) *When Giants Learn to Dance: Mastering the Challenge of Strategy, Management, and Careers in the 1990s*. New York: Simon and Schuster.

Kogut, B. and Zander, U. (1992) 'Knowledge of the firm, combinative capabilities, and the replication of technology', *Organization Science*, 3(3): 383–97.

Kogut, B. and Zander, U. (1993) 'Knowledge of the firm and the evolutionary theory of the multinational corporation', *Journal of International Business Studies*, 24(4): 625–45.

Kostova, T. (1999) 'Transnational transfer of strategic organisational practices: A contextual perspective', *Academy of Management Review*, 24(2): 308–24.

Laffley, A.G. and Charam, R. (2008) *The Game Changer*. New York: Crown Business.

Lane, P. and Lubatkin, M. (1998) 'Relative absorptive capacity and interorganizational learning', *Strategic Management Journal*, 19(5): 461–77.

Lane, P. J., Koka, B.R. and Pathak, S. (2006) 'The reification of absorptive capacity: a critical review and rejuvenation of the construct', *Academy of Management Review*, 31(4): 833–63.

Lazarova, M. and Tarique, I. (2005) 'Knowledge transfer upon repatriation', *Journal of World Business*, 40(4): 361–73.

Lepak, D.P. and S.A. Snell (1999) 'The human resource architecture: Toward a theory of human capital allocation and development', *Academy of Management Review*, 24(1): 31–48.

Levy, O., Beechler, S., Taylor, S. and Boyacigiller, N.A. (2007) 'What we talk about when we talk about "global mindset": managerial cognition in multinational corporations', *Journal of International Business Studies*, 38(2): 231–58.

March, J.G. (1991) 'Exploration and exploitation in organisational learning', *Organization Science*, 2(1): 71–87.

Minbaeva, D. and Michailova, S. (2004) 'Knowledge transfer and expatriation practices in MNCs: the role of disseminative capacity', *Employee Relations*, 26(6): 663–79.

Minbaeva, D., Pedersen, T., Björkman, I., Fey, C. and Park, H. (2003) 'MNC knowledge transfer, subsidiary absorptive capacity and knowledge transfer', *Journal of International Business Studies*, 34(6): 586–99.

Monteiro, L. F., Arvidsson, L. and Birkinshaw, J. (2008) 'Knowledge flows within multinational corporations: explaining subsidary isolation and its preformance implications', *Organizational Science*, 19(1): 90–107.

Moore, K. and Birkinshaw, J. (1998) 'Managing knowledge in global service firms: Centers of excellence', *Academy of Management Executive*, 12(4): 81–92.

Nahapiet, J. and Ghoshal, S. (1998) 'Social capital, intellectual capital, and the organisational advantage', *Academy of Management Review*, 23(2): 242–66.

New York Times (2008) 'Changing the game with innovation', 24 May.

Nonaka, I. (1994) 'A dynamic theory of organisational knowledge creation', *Organization Science*, 5(1): 14–37.

Nonaka, I. and Takeuchi, H. (1995) *The Knowledge-creating Company: How Japanese Companies Create the Dynamics of Innovation*. Oxford: Oxford University Press.

Noorderhaven, N.G. and Harzing, A.W.K. (2009) 'Factors influencing knowledge flows within MNCs', *Journal of International Business Studies*, 40(5): 719–41.

Oddou, G., Osland, J.S. and Blakeney, R.N. (2009) 'Repatriating knowledge: variables influencing the "transfer" process', *Journal of International Business Studies*, 40(2): 181–99.

Paik, Y. and Choi, D.Y. (2005) 'The shortcomings of a global knowledge management system: the case of accenture', *Academy of Management Executive*, 19(2): 81–4.

Polanyi, M. (1967) *The Tacit Dimension*. Garden City, NY: Doubleday.

Probst, G. and Borzillo, S. (2008) 'Why communities of practice succeed and why they fail', *European Management Journal*, 26(3): 335–47.

Simonin, B.L. (1999) 'Ambiguity and process of knowledge transfer in strategic alliances', *Strategic Management Journal*, 20(7): 596–623.

Szulanski, G. (1996) 'Exploring internal stickiness: Impediments to the transfer of best practice within the firm', *Strategic Management Journal* 17(1): 27–43.

Takeuchi, H., Osono, E. and Shimizu, N. (2008) 'The contradictions that drive Toyota's success', *Harvard Business Review*, (June): 96–104.

Tapscott, D. and Williams, A.D. (2007) *Wikinomics: How Mass Collaboration Changes Everything*. New York: Penguin.

Van Wijk, R., Jansen, J. and Lyles, M. A. (2008) 'Inter- and intra-organizational knowledge transfer: A meta-analytic review and assessment of its antecedents and consequences', *Journal of Management Studies*, 45(4): 830–53.

Watanabe, K. (2007) 'Lessons from Toyota's long drive', *Harvard Business Review*, (July–August): 74–83.

Wenger, E.C. and Snyder, W.M. (2000) 'Communities of practice: the organizational frontier', *Harvard Business Review*, 78(January): 139–45.

Zahra, S.A. and George, G. (2002) 'Absorptive capacity: a review, reconceptualization, and extension', *Academy of Management Review*, 27(2): 185–203.

11

The Development of Global Leaders and Expatriates

Yaw A. Debrah and Christopher J. Rees

Contents

Learning Objectives

After reading this chapter you will be able to

- Explain the term global leader with reference to a) the main tasks that global leaders undertake and b) the competencies global leaders need to practice in order to be effective

- Discuss the nature of development programmes for global leaders with reference to the objectives, content and limitations of these programmes

- Critically evaluate the main objectives and effectiveness of cross-cultural skills training for expatriates

- Identify and discuss a range of emerging issues relating to the design, content and delivery of cross-cultural skills training for expatriates

Chapter Outline

The chapter examines the development of global leaders and expatriates. The first section explores definitions of the term global leader, the competencies and tasks associated with their work, and global leadership development programmes. The second section concentrates on issues surrounding cross-cultural training for expatriates.

1 Introduction

In the current dynamic and complex global business environment, organisations need to be able to compete effectively to achieve sustainable growth and indeed survival (Caligiuri, 2006). Globalisation and its attendant global competitiveness is placing increasing pressure on employees working in international organisations to develop a global mindset, regardless of location. As Kedia and Mukherji (1999) propose, the challenge of the global competitive environment requires not only improvement in organisational performance but more importantly in individual development. It has become imperative that organisations develop employees at all levels and in all locations so that they can contribute significantly to the bottom line (Thomas et al., 2005).

This chapter deals with development of global leaders and expatriates in international organisations. International here is defined to include MNCs, joint ventures and other organisations such as international non-governmental organisations (Chang, 2005) including those whose activities may be mainly domestically based, but still are operating within the global environment. The first part of the chapter will focus on the development of global leaders and the second part will concentrate on the development of expatriates.

2 Leading organisations in the global environment

Globalisation is fostered by advances in information and communication technologies (ICT); including internet, advances in transportation, promotion of free trade and the liberalisation of economies. Particularly in developing countries, these changes have created fundamental competitive challenges for most organisations. Operating in the international arena they now have a significant exposure to the global environment in terms of suppliers, customers, employees and other stakeholders (Evans et al., 2002). In Lane et al.'s (1997) view, the world has become a 'global market place' requiring managers to exhibit a global perspective and develop effective strategic responses to the demands of the increasingly competitive global environment (Murtha et al., 1998; Prahaled and Lieberthal, 1998).

Along the same lines, Caliguiri (2006) argues forcefully that concomitant with the changes in the way that business is conducted, leaders need to develop new competencies to succeed. International organisations desperately need globally competent leaders to achieve success (Adler and Bartholomew, 1992; Caligiuri and DeSanto, 2001). In this respect, the development of global leaders is seen as a new source of competitive advantage for organisations (Black et al., 1999; Csoka and Hackett, 1998). The gradual shift towards global leadership development is beginning to generate more interest in the study of human resource development (HRD) practices of international organisations (Thomas et al., 2005). For example, Thomas and Inkson (2004) highlight the urgent need for effective global leaders as an emerging issue for global firms and HRD is increasingly being recognised as a major determinant of the success or failure of global leaders (Deresky, 2008).

Interest in the HRD practices of international organisations is manifested in an emerging body of literature on the subject of international or global HRD (see Wang and McLean, 2007). Global HRD in contrast to comparative HRD and national HRD, is a broad term that concerns processes that address the formulation and practice of HRD systems, practices and policies at the organisational and societal level (Metcalfe and Rees, 2005: 455). It can incorporate comparative analyses of HRD approaches across nations and also addresses how societies develop national HRD policies (see Figure 11.1).

Global HRD involves the development of transnational HRD interventions and is seen as especially important in policy areas of global management development (Metcalfe and Rees, 2005: 456) and in knowledge sharing and learning communities (Iles and Yolles, 2003; OECD, 2000). Global HRD is directly concerned with issues ranging from how governments and international organisations develop global HRD

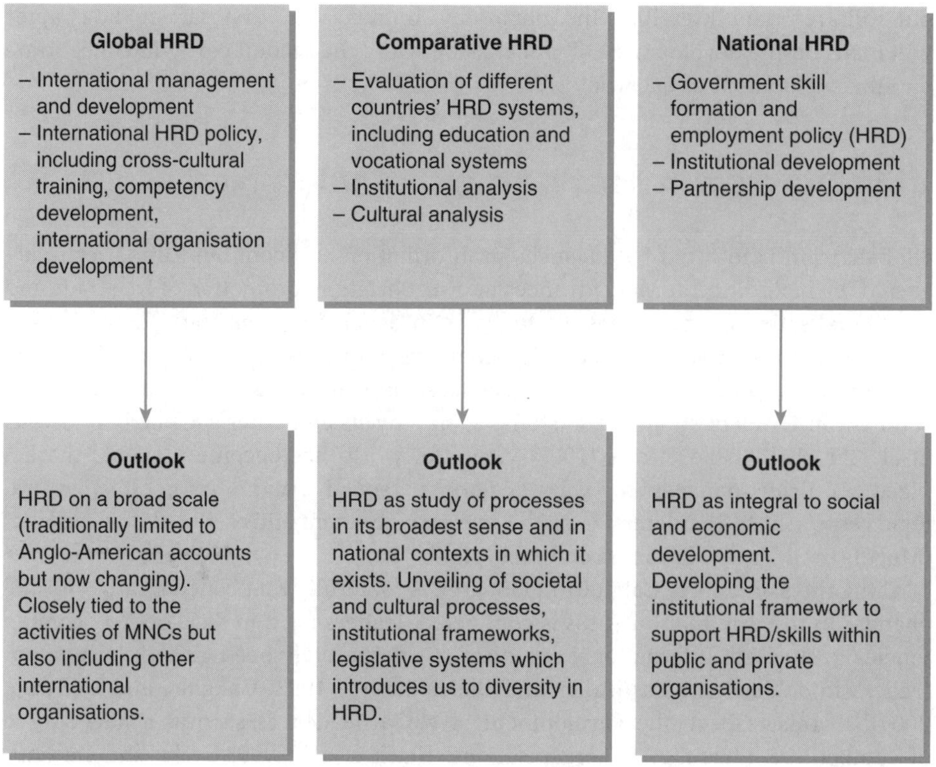

Global HRD	Comparative HRD	National HRD
– International management and development – International HRD policy, including cross-cultural training, competency development, international organisation development	– Evaluation of different countries' HRD systems, including education and vocational systems – Institutional analysis – Cultural analysis	– Government skill formation and employment policy (HRD) – Institutional development – Partnership development
Outlook	**Outlook**	**Outlook**
HRD on a broad scale (traditionally limited to Anglo-American accounts but now changing). Closely tied to the activities of MNCs but also including other international organisations.	HRD as study of processes in its broadest sense and in national contexts in which it exists. Unveiling of societal and cultural processes, institutional frameworks, legislative systems which introduces us to diversity in HRD.	HRD as integral to social and economic development. Developing the institutional framework to support HRD/skills within public and private organisations.

Figure 11.1 Mapping the boundaries of global HRD

Source: abridged from Metcalfe and Rees (2005).

systems, to the development of global leaders via activities such as cross-cultural training, cultural reorientation, foreign language and relocation services (see figure 11.1). In the following sections of this chapter, we seek to explore the notion of a global leader, the competencies required by global leaders, and global leadership development programmes.

3 Global leaders

There is a shortage in available global leaders

The changing business environment makes it abundantly clear that international organisations need to develop effective global leaders in the quest to achieve competitive advantage and survival. Gregersen et al's. (1998) study revealed, however, the lack of an adequate number of globally competent executives. Almost all of the companies that participated in the study indicated that they required more global managers with high quality global leadership capabilities. This reflects a shortage of global leaders in international firms and the need for focused HRD strategies to tackle the problem.

Defining the term global leader

In recent years, considerable effort has gone into attempts to define, explain, develop and illuminate our understanding of what constitutes a global leader. At the outset, we reinforce the view expressed by Jokinen (2005: 201) that terminology surrounding global leadership is 'characterized by missing consensus on concise definitions and classification of such fundamental terms as global, management, leadership and competency'. Arguably, it is counter-intuitive to expect otherwise given the extensive literature that explores similarities and distinctions between terms such as leadership, management, competency and competencies.

Spreitzer et al. (1997) define global leaders as executives who are in jobs with duties and responsibilities which encompass some international scope, and must operate effectively, and competently in an ever-changing, complex and ambiguous global business environment (McCall, 1998). Global leaders are seen as people who must be capable of extending business into foreign markets, initiating and developing global strategies, and managing and motivating geographically dispersed and diverse teams (Bartlett and Ghoshal, 1992; McCall et al., 1988).

Caligiuri and Tarique (2009: 1) offer a helpfully succinct definition of the term global leader. Citing Suutari (2002) and Bartlett and Ghoshal (1992), they state that global leaders are: ' ... high level professionals such as executives, vice presidents, directors, and managers who are in jobs with some global leadership activities such as global integration responsibilities'. It can be seen that this approach to defining global leadership places a heavy emphasis on the organisational seniority of global leaders as well as on the types of leadership activities in which they engage.

The definitions cited above provide some insight into the nature of global leadership. In order however to address a series of issues surrounding the identification and development of global leaders, there are two key questions that researchers have considered over recent years: a) what are the main tasks that global leaders undertake?; and b) what competencies do global leaders need to practice in order to be effective?

The tasks associated with global leadership

Definitions of global leaders such as those cited above tend to employ general phrases such as 'initiating and developing global strategies', 'motivating geographically dispersed and diverse teams' and 'global integration responsibilities'. These phrases provide a valuable flavour of the activities and tasks associated with the role of global leaders, however some researchers have sought to isolate in more depth the generic tasks carried out by global leaders, with a view to influencing the design

	GLOBAL LEADERSHIP ACTIVITIES
GLOBAL LEADERSHIP	• Work with colleagues from different countries • Interact with external clients from different countries • Interact with internal clients from different countries • May need to speak in a language other than their mother tongue at work • Supervise employees who are of different nationalities • Develop a strategic business plan on a worldwide basis for their unit • Manage a budget on a worldwide basis for their unit • Negotiate in other countries with people from other countries • Manage foreign suppliers or vendors • Manage risk on a worldwide basis for their unit

Figure 11.2 Tasks and activities associated with global leadership
Source: derived from Caligiuri (2006).

of global leadership development activities and programmes. For example, in one such study involving focus group meetings and surveys of leaders from European and North American firms, Caligiuri (2004, 2006), identified ten tasks or activities that are common among, and unique to, those occupying global leadership positions (see Figure 11. 2).

Given the radical change environments in which global leaders operate, it is difficult to outline a more detailed typical job description for global leaders than that presented in Figure 11.2. This reflects a more general trend in HRM theory and practice that has seen a move away from traditional HRM selection activities which sought to construct precisely written task-based job descriptions to select and subsequently develop employees (Rees and Doran, 2001). In rapidly changing environments, it is more realistic to identify the behaviours associated with effective performance as opposed to detailing the day-to-day tasks associated with a role, as these tasks are likely to change on a relatively frequent basis. In fact, inspection of the literature on global leaders reveals the relative lack of attention that has been given to defining the precise tasks associated with global leadership. The field has increasingly focused upon identifying the behaviourally linked competencies that are associated with effective global leadership, as opposed to attempting to construct comprehensive task-based job descriptions for global leadership positions within organisations.

The competencies of global leaders

Before examining emerging themes on the competencies of global leaders, it is worthwhile considering the nature of a competency. In his seminal work entitled *The Competent Manager*, Boyatzis (1982: 21) defines a competency as: '... an underlying characteristic of a person ... that could be a motive, trait, skill, aspect of one's self-image, ... or a body of knowledge that he or she uses'. Woodruffe (1993: 29) defines a competency more directly in relation to behaviours and task performance as 'the set of behaviour patterns that the incumbent needs to bring to a position in order to perform its tasks and functions with competence'. Both of these definitions emphasise in common that there are a set of personal characteristics that a position holder needs to demonstrate in order to perform effectively. Such personal characteristics, which are likely to involve specific skills, knowledge and personality variables, will vary according to the demands of a position. Thus, while there may be a set of common (or generic) competencies that are required for all mainstream management and leadership positions, the performance of specific management and leadership roles are likely to require distinctive competencies.

The difference between generic and distinctive competencies is crucial to this discussion, for it raises questions as to whether there is a set of distinctive competencies required by those occupying positions of global leadership. For example, in introducing her review of global leadership competencies, Jokinen (2005: 200) notes the fact that many managers who are successful in domestic operations do not, for various reasons, succeed in the international arena. The explanation for this lack of transferrable success is not altogether clear but calls for a better understanding of what competencies effective domestic managers lack when they prove to be less successful in global leadership positions. Hence, despite ongoing debate about the value of leadership competency models (Hollenbeck et al., 2006), general uncertainty in this area has led to a burgeoning body of research literature which aims to identify the competencies that global leaders should possess in order to undertake their work effectively. In expressing the view that the search for these competencies is elusive yet critical, Mendenhall (2006: 423) states: 'It has only been recently ... that social scientists have begun to conduct research with the aim of delineating the competencies that constitute that construct of global leadership'.

In terms of HRD, understanding the competencies associated with effective global leadership would provide valuable guidance for leader selection, preparation and development. It is not within the scope of this chapter to provide a comprehensive analysis of emerging work on the competencies of global leaders (see, for example, Adler and Bartholomew, 1992; Caligiuri and DeSanto, 2001; Gregersen et al., 1998; Kedia and Mukherji, 1999; Rhinesmith, 1996). Nevertheless, the themes of a number of key contributions in this area can be summarised at this juncture.

According to Gregersen et al. (1998) global leaders exhibit character, embrace duality and demonstrate savvy. The character aspect involves ability to attain an emotional connection with people from various backgrounds while at the same time maintaining an uncompromising degree of personal integrity. In addition, global leaders seem to embrace duality in the management of uncertainty. This involves competences in acting at the appropriate time, balancing tensions, and understanding change and continuity in various countries and regions. Global leaders also exhibit savvy in both business and organisational matters. They demonstrate a great deal of understanding of the competitive business environment, and identify and take advantage of opportunities in the market. They are familiar with the firm's SWOT, its competitive position and are capable of capitalising on the organisation's capabilities to capture market opportunities. One strength underlying global leaders' acquisition of such skills is inquisitiveness. This often means that global leaders possess a spirit of adventure and desire to see and experience new things. In essence, they possess adventuresome characteristics, such as curiosity and open-mindedness (Gregersen et al., 1998).

Kedia and Mukherji (1999) argue that global leaders need to acquire knowledge not just in areas such as cross-cultural management, socio-political and economic effectiveness, but also mastery of technology. The global mindset extends beyond knowledge of ICT to include the management information system and the impact of technology on the global operations of the organisation. Skills in global leadership represent the ability to put knowledge into action. These include acculturation and leadership skills for leading and motivating a diverse workforce. They note in addition that the current competitive global environment requires managers to be flexible and responsive.

In addition, organisations increasingly rely on global management teams to manage their global operations and, as a result, global leaders need to possess a range of competencies to enable them to be effective actors in global management teams (Gupta and Govindarajan, 2002). These teams aim to share resources and manage the transnational including the transfer of knowledge (Deresky, 2008). Deresky defines global management teams as collections of managers in or from several countries who must rely on group collaboration if each member is to experience optimum success and goal achievement. She cites companies as diverse as Whirlpool International and Timberland UK, and Honeywell Bull (HBI). Global management teams are often multicultural and operate from different countries. They include virtual teams, whose geographically dispersed members interact and coordinate their work through computer mediated communication (CMC) technologies. These technologies, such as desktop videoconferencing systems, internet and intranets, group support systems, are linked together across time, space and organisational boundaries (Deresky, 2008; Hertel et al., 2005) and make it possible for global leaders to make more effective use of their talents irrespective of location (Collings et al., 2007; Dowling and Welch, 2004). Clearly, there are some serious challenges associated with leading and participating in global teamwork, not least problems relating to geographical dispersion, cultural differences, language and communication difficulties associated with electronic media such as email, telephone and videoconferencing (Deresky, 2008; Hertel et al., 2005; Maznevski et al, 2006).

It is apparent from the above discussion that many distinctive competencies potentially may be associated with effective global leadership. In one review of the field, Mendenhall and Osland (2002) identified 53 competencies associated with the construct of global leadership, a finding however which is 'hardly a helpful boon to those assigned to develop corporate global management development programmes' (Mendenhall, 2006: 423). Consequently, some of the research work in this field mirrors approaches in occupational psychology which seek to reduce numerous overlapping personality traits into fewer and more coherent personality dimensions. A number of typologies of global leadership competencies have been constructed and four such examples are summarized in Figure 11.3.

Brownell (2006)

- **Intercultural**: cultural sensitivity, cultural intelligence, global mindset
- **Social**: emotional intelligence, empathy, self-control
- **Creativity/resourcefulness**: breakthrough-thinking, innovativeness, synergistic orientation
- **Self-knowledge**: self-efficacy, self-reflective
- **Positive outlook**: vision, passion, optimism
- **Responsiveness**: flexible, agile, opportunistic
- **Decision-making**: decisive, sound judgment, intuitive

Connor (2000)

- **Business savvy:** global leaders are results driven and they achieve outstanding business results. They have a broader view of the business and the world, and an extensive knowledge of the business. They adapt well to new situations, new cultures and new bosses.
- **Knowledge of how to use their personal influence:** global leaders know how to tap into and leverage corporate resources including formal and informal networks. They know how to use teams and how to work well with others. They have strong influencing skills. Their communication skills are excellent.
- **Global perspective:** global leaders understand the global marketplace. They have a high degree of cultural sensitivity. When they move to a new country they make a serious effort to fit in, respect the culture, and learn the language.
- **Strong character:** global leaders talk about vision, purpose and values with clarity. They can be counted on to do what is right and to resist something they oppose. They understand there are changing employee expectations, they inspire trust, and they value and respect the differences each person brings to the workplace. Global leaders meet commitments, act consistent with their words, and are interested in the well-being of others.
- **Knowledge of how to motivate others:** global leaders understand that employees want direction from above and want opportunities for growth and development. They have vision and communicate a clear sense of direction. They are role models. They are comfortable with conflict and know how to deal constructively with conflict among their people.
- **Act like entrepreneurs:** global leaders understand that international competition is challenging companies to act faster and smarter. They put greater emphasis on new product development, standardisation of business processes, and speed to the market. They are creative and encourage others to be innovators. They take risks and have become skilled at overcoming obstacles. They have a sense of urgency. They are self-starters committed to their work.

(Continued)

(Continued)

[Jokinen (2005)]

- **Core global leadership competencies:** self awareness, engagement in personal transformation, and inquisitiveness.
- **Desired mental characteristics of global leaders**: optimism, self-regulation, social judgment skills, empathy, motivation to work in an international environment, cognitive skills, acceptance of complexity and its contradictions.
- **Behavioural level global leadership competencies**: social skills, network management skills and knowledge.

Mendenhall and Osland (2002)

- **Relationship**: close personal relationships, cross-cultural communication skills, 'emotionally connect' ability, inspire/motivate others, conflict management, negotiation expertise, empowering others, managing cross-cultural ethical issues, social literacy, and cultural literacy.
- **Traits/dispositions:** curiosity, inquisitiveness, continual learner, accountability, integrity, courage, commitment, hardness, maturity, results-orientation, and personal literacy.
- **Business expertise**: global business savvy, global organisational savvy, business acumen, total organisational astuteness, stakeholder orientation, and results-orientation.
- **Cognition:** environmental sense-making, global mindset, thinking agility, improvisation, pattern recognition, cognitive complexity, cosmopolitanism, managing uncertainty, local vs. global paradoxes, and behavioural flexibility.
- **Organising expertise**: team building, community building, organisational networking, creating learning systems, strong operational codes, global networking, strong customer orientation, and business literacy.
- **Visioning:** articulating a tangible vision and strategy, envisioning, entrepreneurial spirit, catalyst for cultural change, change agency, catalyst for strategic change, empowering, and inspiring.

Figure 11.3   Competency typologies of global leaders

Source: derived and abridged from Brownell (2006), Connor (2000), Jokinen (2005), Mendenhall and Osland (2002), and Mendenhall (2006).

The frameworks summarised in Figure 11.3 reveal the extent to which intrapersonal and interpersonal attributes (perhaps as opposed to highly developed technical skills in areas such as ICT, law and finance) are central to effective global leadership. Nevertheless, in discussing distinctive competency clusters, Brownell (2006: 320) argues that competency requirements for global leaders are heavily influenced by features of the task, organisation and environment in any given context. For example, she proposes that in situations of high task complexity, it is likely that there will be a priority need for the global leader to display highly developed decision-making competencies such as decisiveness and sound judgment. Similarly, in situations where there is a weak organisational culture, there is likely to be a priority need for the global leader to display positive outlook competencies such as vision,

Competencies depend on the task, org. & environment.

passion and optimism. When discussing cross-cultural competence, Johnson et al. (2006: 537) also acknowledge the effects of external factors such as the physical, economic, political and legal environments which moderate and affect the performance of individuals who are working in international business settings. They state that even a culturally competent individual might not be successful in, for example, a company '... that manufactures products that are unsuited to the local market and/ or is located in a country that is experiencing a deep economic recession'.

4 The development of global leaders

Reflecting the current emphasis on competencies, some international organisations are ditching their traditional HRD policies and practices and adopting new approaches capable of equipping their staff with the competencies needed by global leaders to deal with the demands of this era (Tichy et al., 1992). In spite of such emerging trends, Caligiuri (2006) argues that much of the research focusing on global leaders is still based on expatriate assignment management. However, the development of global leaders is emerging as a new area of research. As Caligiuri (2006) points out, expatriates are not the only people within international organisations who carry out global leadership activities. Indeed, there are many global leadership activities that require international business savvy without the experience of living internationally or working in a foreign country. In a dynamic competitive environment, Caligiuri (2000) proposes that even domestic organisations need their managers/leaders to have global knowledge and cross-national skills to handle business transactions.

Research evidence indicates that successful international organisations are often those that equip their global leaders with global perspectives (Stroh and Caligiuri, 1998a, 1998b). Here the research focuses on the links between the development of leaders and the bottom-line performance of their organisations. For instance, Stroh and Caligiuri's (1998a, 1998b) research found that the most successful international organisations are those that support their leaders with HRD practices that provide opportunities to develop a global orientation and, in effect, global leadership skills. This study also reveals that developing leadership cross-cultural competence was identified as among the top five organisation-wide practices influencing their effectiveness. They conclude from the results that there is a positive relationship between an organisation's bottom line financial success and its ability to successfully develop leadership competencies. This implies that for an organisation to sustain its competitiveness, it must continually develop its leaders and prepare them for future challenges in its business environment (Adler and Bartholomew, 1992). In fact, Black and Gregerson (2000: 175) state that: 'the primary objective of global leadership training is stretching someone's mind past narrow domestic borders and creating a mental map of the entire world'. Thus, while there may be similarities between global and domestic leadership, Black and Gregorson (2000: 174) argue strongly that the difference between the two is based: '... in the worlds themselves. A domestic leader need only put his/her mind around one country, limited cultural paradigms, one political system and one set of labor laws. A global leader must stretch his/her mind to encompass the entire world with hundreds of countries, cultures, and business contexts'.

Caligiuri and DeSanto (2001) assert that there are two assumptions underpinning the development of global leadership programmes. The first assumption is that global competence can be defined in terms of developmental dimensions and the second assumption is that once defined these dimensions are amenable to development through global experience. These assumptions manifest themselves in the design of training programmes for global leaders, which are clear evidence that international organisations are increasingly making use of global (as opposed to domestic) leadership development programmes to groom future leaders (for example, see Box 11.1).

Box 11.1   An example of a development programme for global leaders

Automatic Data Processing, Inc. (NASDAQ: ADP), with nearly $9 billion in revenues and over 585,000 clients, is one of the world's largest providers of business outsourcing solutions. ADP's Global Leadership Development Programme (GLDP) is designed to provide high potential individuals with a combination of stretch assignments, development, coaching and mentoring. Upon successful completion of the programme, participants will be positioned to assume a domestic or international leadership role in one of ADP's growing business units.

The GLDP is centred on three key elements: a) challenging rotational assignments, b) leadership support and c) hands on coaching and development.

- Challenging rotational assignments: delegates receive opportunities to rotate across different functions, geographies, business units and various business situations (e.g. start-up, realignment, sustaining success and turnaround)
- Leadership support: delegates are provided with leadership support designed to help them to navigate successfully through the programme. This consists of support from senior management, the host manager, an assigned talent manager and a mentor.
- Hands on coaching and development: delegates are assigned a talent manager who provides coaching that focuses on strengths and leadership potential.

Source: http://www.adp.com/careers/global-leadership-development-programme.aspx, accessed 23 March 2009.

Many global leadership development programmes have been designed to offer individuals the opportunity to work in different countries (Rhinesmith, 1996; Suutari, 2002; Thaler-Carter, 2000). Developing global leaders, however, does not have to focus only on training or preparing employees for overseas assignments (Neary and O'Grady, 2000). As was noted earlier, Stroh and Caligirui (1998a) assert that the development of global leadership skills should not be limited to expatriates from the home country. Rather it should include both host country and third country nationals and a proactive implementation of 'inpatriation' where host country talents work at corporate head office as well as in other subsidiaries around the world.

development of Global leaders should include employees from allover.

What, however, are the precise objectives of global leadership development programmes? Following their analysis of the global leadership training programme delivered by TRW Inc., Neary and O'Grady (2000: 190–1) offer some insights into the design, delivery and, importantly, the objectives of global leadership development programmes:

- Global leadership programmes are not designed to develop leaders from scratch but rather to enhance the skills of existing outstanding leaders to help to make them outstanding global leaders as well
- Global leadership programmes should encourage leaders to be sensitive to their own assumptions and the assumptions of those around them. Global leaders may not be familiar with the cultural assumptions of the people with whom they are working, so they need to develop the ability to a) adapt multiple leadership styles and b) to adapt to an unfamiliar environment
- Global leadership programmes should help global leaders to exploit diversity by helping them to understand that a wide range of heritages and experiences also supplies a larger pool of business solutions
- Global leadership programmes should help delegates to tolerate and address ambiguity in order to adapt appropriately. There is an increased necessity for global leaders to move effectively between cultures and countries and this requires greater flexibility in terms of style.

It is evident that training and development objectives of this nature are likely to be achieved using a variety of different techniques. Suutari (2002) suggests that specific techniques used for the development of global leaders may, as noted above, include international assignments, but they may also include techniques such as short-term development assignments, international training and development, international meetings and forums, participation in international or global teams, the application of action learning, and international travel.

The limitations of global leadership development programmes

Perhaps the most contentious aspect of the literature on the development of global leaders/managers is the issue of whether all managers can be trained and developed to acquire global perspectives. On this issue, Caligiuri (2006) maintains that managers differentially benefit from participation in intercultural training or development exercises, depending on their individual aptitude, knowledge, skills, abilities and other personality characteristics. The assumption here is that organisations should be selective in terms of who they offer opportunities for development as global leaders. In particular, it is argued that although certain personality characteristics are needed for global leadership they cannot be developed through global assignments, that is, some KSAOs (knowledge, skills, abilities and other characteristics such as personality dimensions of openness and flexibility) are relatively immutable. Consequently, global leadership programmes may not be able to achieve their objectives if they depend on global assignments to shape the aspects of global competence and capability that are influenced by personality (Caligiuri and DeSanto, 2001). On the issue of knowledge development, Caligiuri and DeSanto's findings are consistent with that of the extant literature (Adler, 1981, 1997; Baughn, 1995; Black, 1992; Napier and Peterson, 1991; Osland, 1995) in the sense that it can be developed through global assignments.

Caligiuri and DeSanto (2001) in their attempt to determine the competencies required by global managers defined global competence in terms of KSAOs. Their study revealed that while the knowledge dimensions can be developed through global assignments, personality characteristics are highly resistant to change. In view of the difficulties involved in changing personality characteristics, Gregersen et al. (1998) also conclude that not everyone has the ability to acquire the competencies that are needed to become a global leader. Hence, they suggest that organisations should be selective in their provision of developmental opportunities.

If not everybody can be trained to become a global leader then it follows that training opportunities should only be provided to those whom it is perceived can benefit from such training. This is consistent with Caligiuri's (2006) view that the requisite immutable attributes must be present before training and development interventions can improve or equip individuals with global leadership skills. Where these attributes are not present it may be more effective for organisations to buy-in such people rather than attempt to develop employees who do not have the prerequisite attributes. Nevertheless, even those managers with the right attributes or required immutable attributes still need development. Gregerson et al. (1998) recommend strategies along the lines of: (a) travel; (b) teams; (c) training and (d) transfer to develop global leaders. Similarly, Caligiuri (2006) has identified some HRD strategies for global leaders based on 'Knowledge, skills, abilities and personality characteristics, their relative immutability and suitable developmental interventions'. These HRD strategies incorporate: 'didactic learning opportunities' (such as cross-cultural communication training and training in conflict resolution techniques); 'experimental interventions' (such as cultural immersion programmes and attending global meetings); and 'intensive experience' (such as international assignments and salient non-work cultural experience).

5 Expatriate development

Caligiuri et al. (2005a) argue that while it is true that training and development for global competencies should be present throughout many levels in global organisations, special attention should still be given to expatriates living and working outside their own national boarders. Mendenhall et al. (2008: 20) offer a helpfully succinct definition of the term expatriate when they state that: Expatriates are employees who have been sent by their employers to reside and work outside of their home country on temporary assignment. The term includes expatriate businesspeople, diplomats, employees of international nonprofit organisations, military personnel and missionaries, among others. Thus, to clarify, while global leaders have, for example, some level of global responsibilities regardless of location, a 'global leader is not necessarily an expatriate and vice versa' (Jokinen, 2005: 200). We wish to broaden the scope of the chapter at this point in order to consider the development of expatriates in general.

As indicated in the first part of this chapter, globalisation and the increasingly competitive global business environment has ensured a continuing need for expatriates working on global assignments. In spite of the use of global virtual teams, advances in ICT such as mobile phones and the internet, organisations still face the need to send expatriate managers on international assignments. Bennett et al. (2000) note that global companies compete for markets, technologies, products and investors, as well as seeking the best talent; overall there is an increasing demand for cross-border deployment of people both for short-term and long-term foreign assignments.

Organisations continue to use expatriates for a myriad of reasons, for example, to train host country nationals and to transfer knowledge and technologies; to manage a joint venture or merger: to set up and manage a subsidiary; to ensure effective control of subsidiaries through the transmission of corporate culture, mission and vision; to enter new markets through sales and market presence; to fill staff positions and vacancies; to improve the flow of communication between headquarters and subsidiaries; to develop global leadership competencies; to foster international skills, awareness, sensitivity and knowledge throughout the organisation and to increase efficiency and profits (Au and Fukuda, 2002; Bender and Fish, 2000; Bennett et al., 2000; Bonanche and Brewster, 2001; Caligiuri and Tarique, 2006; Dowling et al., 2008; Gupta and Govindarajan, 2002; Harzing, 2001; Mendenhall, 2000; Mendenhall et al., 2002; Stroh and Caligiuri, 1998a, 1998b; Tarique and Caligiuri, 2004; Tung, 1998).

In what is described by Collings et al. (2007: 200) as their 'landmark study', Edström and Galbraith (1977) helpfully summarise the reasons for using expatriates into three broad areas (see Chapter 6). First, expatriates are used as position fillers, that is, to occupy positions that for various reasons cannot be filled by the indigenous workforce. Second, expatriates are used as agents of management development, that is, to increase the organisation's bank and repertoire of managerial skills. Third, as a means of organisational development, that is, to diffuse specialist knowledge and skills through the organisation in a way that is not limited by geographical locations and contexts.

The role of the expatriate is thus crucial to the achievement of international organisations' global strategic objectives (Caligiuri and Colakoglu, 2007; Mendenhall and Stahl, 2000; Mendenhall et al., 2002; Stroh and Caligiuri, 1998a, 1998b). Moreover in view of the expensive nature of expatriate assignments, it is in the interest of international organisations to ensure that adequate training is given to expatriates and their families to minimise the risk of failure. This is all the more important because one factor that contributes to success or failure of international assignments is the nature and extent of cross-cultural training provided (Black and Mendenhall, 1990). In order to be able to work effectively expatriates need to be trained in amongst other things, cross-cultural management issues (see Chapter 3). As Molinsky (2007: 622) states: 'A critical practical challenge that organizations face in the increasingly inter dependent global economy is the ability to function effectively across national cultural boundaries. Individuals must now be capable of functioning appropriately in a wide variety of foreign cultural situations...'.

Cross-cultural training and development for expatriates

Cross-cultural training is vital if organisations are to avoid high levels of expatriate failure rates (premature returns). Cross-cultural training facilitates the expatriate's cross-cultural adjustment in the host country and hence minimises problems of adjustment (Black and Mendenhall, 1990; Brislin, 1981; Kealey and Protheroe, 1996; Mendenhall and Oddou, 1986; Kealey and Protheroe, 1996; Tung, 1981). In particular, it helps employees to become effective in their jobs within the host country as quickly as possible (McFarlin and Sweeney, 2006) because it provides coping techniques relevant to living and working in a specific foreign environment (Earley, 1987). Cross-cultural training has been formally defined as: '...the educative processes used to improve intercultural learning via the development of the cognitive, affective and behavioral competencies needed for successful interactions in diverse cultures' (Littrell et al., 2006: 356). In essence, cross-cultural training fosters appropriate transitions, adjustment and general adaptability skills (Forster and Johnsen, 1996; Sappinen, 1993).

While our focus here is on expatriates, Adler and Bartholomew (1992) highlight that, for organisations operating worldwide, cross-cultural skills are essential throughout the organisation, not just for those few employees leaving for expatriate assignments. They further contend that both 'expatriates' and 'inpatriates' should become well versed in cultural adaptation skills as well as specific local knowledge, but these are not the only skills managers should possess. In global organisations all managers need broader international, cross-cultural and diversity skills, and a global mindset; what has been referred to by Caligiuri and DeSanto (2001) as a form of 'cosmopolitanism'. Similarly, Adler and Bartholomew (1992) state that whilst organisational and career development programmemes should be components of foreign assignments, such HRD opportunities should not be limited to expatriates. Rather international organisations should send 'transpatriates' all over the world to equip them with global perspectives, orientation, mindsets and awareness as well as cross-cultural skills appropriate for a cadre of globally sophisticated managers. This approach, then, downplays the distinction between expatriation and inpatriation and uses international assignments to encourage and enhance both individual and organisational leadership throughout the organisation. Furthermore, it serves a dual purpose of fulfilling technical and managerial needs as well as providing developmental experiences for potential leaders (Stroh and Caligiuri, 1998a).

In their recent review of research on expatriate preparation, Littrell et al. (2006: 338), drawing upon Cushner and Brislin (1997) identify the following as key objectives for cross-cultural training in personal adjustment, work adjustment and interactions with host nationals:

- **Learning to learn** This objective draws attention to the fact that no training is likely to prepare the expatriate for every eventuality that will be encountered in the new culture. Hence, cross-cultural training needs to assist the expatriate to learn how to acquire information about another culture
- **Making isomorphic attributions** Isomorphic attributions occur when the expatriate makes the same judgments and decisions regarding behaviour as do host nationals. Thus, a key objective of cross-cultural training is to help equip the expatriate to recognise, understand and act upon cultural nuances surrounding behaviours in another culture
- **Overcoming difficulties** that undermine effectiveness while in another culture
- **Developing positive relationships** This relates particularly to expatriates relationships with host nationals
- **Accomplishing work–related tasks** For example, the expatriate may require certain technical skills that relate specifically to work in another culture
- **Coping with stressors** This objective is recognition of the fact that expatriate work is often associated with a range of task and family pressures that can lead to stress.

The effectiveness of cross-cultural training and development for expatriates

In Harrison's (1994) view, the need for cross-cultural management training to facilitate adjustment and performance is essential for financial and strategic reasons. This is because the expatriate's inability to adjust to the foreign environment can have many negative implications for the international organisation. Quite apart from the cost implications mentioned earlier, lack of proper adjustment of an expatriate can result in poor work performance with associated issues of low self-esteem, self-confidence and loss of respect or prestige among colleagues (Caligiuri, 2000). Moreover, an MNC, for example, can also suffer loss of business and damage to corporate image if an expatriate does not adjust appropriately to the new environment (Aycan, 1997; Caligiuri, 2000; Mendenhall and Oddou, 1985; Tung, 1987).

International human resource development (IHRD), much of it embodied in cross-cultural training, focuses on the practical matters of training managers to be posted to foreign countries (Osman-Gani, 2000). Appropriate cross-cultural skills facilitate more effective interaction among people from diverse national and cultural backgrounds. For over three decades researchers have studied how organisations develop their international managers (Forster and Johnsen, 1996; Tung, 1982) and the effects of training on expatriates' adaptation as well as expatriates' adaptability to new environments (Kealey and Protheroe, 1996; Mendenhall and Oddou, 1985; Selmer, 2001). Regardless of the fact that there is evidence beyond reasonable doubt that intercultural awareness, sensitivity and communication skills are essential to the success of international assignments (Kealey and Protheroe, 1996) there are still some organisations that do not provide training to their employees going abroad (Dowling et al., 2008). This lack of cross-cultural management training undermines the effectiveness of their employees working and living outside of their own cultures.

The literature is replete with statistics and comparisons between organisations that offer expatriate training with those that do not. Brewster and Pickard (1994) present an excellent review of the findings of some of these studies. They mention that the early literature was mainly based on expatriates from the USA and was also somewhat anecdotal and prescriptive in nature. The general conclusion from the research was that little preparation takes place before the expatriate departs for an international assignment. In the 1970s, studies of US MNCs revealed that only two-thirds provided any training and less than a quarter provided formal orientation training (Baker and Ivancevich, 1971; Brewster and Pickard, 1994; Rahim, 1983). The picture did not differ much during the 1980s since only 25 per cent of the largest US multinationals provided extensive pre-departure orientation training programmemes to their expatriates (Baliga and Baker, 1985).

In a survey of MNCs in Europe, USA and Japan, Tung (1982) found that whereas only 32 per cent of the US firms provided training, 69 per cent and 57 per cent of European and Japanese firms respectively provided training for their expatriates (Brewster and Pickard, 1994; Forster and Johnsen, 1996). Thus, the research evidence indicates that in the 1970s and 1980s European firms delivered more formal training for their expatriates than did the US firms (Brewster, 1988). In the 1990s, however the European firms appear to have reduced their training activities. Survey evidence indicates that only 13 per cent of European firms provided some form of cross-cultural training to their expatriates although a further 47 per cent provided briefings for culturally 'challenging' international assignments (Dowling et al., 2008).

It is not clear from the literature whether MNCs' reluctance to offer cross-cultural training for their expatriates is due to a lack of access to such training programmes or sheer misgivings about the value and necessity of such training for expatriate managers or perhaps both. There is some evidence from the literature to support either interpretation. Osman-Gani (2000) states that the main reason for the lack of provision of cross-cultural training appears to be the assumption that 'good management is good worldwide'. Senior managers and CEOs supposedly hold two views on this issue. The first is related to the transferability of management skills. The assumption here is that if a manager with general management skills is effective in his/her own country and culture then that person will inevitably be effective in any other country or culture. In other words, the location of the international assignment is immaterial to the effectiveness of the manager. Consequently, no preparation would be required for an expatriate before taking up an international assignment. Drawing from research on the transferability of management practices and in particular the experiences of expatriate managers in Asia, Osman-Gani (2000) debunks this view.

The second view relates to lingering doubts about the value of training for international assignments. Essentially, it asserts that good management skills are important but they do not in themselves guarantee the future effectiveness of managers on international assignments (Osman-Gani, 2000). There is ample evidence from the literature to refute this second viewpoint. For example, Earley (1987) argues that cross-cultural training facilitates an individual's ability to cope and work in a foreign environment. Similarly, evidence from the extant literature leads us to conclude that by virtue of their lack of international experience and cultural skills in foreign societies, these managers will almost inevitably be deficient in some cross-cultural knowledge and skills that they need to perform their duties efficiently (Barratt, 1995; Black and Mendenhall, 1989).

Nevertheless, it is apparent that many international organisations do acknowledge and appreciate the usefulness of training programmes for expatriates and in recent years have supported it. Dowling et al. (2008) attributes this development partly to the increasing provision of internal and external training programmes that are available to MNCs. Evidence from the Global Relocation Trends Survey Reports (conducted by GMAB Global Relocations together with the US National Foreign Trade Council and the SHRM Global Forum) indicates that 64 per cent and 62 per cent of companies offered or made available cross-cultural training in 2002 and 2004 respectively. Despite this development, 76 per cent and 74 per cent of the firms surveyed made cross-cultural training optional in 2002 and 2004 respectively. This suggests that perhaps there are expatriates working for international organisations who still do not receive any cross-cultural training before embarking on international assignments (Dowling et al., 2008).

In spite of some lingering doubts, there is substantial evidence on the positive outcomes of cross-cultural training. In fact, many studies have assessed the effectiveness of cross-cultural training and shown the numerous benefits that expatriates derive from cross-cultural training (Eschbach et al., 2001; Morris and Robie, 2001; Selmer et al., 1998). Tung (1982), Black and Mendenhall (1990), Earley (1987), Deshpande and Viswesvaran (1992), and Harrison (1994) all report that cross cultural training has a strong and positive impact on cross-cultural skills development, adaptation, adjustability and job performance. In addition to improving performance in international organisations, cultural training facilitates the transition and adjustment of expatriates and their families (Cavusgil et al., 1992). Harrison (1994) reports that a number of companies (for example, Fortune 500 firms such as Motorola Inc, Dupont, and IBM and MNCs including BP, Johnson Wax, Shell Oil) now routinely provide cross-cultural training to their expatriates. These programmes are designed to make the managers 'trans-culturally competent' (Callahan, 1989) and intended to reduce expatriate failure rates (Caudron, 1991) and to maximise organisations' competitive advantage.

Harrison (1994) contends that cross-cultural training helps to develop a more cosmopolitan outlook and gives managers a deeper understanding and appreciation of cross-cultural situations. It also can help employees to learn about the culture, its values, and norms as well as appropriate and acceptable behaviours in the society and how that affects the performance of duties in organisations (Black and Mendenhall, 1990; Kealey and Protheroe, 1996). Furthermore, it helps expatriates to minimise the effects of cultural shock, by developing coping methods to deal with new and unforeseen or unpredictable events in the culture and to reduce conflict arising from new, unexpected and unfamiliar encounters (Earley, 1987; Harrison, 1994). Cross-cultural preparation and training also facilitates the international assignment and expatriate adaptation by helping them to form realistic expectations about living and working in a foreign country (Black and Mendenhall, 1990).

Finally, in line with the current vogue, we note that cross-cultural training is often carried out alongside diversity management training. We highlight, however, that there has been a longstanding concern that the selection and development of expatriates is an area imbued with gender and race stereotyping. For example, De Cieri et al. (2007: 288) note that 'gender discrimination has been an issue in expatriate selection and career development, excluding women on the basis of oversimplifications and myths concerning sex-role stereotypes in host countries'. In some cases, these oversimplifications may involve false assumptions that women will not be accepted as expatriate workers in host countries (Varma et al., 2006). While international cultural differences inevitably impact the manner in which expatriates of different genders and races are received by host countries, the situation is highly complex and may even involve interactions between gender and race (Tung, 2008). This complexity may also lead to unfounded assumptions about the developmental readiness of potential expatriates to undertake international assignments. For example, in one recent study (Connerley et al., 2008) it was found that women were rated lower by their supervisors than men on perceptions of expatriate readiness for international assignments.

Emerging themes in expatriate training and development

In spite of the enormous importance of cross-cultural management programmes, it is undeniably only one aspect of an effective expatriate training programme. Although cross-cultural management training has traditionally been the main focus of training expatriates, it is argued that on its own it is not sufficient to ensure the success of an assignment (Dowling et al., 2008).

Over-reliance on pre-departure training programmes As an aspect of broader cross-cultural training, pre-departure training programmes tend to predominate. As Dowling et al. (2008) point out the essential components of a pre-departure programme that contribute to a smooth transition to a foreign location include: (a) cultural awareness training, (b) preliminary visit, (c) language instruction and (d) assistance with practical, day-to-day matters. Commonly used international HRD techniques and practices for expatriates include language training, area/national/country briefings and assistance with day-to-day matters (Mendenhall et al.,1987) and according to Caliguiri et al. (2005a) there are essentially three broad ways of equipping employees of global organisations with cross-cultural skills. These are formal education programmes, individual coaching/mentoring, and immersion programmes:

- Formal education programmes include classroom seminar or lecture-based teaching both off-site and in-house and employer sponsored management development programmes. These programmes also include self-study courses offered electronically by distance-education providers (Gupta and Govindarajan, 2002).
- Individualised coaching/mentoring programmes for global assignees provide them with tailored programmes in response to a specific need or requirement.
- Immersion programmes are developed by experts both within and from outside the organisation. These programmes provide opportunities for expatriates to acquire cross-cultural awareness and facility in some specialised foreign language skills. They are designed to give the expatriate the opportunity to live in a local community in the host country, to experience the foreign culture, interact with the people and participate in local traditions and customs. The ultimate objective is for the expatriate to gain an understanding of the culture and hence appreciate how it impacts on work relations and work practices in organisations in that country.

At another level, Scullion and Brewster (2001) draw attention to emerging European research which attacks the conventional wisdom behind expatriate training and development programmes. This research questions the validity of the assumption that cross-cultural training should take place only before the international transfer. It appears that there is still much informality in training (Celeya and Swift, 2006) and it is suggested that HRD for future expatriate managers is more likely to involve frequent cross-border job swaps, and short assignments working in global multicultural teams (Forster, 2000; Scullion, 2001).

Tailored expatriate training After reviewing the models of expatriate training and development originating from the USA including contingency models where the types of training provided depends on the task, the individual and the environment, Scullion and Brewster (2001) propose that it may be worthwhile examining further some of the European models. In particular, they point to the integrated frameworks for pre-departure training developed by European researchers which make it possible for organisations to tailor programmes that suit the needs of the individual expatriate, taking into consideration both job and individual variables, in addition to assessment of existing levels of competence. Scullion and Brewster contend that in the future a more tailored approach to expatriate training is likely to be the way forward particularly in light of the rapidly changing training needs of expatriates (Collings et al., 2007). This tailored approach may include, for example foreign language training to enable expatriates to participate fully in meetings and official communications (Maclean, 2006; Rees and Rees, 1996; Swift and Huang, 2004).

Use of short-term overseas assignments Collings et al. (2007) argue that the requirements of cross-cultural training to support alternative forms of international assignments have not received adequate consideration in the extant literature. It is observed that more and more large firms are increasing relying on short-term overseas assignments instead of the traditional expatriate postings (Collings et al., 2007; Morley and Heraty, 2004). These developments and initiatives suggest new ways of developing international assignees and expatriates. Even so, most organisations that provide training tend to focus solely on traditional expatriates. In many respects, it is assumed that short-term assignees and international business travellers (IBTs) should develop themselves (Mayerhofer et al., 2004) supposedly so because they usually do not spend enough time in one location to have to adjust to the culture. Research evidence indicates that even where training is provided to short-term assignees, it is not so specific to the country and involves less extensive cross-cultural training than is offered to expatriates (Tahvanainen et al., 2005). However, traditional expatriates, IBTs and short-term assignees likewise all experience adjustment problems and may suffer from a lack of cross-cultural awareness (Collings et al., 2007; Welch and Worm, 2006). In view of this, it is argued that they all will benefit from provision of cross-cultural training and development (Collings et al., 2007).

Real-time training Mendenhall and Stahl (2000) direct attention away from the traditional topic of cross-cultural training to discuss future training needs that organisations must focus on. They argue that it is erroneous to think that the pre-departure cross cultural training is sufficient to equip expatriates with the knowledge and skills they will need to perform their duties effectively. Mendenhall and Stahl (2000) distinguish between two types of in-country training delivery methods: 'traditional' and 'real-time'. The traditional format is akin to a classroom lecture where all the expatriates receive the same content; hence it is inflexible and does not meet the needs of individual assignees. The 'real-time' delivery on the other hand, is tailored to the needs of the individual in the form of personal counselling or coaching by experts. Given the advantages of personal coaching, it is recommended that organisations consider incorporating it into their cross-cultural training and development programmes. Ideally, organisations can combine the traditional and real-time cross-cultural training (Mendenhall and Stahl, 2000).

Assessment and development centres Another emerging issue in the development of expatriates is the use of assessment centres. Assessment centres are increasingly being used to equip expatriates with global management skills and cross-cultural competency (Stahl, 2001). They are designed to evaluate managers who are nominated for an international assignment on their cross-cultural skills and provide detailed feedback on their strengths and weaknesses for such assignments. Assessment centres often include a variety of exercises including cross-cultural role plays, case studies, and simulations of international negotiations to enhance their tolerance of ambiguity, behavioural flexibility, suitability, empathy and cross-cultural communication skills. Moreover, the feedback from the assessment centre session enables managers to develop tailor-made training programmes to address the needs of individual and groups. In the view of Mendenhall and Stahl (2000), then, internationally focused assessment centres provide an excellent avenue to systematically develop expatriates and to equip them with a global outlook and mindset. In cases where assessment centres provide genuine opportunities for expatriates to enhance their global outlooks, mindsets and cross-cultural skills, then these events may legitimately be referred to as development centres as opposed to selection-based assessment centres (Vloeberghs and Berghman, 2003).

Self-training using electronic media Another emerging area in HRD for expatriates is self-training based on electronic media such as software and the internet. Currently available on the market are software-professional multimedia packages (for example, CDs, DVDs and videos) designed to provide self-training for people intending to travel and or live and work in foreign countries. In some cases, this electronic training media is highly suitable for expatriates' families and other dependents who may not be participating in pre-departure training programmes offered by the employing organisations (Mendenhall and Stahl, 2000). Software packages are essentially computer-aided international sensitisers or culture assimilators designed to teach members of one culture information about another culture. The internet is also a useful source of training and development information for expatriates (Mendenhall and Stahl, 2000). For example, fee-based information is available from consulting and commercial firms. Expatriates themselves have also developed websites and blogs to share their experiences and offer advice.

International job rotation International job rotations and cross-border meetings are also designed to provide expatriates with cross-cultural competencies. International job rotation involves sending employees on a series of short-term assignments to different countries, whereas cross-border meetings involve sending employees to meetings that take place in different geographic locations (Caligiuri et al., 2005b). Although these training and development initiatives were originally designed for expatriates, increasing globalisation and the need for cross-cultural skills is making it more relevant for all employees involved in international work whether they are based in the home country or a subsidiary in a host country (Caligiuri et al., 2005b; Harvey, 1997).

Personal security Finally, we highlight the issue of personal security, particularly in relation to global terrorism, as an emerging issue in the area of expatriate training and development. Research in the field of expatriate management already highlights, for example, health and safety issues such as potential health problems linked to business travel, as highly relevant to expatriate assignments (Collings et al., 2007). Further, extant literature (for example, see Scullion et al., 2007) specifically explores the potential impact of the threat of global terrorism to the recruitment of expatriates. However, we wish to draw attention to the increasing relevance of global terrorism to expatriate training and development programmes. We do so partly because this is such a sensitive and complex issue which various stakeholders might find difficult to broach. For example, during cross-cultural training programmes, employing organisations do not want to raise unnecessary fears and anxieties among expatriates about the potential for terrorist activity in particular locations. Similarly, nationals from destination countries who are providing inputs to the design and delivery of expatriate training programmes may not necessarily be the best people to advise expatriates about the risk of terrorism to non-nationals working in the destination countries. Even some expatriates themselves may not encourage discussion of this subject in pre-assignment training, fearing that this discussion may heighten the anxieties of family members who would not necessarily be travelling to the destination countries.

Traditionally, security concerns of this nature were associated with expatriates working in so-called high risk contexts such as certain countries in the Middle

East, Latin America and Africa. However, references to sources of information on this subject, such as the foreign office websites of governments around the world, indicate that the subject of global terrorism, as well as business crime (Bhanugopan and Fish, 2008), is becoming increasingly relevant to training and development programmes for expatriates working in diverse locations including in developed countries in the western world. The main implication for expatriates may be a requirement that the assessment and management of risks associated with global terrorism become a standard component of expatriate training and development programmes.

6 Summary and conclusions

In recent years, the changing global environment has led to an increasing focus in international HRD on the need for organisations to employ competent global leaders and expatriates. This chapter has explored the development of global leaders and expatriates by international organisations.

While various definitions of the term global leader have been offered, it is concluded that global leaders are executives who operate at a very senior level within international organisations and who engage in activities such as developing global strategies, integrating global activities and leading diverse teams. Literature on the subject of the effectiveness of global leaders places a relatively strong emphasis on the competencies of global leaders as opposed to seeking to describe in detail the precise tasks that they undertake. These competencies are developed through global leadership development programmes which include activities such as international assignments, participation in global teams, and cross-cultural sensitivity training. There is some debate in the literature, however, about the extent to which all managers can be trained and developed to acquire global leadership perspectives.

In the later sections of this chapter, the discussion was broadened to consider not just the development of global leaders but the development of expatriates in general. It is evident that many international organisations provide intensive cross-cultural training for expatriates which is focused upon cross-cultural learning and adjustment. There is also, however, evidence to suggest that some international organisations neglect this training perhaps due to the untested premise that managerial effectiveness is cross-culturally transferable almost regardless of training. In the final sections of the chapter, a number of emerging themes in expatriate training and development were considered. These themes include the need for ongoing cross-cultural training throughout an expatriate's overseas assignment, the use of assessment centres, self-training using electronic media, international rotation and personal security.

Discussion questions

1 You work as the HRM director for an international organisation based in Germany. The marketing director needs to recruit someone to manage the section of her department which is responsible for advertising the organisation's products in Germany. She tells you that her idea is to advertise in top international publications for a 'global leader' to ensure that a candidate of the highest quality is appointed. You discuss this idea with her and it soon becomes clear that the two of you have a difference of opinion about the meaning of global leadership. As a result, you agree to send her a summary of your understanding of the term global leader. What will you include in your summary of this term?

2 You are the HRM director employed in a European manufacturing organisation with its headquarters in London. The Board of Directors has decided to open two subsidiaries in Belgium and France. In order to inform the search for a global leader who will oversee this growth and expansion strategy and subsequently direct the subsidiaries in Belgium and France, the Board of Directors has asked you to advise them on the competencies that the global leader will need to posses to undertake the role successfully. What competencies do you think are essential for this executive role?

3 In the past, the MNC you work for has filled overseas positions by identifying effective leaders in the home country and then encouraging/pressurising them to complete overseas assignments lasting approximately 18 months. As the HRM director, you have some concerns about this policy and suspect that it may not be working very well. What information would you seek, and from whom, in order to evaluate this approach to HRM planning?

4 The international organisation for which you work employs approximately 180 expatriates based in Africa, Asia and Europe. As a cost-cutting exercise, the organisation is considering setting up virtual global teams using ICT. What do you think will be the main communication issues associated with this initiative?

5 What would you regard to be the essential features of a cross-cultural training and development programmeme intended for a group of 20 male and female expatriates from England who will be taking up international assignments in the hotel sector in the Middle East?

Closing the Gulf – preparing US executives for assignments in Mexico

Background information

On a summer's day in 2008, Charles Ramoz-Ramírez was chairing a meeting of the six most senior employees of the HR consultancy he established almost five years ago. His decision to establish the consultancy was an extremely difficult one for him, as he held a senior, well-paid, and secure position as an HR executive within an MNC based in New York. This HR position within the MNC involved training and developing professional executive staff such as engineers and project managers to undertake overseas assignments mainly in Spanish speaking countries of South America.

At this meeting with his senior staff, Charles reminded them about the history of the consultancy for which they now work. He reminded them that there were two main reasons which underpinned his decision to leave the employment of the MNC and set up the consultancy business. First, he found himself being invited to deliver, on an increasingly frequent basis, specialised training sessions on expatriate programmes organised by independent training organisations and even other MNCs. He concluded from the frequency of these requests that there was a scarcity of HR professionals who possessed genuine expertise in preparing US executives for assignments in Mexico. Second, he did not agree with his HR director's view of expatriate training which was very much a case of 'send them and see'. That is, his HR director did not doubt that pre-departure training for expatriates was helpful but she did not see it as a critical success factor. Charles's view was that pre-departure training of expatriates was not just helpful; he saw it as a prerequisite for any overseas assignment no matter what its duration. His belief in the value of pre-departure training thus became a key operating principle of the CRR Expatriate Development consultancy organisation which he formed on the day he left the employment of the MNC. In essence, Charles established a consultancy which aimed to design and deliver in-house pre-departure training programmes for employees of US MNCs who would be taking up assignments in Spanish-speaking countries in South America.

The approach by the MNC: problems with employees' pre-departure training

After reminding his senior staff of how the consultancy came into being, Charles explained to them that a recent event had served to convince him that the emphasis he placed on the training of expatriates was fully justified. Charles informed them that he had recently been approached by the current HR director of the MNC which had previously employed him. (The previous HR director for whom Charles worked had retired approximately two years ago.) The current HR director told Charles that, over the last 12 months, the senior management of the MNC had become increasingly concerned about the general failure of its expatriate workforce to adjust to life in Mexico. As a result, the HR department had commissioned an independent training needs analysis. Part of this analysis was based on responses from 40 engineers who had returned home in the last two years from assignments in Mexico. Charles proceeded to inform his staff about the findings of this analysis which were supplied to him by the HR director of the MNC.

The independent analysis provided a fascinating insight into the pre-departure training that the 40 employees had received. Notably, only 25 of them had received any formal pre-departure training at all. Subsequent investigations revealed no obvious explanation as to why the remaining 15 staff had received no formal training. Further, when the MNC's training records were examined, they showed that the duration of the training received by the 25 staff varied tremendously (see Table 11.1).

Table 11.1   Length of pre-departure training received by the 25 employees

	1 to 5 days	6 to 10 days	11 to 15 days	More than 15 days
Number of employees	6	3	11	5

Again, organisational records offered no obvious explanation as to why these 25 employees received training which varied so much in terms of duration.

The training needs analysis document proceeded to report further information about the nature of the pre-departure training received by the group of 25 employees. The 25 employees experienced various pre-departure training methods such as lectures and tutorials including basic language classes, access to online material about Mexico, and cultural awareness workshops delivered by an outside training agency. Prior to their assignments, four of the 25 employees were offered the opportunity to undertake seven day field visits to Mexico. These visits enabled them to meet colleagues already based in Mexico and to visit organisations and places in Mexico that were linked to their assignments. The variation in the pre-departure training received by the 25 employees made it difficult to evaluate the employees' views about the effectiveness of the pre-departure training they had received. Some anecdotal evidence presented in the analysis did, however, indicate that seven employees who accessed online training material found it to be of little value in terms of cultural preparation for their assignments.

Finally, with an eye on future training, the 40 employees who had returned from assignments in Mexico were asked to identify the two biggest challenges that they had faced when working in Mexico. A summary of their responses to this question is presented in Table 11.2.

Table 11.2   The 'two biggest challenges' faced by the employees (N = 40) during their assignments in Mexico

'Biggest Challenge'	Number of employees citing this challenge*
Communication problems with local workers	28
Technical issues relating to their work	15
Travelling within Mexico	10
Health and diet issues	10
Accommodation issues	6
Loneliness/boredom	4
Safety including crime	3
Pressure from family in USA	2
Other challenges cited by only 1 employee	2

*Total number of responses is 80, that is, two responses per employee)

The implications of the analysis

At this point of the meeting, Charles revealed to his team that, on reading the fairly scathing independent report on pre-departure training, the Board of Directors of the MNC reached the conclusion that training for employees undertaking assignments in Mexico was a priority issue. The members of the Board decided that they wanted to bring in an external consultancy with real expertise in this area. It was opportune that the independent investigation into current training arrangements had unearthed a number of documents in which Charles, during the time he was employed by the MNC, had expressed his concern with the training that employees were receiving to prepare them for their overseas assignments. It was quickly established that Charles had left the MNC in order to open a consultancy specialising in this very issue.

Charles then informed his colleagues: 'The HR director of the MNC is commissioning CRR Expatriate Development to design and facilitate a 10-day long pre-departure programme for 30 engineers and project managers who will be taking up medium term (that is, six months to one year) assignments in Mexico over the next year. Using the information we already have from the independent analysis, I want us to put together an initial draft of what this training programme should look like.'

Case questions

1 Assume that you are a member of the senior team of CRR Expatriate Development. On the basis on the case study material and also your wider knowledge of the subject area, highlight what you think should be included in the content of the new 10-day pre-departure programme for the 30 engineers and project managers.
2 Having drawn up your list of the essential elements of this programme, a) explain why you think that each element is necessary, and b) state how much programme time you would devote to each element.

3 Assuming that you were permitted access to the 40 employees who have already completed their assignments in Mexico, state what further information you would seek from them to help you to design the 10-day pre-departure programme.

Case questions for further study and reflection

1 Highlight what further information you would seek about a) the 30 engineers and project managers and b) their forthcoming assignments in Mexico, before finalising the design and content of the pre-departure programme.
2 Explain how you would seek to augment the content of a programme, such as the one you are proposing, with ongoing cultural training during an expatriate's assignment.

Further reading

- Brownell, J. (2006) 'Meeting the competency needs of global leaders: a partnership approach', *Human Resource Management*, 45(3): 309–36

This article is likely to be of interest to readers who want to examine, in more detail, the design of development programmes for global leaders. In one section, the article specifically examines the complementary role that HR professionals can play in identifying and developing leadership talent by focusing upon issues such as graduate admissions processes, curriculum content, out-of-class leadership experiences, guest speakers, research partnerships and performance management.

- Guirdham, M. (2005) *Communicating Across Cultures at Work*, (2nd edn). Hampshire and New York: Palgrave.

This textbook explores, in some detail, a range of issues involved with interpersonal communication in international settings. The chapters on subjects such as 'communicating interculturally' and 'skills for working abroad' build upon some of the work on the development of global leaders and expatriates which is covered in this chapter.

- Jokinen, T. (2005) 'Global leadership competencies: a review and discussion', *Journal of European Industrial Training*, 29(3): 199–216.

This article focuses specifically on global leadership competencies. It reviews global leadership competency frameworks which have been published in previous literature and, in doing so, concludes that there is little agreement among researchers about the nature of the term global competence. The article is well researched and clearly written; it provides an excellent source of information about previous studies and possible directions for future research.

- Littrell, L.N., Salas, E., Hess, K.P., Paley, M. and Riedel, S. (2006) 'Expatriate preparation: a critical analysis of 25 years of cross-cultural training research', *Human Resource Development Review*, 5(3): 355–88.

In reviewing an extensive body of research literature on cross-cultural training, this article is likely to be of real interest to readers who are seeking to establish how the field has developed over the last 25 years. It offers helpful summaries of key studies and explores various theoretical frameworks which have been proposed by researchers investigating the subject of cross-cultural training.

- Mendenhall, M. (2006) 'The elusive, yet critical challenge of developing global leaders', *European Management Journal*, 26(6): 422–9.

This article reviews academic literature on the subject of global leadership and places a focus upon competencies that may be considered when developing global leadership training programmes. Appendix 1 of this paper provides a helpful list of inventories and scales that are used to assess competencies related to global leadership.

- Mendenhall, M.E., Osland, J.S., Bird, A., Oddou, G.R. and Maznevski, M.L. (2008) *Global Leadership: Research Practice and Development.* London and New York: Routledge.

This textbook offers an excellent review of a wide range of literature on the subject of global leadership. Subjects that are covered include: assessing global leadership competencies, leading global teams and global leadership development.

Internet resources

1 Outpost Expatriate Network (www.outpostexpat.nl): An excellent example of an MNC website that is designed to provide practical help and personal advice for the organisation's expatriates and their families. The site emanates from the Global Expatriate Policy Department within the Central Human Resource function of Shell Global.

2 The Associates of the American Foreign Service Worldwide (www.aafsw.com): A non-profit organisation that has been representing Foreign Service spouses, employees and retirees since 1960 and provides practical information for the expatriate. The website provides an interesting insight into the wide range of work and personal issues that are associated with expatriate living such as thrift shopping, voting rights and giving birth abroad. The scope of the website draws attention to the need for organisations to provide thorough cross-cultural training and development for expatriates.

3 Organisations offering training and development programmes for global leaders and expatriates (e.g. www.global-dynamics.com/services/expatriate.htm; www.global-integration.com; and www.mercer.com/expatmanagement). These provide relevant information about the types and content of training and development programmes designed for expatriates.

4 Newspaper websites such as Expat Weekly Telegraph (www.telegraph.co.uk/expat) and Guardian Abroad Global Community (www.guardianabroad.co.uk/expat). Provide in-depth information about expatriate issues from various perspectives including blogs from those actually working abroad.

Self–assessment questions

Indicative answers to these questions can be found on the companion website at www. sagepub.co.uk/harzing3e.

1 **What are the main arguments for focusing on how global leaders undertake their work as opposed to what work they actually do?**
2 **Using Neary and O'Grady's (2000) work, how would you summarise the goals of global leadership development programmes?**
4 **There is evidence to indicate that cross-cultural training is vital in order for expatriates to perform effectively. There is also evidence that some MNCs are reluctant to offer cross-cultural training. What are some of the arguments used to support this reluctance?**
5 **According to Caliguiri et al. (2005a), what are the three main ways of developing expatriates' cross-cultural skills?**
6 **What are some of the key considerations surrounding the inclusion in a cross-cultural training programmeme of a session on the dangers of terrorism?**

References

Adler, N.J. (1981) 'Re-entry: managing cross-cultural transitions', *Group and Organisational Studies*, 6 (3): 341–56.

Adler, N.J. (1997) *International Dimensions of Organisational Behaviour*, 3rd edn. Cincinnati, OH: South-Western College.

Adler, N.J and Bartholomew, S. (1992) 'Managing global competent people', *Academy of Management Executive*, 6 (3): 52–65.

Au, K.Y. and Fukuda, J. (2002) 'Boundary spanning behaviour of expatriate', *Journal of World Business*, 37: 285–96.

Aycan, Z. (1997). Acculturation of Expatriate Managers: A process model of adjustment and performance, in Z. Aycan (ed.), Expatriate Management: Theory and Research. Greenwhich, Connecticut: JAI Press, pp. 1–41.

Baligi, C. and Baker, J. (1985) 'Multinational corporate policies for expatriate managers: selection, training, evaluation', *SAM Advanced Management Journal*, 50(4): 31–8.

Baker, J.C. and Ivancevich, J.M. (1971) 'The assignment of American executives abroad: systematic, haphazard, or chaotic?', *California Management Review*, 13: 39–44.

Barratt, A. (1995) 'Training and development of expatriates and home country nationals', in O. Shenkar (ed.), *Global Perspectives of Human Resource Management*. Englewood Cliffs, NJ: Prentice Hall. pp. 132–46.

Bartlett, C.A. and Ghoshal, S. (1992) 'What is a global manager?', *Harvard Business Review*, Sept/Oct.: 124–32.

Baughn, C. (1995) 'Personal and organisational factors associated with effective repatriation', in J. Selmer, (ed.), *Expatriate Management: New Ideas for International Business*. pp. 215–30. Westport, CT: Quoram Books.

Bender, S. and Fish, A. (2000) 'The transfer of knowledge and the retention of expertise; the continuing need for global assignments', *Journal of Knowledge Management*, 4: 125–31.

Bennett, R., Aston, A. and Colguhun, T. (2000) 'Cross-cultural training: a critical step in ensuring the success of international assignments', *Human Resource Management*, 39: 239–50.

Bhanugopan, R. and Fish, A. (2008) 'The impact of business crime on expatriate quality of work-life in Papua New Guinea', *Asia Pacific Journal of Human Resources*, 46(1): 68–84.

Black, J.S. (1992) 'Coming home: the relationship of expatriate expectations with repatriation adjustment and job performance', *Human Relations*, 45(2): 172–92.

Black, J.S. and Mendenhall, M. (1989) 'A practical but theory-based framework for selecting cross-cultural training methods', *Human Resource Management*, 28(4): 511–39.

Black, J. and Mendenhall, M. (1990) 'Cross-cultural training effectiveness: a review and theoretical framework for future research', *Academy of Management Review*, 15: 113–26.

Black, J.S., Gregerson, H.B., Mendenhall, M.E. and Stroh, L.K. (1999) *Globalizing People Through International Assignments*. New York: Addison-Wesley/ Longman.

Bonache, J. and Brewster, C. (2001) 'Knowledge transfer and the management of expatriation', *Thunderbird International Business Review*, 43: 145–68.

Boyatzis, R. (1982) *The Competent Manager*. New York: Wiley.

Brewster, C. (1988) *The Management of Expatriates*. Human Resource Centre Monographs Series No. 2. Bedford, UK: Cranfield Institute of Technology.

Brewster, C. and Pickard, J. (1994) 'Evaluating expatriate training', *International Studies of Management and Organisation*, 24(3): 18–35.

Brislin, R. (1981) *Cross-Cultural Encounters*. New York: Pergamon.

Brownell, J. (2006) 'Meeting the competency needs of global leaders: a partnership approach', *Human Resource Management*, 45(3): 309–36.

Caligiuri, P.M. (2000) 'Selecting expatriates for personality characteristics: a moderating effect of personality on the relationship between host national contact and cross-cultural adjustment', *Management International Review*, 40(1): 61–80.

Caligiuri, P.M (2004) Global Leadership Development Through Expatriate Assignments and Other International Experiences. Paper presented at the Academy of Management New Orleans Symposium on Expatriate Management: New Directions and Pertinent Issues.

Caligiuri, P.M. (2006) 'Developing global leaders', *Human Resource Management Review*, 16: 219–28.

Caligiuri, P.M. and Colakoglu, S. (2007) 'A strategic contingency approach to expatriate assignment strategy', *Human Resource Management Journal*, 17(4): 393–410.

Caligiuri, P.M. and DeSanto, V. (2001) 'Global competence: what is it, and can it be developed through global assignments?', *Human Resource Planning Journal*, 24(3): 27–38.

Caligiuri, P. and Tarique, I. (2006) 'International assignee selection and cross-cultural training and development', in G. Stall and I. Bjorkman (eds), *Handbook of Research in International Hunan Resource Management*. pp. 302–22. Cheltenham: Edward Elgar.

Caligiuri, P. and Tarique, I. (2009) 'Predicting effectiveness in global leadership activities', *Journal of World Business*, 44(3): 336–46.

Caligiuri, P., Lazarova, M. and Tarique, I. (2005a) 'Training, learning and development in multinational organisations', in H. Scullion and M. Linehan (eds), *International Human Resource Management: A Critical Text.* pp. 71–90. Basingstoke: Palgrave Macmillan.

Caligiuri, P., Lazarova, M. and Zehetbauer, S. (2005b) 'Top managers' national diversity and boundary spanning: attitudinal indicators of a firm's internationalization', *Journal of Management Development*, 23: 848–59.

Callahan, M. (1989), 'Preparing the new global manager', *Training and Development Journal*, March: 29–32.

Caudron, S. (1991) 'Training ensures overseas success', *Personnel Journal*, December: 27–30.

Cavusgil, T., Yavas, U. and Bykowicz, S. (1992), 'Preparing executives for overseas assignments', *Management Decision*, 30(1): 54–8.

Celeya, L. & Swift, J. (2006) 'Pre-departure cultural training: US managers in Mexico', *Cross-Cultural Management: An International Journal*, 13(3): 230–43.

Chang, W. (2005) 'Expatriate training in international nongovernmental organisations: a model for research', *Human Resource Development Review*, 4(4): 440–61.

Collings, D.G., Scullion, H. and Morley, M. J (2007) 'Changing patterns of global staffing in the multinational enterprises: challenges to the conventional expatriate assignment and emerging alternatives', *Journal of World Business*, 42: 198–213.

Connerley, M.L., Mecham, R.L. and Strauss, J.P. (2008) 'Gender differences in leadership competencies, expatriate readiness, and performance', *Gender in Management: An International Journal*, 23(5): 300–16.

Connor, J. (2000) 'Developing the global leaders of tomorrow', *Human Resource Management*, 39(2/3): 147–57.

Csoka, L. and Hackett, B. (1998) *Transforming the HR function for Global Business Success.* New York: Conference Board (Report No. 1209-98-RR).

Cushner, K. & Brislin, R. (1997). Key Concepts in the Field of Cross-Cultural Training: An Introduction in K. Cushner & R. W. Brislin (eds), *Improving Intercultural Interactions: Modules for Cross-Cultural Training Programs* (Vol. 2, pp. 1–17). Thousand Oaks, C.A.: Sage.

De Cieri, H., Cox, J.W. and Fenwick, M. (2007) 'A review of International Human Resource Management: integration, interrogation and imitation', *International Journal of Management Reviews*, 9(4): 281–302.

Deresky, H. (2008) *International Management: Managing Across Borders and Cultures.* New Jersey: Pearson Prentice-Hall.

Deshpande, S.P. and Viswesvaran, C. (1992) 'Is cross-cultural training of expatriate managers effective: a meta analysis', *International Journal of Intercultural Relations*, 16: 295–310.

Dowling, P.J. and Welch, D.E. (2004) *International Human Resource Management: Managing People in a Global Context* 4th edn. London: Thomson Learning.

Dowling, P.J., Festing, M. and Engle, A.D (2008) *International Human Resource Management: Managing People in a Multinational Context.* London: Cengage/South-Western.

Earley, P. (1987) 'International training for managers: a comparison of documentary and interpersonal methods', *Academy of Management Journal*, 30(4): 19–35.

Edström, A. and Galbraith, J.R. (1977) 'Transfer of managers as a coordination and control strategy in multinational organisations', *Administrative Science Quarterly*, 22: 248–63.

Eschbach, D.M., Parker, G.E. and Stoebert, P.A (2001) 'American repatriate employees' retrospective assessments of the effects of cross-cultural training on their adaption to international assignments', *International Journal of Human Resource Management*, 12: 270–87.

Evans, P., Pucik, V. and Barsoux, J.L. (2002) *The Global Challenge: Frameworks for International Human Resource Management.* Boston MA: McGraw Hill.

Forster, N. (2000) 'The myth of the international manager', *International Journal of Human Resource Management*, 11: 126–42.

Forster, N and Johnsen, M. (1996) 'Expatriate management policies in UK companies new to the international scene', *International Journal of Human Resource Management*, 7(1): 177–205.

Gregersen, H.B., Morrison, A. and Black, J.S. (1998) 'Developing leaders for the global frontier', *Sloan Management Review*, 40: 21–32.

Gupta, A. and Govindarajan, V. (2002) 'Cultivating a global mindset', *Academic of Management Executive*, 16: 116–26.

Harrison, J.K. (1994) 'Developing successful expatriate managers: a framework for the structural design and strategic alignment of cross-cultural training programmes', *Human Resource Planning*, 17(3): 17–35.

Harvey, M.G. (1997) 'Inpatriation training: the next challenge for International Human Resource Management', *International Journal of Intercultural Relations*, 21(3): 393–428.

Harzing, A. (2001) 'Of bear, bumble-bees, and spiders: the role of expatriates in controlling foreign subsidiaries', *Journal of World Business*, 36: 366–79.

Hertel, E., Geister, S. and Konradt, U. (2005) 'Managing virtual teams: a review of current empirical research', *Human Resource Management Review*, 15: 69–95.

Hollenbeck, G.P., McCall, M.W. and Silzer, R.F. (2006) 'Leadership competency models', *The Leadership Quarterly*, 17: 398–413.

Iles, P. and Yolles, M. (2003) 'International HRD alliances in viable knowledge migration and development: the Czech Academic Link project', *Human Resource Development International*, 6(3): 301–24.

Johnson, J.P., Lenartowicz, T. and Apud, S. (2006) 'Cross-cultural competence in international business: toward a definition and a model', *Journal of International Business Studies*, 37: 525–43.

Jokinen, T. (2005) 'Global leadership competencies: a review and discussion', *Journal of European Industrial Training*, 29(3): 199–216.

Kealey, D. and Protheroe, D. (1996) 'The effectiveness of cross cultural training for expatriates: an assessment of the literature on the issue', *International Journal of Intercultural Relations*, 20: 141–65.

Kedia, B.L. and Makherji, A (1999) 'Global managers; developing mindset for global competitiveness', *Journal of World Business*, 34(3): 230–42.

Lane, H.W., DiStefano, J.J. and Maznevski, M.L. (1997) *International Management Behaviour*, 3rd edn. Cambridge, MA: Blackwell Publishers.

Littrell, L.N., Salas, E., Hess, K.P., Paley, M. and Riedel, S. (2006) 'Expatriate, preparation: a critical analysis of 25 years of cross-cultural training research', *Human Resource Development Review*, 5(3): 355–88.

Maclean, D. (2006) 'Beyond English: transnational corporations and the strategic management of language in a complex multilingual business environment', *Management Decision*, 44(10): 1377–90.

Mayerhofer, H., Hartmann, L.C., Michelitsch-Riedl, G. and Kollinger, I. (2004) 'Flexpatraite assignments: a neglected issue in global staffing', *International Journal of Human Resource Management*, 15(8): 1371–89.

Maznevski, M.L., Canney-Davison, S. and Karsten, J. (2006) 'Global virtual team dynamics and effectiveness', in K.G. Stahl and I. Bjorkman (eds), *Handbook of Research in International Human Resource Management*. pp. 364–84. Cheltenham: Edward Elgar.

McCall, M.W. (1998) *High Fliers: Developing the Next Generation of Leaders*. Boston: Harvard Business School Press.

McCall, M.W., Lombardo, M. & Morrison, A. (1988) *The Lessons of Experience*. Boston: Lexington Books.

McFarlin, D.B. and Sweeney, P. D (2006) *International Management: Strategic Opportunities and Cultural Challenges*. New York: Houghton, Mifflin.

Mendenhall, M. (2000) 'New perspectives on expatriate adjustment and its relationship to global leadership development', in M.E Mendenhall, T.M Kuhlman, and G.K Stahl (eds), *Developing Global Leaders: Policies, Process and Innovations*. Westport, CT: Quoram.

Mendenhall, M. (2006) 'The elusive, yet critical challenge of developing global leaders', *European Management Journal*, 26(6): 422–9.

Mendenhall, M. and Oddou, G. (1985) 'The dimension of expatriate acculturation: a review', *Academy of Management Review*, 10: 39–47.

Mendenhall, M. and Osland, J.S. (2002). An Overview of the Extant Global Leadership Research. Symposium Presentation, Academy of International Business, Puerto Rico, June.

Mendenhall, M. and Stahl, K. (2000) 'Expatriate training and development: where do we go from here?', *Human Resource Management*, 39: 251–365.

Mendenhall, M., Dunbar, E. and Oddou, G. (1987) 'Expartriate selection, training and career pathing: a review and critique, Human Resource Management, 26(3): 331–45.

Mendenhall, M., Kuhlmann, T.M., Stahl, G.K. and Osland, J.S. (2002) 'Employee development and expartriate assignments', in M. Gannon, and K. Newman,(eds), *Handbook of Cross-Cultural Management*. London: Blackwell.

Mendenhall, M.E., Osland, J.S., Bird, A., Oddou, G.R. and Maznevski, M.L. (2008) *Global Leadership: Research Practice and Development*. London: Routledge.

Metcalfe, B.D. and Rees, C.J. (2005) 'Theorizing advances in International Human Resource Development', *Human Resource Development International*, 8(4): 449–65.

Molinsky, A. (2007) 'Cross-cultural code-switching: the psychological challenges of adapting behavior in foreign cultural interactions', *Academy of Management Review*, 32(2): 622–40.

Morley, M. and Heraty, N. (2004) 'International assignments and global careers', *Thunderbird International Business Review*, 46(6): 633–46.

Morris, M.A. and Robie, C. (2001) 'A meta-analysis of the effects of cross-cultural training on expatriate performance and adjustment', *International Journal of Training and Development*, 5: 112–25.

Murtha, T.P., Lenway, S.A. and Bagozzi, R.P. (1998) 'Global mind-sets and cognitive shift in a complex multinational corporation', *Strategic Management Journal*, 19(2): 97–114.

Napier, N. and Peterson, R. (1991) 'Expatriate re-entry: what do expatriates have to say', *Human Resource Planning*, 14(1): 19–28.

Neary, D.B. and O'Grady, D.A. (2000) 'The role of training and developing global leaders: a case study at TRW Inc.', *Human Resource Management*, 39(2/3): 185–93.

OECD (2000) *Knowledge Management in Learning Society*. Paris: OECD.

Osland, I. (1995) *The Advantages of Living Abroad: Hero Takes from the Global Frontier*. San Francisco CA: Jossey Bass, Inc.

Osman-Gani, A. (2000) 'Developing expatriates for the Asia-Pacific region: a comparative analysis of multinational enterprise managers from five countries across three continents', *Human Resource Development Quarterly*, 11(3): 213–35.

Prahaled, C.K. and Lieberthal, K. (1998) 'The end of corporate imperialism', *Harvard Business Review*, 76: 69–79.

Rahim, A. (1983). 'A model for developing key expatriate executives', *Personnel Journal*, 62: 312–17.

Rees, C.J. and Doran, E. (2001) 'Employee selection in a TQM context: taking a hard look at a soft issue', *Total Quality Management*, 12(7/8): 855–60.

Rees, J.I. and Rees, C.J. (1996) 'Lost for words and losing business', *Industrial and Commercial Training*, 28(3): 8–13.

Rhinesmith, S. (1996) *A Manager's Guide to Globalization*, 2nd edn. New York: McGraw-Hill.

Sappinen, J. (1993) 'Expatriate adjustment on foreign assignment', *European Business Review*, 93 (5): 3–11.

Scullion, H. (2001) 'International Human Resource Management', in J. Storey (ed.), *Human Resource Management*. London: International Thompson.

Scullion, H. and Brewster, C. (2001) 'Managing expatriates: messages from Europe', *Journal of World Business*, 36: 346–65.

Scullion, H., Collings, D.G. and Gunnigle, P. (2007) 'International Human Resource Management in the 21st century: emerging themes and contemporary debates', *Human Resource Management Journal*, 17(4): 309–19.

Selmer, J. (2001) The preference for pre-departure or post-arrival cross-cultural training: an exploratory approach', *Journal of Managerial Psychology*, 16: 50–58.

Selmer, J., Torbiorn, I and de Leon, T. (1998) 'Sequential cross cultural training for expatriate business managers: predeparture and post-arrival', *International Journal of Human Resource Management*, 9: 831–40.

Spreitzer, G.M., McCall, M.W. and Mahoney, J.D. (1997) 'Early identification of international executive potential', *Journal of Applied Psychology*, 82(1): 6–29.

Stahl, G.K. (2001) 'Using assessment centres as tools for global leadership development: an exploratory study', in M.E. Mendenhall, T.M. Kühlmann, G.K. Stahl (eds), *Developing Global Business Leaders: Policies, Processes and Innovations*. pp. 197–210. Westport: Quorum.

Stroh, L.K. and Caligiuri, P.M. (1998a) 'Increasing global competitiveness through effective people management', *Journal of World Business*, 33(1): 1–16.

Stroh, L.K. and Caligiuri, P.M. (1998b) 'Strategic human resource: a new source of competitive advantage in the global arena', *International Journal of Human Resource Management*, 9(1): 1–17.

Suutari, V. (2002) 'Global leader development: an emerging research agenda', *Career Development International*, 7(4): 218–33.

Swift, J. and Huang, Y. (2004) 'The changing nature of international business relationships and foreign language competence', *International Journal of Management Practice*, 1(1): 21–40.

Tahvanainen, M., Welch, D. and Worm, V. (2005) 'Implications of short-term international assignments', *European Management Journal*, 23: 633–73.

Tarique, I. and Caligiuri, P.M. (2004) 'Training and development of international staff', in A.W. Harzing and J. Van Ruysseveldt (eds), *International Human Resource Management*. pp. 283–306. London: Sage.

Thaler-Carter, R.E. (2000) 'Whither global leaders', *HR Magazine*, 45 (5): 83–8.

Thomas, D.C. and Inkson, K. (2004) *Cultural Intelligence: People Skills for Global Business*. San Francisco, CA: Berrett.

Thomas, D.C., Lazarova, M.B. and Inkson, K (2005) 'Global careers: new phenomenon or new respectives?', *Journal of World Business*, 40: 340–7.

Tichy, N.M., Brimm, M.I., Charan, R. and Takeuchi, H (1992) 'Leadership development as a lever for global transformation', in V. Pucik, N.M. Tichy and C.K. Barnett (eds),

Globalizing Management: Creating and Leading the Competitive Organisation. pp. 47–60. New York: Wiley.

Tung, R. (1981) 'Selecting and training for overseas assignment', *Columbia Journal of World Business*, 16: 68–78.

Tung, R. (1982) 'Selection of training procedures of U.S. and Japanese multi-nationals', *California Management Review*, 25(1): 57–81.

Tung, R. (1987) 'Expatriate assignments: enhancing success and minimizing failure', *Academy of Management Executive*, 10: 17–26.

Tung, R. (1998) 'A contingency framework of selection and training of expatriate revisited', *Human Resource Management Review*, 8 (1): 23–37.

Tung, R. (2008) 'Do race and gender matter in international assignment to/from Asia Pacific: an exploratory study of attitudes among Chinese', *Human Resource Management*, 47(1): 91–110.

Varma, A., Toh, S.M. and Budhwar, P. (2006) 'A new perspective on the female expatriate experience: the role of host country national categorization', *Journal of World Business*, 41(2): 112–20.

Vloeberghs, D. and Berghman, L. (2003) 'Towards an effectiveness model of development centres', *Journal of Managerial Psychology*, 18(1): 511–40.

Wang, X. and McLean, G.N. (2007) 'The dilemma of defining international human resource development', *Human Resource Development Review*, 6(1): 96–108.

Welch, D.E. and Worm, V. (2006) 'International business travellers: a challenge for IHRM', in G.K. Stahl and I. Björkman (eds), *Handbook of Research in International Human Resource Management*. Cheltenham, UK: Edward Elgar.

Woodruffe, C. (1993) 'What is meant by a competency?', *Leadership and Organisation Development Journal*, 14: 29–36.

12

Global and Local Resourcing

Ying Zhu, Chris Rowley and Malcolm Warner

Contents

Learning Objectives

After reading this chapter you will be able to

- Understand and evaluate the HR competencies approach

- Rationalise and illustrate the political economy and strategic choice approaches

- Identify the key external factors that determine change in recruitment and retention

- Differentiate between the key characteristics of capitalist market economies and socialist market economies in Asia

- Critically evaluate the reasons for economic reform and adoption of HR policies and practices in Asia

Chapter Outline

This chapter discusses recent changes to labour market policy and regulations and assesses their impact on enterprises' HRM policies and practices in Asia, in particular in the areas of recruitment and retention. Four significant Asian economies are used as examples to represent the range of different economic systems, namely Japan, Taiwan, China and Vietnam.

1 Introduction

This chapter identifies recent changes in labour market policy and regulations and assesses their impact on enterprises' HRM policies and practices in Asia, in particular in the areas of recruitment and retention. Four significant Asian economies are used as examples, namely Japan and Taiwan representing 'capitalist' market economies, and China and Vietnam representing 'socialist' market economies (for other Asian examples, see Rowley and Abdul-Rahman, 2008). The chapter commences with an overview of literature related to the HR competency approach in the areas of 'recruiting and retaining competencies' and then examines the interaction between external changes in political, economic and labour market policy and internal enterprises' strategic adaptation and adjustment of HR policy and practices. Then we review these systems in Japan, Taiwan, China and Vietnam focusing on their impact on enterprises' HR practices in recruiting and retaining people. The final section illustrates the policy implications for government policy regulators and enterprise management in Asia and also considers its significance elsewhere for achieving an appropriate degree of 'fit' between external changes and the internal strategic adaptation and adjustment of HR policies and practices.

2 Review of HR competencies approach

Increasing competition in global markets has encouraged management to pay greater attention to improving 'employee competencies'. After the 1997 Asian Crisis, most Asian economies systematically introduced a competency model incorporating the main activities for HRM (see Bae and Rowley, 2004). The conception of competencies has undergone quite a dramatic change. In the past, the notion of competencies was used only in the areas of vocational training and education. The concept has since gradually become embedded in the field of HRM with a broader domain beyond the 'narrow' view of 'following rules and procedure and performing limited and routine tasks'.

No matter what models and perspectives on HRM are used, recruitment and selection policies and practices can be perceived as integral. In fact, recruitment and selection not only seeks to attract, obtain and retain the human resources the organisation needs to achieve its given strategic goals, but also aims to have a significant impact on the composition of the workforce, the ultimate 'fit' with the organisation's needs and culture, and long-range employment stability (Beer et al., 1984). This chapter examines HR practices in recruitment and talent management in Asia and adopts two elements of the model of four HR competencies constructed by Bae and Rowley (2004) (see Box 12.1), namely 'recruiting competency' and 'retaining competency'. The first element, 'recruiting competencies', consists of recruitment and selection activities. The second one, 'retaining competencies', includes two activities, namely training/development and job design.

Box 12.1   Theoretical perspectives of HR competencies

- Recruiting competencies – consists of recruitment and selection activities.
- Reinforcing competencies – encompasses evaluation and rewards.
- Retaining competencies – includes two activities, namely training/development and job design.
- Replacing competencies – through employment flexibility and outplacement.

Source: Bae and Rowley, 2004.

This model is selected for two reasons. First, the model emerged from empirical research aimed at capturing the changes in HRM activities conducted among Asian economies (see Rowley and Benson, 2004). Second, it groups HRM activities in a systematic way that enables a more integrated analysis. Further, in line with the central theme of this chapter on recruitment and retention, these two elements of competency are addressed in detail.

3 External labour market changes and internal strategic choice

In the past two decades research has focused on the specific circumstances of individual countries and their impact on HR practices at the enterprise level. Two major approaches dominate the debate about the factors that influence HR functions in different political, social and economic environments – the political economy approach (external factors) and the strategic choice approach (internal factors) (Martin and Bamber, 2005; Warner, 2000) (see Box 12.2).

As for the influence of external factors, the political economy approach illustrates the integration of a 'system of production, the role of government, the broader social and economic environment under globalization, labour market regulations and employment relations institutions and their impact on enterprises' development' (Martin and Bamber, 2005: 381). The international political economy has changed dramatically during the last few decades and HR systems have adjusted accordingly. In general there are three main trends: the intensification of international competition, widespread deregulation across industrialised countries and the collapse of communism that boosted the confidence of neo-liberal ideologues (Martin and Bamber, 2005). Murray et al. (2000) claim that this approach involves analysing the interaction between interest groups and institutions. This interaction influences the manner in which nations integrate with the international political economy and ultimately determines the impact of globalisation in each country and region, with their HR systems being influenced accordingly (Van Ruysseveldt, 1995). The strands of this debate lead our research to study the factors that influence enterprises with different ownership forms to adopt specific dimensions of HRM.

Box 12.2   Theoretical perspectives of external and internal factors

- External factors – the political economy approach illustrates the integration of a system of production, the role of government, the broader social and economic environment under globalisation, labour market regulations and employment relations institutions and its impact on enterprises' development.

- Internal factors – the strategic choice approach identifies key elements of internal factors for business success and focuses on choice in terms of organisations' business strategies and their links with HR practice.

Source: Martin and Bamber, 2005

In relation to internal factors, the strategic choice approach identifies key elements for business success and since the 1980s has been part of the vocabulary for many comparative studies (see Chapter 2) of HR practices (Martin and Bamber, 2005). The focus of strategic choice is on organisations' business strategies, in which the relationship between HR practice and business strategies is the major concern (Boxall and Purcell, 2003; Martin and Bamber, 2005). This approach emphasises the role of management initiative (Kochan et al., 1986) and the integration of HR practices with business strategies (Guest, 1989; Storey and Sisson, 1993). It favours increased management autonomy, rejection of collective bargaining and a reduced union role in employment relations (Beer et al., 1984; Dowling and Welch, 2004). In the next section we apply these theoretical perspectives to HR transformation and to debates on the factors influencing adoption of HR practices.

As explained earlier, we chose four Asian economies to represent both developed and developing nations in terms of their economic and labour market policies and consequently their impact on HR practices at the firm level.

4 Capitalist market economies: Japan and Taiwan

It is useful to group Japan and Taiwan together – given each is an island economy, although their populations are different in size and origins. Historically, Japan colonised Taiwan for the first half of the twentieth century and both of them were dominated by a feudalist system and have since transformed to state-led capitalism and industrialisation, and more recently to a more open capitalist market economy. Hence, similarities as well as differences can be found, as we shall see.

Japan

Japan is the leading developed economy in East Asia with many unique management characteristics. Its HRM has been identified as the 'Japanese style of people management' due to the mix of its Confucian legacy with a modern welfare corporatist system (Benson and Debroux, 2004). By facing the challenges of globalisation and regional competition, the Japanese HRM system has undergone a process of transformation that has become known as 'a Japanese model with a more individualistic focus' (ibid.). However, this emerging model is inherently unstable and contradictory and the following section will address those changes in relation to the central theme of this chapter.

Two major aspects are under consideration here. The first is the changes in labour market policy and its impact on HR practices at firm level and the second is the changes in employee resourcing and HRM. The key elements of government labour market policy are related to the changing realities of the economy and labour market. For most of the 1990s and 2000s, the Japanese economy moved between periods of recession and extremely low rates of economic growth. This economic downturn has had a negative impact on employment with relatively high rates of unemployment such as the peak of 5.3 per cent in 2003 (Benson, 2005). The adverse economic situation has built up pressure on the labour market. The key elements of labour market policy have been implemented by the government with the consideration of reducing unemployment and the cost of employment, improving labour productivity, and managing the problems associated with an aging workforce. Relevant policies have been introduced with the purpose of providing incentives for firms to employ more people, in particular young people, and discourage employers to dismiss people and to support labour flexibility. At the same time, the government has provided more funding for training and development, and pension and unemployment benefits, while extending the retirement age to retain relatively older employees within the workforce.

During the first half of the 1990s, the ratio of openings to applicants remained quite high for professional and technical occupations (Benson and Debroux, 2004). Large companies that formerly had recruited many high school graduates started to reduce the amount of employment (ibid.), in addition, many companies reduced the size of their workforce by transferring manufacturing abroad and resorting to new employment policies that relied on atypical work contracts and arrangements. After the 1997 Asian Financial Crisis, poor economic conditions coupled with an acceleration of the restructuring process, brought about a fall in the demand for labour and reduced recruitment of young graduates from both high schools and universities. Following the redundancies of mid-career employees during the recession and business closures, other companies started to recruit more experienced mid-career employees who had been sacked during the downturn (Zhu, 2004a).

This late 1990s economic downturn forced Japanese companies to adopt a more flexible employment arrangement – by dividing the workforce into three categories

1 a core-group with long-term employment
2 a contractor-group of specialists with mid-term employment
3 a peripheral group of employees undertaking simple and routine tasks with short-term employment (Benson, 2005).

Each of these groups exhibited a pattern of distinct recruitment, remuneration, welfare, training and promotion schemes (Benson and Debroux, 2004).

The second area, namely HR retention, covers two elements: job design, and training and development. In order to develop a system that realised 'talent-value' as well as retained capable people within the organisation, most companies have had to re-assess their HR retention policy. In fact, the current generation of Japanese employees has developed a new set of work-values and beliefs that flexible, ability-based, and performance-oriented job design, evaluation, incentives and promotion will benefit their careers (see Chapter 13). Consequently, there has been a gradual shift away from traditional seniority-based ranking, promotion and incentive systems towards meritocratic values and approaches.

As for training and development, Zhu's (2004a) research demonstrates that under the influence of both external and internal factors, such as global competition, technological changes and innovation, and domestic and regional economic down turns, pressure has built up on both the government and industries to pay more attention to HRD. Both national and prefectural governments in Japan have had to allocate more funds for establishing more public HRD facilities throughout the country, targeting unemployed people and graduate students assisting them to gain new jobs and acquire new skills. As for industry, there has been an uneven distribution of job-based training opportunities in terms of size and sector. Generally speaking, large companies provide more training opportunities than small and medium size companies. For instance, companies with 1,000 or more employees are reported to have had a 99 per cent rate of implementation of job-related training programmes, in contrast to 66 per cent of companies with less than 99 employees (Zhu, 2004a).

As for industry sector, finance, insurance and real estate attain the highest percentage (94 per cent) of firms implementing job-training, followed by services (76 per cent), construction (75 per cent), manufacturing (71 per cent), wholesale and retail trades (61 per cent), and finally transport and communications (51 per cent) (Zhu, 2004a). In addition, through formal and informal on-the-job training (OJT) that has been widespread in Japan, off-the-job training (Off-JT) in special skills and knowledge was not widely adopted among employees due to lack of employer uptake. This indicates that even if the Japanese economy has shifted towards a more knowledge-based focus, the reality of HRD policy and implementation still lags far behind. In fact, there are multiple challenges facing the government and industry that require not only training in basic knowledge and skills, but also other programmes, such as improving special skills, responses to technology changes, improvements in business and economic literacy, handling market competition and globalisation, and developing specific competencies within the workforce (ibid.).

Taiwan

Since the 1960s, Taiwan, the self-styled Republic of China (ROC), has experienced many complex political and economic developments. On the political front, the pressure for democratisation became overwhelming during the late 1980s and early 1990s. Over the last three decades, the political system has become more complex and government policy has shifted towards a more pro-labour orientation following the process of democratisation (Zhu, 2004b). The outcome was that the government amended several labour laws in the 1980s; including the Collective Agreement

Law in 1982, the Labour Disputes Law and the Labour Insurance Act in 1988, and the Vocational Training Act in 1983 (Chen, 1998: 155–6; Lee, 1995: 101). New laws were also enacted, such as the Labour Standards Law in 1984 (amended in 1996), the Employment Service Act in 1992, and the Equal Rights in the Workplace Act in 1993 (Chen, 1998: 155–6; Lee, 1995: 101).

The government also expanded the range of worker benefits through the creation of a social welfare system. For instance, the National Health Insurance Law of 1994, the Law for the Protection of People with Mental and Physical Disabilities of 1997, and the Rules for the Implementation of the Payment of Unemployment Insurance Benefits of 1998 were implemented in the 1990s (Wang and Cooney, 2002). Some of the laws, for instance, the rules on unemployment benefits, were a direct response to the effects of the 1997 Asian Crisis.

On the economic front, the different stages of economic development have been accompanied by specific management patterns. In Taiwan, for instance, economic development since the 1960s can be divided into two stages: the 'export' expansion period between 1961 and 1980 and the 'technology-intensive industries' expansion period from 1981 to 1997 before the Asian Crisis (Lee, 1995; Zhu and Warner, 2004; Zhu et al., 2000).

In the labour market, important changes have also taken place (Chen, 1997; Lee, 1995; Zhu et al., 2000; and Wang and Cooney, 2002). In the 1980s, after three decades of rapid industrial expansion, the supply of land and labour reached limits and constraints, causing a rapid increase in labour costs and land prices. As a consequence, many labour-intensive industries relocated from Taiwan to low-cost countries, especially in South East Asia and Mainland China. Government policy also shifted from developing labour-intensive industries to encouraging the development of technology-intensive and service industries in order to maintain the momentum of economic development.

Since the 1997 Asian Crisis, Taiwan's economy has experienced economic slowdown during the 2000s. Unemployment has increased and reached the high level of 7.5 per cent (a total of 765,000 people) in November 2002 (Zhu, 2005). Generally speaking, changes in the economy and labour market, the challenges of the Asian Crisis and more broadly, global economic competition produced different HRM responses from Taiwanese enterprises.

Regarding the central theme of this chapter on recruitment and retention, HR practices have changed from the early years of an export expansion-related policy to the more recent technology-intensive industry policy. During the export-expansion period, recruiting blue-collar workers relied heavily on informal channels, i.e. employee referral and company networks. For the recruitment of white-collar workers, such as managers and public servants, formal channels and recruitment procedures were used. In fact, colleges and universities' graduate recruitment was one of the major sources of applicants for filling those positions. Due to long-term employment conditions and seniority-based employment systems, there was little extensive mid-career recruitment in the labour market during this period.

HR retention policy was based on long-term employment and seniority-based job design and promotion. With the traditional culture of avoiding conflict between management and employees, most employees would be promoted along the grades of their job titles only if their annual performance was classified as 'above-average' (Chen, 1998). However, company-sponsored training was not popular during this period and apprenticeships were not common in Taiwan. Often, in practice more skilled workers received formal OJT than did semi-skilled and unskilled workers (Zhu and Warner, 2004). Moreover, foreign-owned enterprises offered more OJT programme than did local companies (Lee, 1995).

During the technology-intensive industries' period of expansion, the industrial system became more complex and formal, and government policy shifted towards a more pro-labour orientation. The development of the labour market and growing demand for more skilled workforce lead to more formal recruitment and selection procedures among both public and private sectors, as well as performance-based compensation, job promotion and design with less emphasis on seniority (Hsu and Leat, 2000). However, internal recruitment methods such as 'promotion-from-within', 'transfers' and 'job rotations' are still commonly used by the majority of Taiwanese enterprises. External recruitment methods are mainly used for obtaining potential candidates with specialist knowledge, technical or managerial skills for appointments to middle and senior posts (ibid.). In terms of selection practices, 'knowledge or skill tests' and formal interviews are most frequently used, whereas 'psychometric tests' and 'assessment centres' are less common (ibid.).

Training and development became a key element for upgrading skills in the more technology-intensive industries. Given the trends towards developing learning organisations and the shift towards the knowledge economy, many Taiwanese enterprises adopted organisational learning strategies by a) individual learning focusing on and diffusing it with team learning and organisational learning, and b) using the knowledge management system to create an opportunity for individuals, teams and the organisation to learn (Lien et al., 2007: 219). In fact, after the 2008 Global Financial Crisis, the Taiwanese government and industry community have been collaborating to invest more in training and development, while also reducing salary levels and encouraging employees to take non-paid leave in order to avoid creating more unemployment. Therefore, in Taiwan new retention policies became one way of reducing unemployment and maintaining social stability.

5 Socialist market economies: China and Vietnam

The People's Republic of China (PRC) and the Socialist Republic of Vietnam (SRV) represent a different kind of political and economic system. Both countries have been transformed from centrally planned socialist systems to more market oriented economies, while still retaining some 'socialist characteristics'. Economic reforms and an open door policy have led to significant changes in these socialist market economies. The emergence of new interest groups, the inflow of foreign capital and the diversity of ownership of enterprises, combined with a large and floating population moving from the countryside to the cities, have accentuated conflicts of interest and require a more relevant labour market policy at the macro-level and HRM strategies at the micro-level to cope with these challenges.

China

After 'Liberation' in 1949, China laid the foundations of its industrial and labour relations system, particularly during the 1950s. However, there was great turbulence and upheavals over the decades following the establishment of these foundations. China was turned 'upside-down' by the ebbs and flows of radical change that occurred at that time, during the Cultural Revolution. In the 1960s, Mao tried to undermine what he originally thought was the right path to take when he partially emulated Soviet practices, as had been the case during the formative years of the 1950s.

The year of 1976 marked the end of an era: Mao Zedong died and the fall of the 'Gang of Four' occurred. After ten years of the 'Cultural Revolution', China still faced sharp tensions, both politically and economically. At the end of the Cultural Revolution, almost 100 million people had barely enough food and clothing. The level of enterprise performance was weak and unlikely to improve greatly under a system in which the workers were not strongly motivated. Outside, China was challenged by other Asian economies led by Japan and the four so-called 'Little Tiger' economies which had experienced rapid development over the 1960s and 1970s. In order to catch up with their development, China not only set out to encourage Western technological (and managerial) transfer by way of the new 'Open Door' policy (see Child, 1994), but also looked eastwards to the Japanese pattern of economic development and management in particular, as a possible route for modernisation.

The main reforms of labour market policy in general and HRM policy and practice in particular, reflect strategies of marketisation set within the overall national economic development policy. The major changes include the following (see Zhu and Warner, 2004):

1 New policies that were mainly centred on the reform of wages, employment, welfare and management.
2 Reform initiatives of the government that have been broadly defined as breaking the 'three irons' ('iron rice-bowl', 'iron wages', 'iron position'), and establishing three new systems (labour contract system, floating wage system, and a cadre or manager engagement system) with the purpose of increasing labour flexibility and competition.
3 Under Deng Xiaoping's new reformist ideological position, policy aimed to restore the principle of 'distribution according to work' and link individuals' performance,

skills and position with their income in order to generate individuals' motivation for greater production.

4 New types of wage system were introduced such as the 'piece(-work) wage system', 'bonus system' and later the 'structural wage system', 'floating wage system' and 'post plus skills wage system'.

5 Allowing variations in rewards based on productivity was 'part and parcel' of this reform. Moreover, labour was to be encouraged to move from less productive firms to more efficient ones.

6 Immobility of labour has been a feature of the old system dominated by state-owned enterprises (SOEs), where there was over-manning and zero turnover of workers.

Establishment of a new labour market was therefore high on the reformers' agenda. However, improvements in labour mobility did not take place overnight. Even by the later 1990s, the level of job mobility was relatively low in many SOEs although rising in the non-State sector such as in domestic private enterprises (DPEs), joint ventures (JVs) and foreign-owned enterprises (FOEs).

In terms of employment in the early 1980s, many young graduates from school could no longer obtain the guaranteed employment opportunity their parents had enjoyed in the past and in fact became temporarily unemployed. The practice of job inheritance ('dingti'), with posts passing from parents to offspring, was gradually phased out. In addition, many young people who came back to the cities after several years of settlement in the countryside and obtaining their education from peasants ('cha dui') could not find jobs. However, this situation was described by the officials as waiting to be employed ('daiye') but not as unemployment ('shiye') (Zhu and Warner, 2004). It could not be admitted openly that a socialist society might have 'unemployment', which was formerly associated with capitalism.

The boundary of the term of 'daiyie' was even expanded to include the workers who were laid-off from factories throughout the late 1980s and early 1990s (ibid.). Since the mid-1990s, unemployment has been used to refer to people who have not been employed for several years and now unemployment benefit is available for some of them (ibid.). In fact, the level of unemployment has grown steadily as the reforms have deepened and downsizing has taken place (ibid.); many young workers have been forced into spurious forms of 'self-employment' such as street-hawkers. Given the current global financial crisis and economic turbulence, this kind of unemployment has increased and become worse, in particular among college and university graduates, as well as migrant workers ('mingong').

The term HRM is in fact mostly *de rigueur* in the more prominent Sino-foreign JVs and FOEs, particularly the larger ones (see Warner, 2008). Even in these types of firm, management seems to be more inward-looking, with a focus on issues like wages, welfare and promotion, as found in the conventional personnel arrangements, rather than strategic ones like long-term development normally associated with HRM.

One survey based on case studies of Special Economic Zones (SEZs) (see Zhu and Warner, 2002) shows that the market-oriented economy reforms have had a profound impact on organisational changes and HRM practices in enterprises. The pressure towards being competitive and flexible has created a diverse pattern of HRM in relation to individual companies' culture, based as it is on their history and values. The case studies reflect the competition in the HR arena for recruiting and retaining skilled and capable employees. Better work organisation has lead to higher productivity and competitiveness, and helped to manage the workforce, achieve higher commitment and realise individual's values within the organisation. Improved teamwork, quality control circles, and adopting new technology have enabled these Chinese companies to achieve their business goals.

A number of factors influence the ways enterprises are recruiting their employees, as summarised by Cooke (2005). First, there was the gradual withdrawal of the government from direct intervention in the state sector and direct recruitment of people from the external labour market. Second, there was labour market segmentation – with a shortage of skilled labour and oversupply of unskilled/semi-skilled labour that forced enterprises to adopt a more sophisticated recruitment strategy to compete for talent from more diverse sources including expatriates and overseas Chinese graduate-returnees. Third, the common recruitment methods for the low-paid and low-skilled jobs was mainly through family, friends and village networks, in contrast to the more formal, skilled or white-collar jobs with more formal labour market advertising and recruitment procedures (for HRM in small enterprises see Rowley and Li, 2006, 2008).

Training and career development are important means for retaining capable employees and for encouraging employees' commitment to higher productivity and their organisational well-being. Enterprise-based training often reflects two different systems: positional training and vocational competency-based training (Cooke, 2005). The former offers workers positional training and continuous education that enable them to perform in specific jobs and positions within enterprises. As for the latter, it was designed based on national vocational competency tests by the Labour and Social Security authorities at all levels (ibid.). Since the late 1990s, when further reform of the SOEs was implemented, retraining of redundant workers in this sector became one of the main training activities in China to increase their employability. Other areas of management and HRM in China, such as pay (see Wei and Rowley, 2009) and other HR activities (see examples in Rowley and Cooke, 2009) also have been changing.

Vietnam

Economic reform in Vietnam likewise aims to replace direct government administration at the enterprise level with government management of the economy and enterprise autonomy oriented to a market economy (Zhu and Fahey, 2000). Major tasks of reform have included the rationalisation of SOEs into joint stock companies (JSCs) and the introduction and expansion of private enterprises, which extends to DPEs and FOEs (ibid.). Among the reform's initiatives, changing HRM is the 'critical point' at which economic imperatives spill over into social and political considerations.

The pre-reform system Under the pre-reform system, SOEs were integrated into a system of mandatory state planning. Enterprise inputs, including labour, were assigned by government plans. Enterprises did not necessarily acquire labour with the right set of skills and were invariably over-staffed because the labour administration recruited and selected employees for individual firms (Doanh and Tran 1998). In addition, enterprises had few methods available to motivate or discipline employees. The rewards system had only an indirect relation to enterprise efficiency and individual labour effort. It was based on a narrowly defined egalitarianism, as well as the tendency to reward labour on the grounds of seniority and contribution to the Party, as well as to the war-effort in the past.

Personnel management was a rigid function confined to areas such as allocating jobs and managing personnel files. Due to the absence of labour markets, pre-reform personnel management was inward-looking and concentrated on issues such as distribution of wages, provision of welfare and routine promotion of workers and cadres from lower ranks to higher ranks according to the regulations.

The reform of the HR system In the early stages of 'doi moi' (1988–91), reform of the SOEs was intensified owing to the loss of financial assistance from the former Soviet Union (Zhu and Fahey, 2000). In order to create a more flexible HR system, the government relinquished its control over the recruitment and employment of workers. Therefore, individual firms gained more autonomy to decide on the number of workers hired, the terms of employment and release of employees.

The pace of transforming life-time employment into a new contract-employment system has been relatively slow and the dominant change has been the fixed-term contract of employment that was initially introduced in 1987. Since the late 1990s, there have been further changes, with three types of contracts covering different types of employees: first the unlimited-term contract for employees who joined the work unit before the introduction of the new system; second the fixed-term contract with a duration of one to three years for employees who joined the work unit after the introduction of the new system; and third the temporary contract with a duration of less than one year for casual workers or seasonal workers. However, due to the economic difficulties in a large number of SOEs, many so-called 'permanent employees' who are on unlimited-term contracts have been retrenched through further restructuring of SOEs in recent years. Therefore, the term 'unlimited-term contract' nowadays has lost any real meaning.

Generally speaking, staffing activities in local enterprises are considered to be not as effective as they are in FOEs (Thang and Quang, 2005). FOEs tend to extend their search efforts in recruitment and to apply a rigorous selection process to acquire the most appropriate candidates for the job. Among the local enterprises, SOEs have an excessive number of workers due to historical factors and struggles, and most are preoccupied with reducing the burden rather than engaging actively in recruitment and selection of new personnel. As for the JSCs and DPEs, their business started more recently and business growth led to them relying on more capable people. Therefore, JSCs and DPEs are likely to pay more attention to recruitment and selection than are SOEs (ibid.).

For many years, Vietnam has been seen as a place with cheap labour as a source of competitive advantage. However, its relatively lower skills and productivity can raise the alarm bells for foreign companies when they assess its opportunities and threats as a country for potential investment. As a result, many people in government and the business community appreciate the importance of upgrading the workforce's skills through training and development. Full-scale training activities were initiated within the FOE group due to common agreement that their technical and managerial skills amongst employees were insufficient. In contrast, local enterprises have become left behind due to traditional considerations that it is the government's responsibility to ensure adequate training and development. In recent years, some JSCs and DPEs have become more keen to invest in employees through training, in addition, DPEs have continued to seek to recruit experienced employees for their organisations' needs (Thang and Quang, 2005). Under increasing competition, local companies have begun to experiment with innovative measures of acquiring high-quality management expertise. Other areas of management in Vietnam have also been changing (see examples in Rowley and Quang, 2009). Some enterprises have tried to hire foreigners, even as CEOs, for the top jobs that are currently in short demand (Quang et al., 2008).

6 Summary and conclusion

This chapter has provided an overview of key elements related to employee recruitment and retention. Through theories and practical examples of four Asian economies, we have endeavoured to develop knowledge and understanding of the key factors determining the outcomes of HR policies and practices. Regarding the factors that influence enterprises to adopt specific HR practices, the findings in the research literature indicate that government policy on economic reform has a fundamental influence on these changes. Under the reform agenda, management at enterprise level adapted their decisions and practices to meet the more competitive external competitive challenges. The subsequent internal strategic shift, including the adjustment of

HR practices has a clear purpose which is to improve the level of productivity and efficiency of these businesses.

The study has some implications for both HRM theory and practice with the challenges of globalisation, greater market competition, and enhanced economic reform and transition. First, the development of 'people management' is a process of integration involving a number of factors, including political economic changes and enterprise management reform. In fact, a combination of the political economy approach and strategic choice approach can be used to analyse the phenomenon of people-management reform in the context of economic transition and globalisation, and these two approaches can be applied in ways that are *inclusive* rather than *exclusive*.

Second, the implications for policy makers are also significant. The government's purposes in economic reform in general and 'people management' reform in particular are two-fold: on the one hand, economic reform might lead to the improvement of economic growth and living standards; on the other hand, if people benefit from the reform then they may more strongly support economic reform policy and in return, social stability can be maintained and the government sustain its 'legitimacy' to rule the society.

Finally, the implications for enterprise management are also clear. Under the current process of globalisation and market competition, now accompanied by global financial crisis and economic uncertainty, individual enterprises have to find ways to survive. Adequate HR policies and practices are a crucial part of business survival strategies. 'Downsizing' and 'retrenchment' could well be the dominant dimension for HR policy when enterprises experience an economic downturn. However, a *balanced* approach is necessary – not only with the focus on the short-term outcome – but also *vis-à-vis* the long-term well-being of enterprises. Recruitment and retention are important – given that finding the right people with adequate skills may reduce costs and improve efficiency, while job design/training and development can be crucial for the successful achievement of business outcomes, particularly given the continuing demand for high quality work outcomes and better skills and knowledge. Enterprises, therefore, will suffer in the long run if they do not manage HR policy and practices in a balanced way.

Discussion questions

1 With the increasing economic uncertainty and problems of the 2008 global financial crisis, enterprises should focus their HR policy solely on downsizing and retrenchment, rather than other activities such as recruitment and retention. Comment on this statement.

2 How do we identify the key factors influencing enterprises' adoption or adjustment of specific HR policies and practices?

3 With regard to recruitment and selection, actual practice in these four Asian economies seems to be different. Identify the reasons why you think this is so.

4 What is the purpose of enterprises adopting a more advanced training and development policy and practices?

5 What is the role of the government in labour market development at the macro level and in reforming HR policy and practices at the enterprise level?

ITOCHU – a Japanese firm in the era of retrenchment and reform

The Japanese economy has been experiencing severe problems since the early 1990s, when its long-term national economic recession began to emerge. Enterprises have been under tremendous pressure since then to restructure their organisations and reform their people management systems. As one of the leading Japanese MNCs, ITOCHU may be seen as a leader in this era of Japanese reform and has adopted many new ways of people management into the company's routine HR practices. The areas of recruitment and retention, for instance, have been crucial aspects for developing innovative management practices and ensuring business survival. The following case is used as an example showing what changes have been made in adopting new ways of people management and in organisational restructuring. It covers changes that have been introduced up to the 150th anniversary of the company's founding.

Company Background

The history of ITOCHU Corporation dates back to 1858 when the founder Chubei Itoch commenced linen-trading operations. Since then, ITOCHU has evolved and grown into a 'sogo shosha' (general trading company), engaging in domestic trading, import/export, and overseas trading of various products, such as textiles, machinery, information and communications-related products, metals, products related to oil and other energy sources, general merchandise, chemicals, and provisions and food. In addition, ITOCHU has made multi-faceted investments in insurance, finance, construction, real estate trading and warehousing, as well as operations and businesses incidental or related to those fields (http://www.itochu.co.jp/). The total number of employees at the Tokyo headquarters was reduced from over 5,000 people in the early 2000s to the current level of 4,222 (excluding local employees working at overseas branches, offices and other subsidiaries), with a more robust organisational structure (see Figure 12.1) and an extensive global network (see Figure 12.2). The combined sales of Mitsubishi, Mitsui, ITOCHU, Sumitomo, Marubeni, and Nissho Iwai, Japan's top six *sogo sosha*, are nearly equivalent to the combined GDP of all of the countries in South America, and our case example is the third largest of these companies.

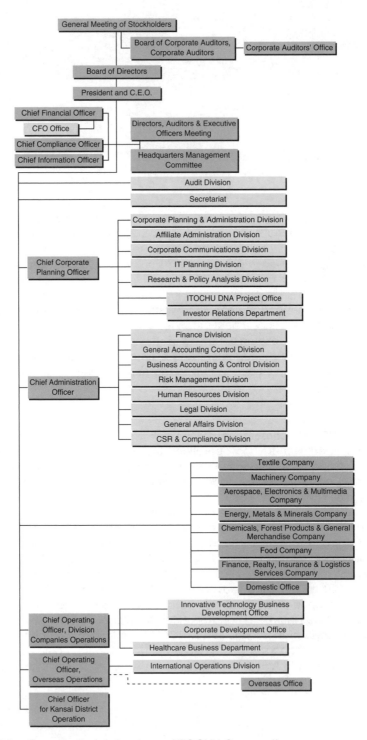

Figure 12.1   Organisational structure of ITOCHU Corporation

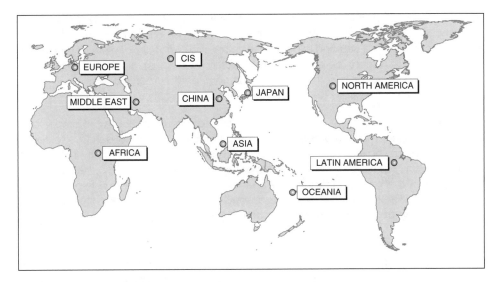

Figure 12.2   ITOCHU: global network

Under a former mid-term management plan 'Frontier-2006', ITOCHU obtained its objective of becoming a highly profitable corporate group achieving over ¥100 billion (the yen has been trading at around 92 to the US dollar at the time of writing) in consolidated net income in a steady and sustainable manner. ITOCHU then moved forward with the implementation of its new mid-term management plan, 'Frontier+ 2008', under which the management hope to adopt an even more aggressive management policy striving to enhance corporate value on the world stage, in order to become a global enterprise that is 'highly attractive to all stakeholders.'

As the President and CEO, Eizo Kobayashi pointed out:

> In the fiscal year ended March 2008, the Company posted consolidated net income of ¥218.6 billion – achieving record earnings for the fourth consecutive year. Without a doubt natural resource price hikes contributed to that favourable performance, but in addition, our growth strategies are steadily bearing fruit … Our medium-term management plan, *Frontier+ 2008* – Enhancing Corporate Value on the World Stage, will be ending in the fiscal year ending March 2009. We will be stepping up the pace of *aggressive* corporate management – based on measures for maintaining a global perspective, creating new initiatives, and enhancing human resources – to dramatically increase earnings.

Recruitment

The change in the area of employee resourcing and in particular recruitment is widespread. Generally speaking, two types of recruitment belong to the traditional system, namely: a) high school and vocational school graduate recruitment and b) college and university graduate recruitment. In recent years, new types of recruitment have emerged as part of HR policies to deal with unemployment, the ageing population and organisations' needs for special skills and experiences under circumstances of global competition and economic recession. These new types of recruitment are: c) mid-career professional recruitment, d) late-career (semi-retiree) recruitment, and e) foreign professional recruitment for special positions.

In recent years, government policy set out to promote greater mobility of employees. Two important schemes have been introduced, namely the 'shukko' scheme (external mobility) and the 'haken' scheme (internal mobility). This step has had its impacts on companies such as ITOCHU. Use of the schemes has gradually reduced the number of employees at the headquarters level. A number of people have been relocated into subsidiaries and more capable and experienced people have been recruited externally through the mid-career professional recruitment system.

HR retention

In recent years, HR retention policies have been re-designed through job allocation/ design and training and development. In ITOCHU, each department was in charge of job allocation and line managers made decisions on tasks and employees' responsibility. The more recent focus was on specialisation rather than job rotation and multi-tasking. Each department had HR personnel who had facilitating roles to support the line managers to handle the issues related to HR. The HR department at the top level of the company was only in charge of HR planning and other general issues, and not responsible for detailed job allocation.

In addition, in order to attract capable young people to join the organisation and promote long-term commitment, ITOCHU changed its ranking system from 9 grades into 6 grades. The company also made it possible for young talented people to be placed on a fast track for early promotion. The new systems of job design and promotion were based on performance assessment rather than seniority. Furthermore, training and development become the key element for people developing their skills and in return motivate higher commitment to the organisation. The most common practices include orientation training, formal and informal OJT and off-the-job training (OFJT). In ITOCHU, orientation training and formal OJT were compulsory with the former lasting 3 weeks and the latter lasting a year. Informal OJT was encouraged through team-based discussion and peer assistance. Specialist and managerial training programmes normally took OFJT forms that enabled the core technicians and managerial staff to enrol in professional training centres or institutions. Overseas training was also common and the company sent 30–40 young people to the US for three to four months training every year.

Discussion

The change in the macro-economic environment, in particular the global financial crisis of 2008, has been an important influence on the kind of HRM changes adopted in Japanese companies. As a leading MNC in Japan, ITOCHU has adopted some new practices alongside preserving conventional good practices. The case shows that substantial changes can occur in the areas of recruitment, job allocations, labour mobility as well as training and development. We see an increasing combination of 'East' and 'West' concepts of people management being adopted in such leading MNCs. In fact, the management philosophy has been adjusted to consider the 'traditional' dimensions of the well-being of stakeholders and company, as well as the new dimensions of market competition and foreign influence. This finding once again is consistent with our previous research on hybrid HRM systems – with a sense of balance between improving short-term efficiency, flexibility and competitiveness under the influence of globalisation and market-driven economy on the one hand, and maintaining a long-term humanist management philosophy with an Asian emphasis on harmony, care and equality, and a community orientation, on the other. This pattern seems to be a logical outcome of the on-going management transition in general in East Asia.

Sources: Company websites, reports and interviews.

Case questions
1 What are the key changes in the area of employee resourcing at ITOCHU during the recent economic restructuring?
2 How would you evaluate the effectiveness of the new HR retention policy at ITOCHU?
3 What are the driving forces for ITOCHU to adopt these changes?

Case questions for further study and reflection
1 Imagine you are the HR manager at ITOCHU. What would be your HR strategy to maintain the balance between traditional management philosophy and current market-oriented management practices?
2 Imagine you are the HR manager at ITOCHU. How do you introduce and develop the strategic role in the current HR management system?

Further reading

Journal articles
* Rowley, C. and Benson, J. (2002) 'Convergence and divergence in Asian HRM', *California Management Review*, 44 (2): 90–109.
This article provides a overview on similarity and difference of HR policy and practices among Asian countries.

* Rowley, C. and Warner, M. (2004) 'The Asian financial crisis: The impact on human resource management', *International Studies of Management and Organization*, 34: 3–9.

This article illustrates the impact of the Asian financial crisis on changes in HRM in Asia. It is useful for considering the current HR strategies used to cope with the economic crisis.

- Warner, M. (2000) 'Introduction: The Asia-Pacific HRM model revisited', *International Journal of Human Resource Management*, 11: 171–82.
This article highlights many of the key elements related to HRM practices in the Asia-Pacific region.

- Zhu, Y. (2004) 'Responding to the challenges of globalization: Human Resource Development in Japan', *Journal of World Business,* 39 (4): 337–48.
This article examines the changes in HRD policies and practices in Japan.

- Zhu, Y., Collins, N., Webber, M and Benson, J. (2008) 'New forms of ownership and human resource practices in Vietnam', *Human Resource Management*, 47: 157–75.
This article provides case studies of recent HR practices in Vietnamese enterprises with different systems of ownership.

Books and chapters in books

- Bae, J. and Rowley, C. (2004) 'Changes and continuities in South Korean HRM', in C. Rowley and J. Benson (eds), *The Management of Human Resources in the Asia Pacific Region: Convergence Reconsidered*. pp. 76–105. London: Frank Cass.
This chapter explains the concepts of HR competencies and employs the competency-based approach to analyse the company cases in South Korea.

- Beer, M., Spector, B., Lawrence, R., Quinn, M.D. and Walton, E. (1984) *Managing Human Assets*. New York: Free Press.
This book analyses strategic HR policy and emphasises the significance of its 'fit' with individual, organisational and societal needs and culture, and its importance for achieving long-range employment stability.

- Benson, J. (2005) 'Unemployment in Japan: globalization, restructuring and social change', in J. Benson and Y. Zhu (eds), *Unemployment in Asia*. pp. 39–57. London and New York: Routledge.
This chapter examines the background and factors influencing economic restructuring, change to government labour market policies and the unemployment problem in Japan.

- Boxall, P. and Purcell, L. (2003) *Strategy and Human Resource Management*. Basingstoke: Palgrave.
This book provides a comprehensive review of strategic HRM, its policies and practices.

- Storey, J. and Sisson, K. (1993) *Managing Human Resources and Industrial Relations*. Milton Keynes: Open University Press.
This book illustrates the relations between HRM and IR under the influence of globalisation and industrial restructuring.

Internet resources

1 Asian Business Management (www.apmforum.com/emerald/human-resource-asia.html): An archive of weekly themed reviews of free research articles on Asian business management.

2 Change and Diversity of HRM in Asia (www.apj.sage pub.com/cgi/content/): An online provider of research results for comparative HRM research in the Asia-Pacific region.

3 Asian Human Resource Sites (www.hrmguide.net/hrm/links/asia.html): An online provider of links with issues on HRM in Asia.

4 Employment Retention (www.themanager.org/Knowledgebase/HR: An online provider of useful information on employee retention.

5 Training, Development and Education for Employees (human resources.about.com/.../training/): An online provider of employee's training and development for organisations.

Self-assessment questions

Indicative answers to these questions can be found on the companion website at www.sagepub.co.uk/harzing3e.

1 **Why is it more important to adopt the HR competencies approach in HR policy formation?**
2 **What are the key external and internal factors influencing HR policy?**
3 **What are the labour market pressures in Japan forcing companies to adopt a more flexible HR policy?**
4 **What are the interrelationships between economic development stages and HR recruitment policy in Taiwan?**
5 **What are the key factors that influence HR policy under the economic reform in China?**

References

Bae, J. and Rowley, C. (2004) 'Changes and continuities in South Korean HRM', in C. Rowley and J. Benson (eds), *The Management of Human Resources in the Asia Pacific Region: Convergence Reconsidered*. pp.76–105. London: Frank Cass.

Beer, M., Spector, B., Lawrence, R., Quinn, M.D. and Walton, E. (1984) *Managing Human Assets*. New York: Free Press.

Benson, J. (2005) 'Unemployment in Japan: globalization, restructuring and social change', in J. Benson and Y. Zhu (eds), *Unemployment in Asia*. pp. 39–75. London and New York: Routledge.

Benson, J. and Debroux, P. (2004) 'Flexible labour markets and individualized employment: the beginnings of a new Japanese HRM system?', in C. Rowley and J. Benson (eds), *The Management of Human Resources in the Asia Pacific Region: Convergence Reconsidered*. pp. 55–75. London: Frank Cass.

Boxall, P. and Purcell, L. (2003) *Strategy and Human Resource Management*. Basingstoke: Palgrave.

Chen, S.J. (1997) 'The Development of HRM practices in Taiwan', *Asia Pacific Business Review*, 3(4): 152–69.

Chen, S.J. (1998) 'The development of HRM practices in Taiwan', in C. Rowley (ed.), *Human Resource Management in the Asia Pacific Region: Convergence Questioned*. pp.152–69. London: Frank Cass.

Child, J. (1994) *Management in China During the Age of Reform*. Cambridge: Cambridge University Press.

Cooke, F.L. (2005) *HRM, Work and Employment in China*. London and New York: Routledge.

Doanh, L.D. and Tran, T. C. (1998) 'The SOE reform policies in Vietnam and their implementation performance', in Ministry of Planning and Investment: Study on *Economic development policy in the transition toward a market-oriented economy in Vietnam, phase 2*. Hanoi: Ministry of Planning and Investment and Japan International Cooperation Agency, 4: 19–49.

Dowling, P. and Welch, E. (2004) *International Human Resource Management: Managing People in a Multinational Context*. Cincinnati, OH: South-Western.

Guest, D. (1989) 'Human resource management: Its implications for industrial relations and trade unions', in J. Storey (ed.), *New Perspectives on Human Resource Management*. pp. 41–55. London and New York: Routledge.

Hsu, Y. and Leat, M. (2000) 'A study of HRM and recruitment and selection policies and practices in Taiwan', *International Journal of Human Resource Management*, 11: 413–35.

Kochan, T.A., Katz, H.C. and McKersie, R.B. (1986) *The Transformation of American Industrial Relations*. New York: Basic Books.

Lee, J.S. (1995) 'Economic development and the evolution of industrial relations in Taiwan, 1950–1993', in A. Verma, T.A. Kochan and R.D. Lansbury (eds), *Employment Relations in the Growing Asian Economies*. pp. 88–118. London: Routledge.

Lien, B., Hung, R. and McLean, G. (2007) 'Organizational learning as an organization development intervention in six high-technology firms in Taiwan: An exploratory case study', *Human Resource Development Quarterly*, 18: 211–28.

Martin, R. and Bamber, J. (2005) International differences in employment relations: What are the relative merits of explanation in terms of strategic choice or political economy? Paper presented at the 19th Conference of the Association of Industrial Relations Academics of Australia and New Zealand, Sydney.

Murray, G., Levesque, C. and Vallee, G. (2000) 'The re-regulation of labour in a global context: conceptual vignettes from Canada', *Journal of Industrial Relations*, 42: 234–57.

Quang, T., Thang, L.C. and Rowley, C. (2008) 'The changing face of human resource management in Vietnam', in C. Rowley and S. Abdul-Rahman (eds), *The Changing Face of Management in South East Asia*. pp. 186–220. London: Routledge.

Rowley, C. and Abdul-Rahman, S. (eds) (2008) *The Changing Face of Management in South East Asia*. London: Routledge.

Rowley, C. and Benson, J. (eds) (2004) *The Management of Human Resources in the Asia Pacific Region: Convergence Reconsidered*. London: Routledge.

Rowley, C. and Cooke, F. (eds) (2009) *The Changing Face of Management in China*. London: Routledge.

Rowley, C. and Li, X. (2006) 'Chinese SMEs: development and HRM', in E. Mrudula and P. Raju (eds), *China: Trading Empire of the New Century*. pp. 108–19. India: ACFAI Press.

Rowley, C. and Li, X. (2008) 'The development of Chinese SMEs and HRM, *Asia* Pacific Journal of Human Resources, 46, (3): 353–79.

Rowley, C. and Quang, T. (eds) (2009) *The Changing Face of Management in Vietnam*. London: Routledge.

Storey, J. and Sisson, K. (1993) *Managing Human Resources and Industrial Relations*. Milton Keynes: Open University Press.

Thang, L.C. and Quang, T. (2005) 'Antecedents and consequences of dimensions of human resource management and practices in Vietnam', *International Journal of Human Resources Management*, 16: 1830–46.

Van Ruysseveldt, J. (1995) 'Growing cross-national diversity or diversity tout court? An introduction to comparative industrial and employment relations', in J. Van Ruysseveldt, R. Huiskamp and J. Van Hoof (eds), *Comparative Industrial and Employment Relations*. pp.1–15. London: Sage.

Wang, H.L. and Cooney, S. (2002) 'Taiwan's labour law: The end of state corporatism?', in S. Cooney, T. Lindsey, R. Mitchell and Y. Zhu (eds), *Law and Labour Market Regulation in East Asia*. pp. 185–214. London and New York: Routledge.

Warner, M. (2000) 'Introduction: The Asia-Pacific HRM model revisited', *International Journal of Human Resource Management*, 11: 171–82.

Warner, M. (ed.) (2008) *Human Resource Management 'with Chinese Characteristics'*. London and New York: Routledge.

Wei, Q., and Rowley, C. (2009) 'Changing patterns of rewards in Asia: A literature review', *Asia Pacific Business Review*, 15(4): 489–506.

Zhu, Y. (2004a) 'Responding to the challenges of globalization: Human resource development in Japan', *Journal of World Business*, 39(4): 337–48.

Zhu, Y. (2004b) 'The post Asia financial crisis: changes in HRM in Taiwanese enterprises', in C. Rowley and J. Benson (eds), *The Management of Human Resources in the Asia Pacific Region: Convergence Reconsidered*. pp. 147–64. London: Frank Cass.

Zhu, Y. (2005) 'Unemployment in Taiwan: Globalization, regional integration and social changes', in J. Benson and Y. Zhu (eds), *Unemployment in Asia*. pp. 79–96. London and New York: Routledge-Curzon.

Zhu, Y. and Fahey, S. (2000) 'The challenges and opportunities for the trade union movement in the transition era: two socialist market economies – China and Vietnam', *Asia Pacific Business Review*, 6: 282–99.

Zhu, Y. and Warner, M. (2002) 'Human resource management in China's 'frontier' special economic zone: A study of selected enterprises on Hainan Island', *International Journal of Employment Studies*, 10: 75–104.

Zhu, Y. and Warner, M. (2004) 'HRM in East Asia', in A.W. Harzing and J.V. Ruysseveldt (eds) *International Human Resource Management, 2nd ed.*, pp. 195–220. London: Sage.

Zhu, Y., Chen, I. and Warner, M. (2000) 'HRM in Taiwan: An empirical case study', *Human Resource Management Journal*, 10: 32–44.

13

Global Performance Management

Arup Varma and Pawan S. Budhwar

Contents

Learning Objectives

After reading this chapter you will be able to

- Identify the key components of an effective performance management system (PMS)

- Explain why PMSs developed for domestic employees aren't automatically usable at international locations

- Explain the role that a nation's culture plays in the effective execution of PMSs

- Compare and contrast PMSs in some leading world economies

- Design a comprehensive and effective PMS for an MNC

Chapter Outline

This chapter discusses the key issues related to performance management systems, with a special emphasis on performance evaluation. It also reviews the factors affecting PMSs, especially in global organisations, and presents the key features of PMSs in four leading economies.

1 Introduction

This chapter discusses performance management systems (PMS) in a global context, by identifying the key components of such systems. Next, we consider the key factors that can impact on organisational objectives of ensuring that managerial decisions are both consistent with corporate strategy and meet local contexts and needs. Then we review the role that a nation's culture can play in the effective execution of PMS, followed by a description of PMS in a few leading economies (e.g. USA, UK, China and India). This is followed by an overview of the unique nature and requirements of expatriate evaluation. Throughout the chapter, we present relevant research on PMS, with a special emphasis on MNEs. Finally, we end the chapter with a discussion of the reasons why organisations need to develop unique systems for each country and its cultural context, rather than simply implementing systems in the host country that were initially developed for the home country.

2 Key components of PMS

From a broad theoretical perspective, performance management systems (PMS) are designed to help organisations draw the best out of their employees, by enabling individual employees to perform at optimal levels. However, as we shall see, the execution of such systems is not always easy, and thus performance management practices frequently do not achieve their goals, with the result that both employees and their supervisors are often dissatisfied with the system. Indeed, as Deming (1986) argued (see Box 13.1), performance appraisals often have the opposite of their intended effect. In other words, if the system is not used properly, evaluations can lead to frustration, anger, and reduced motivation levels, rather than motivating employees to perform better!

Box 13.1   Performance appraisal (Deming, 1986)

The process of performance appraisal 'nourishes short-term performance, annihilates long-term planning, builds fear, demolishes teamwork, nourishes rivalry and politics ... It leaves people bitter, crushed, bruised, battered, desolate, despondent, dejected, feeling inferior, some even depressed, unfit for work for weeks after receipt of rating, unable to comprehend why they are inferior. It is unfair as it ascribes to the people in a group differences that may be caused totally by the system they work in.'

It should be clarified that while performance appraisals form a major part of performance management systems, and the terms are often used interchangeably, effective performance management comprises several other activities, including (i) setting goals/objectives, (ii) providing feedback, and (iii) motivating employees. We discuss these activities later in this chapter.

In terms of practice, performance evaluations traditionally have two main functions: first, they are often used for administrative decisions such as promotions, and merit raises, etc., and second, for developmental purposes such as coaching and feedback (Murphy and Cleveland, 1995). Thus, organisations typically require an individual's direct supervisor to evaluate the subordinate's performance once a year, and determine his/her ratings. These ratings form the basis for individual pay awards based on merit and may also be used to allocate bonuses. While most organisations have some form of performance management system in place, managers and employees often treat the process more as an administrative burden than a developmental tool. Indeed, the developmental role of such systems can provide managers with an effective mechanism to monitor and help improve employee performance levels, through continuous feedback and discussion. However, most managers are reluctant to give performance-based feedback to employees, as these discussions can often become uncomfortable and lead to participants being defensive.

In order for performance management systems to be effective, several key issues need to be addressed, and organisations have to ensure that critical components of such systems are in place. We discuss these below.

Goal-setting

First, it is critical that the supervisor set individual employees' goals for the coming year, through discussions with subordinates, keeping in mind the organisation's business strategy, and ensuring alignment of these goals with the department or business unit's objectives. Goals help employees to understand what is expected of them, and assist them in planning and prioritising their work accordingly. It is well-documented that individuals who have goals work better and are more productive than those who are not given goals, and must rely on their understanding of the job, and their title, to work on a day-to-day basis (Locke, 1968). Further, in order for goal-setting to be effective and for the individual to be able to use the goals in accomplishing his/her work, these goals should be (i) specific, (ii) measurable, (iii) attainable, (iv) relevant, and realistic, and (v) timely.

Feedback

In order for an individual to know how he/she is doing on the job, it is critical that supervisors provide regular feedback to employees (see Murphy and Cleveland, 1995). However, as we note above, the feedback process is rather complicated, and is often avoided by both managers and employees, especially in cases where the manager is required to give constructive or negative feedback. Timely feedback can help employees correct performance deficiencies and prevent errors from increasing. Thus, it is clear that, in spite of some reluctance, it is very important that managers provide feedback on a consistent basis, and deliver it in a spirit of constructive counselling. As such, organisations need to create a culture where feedback is easily accepted by all people concerned, and is seen as a critical part of the performance management process. In cases where managers deliver insufficient feedback, human resource departments may need to institute policies that mandate feedback-giving for managers, perhaps by requiring documentation of their feedback meetings.

Performance evaluation process guidelines

In order for annual evaluations to proceed smoothly and serve their critical purpose, it is essential that organisations establish comprehensive processes that are clearly spelt out in organisational handbooks or operating manuals. Further, all

Table 13.1   PMS tips for organisations

1 Decide, design and publicise the evaluation process
2 Clearly set the timing
3 Inform employees of the judgment criteria
4 Clarify individual roles in the PMS
5 Ensure clear and obvious links between performance and ratings; and ratings and outcomes.

employees should be made familiar with the form and content of the performance evaluation system in place in their organisation, so that they know what to expect, when to expect it, and how to go about achieving a fair and timely evaluation of employees' performance. The evaluations guidelines should clearly spell out the key features of the process, including (i) how the evaluation will be conducted (i.e., employee input, types of forms to be used, etc.), (ii) who will conduct the evaluation (i.e., immediate supervisor, divisional head, corporate office, etc.), (iii) when the evaluation will be conducted (i.e., annually, bi-annually, etc.), (iv) what is to be evaluated (traits, behaviours, outcomes), and (v) the potential rewards/penalties for the ratings received by the individual (i.e., merit raises, bonuses, promotions, terminations, etc.).

Each of the five steps shown in Table 13.1 is critical to the proper and fair execution of the appraisal process, and thus worthy of further discussion.

1 *How will the evaluation be conducted?* The process for conducting the evaluation should be spelt out clearly, with information on manager and employee responsibilities, dates and venues, and specific steps. The essence of this recommendation is that the performance appraisal (and feedback) process should not be a surprise. The employee should be well aware of his/her role – so, for example, if he/she is expected to fill out a self-evaluation, he/she can start well in advance of the scheduled meeting date, and not have to rush through the process. In addition, being aware of the process and the schedule can allow the employee to be prepared to explain any deviation in performance, and support his/her arguments with facts and figures.

2 *Who will conduct the evaluation?* This is an integral part of the process, and needs to be clearly articulated. From the perspective of fairness, it is important that the employee knows who is ultimately responsible for evaluating his/her performance, as this will help the employee to focus his/her efforts, as well as seek guidance and coaching from the supervisor. Too often, we hear complaints from individuals about having 'ten different bosses', all claiming that his/her tasks should be treated as priority. In the case of expatriates, this issue has added significance, as very often expatriates may report to someone at their location in terms of their day-to-day operational activities, and concurrently report to someone at

headquarters, on their strategic objectives. While organisational or departmental objectives sometimes make it necessary for an individual to work and report to several managers, such demanding situations can create confusion for individuals, thus resulting in lowered performance and motivation levels, unless the reporting relationship(s) is clearly laid out.

3   *When will the evaluation be conducted?* While most traditional PMS rely on the annual evaluation, there are numerous different models practised by organisations, including (a) quarterly evaluations, (b) bi-annual evaluations, (c) evaluations at the end of a project and (d) evaluations conducted when the manager has time or (e) no formal evaluations. Indeed, even the annual evaluation has different versions in practice, with some organisations evaluating all employees on or around a particular date, every year, while others conduct staggered evaluations, with individual employees evaluated yearly on the anniversary of their date of joining the organisation. Whichever method is followed, it is important that the employees be well aware of the timing. This will help them prepare for the evaluation, and be able to collect relevant performance information, for discussions. Too often, managers rely on conducting the evaluation when they find some time available. This *ad hoc* scheduling does not allow the employee to be mentally prepared for the evaluation; it often comes as a surprise, and does not support the seriousness and significance of the process.

4   *What will be evaluated?* The performance appraisal literature has continued to debate the merits of evaluating traits, behaviours and outcomes for several decades, without arriving at a definite conclusion (see DeNisi, 1996). Those in favour of evaluating traits argue that if an individual has the right traits, performance will automatically follow. As an example, if we believe an employee has high levels of sincerity and conscientiousness, he or she is likely to perform well. Those that are in favour of evaluating behaviours argue that possessing certain desirable traits does not automatically guarantee acceptable or higher levels of performance. Thus, an individual may be very sincere and loyal, but may consistently produce sub-standard work, though it might be completed well before the deadline. In addition, some have argued that evaluating personality traits like sincerity is akin to passing judgment on an individual, and that it is preferable to restrict judgments to an employee's work. The third option is often popular with managers who are primarily, if not solely, driven to achieve revenue targets – thus the exclusive emphasis on outcomes and results. The danger of the third option is that employees may be driven to cheat, as they are aware that they will only be evaluated on their results, and not how they achieved them. Further, this option does not allow managers to use the high performers' behaviours to develop new employees, as the primary information available is all about outcomes. In addition, there are numerous jobs where results are not immediately available, and thus behaviours, and sometimes traits, are what can be evaluated. For example, for over 20 years now, thousands of researchers around the world have been working on finding a cure for AIDS. While a cure hasn't been found yet, this

does not imply that the individuals have not performed at acceptable levels, or even exceeded expectations, for that matter. So, the question is – what should be evaluated – just traits, just behaviours, or just outcomes – or, all three? This decision will depend on the organisation's culture, its objectives and its management philosophy. In addition, the national culture will also have an impact, since many countries emphasise traits over behaviours and/or results. What is important is that companies decide what will be evaluated, and share this information with their employees.

5 *Potential consequences of evaluation* One of the reasons employees often dislike PMS, and more specifically their evaluations, is that they don't see any connection between their performance and the rewards obtained. In order for employees to take the process of evaluation and feedback seriously, it is critical that they see a logical and causal relationship between the PMS and the outcomes. So, if an employee is evaluated as having exceeded performance expectations, he/she should receive rewards that are commensurate with that level of performance. As reinforcement theory (Skinner, 1953) suggests, desired levels of performance will be repeated if the outcomes are seen as positive, while neutral or negative outcomes will lead to the likelihood that the behaviour is not repeated.

Another way that this phenomenon often plays out is when the ratings themselves do not reflect the actual performance level(s). This is most often seen in organisations that have implemented forced distribution of ratings, whereby no more than a certain percentage (say, 10 per cent) of a manager's direct reports (or a department's workforce) can be rated as having exceeded expectations, and roughly the same percentage (i.e., 10 per cent) must be rated as having performed below expectations. In theory, this sounds like a great system, as it will motive everyone to work harder, since (i) they know that slots in the top category are limited, and (ii) they presumably will want to avoid being placed in the low category. In addition, it enables the organisation to identify its top performers and concentrate efforts on retaining them, and the organisation might also replace the bottom 10 per cent with better performers or new recruits.

In practice, this does not work out so well, and it is easy to see why. Let's say a manager objectively evaluates his/her staff, and finds that 30 per cent have performed in an outstanding fashion and thus have exceeded expectation. In the true spirit of reinforcement, he/she must rate them accordingly, and recommend commensurate merit-based rewards. However, the forced distribution will allow him/her to rate only 1/3rd of this high performing group at that level – the others will be told to continue to work hard, and hope they get into the top 10 per cent the following year. Not only does this lead to a system-sponsored distortion of ratings, the individuals who are not rated as deserved have an incentive to work less hard the next year, as they will lose confidence in the validity of the PMS.

Training

For efficient and effective conduct of the performance management process, it is critical that organisations train all managers who are responsible for supervising individuals. The training should familiarise managers with (i) the performance management process at the organisation, (ii) the objectives and philosophy behind the process, and (iii) the tools used in the process (i.e., rating forms and scales, etc.). In addition, training can help managers learn how to avoid potential biases and errors, such as halo and recency effects. Where relevant, organisations should also provide training for employees, so that they may play a participative role in the performance management process, rather than be passive recipients. Thus, for example, if the organisation provides employees the opportunity for self-evaluation, they should be trained in how to complete the form objectively, using relevant performance data. In addition, performance management training can be very helpful in preparing both managers and employees for a meaningful and productive exchange during feedback meetings.

3 Key factors affecting PMS

While the above guidelines apply to all organisations, it should be noted that performance management does not occur in a vacuum, and that there are numerous factors that can affect the success or failure, no matter how well-intentioned or well-designed the systems. In their recently published comprehensive model of the appraisal process, Murphy and DeNisi (2008) have identified several key factors that can directly or indirectly affect the performance management process in any organisation. The authors group these factors under five categories: (i) distal factors (e.g., national or cultural norms, technology), (ii) proximal factors (e.g., purpose of appraisal, and organisational norms), (iii) judgment factors (e.g., time pressures and availability of standards), (iv) intervening factors (supervisor–subordinate relationships and rater motivation), and (v) distortion factors (e.g., consequences of appraisal and reward systems).

We draw upon the authors' model to emphasise five critical issues (one from each of the authors' five factor-groups) that, in our opinion, need to be addressed by human resource managers, in order to design and execute successful PMS, *especially* in global organisations.

Technology

The technological advances made over the last three decades have had a clear impact on human resource systems in organisations. In many cases, technology has made the work of HR departments easier and faster. So, for example, HR professionals

Table 13.2 Key factors affecting PMS

1 Technology
2 Purpose
3 Performance standards
4 Supervisor–subordinate relationships
5 Reward systems

no longer need to wade through numerous employee files to identify how many employees have college degrees or a specific skill that the organisation needs. Human Resource Information Systems (HRIS) are commercially available that enable the HR professional to access such information from the company's database in seconds. Needless to say, technology has also made inroads into PMS, with several software applications available to track, monitor, record and rate employees' performance, often on an on-going basis. In addition, global organisations can now receive almost instant information on individual performance, through computer-monitoring for example, and provide necessary feedback in a timely manner, thus avoiding the traditional problems of time delay in communications between locations. However, caution needs to be exercised in the use of technology for performance management systems and processes. First, no amount of sophistication in technology can replace the value of face-to-face interaction between an employee and his/her manager. Next, managers should be careful not to become overly reliant on computer-generated data for making judgments, and must ensure the individual is given an opportunity to explain any variance in performance. Finally, the quality and reach of technology vary substantially between nations and across regions, so managers should ensure that employees throughout the organisation are able to access and use computer-based systems with equal ease.

Purpose of appraisal

The purpose of the appraisal can have significant impact on the conduct and acceptance of the appraisal system and results. Thus, if the appraisal is designed for administrative purposes, such as performance evaluation and pay increases, the individual's immediate supervisor is most likely going to be responsible for evaluating the employee, and determining merit awards. Further, the purpose of the appraisal is also likely to impact on the manager's use of data, and may influence his/her motivation to be objective in conducting the evaluation. Thus, if the manager is interested in getting one of his/her subordinates promoted or awarded a substantial merit increase, it is possible that he/she could distort the data and its interpretation in order to justify his/her recommendations. In addition, the manager is likely to rely heavily on performance data available, and collected by him/her. On the other hand, if the purpose of the appraisal is to provide developmental feedback to subordinates, managers are more likely to try and supplement their evaluation with information from the employee's peers, and subordinates, clients and customers, where relevant. In 360 degree appraisal, the manager has the benefit of multiple sources and raters and may be more motivated to analyse and interpret the data more objectively, when preparing feedback for the employee. Finally, in countries where the appraisal might be seen as a mere formality, and where the manager might be motivated more by the need to 'take care'of his/her team members (Varma, et al., 2005a) than provide objective evaluations, the whole process may lose its original objective.

Performance standards

In addition to setting objectives, it is essential that performance standards be established and shared with the employee at the beginning of the performance period. Once performance standards are established (i.e., acceptable vs. unacceptable performance, etc.) and shared with the employee, subsequent evaluations of the candidate can then be measured against these standards (see also, Bobko and Colella, 1994). Thus, an employee will know before he/she begins work how it will be judged at the conclusion of the period under review. So, for example, let us say it is established that a rating of 5 on the dimension 'quality of customer service' (on a 5-point scale, with 5 being the highest possible level of performance and 1 being the lowest possible level) can only be obtained by individuals who have zero customer complaints during the evaluation period. An individual who has even a single case of a customer complaint should know that the best rating he/she can achieve on this dimension is a 4. Providing clear standards reduces unpleasant surprises and makes it easier for employees to keep track of how they are performing, by periodically measuring their achievements against the established standards. In addition, this practice can motivate employees to be more proactive and seek out feedback, so they know more about which dimensions they should improve on their performance.

Supervisor–subordinate relationships

The leader–member exchange theory (Graen and Cashman, 1975) posits that most individuals in managerial roles do not treat all their subordinates the same. Instead, consciously or sub-consciously, managers create in-groups and out-groups among those who report to them. The managers' relationships with individuals in his/her in-group are characterised by higher quality interactions and more attention and support from the supervisor, as compared to his/her relationship with subordinates in the out-group. Further, research has also consistently shown that individuals in a manager's in-group receive significantly higher performance ratings than those in the out-groups, even when they have performed at the same level (Varma and Stroh, 2001). It is worth noting here that while the initial research on leader–member exchange was conducted in the United States, empirical trials of this theory in other countries (e.g., India and Japan) have also reported the same pattern of results (Wakabayashi et al., 1988; Varma et al., 2005b). Thus, it is critical that the training that managers receive on performance management actually includes information on (i) the potential for them to create in-groups and out-groups, (ii) advice on how to avoid creating preferential groups, and (iii) specific means of ensuring that evaluations are based on objective performance data and are not biased by their relationships with their subordinates.

Reward systems

In relation to reward systems, Murphy and DeNisi (2008) have argued that organisations often punish managers for providing accurate ratings, and reward them for distorting ratings, thus leading managers to avoid giving accurate ratings. Specifically, in organisations that practice forced distribution of ratings, managers are required to assign a fixed percentage of their team members into set categories. So, for example, a manager might be required to place a minimum of 10 per cent of his direct reports as having performed at 'unacceptable' levels, and no more than 10 per cent at levels 'exceeding expectations', with the remaining 80 per cent being rated as having performed at 'acceptable' levels. Clearly, it is very rare that the performance of individuals on any manager's team will follow the exact proportions mandated by a pre-established system of forced distribution. For example, one manager may have a situation where half his team has performed outstandingly exceeding performance expectations. However, if he/she were to rate all of them at the highest level, the HR department will most likely return the set of ratings back to the manager, and ask him/her to 'fit' the individuals into the required pattern of distribution. In reality, in this situation the manager is required to distort the assessment by presenting inaccurate ratings. If the manager then refuses to adjust the ratings to fit the distribution, he/she might even be 'punished' for this transgression. Clearly, such reward/punishments systems lead managers to distort their ratings – in other words, providing ratings that 'do not reflect the judgment made about the subordinate's performance'.

We believe that there is another way that reward systems can work – as a motivating tool to ensure that managers take the performance management process seriously (thus, an intervening factor, in Murphy and DeNisi's typology). It is well known that most managers consider the performance management process a 'necessary evil', and many believe that the system is kept alive by HR departments to justify their existence. Here, managers look to the organisation's senior management team to get a sense of how they view performance management, and the importance they attach to the process and its outcomes. While organisational handbooks and policy manuals may detail how the PMS works, and the manager's role in executing it, managers are unlikely to take the process seriously unless there are rewards and/or punishments associated with the process. Thus, if an organisation wants its managers to treat the process as an integral part of their own roles, it should allot a certain percentage of the manager's own evaluation to how well he/she conducts the PMS with his/her team members. Here, organisations could track (i) whether goals and objectives were provided to each subordinate at the beginning of the year, (ii) how often managers meet with their team members to provide feedback, (iii) whether appraisals are given on time, and (iv) the extent that the administrative decisions recommended by the manager reflect the subordinate's actual performance. Ironically, in most cases, the manager's own evaluation is based solely on his/her ability to meet revenue targets and generate profits. Unless managers are formally evaluated for their conduct within the performance management of their subordinates, they will continue to treat PMS more or less as an unnecessary burden.

4 The impact of culture on PMS

Following the publication of Hofstede's classic treatise on cultural comparisons of various nations (1980), management scholars have paid close attention to the impact of national culture on organisations. While Hofstede's methods have subsequently been criticised (all his data were collected from employees of one organisation – IBM), there is no denying the fact that he alerted both scholars and practitioners to the critical role of culture, especially in international organisations.

Specifically, Hofstede proposed five dimensions of culture:

1　Power distance – the degree to which people accept status and authority differences between themselves and their supervisors
2　Individualism vs. collectivism – the degree to which people find their identity, or define themselves, as unique individuals, versus seeking group-identity
3　Masculinity versus femininity – where masculine cultures are defined by assertiveness, competitiveness, success, etc., and feminine cultures are known for being relationship-oriented and valuing quality of life issues
4　Uncertainty avoidance – the degree to which people seek structure versus their willingness to accept unstructured situations
5　Long-term versus short-term orientation – deals with whether the culture emphasises long-term commitments and respect for tradition, while short-term orientation emphasises the now and here, and change is more readily acceptable.

Drawing upon the Hofstede typology, it is easy to see how a nation's culture might impact on practices related to PMS. For example, the United States scores 40 on power distance, meaning low acceptance of status and hierarchy differences, while India scores a rather high 77 when measured against the world average of 56.5. Thus, in this instance, individuals are more likely to accept, often without argument, downward supervisor feedback in India, than they are in the United States. So, a company that operates in both nations will have to adapt its PMS practices and feedback mechanism, as managers are less likely to be willing to receive upward feedback in India. Similarly, in a country like China, that is known for collectivistic values, people prefer group-based, rather than individual-focused training (Earley, 1994) and may respond better to group-based, rather than individual-focused feedback (van de Vliert et al., 2004).

Culture can also influence how supervisors evaluate their subordinates. For example, Varma et al. (2005a) reported that managers in India gave significantly higher ratings to employees that they liked, awarding much beyond the level warranted by their performance. Such behaviour is often motivated by culturally accepted practices, such as the need to protect and support members of one's in-group, even though the performance of such members may not warrant the high ratings awarded to them. In a similar vein, Law et al. (2000) reported that managers in China are likely to go out of their way to help subordinates with whom they share high quality relationships.

Clearly, the culture of a nation can have a significant impact on how performance is viewed, evaluated and managed. Thus, organisations would do well to take this into account in designing their PMS for different cultures. A word of caution is appropriate here – as is well-known, culture is not a static concept, and keeps changing, with the rate of change dependent on a number of factors. For example, the recent economic growth of China is creating a group of individuals who are slowly moving away from collectivistic values – this shift is often seen among those working for MNCs. Thus, organisations need to attend to the shifts in culture, as they attempt to adjust and adapt their HR systems – and, clearly, these systems need to be audited on a continuous basis, to ensure that they accurately reflect the times.

5 PMS in four leading economies (USA, UK, China, India)

In this section, we present some of the key features of PMS in some of the world's leading economies, specifically the United States, the United Kingdom, China and India. We recognise that this is a short and incomplete list – however, our purpose here is to demonstrate some of the differences in how PMS operate in these countries, and thus emphasise the general importance of creating systems that serve corporate objectives while at the same time ensuring they remain consistent with local realities.

PMS in the USA

In their comprehensive summary of PMS in the USA, Pulakos and colleagues (2008) argue that history of the USA, and its fundamentally individualistic culture have had a significant impact on the workplace and performance management practices. Thus, individual performance, accountability and performance-linked rewards, form an integral part of the performance management process. As the authors argue, it is difficult to identify a single PMS as being the American system, given that almost every type and size of business exists in the US. However, there are some clear themes that emerge from a review of the PMS in the US.

1 PMS are primarily used for administrative purposes, such as awarding merit raises, and informing promotion decisions, with the use of PMS for developmental purposes remaining rather limited.
2 There is a very strong focus on results – thus, performing the desired behaviours, or demonstrating the right traits will not suffice.
3 The legal system is very well attuned to organisational issues – and there are numerous reported instances of individual legal challenges to performance-related decisions.
4 There is an ongoing emphasis on the use of technology in PMS, thus facilitating the easy access and sharing of performance information.
5 Acceptance of, and trust in, PMS continues to be rather low, and both managers and employees report dissatisfaction with the process and its outcomes.

PMS in the UK

PMS in the United Kingdom have a long history, and most UK organisations use some form of PMS. As Sparrow (2008) notes, PMS in the UK may be classified as being 'mature', with the ability to adapt to changes in UK's socio-economic, political and legal frameworks.

The key features of PMS in the UK are:

1 There is significantly more emphasis on the developmental aspect of performance management, as compared to the US.
2 There is an on-going emphasis on cost effectiveness.
3 A recent emphasis on 'talent management' requires PMS to be able to identify and reward 'high talent' employees.
4 There is a new emphasis on total rewards management, which has led to the development of PMS that assess and reward individual performance, in terms of both monetary and non-monetary rewards.
5 There is, however, an ongoing need to address issues such as work-life balance, rater bias and diversity.

PMS in China

The next two countries included in this section are known to be culturally very different from the two discussed above. Both China and India are relatively collectivist nations, with an emphasis on relationship-building in the workplace. Interestingly, PMS have existed in both these countries for much longer than one might expect. As Cooke (2008) notes, a Chinese version of assessment tools performance appraisal has been practised in China for a very long time. The key features of current PMS practice in China follow.

1 Since the late 1980s there has been widespread implementation of performance management systems, both in the private and the public sectors.
2 PMS in China continue to have strong influences from the culture, including respect for age and seniority, and the emphasis on harmony and face.
3 The collectivist nature of society means that group-based evaluations and feedback are often preferred to individual evaluations and feedback.
4 However, there is still a strong emphasis on traits and behaviours, and less on outcomes, as opposed to PMS in the US.
5 PMS are often seen as an administrative formality.
6 The validity and reliability of these systems often suffer from high levels of subjectivity in the evaluations exercised by managers.

PMS in India

As we note above, PMS have existed in India for rather a long time. Indeed, the public sector has used confidential evaluations of civil servants and other government employees for over a century. Several private sector organisations (e.g., Tata Steel) have also had formal evaluations in place for the same period. However, the PMS keep evolving with socio-economic and cultural changes, and the key features of current PMS include:

1 The recent advent of numerous MNCs into Indian business has caused many domestic firms to review their PMS, and many report revising and upgrading their existing systems.
2 There is a clear shift in the workplace, from traditional collectivist values to more of an individual orientation.
3 Individual employees often expect and appreciate immediate and short-term rewards.
4 The paternalistic nature of the culture continues to influence PMS, as many blue-collar employees rely on their supervisors to 'take care of them'. As we discussed above, this can often lead to inflated ratings being awarded by managers.
5 On the other hand, white-collar professionals, especially those working in technology-related jobs, pride themselves in having the skills to manage their careers.
6 One of the significant challenges faced by organisations in designing PMS for their Indian operations is the significant diversity of the Indian workforce, which comprises individuals who belong to numerous different ethnicities and religions, and speak a variety of different languages.

6 PMS for expatriates

Expatriate assignments play a critical role in multinational organisations, and thus it is imperative that organisations find ways to ensure they have high rates of success.

Expatriate PMS can provide critical measures of the success of an organisation's strategic objectives, as well as be an important means of evaluating the expatriate's actual on-the-job performance. However, as Tung and Varma (2008) have noted, it seems that expatriate performance evaluations are based primarily on systems developed for domestic purposes, both in US and non-US MNCs. Clearly, this is an issue that warrants attention both from MNC executives and scholars, as performance issues are context-driven and should be evaluated accordingly (Murphy and Cleveland, 1995). In addition, it is important that MNCs clearly define the parameters of expatriate performance (Shaffer et al., 2006). Hitherto, several different criteria have been used to measure expatriate effectiveness, although these are not consistent across organisations (Gregersen et al., 1996; Shih et al., 2005). Finally, as Yan and colleagues (2002) argue, the expatriate's own goals should also form an integral part of the evaluation system.

In addition to designing appraisal systems based on the expatriate's specific job objectives, expatriate PMS should incorporate the unique environmental factors related to the host country, such as laws, technology (Shen, 2005) and cultural norms (Tahvanainen, 2000). Another issue that needs to be addressed is the issue of host country national (HCN) categorisation. Several scholars (see, for example, Toh and DeNisi, 2007) have argued that expatriates often have to rely on HCNs for information that can help them on their assignments. However, as Toh et al., (2004) argue, HCNs are likely to share information only with those expatriates whom they accept into their in-groups, due to perceived shared values, or other similarities. Indeed, HCN categorisation of expatriates can be based on a whole range of factors, such as collectivism and ethnocentrism (Zeira, 1979), etc. Recent empirical investigations of HCN categorisation have reported that this phenomenon operates in numerous countries, and thus clearly is worthy of further attention. For example, Varma and colleagues (2006) examined HCN attitudes towards expatriates in India and the United States. These authors found that Indian HCNs (both male and female) would prefer to work with female expatriates from the US rather than male expatriates. In another study, Varma and colleagues (2009), found that Chinese HCNs categorised expatriates from both the US and India into in-groups and out-groups, based on their personal levels of collectivism, and guanxi. Finally, Varma and colleagues (in press) report similar results from their investigation in the United Kingdom. Clearly, the conditions on the ground in the host country are likely to be different, depending on the location of the expatriate's assignment, and have a significant impact on the expatriate's ability to do his/her job. Further, since the goals of expatriate assignments vary between locations, it is clear that expatriate evaluation mechanisms should incorporate the context or unique circumstances of the expatriate's assignment. After all, performance management is the medium through which the organisation can assess the expatriate's performance, and thus gauge the success of the organisation's strategic objectives (Dowling and Schuler, 1990).

7 Summary and conclusions

In this chapter, we have discussed PMS in a global context, and tried to emphasise the unique nature of such systems. We commenced by discussing the core components of PMS, followed by a discussion of the key factors that can impact on such systems. We included the all-important discussion of national culture, especially as it relates to people-related systems. We also provided an overview of PMS in four leading economies (USA, UK, China and India), to establish the principal differences that one might see in PMS implemented in different cultures. This was followed by a review and assessment of the unique nature and requirements of expatriate evaluations. Throughout the chapter, we have presented relevant research on PMS, with special emphasis on multinational corporations (MNCs). We concluded our discussion by emphasising the main reasons why organisations need to develop unique systems for each country in which they operate, rather than simply transferring systems developed for the home country environment.

As Tung and Varma (2008) have argued, globalisation is here to stay, and will continue to grow for the foreseeable future. This makes the role of the multinational corporation (MNC) critical in the economic and socio-political well-being of nations around the world. While organisations may be able to adapt home-based financial and technical systems to the new location, people-related systems do not lend themselves so easily to cross-national transfer, as they are the most context-driven of all organisational systems. Specifically, the subject of performance management presents unique challenges, as it is heavily impacted by local issues, such as national culture and practices – yet, performance management is the primary process through which organisations set goals, assign and evaluate work, and measure successful implementation of business strategy. While all organisations face similar challenges, the strategies adopted to address the challenges will often depend on the organisation's home country and host countries. In other words, the differences in culture, laws, technology, or simply past practices, makes it very difficult to directly apply systems from one setting to another.

We concentrated on MNCs in our discussion above, as these organisations are the ones most affected by the issues. For organisations that operate solely in a domestic region, the issues are different and much more localised. Setting aside the necessity of competing on PMS, they have the luxury of deciding whether to develop their own systems, adopt foreign-developed systems, or even having no system at all. As long as their practices conform to local legal and social requirements, they are not 'burdened' by the necessity to adapt or adopt other systems. Due to their global reach and diversity, MNCs need to operate according to a different set of principles and rules.

At first sight, it may seem that the transfer of PMS across countries is relatively easy, since the majority of MNCs originated in the US, and the majority of other nations seem to have adopted some version of PMS first developed in the US. Thus, one might suggest that all MNCs have to do is to take their existing systems and tweak them slightly to account for cultural differences. However, this is an overly simplistic view. First, it is reasonable to assume that as economies like China and India grow and become leaders, some influential individuals and groups in these nations will demand more 'local' systems that address locally relevant issues such as collectivism, deference to seniority and issues of face. At the same time, employees of MNCs in these and other similar nations will also demand that they be treated on par with their counterparts in western nations, in terms of compensation, and evaluation and promotion practices. Coordinating and satisfying this set of conflicting demands placed on organisations and their HR departments will require the finesse of a fine balancing act. These systems cannot be developed and left alone to run themselves, they have to be maintained and improved to ensure that they remain current and appropriate. This is not to say that MNCs have solely emerged from the west or the US in particular, but there is no denying that such MNCs have dominated global business for more than 50 years. Indeed, there is a new generation of MNCs emerging on the global business scene – demonstrated by acquisitions such as the purchase of IBM's personal computer division by China's Lenovo, and India's Tata group acquiring Jaguar and Land Rover. This new trend of MNCs arising from countries around the world is adding a new and somewhat complex dimension to the development and implementation of appropriate systems for managing people.

We hope we have been able to make it clear why PMS should be adopted following critical evaluation and after making appropriate modifications. As should be clear by now, in addition to ensuring that organisations have proper PMS in place, it is critical that the PMS be relevant to the environment – especially in the case of global organisations. As Goderis of Underwriters Laboratories Inc. notes, the emphasis on having a sophisticated system should not override the practical need to have a system that is appropriate to the location (see Box 13.2), and emphasises the main purpose of PMS – which is to encourage optimal levels of performance.

Box 13.2 Global PMS according to Goderis

'As someone directly involved in global PMS design and implementation for over a decade, I have seen everything – from manager and employee apathy, to engagement, tears, frustration, disbelief, and yes performance excellence too. As our organisation and culture has evolved, we have modified our PMS to align with, and support

(Continued)

(Continued)

business changes while balancing the needs and concerns of our employees. Over the years, our PMS has evolved, along with the business – today we have a simple, single globally consistent approach, anchored by a strong set of global behavioural competencies, supported by a robust and flexible HRIS tool. Of course, we will make changes again – if anyone could design the perfect PMS, history would be made and we would all be wealthy ... but human beings, even more so than MNEs, are complex entities, and never perfect, so my recommendation to HR professionals in MNEs is not to spend their time trying to come up with a perfect global PMS – instead, what we need is simplicity, with a 'glocal' (globally consistent and locally appropriate) flavour, in an effort to continually motivate the best employee performance possible. Therein lie our challenge, and our future.'

Josh Goderis, CCP, PHR
Director Global Talent Management
Underwriters Laboratories Inc.

Indeed, it is critical that HR practitioners everywhere critically evaluate the PMS before adopting it – systems developed in the US, or elsewhere, may not be automatically appropriate for implementation in other locations. Most HR systems and practices are context-specific, but performance-related systems are even more so, as performance may not be defined the same way in different locations and in different organisations. Practitioners should judge the suitability of the systems and adapt/modify them, as necessary. As has been noted above, feedback systems designed for a low power distance culture like the US will likely fail in high power distance cultures like China and India, unless the systems are modified to reflect local realities.

As more and more organisations around the world begin to introduce and implement performance management techniques, it is important that HR professionals do not uncritically import a policy or practice simply because it has worked somewhere else. Such a strategy is likely to be counter-productive, as it will fail to yield the desired results, and may even end up negatively impacting on performance. If creating a home-grown system is not practical, and one must import the PMS from headquarters, the key is to select the best of the system, and modify it such that it is like it was developed for local needs.

As DeNisi and colleagues (2008) note, 'Visitors to India will find that McDonalds doesn't sell hamburgers but sells vegetable burgers. This "Indianization" of the hamburger seems to be exactly the approach we need in the area of performance management. As countries develop more sophisticated systems they should learn from other countries, but also make sure that, where needed, they modify existing programmes to fit with local "tastes."'

Discussion questions

1 Assume you are a management consultant to a leading MNC. The senior management team there insists that performance management is a waste of time. How would you convince them of the importance of PMS?

2 Many managers argue that they should have the same PMS (including having the same appraisal forms) across all international locations, for purposes of consistency. What is your reaction to this assertion? Please justify your response with specifics.

3 Almost every article on global performance management emphasises the critical role played by the culture of the host countries in the conduct of PMS. Provide some examples of how culture impacts PMS.

4 'Given the unique situation under which expatriates operate, and the fact that they are often sent on fixed-term assignments, there is no need to conduct formal PMS for expatriates. One can simply judge their performance by whether or not they completed the assignment.' Discuss this statement, and justify your responses.

V-Pharmel Performance Management Case

V-Pharmel is an integrated consumer products company, producing a wide range of quality, affordable household products, with a mission to provide a better life for citizens of the world. It has been ranked on numerous lists amongst the top 100 'preferred employers'. The company has manufacturing facilities in 14 countries, and its products are sold in over 90 countries around the world. The excerpt below, from the company's website, is intended to demonstrate its management philosophy.

> V-Pharmel is committed to values-based leadership, and the ethical treatment of all its constituencies. In keeping with our philosophy, we will uphold the highest ethical integrity in all business transactions, and practise the following values in all our transactions, both inside and outside the company:
>
> 1 Honesty and integrity in all our dealings – with co-workers, customers, clients, and all others.
> 2 Respect for each other's individuality, and diversity in all its forms.
> 3 Being a responsible corporate social citizen.
> 4 Maintaining a profit-orientation, without compromising our values.

The case of the management trainee

V-Pharmel has a comprehensive Management Trainee (MT) scheme, whereby they hire MTs from the top-ranked business schools in the US, and put them through a 2-year training programme, after which the trainee is assigned to a functional area, and assigned the title of Specialist.

In August 2007, they hired five MTs for the Marketing department – four from schools in the US, and one from Singapore. This was the first time they had hired internationally for the MT scheme, and AJ was the only 'foreigner' in the Marketing department. The MTs had similar backgrounds, in that they had Bachelor's degrees in the arts, and had specialised in Marketing in their graduate studies. However, AJ, the MT from Singapore, was the only one in the group who had worked in consumer products sales for four years, inbetween his Bachelor's and Master's. The other four had gone straight from undergraduate to graduate studies. Due to AJ's experience, he was assigned to work directly with Scott, the head of Marketing, while the other four were assigned to heads of product development teams within the marketing department. The MT scheme was supervised by Jim, the head of HR.

AJ's evaluation experience

According to AJ, Scott was very polite and respectful towards him, and often told him that the first year of an MT's career should be spent learning the ropes and getting to know the people. However, Scott rarely gave him any work of substance, and whenever AJ stopped by to speak with Scott, he was asked to come by later, as Scott was 'busy'. AJ remarked that, very often, when he stopped by to speak with Scott, he could hear Scott chatting about movies or dinners with other colleagues.

Sometime in March 2008, six months into the probationary period for the MTs, the five supervisors met with Jim, to discuss the progress of the MTs. Each supervisor spoke briefly about the MT assigned to him/her, and then filled out the appraisal form, and submitted it to Jim. Normally, the MTs were not invited to this meeting. Instead, Jim met with them individually, and gave them a letter he had written, based on the supervisor's comments. After the conclusion of the March meeting, one of the supervisors, Susan, stopped by AJ's cubicle, and informed him that Scott had given him a very negative report at the meeting, and that he should expect a 'tough' meeting with Jim, with the high probability that his contract might be terminated.

AJ approached Jim, and wanted to talk about what 'he had heard' (since he did not want to reveal Susan's name). Jim told him there was 'nothing to worry about', and that he would meet with him (and the other MTs) in a few days. Over the next week, Jim met with the MTs individually, and gave them feedback about their performance to this point. AJ was scheduled to be the last one to meet with Jim. AJ checked with the other MTs about their meetings, and they all reported being very pleased with their reports, having received all fours and fives on their forms. On Friday at 4, AJ met with Jim in his office, and Jim presented him with a two-page letter, detailing Scott's evaluation of AJ's performance. While AJ was prepared for a somewhat negative report, based on Susan's friendly warning, he was shocked to see that he had been rated one on all five categories (see sample form below).

AJ tried to explain to Jim that he had never been given any indication of problems with his performance, and that Scott was always very pleasant to him, and kept telling him that he needed to 'get his feet wet' the first year, as later on he would be swamped with work. Jim told AJ not to worry about the report – that he was confident that subsequent reports would be much better. Over the weekend, AJ kept wondering what had gone wrong, and why he had received such a big surprise. He had always been to work on time, often stayed late reading company manuals and reports, and since Scott barely gave him any work, he spent a lot of time speaking to other managers and taking copious notes, to learn about the company. Yet, he had been evaluated so poorly, that he began to wonder if he had chosen the wrong company – indeed, he wondered, if he had chosen the wrong profession.

He kept looking at the letter, written and signed by Jim, whom he considered a friend, yet the contents were not friendly, by any stretch of imagination. As he pored over the form one more time, he started to get upset and angry, not knowing what to do next. All the other MTs had received good ratings, and he did not believe they were too different from him – either in background (he was the one with real experience!), or in the way they had worked over the last six months. As he looked more the form one more time, he suddenly realised that he had never written anything for Scott, so it made no sense that Scott had rated him on that category. On Monday, he approached Jim with this information, but Jim told him to just forget about it, as no one else would see the file, and in any case, Jim said 'I think very highly of you'.

Over the next three months, AJ kept approaching Jim, with the same issue, but each time Jim told him not to worry. During these meetings, AJ also realised that even though Jim would not budge on the Scott issue, he did indeed respect AJ, and they were becoming quite friendly and collegial. Also, during these three months, Scott stopped talking to AJ completely, and gave him no work at all.

Ultimately, AJ decided he had no option left, but to quit the company and move back to Singapore. When AJ approached Jim to share his decision, Jim expressed surprise, but accepted AJ's resignation, and wished him all the best 'in his future endeavours'.

Attachment 1

V-Pharmel
Document 07PMS
Management Trainee Evaluation Form
(To be completed every 6 months for the first 2 years)

Name of Trainee _____

Date of Joining _____

Division _____

Supervisor Name _____

To the rater: Please use the following scale to evaluate the Management Trainee

1 = Poor; 2 = Below Average; 3 = Average; 4 = Above Average; 5 = Outstanding

Initiative	1	2	3	4	5
Attendance	1	2	3	4	5
Timeliness	1	2	3	4	5
Written Communication	1	2	3	4	5
Verbal Communication	1	2	3	4	5

Signature of HR head _____

Signature of Management Trainee _____

Date _____

Note: This form is to be placed in trainee's file after completion, and becomes a part of his/her permanent record.

Case questions
1 Critique the MT performance evaluation process at V-Pharmel. What could have been done differently?
2 What, in your opinion, was the purpose of the supervisors meeting as a team to evaluate all of the MTs?
3 In your opinion, what role did AJ and Scott's backgrounds play in this case?
4 How would you rate the form used to evaluate the MTs?
5 Please critique the role played in this scenario, by all the major players – i.e., AJ, Scott, Jim, and even Susan.

Case questions for further study and reflection
1 If you were invited by V-Pharmel management to help revise the Management Trainee scheme, what changes would you institute?
2 Imagine you are AJ. What could you have done differently?
3 Most organisations nowadays have a set of values that they claim guide their professional behaviour. To what extent did the managers at V-Pharmel practise the company's stated values? If they had truly internalised those values, would AJ's experience have been different? How? Why?

Further reading

- DeNisi, A.S. and Pritchard, R.D. (2006) 'Performance appraisal, performance management, and improving individual performance: A motivational framework', *Management and Organizational Review*, 2(2): 253–77.

This article goes beyond addressing the common measurement issues – instead, the authors emphasise the role of PMS in improving individual performance. Included are specific recommendations on designing such systems.

- Feldman, J.M. (1981) 'Beyond attribution theory: Cognitive processes in performance appraisal', *Journal of Applied Psychology*, 66: 127–48.

A landmark article on performance appraisal, which covers key issues in PA, such as attention, categorisation, recall, and information integration, and the processes used by raters for these processes.

- Claus, L. and Hand, M.L. (2009) 'Customization decisions regarding perform-ance management systems of multinational companies', *International Journal of Cross-Cultural Management*, 9(2): 237–58.

The authors report the results of a survey conducted to ascertain the extent of customisation of PMS in MNCs and delineate the main factors that influence customisation decisions. Based on the survey of top HR professionals in 100 leading companies in Bulgaria and Romania, the authors conclude that MNCs are already aware of the need for cultural adaptations of PMS, and that global integration strategy, power distance, and masculinity impact PMS customisation decisions significantly more than cultural distance.

- Tung, R.L. and Varma, A. (2008) Expatriate selection and evaluation', in P.B., Smith, M.F. Peterson, and D.C. Thomas (eds), *Handbook of Cross-Cultural Management Research*. pp. 367–78. London: Sage.

In this book chapter, the authors review almost a quarter century's worth of research on selection and performance evaluation of expatriates. The authors note that there is extremely limited empirical work on PMS for expatriates, and that the limited information that is available leads them to conclude that most organisations either simply use domestic systems for expatriate performance management, or no system at all.

- DeNisi, A.S. (1996) *Cognitive Processes in Performance Appraisal: A Research Agenda with Implications for Practice*. London: Routledge.

This research-oriented book provides a comprehensive overview of the cognitive processes involved in the performance appraisal process, including (i) information-processing models, (ii) information storage, (iii) recall, (iv) managerial judgments, and (v) issues with memory-based judgments.

- Murphy, K.R. and Cleveland, J.N. (1995) *Understanding Performance Appraisal: Social, Organizational, and Goal-based Perspectives*. Thousand Oaks, CA: Sage.

This book provides a comprehensive overview of the performance appraisal process, sum-marising and critiquing relevant research. In addition, the authors discuss the impact of (i) social norms, (ii) organisational objectives, and (iii) linking individual performance goals to strategic objectives.

- Varma, A., Budhwar, P.S. and DeNisi, A (eds) (2008) *Performance Management Systems: A Global Perspective*. Global HRM Series. London: Routledge.

This edited volume takes an international perspective to the study of PMS. The initial chapters discuss some critical issues relating to PMS, such as motivation and rewards. The book also examines PMS in 11 different countries, including France, Germany, Turkey, and Japan.

Internet resources

1 Society for Human Resource Management (www.shrm.org): The website of the pre-mier professional organisation for HR professionals. An excellent resource which

provides continuous updates on developments in the field, and numerous 'white papers' on various topics in HR. Access to some sections may require membership. (See also www.shrimindia.org.)

2 www.performance-appraisal.com: Provides a complete online guide for performance appraisals, including access to several tools and forms, etc.

3 www.worldatwork.org (formerly American Compensation Association): Particular focus on issues related to attracting, motivating and retaining employees. Also provides publications and knowledge resources. Recently launched online community is open to all.

Self-assessment questions

Indicative answers to these questions can be found on the companion website at www.sagepub.co.uk/harzing3e.

1 **What is the difference between performance appraisal and performance management?**
2 **What are the critical features of an effective performance appraisal process?**
3 **What are the key issues in global performance management, as distinct from domestic performance management systems?**
4 **How are expatriate appraisals different from appraisals of HCNs (i.e., local employees)?**

References

Bobko, P. and Colella, A. (1994) 'Employee reactions to performance standards: A review and research propositions', *Personnel Psychology*, 47(1): 1–29.

Cooke, F.L. (2008) 'Performance management in China', in A. Varma, P.S. Budhwar and A.S. DeNisi (eds), *Performance Management Systems: A Global Perspective*. Global HRM Series. London: Routledge.

Deming, W.E. (1986) *Out of the Crisis*. Cambridge, MA: MIT Press.

DeNisi, A.S. (1996) *Cognitive Processes in Performance Appraisal: A Research Agenda with Implications for Practice*. London: Routledge.

DeNisi, A.S., Varma, A. and Budhwar, P.S. (2008) 'Performance management around the globe: What have we learned?', in A. Varma, P.S. Budhwar and A.S. DeNisi (eds), *Performance Management Systems: A Global Perspective*. Global HRM Series. London: Routledge.

Dowling, P.J. and Schuler, R.S. (1990) *International Dimensions of Human Resources Management*. Boston, MA: PWS Kent.

Earley, P.C. (1994) 'The individual and collective self: An assessment of self-efficacy and training across cultures', *Administrative Science Quarterly*, 39: 89–117.

Graen, G. and Cashman, J. (1975) 'A role-making model of leadership in formal organizations: A developmental approach', in J.G. Hunt and L.L. Larson (eds), *Leadership Frontiers*. pp. 143–65. Kent, OH: Kent State University Press.

Gregersen, H.B., Hite, J.M. and Black, J.S. (1996) 'Expatriate performance appraisal in U.S. multinational firms', *Journal of International Business Studies*, 27: 711–38.

Hofstede, G.H. (1980) *Culture's Consequences: International Differences in Work-related Values*. Beverly Hills, CA: Sage.

Law, K.S., Wong, C.S., Wang, D. and Wang, L. (2000) 'Effect of supervisor–subordinate guanxi on supervisory decision in China: an empirical investigation', *International Journal of Human Resource Management*, 11(4): 751–65.

Locke, E.A. (1968) 'Toward a theory of task performance and incentives', *Organizational Behavior and Human Performance*, 3: 157–89.

Murphy, K.R. and Cleveland, J.N. (1995) *Understanding Performance Appraisal: Social, Organizational, and Goal-based Perspectives*. Thousand Oaks, CA: Sage.

Murphy, K.R. and DeNisi, A.S. (2008) 'A model of the appraisal process', in A. Varma, P.S. Budhwar and A.S. DeNisi (eds), *Performance Management Systems: A Global Perspective*. Global HRM Series. London: Routledge.

Pulakos, E.D., Mueller-Hanson, R.A. and O'Leary, R.S. (2008) 'Performance management in the United States', in A. Varma, P.S. Budhwar and A.S. DeNisi (eds), *Performance Management Systems: A Global Perspective*. Global HRM Series. London: Routledge.

Shaffer, M.A., Harrison, D.A., Gregersen, H., Black, J.S. and Ferzandi, L.A. (2006) 'You can take it with you: Individual differences and expatriate effectiveness', *Journal of Applied Psychology*, 91: 109–25.

Shen, J. (2005) 'Effective international performance appraisals: Easily said, hard to do', *Compensation & Benefits Review*, 37(4): 70–9.

Shih, H.A., Chiang, Y.H. and Kim, I.S. (2005) 'Expatriate performance management from MNEs of different national origins', *International Journal of Manpower*, 26: 157–76.

Skinner, B.F. (1953) *Science and Human Behavior*. New York: Macmillan.

Sparrow, P. (2008) 'Performance management in the UK', in A. Varma, P.S. Budhwar and A.S. DeNisi (eds), *Performance Management Systems: A Global Perspective*. Global HRM Series. London: Routledge.

Tahvanainen, M. (2000) 'Expatriate performance management: the case of Nokia Telecommunications', *Human Resource Management*, 37: 267–75.

Toh, S.M. and DeNisi, A.S. (2007) Host country nationals as socializing agents: A social identity approach', *Journal of Organizational Behavior*, 28: 281–301.

Toh, S.M., Varma, A. and DeNisi, A.S. (2004) 'Host Country National Helping on the Adjustment of Expatriates. Paper presented at the conference of the Society for Industrial/Organizational Psychology, Chicago, IL.

Tung, R.L. and Varma, A. (2008) 'Expatriate selection and evaluation', in P.B. Smith, M.F. Peterson and D.C. Thomas (eds), *Handbook of Cross-Cultural Management Research*. pp. 367–78. London: Sage.

Van de Vliert, E., Shi, K., Sanders, K., Wang, Y. and Huang, X. (2004) 'Chinese and Dutch interpretations of supervisory feedback', *Journal of Cross-Cultural Psychology*, 35: 417–35.

Varma, A. and Stroh, L.K. (2001) 'The impact of same-sex LMX dyads on performance evaluations', *Human Resource Management*, 40: 309–20.

Varma, A., Pichler, S. and Srinivas, E.S. (2005a) 'The role of interpersonal affect in performance appraisal: Evidence from two samples – U.S. and India', *International Journal of Human Resource Management*, 16: 2029–44.

Varma, A., Srinivas, E.S. and Stroh, L.K. (2005b) 'A comparative study of the impact of leader member exchange relationships in U.S. and Indian samples', *Cross-Cultural Management: An International Journal*, 12(1): 84–95.

Varma, A., Toh, S.M. and Budhwar, P.S. (2006) 'A new perspective on the female expatriate experience: The role of host country national categorization', *Journal of World Business*, 41: 112–20.

Varma, A., Pichler, S., Budhwar, P.S. and Biswas, S. (2009) 'Chinese host country nationals' willingness to support expatriates: The role of collectivism, interpersonal affect, and guanxi', *International Journal of Cross-Cultural Management*, 9(2): 199–216.

Varma, A., Pichler, S. and Budhwar, P.S. (in press) 'The relationship between expatriate job level and host country national categorization: An investigation in the United Kingdom', *International Journal of Human Resource Management*.

Wakabaysahi, M., Graen, G., Graen, M. and Graen, M. (1988) 'Japanese management progress: Mobility into middle management', *Journal of Applied Psychology*, 73: 217–27.

Yan, A., Zhu, G. and Hall, D.T. (2002) 'International assignments for career building: A model of agency relationships and psychological contracts', *Academy of Management Review*, 27: 373–91.

Zeira, Y. (1979) 'Ethnocentrism in host-country organization', *Business Horizons*, 22(3): 66–75.

14

Total Rewards in the International Context

Meredith Burnett and Mary Ann Von Glinow

Contents

Learning Objectives

After reading this chapter you will be able to

- Understand the complexities faced by IHR managers

- Identify the international total rewards objectives for the MNC and the employee

- Differentiate between the key components of global total rewards

- Explain the going rate and balance sheet approaches to international compensation and their advantages/disadvantages

- Explain the current best practices to the tax equalisation and tax protection approaches to international taxation

Chapter Outline

We examine the complex issues that international human resource (IHR) managers face when creating international total rewards systems. This chapter provides comprehensive examples of rewards policies and practices, and for the sake of simplicity concentrates on examples from US MNCs and expatriates. First, we discuss the intricacies that arise when firms design total rewards systems for an international assignment (IA) versus the typical headquarters assignment. We briefly highlight traditional and newer forms of IAs since rewards are often a function of the type of IA (i.e., 3-year vs. 6 week vs. commuter assignment). Second, we outline the key components of an international total rewards programme, namely, base salaries, hardship premiums, allowances and benefits. Third, we discuss the Going Rate and Balance Sheet Approach to total rewards, followed by a discussion of their advantages and disadvantages. Fourth, we examine international taxation in total rewards systems by focusing on current best practices. For practical reasons, we present current international cost-of-living data which are useful for IHR managers who face problems associated with limited information/ statistics on cross-country comparisons. We also discuss the specific problems that IHR managers face when compensating third country nationals relative to those they face with host country nationals. Finally, we close our discussion by elaborating on recent international trends in global total rewards.

1 Recap

We primarily rely on use of the term expatriate to describe employees working internationally, although multinational companies (MNCs) may assign either parent country nationals (PCNs) or third country nationals (TCNs) to work on foreign assignments depending on the type of staffing policy within the MNC (Moshe and Sama, 2000). PCNs are employees hired by the MNC at the headquarter's location and assigned to a foreign location for a period usually lasting 2–5 years (see Chapter 6). MNCs following an ethnocentric approach (i.e., appreciation for the cultural values and business practices in the MNC's home country) have a predisposition to reject employees from other countries. Thus, MNCs with an ethnocentric policy may prefer PCNs because they have a high degree of familiarity with the MNC's national compensation and benefits practices. However, the cost associated with maintaining these employees and their families abroad can be excessive. TCNs are foreign nationals hired by the MNC to work in any of their foreign locations with the exception of the TCN's own home country. For example, an Australian citizen working in the UK for a US-based MNC is a third country national. MNCs with a geocentric staffing approach (i.e., an appreciation for the cultural values and business practices in the MNC's home country and in the foreign location) believe that nationality does not matter when selecting the best people for an overseas assignment. MNCs with a geocentric staffing policy believe that they will choose the best people for the job, regardless of their home country. However, MNCs with a geocentric policy may prefer TCNs because they have a high degree of familiarity with various types of compensation and benefits practices. TCNs typically work in areas usually less expensive to maintain than PCNs. TCNs may work in various international business settings for their MNC throughout their careers. However, they may experience perceptions of inequality as they move between foreign locations. Host Country nationals (HCNs) are employees hired by the MNC at a foreign location. MNCs with a polycentric approach (i.e., an appreciation for the cultural values and business practices in the foreign location) believe that local foreign nationals are the best people to manage their foreign subsidiary. Thus, MNCs with a polycentric policy may prefer HCNs because they have a high degree of familiarity with the compensation and benefits practices in the foreign location, unlike PCNs.

2 Introduction: The current state of total rewards

International compensation has quickly moved beyond the limited domain of expatriate pay. Worldwide total rewards now more commonly refers to a mechanism through which organisations' IHR managers can perform a number of critical activities including:

1 combining MNC's local and global data in order to develop appropriate compensation packages for a global workforce
2 using centralised total rewards systems in order to maintain financial control over compensation and benefits programmes that span multiple geographic locations
3 linking global financial outcomes with geographically dispersed costs.

Among the many complexities that are often associated with growing international total rewards programmes include organisations' use of outsourcing activities in order to further their corporate interests abroad. Certainly, these international total rewards programmes are of strategic value to most MNCs due to their interest in establishing operations in desirable emerging foreign markets such as China, India, Pakistan, Mexico and Brazil. A second complexity that is often associated with using international total rewards programmes includes the increasing attractiveness of foreign assignments to employees. International opportunities are generally appealing to employees since they send signals to employees that such opportunities may improve their financial situation and/or improve their upward career progression or status in the organisation. Although employess and MNCs face difficulties they assure many benefits. For instance, MNCs are confronted with balancing incentive, benefit and pension programmes that may span degrees of centralisation and decentralisation resulting from managing employees across multiple geographic locations. MNCs must also deal with repatriation as employees move from an international assignment to a domestic assignment in their home country.

3 Complexities faced by IHR managers

Increased use of outsourcing

One of the complexities faced by IHR managers as a result of the challenge associated with placing employees in foreign assignments is the increase in the total number of outsourced employees and activities (Brewster and Harris, 1999). In fact, according to some reports, up to 90 per cent of US MNCs outsource at least one HR activity (Galanaki and Papalexandris, 2007). When outsourcing HR activities, IHR managers may contract with another company to engage in work that they might typically perform in-house. Outsourcing HR activities is beneficial to IHR managers because it may reduce costs, even though outsourcing HR activities is complicated by the fact that contractors may lack firm-specific knowledge (Klaas et al., 1999).When outsourcing employees, IHR managers either source offshore or relocate some of their employees to companies in other countries. Outsourcing employees abroad challenges IHR managers since offshoring may undermine employees' perceptions about their MNC's total rewards programme (cf. Kessler et al, 2006).

Decentralisation of incentives

A second complexity faced by IHR managers resulting from placing employees in foreign assignments is the decentralisation of incentives. By decentralising their incentives away from headquarters, IHR managers are able to move their incentive programmes closer to employees working abroad. An added benefit of decentralising their incentives is that IHR managers are also able to move decision making closer to employees. Despite the benefits of moving incentive systems and the decision regarding the global distribution of those systems abroad, IHR managers still face two challenges when decentralising incentives. First, such systems become increasingly complex since HR managers are often faced with growing numbers of outsourced employees. Second, outsourced incentive systems may require the disclosure to external parties of proprietary information conducted within an organisation (Dickmann and Tyson, 2005).

Balancing performance metrics

A third complexity faced by IHR managers resulting from placing employees in foreign assignments is the balancing of performance metrics (see Chapter 13). Traditionally, HR managers focused on developing performance metrics that maximise outcomes in a domestic environment. Recently, however, there is greater focus on understanding the influence of employee differences in cultural orientations and their preferences for particular HRM practices and policies (Aycan et al., 2007). IHR managers now must understand how the barriers they encounter when operating in non-domestic contexts influence their domestic HRM practices (Leat and El-Kot, 2007). Despite the complexities that IHR managers face, they must manage the highly complex nuances between their MNCs and expatriates in order to meet the objectives of both.

4 International total rewards objectives for the MNC and the employee

MNC objectives

Ensuring that total rewards policies are consistent with business strategies

One objective of MNCs when developing an international total rewards system is to ensure that HRM compensation and benefits policies are consistent with business strategies (see Chapter 1). Many MNCs pursue a low-cost strategy and thereby create offshore facilities in countries (e.g., India, China, Mexico, etc.) where labour is less expensive than in the United States. As an example, US technology MNCs are attracted by low labour costs and high-quality technical and professional employees working in India. MNCs also want to capitalise on the absence of labour unions by creating facilities in emerging markets. With union membership in many emerging nations declining, MNCs are attracted to those areas because they provide MNCs with critical information about restrictions on planned compensation and benefit programme modifications as well as potential liabilities (Fealy and Kompare, 2003). MNCs that pursue a differentiation strategy by offering unique products and/or services may create opportunities in countries by ensuring that their HR policies, programmes and practices are consistent with product attributes and brand names as well as the needs of local consumers. As an example, US MNCs are attracted by innovative and creative employees working in Finland, Ireland, Sweden and Switzerland due to their ability to develop new products. MNCs are also attracted to those areas because employees working there provide MNCs with ideas about how to create novel total reward systems that effectively motivate and reward employee success.

Developing total rewards policies that maximise recruiting and retention efforts A second objective of MNCs when developing their international total rewards system is to ensure that compensation and benefits policies maximise recruitment and retention efforts. Here, most MNCs want to make sure that they assign the right people to international operations. For example, when assigning employees to work in foreign nations, MNCs want employees who are sensitive to numerous cultural norms (i.e., dress, display of affection, alcohol usage). Furthermore, IHR managers also want to make sure that employees are open to non-traditional ways of approaching work-related problems. By guaranteeing that there is little turnover resulting from insensitivity and lack of openness, MNCs are able to address the needs of expatriates and take advantage of opportunities while doing business in foreign locations (cf. Birdseye and Hill, 1995).

Developing cost-effective global total rewards policies A third objective of MNCs when developing their international total rewards system is to ensure that compensation and benefits policies are cost effective. Here, MNCs make sure that employees receive incentives or premiums for their foreign service, reimbursements for reasonable costs (e.g., relocation assistance or education reimbursement), and tax equalisation when discrepancies exist.

Creating global total rewards policies that result in fair processes and outcomes A fourth objective of organisations when developing their international total rewards system is to ensure that compensation and benefits policies result in fair processes and outcomes (cf. Chen et al., 2002). Here, most MNCs design programmes so that employees are treated with procedural fairness with regard to their overseas assignment, namely, 'the ability to voice one's views and arguments during a procedure' and 'the ability to influence the actual outcome itself' (Colquitt, 1999: 388). The consequences of fair processes are that employees are likely to have higher levels of job satisfaction and performance while on their overseas assignment and are likely to remain with their MNC (cf. Colquitt et al., 2001).

Employee goals

Creating HR policies that provide financial protection Employees have goals and objectives that they too need to have met in order for their international assignment to be a success. First and foremost, employees want their MNC's HR policies to provide financial protection by enabling them to maintain the same standard of living and purchasing power as they would receive when working in the domestic country. Employees generally look for key elements in their compensation package and expect to receive particular tax considerations when working overseas.

Creating HR policies that offer opportunities for financial growth and career advancement A second goal of employees is that the MNC's HR policies offer them opportunities for financial growth and career advancement. Financial growth, which refers to the opportunity to save and/or receive additional income, gives employees a chance to move forward monetarily subsequent to returning to headquarters. If an employee is able to save substantially when working abroad, then s/he might have a higher quality of living upon repatriation than when s/he left for the foreign assignment. Training and mentoring opportunities may provide expatriates with career advancement opportunities and the chance to experience enhanced responsibilities that may not have been available in the home country (Downes et al., 2002). Consequently, if an employee is able to successfully fulfil more complex duties and develop more enhanced skill sets while working abroad, then s/he might gain an opportunity to take on new duties and tasks upon return to headquarters.

Creating HR policies that ease repatriation A third goal of employees is that the MNC's HR policies remove complexities associated with repatriation (Harvey, 1989). Here, effective total rewards programmes should help address expatriates' experiences associated with receiving substantially less pay when they return to headquarters since they might forfeit premiums, allowances and other perks associated with the expatriate assignment, particularly if they have been abroad for a 3-year assignment. Given that many expatriates might take on additional tasks and duties while working abroad, they might feel more valuable and as a consequence should receive more pay. Effective total rewards programmes should also address expatriates' inability to work collaboratively with colleagues. Since many expatriates might have, out of necessity, worked collaboratively abroad, they might experience difficulties re-acclimating themselves to less team-oriented work norms prevalent in some home countries. Effective total rewards programmes should address the possibility that expatriates might seek employment with competitors upon their return to headquarters. In order to overcome each of these possibilities, MNCs should implement career development programmes to send a signal to employees that they will be valued upon repatriation. In addition, MNCs should collect information from expatriates before, during and after their assignment in order to determine employees' levels of international compensation satisfaction and their levels of satisfaction with their foreign experience.

5 Traditional versus newer forms of International Assignments (IAs)

Commuter IAs

The length of an international assignment can vary drastically depending on the nature of the job and the proximity of the foreign assignment to the home country. Assignments that are expected to last for less than six weeks are known as commuter assignments. When expatriates are only expected to remain in the foreign location for six consecutive weeks or are expected to travel back-and-forth during their short stay, these assignments are often treated like business travel. If this is the case, then MNCs will determine foreign living costs for short-term assignees (e.g., per diem restaurant meals, local transportation, hotels, etc.) and then reimburse employees for their expenses as they would if they were travelling domestically.

The US State Department (www.state.gov) publishes a monthly schedule of foreign per diem rates for nearly 1,100 foreign locations. Their table includes not only a per diem rate for civilians travelling in foreign areas but also breaks down their rate by lodging, meals and incidentals. As an example, until December 2008, the maximum per diem rate including lodging, meals and incidentals for individuals employed with the US government travelling to Brazil is $348.00 (US). Similarly, the Australian Taxation Office (www.ato.gov.au) publishes a schedule of daily travel allowance expenses that vary according to salary levels and destinations. As an example, until December 2008, the maximum per diem rate including lodging, meals and incidentals for individuals employed with the Australian government travelling to Brazil is $165.00 (AUS) for salaries of $87,200.00 (AUS) and below, $205.00 (AUS) for salaries between $87,201.00 (AUS) and $155,000.00 (AUS), and $240.00 for salaries between $155,001.00 (AUS) and above. The Treasury Board of Canada Secretariat National Joint Council (www.tbs-sct.gc.ca) publishes a schedule of per diem rates that includes meals and incidentals for individuals travelling abroad. As an example, since 1 October 2008, the maximum per diem rate for individuals travelling to Brazil and residing in commercial and non-commercial accommodation is $190.40 ($142.80 after 30 days) and $170.00 ($127.50 after 30 days), respectively. Indeed, most countries publish their allowable per diem rates, which helps the IHR managers in MNCs make accurate travel allowances (for an extensive review of the IA literature, see Meyskens, et al., (in press).

6-week IAs

If expatriates are expected to remain in the host country for up to six weeks then IHR managers expect that the employee's family will remain home during that time period. Generally speaking, they anticipate that expatriates will spend less on local transportation costs and more on transportation home than with commuter assignments. Here, expatriates are expected to spend more on groceries and less on restaurant meals than with a commuter assignment. MNCs are not likely to adopt an expatriate pay package since the employee's home pay package is likely to be less expensive.

3-year IAs

If expatriates are expected to become permanent assignees, they will receive an international compensation package consisting of base pay, premiums, allowances and benefits. We now turn our discussion to each of these components.

6 Key components of global total rewards programmes

Base salary

Base pay is the building block of employees' compensation package both domestically and internationally, and it takes on new meaning when employees are working abroad. In a domestic setting, the term base salary refers to the amount of pay (e.g., hourly pay or salary) that employees earn on a regular basis for performing their jobs. In turn, the base pay serves as a benchmark for other forms of discretionary compensation that employees may receive such as merit pay, bonuses and incentives. In contrast, for employees working abroad, base salary may be either the comparable pay that s/he would receive for performing the same job in his/her home country or the amount of pay that s/he would receive for performing the job in the host country. Adjustments are then made to expatriates' base salary for their accepting a foreign assignment, hardships they may encounter, and their willingness to move from one assignment to another. Stark discrepancies can occur in an employee's compensation package depending on whether the employee's base pay is linked to the home or host country.

Levels of base pay vary depending on the MNC's headquarters location. The compensation mix for managerial employees working for MNCs headquartered in countries such as Australia, New Zealand, Austria, Finland and France is comprised of over 80 per cent of base pay (Mercer International, 2008). By comparison, the compensation mix for managerial employees working for MNCs headquartered in India is less than 40 per cent base pay (Mercer International, 2008). Base salaries may also differ substantially between management- and professional-level expatriates working for MNCs within the same country. Base pay for professional-level employees working for MNCs headquartered in Italy exceeds 80 per cent while base pay for management-level employees working for MNCs headquartered in Italy is less than 70 per cent (Mercer International, 2008).

Many MNCs also provide additional salary payments to expatriates that are independent of performance. Brazilian MNCs are required by law to provide a thirteenth month salary which is partially paid at vacation and at Christmas (i.e., 50 per cent is paid at vacation and 50 per cent is paid at Christmas) (Mercer International, 2009). In Mexico, 15 days of base pay are mandated as Christmas bonuses. In addition, Mexico also has laws mandating profit sharing whereby companies must distribute an equivalent of 10 per cent of their pre-tax profits among employees (Mercer International, 2008). In Australia, MNCs are required to pay Employer Retirement contributions equal to 9 per cent of employees' earnings up to a maximum of $38,180 per year.

Foreign service inducements: foreign service premiums, mobility premiums, hardship premiums and danger pay

There are four types of foreign service inducements and each has a different goal. The first type, a foreign service premium, is given to expatriates in order to encourage them to accept assignments in other countries. Until recently, nearly all employees working in assignments expected to extend beyond one year received a foreign service premium. However, only 37 per cent of US MNCs currently offer expatriates a foreign service premium (Culpepper and Associates, 2008). Foreign service premiums vary depending on the expatriates' base pay, and typically range between 10 per cent and 30 per cent of base salary, and these are disbursed incrementally as a reminder to employees of the reward that they are receiving for their assignment. Short-term premiums differ from MNC to MNC depending on where the MNC is headquartered. Nearly all MNCs headquartered in Brazil provide short-term premiums that range between 8 per cent and 50 per cent of base pay to expatriates working at the professional (e.g., non-managerial sales positions) level and above (managers and executives). By comparison short-term premiums are also prevalent for expatriates working at the professional level and above in Germany and Japan but range from 53 per cent to 95 per cent, and from 63 per cent to 71 per cent of base pay, respectively (Mercer International, 2009).

Second, mobility premiums are lump-sum cash bonuses paid to employees for their willingness to move between two foreign posts. Twenty-six percent of US MNCs pay mobility premiums to expatriates assigned to both short- and long-term assignments (Culpepper and Associates, 2008). In addition to mobility premiums, 25 per cent of US MNCs also provide expatriates with field allowances in order to cover the additional costs that they incur simply by travelling and working in numerous locations (Culpepper and Associates, 2008).

Third, hardship premiums are lump-sum cash bonuses paid to expatriates for the adversities that they may face experiencing difficult conditions. The US Government pays hardship premiums to employees assigned to locations where living conditions are tough or unhealthy and/or physical hardships are excessive. Depending on the total hardship rating (based on a standard evaluation of environmental conditions), employees are paid differentials of 5 per cent to 35 per cent of base salary. The maximum amount that Federal employees can currently receive as combined annual base salary and hardship differential is $186,600. Column 1 of Table 14.1 shows a list of selected posts adapted from the US Department of State Hardship Differentials Pay table (www.state.gov). Column 2 shows the percentage of hardship pay allowed for each city listed in Column 1.

Table 14.1   Hardship differentials and danger pay, January 2008

Country and city	Hardship pay (per cent)	Danger pay (per cent)
Afghanistan: Kabul	35	35
Algeria: Algiers	25	15
Chad: N'Djamena	30	
China: Shenyang	30	
Colombia: Barranquilla	10	15
Cote d'Ivoire: Abidjan	20	15
Equatorial Guinea: Malabo	35	
Ethiopia: Addis Ababa	30	
Haiti: Port-au-Prince	25	20
India: Calcutta	25	
Indonesia: Bandung	30	
Iraq: Baghdad	35	35
Israel: Tel Aviv	0	20
Jerusalem	5	20
Kenya: Nairobi	30	
Lebanon: Beirut	25	30
Liberia: Monrovia	30	15
Nigeria: Abuja	30	
Pakistan: Karachi	30	35
Russia: Vladivostok	30	25
Sierra Leone: Freetown	30	25
Somalia: Mogadishu	20	
Sudan: Juba	25	
Turkmenistan: Ashgabat	30	
Uganda: Kampala	25	
Uzbekistan: Tashkent	30	
Vietnam: Hanoi	30	
Yemen: Sanaa	20	
Zimbabwe: Harare	30	20

Source: US Department of State (2008).

The fourth type of foreign service inducement that is included in international total rewards programmes is given to expatriates in order to compensate them for working in situations where they are exposed to either hazards or danger. Imminent danger pay is provided to members of the US uniformed services and reserves who work in foreign areas where there is a threat of physical harm due to civil disobedience, civil war, terrorism or wartime conditions. Depending on the level of danger exposure, employees are paid differentials of 5 per cent to 35 per cent of base salary, similar to hardship premiums discussed above. Column 3 of Table 14.1 shows the percentage of base pay allocated to employees for danger (in addition to hardship) for each city listed in Column 1. Currently, US uniformed servicemen are eligible to receive a $225 per month premium. In comparison to the premiums given to

US uniformed service employees and federal employees, only 21 per cent of private US MNCs provide hardship or danger pay premiums (Culpepper and Associates, 2008). The cities listed in Table 14.1 are also consistent with other reports such as the Mercer Global Compensation Planning Report (Mercer International, 2009) which lists Helsinki, Finland and Geneva, Switzerland among the top cities for personal safety and Baghdad, Iraq as the bottom city for personal safety.

Allowances

Discretionary payments are also given to expatriates in order to attract and retain those most qualified. There are three goals of discretionary allowances. The first objective is to promote a sense of well-being among expatriates and their families, the second is to maintain their standard of living, and the third is to prevent their purchasing power from declining.

Cost-of-living allowance (COLA) The most widely used discretionary allowance, COLA, is given to compensate expatriates for differences in expenditures between the home country and the foreign country. COLAs are currently offered to expatriates by nearly 80 per cent of US MNCs. A city is considered high cost if the cost-of-living for the area exceeds 108 per cent of the national average of non-housing costs and when the local taxes are considered excessively high. For example, Fairbanks, Alaska and Flagstaff, Arizona are high cost areas since their cost-of-living indices are 136.4 per cent and 118.4 per cent, respectively, of the US national average (The Council for Community and Economic Research, 2008). Typically, employees are only eligible to receive COLAs when they are assigned to an area where the cost-of-living is higher than it would be in the city where their organisation is headquartered in the United States. COLA rates are typically based on base salary.

Goods and services allowance Goods and service allowances are given to expatriates to compensate for differentials in the price of merchandise (e.g., grocery, devices, etc.) or activities (e.g., lessons, repair work, etc.) they may need while working abroad. As shown in Table 14.2, the US Department of State publishes a quarterly *Indexes of Living Costs Abroad*. Their index compares the costs of goods and services in the Washington, DC area to similar goods and services in foreign locations. The table contains six columns of pertinent information. The survey date column represents the month and year that the US Department of State received the cost data. The exchange rate column represents the number of each country's foreign currency units traded in exchange for $1 US, as of the writing of this chapter. The local relative column is a comparison of goods and service prices between the foreign country and Washington, DC with the price ratios weighted by the pattern of expenditures in Washington, DC. The local index column is a straightforward

Table 14.2 Index of living costs abroad (Washington, DC = 100), January 2008

Country and city	Survey date	Foreign unit	Number per US$	Relative	Index	Relative	Index
		Exchange rate		**Local**		**US Government**	
Australia: Canberra	6/27/2006	Dollar	1.35	130	126	120	116
Brazil: Rio de Janeiro	11/20/2005	Real	2.17	123	124	113	113
Canada: Toronto	02/15/2007	Dollar	1.17	132	131	126	126
China: Beijing	07/27/2007	Renminbi	7.57	124	130	107	113
Cuba: Havana	8/1/2005	Chavitos	0.9259	143	151	124	129
Denmark: Copenhagen	6/28/2006	Kroner	5.91	163	166	152	155
Egypt: Cairo	3/13/2006	Pound	5.73	91	96	76	83
El Salvador: San Salvador	01/25/2007	Dollar	1.00	100	108	95	103
France: Paris	04/19/2007	Euro	0.74	192	190	162	165
Germany: Munich	04/10/2007	Euro	0.73	175	166	148	143
Greece: Athens	7/20/2005	Euro	0.8	154	154	129	129
Haiti: Port-au-Prince	1/6/2005	Gourde	35.8	118	121	110	112
Hong Kong	07/13/2007	Dollar	7.82	157	154	142	143
India: New Delhi	10/16/2006	Rupee	45.5	93	97	93	99
Israel: Tel Aviv	11/15/2006	New Shekel	4.27	139	138	121	120
Italy: Milan	3/12/2007	Euro	0.74	184	178	159	156
Jamaica: Kingston	03/01/2007	Dollar	67.4	101	103	98	100
Japan: Tokyo City	1/23/2006	Yen	113	177	177	146	149
Korea: Seoul	3/7/2006	Won	934	139	148	104	114
Mexico: Mexico City, DF	03/07/2007	Peso	10.8	114	123	104	113
New Zealand: Wellington	10/6/2005	Dollar	1.37	145	144	132	132
Nigeria: Lagos	12/20/2005	Naira	129	144	161	122	137
Pakistan: Islamabad	12/10/2004	Rupee	59.5	98	102	93	98
Philippines: Manila	04/16/2007	Peso	48	94	97	91	95
Poland: Warsaw	3/17/2006	New Zloty	3.18	129	127	119	117
Russia: Moscow	12/20/2006	Ruble	26.3	162	164	134	138
Saudi Arabia: Riyadh	5/8/2006	Riyal	3.75	108	114	103	114
Singapore	04/09/2007	Dollar	1.52	140	140	127	127
S. Africa: Johannesburg	07/20/2007	Rand	7.13	119	121	116	117
Spain: Madrid	4/17/2006	Euro	0.8	152	150	133	132
Sweden: Stockholm	3/19/2006	Kroner	7.92	164	162	144	142
Switzerland: Geneva	3/30/2006	Franc	1.31	178	177	161	161
Thailand: Bangkok	2/3/2006	Baht	39.6	90	98	85	94
Turkey: Istanbul	02/11/2007	New Lira	1.42	162	156	122	119
United Kingdom: London	10/18/2006	Pound	0.5199	177	183	145	155
Venezuela: Caracas	08/15/07	Bolivar	2150	111	131	101	121
Vietnam: Hanoi	1/31/2005	N Dong	15769	96	98	90	94

Source: US Department of State (2008)

measure comparison of goods and services prices between the foreign country and Washington, DC with the price ratios weighted by the pattern of expenditures in the foreign country. The local index is most appropriate for US MNCs to establish cost-of-living allowances for their US-based employees working abroad. The US Government relative and index columns are calculated in the same way as the local indexes but they also include prices of goods imported to the post and price advantages available only to US Government employees. The US Government index is useful in order to establish cost-of-living allowances for both public and civilian employees working abroad (www.state.gov).

Exchange rate protection programmes Thirty-nine per cent of US MNCs offer expatriates exchange rate protection programmes (Culpepper and Associates, 2008). These programmes, which are increasing in number, are becoming more popular in the US due to the volatility of the dollar against other currencies.

Housing and utilities allowance Sixty-two percent of US MNCs provide housing and utilities allowances to expatriates to compensate for differentials in the cost of lodging, electricity, gas, fuel, water, garages, furniture, and housing-related taxes and insurance premiums required by local law or custom in the foreign country. Housing allowances are designed so that employees will be able to maintain their home country living standards. Housing allowances are handled on a case-by-case basis and may include provisions for payments for either assessed or actual costs in order to make-up for differences in the cost of housing. These costs may be fixed or variable and are paid on an incremental basis. Fifty-two percent of MNCs headquartered in the US provide free housing. Similarly, approximately 50 per cent of MNCs headquartered in Japan provide free housing for relocated employees (Mercer International, 2009).

As shown in Table 14.3, the US Department of State publishes a quarterly 'Quarters Allowances' table. Their indexes compare the costs of goods and services in the Washington, DC area to those similar goods and services in foreign locations. The table contains five columns of pertinent information. The number per US $ column shows the rate used to compute the quarters allowances as of the effective date. The family status column shows whether the allowance is for a single employee or an employee with a family of two or more persons. The table does not show that employees with larger families living with them at post receive supplements of 10, 20, or 30 per cent of the 2-person allowance (for families of 3 to 4 persons, 5 to 6 persons, or 7 or more persons, respectively). The last three columns show the annual maximum allowances paid for employees earning less than $51,738, between $51,739 and $81,092, and $81,093 and above, respectively. The quarters allowance paid to government employees is either the amount of actual expenditures or the allowance maximum, whichever is less.

Table 14.3   Quarters allowances, January 2008

Country and city	Survey date	Exchange rate			Annual allowances by family status and salary range			
		Effective date	Foreign unit	Number per US$	Family status	Less than $51,738	$51,739 to $81,092	$81,093 and above
Canada: Toronto.	Dec-06	Nov-07	Euro	0.93	Family	45,000	50,000	50,500
					Single	38,700	45,000	50,300
France: Paris.		Nov-07	Euro	0.68	Family	58,700	65,100	89,800
					Single	52,100	58,700	68,100
Greece: Rome.		Nov-07	Euro	0.68	Family	40,900	45,100	59,800
					Single	36,200	40,900	59,100
Japan: Tokyo City		Nov-07	Yen	112	Family	69,100	80,100	85,700
					Single	61,200	69,900	80,400
Korea: Seoul.		Nov-07	Won	870	Family	59,400	63,300	66,900
					Single	56,600	59,400	63,300
Mexico: Mexico City.	May-07	Nov-07	Peso	10.5	Family	35,500	39,500	43,200
					Single	31,600	35,500	41,200
Netherlands: Hague, The.		Nov-07	Euro	0.68	Family	54,700	54,700	61,400
					Single	40,600	54,700	58,300
Singapore: Singapore.	Apr-07	Nov-07	Dollar	1.45	Family	48,000	53,000	59,000
					Single	44,300	50,400	53,900
Switzerland: Geneva.		Nov-07	Franc	1.16	Family	61,000	67,400	74,600
					Single	54,300	61,000	67,400
United Kingdom: London.		Aug-07	Pound	0.4739	Family	63,800	74,300	77,800
					Single	56,800	68,700	74,300

Source: US Department of State (2008)

Home leave allowance Home leave allowances cover employees' expenses for making trips back to their home country. This paid time-off is designed to assist employees with maintaining both family and business ties so that they will have fewer adjustment problems during the repatriation process. Most MNCs restrict home leave allowances to trips home; however, some firms also give expatriates the opportunity to use their allowance for foreign travel rather than travel home.

Home leave benefits to a great extent vary from MNC to MNC. However, benefits typically apply to both employees and their family members living abroad. Employees are expected to continue working abroad for at least six additional months beyond the date of expected return from each leave. Employees are eligible to take home leave once every twelve months. Expenses are usually limited to round-trip air fare tickets, ground transportation and accommodation.

Rest, relaxation and rehabilitation leave and allowance Many expatriates who work in designated hardship or danger areas receive rest, relaxation and rehabilitation leave and allowance benefits. Rest, relaxation and rehabilitation leave and allowance represents paid time off given because employers that are more progressive understand that expatriates may need a break from unpleasant and/or dangerous working conditions in order to re-energise themselves. Rest, relaxation and rehabilitation leave should not be confused with regular vacation benefits because leave locations are designated by the employer. For instance, service members and US Defense Department civilians on 12-month orders in Iraq and Jordan supporting Operation Iraqi Freedom now have a rest and recuperation leave programme that will allow them to take up to 15 days, excluding travel time, to visit family or friends in the United States or Europe (Banusiewicz , 2005).

Rest, relaxation and rehabilitation leave and allowance programmes may also include allowances to cover travel expenses incurred when travelling from their foreign post to the designated leave location. For instance, service members on leave from Operation Iraqi Freedom have the choice of travelling free from Iraq to gateway airports in Atlanta, Baltimore, Dallas, Los Angeles or Frankfurt, Germany (Banusiewicz, 2005). Service members are responsible for their own expenses when travelling from the gateway airports to their final destination. MNCs typically pay expatriates standard allowances for costs that they incur that are associated with food, lodging and transportation to and from their leave location.

Education allowance for expatriate's children Sixty-eight percent of US MNCs extend education allowances to expatriates to cover the schooling costs associated with placing their children in private schools designed for English speaking students or home country schools. Since the cost of tuition in foreign countries is often much

Table 14.4 Education allowances, August 2008

Location	Grade level			
	K	1–5	6–8	9–12
Rio de Janeiro, Brazil	26,300	26,300	28,350	31,950
Cairo, Egypt	15,000	15,000	14,850	15,500
Addis Ababa, Ethiopia	17,200	17,200	18,950	19,350
Athens, Greece	16,650	19,900	21,300	23,150
Jakarta, Indonesia	22,400	22,400	24,650	24,650
Tel Aviv, Israel	19,100	19,100	20,100	21,400
Tokyo City, Japan	24,650	24,650	24,650	24,650
Amsterdam, Netherlands	25,650	28,150	32,400	33,650
Lima, Peru	10,300	11,100	11,550	11,550
Doha, Qatar	14,500	14,500	17,600	17,600
Johannesburg, South Africa	19,700	19,700	22,600	24,750
Bangkok, Thailand	22,300	22,300	24,700	25,700

Source: US Department of State (2008)

more expensive than tuition for private schools in the US, expatriates are reimbursed rather than given a percentage of their base salary depending on the differential. Table 14.4 shows selected data from the US Government's education allowance rates. The rates range from $10,300 US to $33,650 US. Primary school allowances and nursery tickets are also commonly granted in countries such as Portugal, Spain, and Hungary by many MNCs (Mercer International, 2009).

Relocation allowance Relocation allowances are given to expatriates in order to compensate them for costs associated with moving. One category of relocation expenses includes actual moving transportation charges, shipping and packaging charges associated with moving household goods to the foreign location. Related to the latter category, many MNCs also reimburse for storage charges associated with holding goods in the home country until they are ready for shipment. A second category of relocation expenses includes reimbursement for temporary living costs accrued while waiting for delivery of goods or while looking for permanent housing. Related to the latter category, many organisations also reimburse for temporary housing prior to departure to the foreign post when the expatriate's house has been rented or sold. Furthermore, many MNCs will also reimburse for household appliances in the foreign location since many expatriates may have left those items behind due to a lack of compatibility with utilities in the foreign country. A third category of relocation expenses includes reimbursement for travel to the foreign post for employees and their families. These reimbursements will also typically cover the costs associated with relocating expatriate's automobiles to the foreign post as well as reimbursement for reasonable expenses incurred by the family during their travel to the foreign post. Ninety-two percent of US MNCs offer relocation allowances to their expatriates (Culpepper and Associates, 2008).

Spouse/family allowance Increasingly, many organisations are also providing spousal assistance to help defray the income lost by a spouse as a result of relocating abroad. Spousal and family allowances are also provided in many locations as a means to countermeasure falling birth rates (Mercer International, 2009). Some MNCs may also provide marriage allowances to blue-collar workers while working abroad in countries such as Turkey (Mercer International, 2009).

Benefits

International benefits programmes often present complexities above-and-beyond those associated with international compensation. Pension plans and saving and investment plans are difficult to manage between countries due to variations in national rules and regulations. There is also very little portability of retirement plans and health insurance programmes. Furthermore, required benefits arising from national labour or employment legislation such as workers' compensation plans have no applicability in foreign environments. Social security programmes and medical leave exist in many countries, however those programmes are not simple replications of schemes in the home country. As a result, MNCs must address many important questions when designing foreign benefits programmes such as: (1) Considering tax deductions, should an expatriate's home country benefit programme be maintained? (2) Should the firm enrol expatriates in the host country benefits programme? (3) Should expatriates be given home country or host country social security benefits? (The tax implications will be considered later, see pp. 491–492.)

Benefit levels vary extensively depending on the MNC's headquarters location. Generally, benefits comprise less than 20 per cent of expatriates' compensation mix. However, the compensation mix for professional employees working for MNCs headquartered in Venezuela is comprised of over 40 per cent benefits (Mercer International, 2008). By comparison, the compensation mix for professional employees working for MNCs headquartered in Finland is comprised of only 2–3 per cent benefits (Mercer International, 2008). Benefits may also differ substantially between management- and professional-level expatriates working for MNCs within the same country. As previously mentioned, benefits for professional-level employees working for MNCs headquartered in Venezuela exceed 40 per cent; however, benefits for management-level employees working for MNCs headquartered in Venezuela is only 23–24 per cent (Mercer International, 2008).

Protection programmes In the US, the Social Security Act of 1935, The Family Medical Leave Act of 1993, and state worker's compensation programmes direct

MNCs to provide expatriates and their families with standard benefits. Despite their foreign assignments, if expatriates are US citizens they are able to continue to participate in the US Social Security Programmes (retirement-, survivor-, and disability-insurance, supplemental security income, and Medicare) as long as they are eligible. US Treasury Department regulations do not allow payments to eligible US citizens residing in Cuba or North Korea. Regulations also prohibit sending payments to expatriates in Cambodia, Vietnam or many areas that were in the former Soviet Union; however, exceptions are made. US expatriates younger than full retirement age should contact the Social Security Administration in order to avoid penalties or even the loss of future benefits (www.ssa.gov.). Expatriates are expected to report changes in family status when working on foreign assignments. Expatriates generally do not receive Medicare since it does not apply to health services outside of the US. Thus, no monthly premium is withheld for Medicare. The hospital insurance part of Medicare is available to expatriates when they are in the US. More information regarding expatriates' social security benefits is available at www.socialsecurity.gov. Expatriates working abroad for US public organisations and MNCs with 50 or more employees are eligible to receive up to 12 weeks of unpaid, job-protected leave per year as regulated by The Family and Medical Leave Act (FMLA). More information regarding FMLA is available at www.dol.gov. State workers' compensation laws generally do not apply to expatriates. Instead, expatriates must rely on their MNC's private insurance for expenses that they incur during work-related accidents.

In Canada, The Old Age Security Act, which came into force in 1952 directs MNCs regarding how to compensate expatriates with standard benefits. Typically, expatriates working abroad in Canada are eligible to receive coverage under Canada's Social Security programme for physician visits and hospitalisation. Furthermore, Social Security also provides limited benefits for long-term disability and a death benefit. For more information on the regulations regarding contributions to Canada's Old Age Security Programme please visit www1.servicecanada.gc.ca.

Paid time-off Similar to employees working domestically, expatriates are eligible to receive time-off for annual vacations, holidays and emergency leave. Expatriates typically do not receive extended periods of annual vacation relative to their domestic counterparts. However, US MNCs must comply with foreign laws regarding the amount of time that employees are given for vacation. Thus, as shown in Table 14.5, in many European countries (e.g., Austria, Denmark, France and Spain) where employees receive as many as 30-days minimum annual leave by law, US expatriates are also required to receive the same minimum number of annual vacation days even though the US has no minimum number of annual vacation days required by law. Many countries also have laws governing vacation

Table 14.5 Vacation days

Country	Days required by law	Average number of days taken
China	15 days	15 days
France	25 days	35–42 days
Italy	20 days	30 days
Japan	10 days	17.5 days
Spain	25 days	30 days
UK	20 days	25 days
USA	0 days	10.2 days (14)
Germany	30 days	37–47 days

Source: List of statutory minimum employment leave by country.

bonuses. For instance, MNCs headquartered in Brazil are required to pay a vacation bonus equivalent to one-third of the expatriate's monthly wage at the time of vacation. Expatriates do receive paid time-off for local and national holidays that are observed in the geographic area of their work assignment. In addition, US expatriates are also given time-off for nationally observed US holidays. Expatriates may also receive time-off for family emergencies such as those involving critical-illnesses and/or deaths of family members. When these events occur, MNCs may provide expatriates with either paid time-off emergency leave or an unpaid leave of absence.

Pension contributions The US Employee Retirement Income Security Act of 1974 (ERISA) protects the integrity of pensions for expatriates. Despite their foreign assignments, US expatriates are allowed to continue to participate in their company's pension plan as long as they are eligible. For more information regarding the fiduciary responsibilities of US MNCs regarding their employees' pension plans see the Employee Benefits Security Administration (https://www.dol.gov/ebsa/) or the Pension Benefit Guaranty Corporation (PBGC) (http://www.pbgc.gov/) websites. Similarly, The Canadian Pension Plan (CPP) and The Department for Work and Pensions (DWP) govern these matters for residents of Canada (www.hrsdc.gc.ca) and the UK (http://www.dwp.gov.uk/), respectively.

Other benefits Increasingly, many US MNCs also offer additional perquisites to expatriates in order to accommodate them during their overseas assignments including: (a) making contributions to savings and investments plans and equity portions of mortgage payments and (b) paying insurance premiums, alimony, child-support, student loans, and car subsidies particularly in hardship and danger situations. In some areas, such as Brazil, Norway, and Israel MNCs are mandated by the government to provide transportation allowances. Company cars are also common perquisites in Brazil (Mercer International, 2009). Other perquisites such as allowances for meals, clothing, club memberships, domestic help, medical, telecommunications, and security are provided on a case-by-case basis.

7 Approaches to international compensation

In the following section, we discuss the two main methods of international compensation. First, we discuss the going-rate approach which is also referred to as the market-rate approach. Second, we discuss the balance sheet approach which is also known as the build-up approach.

The going-rate approach

The going-rate approach is based upon typical market values found in the foreign country. In order to establish the expatriates' base salary and benefits, MNCs gather compensation information from local sources in the foreign environment in order to determine the best method of benchmarking. Once the information is collected, organisations determine whether the referent for determining their expatriates' salary will be: (1) employees of local companies, (2) expatriates of domestic competitors, or (3) expatriates' international global competitors working in the foreign location and performing similar work tasks. Typically, the MNC will supplement both pay and benefits if the foreign location is considered a low pay country.

An advantage to MNCs of using the going-rate approach is that it is easy to understand. It is also commonly used because of the perceived equality that exists between expatriates and local nationals. The perception of equality is very attractive to both parent- and third-country nationals in locations where local nationals receive higher salaries than those received in the expatriate's home country. When expatriates perceive that equality exists, they also adapt easily to the host country work norms and culture. Furthermore, there is impartiality in pay among expatriates of all nationalities.

There are many advantages to the going-rate approach, but it still has its shortcomings. Variations may exist in compensation when an expatriate moves between assignments in different countries. Expatriates' pay can fluctuate considerably due to disparities in pay between low- to high-pay countries. Such variations can also occur when an expatriate moves between assignments in a single country. Here an expatriates' pay might change due to vast differences in non-supervisory and managerial salaries in advanced economies. A second drawback to the going-rate approach is that variations may exist in compensation between expatriates of the same nationality working in different locations. This distinction can lead to competition between expatriates striving to accept assignments in high-pay foreign locations.

Balance sheet approach

Home country-based balance sheet approach The home country-based balance sheet approach is the most widely used approach and is based upon typical market values found in the home country area. It is the most common method because it ensures that expatriates are able to preserve the standard of living that they experience in their home country and prevents them from experiencing important losses due to their foreign assignment. In order to establish expatriate base salary and benefits, MNCs gather compensation information only from home country sources. Once baseline pay and benefits are established, adjustments are then made to balance additional expenses that expatriates will face in the foreign country. In order to appeal to employees, the home country-based balance sheet approach also provides expatriate and/or hardship premiums to the international assignment packages in addition to base salary.

The home country-based balance sheet approach is designed to cover four categories of expenses that are met by MNCs and expatriates in locations where costs exceed equivalent costs in the parent country. First, MNCs share costs associated with goods and services, namely expenditures associated with food, personal care, clothing, household furnishings, recreation, transportation and medical care in the foreign location. These costs may be typically reimbursed in the form of a cost-of-living allowance. Second, MNCs share costs associated with housing in the foreign location. These costs may be covered in the form of a housing deduction. Third, MNCs share costs associated with income taxes in both the expatriates' home- and host-country. These costs may be covered in the form of a tax deduction. Fourth, and finally, MNCs provide what are known as reserves to expatriates. These allowances may be in the form of investments, savings and/or pension contributions, payments for benefits, education expenses and taxes.

There are four advantages to MNCs of using the home country-based balance sheet approach. First, it creates perceptions of equity regarding foreign assignments for employees faced with choosing among locations. As a result of their perceived equity, expatriates will tend to view foreign locations in the same way with regard to levels of attractiveness. Second, the home country-based balance sheet approach creates perceptions of equity between parent country nationals since those working at or near headquarters and those on foreign assignments are compensated equally. Third, the home country-based balance sheet approach facilitates re-entry for expatriates. Repatriation is less arduous because employees' standard of living during their foreign assignment is not compromised under the home country-based balance sheet approach. Fourth and finally, this is easy to communicate to employees.

Whereas there are advantages to the home country-based balance sheet approach, it also has its disadvantages. Specifically, the home country-based balance sheet approach may create great disparity among parent country nationals and local nationals. Feelings of disparity might occur if expatriates discover that local nationals receive significantly more pay for performing the same job. For instance, this often happens when non-US-based MNCs establish subsidiaries in the US where employees receive among the highest levels of compensation in the world. However, the opposite is also true since US local nationals might also feel disparity when they discover that their US-based MNC is helping foreign expatriates to cover costs associated with goods and services, housing, income taxes and other reserves. The home country-based balance sheet approach may also create disparity among parent- and third-country nationals. For instance, in the Hong Kong regional office of a US MNC, a US-based expatriate and a Beijing third-country national performing the same job duties may have huge disparities in salary arising from the differences in US and Beijing base salaries. Lastly, the home country-based balance sheet approach may present MNCs with difficulties associated with helping expatriates to cover goods and services, namely those regarding tax deductions and pension contributions.

Headquarters-based balance sheet approach The headquarters-based balance sheet approach makes reference to the country where the MNC is headquartered rather than the expatriates' home country when estimating living standards. MNCs then pay the differential between the headquarters normal costs and the assignment costs. The headquarter-based balance sheet approach is an alternative for many MNCs because, similar to the home country-based balance sheet approach, it is simple for expatriates to understand and it allows them to maintain their purchasing power. It is also attractive because it is simple for the MNC to administer since all of the comparisons made refer to the headquarters' locale and promote perceptions of equity among assignees of different nationalities working in the same foreign location.

However, the headquarter-based balance sheet approach presents many obstacles to MNCs. It is more costly to administer with respect to assignees from low salary countries since their compensation is raised to meet the salaries of those working in close proximity to headquarters. The salary raises given to expatriates from MNCs located in low salary countries may be undesirable. They may create a disincentive for MNCs to repatriate for those expatriates and/or create a sense of entitlement among expatriates from low salary countries. The headquarter-based balance sheet approach may also be unfair to assignees from countries in which tax and cost-of-living expenditures are vastly different from headquarters.

Modified home country-based balance sheet approach The modified home country-based balance sheet approach gives reference to the expatriate's home country with regard to pay. However, unlike the home country-based balance sheet approach, reference is given to the host country with regard to payment of expenditures for housing and/or goods and services. Thus, the modified home country-based balance sheet approach offers a compromise between home country- and headquarter-based balance sheet approaches. Essentially, the modified home country-based balance sheet approach equalises cost-of-living adjustments for all expatriates working in the same host country while preserving their home country base pay. Similar to other balance sheet approaches, the modified home country-based balance sheet approach is challenging to administer and can lead to a sense of entitlement.

8 Current best practices to international taxation

The issue of taxation is perhaps the most emotional issue for international total rewards managers and expatriates. For IHR managers, resolving expatriate-related taxation concerns may be exceedingly time consuming and may present legal obstacles. For parent- and third-country nationals, taxation issues can evoke negative emotions since they may involve significant financial obligations. The burdens for parent- and third-country nationals are created since they are required to pay income tax returns in the same way as those residing in the United States and they may also be expected to pay income tax returns in their foreign location. As a result of expatriates paying taxes in two locations, MNCs usually select one of four approaches for handling international taxation. One of the less commonly used approaches is the *ad hoc* approach in which MNCs handle each expatriate differently. A second less commonly used approach is the *laissez-faire* approach in which employees are left to comply with taxation rules and regulations without any assistance from their MNC. Many expatriates respond to the *laissez-faire* approach by employing the services of an international tax accountant. The two most frequently used approaches are tax equalisation and tax protection (Latta and Danielsen, 2003), now discussed.

Tax equalisation
The underlying principle of tax equalisation is that expatriates neither gain nor suffer undue burden as a result of taxation issues while working abroad (Latta and Danielsen, 2003). There are two underlying premises of the tax equalisation approach. First, the MNC withholds an estimated amount equal to the home country tax obligation from the parent country national's pay. Second, the MNC pays actual taxes in the host country on behalf of the parent country national. The tax equalisation approach is used by MNCs because it does not impede the mobility of employees. It is also chosen by MNCs because it helps to facilitate tax planning and minimises expatriate non-compliance with their tax obligation. According to Latta and Danielsen (2003), 87.7 per cent of US, 73.7 per cent of Canadian, and 66.1 per cent of UK companies follow tax equalisation. Thus, US companies are more likely to use the tax equalisation approach than both Canadian and UK companies.

Tax protection
Tax protection is the most commonly used approach to taxation in the US. MNCs calculate a hypothetical tax (excluding foreign allowances) based upon the expatriates' home and foreign country income tax laws. The expatriate then pays the estimated

tax amount to both the home and host country. Thus, the expatriate's income is subject to taxes in the same way as home country and local nationals. Once the MNC is in receipt of the tax obligation funds, the expatriate is reimbursed for the difference if their actual taxes are less than the hypothetical tax. They are allowed to keep the difference if the actual tax is less than the hypothetical tax. The process of collecting tax liabilities from expatriates has become increasingly complex as MNCs operate in more and more countries with varying tax rates. In reaction to the added complexities that are associated with providing tax protection to employees working across multiple geographic areas, many MNCs have sought the advice and services of international accounting firms. They also respond by outsourcing one-of-a-kind components of expatriates' compensation packages that are too cumbersome to administer on a case-by-case basis. Outsourcing is particularly pertinent with regard to employee benefits, namely, pension plans, medical coverage and social security. However, even though outsourcing makes the latter issues more manageable, there are many remaining questions for MNCs regarding expatriate benefits. These questions include whether or not to enrol expatriates in-country or host country benefits programmes and whether expatriates should receive in-country or host country social security benefits. The intricacies associated with taxation and benefit administration are expected to continue as expatriate assignments become more increasingly prevalent. According to Latta and Danielsen (2003), 4.5 per cent of US companies and 13.2 per cent of both Canadian and UK companies follow tax protection. Thus, UK and Canadian companies are more likely to use tax protection than US companies.

9 International cost-of-living data

A particular challenge for MNCs is obtaining up-to-date and accurate international cost-of-living data. Due to the difficulties associated with gathering such data, many firms seek the advice of consulting compensation firms (e.g., Economic Research Institute, SalariesReview.com, SalaryExpert, Runzheimer International, etc.). Compensation firms offer cost-of-living indices based on the US Dollar which can be uploaded electronically by MNCs. For instance, The World Salaries Group publishes cost-of-living indices based upon Interbank exchange rates and IMF purchasing power parity exchange rates. As shown in Table 14.6, Switzerland has the largest cost-of-living index based upon the World Salaries Group estimation. Mercer Consulting conducts the most comprehensive comparisons of costs-of-living indexes in major international cities. Their survey is based on 200 items including housing, transportation, food, clothing, household goods and entertainment. According to their 2008 survey, Moscow topped their list of 143 cities as the world's most expensive for expatriates for the third consecutive year. Moscow is followed in rank by Tokyo, London, Oslo and Seoul respectively. The city of Asunción, Paraguay, is the least expensive city of those

Table 14.6   International average cost-of-living country comparison (US = 1.000)

Country	2005	2004	2003	2002	2001
Switzerland	1.505	1.522	1.421	1.257	1.166
Norway	1.487	1.366	1.254	1.105	1.010
Sweden	1.293	1.305	1.190	0.982	0.920
UK	1.240	1.240	1.090	0.989	0.932
Netherlands	1.224	1.219	1.108	0.913	0.847
Finland	1.184	1.194	1.110	0.955	0.915
Ireland	1.177	1.160	1.067	0.888	0.817
France	1.161	1.158	1.055	0.886	0.834
Japan	1.150	1.210	1.170	1.130	1.200
Belgium	1.132	1.132	1.032	0.863	0.813
Germany	1.130	1.133	1.040	0.878	0.829
Austria	1.095	1.097	1.002	0.843	0.796
New Zealand	1.069	1.001	0.876	0.710	0.651
Australia	1.062	1.021	0.891	0.731	0.688
Italy	1.042	1.049	0.952	0.789	0.736
Spain	1.019	1.000	0.897	0.734	0.678
Canada	1.006	0.935	0.866	0.761	0.773
US	1.000	1.000	1.000	1.000	1.000
Singapore	0.933	0.917	0.879	0.867	0.881
Greece	0.894	0.881	0.792	0.651	0.604
Portugal	0.890	0.881	0.796	0.659	0.604
Israel	0.810	0.819	0.825	0.811	0.884
Korea	0.780	0.720	0.690	0.660	0.630
Hong Kong	0.751	0.765	0.810	0.881	0.929
Mexico	0.640	0.610	0.631	0.692	0.690
Hungary	0.635	0.622	0.549	0.456	0.382
Czech Republic	0.622	0.573	0.513	0.442	0.371
Poland	0.604	0.536	0.494	0.477	0.473
Taiwan	0.554	0.535	0.524	0.535	0.562
Slovakia	0.543	0.514	0.436	0.340	0.309
Romania	0.513	0.432	0.378	0.315	0.289
Lithuania	0.505	0.500	0.450	0.381	0.352
Brazil	0.493	0.395	0.362	0.346	0.387

(Continued)

Table 14.6   *(Continued)*

Country	2005	2004	2003	2002	2001
Russia	0.480	0.400	0.320	0.280	0.270
Peru	0.459	0.448	0.438	0.432	0.425
Latvia	0.444	0.458	0.428	0.389	0.381
Thailand	0.319	0.311	0.299	0.289	0.282
Philippines	0.226	0.218	0.221	0.229	0.224
China	0.217	0.215	0.214	0.213	0.216

Source: worldsalaries.org (2008); reproduced with permission.

included on the survey. As shown in Table 14.7, only New York City, of 20 US cities included in Mercer's list, is among the top 50 most expensive world cities.

10 Repatriation issues

Perhaps the biggest obstacle that expatriates face is readjusting to work at head-quarters once their overseas assignment has ended. Even when MNCs expend an enormous amount of effort to meet the compensation and benefits needs of expatriates, they must apply the same amount of energy to ensure that expatriates' concerns are met once they return to their home country. First, IHR managers must ensure that repatriates are satisfied with their base salaries when they return to their home country. Specifically, upon return, repatriates might develop negative attitudes toward their MNC if they compare their work inputs and resulting outputs to the work inputs and resulting outputs of co-workers. If repatriates perceive an imbalance, they will likely develop perceptions of inequity (Bonache, 2005). This may occur when the repatriate has been assigned to foreign environments where work norms regarding the amount of activity and effort that employees contribute in order to complete work tasks are different from the norms in the expatriates' home country.

11 International trends in global total rewards

Three international trends in global total rewards have resulted in increased complexities for MNCs. The first trend is the increase in GDP growth rates which result from the influx of foreign investment. The latter increases ultimately place demands on the number of HCNs available to work in a particular area. The second trend is the ageing workforce which complicates how MNCs must handle pensions and other protection programmes such as social security. The third trend is the exchange rate,

Table 14.7   International average cost-of-living city comparison (New York City, US = 1.000)

1	Moscow	Russia	142.4
2	Tokyo	Japan	127
3	London	UK	125
4	Oslo	Norway	118.3
5	Seoul	South Korea	117.7
6	Hong Kong	China	117.6
7	Copenhagen	Denmark	117.2
8	Geneva	Switzerland	115.8
9	Zurich	Switzerland	112.7
10	Milan	Italy	111.3
11	Osaka	Japan	110
12	Paris	France	109.4
13	Singapore	Singapore	109.1
14	Tel Aviv	Israel	105
15	Sydney	Australia	104.1
16	Dublin	Ireland	103.9
16	Rome	Italy	103.9
18	St. Petersburg	Russia	103.1
19	Vienna	Austria	102.3
20	Beijing	China	101.9
21	Helsinki	Finland	101.1
22	New York City	US	100
23	Istanbul	Turkey	99.4
24	Shanghai	China	98.3
25	Amsterdam	Netherlands	97
25	Athens	Greece	97

Source: Mercer LLC (http://www.mercer.com/costofliving); used with permission.

and thus, the rate of pay in a foreign area relative to inflation rates. In 2007, the US dollar weakened against most of the currencies being compared and has been the dominant force behind changes in comparative unit labour costs and international competitiveness. Towards the end of 2008, the US dollar strengthened substantially, but its global role as a key peg for a number of other currencies is becoming increasingly questioned as more countries move towards baskets of currencies so as to reduce the risk of exposure to currency fluctuation. Each of these factors is likely to affect how MNCs reward their expatriate employees.

12 Summary and conclusion

In conclusion, we have tried to highlight the most important issues associated with a total rewards programme in the international arena. We began by examining the complex issues that IHR managers face when creating international total rewards systems. We then discussed the intricacies of the design process of a total rewards system for an international assignment (IA) versus the typical headquarters assignment. We highlighted traditional and newer forms of IAs since rewards are often a function of the type of IA (i.e., 3-year vs. 6-week vs. commuter assignment). We outlined the key components of an international total rewards programme, namely, base salaries, hardship premiums, allowances and benefits. We discussed the going rate and balance sheet approach to total rewards, followed by a discussion of their advantages and disadvantages. We examined international taxation in total rewards systems by focusing on current best practices. Unique to this analysis, we presented current international cost-of-living data which are useful for IHR managers who face problems associated with limited information/statistics on cross-country comparisons. We also discussed the specific problems that IHR managers face when compensating third country nationals relative to those they face with host country nationals. Finally, we closed our discussion with recent international trends in global total rewards.

Discussion questions

1 With the increase in use of outsourcing activities to further corporate interests abroad, all MNC employees are likely to work as expatriates during their careers! Comment on this statement.

2 Imagine an American MNC having to staff one of its subsidiaries in The Republic of Colombia. Which staffing approach would you chose? Explain why.

3 Stark discrepancies can occur in an employees' compensation package depending on whether employees' base pay is linked to their home or host country. How can MNCs ensure that these differences are justifiable?

4 There are two main methods of international compensation. Under which circumstances does each work best and why?

5 One of the most emotional issues for international total rewards managers and expatriates is taxation. Discuss in class ways in which both parties can overcome the challenges they are likely to face.

In a World of Pay

This case is adapted from "In a World of Pay" by Bronwyn Fryer, Harvard Business Review (HBR), November, 2003. Reproduced by permission of HBR.

Renate Schmidt, head of human resources, stood near her office window. Jürgen Mehr, Typware's head of marketing, had called to voice his displeasure about hiring Anne Prevost, director of marketing, at Xon Technologies, an American software company. Jürgen had been impressed with Anne's deep understanding of the global software industry. When Jürgen heard what the company was offering her, he lost his temper: 'Renate, € 244,000 is exorbitant!' 'She has another offer from Seistrand Systems. Our global head of marketing's eager to hire her, and I think Thomas will say that we should consider what she's worth.'

During dinner, Thomas, the CEO, had told Renate and Jürgen that Anne would be a fine addition. 'But this salary is too high.' 'We're trying to match the stock options that Seistrand is offering. The amount is not out of line when you consider things are more expensive in Europe than in the US', Renate explained. Jürgen was conservative about salaries, particularly in international negotiations. 'You know our strategy is to increase our international revenues by 10 per cent. 'Remind me why she is so interested in joining us?' Jürgen grumbled. 'There's no upward mobility for her at the company, and she's not satisfied with the lateral position she has been offered. Seistrand wants her, but the company is small and its stock is highly leveraged. And she's very interested in the idea of educating her sons in Europe.' 'And is her husband being transferred?', Jürgen asked. 'No husband.' 'All right, Renate,' Jürgen said finally.

The View from the top

'You want to talk with me about the American hire,' Thomas began. 'This salary request is for nearly as much as Jürgen himself makes. It will make others feel that we don't care about them.' 'Prevost is probably trying to figure in differences in tax rates, inflation, benefits, and floating currencies. She probably has stock options and a bonus package that she would give up. And, as you know, the United States does not have subsidised health care or educational support. 'I am concerned that too many people are already asking for much more than the job warrants.'

What's fair?

'Things were never this complicated at Lesom,' Renate thought. Typware was the opposite. Pay was not rationalised, and Renate noticed increasingly troublesome salary and benefit disparities among the managerial ranks. Female and minority employees made less than their white male counterparts. While Thomas had agreed to rectify the most glaring disparities, he seemed uninterested in stabilising salaries.

Of the company's 4,800 employees, 85 per cent were in Germany and were paid according to market rates. But since 1996, Typware had ventured aggressively into international markets. Most expatriates received the equivalent of their German salary, enrolment in local health care programmes, contributions to their German social security, and retirement plans. In most cases, the salary had been sufficient, given Germany's high cost of living. Nevertheless, individual expatriate packages had become complicated over the years. Per diem expenses varied according to country. Colombia's country manager had insisted on a 15 per cent 'danger pay' salary increase, more money for a German–Spanish private school, bodyguard protection, and additional household help. Moscow's manager of operations had insisted on a chauffeur. The Chicago regional director required college tuition fees for his son, since universities were paid for in Germany. The manager in India wanted compensation for premium health care. Some expatriates had boosted their total salary and benefits by more than 30 per cent, while others had seen their compensation fall.

All good questions

'Rainer,' Renate began, 'I would be very grateful for some advice.' 'What kind of retirement plan does she have in the US?' 'American social security, of course. And Xon probably contributes to a plan.' 'She will not be able to contribute to her US social security if she comes here. And she may not qualify for a German social security plan. So you will want to offer her a pension plan. Is Anne married? Does she have any children?' 'She is divorced and has two sons, 7 and 11,' Renate said. 'And they will enroll in a German school?' 'I assume so.' 'It would be free if they enroled in a German school. If she prefers a private school, or if they go to college in the US, she may want you to contribute something to their tuition. Does she have older parents? If she pays for a retirement home, you must consider that it costs very little here. She probably has executive medical coverage, which we do not have here. Find out whether anyone in the family has a health condition. US medical care is superior to what we offer here.' 'Rainer,' Renate said, 'These extra things will mean she is paid more in the end than her peers and perhaps even than her boss.'

Past the eleventh hour

Renate phoned Anne and ran through the questions. Anne said she had assumed her children would attend a German gymnasium. Anne added that she was paying the $3,000-per-month fee for an assisted living facility for her mother and was concerned about receiving good asthma health care for her 7 year-old. 'We hope that you will be willing to compromise on some issues and to be patient for a while longer.' 'I have another very good offer and can't keep them waiting forever. When can I expect to hear from you?' 'Soon.'

No easy answers

Rainer called the next morning. But the information he had was not helpful. 'It seems no one here has come up with a solution to the situation you are facing.' 'So I am pulling together a quick benchmark analysis on your broader issue.' 'It looks as if I'll have to sort this out myself.' 'I wish I could be of more help,' Rainer said. The thought occurred to Renate that, as a client, Typware might be more trouble than it was worth. 'I'll keep researching this problem if you want.' 'No, thank you,' Renate said. 'I need to get this report to the CEO soon. I'll figure something out.'

Case questions

1 What information does Typware need about Anne Prevost's current package at Xon Technologies in order to arrive at an appropriate offer?
2 Which components of global total rewards do you believe are essential for Typware to offer in order to keep Anne Prevost in Germany for several years?
3 Which approach to international taxation will ensure that Anne Prevost does not face double taxation issues?

Case questions for further study and reflection

1 Imagine you are offered an international assignment with your current employer. What are the main issues you need to negotiate with your employer prior to accepting the offer?
2 Imagine you have just completed your studies and are looking for an international job working in the technology industry. Would you work for Typware?

Further reading

- Bonache, J. and Fernandez, Z. (1997) 'Expatriate compensation and its link to the subsidiary strategic role: A theoretical analysis', *The International Journal of Human Resource Management*, 8(4): 457–75.

This article examines the connection between international strategy and strategic design of expatriates' salaries.

- Chen, C., Choi, J. and Chi, S-C. (2002) 'Making justice sense of local-expatriate compensation disparity: Mitigation by local referents, ideological explanations, and interpersonal sensitivity in China-foreign joint ventures', *Academy of Management Journal*, 45(4): 807–17.

This article focuses on how local employees of international joint ventures (IJVs) perceived disparity between their compensation and foreign expatriates' compensation from equity theory and social justice perspectives.

- Herod, R. (2009) *Expatriate Compensation: The Balance Sheet Approach (Global HR Management Series)*. Alexandria: Society for Human Resource Management (SHRM).

This book discusses the most important issues involved in developing a total rewards system for international expatriates, with an emphasis on the differences in the cost of goods and services, housing and income taxes in international assignments.

- Hodgetts, R.M. and Luthans, F. (1993) 'US multinationals' expatriate compensation strategies', *Compensation & Benefits Review*, 25(1): 57–62.

This article examines the compensation challenges faced by businesses expanding globally by describing the basic components of expatriate compensation and providing examples of strategies.

- Lomax, S. (2001) *Best Practices for Managers and Expatriates: A Guide on Selection, Hiring and Compensation*. New York: John Wiley & Sons, Inc.

This book describes the best practices for expatriate assignments, covering the entire process from tips on negotiating the best terms and conditions in such critical areas as compensation, benefits, housing and career planning to repatriation.

- Meyskens, M., Von Glinow, M.A., Werther, W. and Clarke, L. (in press) 'The paradox of international talent: alternative forms of international assignments', *International Journal of Human Resource Management*.

This article examines the different forms of international assignments, and how sourcing talent is often contingent on the length of assignment abroad.

- Paik, Y., Parboteeah, K.P. and Shim, W. (2007) 'The relationship between perceived compensation, organizational commitment and job satisfaction: The case of Mexican workers in the Korean Maquiladoras', *International Journal of Human Resource Management*, 18(10):1768–81.

This article uses equity theory to examine the effects of perception gaps in compensation between host country nationals and expatriates on organisational commitment and its impact on job satisfaction and job performance.

- Suutari, V. and Tornikoski, C. (2001) 'The challenge of expatriate compensation: the sources of satisfaction and dissatisfaction among expatriates', *International Journal of Human Resource Management*, 12(3): 389–404.

This article examines the sources of satisfaction and dissatisfaction relative to issues of taxation, availability of information about local cost levels, standard of living, currency rate risks, social security and pension issues, and spouse-related issues among expatriates.

- Wentland, D.M. (2003) 'A new practical guide for determining expatriate compensation: the comprehensive model', *Compensation & Benefits Review*, 35(3): 45–50.

This article discusses a model of expatriate compensation that incorporates and combines an expatriate selection process with a detailed foreign assignment evaluation and then links that situational analysis with a specific compensation package. The article also describes the recommended compensation approaches for each situational analysis.

Internet resources

1 International Average Salary Income Database (www.worldsalaries.org): An online provider of an international comparison of average salary for various professions and an international comparison of average personal income and expenditure.

2 US Department of State (www.state.gov): A United States federal department that publishes average costs of subsistence expenses outside of the United States.

3 Australian Taxation Office (www.ato.gov.au): An Australian office that publishes a schedule of daily travel allowance expenses that vary according to salary levels and destinations.

4 The Treasury Board of Canada Secretariat National Joint Council (www.tbs-sct. gc.ca): A Cabinet committee of the Queen's Privy Council of Canada that publishes a schedule of per diem rates that includes meals and incidentals for individuals travelling abroad.

5 Social Security Administration (www.ssa.gov): An independent agency of the United States federal government that administers a social insurance programme consisting of retirement, disability and survivors' benefits that US expatriates should contact in order to avoid penalties, avoid the loss of future benefits, and to report changes in family status when working on foreign assignments.

6 Service Canada (www1.servicecanada.gc.ca): A part of a Government of Canada-wide service transformation initiative aimed at responding to Canadians' expressed desire for better, more responsive, less cluttered service from Canadian governments, that Canadian expatriates should contact in order to avoid penalties, avoid the loss of future benefits, and to report changes in family status when working on foreign assignments.

Self-assessment questions

Indicative answers to these questions can be found on the companion website at www. sagepub.co.uk/harzing3e.

1 **How does an MNC that pursues a differentiation business strategy ensure that its HRM compensation and benefits policies are consistent?**

2 How might MNCs ensure that their total rewards policies maximise recruiting and retention efforts?

3 Why is it important for MNCs to develop compensation and benefits policies that result in fair processes and outcomes?

4 What are the complexities of international benefits programmes above-and-beyond those associated with international compensation?

5 How does employees' domestic base pay differ from employees' international base pay?

References

Aycan, Z., Al-Hamadi, A.B., Davis, A. and Budhwar, P. (2007) 'Cultural orientations and preferences for HRM policies and practices: The case of Oman', *International Journal of Human Resource Management*, 18: 11–32.

Banusiewicz , J.D. (2005) 'R&R leave program begins for service members, civilians in Operation Iraqi Freedom', First US Army in the News. American Forces Press Service.

Birdseye, M.G. and Hill, J.S. (1995) 'Individual, organizational/work and environmental influences on expatriate turnover tendencies: an empirical study', *Journal of International Business Studies*, 26: 787–813.

Bonache, J. (2005) 'Job satisfaction among expatriates, repatriates and domestic employees', *Personnel Review*, 34: 110–24.

Brewster, C. and Harris, H. (1999) *International HRM: Contemporary Issues in Europe*. London: Routledge.

Chen, C., Choi, J. and Chi, S-C. (2002) 'Making justice sense of local-expatriate compensation disparity: Mitigation by local referents, ideological explanations, and interpersonal sensitivity in China–foreign joint ventures', *Academy of Management Journal*, 45: 807–17.

Colquitt, J.A. (1999) 'On the dimensionality of organizational justice: A construct validation of a measure', *Journal of Applied Psychology*, 86: 386–400.

Colquitt, J.A., Conlon, D.E., Wesson, M.J., Porter, C. and Ng, K.Y. (2001) 'Justice at the millennium: A meta-analytic review of 25 years of organizational justice research', *Journal of Applied Psychology*, 86: 425–45.

Culpepper and Associates (2008) *Compensation and Benefite Survey*. Alpharetta, GA: Culpper and Associates.

Dickmann, M. and Tyson, S. (2005) 'Outsourcing payroll: Beyond transaction-cost economics', *Personnel Review*, 34: 451–67.

Downes, M., Thomas, A.S. and Singley, R.B. (2002) 'Predicting expatriate job satisfaction: The role of firm internationalization', *Career Development International*, 7: 24–36.

Fealy, L. and Kompare, D. (2003) 'Forging new territory – people challenges of emerging markets', *The Journal of Business Strategy*, 24: 9–13.

Galanaki, E. and Papalexandris, N. (2007) 'Internationalization as a determining factor of HRM outsourcing', *International Journal of Human Resource Management*, 18: 1557–67.

Harvey, M.G. (1989) 'Repatriation of corporate executives: An empirical study', *Journal of International Business Studies*, 20: 131–44.

Kessler, I., Coyle-Shapiro, J. and Purcell, J. (2006) 'Outsourcing and the employee perspective', *Human Resource Management Journal*, 9: 5–19.

Klaas, B.S., McClendon, J. and Gainey, T.W. (1999) 'HR outsourcing and its impact: The role of transaction costs', *Personnel Psychology*, 52: 113–36.

Latta, G.W. and Danielsen, T.A. (2003) 'Treatment of expatriate tax: A look at US, UK and Canadian practices', *Compensation and Benefits Review*, 35: 54–9.

Leat, M. and El-Kot, G. (2007) 'HRM practices in Egypt: The influence of national context', *International Journal of Human Resource Management*, 18: 147–58.

Mercer International (2008) *Compensation Plans around the World: A Guide for Multinational Employers*, August. New York, NY: Mercer International.

Mercer International (2009) *Global Compensation Planning Report*. New York, NY: Mercer International.

Meyskens, M., Von Glinow, M.A., Werther, W. and Clarke, L. (in press) 'The paradox of international talent: Alternative forms of international assignments', *International Journal of Human Resource Management*.

Moshe, B. and Sama, L.M. (2000) 'Ethical dilemmas in MNCs' international staffing policies – a conceptual framework', *Journal of Business Ethics*, 25: 221–35.

The Council for Community and Economic Research (2008) *ACCRA Cost of Living Index: Comparative Data for 318 Urban Areas*, 41.

US Department of Strate (2008) *Indexes of Living Cots Abroad*. Washington, DC: US Government Printing Office. (Available online at www. state.gov.)

World Salaries.Org (2008) *International Cost of Living Comparison*. Retrieved 23 December 2008 from http://www.worldsalaries.org/cost-of-living.shtml.

Part 4
Developments in IHRM Policy and Practice

15

Women Leading and Managing Worldwide[3]

Nancy Adler

Contents

Learning Objectives

After reading this chapter you will be able to

- Understand some of the recent changes for women in leadership and management

- Assess the past and present roles of women in international assignments and management

- Identify different ways of developing women for leadership and international management

- Explain why cross-cultural communication is an integral part of international management

- Critically evaluate the success of international assignments from the perspectives of the individual assignee and the company

Chapter Outline

The chapter reviews the increase of women expatriates and examines why in the past few women were selected for international assignments. A case study is presented of one organisation's approach to developing women for leadership and international management roles. The case emphasises the importance of continually improving employees' cross-cultural communication skills.

1 Introduction

This chapter considers women's increasing role in international management. Section 2 on 'women managing across borders' identifies the growing demand for women in international management and expatriate assignments. It argues that this demand arises from a number of factors and especially is due to global competitiveness and developments in societal norms and individual viewpoints. Section 3 discusses the results from various research studies and reports which demonstrate that the proportion of women employed on expatriate assignments and in leadership positions, whether in government or business, was very low until shifts in the global economy caused the increased pace of change since the 1980s. The global trend is one of increasing representation of women in senior positions in organisations and a growing proportion of women receiving expatriate assignments. Section 4 reflects on the reasons why there were so few women in international management roles and seeks to understand how a fairer and more meritocratic distribution of roles and responsibilities can be sustained in the future. Major themes include: companies recognising women's interest in international management; facilitating women's involvement in international management and career progression into leadership positions; as well as dealing with sources of reluctance and negativity especially when these reside inside the company's management ranks rather than, as is more often claimed, in other countries or organisations. This section ends with an investigation of some of the challenges and opportunities of dual-career families. Then, section 5 identifies some of the anticipated developments in the forseeable future and argues for greater sensitivity, corporate, social and ethical responsibility. Finally, a major case study is presented on one company's proactive and strategic approach to global leadership and management development for women.

2 Women managing across borders

Given the globalisation of the world economies, it is essential that managers who are prepared to assume significant leadership roles develop a global worldview based on international experience. Whereas the proportion of women managers working domestically within such countries as the United States has increased markedly over the last few decades, the number of women working outside their home country has not increased to the same degree. It was not until 2000 that many companies began to realise that women were as interested as their male colleagues in international careers (Caligiuri and Tung, 1999; Stroh et al., 2000b). Many women, however, continue to doubt their companies' commitment to act on such changed beliefs (Stroh et al., 2000a, 2000b).

There has been a longstanding belief in many countries that women don't want international careers. However, women have been shown to be just as interested in international careers and expatriate assignments as their male counterparts, and slightly more prepared (Adler, 1984b, 1994). Not surprisingly, the level of women's interest varies, as does that of their male colleagues, depending on the region of the world in which the foreign assignment is located (Lowe et al., 1999). In the decades to come, it is highly likely that companies will increasingly draw on their most talented men and women for global leadership and careers. Women will therefore have more opportunities to succeed on global assignments and as global leaders in the twenty-first century than in any prior era (see, among others, Caligiuri and Cascio, 1998).

3 The number of women expatriates is increasing

How many women are sent by their companies on assignments abroad? In the 1980s, only 3 per cent of North American expatriate managers were women (Adler, 1984c). At that time, no higher percentage existed anywhere else in the world. By the early 1990s, a survey of Asian, European and North American expatriate managers revealed that the proportion of women had risen to 5 per cent (ORC, 1992). A few years later, a 1995 UK survey (UMIST et al., 1995) documented that just under 9 per cent of expatriates were women. At about the same time, a 1996 US survey found that 14 per cent of American expatriate managers were women (Windham and NFTC, 1997). By 2002, data from Asia, Europe and the United States revealed that the proportion of women among expatriate managers in all three regions was 14 per cent (ORC, 2002). Although these surveys cannot be meaningfully compared due to varying methodologies, the proportion of women expatriates has clearly risen and can be expected to continue to do so. Selmer and Leung (2003c), among others, attribute this increase to the escalating intensity of worldwide economic competition, along with changes in corporate business strategies and changes in the women professionals themselves.

During the same period that the proportion of women expatriates was increasing, the work performed by expatriates and their role within multinational companies' overall business strategy also evolved. Through most of the twentieth century, most companies viewed expatriates, as well as the international operations within which they worked, as marginal to their overall business strategies (see Adler, 2002). By the end of the twentieth century, however, most companies recognised that their industries and companies had gone global, and, for the first time, expatriates were viewed as central to business success (Adler, 2002). Moreover, by the close of the twentieth century, the success of global operations was no longer seen as primarily the concern of expatriates, but rather, it was viewed as part of almost every manager's responsibility. As historic patterns of domestic and multi-domestic management became a relic of the past, virtual and co-located global teams, international business travel, international commuting, and both shorter- and longer-term global assignments emerged as part of most successful managers' business careers (see, among others, Adler, 2000; Adler and Ghadar, 1990, 1993; Mayerhofer et al., 2004). For women, this means that what had been a nice-to-have international experience that was often denied to them and then became a must-have international experience that was often denied to them, became a must-have career experience that was becoming somewhat more open to them, but which was still more frequently offered to men.

Some scholars are even predicting that women will be more in demand than men (among others, see Guthrie et al., 2003). Among other reasons given are that women are model global managers (Tung, 2004), women have more experience working as outsiders (Altman and Shortland, 2001), and as relative remuneration decreases for expatriation – as is currently the case – the proportion of women working abroad will rise (Selmer, 2001).

4 Myths and reasons explaining why multinational and global companies sent so few women on expatriate assignments

Why have multinational and global companies sent so few women on expatriate assignments? The most commonly believed reasons (Adler, 1994; also see Harris, 1995, 2004) are that:

1 women don't want to go abroad
2 companies do not want to send women abroad
3 foreigners are so prejudiced that women would not succeed even if sent
4 dual-career marriages make expatriation impossible for most women

Women don't want to go abroad?

One demonstration of women's interest in working internationally that was identified in early research studies is that most women expatriates, unlike their male counterparts, asked to be sent abroad (Adler, 1987). By contrast, up through the 1980s, most men waited for their company to ask them to consider a foreign assignment. Most women in the same era who were successful in being sent abroad initiated their assignments by going to their boss or other relevant decision-maker within the company and expressing interest in a foreign posting. If the woman failed to initiate a conversation in which she expressed interest in expatriation, it would often not occur to her company that they could consider her as a potential candidate. A recent study conducted in Hong Kong found that women who take the initiative to secure global assignments usually succeed in being sent (Selmer and Leung, 2003a). Given that the historical expatriate literature shows that the desire to go abroad is one of the best predictors of success on an expatriate assignment, it is particularly encouraging to learn that most women who are selected for international assignments desire to go. Historically, this has never been the case for the majority of male expatriates (see Adler, 2002).

Companies do not want to send women abroad?

How prepared are CEOs to recognise that their global competitiveness depends on including the most talented people in the world on their executive teams, women as well as men? Based on history, many believe the answer to be *not very*. In the United States at the beginning of this century, only two CEOs of *Fortune 500* companies were women (*Catalyst*, 2000). Among *Fortune 500* firms, women held only 6.1 per cent of the highest corporate titles and represented only 4.1 per cent of the top earners; while simultaneously holding half of all managerial and professional positions at lower levels (*Catalyst*, 2000). Similarly in Europe, women held less than 2 per cent of all senior management positions (Dwyer et al., 1996). Can companies – or countries – afford to continue their historic pattern of male-dominated leadership? As global competition intensifies, the opportunity cost of such traditional patterns escalates.

Research in the late 1970s first confirmed that companies do, in fact, hesitate to send women abroad (Izraeli et al., 1980; Thal and Cateora, 1979). This hesitation was reconfirmed by Adler (1984a) in the early 1980s. More than half the international HR managers surveyed in the early 1980s expressed hesitation, if not outright resistance, to selecting women as expatriate managers. A woman who was not considered for an assignment in Malaysia had this to say: 'Management assumed that women don't have the physical stamina to survive in the tropics. They claimed I couldn't hack it.'

Several women were offered positions, but only when there were no suitable male candidates for the assignment. Another woman who eventually obtained a position in Japan explained how she initially obtained the posting when management as more or less forced to send her out: 'They never would have considered me. But then the financial manager in Tokyo had a heart attack and they had to send someone. So they sent me, on a month's notice, as a temporary until they could find a man to fill the permanent position, it worked out and I stayed.' Firms often expressed their hesitancy by sending women in temporary or lower-status positions, for example, a woman reflecting on how she first gained her position in Hong Kong : 'After offering me the job, they hesitated, "Could a woman work with the Chinese?" So my job was defined as temporary, a one-year position to train a Chinese man to replace me. I succeeded and became permanent' (Adler, 1984a).

The primary reasons companies gave for their hesitancy, as expressed by three-quarters of the surveyed International HR managers, were that they believe that foreigners would not accept or sufficiently respect women expatriate managers for them to succeed abroad and that dual-career marriages would make it impossible for married women to move abroad (Adler, 1984a). Both concerns will be discussed in the following sections.

In the 1990s, further research confirmed similar results: companies continued to discriminate against women in their selection of expatriate managers (see Stone, 1991 and Punnett et al., 1992, among others). Some companies claimed that there were insufficient women available to send abroad (Izraeli and Zeira, 1993). Other companies required higher qualifications for women than for men before they would consider selecting a woman for an international assignment, including requiring women to have a higher level of education, greater technical competency, and more senior experience than their male colleagues prior to being sent abroad (Linehan and Walsh, 1999, 2000). Vague selection criteria gave still other companies the leeway to deselect women for a variety of unspecified reasons (see Harris, 1999, 2002). By contrast, companies using transparent and formal selection processes for men and women, based on job-specific criteria, select more women for international assignments (see Harris, 1999, 2002).

Foreigners are so prejudiced that women would not succeed even if sent?

One of the most common reasons companies give for hesitating to send women abroad on expatriate assignments is that foreigners are so prejudiced against women that it would be impossible for female expatriate managers to succeed abroad. The evidence, however, reveals that their fears are unwarranted (and are often, unfortunately, a naïve projection of their own belief systems onto foreigners). The first study of women expatriate managers' ability to succeed abroad was conducted in the 1980s and showed that North American women were slightly more successful than their male counterparts when working in Asia on expatriate assignments for North American multinational companies (Adler, 1987). In the 1990s, Caligiuri and Tung (1999) found that performance on expatriate assignments, as assessed by supervisors and as reflected in the proportion of expatriates who wanted to return home early, was equivalent for men and women. More recent studies have confirmed that expatriate women, although facing varying challenges, have succeeded in countries as varied as China, Japan and Turkey (Napier and Taylor, 2002; Taylor and Napier, 1996, 2001). Similar to their North American counterparts, European women have also succeeded when sent abroad as expatriate managers (Linehan and Scullion, 2004; Van der Boon, 2003) as have female Japanese expatriates (Thang et al., 2002).

Paik and Vance's research (2002) established that American women expatriates sent abroad by US multinationals were perceived more negatively by their American colleagues than by their Mexican, Korean and German colleagues; thus strongly suggesting that the problem is much more an issue of home-country prejudice and stereotyping than one of prejudicial behaviour on the part of host-country nationals. For years, anecdotal evidence has suggested that the problem of discrimination and prejudice resides at home, but is attributed to foreigners living abroad. As a number of North American women expatriates have stated, 'The hardest job on an international assignment is getting sent, not succeeding once sent' (Adler, 1987, 1994). Paik and Vance's 2002 research was the first to confirm the truth of such anecdotes (also see Van der Boon, 2003).

Dual-career marriages make expatriation impossible for most women?

Most, although not all, challenges facing dual-career expatriate couples are either caused or exacerbated by companies using traditional single-career paradigms rather than approaches designed for dual-career couples.

Historically, when most companies' expatriate policies were developed, they assumed that the husband was the expatriate manager and that his wife would accompany him, but would not work outside the home. Such companies traditionally offered expatriates extra money – so, among other things, the wife could enjoy the international club while not working. When the topic of employment for the wife came up, companies usually pointed out that the foreign country did not offer working permits to spouses. In some cases, companies attempted to secure low-level positions for the wife at a partner company (thus implicitly assuming that the wife neither had nor wanted a higher level position). In other cases, companies suggested that the wife forgo employment and involve herself in volunteer activities. Other companies offered to replace the salary of wives who had worked at home but couldn't work abroad. In almost all such cases, however, the company assumed that the wife's replacement salary would be insignificant when compared with that of her expatriate manager husband. None of these solutions are a good fit for today's dual-career couples. Each assumes that the wife was either not previously employed, did not previously hold a high-ranked professional position, had a job (not a career), was willing to give up her job, did not want to work abroad, or could not work abroad (see Adler, 2002).

Today, whether the trailing spouse is male or female, what dual-career couples need from the companies that wish to send them abroad are: (1) career counselling so that the trailing spouse (whether husband or wife) can think through the options that might work at his or her particular career stage and in the part of the world where the potential expatriate assignment is to be located; (2) international executive search services to help the trailing spouse locate appropriate professional positions abroad and learn to present themselves in ways that are attractive to potential foreign-based employers; and (3) flexible benefits packages.

Different couples make different decisions about what will work for them. Many expatriate couples choose to commute, rather than both co-locate in the same foreign city. In such cases, couples need their expatriate package to cover 'staying connected' costs (primarily airline tickets and phone bills). Other couples choose to both move into the same region, but are unable to co-locate in the same city. They too need staying-connected costs reimbursed. Still other couples prefer to have the trailing spouse take primary responsibility for the children, the home and social functions rather than taking paid employment.

Whereas staying at home had been the conventional choice when the trailing spouse was a woman, it becomes a more challenging choice when the trailing spouse is a man. Few societies readily respect men who take primary responsibility for the home and children and who are financially supported by their wife. If such culturally generated stresses are not explicitly addressed, they can easily damage both the marriage and the expatriate manager's productivity.

Company support is critical for female expatriate managers, no matter what the family situation (see Caligiuri et al., 1999; Selmer and Leung, 2003b; Westwood and Leung, 1994, among others). It should be noted that single women who go abroad as expatriate managers, similar to men who find themselves in the role of a trailing spouse, face challenges that most of their predecessors never considered. The issue is not that such problems are insoluble, but rather that reality-based creativity is needed to solve them.

5 Conclusion: The future – women leading and managing worldwide

As scholars seek to understand better the role of women managers and leaders in the twenty-first century, it will be important to go beyond the twentieth-century models based on the personal and professional lifestyles of men. Equally, it will be important to go beyond models based primarily on the experiences of multinational companies headquartered in traditionally prosperous countries. We need to understand better the experience of women from economically developing and transitional economies who seek international careers. More broadly, we need to understand the global business and HR strategies of companies headquartered outside of North America, Europe and Japan. As our global understanding increases, it will become easier to provide nuanced descriptions of women's managerial and leadership styles, rather than continue to assume that women's contexts and experience are similar worldwide. Lastly, given the competitive intensity of the global economy, we should strive to learn more about the complementary and synergistic possibilities inherent to women and men working together.

The most important question for the future is not simply how we can increase the proportion of women leaders, executives and managers. Rather, the crucial twenty-first century question is how we can create a society worthy of being bequeathed to future generations (see Adler, 1998b). To create such a society, we need corporations worldwide to understand that the most effective leadership comes from women and men. The world will not benefit if we simply substitute ineffective, greedy women for similarly ineffective, greedy men. The goal is not to have the next Enron led to its demise by Katrina Lay rather than Ken Lay. Equity is only sustainable within a larger system of purpose and meaning.

Discussion questions

1 Assuming that over the next two decades an ever increasing number of women are employed on expatriate assignments, what changes will have to be made in corporations and societies for this development to be properly supported?

2 What IHRM policies and practices should companies consider to maximise the benefits for women's careers within the company?

3 What initiatives should be implemented in schools and universities to encourage men to improve their contribution to dual-career families?

4 The chapter reports massive and recent change in women's opportunities for jobs in leadership and management roles. What further change do you hope will occur during your working life?

5 Create and discuss ten recommendations for women on: a) Cross-cultural communication competences; and b) Preparation for an expatriate assignment.

The Women's Global Leadership Forum
Nancy J. Adler, Laura W. Brody and Jayca S. Osland

Anytime you have a fiercely competitive, change-oriented growth business where results count and merit matters, women will rise to the top. (Carly Fiorina, CEO, Hewlett Packard, 1998)

Case Study – The women in global leadership forum

Adapted from: Nancy J. Adler, Laura W. Brody and Joyce S. Osland, 'Going beyond twentieth century leadership: a CEO develops his company's global competitiveness', *Cross-Cultural Management: An International Journal*, vol. 8 (no. 3-4), 2001, pp, 11-34.

Women leaders

Careful observation reveals a rapidly increasing number of countries and companies moving away from the historic men-only pattern of senior leadership. For example, of the 47 women who have served in their country's highest political leadership position by the end of the twentieth century – either as president or prime minister – over 60 per cent have come into office in just the last decade, and all but seven are the first woman her country has ever selected for such a position (for a more in-depth discussion of women political leaders see Adler, 1996, 1997a, 1998a and 1998b. Similarly, among the current women CEOs leading major companies, almost all are the first woman whom her particular company has ever selected (similarly for a more in-depth discussion of global women business see Adler, 1997a, 1997b, 1999a,1999b, and 1999c).

The question is no longer 'Is the pattern changing?' but rather, 'Which companies are taking advantage of the trend and which are falling behind?' and 'Which strategies will prove most effective in moving the best people – women and men – into senior leadership positions?' Led by IBM, a small number of global companies began major initiatives to move the most talented women from around the world into their company's previously all-male senior executive positions. This case study describes one such company's experience in creating an organisational change process designed to increase its overall global competitiveness (Adler, et al., 2000, 2001).

Bestfoods Leadership and Global Competitiveness

By the time Unilever bought Bestfoods in 2000 – immediately after the events described in this article – the company had become one of the most internationally oriented food companies. It was among the largest US-branded food companies, with annual sales in

1999 of $8.4 billion. Bestfoods' return on equity of 56 per cent placed it in the top quartile of its peer group. The company earned 60 per cent of its revenues from non-US sources, operated in more than 60 countries, and marketed products in 110 countries.

Bestfoods' leadership was as global as the company's operations. Almost half of the 20 corporate officers came from outside of the United States, with eight nationalities represented among them. Similarly, on the board of directors, five passports were represented among the 14 members. Two of the CEOs sitting on Bestfoods' board were women. Of the company's 44,000 employees, two-thirds worked outside of the United States.

Similar to many industries, consumer foods was becoming increasingly competitive. Whereas many consumer foods companies used to be able to operate as loose confederations of fairly autonomous individual country operations, global competition was beginning to force all members of the industry, including Bestfoods, to more closely coordinate their operations worldwide to an extent previously found unnecessary.

To succeed in such an environment, companies need to attract and retain the best talent available worldwide, including both women and men from all nationalities. Bestfoods was no exception. Such global talent needs to operate effectively at both global and local levels. Moreover, with women making more than 80 per cent of purchasing decisions for its products, Bestfoods knew that it would not survive if it failed to understand women's needs and priorities.

There is no question that Dick Shoemate, Bestfoods' chairman, chief executive officer, and president, fully understood this competitive necessity and its implications for his company's future. Shoemate had explicitly stated Bestfoods' commitment to actively attract, retain and develop the most highly talented women and men from all parts of the globe. Moreover, he recognised that words were not enough to institute the changes needed for twenty-first century success. By 1997, Shoemate had significantly increased the number of women in executive positions and had placed the first two women on Bestfoods' board of directors. Even though Bestfoods' numbers compared favourably with those of most global companies in the industry, the CEO considered them insufficient to support the future he envisioned for the company.

Bestfoods first Women's Global Leadership Forum

In 1998, Shoemate announced that Bestfoods would hold its first Women's Global Leadership Forum. (For a detailed description of Bestfoods, the process leading up to the Global Women Leader's Forum, and the design of the Forum itself, see Adler et al., 2000.) Similar to other companies confronting such issues, Bestfoods had to make a difficult decision – to hold a women-only event or invite both men and women. There are advantages and disadvantages to both approaches. Women-only events theoretically allow women to discuss issues more openly in a group that understands the context of their remarks without needing much interpretation or explanatory background. The opportunity to discuss the unique aspects of their situation often allows women to form relationships that provide ongoing support. On the other hand, including both women and men provides an opportunity to hear different perspectives and to build a mutual agenda for change. Mixed groups often mitigate the possibility of a backlash. Given the goals of the Forum, Shoemate and Brody opted for a strategy that combined the best of both methods. It was a women-only event when they discussed developmental issues and the women's current situation; however, most key executives, male and female, were invited to and attended the opening and closing of the Forum and selected other sessions. In addition, to symbolically communicate the importance and urgency attached to the issues, Shoemate chose to convene the Forum in the same location used by the company for its most important meetings and leadership development programmes.

As announced, the Forum was to be held for 4½ days under the direction of Laura Brody, Bestfoods' Director of Diversity and Development. (See Osland and Adler, 2001 for an in-depth discussion of the major role Brody played in managing the organisational change effort and in leading the Women's Global Leadership Forum.) The CEO planned to invite the company's most talented and senior women from each region of the world and every functional area. Because he did not want to isolate the women in a women-only event that could be perceived as tangential to the company's core business strategy, Shoemate also invited members of the Corporate Strategy Council – composed of the six most senior corporate officers, all of whom were men – most corporate officers, and both women members of the board of directors to the opening of the Forum, selected sessions and the participants' presentations. Shoemate personally attended the Forum on three of the four days.

The primary purpose of the initiative was strategic – to increase Bestfoods' global competitiveness. The company's other explicitly stated goals were to:

- Develop the global leadership skills of Bestfoods' most highly talented and senior women;
- Create an internal network among Bestfoods' women leaders to facilitate their global effectiveness; and
- Develop both global and local recommendations for enhancing Bestfoods' ability to support the career advancement and success of an increasing number of highly talented and senior women.

The process leading up to the forum: creating an environment for change
The Forum is best understood as part of the larger process of organisational change and development in which it was embedded (see Adler et al., 2000, 2001; Osland and Adler, 2001). The organisational change process was not only a first for Bestfoods; it was one of the first in-company global leadership initiatives in the world to focus on women. Many, primarily American, companies offer women-in-management programmes, but such programmes are usually domestic in focus and rarely include women from around the world. Moreover, in most firms these domestically oriented programmes target lower-level employees – often emphasising entry-level personnel or managers rather than the company's most senior leaders (Adler, 1999a). Similarly, whereas many companies regularly hold global leadership programmes for their senior executives, these programmes rarely include many, if any, women.

The initial step in the organisational change process focused on identifying the company's most talented women and providing visibility for them, both as potential invitees to the Forum and, more importantly, as part of the company's talent pool for current and future leadership positions. To identify such women, Brody solicited nominations from all division presidents and personally reviewed the company's lists of high potential and outstanding employees. The Corporate Strategy Council then ranked the nominees. Final selections maintained an equitable representation from each division and region of the world, with more than half of the invitees coming from outside the United States. (Research based on a wide range of US-based companies suggests that they tend to select the women perceived to be the most masculine for promotion and leadership positions – see Wajcman, 1998)

During the selection process, some members of the Corporate Strategy Council expressed concern about potentially generating negative reactions to holding a global forum for women leaders. Contrary to their fears, the initial response to announcing the Forum was extremely favourable, with every division requesting additional spaces for women from their region. The mere process of identifying high-potential women had immediate, positive outcomes. One country manager, for example, expressed how pleasantly surprised he was to discover many more high potential women working in his affiliate than he had imagined. In another division, the nominations review process led to one woman's immediate promotion.

Following the initial positive response, reactions among both the men and women varied. In the ensuing weeks, some men reacted very positively, believing that such a forum was long overdue, while others expressed scepticism. Still others responded negatively, believing that the very idea of a *women's* forum discriminated against men. The most negative men informally began referring to the upcoming Forum as 'a coffee klatch' and 'the girls' knitting club', and cautioned that the Forum would turn into 'a bitch session'.

Many women in the company responded very positively to the announcement that Bestfoods would be holding a Women's Global Leadership Forum. One senior woman sent a letter to the CEO expressing her amazement, 'I never thought I would live to see the day that this company, or any company, would hold such a forum. ...Congratulations! I am 100 per cent with you.'

The women's reactions, similar to those of the men, also varied, with some more cautious or negative than the majority. Some women were apprehensive about a possible male backlash. Others expressed concern that, in singling them out as women, the company was not recognising their business accomplishments. As one senior European executive commented, 'I am happy to attend the Forum if I'm being invited because of my business acumen as one of the top 100 people in this company; not simply because I am "a girl".'

Bestfoods designed a survey (based loosely on *Catalyst*, 1996) to differentiate people's perceptions from actual competitive advantages and actual obstacles women and men encounter in exercising leadership and achieving career success in global companies. The survey constituted the second major initiative in the company's organisational change process. As such, it was used to more deeply involve Bestfoods' most senior men and women in the competitive challenges facing the company, and, thus to build their support for implementing the recommendations that the Forum would generate.

The confidential survey was sent to 200 men and women, including all corporate offi-cers, the most senior executives, and all women invited to attend the Forum. While iden-tifying some similarities among women's and men's perceptions and their respective recommendations for change, the comprehensive 150-question survey revealed many highly significant differences (see Adler et al., 2000). Most identified issues were in no way unique to Bestfoods but rather echoed general patterns that are well documented in recent organisational research (Ragins et al., 1998).

Given the marked differences – both between perception and experience, and between women's and men's points-of-view – the next step in the organisational change effort was to assist both women and men to better understand each other's reality. As in other companies, the problem was neither singularly women's behaviour nor men's attitudes or vice versa; rather it was for both to learn to see organisational reality more clearly and to begin to work together in new ways. The survey results thus reinforced the need for the Forum as a place where women and senior male executives could better understand each other's reality, and where the women could generate reality-based, rather than myth-based, recommendations to guide Bestfoods' future.

The third major initiative in the organisational change process was the 4½-day Women's Global Leadership Forum. Fifty-five participants came from 25 countries and represented every function within the company. The typical woman participat-ing in the Forum was 41 years old, married, and had at least one teen-aged child. The diversity among the women, however, was significant. There was a 29-year gap between the oldest and the youngest participant, with families ranging from those with grown-up children to toddlers, to single women without any children. The aver-age participant had at least 15 years of professional experience and 10 years working at Bestfoods. The women were highly educated. Most held a bachelor's degree, with almost half having earned a master's or doctorate degree. The typical participant spoke at least two languages, with some Europeans fluently speaking as many as five. Most Americans were monolingual. A quarter of the women had global work experience, with some having lived and worked in as many as five countries. Fewer participants from the United States than elsewhere had benefitted from such global experience.

As described previously, the Forum had four major objectives: enhancing the com-pany's strategic business capability; enhancing participants' global leadership skills; creating a network of women leaders within the company; and producing both glob-ally and locally applicable recommendations. The series of activities planned for the Forum was designed to further all four objectives, with some activities more focused at the individual level, some at the organisational level, and some at the team or network level.

Developing the individual: enhancing global leadership skills
Global leadership is not the same as domestic leadership (Adler, 1997b; Bartlett and Ghoshal, 1989; Dorfman, 1996). Harvard leadership scholar Howard Gardner notes

that global leadership had been '...the most important, but rarest and most elusive, variety of leadership' (Gardner, 1995). As CEO Shoemate appreciated, the 'rarest leadership' of yesteryear has become today's competitive necessity. One of his goals for the Forum, therefore, was to develop the global leadership competencies of Bestfoods' most highly talented and senior women. As CEO, he recognised that the company's current and future senior leaders needed to replace their previously effective domestic and multi-domestic approaches with globally integrated, cross-culturally interactive competencies that would allow them to lead in the twenty-first century (Adler, 1997b; Bartlett and Ghoshal, 1989; Black et al., 1999; Gregerson et al., 1998; Levy, et al., 1999; Mendenhall, 2001; Osland and Taylor, 2001 and Yeung and Ready, 1995), including:

- Personal traits and competencies – Commitment, a cosmopolitan outlook, courage, curiosity, an entrepreneurial spirit, maturity, thinking agility (or cognitive complexity), and the ability both to improvise and to create and maintain a vision.
- Interpersonal competencies – Ability to communicate across cultures, to establish close personal relationships with people from around the world, to motivate colleagues from a wide range of cultures, to manage cross-cultural conflict, to negotiate internationally, to work in multicultural teams, and to build geographically dispersed communities.
- Global business competencies – Ability to demonstrate global business savvy, balance both global and local tensions, simultaneously meet the demands for current performance and continual innovation and learning, and act in environments defined by increasingly high levels of ambiguity and complexity.
- Global organisational competencies – Global organisational savvy, a stakeholder orientation, and the ability to: successfully bring about organisational change, manage uncertainty, create learning systems and manage cross-cultural ethical issues.

Although the full set of global competencies could not be addressed during such a short meeting, the Forum wove together a series of lectures, discussions, exercises and team meetings designed to enhance a number of the participants' global leadership competencies, including, for example, their ability to use a full range of power and influence skills.

In the past, well-run companies were described as those having a unitary command structure. Today, as global organisations flatten into geographically dispersed and flattened networks and project teams, the relevant metaphor has shifted from single-leader models to the *leader-ful* organisation – from leadership as *power over* increasingly to leadership as *power with*. In a global context, being able to work closely with people from different nationalities in situations only minimally defined by hierarchy has become a necessary competence for success. Forum activities focused on enhancing each woman's skills at communicating, mentoring, negotiating, and working in teams with colleagues from around the world. A session was held the last day, for example, in which each woman received cross-cultural feedback on her overall effectiveness at the Forum from her Asian, European, Middle Eastern and North and South American colleagues.

To enhance the women's skills at creating a globally encompassing vision – and thus at enhancing their *power to* skills – the women presented vision statements in the form of news documentaries. During the session, each woman received feedback on the content and delivery of her vision statement from multiple perspectives. Would the message be meaningful to Latin Americans? Would it inspire Europeans? Would it motivate Asians? Would North Americans consider it worthwhile? Would Middle Easterners find it respectful?

With globalisation comes rapidly increasing levels of ambiguity, complexity and uncertainly. *Power within* skills become particularly important in anchoring executives working in such environments. *Power within* derives from leaders' most profound understanding of themselves and their most deeply held personal and spiritual values, commitments and beliefs. Leaders foster *power within* skills by setting aside daily time for reflection (Gardner, 1995). At the Forum, daily time set aside for journal writing encouraged participants to reflect on the relationship among the world's and industry's global challenges, their career aspirations and leadership approaches, and their most deeply held values, beliefs and commitments. In another reflective session, participants clarified their leadership role models by identifying women whom they wished to emulate or whose leadership had influenced them. This *Herstory* session allowed participants to examine more closely the ways in which women worldwide exercise power and influence.

Developing the organisation: enhancing the company's strategic business capability

Numerous aspects of the Forum focused on developing the overall organisation. For example, Laura Brody presented the survey results the first day, followed immediately by global team meetings to begin developing recommendations for increasing the company's opportunities for success in the twenty-first century.

Following a presentation the second morning on *Competitive Frontiers* outlining the experiences companies face in sending women abroad on global assignments, the women identified the conditions Bestfoods needed to create to successfully send both single and married women – either with or without children – abroad (Adler, 1994, 2000). This discussion was particularly important, since most companies still design their expatriate philosophies, policies and benefits packages primarily for married men with stay-at-home wives, rather than for the women represented at the Forum (Adler, 2002; Osland, 1995).

Continuing the organisational theme on the third morning, a lecture on *Global Leadership: A Dialogue with Future History* was planned highlighting the increasing number of women leading global companies and countries and their unique contributions, commitments and paths to power (Adler, 1997a). The discussion was designed to give participants access to a wide range of role models of successful women from around the world who have become global leaders – women whose career paths rarely replicate those of the men who have traditionally led most major companies.

Developing a network of women leaders

Bringing together 55 of the company's most senior and highest potential women was the first step in creating a network to facilitate both the company's and the women's global effectiveness. Most Forum activities were designed to strengthen the network, initially by allowing the women to meet and to learn about each other's unique individual and cultural backgrounds. In the opening *Who Are We?* session, for example, the women introduced themselves by describing one way in which being a woman had helped in achieving company goals. Such stories allowed participants to more fully appreciate the professional impact of being a woman – including, contrary to the popular mythology, that being a woman is often a competitive advantage. Participants also began to understand the ways in which their positive professional experiences were both varied and similar worldwide.

Among other network-building activities, a *How well do you know your global colleagues?* session paired women from various parts of the world in coaching sessions about themselves, their countries and their leadership styles. Beyond increasing understanding of each other's countries, the session encouraged the women to identify opportunities for creating cultural synergy – for combining their unique cultural perspectives for the benefit of the company, society, the network and each individual (see Adler, 2002).

The teambuilding and networking aspects of the design resulted in numerous business and idea-sharing discussions. During the Forum, the women formally created a *Global Women's Network* and committed to staying in touch electronically and in person. Following the Forum, they quickly began using the *Network* for coaching, professional support and notifying each other of career and business opportunities and strategies.

Table 15.1 The Women's Global Leadership Forum

Forum Acitivities		Organizational Development	Team & Network Building	Individuals Leadership Development
Pre-Forum				
	Cross-cultural Facilitator Training			X
Daily:	Daily time for personal reflection, leadership role models, and networking:			
DAY 1	Pre-Form Activities	X	X	
	Reception & Opening Dinner,	X	X	
	with board members, CEO and corporate directors			
DAY 2 a.m.	Global Introductions: Who are we?	X		
	CEO Opening Keynote address		X	
	Retaining Global Talent		X	
	Leadership and Power	X		X

(Continued)

Table 15.1 *(Continued)*

Forum Acitivities		Organizational Development	Team & Network Building	Individuals Leadership Development
Lunch				
p.m.	How Well Do You Know Your Global Colleagues?		X	X
	Building Global Teams: The Perfect Square		X	X
	Leadership & Vision		X	X
	Perceiving a Global Reality	X		X
	Is it True?: Reality & Perception			
	(survey feedback)	X		X
DAY 3 a.m.	Workforce Inclusion: Talent as a Competitive Asset		X	
	Competitive Frontiers: Women			X
	Managers in Global Economy	X		
Lunch	Ethnic lunch		X	X
p.m.	Herstory: The Roots of women's		X	
	Global Leadership			
	Assessing Leadership Excellence			
	The Bottom Line: Women and	X		
	Business Opportunities			X
DAY 4 a.m.	Global Leaders: A Dialogue with Future History			
	Our Best Wisdom:	X		X
	• Men Mentoring Women	X		X
	• Women Mentoring Men	X		X
Lunch	Cross Cultural Coaching		X	
p.m.	Cross-cultural Negotiating and Coaching			X
	Organizational Changes and Development	X		X
	Preparation for team presentations to CEO	X		X
Pre-Forum				
DAY 5 a.m.	The Future: Global Women's Leadership			X
	Network Acts Recommendations presented to			
	CEO & senior executives	X		
	Closing reflection & feedback in global teams	X	X	X
	Response from CEO & senior executives	X		
Lunch	Closing lunch celebration with CEO & executives.		X	

Source: Table 1: The women's global leadership forum, in: Nancy J. Adler, Laura W. Brody and Joyce S. Osland, 'Going beyond twentieth century leadership: a CEO develops his company's global competitiveness', *Crass-Cultural Management: An International Journal*, vol. 8 (no. 3-4), 2001, pp. 11–34.

Organisational change at Bestfoods

On the final morning of the Forum, Shoemate asked the participants to be very honest in their feedback to him and to senior management. The women recommended that the company make changes in three major areas: work/life balance – enabling women to perform to their highest level; diversity – increasing women's representation in senior and high level positions; and career development – enhancing career opportunities. To craft an immediate response, the CEO separated the recommendations into three response categories:

- Current company initiatives. Activities already underway whose progress the company needed to accelerate and to better communicate
- New corporate-wide initiatives with potentially high impact
- New 'local' initiatives best addressed within specific countries, regions or divisions while still at the Forum, the CEO committed to accelerating the company's efforts in the first category.

New corporate-wide initiatives

Before the Forum ended, Shoemate also agreed to place the entire second category of recommendations focusing on new corporate-wide initiatives on the agenda for the next Corporate Strategy Council (CSC) meeting. The new initiatives included:

- Establishing senior management accountability for retaining and developing high-performing women;
- Increasing women's participation in high-visibility assignments and taskforces – especially those with a global focus;
- Creating flexible global assignments of shorter duration as an alternative to traditional expatriate assignments;
- Defining the 'work-day' and 'work-place' more flexibly to avoid the 'all or nothing' ('work or stay home') choice managers currently face when attempting to balance professional with private life and commitments; and
- Expanding global membership on the Diversity Advisory Council.

Less than two months after the Forum, the Corporate Strategy Council approved all the women's corporate-wide recommendations. In addition, the Corporate Strategy Council agreed to take responsibility for oversight of the company's global diversity strategy, thus inextricably linking the company's business and diversity strategies. To more effectively address the many regional and country-level issues, the Corporate Strategy Council members, as division presidents, committed to replicating the corporate diversity council architecture in each of their respective businesses. The Corporate Strategy Council also initiated a company-wide strategy for communicating the results of the Forum throughout the company. One month after the Corporate Strategy Council meeting, at the WorldTeam Meeting (the biannual meeting of the company's 145 most senior executives), the survey results, Forum recommendations and the new company commitments were formally announced.

New 'Local' initiatives

The newly created division councils formulated their own local initiatives, with many Forum participants helping to guide their division's strategy. In Latin America, for example, not only did Argentina, Brazil, Colombia and Mexico form country-level councils, but each country also started benchmarking itself against the diversity initiatives of other multinationals operating in the region. Just three months after the Forum, Argentina mirrored the corporate model and conducted an Argentine Women's Forum for their highest-potential and most senior women. Mexico soon followed. Asia, Europe and corporate headquarters similarly began to more actively use their executive programmes and senior-level positions to improve the retention and development of high-performing women.

Outcomes and responses to Bestfoods' first Women's Global Leadership Forum

As the Forum ended, everyone agreed that it had been a success. The CEO stated that the Forum had exceeded his expectations and that he believed it would make a difference in the company's future. The women participants echoed the same positive sentiments, with one woman exclaiming, 'I had no idea that there were so many talented and outstanding women in this company!' Another woman, who leads a $400 million business, addressed the CEO at the closing session, saying:

> At first I was hesitant about coming to a company forum just for women. Yet this has been a wonderful experience. Mr. Shoemate, this is a group of outstanding business colleagues, each of whom just happens to be a woman.

The women's surprise at the breadth and depth of talented women within the company may reflect the historical invisibility of talented women in most companies, or the extent to which some women, including at Bestfoods, have assimilated the values and perspectives of the dominant male organisational culture. However, the increasing visibility of talented people – both male and female – also probably reflects the shift from a domestic to a global mindset. In domestic companies, it is less necessary to recognise talented people working outside one's own country; in global companies, it is imperative.

Looking beneath the success, an analysis of the Forum reveals the unique challenges of bringing together women from 25 nationalities to address strategic business issues while simultaneously focusing on enhancing individuals' global leadership capabilities. That global leadership requires simultaneous organisational and individual transformation is widely accepted (see Pucik et al., 1993: 206). At the Forum, however, the dual organisation- and individual-level agenda inadvertently raised the question of who was primarily to blame for the under-representation of women leaders within the company. Was it the company – thus implying that the organisational change initiatives should take precedence – or was it some perceived deficiency in the women themselves – thus implying that the leadership development initiatives should take precedence (see Izreaeli and Adler, 1994)? Given their appreciation of the systemic issues, many women's first priority was to recommend ways in which the organisational culture could be changed. Some women consequently viewed the personal development aspects of the agenda as secondary, and, at times, as taking them away from their primary goal of changing the organisation. Perhaps the lesson to be learned regarding first meetings of this sort is that participants – especially those as sophisticated in understanding organisational dynamics as the women attending the Forum – may initially view sessions aimed at individual leadership development as superfluous or even as counterproductive. Designers must take care to ensure that organisational change and individual leadership development goals complement, rather than compete, with each other. As companies shift from multi-domestic to global strategies, this balance becomes particularly important (see Chapter 16), because all managers, whether male or female and whether from Asia, Africa, Europe or the Americas, need to upgrade their global leadership skills.

The second major challenge of recognising and accommodating differences emerged from the implicit expectation that the women attending the Forum would have had similar experiences and therefore would share similar perspectives on most important professional issues, simply because they are women. Given that many women's experiences and opinions are not identical to those of men – as the survey results had clearly documented – it is understandable that some women arrived at the Forum expecting, consciously or otherwise, that they would finally be among a community of professionals who saw the world as they did. Yet, exactly as is true among men, women come from diverse backgrounds and career experiences. As the Forum progressed, the company and the participants learned – not without a certain degree of frustration – to accept that differences in the women's cultural background, age, tenure, rank and personal experience meant that the group could not, and should not, come to a consensus on a uniform 'women's' perspective or position. The women expressed markedly divergent opinions, for example, on the existence, or lack thereof, of a *glass ceiling*. Some of the most senior women, a disproportionate number of whom had begun their professional lives as trail-blazers in a very different social climate than that of the late 1990s, now saw their careers as having plateaued, albeit at a very senior level, below a very real *glass ceiling*. These senior women held attitudes and objectives that differed markedly from those of many younger women whom the company had only recently identified as fast trackers, and for whom the *glass ceiling* held no personal meaning. Moreover, so as not to discourage their younger colleagues, the most senior women chose not to describe their most negative experiences to their junior colleagues. This choice made it easy for some younger women to blame their senior colleagues for not having progressed further and faster, rather than appreciating the systemic barriers these trail-blazing women had faced. Just as one would not expect all male executives to have had identical experiences or to hold identical opinions, a uniform 'women's point of view' seldom exists, and neither companies nor women should expect one.

As highlighted in the Forum, helping people appreciate different realities – not just between women and men, but among the women themselves – is a crucial step in allowing them to move beyond the need to reach consensus on either 'the state of women' or explanations about why women do or do not make it to the top of major companies. A lack of consensus, however, neither indicates that such companies have no systemic issues nor that there is no need for corporate action. Developing an understanding of the range of experiences and explanations makes it more likely that companies can achieve real change.

The third set of challenges involved the impact of cross-cultural differences on Forum dialogue and interaction. The dynamics of global meetings differ from those of domestic meetings for both women and men. At the Forum, communication and behavioural styles varied across cultures and significantly influenced the group's dynamics and learning climate. The cross-cultural differences among participants were often larger and frequently became more important to the success of the meeting than many of the differences usually attributed to gender. Erroneously assuming a level of homogeneity among the women that simply did not exist caused problems in both conducting and interpreting the Forum.

Key cultural differences were evident in problem-solving approaches, agenda preferences and communication styles. The interaction of various cultural dimensions, described below, help to explain the role culture played in the Forum.

- *Problem-solving: Inductive versus deductive approaches* Following the typical cultural pattern of people from the United States and Canada, for example, many North American participants preferred to use a more inductive approach to resolving issues and formulating recommendations. They wanted to start with the specifics of their own and other's personal experience and later arrive at generalisations. Women from many other regions – for example, many Europeans, and especially those from France – preferred to take the opposite, more deductive approach (Hall and Hall, 1990; Samovar et al., 1998). They chose to begin with a general understanding and broad concepts and then work down toward the specifics of their own and others' lives. Both approaches ultimately arrive at an integration of general patterns and specifics. The processes for arriving at integration, however, are culturally defined, opposite, and, if not made explicit, often difficult to bridge. Global leaders need to be able to use the strengths of both inductive and deductive approaches, rather than merely negating one in favour of the other.

- *Power distance: The influence of status and hierarchy* Cultures also vary in their relationship to power and in what cross-cultural management scholars refer to as power distance – the extent to which individual cultures accept the fact that power in society and organisations is distributed unequally (Hofstede, 1980; Hofstede and Bond, 1988). Power distance impacts the degree of respect given to authority, position and hierarchical status. At the end of the second day, a group of primarily American women assertively requested a change in the agenda for the following day to allow participants more time to work in their teams on organisational development issues – a change that they believed would allow them to make best use of their time. It is not uncommon for participants from the United States attending domestic US workshops to 'take over' the agenda – a behaviour that is viewed as a positive sign by some American organisational development consultants. When the Forum organisers announced the schedule changes, some Asian and Latin American women – who come from higher power-distance countries – expressed surprise that participants would attempt to change the agenda. Their reactions are a strong reminder that people from different cultures vary in their perceptions, needs, and reactions, and that it is often difficult to fulfil all needs simultaneously.

- *The source of truth: Experts versus experience* Another cross-cultural difference that global teams frequently experience relates to what anthropologists refer to as the source of truth – how a group seeks the 'right' answer, or in the case of the Forum, the 'right' recommendations. Is truth believed to come primarily from scientific research, legal precedent, the opinion of experts, tradition, personal experience, or trial-and-error experimentation (Phillips and Boyacigiller, 1998)? Participants' varied reactions to changing the Forum agenda, described above, reflects this cultural difference regarding the source of truth. Beyond expressing surprise, some Asian and Latin American women were also disappointed because the new agenda left less time for the originally scheduled presentations by experts. Hearing the opinions of those experts was more salient for these women than for many of their North American colleagues. Whereas Americans also value expert opinion, they are much more likely to question authority than are most other cultures. Influenced by their more inductive approach and greater acceptance of change, most Americans at the Forum welcomed the agenda change, believing it would give them more time to develop recommendations based on their own personal experience. Typical of lower power-distance cultures, the Americans were placing less importance on expert input and hierarchical status than many of their colleagues from other countries. Which approach is correct? Neither – they simply differ. Global leadership involves bridging and integrating diverse approaches, not labelling one culture's approach as superior to that of other cultures.

- *Communication styles: Direct versus indirect*   The most obvious communication differences were rooted in culturally based preferences for direct versus indirect communication (Gudykunst and Ting-Toomey, 1988). The formality and reserved nature of many women from outside the United States contrasted dramatically with the more direct communication style used by the highly verbal Americans. Indirect communicators – most commonly from outside of the United States – were sometimes shocked by the bluntness and greater willingness to confront senior management on the part of their colleagues who were more direct communicators. These indirect communicators felt that many of their North American colleagues expressed themselves too bluntly and directly – taking charge and attempting to solve problems too quickly and without sufficient consultation or reflection. By contrast, some of the direct communicators misinterpreted the more formal respect and deference of participants from indirect cultures as being too accepting of the status quo. The strong emphasis that many indirect-communicator cultures place on relationship building and on putting the needs of the group ahead of one's own opinion or needs, contrasted dramatically with the behaviour of their more direct and individualistic colleagues. The difference is not so much in the level of respect each culture shows, but rather in the ways in which respect is communicated. As is usually true in such situations, a number of cross-cultural influences were operating simultaneously, and, for the most part, below the level of conscious awareness of most of the people involved. At the Forum, as in most global meetings, participants differed in their culturally based orientations toward direct versus indirect communication, group versus individual problem-solving, faster- versus slower-paced decision making, and the proclivity to accept situations versus attempting to change them.

Alerting participants to potential cross-cultural differences increases their ability to manage the impact of culture and benefit from its presence. At a pre-Forum session for team leaders and during the Forum itself, facilitators briefed the women on communication style differences and effective approaches to communicating across cultures, including with non-native English speakers. In retrospect, more cross-cultural training could have been included in the Forum itself. Such presentations do not, however, mitigate cultural differences. When differences are made explicit, however, the inevitable discovery of differing cultural and value-based norms regarding appropriate behaviour and communication styles can, if well managed, become a source of potential synergy, rather than merely a source of frustration, misleading interpretations and inappropriate evaluations.

Conclusion: Women's leadership and international management

In convening the Women's Global Leadership Forum, the CEO invited the most senior and highest-potential women in the company to contribute in ways that had been absent in the past. The organisational change process, the Forum itself, and the outcomes that cascaded throughout the worldwide organisation are proving that neither the company nor the women themselves knew the extent to which they could, should or would collectively contribute. As is true in all highly competitive industries, future success depends on the leadership of both women and men from around the world. The Women's Global Leadership Forum was an experiment in enhancing a company's global leadership capacity by amplifying women's voices. Not only the success of companies in this industry, but the success of twenty-first century society, depends on the voices of such leaders being amplified and heard.

> To...(lead) is not always to succeed, but it is always to learn.
> It is to move forward despite the obstacles. (David Krieger, 1998: 273)

Case questions

1 In your opinion, in what ways was the Women in Global Leadership Forum a success for Bestfoods?
2 What does the Bestfoods case study tell you about the extent of gender equality in the company?
3 In terms of women in leadership, management and international assignments, how does Bestfoods compare with the literature reported in this chapter?
4 Select three events in the Bestfoods case study and evaluate what elements of each situation were: a) specific issues of cross-cultural communication; and b) what were more general matters?

Case questions for further study and reflection

1 Imagine you are offered the opportunity to extend the company's development initiatives in Women in Leadership and Management at Bestfoods? Assume that you have been granted a new, additional budget of 3 million US dollars per annum, what would you recommend?
2 What competencies in cross-cultural communication are most essential for leaders of the Women's Global Leadership Forum? To what extent are these competency requirements the same as for all other participants in the Forum?
3 What preparation and pre-conference development opportunities should Bestfoods provide to female employees in the two year run up to the next Women's Global Leadership Forum?

Further reading

- Alder, N. J. with Gundersen, A. M. (2008) International Dimensions of Organizational Behavior, 5th edition. Cincinnati, Ohio: Cengage
This seminar book reviews the full range of organizational behavior and development issues from a global, cross – cultural perspective.

- Harzing, A.W.K. (2001a) 'Who's in charge: An empirical study of executive staffing practices in foreign subsidiaries', *Human Resource Management*, 40(2): 139–58.
- Harzing, A.W.K. (2001b) 'Of bears, bumble-bees and spiders: The role of expatriates in controlling foreign subsidiaries', *Journal of World Business*, 36(4): 366–79.
The main conclusions of these two articles are summarised in this chapter, but the original articles provide much more detail on recent empirical studies dealing with staffing policies and the functions of international transfers.

- Collings, D.G., Scullion, H. and Morley, M.J. (2007) 'Changing patterns of global staffing in the multinational enterprise: Challenges to the conventional expatriate assignment and emerging alternatives', *Journal of World Business*, 42(2): 198–213.
This article provides a more detailed account of recent changes in the management of international assignments due to supply side issues, cost issues, demand side issues and career issues. It also reviews alternative forms of international assignments that have recently emerged and discusses the implications for the design of international HR policies and practices.

- Shaffer, M.A., Harrison, D.A. and Gilley, K.M. (1999) 'Dimensions, determinants and differences in the expatriate adjustment process', *Journal of International Business Studies*, 30(3): 557–81.
This study provides the most comprehensive and up-to-date empirical test of the expatriate adjustment model by Black, Mendenhall and Oddou. It introduces two new variables in the model – international experience and language fluency – and shows that both variables have an important direct effect as well as a moderating effect on some of the other variables related to adjustment.

- Reiche, B.S. Harzing, A.-W. and Kraimer, M.L. (forthcoming) 'The role of international assignees' social capital in creating inter-unit intellectual capital: A cross-level model', *Journal of International Business Studies*.
This article offers a more complete picture of how international assignees initiate and contribute to knowledge flows in MNCs. It introduces two distinct roles that assignees possess as knowledge agents. First, assignees serve as knowledge brokers by linking their social networks at the home and the host unit, thereby generating access between previously unconnected knowledge resources. Second, assignees also act as knowledge transmitters, both by sharing their home-unit knowledge with host-unit staff and by transferring the knowledge they have acquired during the assignment to their home unit.

- Bonache, J. (2006) 'The compensation of expatriates: A review and a future research agenda', in G.K. Stahl and I. Björkman (eds), *Handbook of Research in International Human Resource Management*. pp. 158–75. Cheltenham: Edward Elgar. This book chapter gives a good overview of issues related to the compensation of international assignees.

- Caligiuri, P.M. (2006) 'Performance measurement in a cross-national context', in W. Bennet, C.E. Lance and D.J. Woehr (eds), *Performance Measurement: Current Perspectives and Future Challenges*. pp. 227–43. Mahwah, NJ: Lawrence Erlbaum. This book chapter discusses performance measurement strategies in MNCs and differentiates performance evaluation instruments with regard to different forms of international assignments.

- Black, J.S., Gregersen, H.B. and Mendenhall, M.E. (1992) *Global Assignments: Successfully Expatriating and Repatriating International Managers*. San Francisco: Jossey-Bass. This book is a good source of reference on issues related to the management of the various phases of the international assignment process, with a particular focus on the balancing of family concerns and the repatriation of assignees.

- Scullion, H. and Collings, D.G. (eds) (2006) *Global Staffing*. Milton Park: Routledge. This is an edited book that provides a wide range of topics on the strategic and operational aspects of staffing in MNCs, including international staff composition, international recruitment, talent management, cross-cultural management and the management of international assignments.

Internet resources

1 GMAC Global Relocation Services (www.gmacglobalrelocation.com): A US-based provider of relocation services and consulting that publishes an annual global relocation trends survey.

2 Delta Intercultural Academy (www.dialogin.com): A knowledge community on culture and communication in international business that maintains online forums on different topic areas, advertises job postings, publishes online articles and book reviews, organises e-conferences etc.

3 Living Abroad (www.livingabroad.com): An online provider of general information, country reports and tools for international assignees.

4 Relocation Journal (www.relojournal.com): An online provider of news and information on global relocation that includes a library of topical articles, informative white papers, a newsletter and general relocation service information.

5 Expatriate Exchange (www.expatexchange.com): An online community for meeting other expatriates, finding international jobs, getting expert advice on living abroad, international schools, taxes, relocation, etc.

Self-assessment questions

Indicative answers to these questions can be found on the companion website at www.sagepub.co./harzing3e.

1 **What are some of the reasons why over recent years the proportion of women on international assignments has increased?**
2 **How do the past and present roles of women in international assignments and management differ?**
3 **Identify different ways of developing women for leadership and international management.**
4 **Explain why inclusive approaches to men and women are an integral part of global leadership and international assignments.**
5 **Critically evaluate the success of international assignments from the perspectives of the individual assignee and the company.**

Notes

Excerpts from the following two articles are included in this chapter: Nancy J. Adler, Laura W. Brody, Joyce S. Osland, (2001) "Going beyond twentieth century leadership: a CEO develops his company's global competitiveness", *Cross Cultural Management: An International Journal*, Vol. 8 Iss: 3/4, pp, 11- 34 © Emerald Group Publishing Limited all rights reserved; Adler, N.J. (2007) 'One World: Women Leading & Managing WorldWide', in: Diana Bilimoria and Sandy Kristin Piderit (eds.), *Handbook on Women in Business and Management*. Cheltenham, U.K.: Edward Elgar, pp. 330-355. With kind permission from Edward Elgar, Diana Bilimoria and Sandy Kristin Piderit.

References

Adler, N.J. (1984a) 'Expecting international success: female managers overseas', *Columbia Journal of World Business*, 19(3): 79–85.

Adler, N.J. (1984b) 'Women do not want international careers: and other myths about international management', *Organizational Dynamics*, 13(2): 66–79.

Adler, N.J. (1984c) 'Women in international management: where are they?', *California Management Review*, 26(4): 78–89.

Adler, N.J. (1987) 'Pacific Basin managers: a gaijin, not a woman', *Human Resource Management*, 26(2): 169–92.

Adler, N.J. (1994) 'Competitive frontiers: women managing across borders', in N.J. Adler and D.N. Izraeli (eds), *Competitive Frontiers: Women Managers in a Global Economy*. pp.22–40. Cambridge, MA: Blackwell.

Adler, N.J. (1996) 'Global women political leaders: An invisible history, an increasingly important future', *Leadership Quarterly*, 7(1): 133–61.

Adler, N.J. (1997a) 'Global leaders: A dialogue with future history', *International Management*, 1(2): 21–33.

Adler, N.J. (1997b) 'Global leadership: Women leaders,' *Management International Review,* 37(1): 135–43.

Adler, N.J. (1998a) 'Did you hear? Global leadership in charity's world', *Journal of Management Inquiry*, 7(2): 21–33.

Adler, N.J. (1998b) 'Societal leadership: the wisdom of peace', in S. Srivastva (ed.), *Executive Wisdom and Organizational Change*. pp. 243–337. San Francisco, CA: Jossey-Bass.

Adler, N.J. (1999a) 'Global entrepreneurs: Women, myths, and history,' *Global Focus,* 1(4): 125–34.

Adler N. J. (1999b) 'Global leaders: women of influence', in S. Srivastva (ed.), *Executive Wisdom and Organizational Change*. pp. 243–337. San Francisco: Jossey-Bass.

Adler, N.J. (2000) 'Coaching global executives: women succeeding in a world beyond here', in M. Goldsmith, L. Lyons and A. Freas (eds), *Coaching for Leadership*. pp. 359–68. San Francisco, CA: Jossey-Bass.

Adler, N.J. (2002) *International Dimensions of Organizational Behavior*, 4th edn. Cincinnati, OH: South Western.

Adler, N.J. and Ghadar, F. (1990) 'Strategic human resource management: a global perspective', in R. Pieper (ed.), *Human Resource Management in International Comparison*. pp. 235–60. Berlin: deGruyter.

Adler, N.J. and Ghadar, F. (1993) 'A strategic phase approach to international human resource management', in D. Wong-Rieger and F. Rieger (eds), *International Management Research: Looking to the Future*. pp. 55–77. Berlin: DeGruyter.

Adler, N.J. and Ghadar, F. (1993) 'A strategic phase approach to international human resource management', in D. Wong-Rieger and F. Rieger (eds), *International Management Research: Looking to the Future*. pp. 55–77. Berlin: DeGruyter.

Adler, N.J., Brody, L.W. and Osland, J.S. (2000) 'The Women's Global Leadership Forum: Enhancing one company's global leadership capability,' *Human Resource Management*, 39(2 & 3): 209–25.

Adler, N.J., Brody, L.W. and Osland, J.S. (2001) 'Advances in global leadership: The Women's Global Leadership Forum', in William H. Mobley (ed.), *Advances in Global Research*, Volume 2. Greenwich, CT: JAI Press.

Altman, Y. and Shortland, S. (2001) 'Women, aliens and international assignments', *Women in Management Review*, 16(3): 141–5.

Bartlett, C.A. and Ghoshal, S. (1989) *Managing Across Borders: The Transnational Solution*. Boston: Harvard Business School Press.

Black, J.S., Morrison, A.J. and Gregerson, H.B. (1999) *Global Explorers: The Next Generation of Leaders*. New York: Routledge.

Caligiuri, P.M. and Cascio, W.F. (1998) 'Can we send her there? Maximizing the success of western women on global assignments', *Journal of World Business*, 33(4): 394–416.

Caligiuri, P.M. and Tung, R.L. (1999) 'Comparing the success of male and female expatriates from a US-based multinational company', *International Journal of Human Resource Management*, 10(5): 763–82.

Caligiuri, P.M., Joshi, A. and Lazarova, M. (1999) 'Factors influencing the adjustment of women on global assignments', *International Journal of Human Resource Management*, 10(2): 163–79.

Catalyst (1996) 'Women in Corporate Leadership: Progress and Prospects', New York City.

Catalyst (2000) '2000 Catalyst Census of Women Corporate Officers and Top Earners of the Fortune 500', New York City.

Dorfman, P.W. (1996) 'International and cross-cultural leadership', in B.J. Punnett and Oded Shenkar (eds), *Handbook for International Management Research*. pp. 267–349. Cambridge, MA: Blackwell.

Dwyer, P., Johnston, M. and Miller, K.L. (1996) 'Europe's corporate women', *Business Week*, 15 April: pp. 40–2.

Gardner, H. (1995) *Leading Minds: An Anatomy of Leadership*. New York: Basic Books.

Gregerson, H.B., Morrison, A.J. and Black, J.S. (1998) 'Developing leaders for the global frontier', *Sloan Management Review*, 40(1): 21–33.

Gudykunst, W.A. and Ting-Toomey, S. (1988) *Culture and Interpersonal Communication*. Newbury Park, CA: Sage.

Guthrie, J.P., Ash, R.A. and Stevens, C.D. (2003) 'Are women better than men? Personality differences and expatriate selection', *Journal of Managerial Psychology*, 18(3): 229–43.

Hall, E.T. and Hall, M.R. (1990) *Understanding Cultural Differences*. Yarmouth, ME: Intercultural Press.

Harris, H. (1995) 'Women's role in (international) management', in A.-W. Harzing and J. Van Ruysseveldt (eds), *International Human Resource Management*. pp. 229–51. London: Sage.

Harris, H. (1999) 'Women in international management – Why are they not selected?', in: C. Brewster and H. Harris (eds), *International HRM – Contemporary Issues in Europe*. pp. 258–76. London: Routledge.

Harris, H. (2002) 'Think international manager, think male: Why are women not selected for international management assignments?', *Thunderbird International Business Review*, 44(2): 175–203.

Harris, H. (2004) 'Women's role in international management', in A.-W Harzing and J. Van Ruysseveldt (eds), *International Human Resource Management*. pp.357–86. London: Sage.

Hofstede, G. (1980) *Culture's Consequences: International Differences in Work-Related Values*. Sage: Beverly Hills.

Hofstede, G. and Bond, M. (1988) 'The Confucius connection: From cultural roots to economic growth', *Organizational Dynamics*, 16(4): 4–21.

Izraeli, D.N. and Adler, N.J. (1994) 'Competitive frontiers: Women managers in a global economy', in N.J. Adler and D.N. Izraeli (eds), *Competitive Frontiers: Women Managers in a Global Economy*. pp. 3–21. Cambridge, MA: Blackwell.

Izraeli, D.N., Banai, M. and Zeira, Y. (1980) 'Women executives in MNC subsidiaries', *California Management Review*, 23(1): 53–63.

Izraeli, D.N. and Zeira, Y. (1993) 'Women managers in international business: a research review and appraisal', *Business and the Contemporary World*, 5(3): 35–46.

Krieger, D. (1998) in F. Franck, J. Roze and R. Connlly (eds), *What Does It Mean To Be Human?* Nyack, NY: Circumstantial Productions.

Levy, O., Beechler, S., Taylor, S. and Boyacigiller, N. (1999) 'What we talk about when we talk about "global mindset". Managerial cognition in multinational corporations', Paper presented the *Academy of Management Meeting*, Chicago.

Linehan, M. and Scullion, H. (2004) 'Towards an understanding of the female expatriate experience in Europe', *Human Resource Management Review*, 14: 433–48.

Linehan, M. and Walsh, J.S. (1999) 'Senior female international managers: breaking the glass border', *Women in Management Review*, 14(7): 264–72.

Linehan, M. and Walsh, J.S. (2000) 'Beyond the traditional linear view of international managerial careers: a new model of the senior female career in an international context', *Journal of European Industrial Training*, 24(2–4): 178–89.

Lowe, K.B., Downes, M. and Kroeck, K.G. (1999) 'The impact of gender and location on the willingness to accept overseas assignments', *International Journal of Human Resource Management*, 10(2): 223–34.

Mayerhofer, H., Hartmann, L.C. and Herbert, A. (2004) 'Career management issues for flex-patriate international staff', *Thunderbird International Business Review*, 46(6): 647–66.

Mendenhall, M. (2001) 'Introduction: New perspectives on expatriate adjustment and its relationship to global leadership development', in M. Mendenhall, T.M. Kuhlmann and G.K. Stahl (eds), *Developing Global Business Leaders: Policies, Processes, and Innovations*. Westport, CT: Quorum.

Napier, N.K. and Taylor, S. (2002) 'Experiences of women professionals abroad comparisons across Japan, China and Turkey', *International Journal of Human Resource Management*, 15(2): 837–85.

ORC (Organisation Resources Counsellors)/CBI (1992) *Update on Survey of Spouses/Partners and International Assignments*. London: ORC Europe and CBI Employee Relocation Council.

ORC (Organisation Resources Counsellors) (2002) *Dual Careers and International Assignments Survey*. London: Organisation Resources Counsellors, Inc.

Osland, J.S. (1995) *The Adventure of Working Abroad: Hero Tales from the Global Frontier*. San Francisco, CA: Jossey-Bass.

Osland, J.S. and Adler, N.J. (2001) 'Women and global leadership at Bestfoods', in J.S. Osland, D. Kolb and I. Rubin (eds), *Organizational Behavior. An Experiential Approach*. pp. 533–55. Upper Saddle River, NJ. Prentice Hall.

Osland, J.S. and Taylor, S. (2001) 'Developing Global Leaders', *HR.com*, 1 February.

Paik, Y. and Vance, C.M. (2002) 'Evidence of back-home selection bias against American female expatriates', *Women in Management Review*, 17(2): 68–79.

Phillips, M.E. and Boyacigiller, N.A. (1998) 'Learning culture: An integrated framework for cultural analysis.' Symposium presentation at the *Academy of Management* Meetings, San Diego, California.

Pucik, V., Tichy, N. and Barnett, C. (1993) *Globalizing Management: Creating and Leading the Competitive Organization*. New York: Wiley.

Punnett, B.J., Crocker, O. and Stevens, M.A. (1992) 'The challenge for women expatriates and spouses: some empirical evidence', *International Journal of Human Resource Management*, 3(3): 585–92.

Ragins, B.R., Townsend, B. and Mattis, M. (1998) 'Gender gap in the executive suite: CEOs and female executives report on breaking the glass ceiling', *Academy of Management Executive*, 12(1): 28–42.

Samovar, L.A., Porter, R.E. and Stefani, L.A. (1998) *Communication Between Cultures,* 3rd edn. Belmont, CA: Wadsworth.

Selmer, J. (2001) 'Expatriate selection: back to basics?', *International Journal of Human Resource Management,* 12(8): 1219–33.

Selmer, J. and Leung, A.S.M. (2003a) 'Expatriate career intentions of women on foreign assignments and their adjustment', *Journal of Managerial Psychology,* 18(3): 244–58.

Selmer, J. and Leung, A.S.M. (2003b) 'International adjustment of female vs. male business expatriates', *International Journal of Human Resource Management,* 14(7): 1117–31.

Selmer, J. and Leung, A.S.M. (2003c) 'Personal characteristics of female vs. male business expatriates', *International Journal of Cross Cultural Management,* 3(2): 195–212.

Stone, R.J. (1991) 'Expatriate selection and failure', *Human Resource Planning,* 14: 9–18.

Stroh, L.K., Varma, A. and Valy-Durbin, S.J. (2000a) 'Why are women left at home: Are they unwilling to go on international assignments?', *Journal of World Business,* 35(3): 241–55.

Stroh, L.K., Varma, A. and Valy-Durbin, S.J. (2000b) 'Women and expatriation: revisiting Adler's findings', in M.J. Davidson and R.J. Burke (eds), *Women in Management.* London: Sage.

Taylor, S. and Napier, N. (1996) 'Successful women expatriates: the case of Japan', *Journal of International Management,* 2(1): 51–78.

Taylor, S. and Napier, N. (2001) 'An American woman in Turkey: adventures unexpected and knowledge unplanned', *Human Resource Management,* 40(4): 347–64.

Thal, N.L. and Cateora, P. (1979) 'Opportunities for women in international business', *Business Horizons,* 22(6): 21–7.

Thang, L.L., MacLachlan, E. and Goda, M. (2002) 'Expatriates on the margin – A study of Japanese women working in Singapore', *Geoforum,* 33(4): 539–51.

Tung, R.L. (2004) 'Female expatriates: the model global manager?', *Organizational Dynamics,* 33(3): 243–53.

UMIST, CBI and CIB (1995) *Assessment, Selection and Preparation for Expatriate Assignments.* London: University of Manchester Institute of Science and Technology, CBI Employee Relocation Council, and the Centre for International Briefing.

Van der Boon, M. (2003) 'Women in international management: An international perspective on women's ways of leadership', *Women in Management Review,* 18(3): 132–46.

Wajcman, J. (1998) *Managing Like a Man: Women and Men in Corporate Management.* University Park, PA: Pennsylvania State University Press.

Westwood, R.I. and Leung, S.M. (1994) 'The female expatriate manager experience', *International Studies of Management and Organization,* 24(3): 64–85.

Windham and NFTC (1997) *Global Relocation Trends 1996 Survey Report.* New York: Windham International and the National Foreign Trade Council.

Yeung, A. and Ready, D. (1995) 'Developing leadership capabilities of global corporations: A comparative study in eight nations', *Human Resource Management,* 34(4): 529–47.

16

Global Work-Life Management in Multinational Corporations

Helen De Cieri and Anne Bardoel

Contents

Learning Objectives

After reading this chapter you will be able to

- Understand key issues for managers dealing with work-life issues in a global context

- Understand some of the major work environment and social factors that affect work-life issues for MNCs

- Understand the substantial challenges managers in MNCs face when balancing the frequently competing pressures for global integration and local responsiveness

- Learn about examples of work-life issues in MNCs

Chapter Outline

In this chapter, we examine the complex issues faced by multinational corporations (MNCs) related to the management of work-life issues in a global context. We begin by defining work-life initiatives as those strategies, policies, programmes and practices initiated and maintained in workplaces to address flexibility, quality of work and life, and work–family conflict. We acknowledge that, while work-life issues have been discussed and investigated in western contexts, less is understood about how these issues are experienced and managed in Asia and developing nations, let alone how MNCs could develop a corporate work-life policy where global consistency is likely to be difficult to achieve. We examine the tensions and dualities in managing work-life initiatives in MNCs. We then develop a framework to inform the allocation of responsibilities for work-life management in MNCs, and assist the application of strategies to resolve tensions. Finally, we discuss the emerging challenges for researchers and practitioners related to global work-life management.

1 Introduction

Globalisation has brought numerous, noteworthy developments in the diversity and complexity of international business and forms of multinational corporations (MNCs). Managers in MNCs face substantial challenges in balancing the often competing pressures for global integration and local responsiveness. Connected with these developments and challenges has been an increasing awareness that management of the global workforce, via an international human resource management (IHRM) system, is a crucial dimension of international business.

The IHRM system is a key driver in a firm's ability to attract, retain and manage talent in global, competitive labour markets. In this chapter, we examine the roles and responsibilities for IHRM in MNCs, with a deliberate focus on work-life management. We define work-life initiatives as those strategies, policies, programmes and practices initiated and maintained in workplaces to address flexibility, quality of work and life, and work-family conflict. We argue that global talent management relies on effective IHRM systems, including a shared understanding of the roles and responsibilities of all managers. The work-life management area is increasingly recognised as an important aspect of IHRM in practice and a major factor in talent and diversity management (see Chapter 18) (Bardoel and De Cieri, 2006; De Cieri and Bardoel, 2009; Poelmans, 2005; Spinks, 2005).

However, research appears to lag behind practice with respect to global work-life management. While leading scholars in IHRM have raised awareness of the constraints and challenges, which we view as tensions, related to managing a global workforce (e.g., Scullion et al., 2007), there has been limited discussion amongst researchers regarding the roles and responsibilities of managers in MNCs (Brewster et al., 2005), and even less attention given to work-life management in the global context (Lewis et al., 2007). By combining these important yet neglected areas, we aim to demonstrate that work-life management is an emerging aspect of IHRM that contributes to organisational and individual performance.

In the western literature there is an abundance of research in the area of work–family conflict and work-life issues (Byron, 2005; Greenhaus and Powell, 2006) which has been largely driven by substantial changes in workforce demography and by increasing recognition that work-life issues are highly salient for many people (Spector et al., 2004). In North America, Australia and Europe there is increasing interest from employers and employees in how to manage the tensions between work and other life demands (Rapoport et al., 2005). However, less is understood about how these tensions are experienced in Asia and developing nations, let alone how MNCs could develop a corporate work-life policy where global consistency or standards are likely to be difficult to implement (De Cieri and Bardoel, 2009).

In this chapter, we first apply a tension-centred approach to global work-life management; second, we discuss how these tensions apply to the HR function in MNCs. Bringing these areas together, we develop a framework to show how these tensions are linked as influences on global work-life management. Our discussion leads to the identification of strategies and responsibilities to manage and resolve the tensions.

2 Tensions in global work-life management

A theoretical perspective that has strong potential for application to the work-life field is the tension-centred approach. Dallimore and Mickel (2006) have suggested that there are inherent tensions in the pursuit of quality of life, and much of the research in this area has explored tensions experienced by individuals in this pursuit. As Trethewey and Ashcraft (2004: 82) explain, 'a tension-centered approach begins with the premise that organisations are conflicted sites of human activity'.

Organisational tensions have been broadly defined by Stohl and Cheney (2001: 353–4) as a 'clash of ideas or principles or actions and the discomfort that may arise as a result'; such tensions are viewed as 'inescapable, normal and, in some cases, to be embraced' (Tracy, 2004: 121). From this standpoint, an understanding of organisational tensions may be used to develop insights into organisational phenomena and change. Tensions in organisational life have been explored in several studies, identifying tensions at both micro- and macro-levels (Dallimore and Mickel, 2006; Stohl and Cheney, 2001; Tracy, 2004). We suggest that tensions will arise in an organisation's pursuit of work-life initiatives, such as those that strive to meet both economic and social goals, or both global and local concerns.

Drawing from the tension-centred research, we propose that tensions exist in individual–organisational interactions such as negotiation of roles and responsibilities related to work-life matters in MNCs. We favour Grzywacz and Carlson's (2007) approach to conceptualising work–family balance which focuses on the accomplishment of role-related expectations that are negotiated and shared between individuals' role-related responsibilities at work and with their family. However we argue that this understanding of role-related responsibilities can be extended to include not only family responsibilities but also include responsibilities to oneself, one's community, and the many priorities that may or may not have to do with family (Bardoel, 2006). The change in terminology from labelling organisational initiatives as work-life instead of work–family reflects a broadening of quality of life issues and career issues for both men and women (see Chapters 11 and 15). It also reflects a call for HR practitioners to play a significant role in encouraging thinking to move beyond merely providing programmes to viewing work-life issues more systemically, so they are included in work process redesign and cultural change processes (Bardoel et al., 2007).

The tension-centred approach informs our understanding of work-life management in MNCs in several ways. As has been well-documented in international business research, there are inherent tensions between priorities and concerns upheld by various stakeholders and drivers in MNCs. Numerous tensions can be identified in the management of work-life in a global context. For example, managers in MNCs need to balance the often conflicting needs of global efficiencies and coordination (integration) with responsiveness to factors such as political pressures in each local market (differentiation) (Doz and Prahalad, 1991; Edwards and Kuruvilla, 2005). The paradox of 'think globally, act locally' is a dilemma for HR professionals working in MNCs especially during periods when there are unprecedented levels of global mergers, acquisitions and international growth. We postulate that these tensions may be expressed as alternative priorities and concerns at different levels (e.g. strategy/policy vs. operational); in different organisational units (e.g., headquarters vs. subsidiary);

in different functions (e.g., HR vs. line management); and between management and employees. Other examples of tensions that may permeate the organisational boundaries of an MNC, include tensions between economic and social/moral concerns, institutional requirements and organisational needs, or between collective and individual concerns (e.g., organisational performance and gender equity).

In addition, we acknowledge that in managing global work-life there exists tension between academic and practical priorities and concerns. Concern about conflict between academic research priorities and management practice is not new; as research technology has become more sophisticated, it has been seen by practitioners as less relevant to solving their organisational problems. Rynes and colleagues (2001) note evidence of the pervasiveness of a management research-practice gap and comment that managers typically do not use academic research or academic research findings when developing their management practices. Scholars have recently argued for evidence-based approaches to HRM and called for the establishment of better links between research and practice (Rousseau, 2006; Rynes et al., 2007), particularly with regard to understanding how HR practices affect performance and organisational outcomes (Rynes et al., 2007). Hence, we argue in favour of better cooperation between scholars and practitioners engaged either in research or in improving practice in work-life management.

Moving beyond the identification of tensions in MNCs, we propose that managers need to understand and develop ways and means to resolve them. According to Bird (2006), the demand by employees and managers for work-life solutions is expanding and it will be one of the issues that executives and HR professionals can be expected to manage over the coming years. Drawing from the literature on managing paradox (Poole and Van De Ven, 1989), we note four potential strategies that may be applicable to tensions in global work-life management:

1 *Opposition – accept that paradox exists and use it constructively*; e.g. the case of the MNC that had made several unsuccessful attempts of trying to develop a global work-life strategy. The company had been operating in its various locations different work-life programmes and the US-based headquarters work-life team received increased requests for help, information and directions from its international locations. In response the headquarters work-life team created an overarching way to help these organisations by communicating a company-wide philosophy of supported work climates. This involved creating a tool that explained the 'philosophy' of work-life demonstrating why the MNC operations in the US were implementing work-life policies and programmes and assessing the implications for locations outside the US.

2 *Spatial separation – clarify level of analysis and connections between them*; e.g. place the responsibility for implementing work-life and diversity initiatives in the hands of the geographic managers. Give them accountability by measuring it on their scorecards. Declare what success looks like.

3 *Temporal separation – take time into account*; e.g. organisations need to consider how far along the globalisation journey their company is and also indicate how

work-life initiatives are part of the global brand. So, if the journey has been long and a strong commitment has been developed over many years (e.g. IBM and Shell) then it is easier to mandate for more standardised work-life policies. Therefore, decisions made on the degree that policies are global need to be based on how 'global' employees are. As an example, if employees are often moving between countries, then there will need to be more consistency.

4 *Synthesis – develop new terms to resolve paradox;* e.g. an MNC developed a long-term leave policy, which came about because the company was losing valuable people. Turnover rates were analysed and in particular 'regretted losses' were identified. The new programme announcement was included on the company website.

It is likely that combinations of the above could be found in practice. While research has begun to explore tensions in work-life management (Dallimore and Mickel, 2006), our research on tensions in global work-life management and the different ways of achieving resolution, breaks new ground.

In this chapter, we focus on the management of a global work-life strategy that will support a global workforce. Despite the potential benefits associated with global work-life initiatives, the specific challenges associated with the development of effective work-life initiatives that balance global and local demands need to be identified and understood. Global work-life initiatives need to be aligned with strategic objectives such as diversity and performance management, recognising the goal for MNCs is to achieve competitive advantage, but not to do so at the expense of human health, well-being and personal lives. In addition, there are specific and unique challenges for managers seeking to attract, retain and manage the talent required to implement a global strategy which is critical to the organisation's long-term survival.

To understand the tensions related to global work-life management, and to point towards ways to resolve these tensions, we propose a framework for global work-life management: its influences, elements and outcomes.

3 A framework for global work-life management

We propose that a viable approach to managing global work-life is to view it as one aspect of a global diversity management agenda and a part of IHRM strategy (Childs, 2005). We note that practitioners such as Childs (2005) seem to be ahead of researchers in recognising the importance of work-life as an aspect of global diversity management (Nishii and Özbilgin, 2007). The framework presented in Figure 16.1 shows the influences on the IHRM system, and specifically depicts the components of global diversity, including work-life management and anticipated outcomes for individuals and MNCs.

Korabik and colleagues (2003) distinguish two different approaches to work–family research that has been carried out globally: micro- and macro-level approaches. First, the micro-level approach emanating mostly from North America has focused mainly

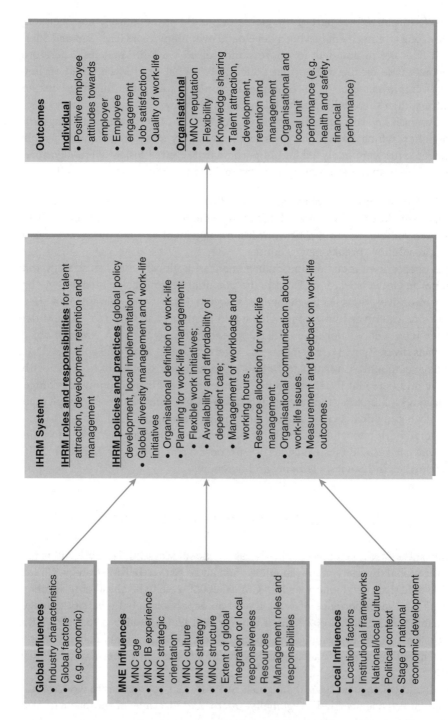

Global Influences
- Industry characteristics
- Global factors (e.g. economic)

MNE Influences
- MNC age
- MNC IB experience
- MNC strategic orientation
- MNC culture
- MNC strategy
- MNC structure
- Extent of global integration or local responsiveness
- Resources
- Management roles and responsibilities

Local Influences
- Location factors
- Institutional frameworks
- National/local culture
- Political context
- Stage of national economic development

IHRM System

IHRM roles and responsibilities for talent attraction, development, retention and management

IHRM policies and practices (global policy development, local implementation)
- Global diversity management and work-life initiatives
- Organisational definition of work-life
- Planning for work-life management:
  - Flexible work initiatives;
  - Availability and affordability of dependent care;
  - Management of workloads and working hours.
- Resource allocation for work-life management.
- Organisational communication about work-life issues.
- Measurement and feedback on work-life outcomes.

Outcomes

Individual
- Positive employee attitudes towards employer
- Employee engagement
- Job satisfaction
- Quality of work-life

Organisational
- MNC reputation
- Flexibility
- Knowledge sharing
- Talent attraction, development, retention and management
- Organisational and local unit performance (e.g. health and safety, financial performance)

Figure 16.1 A framework for global work-life management

on workplaces and the business case for developing more effective management approaches to reducing work–family conflict. Second, the macro-level approach has derived mainly from Europe and has identified the critical importance of public policies in relation to societal expectations about men and women's roles and employment supportive policies such as paid parental leave and benefits (see Chapter 14). We suggest that, for researchers and managers, it is important to consider the potential interactions between micro- and macro-level approaches to work–family issues, and so we seek to integrate these two approaches. Hence, we draw on both micro- and macro-level work–family approaches, in developing our comprehensive framework of work-life issues from a global perspective.

Global and local influences

Michaels (1995) noted that, although many US corporations have been leaders in developing work-life programmes, there is much to be gained by comparing how other countries' values, policies and programmes address work-life issues; in particular the role of stakeholders and possible change agents such as unions, agencies and governments. Hence, we note in our framework that there are numerous global and local factors that are important to recognise as potential influences on global work-life management. As noted earlier, managers in MNCs need to balance the often conflicting global influences (e.g., industry characteristics and global market factors) with local influences (e.g., institutional frameworks, local culture and the stage of local economic development) (Doz and Prahalad, 1991; Edwards and Kuruvilla, 2005).

Box 16.1   The 80/20 rule

A large, US-based, multinational corporation (MNC) has more than 300,000 employees in 170 countries. Interviews conducted with HR managers show that global work-life management can be difficult to manage and there may be very different perspectives held by HR practitioners at global and local levels. The Global Diversity Manager, based at headquarters with global responsibility for work-life management, discussed an '80/20 rule':

> We want to make sure that what we develop at a corporate level can be implemented at the geography level and those individuals are actually a part of [our] team. So we use what we call the 80/20 rule. Eighty per cent is standard and can be implemented across [the MNC]. We want to have some consistency of approach that's based on being able to manage a culture, affordability and

(Continued)

(Continued)

implementation for all, so employees do not get conflicting messages. So that is the 80 per cent. Twenty per cent is driven based on the business needs, local legislations and the culture of the geography.

However, none of the local or regional managers interviewed in this MNC were aware of this 'rule'. Their comments are shown below:

The strategy is a common strategy ... The initiatives and policies are followed too. ... Sometimes there is an initiative that is not adequate for our reality, then we have to say, look, we are not going to implement it because it won't be effective. Then we go back in a structured manner showing why it doesn't make sense. (National Diversity Manager, Brazil)

They're trying to standardise flexible work options ... So for a lot of the Asia region they don't have a lot of these workplace practices, so irrelevant of their culture they actually have to try and implement them and make them part of it. ... [MNC] globally says 'we will become a flexible workforce and you're not and but we're going to help you to do that, it doesn't matter about your culture, you're going to have to sort that out as well'. (National Diversity Manager, Australia)

The different views expressed by HR managers at global headquarters and in local units may indicate that, even in an MNC that is well-advanced in terms of managing diversity and work-life issues, there may be deficiencies in the IHRM system with regard to knowledge transfer and shared understanding of the policy.

Box 16.2 GLBT Posters

Research interviews conducted with HR managers in a large US-based multinational corporation showed that policies planned at global headquarters were not being implemented, and headquarters staff were unaware that their policies were not being followed in local units:

... to give you an example of our diversity ... the gay, lesbian, bi-sexual and transgender [GLBT] constituency ... is also a group where we look into ensuring that the workplace is conducive for employees. So yes we have these challenges ... trying to introduce the same kind of initiatives that we have in US... International Womens Day is celebrated 8 March every year ... in

> all the countries we have posters put up, communication note going out
> to employees .... But the GLBT is not celebrated in the same way. In fact
> the posters are not put up in all locations, it's definitely not in Malaysia or
> Indonesia because they're Muslim countries or rather the majority of the
> place is Muslim... (Diversity Manager, Singapore)

MNC influences

In addition to this global/local dilemma, there are numerous MNC characteristics
that should be recognised as influences on the IHRM system and therefore on global
work-life management; these include the age and international experience of the
MNC, strategic orientation, organisational culture, structure and strategy, and available resources (De Cieri and Dowling, 2006).

IHRM system

We suggest that the roles and responsibilities adopted by all managers across the
MNC will influence the way in which the IHRM system, including work-life initiatives, is developed and implemented (Novicevic and Harvey, 2001). Welbourne
(2005) has argued that top management support for HRM initiatives is critical for
successful talent management, and further, HRM should be recognised as a priority for all managers. IHRM initiatives, including work-life initiatives, will be most
effective when led by senior leaders and supported and understood throughout the
organisation. One implication arising from these ideas is that HR professionals also
have to be proactive and assist the organisation in understanding and adjusting its
mindset, so that human resource practices become a source of competitive advantage. Part of the HR strategy to achieve competitive success often will be to attract
and retain individuals who possess higher quality human capital.

Hence, the IHRM system needs to deliver a strategic approach to HR, since attracting and retaining the people required to implement a global strategy is central to the
organisation's long-term growth and survival (Stroh and Caligiuri, 1998). Scholars
and practitioners have used the phrase 'talent management' to describe a long-term
and integrated approach to managing employees, attracting them into the organisation, providing development and engagement opportunities utilising a sophisticated
system of HR practices, and retaining valued employees in the organisation.

Central to global work-life management is the acknowledgement that, although
there are a number of common issues faced by working women and men and
their families, the global work-life strategy needs to balance shared concerns with
a course of action that is appropriate to each local environment. Global work-life
needs assessments conducted by work-life consultants Shapiro and Noble (2001)
have identified three surprisingly consistent themes in what employees from around
the world identify as being important barriers to reconciling their work and personal

lives. The three issues identified included a lack of flexible work policies and practices, the availability and affordability of dependent care, and the negative impact of work overload and long working hours; hence, we place these at the core of the IHRM system for global work-life management.

Individual and organisational outcomes

Haas and colleagues (2000) have identified a range of positive outcomes that may accrue to employees and organisations that implement work-life practices and policies. First, work-life practices can provide an incentive to increase motivation, job satisfaction and commitment and thus achieve higher levels of engagement and productivity from the current labour pool. Second, these practices can be part of a strategy that supports attracting, managing and retaining the talent. For example, global diversity management and work-life initiatives can provide a means for knowledge sharing across an MNC, leading to reduction of tensions and better understanding of the priorities and concerns of various parties. Third, an effective work-life strategy can enable the best quality people to advance in the organisation. For example, it has been recognised that barriers to women include having to take time out for dependent care responsibilities and a lack of flexibility in career structures. Finally, companies can obtain community recognition and reputation by being seen as a 'good' corporate citizen or caring organisation. As Childs (2005: 113) has stated, 'Leaders must help all people within their business understand that workforce diversity [including work-life management] can be the bridge between the workplace and the marketplace'. Western researchers have reported on a range of potential benefits including: acknowledgement of being a 'good' corporate citizen (Russell and Bourke, 1999); improved organisational commitment (Allen, 2001); increased job satisfaction (Bedeian et al., 1988); improved organisational performance (Perry-Smith and Blum, 2000); increased organisational productivity (Konrad and Mangel, 2000); and, improved staff morale (McCampbell, 1996). Furthermore, both HRM and management consultants suggest that work-life initiatives can enhance the employer brand that will lead to other associated benefits including a broader and better quality labour pool available, improved employee retention and reduced employee turnover (Barrow and Moseley, 2006).

Overall, the complexities and ongoing developments related to global work-life management present many important challenges and opportunities for managers in MNCs, and for researchers who study these firms. However, to-date, few researchers have endeavoured to integrate the micro- and macro-level approaches; nor have they paid much attention to the strategic role of work-life management as a part of IHRM.

4 Resolving tensions

We suggest that there are numerous synergistic strategies, techniques or MNC features that managers could use to resolve tensions, although this is not a conclusive list.

These include strategies that require the attention and support of global headquarters, such as development of clear policies and expectations, resourcing for work-life initiatives and headquarters' respect for local knowledge. We suggest that work-life management should be integrated with other HR practices in the IHRM system. There are also several strategies that should be led by the HR function, such as communication, awareness and support, and gathering information, measurement and feedback on work-life initiatives. There are numerous ways in which HR managers may seek to resolve tensions with line managers, including engagement in decision making, building HR competencies, and providing training, education and advice (for all levels of managers, employees and colleagues). There are also suggestions for all employees, such as developing rapport with one's manager, and respecting and accepting diversity in the workplace.

Overall, our analysis of global work-life management demonstrates that there needs to be a stronger understanding of the tensions between various drivers, and possible responsibilities for resolving tensions and managing work-life in MNCs. Table 16.1 summarises the key responsibilities for work-life management at the global, HR and line management levels. These responsibilities can be adopted by managers as accountabilities for the various elements of our framework of global work-life management (shown in Figure 16.1).

There are several global responsibilities for work-life management. For senior executives, responsibilities include endorsement of work-life initiatives and provision of adequate resourcing (Enns and McFarlin, 2005). The HR professionals in corporate

Table 16.1   Responsibilities for work-life management

Global Responsibilities:	Line Manager Responsibilities:	HR Responsibilities:
<ul><li>Senior level endorsement</li><li>Engagement in decision-making</li><li>Adapt to the needs of each country</li><li>Resourcing</li><li>Gather information (e.g. focus groups)</li><li>Measurement and feedback</li></ul>	<ul><li>Make work place more of an attractive and joyful place</li><li>Management at all levels must understand, accept and support flexibility</li><li>Have conversations with employees around career development and performance reviews, try and open up a dialogue around work life balance</li></ul>	<ul><li>Build HR competencies: HR managers need to have the time and ability to coach line managers</li><li>HR provide formal management training program and implement flexible work options.</li><li>HR to communicate success stories</li><li>Placement of flexible work arrangement advisors</li><li>Communication and support</li><li>Provide a tool kit for employees</li><li>Develop network in HRM community</li></ul>

headquarters will have global responsibility for formulating global policy, yet also must show an overall responsiveness to local concerns (Novicevic and Harvey, 2001). Conversely, implementation relies to a large extent on the engagement, knowledge and competencies of local HRM. We anticipate that global work-life management raises several challenges, particularly for MNCs seeking to operate in developing and growing markets, such as the large emerging markets of Brazil, Russia, India and China (see Chapter 18). First, recruiting and selecting candidates for local HR positions can be difficult, as many employers report difficulty in recruiting people with HR experience and knowledge in emerging markets. A second challenge is to develop talent in the HR function; HR professionals in dynamic markets such as China require competencies such as communication and networking skills in order to build strong relationships with line managers and develop a clear understanding of the IHRM system.

Resolving the global–local tensions within the HR function depends to some extent on the ability to develop a shared view of the IHRM system and increase synergies across levels of the HR function (Bowen and Ostroff, 2004). Building these competencies will help to raise the credibility of HR managers with senior and line managers (Enns and McFarlin, 2005; Farndale, 2005). A third challenge is that HR professionals need to form networks in the wider HRM community outside of their own organisation. Knowledge sharing within the HRM community can be an important mechanism for designing and managing improvements in HRM policies and practices; for example, in China, the importance of networks or *guanxi* has been widely recognised. Finally, HR practitioners must address the challenge of working with line managers and employees to build their competencies, deliver training programmes, and provide advice, support and resources. The above are all examples of the ways in which work-life initiatives can become embedded in an MNC.

5 Directions for research

Von Glinow and colleagues (2002) note that much of IHRM has been parochially focused (mainly on the US, sometimes Europe and occasionally Japan), and has been dominated by the use of quantitative research methods. According to Von Glinow et al. (2002) there is a place for the precision of valid and reliable scales but quantitative methodologies run the risk of masking anomalies and obtaining counter-intuitive findings for different cultural contexts. They recommended that future researchers use broad research lenses and examine multiple embedded contexts when conducting globally distributed IHRM research.

Similarly, work-life scholars have called for future research to address how global organisations can be inclusive of work-life issues in multiple cultural contexts (Poelmans, 2005; Poster and Prasad, 2005). As Poelmans (2005) concludes, there is a need for more qualitative research that includes case studies of international companies to explore the impact of globalisation on work–family policy development in organisations.

To unearth issues involving the key tensions and derived etics related to global work-life management, researchers must have a '... heightened awareness of the poly-contextuality that surrounds all of our IHRM practices' (Von Glinow et al., 2002: 137).

6 Summary and conclusion

This chapter discusses work-life issues in MNCs and across different socio-cultural contexts, and identifies issues hitherto not raised on the research agenda (Poelmans, 2005). We have discussed numerous tensions that need to be resolved in order for global work-life management to be managed effectively. Our framework for global work-life management provides a structure within which responsibilities can be identified and acted upon throughout an MNC.

As Childs has noted, 'The business of workforce diversity is constantly evolving and presents us with new and different challenges, especially as businesses become more global' (2005: 117). We propose that work-life balance is important for talent management and for developing a high performing workforce. Employees around the world are becoming increasingly vocal about their work and family needs and the issue of managing work-life needs is likely to grow. Managers and employees are beginning to recognise the strategic role of global work-life policies and practices in managing a global workforce; this presents significant challenges and opportunities for the HRM function in MNCs.

Discussion questions

1 What's your own definition of work-life balance?

2 Are you clear about all the priorities in your life? Are you expending your energy proportionately on each of them?

3 What currently are your top three work – life issues?

4 What types of internal communications might be helpful in improving work-life balance in teams across an MNC? What would you expect those communications to accomplish? How often would they be issued and what form would they take? (e.g., meetings, e-mail bulletins, etc.)

5 In MNCs that have organised their business lines globally, employees may now find themselves reporting to bosses and colleagues in different cities or countries when previously their supervisors were sitting just a few seats away. What type of work-life challenges can this bring about for employees and managers?

Work-life in the global village

Things used to be so uncomplicated. Before the restructuring, Dandan Yuwen reported to someone in her own office with whom she shared a language, a set of common cultural references, and most importantly, a time zone.

It is 9:30 p.m. on a Thursday night in Shanghai. Yuwen finds herself participating in a conference call with colleagues in Europe. She'd like to do it from home with her husband and daughter. From past experience she knows she will be in for a late night because inevitably, her European colleagues will ask her to send them some kind of report 'by the close of business'. In Europe, it's about 4:30 p.m. – practically the close of business already. Yuwen only has access to the company's public computer drives when she's logged onto the company network. So she's got to be at the office to send the people in Europe whatever they ask for.

Before the company restructured, this would not have happened. Yuwen reported to a supervisor who sat across the room from her – a Chinese man whose language and frame of reference she understands without difficulty. Now she must report in a foreign language to people from a different culture living in a time zone five hours away. She's afraid she won't understand everything that's said, so she takes copious notes. And she stays at the office until 11:00 p.m. to make sure the people in Europe get what they need. Otherwise, they might be unhappy, and Yuwen values her job too highly to allow that. However she did wonder to herself if her global colleagues ever appreciated what time it was in her part of the world.

It is not just the timing of the conference calls that causes Yuwen anxiety. Last week, the US team called a teleconference at 8:00 p.m. Shanghai time. Colleagues from the US, Europe, and Asia participated; Yuwen represented the China business.

A manager from Thailand presented some information and someone from the US asked questions. The phone connection was poor, and although the European colleague was speaking English he was difficult to understand because he had a pronounced accent. Yuwen did not entirely understand some of his questions, but because the call was running overtime and she also did not want to appear impolite she did not ask for clarification.

Then an Australian colleague started discussing an approach considered risky by those in Europe and the US. It turned into a bit of a debate, during which the Japanese man and a colleague from Thailand remained silent.

When things calmed down, the Japanese colleague began to warm up and started making some very good points. But then the meeting's designated timekeeper reminded everyone that it was getting late. Discussion moved on to the next topic. When the conference call ended, Yuwen felt that some good ideas had been raised, but that no one had been able to develop them. Part of it was the phone line, part of it was the time constraint, and part of it was cultural and language barriers. As a result, some good ideas went unused and Yuwen remained puzzled. She felt these meetings often failed to benefit from the collective knowledge of the company's global network of employees.

Case questions

1 Are these issues relevant to work? How do they affect work-life balance?
2 What are the main causes of the issue?
3 Which aspects of the issue are within the individual's control?
4 How could you, as an individual, improve the situation – or avoid it altogether?
5 How can the company support individuals in improving or avoiding the situation?

Case questions for further study and reflection

1 Imagine you are Yuwen's US colleague and you have a feeling that these meetings are not working well. You think it would be useful to get Yuwen's point of view. How would you approach this with Yuwen?
2 Imagine you are designing a cross-cultural training programme to encourage teamwork in this company. What are the main factors you would need to consider in designing this training? Outline the basic components of the training programme.

Box 16.3   Work-life priorities in China

Becoming a leader in working life in China requires companies to place a greater emphasis on understanding and responding to the needs of Chinese employees and considering a range of work-life initiatives that are not necessarily the same initiatives that would apply in western Anglo countries. At the Global Workforce Roundtable organised by Boston College and held in Shanghai, China in February 2008 the focus of discussion was on the role of Work-Life in Recruitment, Retention and Development of Top Talent practitioners in both global and regional positions from around the region. Participants discussed the importance for MNCs of reviewing their own approaches and questioning the tacit assumptions they make about work-life strategies in China. See Table 16.2 for how senior HR Practitioners working in China ranked the key work-life initiatives that were needed.

Table 16.2 Work-life priorities in China

	Work-life policy initiatives for China
First priority	• Assist with educational costs for children, especially when relocating employees within China • Provide flexibility in when and where work is conducted and flexibility in leave policies. • Define clearly the development and promotional opportunities available.
Second priority	• Have initiatives that contribute to the health and well-being of employees.
Third priority	• Enable employees to care for and maintain contact with extended family members • Ensure more financial security through supplemented retirement benefits • Continue to provide work-life policies and programmes equally to men and women.

Further reading

- Bardoel, E.A. and De Cieri, H. (2006) 'Developing a work/life strategy in a multinational enterprise (MNE)', A *Sloan Work and Family Encyclopedia* Entry, Sloan Work and Family Research Network, accessed at http://wfnetwork.bc.edu/encyclopedia_entry.php?id = 3814&area = All.
This article examines issues relevant to how multinational corporations (MNCs) can build a strategic approach to global work-life issues from a human resource management (HRM) perspective.

- Collings, D.G., Scullion, H. and Morley, M.J. (2007) 'Changing patterns of global staffing in the multinational enterprise: Challenges to the conventional expatriate assignment and emerging alternatives', *Journal of World Business*, 42 (2): 198–213.
This article discusses issues related to different types of international assignments, including short-term project work.

- De Cieri, H. and Bardoel, E.A. (2009) 'What does "work-life management" mean in China and Southeast Asia for MNCs?', *Community, Work and Family*, 12 (2): 179–96.
This article discusses the findings of interviews conducted with HR managers in multinational corporations, to explore the meaning and management of work-life issues in the Asian region.

- Lewis, S., Gambles, R. and Rapoport, R. (2007) 'The constraints of a "work-life balance" approach: An international perspective', *The International Journal of Human Resource Management*, 18 (3): 360–73.
This article provides a critique of work-life balance discourses and debates. The authors suggest that more attention should be paid to the implications of the changing nature of paid

work in the global context. The authors advocate increasing attention on the broader social sustainability of working life.

- Ngo, H.-Y., Foley, S. and Loi, R. (2009) 'Family-friendly work practices, organizational climate, and firm performance: A study of multinational corporations in Hong Kong', *Journal of Organizational Behavior,* 30: 665–80.
These authors investigate the relationship between family-friendly work practices and firm-level outcomes in multinational corporations operating in Hong Kong. Their research highlights the importance of top management support for family-friendly initiatives.

- Dowling, P.J., Festing, M. and Engle, A.D. (2008) *International Human Resource Management: Managing People in a Multinational Context,* 5th edn. South-Melbourne, VIC: Thomson.
This text provides an introductory overview of the field of international HRM.

- Komarraju, M. (2006) 'Work and family: Cross-national comparisons', A *Sloan Work and Family Encyclopedia* Entry, Sloan Work and Family Research Network, accessed at http://wfnetwork.bc.edu/encyclopedia_entry.php?id = 2862&area = All
This article examines work–family linkages in national and cross-national settings and discusses historical, economic, political, religious and social factors that influence work–family linkages.

- Poelmans, S.A.Y. (ed.) (2005) *Work and Family: An International Research Perspective.* Mahwah, NJ: Lawrence Erlbaum Associates.
This book addresses work and family issues by addressing a range of international and comparative concerns.

- Poelmans, S. and Caligiuri, P. (eds) (2008) *Harmonizing Work, Family, and Personal Life in Organizations: From Policy to Practice.* Cambridge University Press: Cambridge.
This book addresses a range of issues related to research and practice for organisations dealing with work-life issues.

Internet resources

1 Sloan Work and Family Research Network (http://wfnetwork.bc.edu/): Designed to support research and teaching, promote best practices at the workplace, and inform state policy on issues that affect the lives of working families and the places where they work.

2 Penn State University Work/Family web site (http://lser.la.psu.edu/workfam/): A range of links to websites that provide information on research, work/family activism, US Government Agencies, professional organisations, publications, consultants and professional links.

3 The Work Foundation (United Kingdom) (http://www.theworkfoundation.com/difference/e4wlb.aspx): A not-for-profit organisation that provides answers to practical problems for UK employers and the public sector.

4 The International Center of Work and Family (ICWF) (http://www.iese.edu/en/ Research/CentersandChairs/Centers/ICWF/Home/Home.asp): Located at IESE Business School, University of Navarra, Spain, the ICWF provides information to help organisations create a family-responsible environment.

5 Work-Life Research Programme in the Australian Centre for Research in Employment and Work (ACREW) (http://www.buseco.monash.edu.au/mgt/research/acrew/work-life.html): Based at Monash University in Australia, this provides information about work-life research, education and practice.

Self-assessment questions

Indicative answers to these questions can be found on the companion website at www.sagepub.co.uk/harzing3e.

1 **What is the difference between the terms 'work–family' and 'work-life'?**
2 **What are some examples of 'work-life initiatives'?**
3 **Identify and discuss some of the tensions that can arise in the management of work-life in a global context.**
4 **Identify and discuss four potential strategies that may be applicable to tensions in global work-life management.**
5 **What are the key responsibilities for work-life management at the global, HR and line management levels?**

References

Allen, T.D. (2001) 'Family-supportive work environments: The role of organizational perceptions', *Journal of Applied Psychology*, 81(4): 414–35.

Bardoel, E.A. (2006) 'Work-life and HRD', in P. Holland and H. De Cieri (eds), *Contemporary Issues in Human Resource Development: An Australian Perspective*. pp. 237–59. Sydney, NSW: Pearson Education.

Bardoel, E.A. and De Cieri, H. (2006) 'Developing a work/life strategy in a multinational enterprise (MNC)', A *Sloan Work and Family Encyclopedia* entry, Sloan Work and Family Research Network, accessed at http://wfnetwork.bc.edu/encyclopedia_entry.php?id = 3814&area = All.

Bardoel, E.A., Morgan, L. and Santos, C. (2007) '"Quality" part-time work in Australian organisations: Implications for HRD', *Human Resource Development International*, 10 (3): 281–99.

Barrow, S. and Mosley, R. (2006) *The Employer Brand: Bringing the Best of Brand Management to People at Work*. Chichester, UK: John Wiley & Sons Ltd.

Bedeian, A.G., Burke, B.G. and Moffett, R.G. (1988) 'Outcomes of work-family conflict among married male and female professionals', *Journal of Management*, 14(3): 475–91.

Bird, J. (2006) 'Work-life balance: Doing it right and avoiding the pitfalls', *Employment Relations Today*, 33(3): 21–30.

Bowen, D.E. and Ostroff, C. (2004) 'Understanding HRM-firm performance linkages: The role of "strength" of the HRM system', *Academy of Management Review*, 29: 203–21.

Brewster, C., Sparrow, P. and Harris, H. (2005) 'Towards a new model of globalizing HRM', *International Journal of Human Resource Management*, 16: 953–74.

Byron, K. (2005) 'A meta-analytic review of work-family conflict and its antecedents', *Journal of Vocational Behavior*, 67: 169–98.

Childs, J.T. (Jr.) (2005) 'Workforce diversity: A global HR topic that has arrived', in M. Losey, S. Meisinger and D. Ulrich (eds), *The Future of Human Resource Management*. pp. 110–18. Hoboken, NJ: Wiley.

Dallimore, E.J. and Mickel, A. E. (2006) 'Quality of life: Obstacles, advice, and employer assistance', *Human Relations*, 59: 61–103.

De Cieri, H. and Bardoel, E.A. (2009) 'What does "work-life management" mean in China and Southeast Asia for MNCs?', *Community, Work and Family*, 12(2): 179–96.

De Cieri, H. and Dowling, P.J. (2006) 'Strategic human resource management in multinational enterprises: Developments and directions', in G.K. Stahl and I. Björkman (eds), *Handbook of Research in International Human Resource Management*. pp. 15–35. Cheltenham, UK: Edward Elgar.

Doz, Y. and Prahalad, C.K. (1991) 'Managing DMNCs: A search for a new paradigm', *Strategic Management Journal*, 12: 145–64.

Edwards, T. and Kuruvilla, S. (2005) 'International HRM: National business systems, organisational politics and the international division of labour in MNCs', *International Journal of Human Resource Management*, 16(1): 1–21.

Enns, H. and McFarlin, D.B. (2005) 'When executives successfully influence peers: The role of target assessment, preparation and tactics', *Human Resource Management*, 44: 257–78.

Farndale, E. (2005) 'HR department professionalism: A comparison between the UK and other European countries', *International Journal of Human Resource Management*, 16: 660–75.

Greenhaus, J.H. and Powell, G.N. (2006) 'When work and family are allies: A theory of work-family enrichment', *Academy of Management Review*, 31: 72–92.

Grzywacz, J.G. and Carlson, D.S. (2007) 'Conceptualizing work-family balance: Implications for practice and managing', *Advances in Developing Human Resources*, 9(4): 455–71.

Haas, L.L., Hwang, P. and Russell, G. (2000) *Organizational Change and Gender Equity*. Thousand Oaks, CA: Sage.

Konrad, A. and Mangel, R. (2000) 'The impact of work-life programmes on firm productivity', *Strategic Management Journal*, 21: 1225–37.

Korabik, K., Lero, D. and Ayman, R. (2003) 'A micro-macro approach to cross-cultural work-family research'. Paper presented at the European Academy of Management, Milan, Italy.

Lewis, S., Gambles, R. and Rapoport, R. (2007) 'The constraints of a 'work-life balance' approach: An international perspective', *The International Journal of Human Resource Management*, 18(3): 360–73.

McCampbell, A.S. (1996) 'Benefits achieved through alternative work schedules', *Human Resource Planning*, 19(3): 31–7.

Michaels, B. (1995) 'A global glance at work and family', *Personnel Journal*, 74(4): 85–93.

Nishii, L.H. and Özbilgin, M.F. (2007) 'Global diversity management: towards a conceptual framework', *International Journal of Human Resource Management*, 18(11): 1883–94.

Novicevic, M. and Harvey, M. (2001) 'The changing role of the corporate HR function in global organisations', *International Journal of Human Resource Management*, 12(8): 1251–68.

Perry-Smith, J. and Blum, T. (2000) 'Work-family human resource bundles and perceived organizational performance', *Academy of Management Journal*, 43: 1107–17.

Poelmans, S.A.Y. (2005) 'Organizational research on work and family: Recommendations for future research', in S.A.Y. Poelmans (ed.), *Work and Family: An International Research Perspective*. Mahwah, NJ: Lawrence Erlbaum Associates.

Poole, M.S. and Van De Ven, A.H. (1989) 'Using paradox to build management and organization theories', *Academy of Management Review*, 14: 562–78.

Poster, W.R. and Prasad, S. (2005) 'Work-family relations in transnational perspective: A view from high-tech firms in India and the United States', *Social Problems*, 52: 122–46.

Rapoport, R., Lewis, S., Bailyn, L. and Gambles R. (2005) 'Globalization and the integration of work with personal life', in S.A.Y. Poelmans (ed.), *Work and Family: An International Research Perspective*. pp. 463–84. Mahwah, NJ: Lawrence Erlbaum Associates.

Rousseau, D. (2006) 'Is there such a thing as "evidence-based management"?', *Academy of Management Review*, 31: 256–69.

Russell, G. and Bourke, J. (1999) 'Where does Australia fit in internationally with work and family issues?', *Australian Bulletin of Labour*, 25(3): 229–50.

Rynes, S., Bartunek, J. and Daft, R. (2001) 'Across the great divide: Knowledge creation and transfer between practitioners and academics', *Academy of Management Journal*, 44(2): 340–55.

Rynes, S., Giluk, T. and Brown, K. (2007) 'The very separate worlds of academic and practitioner periodicals in human resource management: Implications for evidence-based management', *Academy of Management Journal*, 50(5): 987–1008.

Scullion, H., Collings, D.G. and Gunnigle, P. (2007) 'International human resource management in the 21st century: emerging themes and contemporary debates', *Human Resource Management Journal*, 17(4): 309–19.

Shapiro, A. and Noble, K. (2001) 'A work/life lens helps bring a global workforce into focus'. *Its about time*, 2 (Spring): 1–2.

Spector, P.E., Cooper, C.L., Poelmans, S.A.Y., Allen, T.D., O'Driscoll, M., Sanchez, J.I., Oi, L.S., Dewe, P., Hart, P., Luo, L., De Moraes, L.F.R., Ostrognay, G.M., Sparks, K., Wong, P. and Yu, S. (2004) 'A cross-national comparative study of work-family stressors, working hours, and well-being: China and Latin America versus the Anglo world', *Personnel Psychology*, 57(1): 119–42.

Spinks, N. (2005) *Work-life Around the World: Building a Global Work-life Strategy*. Toronto, Canada: Work-Life Harmony Enterprises.

Stohl, C. and Cheney, G. (2001) 'Participatory practices/paradoxical practices: Communication and the dilemmas of organizational democracy', *Management Communication Quarterly*, 14: 349–407.

Stroh, L.K. and Caligiuri, P.M. (1998) 'Increasing global competitiveness through effective people management', *Journal of World Business*, 33(1): 1–16.

Tracy, S.J. (2004) 'Dialectic, contradiction, or double bind? Analyzing and theorizing employee reactions to organizational tension', *Journal of Applied Communication Research*, 32(2): 119–46.

Trethewey, A. and Ashcraft K.L. (2004) 'Special issue introduction. Practicing disorganisation: The development of applied perspectives on living with tension', *Journal of Applied Communication Research*, 32(2): 8–88.

Von Glinow, M.A., Drost, E. and Teagarden, M.B. (2002) 'Converging on IHRM best practices: lessons learned from a globally distributed consortium on theory and practice', *Human Resource Management*, 41(1): 123–40.

Welbourne, T. (2005) 'Editor-in-chief's note', *Human Resource Management*, 44: 113–14.

17

Regulation and Change in Global Employment Relations

Miguel Martínez Lucio and Robert MacKenzie

Contents

Learning Objectives

After reading this chapter you will be able to

● Comprehend the complex and varied role of regulation

● Appreciate the competing narratives and approaches to regulation

● Understand the role of organisations and institutional bodies on regulation and the market

● Appreciate the current debate on re-regulation and how the control of business behaviour has re-emerged

● Critically discuss the different levels of re-regulation and their role

Chapter Outline

The chapter studies the ways that businesses are regulated and how this varies. The politics of IHRM and of industrial relations are an ongoing reality and raise important questions of power, control and democracy. The chapter studies the changing nature of the debate on regulation and politics, and raises questions on how we see the future role of regulation: the concept of human rights is becoming increasingly prevalent in current discussions about IHRM.

1 Introduction

There are political and economic dimensions to HRM and IHRM which shape the decision-making processes of management and the strategic choices made by organisations. HRM and IHRM do not exist in a vacuum – rather they exist within different contexts of regulation of local and global employment relations. The very notion of more strategic approaches to the management of people, which is a central tenet of HRM, assumes a degree of managerial autonomy to act. Yet, recipe book approaches to HRM strategy that assume managers and their organisations are wholly free to enact managerial prerogative in their decision making, ignore the complex, changing and contingent reality. Strategic decision making within MNCs is constrained and sometimes determined by the implementation of laws and codes of practice and by pressure from political actors, including national governments, supranational institutions such as the EU and Non-Governmental Organisations (NGOs) operating at various levels.

Moreover, the economic environment and HRM attributes of any given national or regional context influences internal decision making in terms of prevalent rates of pay, levels of skills and training, and the permissiveness of employment contracts in terms of ease of termination. Managers in MNCs have to make strategic choices that are shaped by the nature of government intervention and the local economy, which include both the decision to pursue quality or cost-related advantages, and whether to invest or disinvest in any given national context.

However, it is easy to over-simplify what we mean by the political and economic dimensions of IHRM. This chapter will discuss how these concepts are related and engage a concept of *regulation* which binds the role of political actors with the impact of the economic context. Firstly we explore *how* we should understand the concept of regulation and appraise *why* it is important for HRM/IHRM. This will help us to understand how political actors and institutions frame the behaviour of managers and attempt to influence the nature of HRM both nationally and internationally. We examine how the role of regulation is not solely about government or the state but incorporates a range of players who shape the rules and processes influencing the firm and its decision making. To understand the political dimension of IHRM we therefore must look beyond the national state and government to consider the various public, voluntary and private sector groups that may influence the shape of HRM in national and, increasingly, international contexts. Similarly, in terms of the economic dimension, there is a widening array of organisations shaping the economic context of IHRM, from fair-trade organisations, social lobbies and transnational governmental institutions such as the World Trade Organisation (WTO).

Secondly, the political and economic dimensions are not clearly separated entities, but have a symbiotic and mutually defining relationship. Political agendas are shaped by economic circumstances and perspectives, in turn economic relations are subject to the influence of policy and political pressure. This relationship is absent from much of the IHRM literature, where the conceptual separation of politics and economics has facilitated a downgrading of the notion of regulation. If we are to comprehend the role of these influential political and economic pressures then we need to be aware of the way different views of the role of regulation develop over time in line with various political projects (Jessop, 2002). That is to say, that there are dominant viewpoints within the political contexts of IHRM and HRM that change over time and which frame the way firms will react to economic factors such as wages and employment contracts.

The chapter will explain how the politics *of* economics has changed over time for IHRM. It briefly outlines the shift over the 1980s and 1990s away from a national and legally based view of regulation reflected in national governments' attempts to control MNCs, towards an agenda which gives priority to the de-regulation and removal of constraints on companies, especially MNCs. The ways that different actors were involved in propagating this change are discussed, for example the role of international consultancies, accountancy firms and think tanks. The new agenda represented not just a critique of the role of regulatory actors but a challenge to the idea of regulation itself, albeit often narrowly defined in terms of 'hard' legalistic intervention. In their own terms, these actors were successful in changing the nature of the debate, undermining the political appetite for 'hard' regulation. Indeed, it was not until the international economic crisis emerged in 2008 that more interventionist forms of regulation were rehabilitated in mainstream political narratives.

Yet the failure to win the argument for complete de-regulation left the door open to new forms of 'soft' regulation. Current modes of thinking favour some re-regulation of HRM practices within MNCs, through establishing codes of practice and ethical agendas in the light of a greater interest in worker rights and social responsibility. Whilst ethical and social responsibility issues are discussed in this book (see Chapters 16 and 18), here we focus on the 'shift' in thinking towards a new form of soft regulation that has been developed by a new set of political actors and social movements. Throughout the chapter we will show how ideas and values that frame the economic and political context of IHRM are developed and often contested by a variety of actors and institutions.

2 The centrality of regulation and its political and economic context

When we speak of the political context of HRM and IHRM there is a tendency to think in terms of the legal framework within which companies engage in the labour market. For example, ensuring recruitment practices are consistent with equality and diversity legislation, and the ongoing administration of HRM conforms to the legislation for minimum wages, working time and health and safety. Likewise, when we think of the economic context of HRM we may be drawn to a vision of the quantitative aspects of the labour market in terms of wage rates or levels of skills and training. However, we argue that in order to understand the political and economic dimensions of IHRM it is important to think in terms of the economic purpose of the political process. The link between them is *regulation*, which is a vital concept if we are to understand the political and economic dimensions of HRM and IHRM.

The concept of regulation is perhaps best understood from the perspective of the purpose it serves. The purpose of regulation is to facilitate social and economic reproduction. The logic of reproduction is based on the establishment of order and regularity, in terms of establishing shared rules and sustaining consistent decision-making processes. Regulation provides a stable environment, which offers some predictability regarding the conduct of agents operating within that environment. Whereas the development of standard expectations regarding the behaviour of others provides the basis for social and economic interaction and reproduction (MacKenzie and Martínez Lucio, 2005), it does not imply that regulation is always effective in establishing a basis for economic activity (Jessop, 1990; Peck, 1996). Our understanding of regulation should go beyond viewing it as merely legal enactment (see MacKenzie and Martínez Lucio, 2005; Martínez Lucio and Mackenzie, 2004). In a survey of debates on the conceptualisation of regulation, Baldwin et al. (1998) argue that three key strands of thought on regulation can be detected. The first views regulation in terms of 'targeted rules' 'accompanied by some mechanism, typically a public agency, for monitoring and promoting compliance' (Baldwin et al., 1998: 3). A second view is to be found in the area of political economy, which conceptualises regulation as being the state and its attempt to manage the economy. However, the third view adopts a broader perspective defining regulation to include 'all mechanisms of social control – including unintentional and non-state processes ...' (ibid.: 4).

It has been long recognised that regulation involves a variety of *actors* such as state bodies, trade unions and management networks, to name some key examples (MacKenzie and Martínez Lucio, 2005; Martínez Lucio and MacKenzie, 2004; Regini, 2000). Regulation also consists of a variety of levels and relations between them. The regulatory roles of organised labour and organised capital, for instance, interrelate at various levels: from the macro level peak organisations of national employer federations and trade unions organisations, to regional or sectoral level mechanisms and into the level of company and workplace relations between management and trade unions, which may also include less institutionalised, informal practices. So trade unions and management interact at the level of the workplace and above, and through various mechanisms ranging from formal and informal workplace arrangements, to centralised bargaining and corporatist structures, up to the national and even transnational level. These actors and their interrelations are central to national, and even supranational, systems of regulation.

The actual regulatory actors and the roles they play in the regulation of social and economic relationships vary according to the context. For example, in relation to social resources such as child care facilities, in one location it will be served by the local state, whilst in another it may be dealt with by employers. In other circumstances key regulatory roles may be played by social institutions such as professional bodies and consumer agencies or a combination of these actors. It is important to recognise therefore that the panoply of actors and levels reflects the coexistence of different types of regulation. Indeed, many insist that regulation has formal and informal qualities, reflected in the increasing array of actors involved (Picciotto, 1999). Individuals and organisations may simultaneously operate within and be subject to a multiplicity of regulatory actors in terms of the state, employers, mechanisms of joint regulation, plus social agencies and institutions. In each case these regulatory actors provide a framework of relative stability, a space within which economic and social actors can act with reasonable confidence regarding the actions of others.

3 Political projects and narratives of market de-regulation

Historically, approaches to HRM have been nationally contextualised in terms of government regulatory influence, national cultures and political processes. Overall, from the mid-1940s until the late 1970s most European countries supported an interventionist role for the state and whether effective or otherwise, encouraged systems of regulation through legislation or other institutionalised means (Esping-Anderson, 2000). Taking this generalisation into account, the precise nature and extent of regulation was still somewhat varied. The implementation of worker rights on such issues as participation or dismissal was not the same across these countries nor was protection against discrimination on the basis of gender or ethnicity consistently upheld, and investment in skills differed across systems. Nonetheless from the late 1970 and 1980s onwards these systems experienced common pressures for change which heralded the steady emergence of the neo-liberal and market-led models of reform, which downplayed the role of joint regulation and industrial bargaining.

Regulatory bodies and agencies reflect particular political views and economic orientations which influence their role and impact. Such framing occurs whether they are state agencies or voluntary and social organisations contributing to the system of regulation. For 30 years (mid-1940s onwards and up to the late 1970s) the dominant model of development and regulation in many developed economies was based on the state as the central actor and major regulator. Often associated with Keynesian models of state intervention in the management of the economy and the associated redistributive mechanisms of the Welfare State, this 'Golden Age' began to falter in the European context during the mid- to late 1970s (see Jessop, 2002: 55–79). The critique made was that extensive state intervention in the economy, the increasing rigidity of labour market regulations in terms of hiring and firing workers, and the steadily increasing power of trade unions created an untenable inflationary situation. Whilst much of this critique is disputed, the belief in structured and nationally based systems of regulation as a central feature of economic and social progress became tarnished (see Jessop, 2002: 95–139). The new narrative that emerged portrayed the state as no longer being an effective 'caretaker' for social order and progress (Hall, 1988). Novel and innovative approaches were said to be needed to respond to the economic and social demands of a global order characterised more than previously by cost competition and new market choices (Alonso, 2006).

What began to emerge in the mid- to late 1970s was a political view of regulation *per se* as being costly and prohibitive for the firm and for society in general (Friedman, 1968). The argument is relevant to HRM and IHRM because it underpins a series of narratives around strengthening management prerogative and making workers become more flexible (see Martínez Lucio, 2008 for a discussion). The basic contours of the argument are as follows. The state and regulation should play a less central role in economic management more generally and in circumscribing the operations of the firm, including its HRM practices. In terms of IHRM, the 'market' through the imperative of competition will force organisations to be more efficient and dynamic. This will push firms either toward seeking cost-reduction strategies through forms of flexible employment and restructuring, or quality enhancing strategies through forms of work organisation that capitalise on workers' skills and knowledge. These are also not mutually exclusive strategies and in both cases rely upon the assertion of management prerogative. The internationalised context in which these strategies are pursued means that the former may be controlled through coercive comparisons between national contexts, underpinned by the threat of 'capital flight' (Keenoy, 1990; Martínez Lucio and Weston, 1994; Mueller and Purcell, 1992), and the latter through the emulation of 'best practices' derived from different national systems, for example the adoption of Quality Circles and Team Working practices developed in Japan (Garrahan and Stewart, 1992; Pinnington and Hammersley, 1997). There are therefore economic and resource based advantages to be gained from the new global market and it offers a greater degree of choice for firms. There are also gains of a more indirect nature from this new marketised 'open' order in terms of greater opportunity to draw upon managerial experience and knowledge from different countries. The new learning and ideational networks that emerge from the increasingly international nature of markets and economies (see Chapters 1 and 2) create an environment where national governments and politics are felt to be less important.

For some this marketisation represents an Americanisation of employment strategies (Brewster, 2004; Guest, 1990), where the role of regulation through the state and collective organisation become secondary to management prerogative (Whitley et al., 2005). This model can be juxtaposed against a traditional European model where the state is more interventionist and collective worker rights are more influential in terms of HRM practices and decision making (Communal and Brewster, 2004). The reality is that the vision of the global is configured in terms of different perspectives (Lillie and Martínez Lucio, 2004), and within these general perspectives specific models such as the American model emerge (Boyacigiller and Adler, 1991). The political dimension of IHRM is linked, in rhetorical terms at least, to this policy oriented move away from state-led forms of regulation and towards new flexible, performance-driven paradigms of work.

4 The agents of de-regulation and flexibility: politics and institutions of change

Regardless of the rhetoric of 'market-led' imperatives, the development of IHRM practices and the transmission of 'best practice' ultimately relies upon the agency of management and other actors, therefore its implementation is still essentially a political process – that is to say it is based on struggles between actors regarding the distribution of power. Competing views of a firm's management, based on divergent values pertaining to the market and the individual, exist within the same firm, not only between management and the representatives of labour, but also between different cohorts of management. The process by which models of HRM/IHRM become predominant within firms is often not through evolutionary adaptation but emerges as the outcome of a variety of pressures. These pressures arise in the form of isomorphism, be it *coercive*, whereby companies are forced to comply due to strong sanctions, or *mimetic*, where companies copy practices because they are seen as successful or currently the 'best way' to work (DiMaggio and Powell, 1983). The implementation of IHRM practices is a political process that involves various actors' attempts to impose ideas and practices and is a conscious struggle between them over strategies and ideas, reflecting differences between management cohorts and both cooperative and adversarial relations between management and labour.

In terms of HRM/IHRM developments associated with the *Japanisation* debate in the UK, Stewart (1996) argues that the associated organisational and employment changes were the outcomes of political debates and struggles between unions, employers and even academics. The practices of teamworking and quality management were to a significant degree created not just by overseas MNCs in the early 1990s but also by consultancy firms such as Arthur Anderson. The large international consultancy and accountancy firms were in many ways MNCs in their own right, and were central to the propagation of these new ideas. Consultancies such as Price Waterhouse (now Price Waterhouse Coopers) and McKinsey & Co amongst others developed consultancy and research into flexible systems of employment which influenced the development of HRM concepts in many national contexts. The contribution of other actors was also highly significant, such as the role of the right wing think tanks in the USA (The Heritage Foundation founded in 1973) and the UK (Centre for Policy Studies founded by right wing politicians Keith Joseph and Margaret Thatcher in 1974). These political actors contributed much to the initial development of the reified notion of the 'market', and to the campaign for greater flexibility in the labour market, that were central to the opposition and undermining of state-led regulation (see Klein, 2007: 50–1). Within management and business circles consultancy firms promoted more elaborate and 'scientific' models of management behaviour and organisational strategy. The role of such bodies has grown in significance in the past 20 years as a basis for networking and disseminating views on work and its organisation in terms of HRM (Heller, 2002; Legge, 2002). At the more extreme end, anti-union and union-busting consultancies have become a common feature of such ideational networks.

Within this general framework of ideas and initiatives we also see the development and dissemination of expert knowledge through global university and business school networks. Expert knowledge is being sought in terms of the subject of work (the worker), the psychological framework of employment (motivation and commitment), the organisational context (owners, managers and employees), the social context (gender and ethnicity), the economic and labour market contexts (skills and HRM attributes), and the regulatory environment (legal constraints and rights).

The growth of the consultancies and business schools was due to a range of phenomena, including: new forms of competitive management, new forms of HRM, organisational factors in terms of a mushrooming management constituency, and institutional factors related to the restructuring and commodification of education. Underpinning this has been the fact that the greater degree of management intervention in the administration of businesses (and the social and cultural spaces of organisations) has required initiatives specifically to address the inevitable cognitive gaps arising within management knowledge. This dimension has become central to the mapping of regulatory interventions and the attempts to realign them. These educational and research institutions have been paralleled and supported by more direct intervention from consultancy firms who research, motivate and legitimate organisational change (O'Shea and Madigan, 1997). This has provided the new regulatory actors, be they state agencies or particular consultancy firms, with knowledge resources, technical abilities and competences, and the degree of legitimacy necessary for influencing the terminology and practices of new forms of management strategy within HRM/IHRM. Yet these educational and knowledge-based spaces are changing and becoming the object of greater internal debate and challenge: the realities of what business schools 'do' can vary, especially in light of critical academic traditions within the teaching of HRM and Organisational Studies in many British business schools (Martínez Lucio, 2007). Increasingly, ethical issues, questions of equality and diversity, and CSR are beginning to move up the agenda, as are issues of employment and financial regulation – not least in the light of the economic downturn and problems of global finance since 2008–9.

Even at the macro level of the global political scene, ideas of harder management-led HRM are propagated, both directly and indirectly. The roles of the World Bank and the IMF, as transnational and inter-state publicly funded bodies, have been crucial in extending the idea of free markets, greater competition and the importance of continuous labour and organisational restructuring. The practices of these bodies vary but their role in using debt in developing countries as a vehicle for pushing through restructuring and supporting more managerially driven systems of control and performance management within work is key (Klein, 2007: 267–71; Stiglitz, 2006: 211–44). They link with the harder and more performance-driven aspects of HRM and help to legitimate and propagate the internal debates of governments or MNCs that promote harder and less involvement-based versions of HRM.

What we are arguing here is that the politics and economics of IHRM is as much about a variety of actors disseminating ideas and values, as it is about natural adaptation. Such approaches are forged through agency and political processes, and are not simply the natural or 'best' outcome in the light of the needs of the new global market. In the late 1970s the political project of the new right in the UK and USA defined hegemonic views towards regulation for governments on both sides of the Atlantic for the next three decades. Successive governments elected from either side of the respective political divides did not demur, whether due to ideological commitment or political expediency. Indeed it was not until the international economic crisis emerged in 2008 that the recognised need for government intervention returned to the mainstream political narrative. In the UK this even meant the rehabilitation of the long exiled concept of nationalisation, a word no 'New Labour' Minister would have dared utter over the preceding ten years. Regulation had returned to the political agenda.

5 The new politics of IHRM: projects and narratives of re-regulation

Due to their dynamic nature, the political landscapes of IHRM and the management of labour by MNCs have not stood still. The late 1990s began to see a change in the politics of labour management and a new set of actors emerge who were internationally intent on raising alternative approaches and issues. The cost of unfettered MNC development in terms of uneven and unfair labour standards, the increasing concern with the social condition of employment throughout the world, and the gradual increase in ethical issues placed on the agenda of business management (see Chapters 7 and 8), meant that a new set of discourses began to appear in the discussion of labour management.

Given the legitimacy and historical pre-eminence of the nation state, the role of national governments and government bodies have been central political influences on the firm and its HRM strategies. Extending beyond the nation state there has been a long standing tradition of international regulatory bodies. These organisations took on increased importance during the new wave of internationalisation in the 1980s and the growing concern with setting minimum benchmarks for treatment of workers. It is too soon to talk of a re-regulation of employment given the weak and uneven nature of transnational regulatory bodies, and the fact that the ideas underpinning them are not universally shared. The interaction of formal and informal regulatory processes around legal forms and codes of conduct is increasingly a part of modern business environments (Picciotto, 1999). However, there are three further dimensions which we will now discuss that are important aspects of this partial return to regulation through a growing interest in re-regulation.

Standardisation and labour market knowledge
Firstly, MNCs continue to develop and edge towards the potential of global systems of employment. At the same time migration continues to be a vital part of international labour markets at virtually all skill and educational levels. This prompts the

need to create structures and frameworks that assist in sharing and validating the content of work and the skills of workers. There are extensive government networks across countries throughout the world sharing information about qualifications, apprenticeship systems, and new forms of skills development such as soft skills, which are creating common standards and templates. These can be used to validate the qualifications of students travelling to study or work in different countries and to create common templates for learning. In the European Union there is increasing standardisation of educational systems, especially at the higher and professional level. Employers are thus more able than they were in previous decades to verify the authenticity of skills and qualifications when recruiting from the international pool of labour.

These systems are complemented by international networks in specific sectors with a high level of inter-state activity. In the airlines industry for example there are various international regulatory bodies primarily focused on operational concerns that in addition cover work and employment related issues and standards when addressing health and safety. Here, international regulatory agencies collaborate to influence approaches in safety-related issues and assist in the pooling of knowledge and practice in IHRM. Many of these bodies have questionable regulatory efficacy as they have no form of effective sanction, nevertheless they form part of a tapestry of regulation which although 'soft' in orientation contributes to greater coordination on aspects of labour management and HRM/IHRM.

Labour standards and codes of practice

Secondly, there is increasing interest in labour standards and the behaviour of employers from a range of bodies that are concerned with issues of malpractice, corruption and 'bad' employment practices. The International Labour Organisation (ILO), the United Nations (UN) labour and work related department, was actually established as part of the UN's predecessor, the League of Nations, after the First World War (1919). The ILO historically outlined a basic body of labour codes and rights which whilst often ignored were formally part of the system of inter-governmental relations. Over time it has established more explicit sets of conventions and rules, and a vast array of research and educational activities that map and outline 'good' practices in relation to employment issues. The ILO sets the benchmark against which firms and governments are measured in this area. Political sensitivities around issues such as child labour are directly informed by compliance to ILO standards. Furthermore, the ILO provides standards across the range of everyday employment issues which attract less media attention. Whether these standards are systematically developed or adhered to by member states is another issue. However, they constitute a part of the international dialogue on employment and HRM.

The Organisation for Economic Cooperation and Development (OECD) is a body that has 30 members – mainly developed countries – which broadly share a free market and liberal democratic philosophy. This body has developed a range of economic and social agendas. In relation to MNCs it has produced a set of guidelines establishing a series of principles on the approach of member states to MNCs and the behaviour of MNCs themselves. They cover a range of areas related to employment issues, through to corruption and investment matters. Bodies such as the World Bank and the WTO have also begun to address the issue of labour standards and the basic rights of labour organisations. Whilst such bodies are mainly focused on the economic and developmental aspects of their affiliate nations, they do increasingly address employment and work-related issues, although their prescriptions tend to reflect a particular neo-liberal orientation and vary in their social impact.

These international institutions provide a backdrop of minimum standards and benchmarks which do, on occasion, influence the way that firms behave in relation to their workforce. How much and how often they have an influence depends on the industrial sector and its traditions of labour organisation. However, the main point is that there exists an array of bodies addressing international issues and cross-national labour standards which impact upon HRM practices. They have not possessed a strong regulatory and sanctioning role in many cases, but that does not detract from the fact that there is a tapestry of international labour bodies and HR influencing agencies that challenge the recent vogue for panegyrising globalisation.

Moreover, these developments are not always 'soft' or voluntary and may have the potential for sanctions and a more systematic regulatory process. In some regions of the world countries are beginning to form more permanent systems of supranational economic and social governance. The most developed manifestation of this is the EU – a political structure unifying over 20 European nation states to varying degrees, with a range of social and employment related rules and laws (see Chapter 7). This has included systematic frameworks of HR related regulations on issues such as mass redundancy, health and safety, working hours and discrimination. The European Works Councils Directive provides legislation on worker participation in MNCs, and represents the first supranational employment regulation within the EU. These are all developments that show the necessity of conceptualising regulation within broader transnational frameworks.

The developing tapestry of supranational, transnational and inter-nation state based bodies is creating a framework of regulation affecting firms and their human resource practices. It is part of an evolving international dialogue on labour rights that has emerged since the end of the Second World War, and is underpinned by the Universal Declaration of Human Rights (see Cassese, 1992). There remains a great degree of cynicism regarding the development of such rights due to the highly variable responses of national governments and multinational employers. There is also a concern that the assertion of such rights favours the production regimes of developed countries and disadvantages developing countries where competitive advantage based on low labour costs have become common government strategies for economic development.

Another school of thought in the form of the 'boomerang theory' is more optimistic and argues that governments which ignore the increasing establishment of international rights systems may be shamed and compelled in the longer term to subscribe to them (Risse et al., 1999). Even if this is symbolic in the first instance, over time it establishes expectations within countries, arising from unions or political bodies, as well as pressures beyond from international consumer groups, other nation states (Norway for example has been highly active on such issues) and transnational inter-state organisations such as the EU.

Ethics, values and context

Thirdly, the developments described above dovetail with an increasing interest in social responsibility and ethics within HRM (Pinnington et al., 2007). In relation to major issues such as child labour there is emergent external pressures from NGOs such as OXFAM or War on Want. Movements such as 'Fairtrade', which campaigns for a decent wage for workers in the global agricultural sector, notably coffee, and in the textiles industry have provided a new reference point for ethically based regulation that is of growing importance, although there are views arguing that such initiatives could be more assertive and extensive.

The focus on social issues and the rights to participation at work in MNCs (Wills, 1998) has emerged as a renewed role for international trade union organisations such as the International Trade Union Congress. Whilst these bodies have less resources to access than nation states (Smith et al., 1998), and indeed compete with each other for scarce resources (Claude and Weston, 1992), they do form part of the global set of institutions that contribute to the tapestry of regulation shaping the political and economic context in which IHRM exists. They play a regulatory role in terms of diffusing expert knowledge, and informing and educating public agencies and nation states (Baehr, 1999). They also constitute a counterpoint to the private and market driven networks of consultancies and think tanks. These developments echo the interest in stakeholder theories of ethics and HRM, which espouse a more pluralist understanding of voice and the role of different actors (Greenwood and De Cieri, 2007). What is more, a range of informal and work place activist based union networks have emerged, aimed at exchanging information on campaigns and coordinating across a range of disputes and mobilisations (Wills, 1998). The politics of such networks has given rise to broad coalitions combining trade unions with a diverse range of peace campaigners, environmentalist and anti-capitalist groups, into movements that are both innovative and increasingly entrenched (Thomas, 2007).

The Internet has provided a forum for discussion and a conduit for the transmission of critiques of MNCs and the articulation of alternative, progressive perspectives on consumption. Consumer groups are utilising this medium to bring pressure to bear on the activities of MNCs and the ethicality of their approach to such issues as employment and sustainable resourcing. Whereas there may be a more individualist and consumerist orientation to contemporary capitalism (Alonso, 2006), a new politics of consumption is emerging that places social and employment issues on the agenda.

These three dimensions of transnational regulation are a vital part of the environment that MNCs inhabit. Indeed, they encourage MNCs to internalise regulatory roles themselves, as they increasingly need to ethically police their organisations and create sustainable and legitimate operations.

6 Summary

The chapter has argued that the concept of regulation should be central to any discussion of the politics and economics of IHRM. Regulation involves various levels and actors, and in any given context these will vary. There has also been a shift in the way regulation is viewed and who is involved in it. Where once stood the apparatus of the state and direct forms of intervention, there is now an even more complex scenario. Whilst there has been a move towards more marketised economies where the remit of regulation is limited, this is only part of the story. Firstly, such a shift towards a marketised and more individualistic perspective is itself the political product of a range of actors and knowledge networks – which can be prone to shifting economic and political contingencies, as witnessed in the clamour for regulatory responses to the emergent economic crisis in 2008–9. Secondly, sustaining the hegemony of marketised perspectives has always been a contested process and there is again increasing concern with the need to rebuild regulation and create a more effective platform for regulating international employment issues. That this has emerged is indisputable – whether or not it will be as influential as the more established and traditional forms of regulation remains to be seen.

Conclusion

Increasingly we need to appreciate that the politics of IHRM involves a variety of actors influencing the way that people are managed. The illusion that the emergence of market-oriented HRM strategies would deliver a new world of autonomous managerial decision making has been shown to be questionable and surpassed by processes of re-regulation. There are competing views on how firms should conduct their HR strategies and in the case of MNCs this has now become a question at the centre of a range of policy and social debates (see Klein, 2007). The once dominant view of the reassertion of the prerogative of management, as a new and invigorated actor that can assimilate many of the requirements of regulation and actually regulate in relation to the internal context of the firm, is highly problematic and contested. This is the key challenge for IHRM: as MNCs develop their own geocentric forms of governance (see Chapter 1), which are neither influenced by national systems of origin or the contexts they operate in, it is becoming clear that there is an urgent need for new forms of global regulation. MNCs can create their own idiosyncratic HRM systems that are hybrids of what went before but there are limits to the extent to which they can internalise their strategies to create systems that respond to internal business and operational requirements and minimise external regulatory influences.

Pressures remain in terms of national governments, transnational public bodies, transnational organisations, social movements, consumer organisations, and transnational trade unions structures and networks. This new environment is about setting standards and creating alternative visions of how people should be managed: and, therefore, it presents a whole new challenge to the political dimension of IHRM. This political dimension will be a global struggle of ideas about the way capitalism should be regulated, involving clusters of nation states, national systems and international bodies and networks. Regulation, far from disappearing, has become a significant and ever more complex reality. It would be too easy to dismiss this tapestry of often soft regulation, voluntary codes of practice and pressure groups as not sufficiently coordinated, nor backed by meaningful sanction apparatus, to provide an international equivalence to the regulatory role historically played by nation states. Yet, given the obvious disparities in the geo-political context such direct comparisons become essentially meaningless. Regulation in the current global context involves a move towards combinations of actors at different levels: from nation states, to transnational bodies (both regulatory and voluntary in character) and even social and private associations who lobby and highlight issues. Thus, both hard and soft forms of regulation co-exist.

Discussion questions

1 What are the main political ideologies driving the debates on regulation and de-regulation?

2 What is the purpose of regulation and why does it matter who leads and governs projects of regulation?

3 What are the main features of re-regulation and what kinds of pressures are MNCs experiencing in relation to these features?

4 How sustainable are new forms of regulation and state intervention within a global context?

A motor company in England

'Bartlett Motor Cars' produces some of the most expensive and luxurious cars in the world, and has been long established as a much sought after brand. The workforce was relatively more skilled than the typical industrial car worker due to the craft based expertise that went into production. During the 1960s and 1970s it was known for having a traditional industrial relations approach and strong workplace representation. The company was firmly locked into the national tradition of industrial relations which consisted of informal workplace discussions on operational matters and problems, along with a formal, collective agreement and sets of procedures for the company as a whole. However, the management culture was uncertain about extending a strong system of participation in terms of strategic issues to the workforce, and the lines of communication were limited to dealing with issues and problems as they arose.

Whilst this segment of the car market remained relatively robust over time, the changing industrial relations context of the 1980s brought with it a set of tensions and problems. The Conservative government passed legislation which restricted the role of trade unions and limited their political activity (in theory, although not always in practice). The increasing competition from German high value motor cars, and the move towards new more speed-oriented models, meant that British high status, luxury cars faced new competitive challenges to their sales and position in the market. Restructuring became common but the practices of industrial relations remained adversarial and initiatives to develop new individual HR systems of control and communication challenged the legitimacy and role of unions. There appeared to be a tension between the more collective and standardised system of national industrial relations, with its informal workplace features, and the new pressure for Japanese and American oriented practices as adopted, to some extent, by the firm's management. In many respects it appeared that the local system of regulation through informal and formal processes would be undermined by more market-based and individually oriented approaches.

Case questions
1 Why is there a tension between collective and individual approaches to HRM?
2 How was the national system of regulation put under pressure by global developments in the market and management practices within the workplace?
3 What do you imagine are the trade union's long term prospects?

A European company with subsidiary businesses in the UK and elsewhere

The luxury car company referred to in the previous Case Study was bought by a leading European car manufacturer which we will call People Motors. It became part of a transnational corporation with operations in many parts of the world. Local management was supported in terms of the development of new systems of work-place organisation and operations; although the nature of the car manufactured in the UK was of such a high value-added nature that the local management was able to convince their transnational headquarters of the different challenges facing the local operator. Suddenly, local management in Bartlett Motors found themselves a small player in a much larger pool of senior and international managers, regardless of the strength of their local brand worldwide. They were exposed to new systems of international management control and performance management systems.

At the same time the presence of a European Works Council and a Global Works Council meant that local trade unionists began to have access to a higher tier of negotiation and consultation. This provided them with information that local management did not always obtain. What is more, with the concern with ecological and ethical pressures, a series of projects were developed worldwide which, involved key individuals from the UK factory. Trade unionists began to engage explicitly with the agenda of CSR. The consequence of these developments was that there arose a new, albeit soft, system of regulation and consultation, which provided information and networks to local trade unionists. This was part of the new attempt to set common benchmarks and socially oriented standards of employment.

In some cases members of these councils were used as mediators and 'consultants of sorts' to deal with problems in PeopleMotors production plants in Africa and Latin America. These trade unionists therefore became new players within the firm, linking up with external organisations including the ILO, international union bodies and international social organisations. Through these networks they lobbied for more regulation and negotiation within the wider structures of the MNC. The trade union representatives found themselves travelling throughout Europe, and the world, attending meetings and lobbying. The trade unionists referenced the increasing presence of international frameworks, corporate social responsibility declarations, codified labour standards and even the greater interest in ecological and sustainability issues within their repertoire of actions and narratives.

Roles within the workplace at Bartlett Motor Cars began to change as trade unionists began to engage with such international networks. Trade union representatives faced increased pressure from competing claims on their time and resources in terms of balancing their traditional workplace responsibilities with their new international roles. By their nature such international networks could appear to be somewhat remote from daily experiences of the workplace, which created an additional source of tension for trade union representatives in terms of balancing their roles. This was countered by consciously sustaining a strong dialogue with the range of activists and members within the plant's union structures, and actively encouraging their involvement in these broader processes. The concern was that over the longer term such international developments would require greater resources and time if they were not to evolve at the expense of day to day local union activity.

Case questions

1 Are the new forms of activity by trade unionists soft or hard regulation? Why do you reach this conclusion?
2 What do these new forms of activities and regulation tell us about the political context of MNCs?
3 Is there a risk that such developments may become a form of control over local management (strengthening the role of transnational headquarters)?
4 Is there a risk that trade unionists may be caught in roles that disconnect them from more traditional roles in terms of worker representation?
5 What kinds of work and personal pressures do such new roles bring to individuals involved? What can be done about this issue?
6 What kind of training and preparation is required to sustain and develop effective forms of dialogue and engagement between unions, workers and managers at various levels within these new types of international forums?

Further reading

- Freeman, M. (2002) *Human Rights*. Cambridge: Polity.
This is a good introduction to the concept of human rights. It covers a range of areas that are essential for the study of international human rights issues. This is becoming a key feature of the CSR agenda and students will find no better guide for exploring the competing meanings and the significance of this concept.

- Picciotto, S. and Mayne, R. (eds) (1999) *Regulating International Business: Beyond Liberalisation*. Basingstoke: Macmillan and Oxfam.
The book explores the way the regulation of international business has developed. It offers a set of very detailed chapters on different dimensions of regulation and how they function. It is seen as one of the first real attempts to engage with a broader set of approaches to regulation.

- Pinnington, A.H., Mackin, R.E. and Campbell, T. (2007) 'Introduction' in A.H. Pinnington, R.E. Macklin and T. Campbell (eds), *Human Resource Management: Ethics and Employment*. Oxford: Oxford University Press.

The edited collection is a very informative outline of the different concerns and issues associated with the ethics of HRM. The introduction to this text is a very good starting point for those wishing to develop their understanding of this increasingly important topic.

- Stiglitz, J. (2006) *Making Globalization Work*. London: Penguin.

This book is written by the Nobel Prize winner Joseph Stiglitz. Students will find this to be an important read, which suggests how the new global order needs to be regulated and made to work for social as well as economic reasons. The book was written prior to the financial crisis of 2008 but it serves to help understand how regulation is a key feature of the debate regarding international economic relations.

- Whitley, R., Morgan E. and Moen, E. (2005) *Changing Capitalisms? Internationalization, Institutional Change and Systems of Economic Organization.* Oxford: Oxford University Press.

No discussion of capitalism can proceed without understanding the basic differences in the models of capitalism and the way they are regulated. The book is useful for explaining how capitalism varies and how institutional change is shaped through the system of economic organisation.

- Claude, R.P. and Weston, B.H. (1992) 'International human rights: overviews', in R.P. Claude and B.H. Weston (eds), *Human Rights in the World Community: Issues and Action,* 2nd edn. Philadelphia: University of Pennsylvania Press.

This is a brief and succinct overview of the way international human rights have developed and explores the meaning of its different dimensions. The concept of rights is becoming part of the teaching of business and management – yet we need to be clearer how this concept evolves and how it varies.

- Greenwood, M. and De Cieri, H. (2007) 'Stakeholder theory and the ethicality of human resource management', in A.H. Pinnington, R.E. Macklin and T. Campbell (eds), *Human Resource Management: Ethics and Employment*. Oxford: Oxford University Press.

The paper points to the importance of democratic participation within the firm and the importance of a stakeholder approach. It is part of a set of positions which argue that the question of ethics necessitates a more open view of organisations.

- Giddens, A. and Hutton, W. (2000) 'Anthony Giddens and Will Hutton in conversation', in W. Hutton and A. Giddens (eds), *Global Capitalism*. New York: New York Press.

Put two visionaries on a park bench to talk about capitalism and this is what emerges. This is a vivid insight into the views of two significant commentators on what has been happening in the past 20 years.

- MacKenzie, R. and Martínez Lucio, M. (2005) 'The realities of regulatory change: beyond the fetish of deregulation', *Sociology* (39) 3: 499–517.

If we are to talk about regulation then we cannot simply think in terms of it as legal systems. Regulation is a broad process involving many players and processes. The employment relation is regulated in a variety of ways, and this article points to how this can be understood, and how the politics of regulation is itself a matter for discussion.

- Wills, J. (1998) 'Taking on the Cosmocorps: Experiments in transnational labor organization', *Economic Geography*, 74: 111–30.

One of the first pieces to systematically discuss the way organised labour is developing in international terms and as part of a broader alternative in global capitalism. It provides the student with a discussion of how unions and workers are active and essential to a global social order and locates this within an effective historical analysis.

- Wills, J. (2000) 'Great expectations: Three years in the life of a European Works Council', *European Journal of Industrial Relations*, 6(1): 85–107.

The paper is a detailed case study of the life of a European Works Council. It is a seminal study which critiques such developments and highlights how they are constrained and limited within the context of industrial relations structures. It is a good case of why such structures need a broader more independent union approach to internationalism. It contrasts and compliments the next reading.

- Whittall, M., Knudsen, H. and Huijgen, F. (2009) 'European Works Councils: Identity and the role of information and communication technology', *European Journal of Industrial Relations*, 15(2): 167–85.

This is a series of case studies on European Works Councils that argues that with regards to any formal system of transnational representation and union activity within firms we must account for the important way in which Information and Communication Technology impacts on and moulds developments. The current context of the Internet has added a strong dimension of support in terms of how trade unionists manage to coordinate activity across national boundaries within MNCs.

- Thomas, N.H. (2007) 'Global Capitalism, the anti-globalisation movement and the Third World', *Capital and Class*, 92, Summer: 45–80.

This article is a good introduction to debates about alternatives to the neo-liberal global order. It is a strong stand for a more mobilisation-based response to the problems of contemporary capitalism. The analysis is forthright and marks the kind of literature that is becoming more common due to the negative consequences of global capitalism and the behaviour of MNCs.

- Martínez Lucio, M. (2010) 'Dimensions of internationalism and the politics of the labour movement: Understanding the political and organisational aspects of labour networking and co-ordination', *Employee Relations*.

The article is concerned with labour internationalism and debates about how it is developing. It argues that trade union coordination at an international level is framed by competing projects, national/regional traditions, and sector based factors. In effect, there are different internationalisms and a politics of internationalism.

Internet resources

1 OECD – Organisation for Economic and Cooperation and Development (http://www.oecd.org/home/): Plenty of material on MNCs and you can search for the OECD's voluntary codes of conduct which are a basic outline for the governance of MNCs within an ethical context.

2 International Labour Organisation (http://www.ilo.org/global/lang--en/index.htm): As the labour department of the ILO this is a significant organisation. The website has many national and international reports and research papers. It also has a series of outlines and codes on MNCs and their behaviour.

3 International Trades Union Congress (http://www.ituc-csi.org/): Website of the organisation that represents most national unions at an international level. It has many resources and links. It will show how unions approach the issues at hand and are responding to greater internationalisation and the need for new forms of regulation.

4 Labour Start (http://www.labourstart.org/): An important and independent source of information about union activity supported by trade unionists. It provides insight into developments around national and international labour related agendas. There are many campaigns around MNCs reported here.

Self-assessment questions

Indicative answers to these questions can be found on the companion website at www.sagepub.co.uk/harzing3e.

1 **Given the growth of MNCs what are the possibilities of effectively regulating them?**
2 **What are the chances of global forms of governance and regulation in terms of employment related issues developing in the coming years?**

3 **Do Non-Government Organisations have a role to play?**
4 **Do voluntary codes of conduct have a realistic chance of influencing IHRM or should a stronger form of regulation develop?**
5 **How would you design into your learning within business schools and universities greater sensitivity concerning international regulation and rights, and the role of broader social organisations?**

References

Alonso, L. (2006) 'The Fordist cycle and the gensis of the post-Fordist society', in L.E. Alonso and M. Martínez Lucio, (eds), *Employment Relations in a Changing Society*. London: Palgrave.

Baehr, P.R. (1999) *Human Rights: Universality in Practice*. Basingstoke: Macmillan

Baldwin, R., Scott, C. and Hood, C. (1998) 'Introduction' in R. Baldwin, C. Scott and C. Hood (eds), *A Reader on Regulation*. Oxford: Oxford University Press.

Boyacigiller, N.A. and Adler, N.J. (1991) 'The parochial dinosaur: organizational science in a global context', *Academy of Management Review*, 16(2): 262–90.

Brewster, C. (2004) 'European perspectives on Human Resource Management', *Human Resource Management Review*, 14(4): 365–82

Cassese, D. (1992) 'The General Assembly: Historical perspective 1945–1989', in P. Ashton, *The United Nations and Human Rights: A Critical Appraisal*. New York: Cambridge University Press.

Claude, R.P. and Weston, B.H. (1992) 'International Human Rights: overviews', in R.P. Claude and B.H. Weston (eds), *Human Rights in the World Community: Issues and Action*, 2nd edn. Philadelphia: University of Pennsylvania Press.

Communal, C. and Brewster, C. (2004) 'HRM in Europe', in A-W. Harzing and J. Van Ruysseveldt (eds), *International Human Resource Management*. London: Sage.

DiMaggio, P.J. and Powell, W. (1983) '"The iron cage revisited": institutional isomorphism and collective rationality in organizational fields', *American Sociological Review*, 48: 147–60.

Esping-Anderson, G. (2000) 'Who is harmed by labour market de-regulation', in G. Esping-Anderson and M. Regini (eds), *Why Deregulate Labour Markets*. Oxford: OUP.

Friedman, M. (1968) 'The role of monetary policy', *American Economic Review*, March: 1–17.

Garrahan, P. and Stewart, P. (1992) *The Nissan Enigma*. London: Mansell.

Greenwood, M. and De Cieri, H. (2007) 'Stakeholder theory and the ethicality of human resource management', in A.H. Pinnington, R.E. Macklin and T. Campbell (eds), *Human Resource Management: Ethics and Employment*. Oxford: Oxford University Press.

Guest, D. (1990) 'Human resource management and the American Dream', *Journal of Management Studies*, 27(4): 377–97.

Hall, S. (1988) *The Hard Road to Renewal*. London: Verso.

Heller, F. (2002) 'What next? More critique of consultants, gurus and managers', in T. Clark and R. Fincham, *Critical Consulting: New Perspectives on the Management Advice Industry*. Oxford: Blackwell.

Jessop, B. (1990) *State Theory.* Oxford: Polity.

Jessop, B. (2002) *The Future of the Capitalist State.* Cambridge: Polity.

Keenoy, T. (1990) 'HRM: A case of wolf in sheep's clothing', *International Journal of Human Resource Management,* 11(5): 4–10.

Klein, N. (2007) *The Shock Doctrine.* London: Penguin.

Legge, K. (2002) 'On knowledge, business consultants and the selling of Total Quality Management', in T. Clark and R. Fincham, *Critical Consulting: New Perspectives on the Management Advice Industry.* Oxford: Blackwell.

Lillie, N. and Martínez Lucio, M. (2004) 'International trade union revitalization: the role of national union approaches', in C. Frege and J. Kelly (eds), *Labour Movement Revitalization in Comparative Perspective.* Oxford: Oxford University Press.

Mackenzie, R. and Martínez Lucio, M. (2005) 'The realities of regulatory change: Beyond the fetish of deregulation', *Sociology* 39(3): 499–517.

Martínez Lucio, M. (2011) 'Dimensions of internationalism and the politics of the labour movement: understanding the political and organisational aspects of Labour networking and

Martínez Lucio, M. (2007) '¿Neoliberalismo y neoconservadurismo interrumpido? El porqué de la existencia de una tradición crítica en las escuelas de dirección de empresas británicas', in C. Fernandez (eds), *Estudios Sociales de la Organización: El Giro PostModerno.* Madrid: Siglo VeintiUno.

Martínez Lucio, M. (2008) 'The organization of human resource strategies: Narratives and power in understanding labour management in a context of change', in Stewart Clegg (ed.), *Oxford Handbook of Organisational Behaviour.* Oxford: OUP.

Martínez Lucio, M. and MacKenzie, R. (2004) 'Unstable boundaries? Evaluating the 'new regulation' within employment relations', *Economy and Society,* 33(1): 77–97.

Martínez Lucio, M. and Weston, S. (1994) 'New management practices in a multinational corporation: the restructuring of worker representation and rights?', *Industrial Relations Journal,* 25(2): 110–21.

Mueller, F. and Purcell, J. (1992) 'The Europeanization of manufacturing and the decentralization of bargaining: multinational', *International Journal of Human Resource Management,* 3(2): 15–34.

O'Shea, J. and Madigan, C. (1997) *Dangerous Company: The Consulting Powerhouses and Businesses They Save and Ruin.* New York: Times Business.

Peck, J. (1996) *Workplace: the Social Regulation of Labour Markets.* New York: Guilford Press.

Picciotto, S. (1999) 'Introduction: What rules for the world economy', in S. Picciotto and R. Mayne (eds), *Regulating International Business: Beyond Liberalisation.* Basingstoke: Macmillan and Oxfam.

Pinnington, A.H. and Hammersley, G.C. (1997) 'Quality circles under the new deal at Land Rover', *Employee Relations,* 19(5): 415–29.

Pinnington, A.H., Mackin, R.E. and Campbell, T. (2007) 'Introduction' in A.H. Pinnington, R.E. Macklin and T. Campbell (eds), *Human Resource Management: Ethics and Employment.* Oxford: Oxford University Press.

Regini, M. (2000) 'The dilemmas of labour market regulation', in G. Esping-Andersen and M. Regini (eds), *Why De-regulate Labour Markets.* Oxford: OUP.

Risse, T., Ropp, S.C. and Sikkink, K. (eds) (1999) *The Power of Human Rights: International Norms and Domestic Change.* Cambridge: CUP.

Smith, J., Pagnuncco, T. and Lopez, G.A. (1998) 'Globalising human rights: The work of trasnational human rights NGOs in the 1990s', *Human Rights Quarterly,* 20(2): 379–412.

Stewart, P. (1996) *Beyond Japanese Management.* London: Taylor and Francis.

Stiglitz, J. (2006) *Making Globalization Work.* London: Penguin.

Thomas, N.H. (2007) 'Global capitalism, the anti-globalisation movement and the Third World', *Capital and Class,* 92 (Summer): 45–80.

Whitley, R., Morgan E. and Moen, E. (2005) *Changing Capitalisms? Internationalisation, Institutional Change and Systems of Economic Organization.* Oxford: Oxford University Press.

Wills, J. (1998) 'Taking on the Cosmocorps: Experiments in transnational labor organization', *Economic Geography,* 74: 111–30.

18

Social Responsibility, Sustainability and Diversity of Human Resources

Fang Lee Cooke

Contents

Learning Objectives

After reading this chapter you will be able to

- Understand the concepts of ethics, corporate social responsibility, equal opportunity and diversity management

- Differentiate perspectives of corporate social responsibility and diversity management

- Explain how ethical employment practices can contribute to sustainable business success and social development

- Critically evaluate the gaps between the aspirations of corporate social responsibility and diversity management and actual practices in workplaces

- Appreciate the global challenges to MNCs in developing and implementing equality and diversity management strategies

Chapter Outline

This chapter provides an overview of the emergence of the concepts of corporate social responsibility, equal opportunities, and diversity management and describes how they gain popularity as part of SHRM for firms seeking to gain a competitive advantage. It critically analyses how different societal contexts may influence the way these notions are understood and discusses related issues managed at workplaces.

1 Introduction

> Corporate social responsibility is a concept whereby companies integrate social and environmental concerns in their business operations and in their interaction with their stakeholders on a voluntary basis. (European Commission, 2008)

Issues related to labour standards, employment ethics, equal opportunities (EO) and diversity management (DM) have been topics for studies in the field of employment and HRM. Whilst international labour standards have attracted much attention as part of corporate social responsibility (CSR), few studies, if any, have looked at these issues together from the CSR perspective and in the international HRM context. Firms face increasing pressure, on the one hand, to act in a socially responsive way towards their stakeholders, including their investors, shareholders, employees, trade unions, customers and the local community, and to pursue socially responsible behaviour from them on the other (e.g. Bhattacharya and Sen, 2004; Brammer et al., 2007).

This chapter provides an overview of the international context in which the notions of CSR, employment ethics, labour standards and diversity management have emerged and been debated by some as part of SHRM and a potential source of competitive advantage. Different societal contexts may influence the way these notions are understood and managed in workplaces. Informed by primary and secondary empirical data, the chapter presents examples from different countries to demonstrate the complexity of these issues and challenges that MNCs can encounter. The chapter also examines the extent to which firms have moved on from the EO approach (compliance approach) to a value added approach (business case) to CSR and DM.

We begin the chapter with a section that discusses corporate ethical and social responsibility generally and employment ethics more specifically. This is followed by sections that discuss international labour standards, equal opportunities and diversity management respectively as pertinent issues of CSR. Finally, the chapter provides an integrated framework within which the relations of CSR, labour standards, EO and DM can be understood and their implications for HRM and organisational outcomes assessed. In particular, the chapter highlights the two related aspects of HRM in CSR. One is how HR initiatives, such as employee involvement (EI), may facilitate firms to fulfil their CSR tasks. The other is how firms may adopt ethical HR practices as part of their CSR. It argues that the integration of HR policy with CSR policy will contribute to the sustainability of businesses and the social and economic development of society, particularly in the less developed countries.

2 Corporate ethical and social responsibility

Issues related to business ethics and CSR have been the subject of growing debate across an increasingly wide range of disciplines in the social sciences and business and management studies (see Egri and Ralston, 2008 for a comprehensive review). Business ethics and CSR are distinctive concepts, but they share in common a concern for the ethical dimension (Cacioppe et al., 2008). CSR has an expanding focus in both academic studies and business practices in different parts of the world, with some countries advancing at a more rapid pace than others.

Theoretical perspectives of CSR

The study of CSR dates back to the 1950s and initially it focused primarily on philanthropy (see Carroll, 1979; Garriga and Melé, 2004 for more detailed reviews). Despite more than four decades of debate, there is still no consensus on what the concept of CSR really means (e.g. Bhattacharya and Sen, 2004; Carroll, 1979, 1999;

PHILANTHROPIC
Responsibilities

Be a good corporate citizen.
Contribute resources
to the community;
improve quality of life.

ETHICAL
Responsibilities

Be ethical.
Obligation to do what is right, just,
and fair. Avoid harm.

LEGAL
Responsibilities

Obey the law.
Law is society's codification of right and wrong.
Play by the rules of the game.

ECONOMIC
Responsibilities

Be profitable.
The foundation upon which all others rest.

Figure 18.1   The pyramid of CSR

Source: Reprinted with permission from The pyramid of corporate social responsibility: Toward the moral management of organizational stakeholders by Archie B. Carroll; Business Horizons. Copyright © Elsevier.

Crowther and Capaldi, 2008). Corporate responsibility, corporate citizenship, responsible business and corporate social opportunity are some of its variant terms. Carroll (1991: 42) argued that CSR is a multidimensional construct embracing four sets of responsibilities: economic, legal, ethical and philanthropic. Through representing the four components of total CSR in a pyramid (see Figure 18.1), Carroll (1991) proposed that each of these responsibilities should be fulfilled together and in parallel rather than within a sequence.

The growing interest in corporate ethical and social responsibility in recent years has led to the proliferation of theoretical perspectives. Two commonly debated ethical theories (see Ackers, 2006) are Utilitarianism and Kantianism. Proponents of Utilitarianism hold the view that whichever action gives the greatest happiness or

Table 18.1 Means and ends in ethical theories

Consequentialist	Non-consequentialist
Utilitarianism	Kantianism
Happiness of the greatest number	Human dignity an end in itself
The end justifies the means	Universal moral rules
Language of economic utility	Language of human rights

Source: adapted from Ackers, 2006: 429. With kind permission of Peter Ackers.

utility is to be preferred. In other words, ultimately the end justifies the means. By contrast, proponents of Kantianism believe that the imperative to respect everybody is the means as well as the end and that what is right for one person is right for everybody (see Table 18.1).

Garriga and Melé (2004: 52–53) divide CSR theories into four groups:

1 *Instrumental theories*: This group of theories understands CSR as a mere means to the end, which is profits. It is assumed that the corporation is an instrument for wealth creation and that this is its sole social responsibility. Only the economic aspect of the interactions between business and society is considered. So any social value or activity is accepted if, and only if, it is consistent with wealth creation.
2 *Political theories*: The social power of the corporation is emphasised in this group of theories, specifically in its relationship with society and its responsibility in the political arena. This leads the corporation to accept social duties and rights or participate in activities requiring social cooperation.
3 *Integrative theories*: This group of theories argues that business depends on society for its continuity and growth and even for the existence of business itself. Therefore, business ought to be integrated with social demands.
4 *Ethical theories*: A fourth group of theories understands that the relationship between business and society is embedded with ethical values. This leads to a vision of CSR from an ethical perspective and as a consequence, firms ought to accept social responsibilities as an ethical obligation above any other consideration.

Whilst acknowledging the comprehensiveness of Garriga and Melé's (2004) review, Secchi (2007) pointed out a number of weaknesses in their way of grouping. Secchi (2007: 347) proposed an alternative way of categorising the CSR literature into three major groups based on their theoretical perspectives, and with each consisting of some sub-groups (see Figure 18.2):

1 The Utilitarian group, in which the corporation is intended as a maximising 'black box' where problems of externalities and social costs emerge;
2 The managerial category, where problems of responsibility are approached from inside the firm (internal perspective);

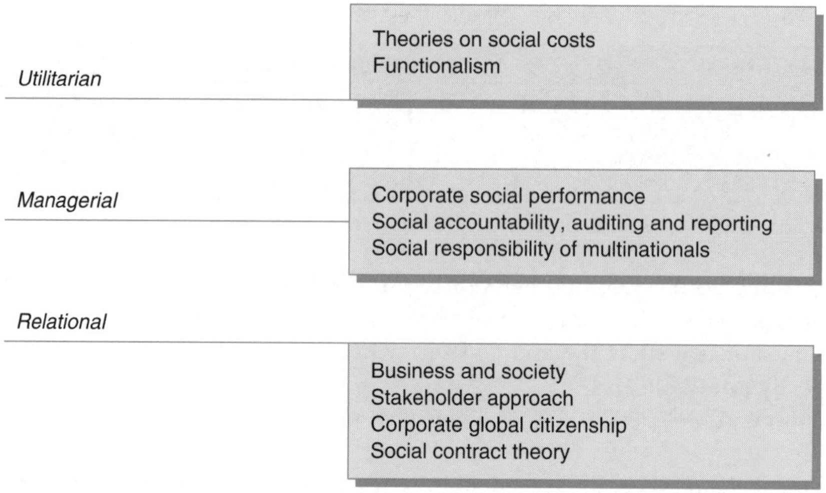

| Utilitarian | Theories on social costs |
| | Functionalism |

Managerial	Corporate social performance
	Social accountability, auditing and reporting
	Social responsibility of multinationals

Relational	
	Business and society
	Stakeholder approach
	Corporate global citizenship
	Social contract theory

Figure 18.2   Utilitarian, managerial and relational theories of CSR

Source: Secchi, 2007: 350 With kind permission. (Granted by David Secchi- Wiley Journal Rights aware).

3 Relational theories, in which the type of relations between the firm and the environment are at the centre of the analysis.

Two schools of thought have been influential in the debate on corporate ethical and social responsibility: the efficiency theory and the social responsibility theory. The efficiency perspective, as represented by Milton Friedman, has a utilitarian and narrow focus on the shareholder value. According to Friedman (1962: 133):

There is one and only one social responsibility of business – to use its resources and engage in activities designed to increase its profits so long as it stays within the rules of the game, which is to say, engages in open and free competition, without deception or fraud.

By contrast, the social responsibility theory, or the integrated-strategy perspective (Baron, 2001), adopts a much broader focus that emphasises stakeholder value (e.g. Freeman, 1984). It argues that corporations should take into account the interests of different stakeholders, such as employees, customers, suppliers and communities when making business decisions:

Socially responsible companies not only try to be economically sustainable and profitable, but also endeavour to work with their employees, families, local communities and nation states to improve the quality of life in ways that are both ethical and sustainable in relation to society and the environment. (Cacioppe et al., 2008: 684)

Table 18.2 Issues covered by CSR

• Environmental	• Concern for human rights
• Fair trade	• Philanthropic history
• Organic produce	• Cooperative principles
• Not tested on animals	• Support for education
• Community involvement	• Participates in local business initiatives
• Cause related marketing	• Supports national business initiatives
• Charitable giving	• Commitment to reporting
• Religious foundation	• Employee schemes
• Support for social cause	• Refusal to trade in certain markets

Source: Howard and Willmott (2001), cited in Sachdev (2006: 264). With kind permission.

The stakeholder concept is highly relevant to HRM, since looking after employees' welfare is an important part of a company's social responsibility. As employers, firms have the responsibility to ensure the quality of their employees' working life, which includes job quality, work-life quality and personal well-being associated with work. This calls for an approach that promotes EI and participation in organisational decision making. It also requires firms to take employees' interests into consideration when formulating HR policy.

CSR in practice

Companies may adopt different approaches to CSR in practice. Table 18.2 summarises some of the issues on which companies may choose to focus their CSR activities, depending on the nature of the business, the environment in which the business operates, management cognition and business priorities.

Firms may be influenced to adopt CSR practices by several driving forces, some of which are related. One is the rising awareness of ethical consumerism, particularly related to environmental issues, health concerns, and human and animal rights. Another driving force comes from international and domestic pressure groups. As business competition intensifies globally and MNCs are under increasing pressure to reduce their costs, they are simultaneously under growing demand to review their labour standards, sourcing strategy, environment policy and their wider role in the economic and social development of developing countries. Many MNCs now have an espoused CSR policy and publish it on their corporate websites. As part of CSR initiatives, employees are encouraged to participate in community projects and charity activities, and they may be supported by their employer through sponsorship and time off for engaging in these activities.

CSR and business benefits

Opinions on the perceived benefits of CSR activities differ widely. Some argue that there is a strong business case for CSR and that adopting a proactive CSR approach can help companies:

- avoid business risks such as corruption scandals or environmental accidents;
- have greater access to capital through distinctive ethical values that appeal to particular types of investors;
- attract and retain customers through enhanced brand image and corporate reputation;
- legitimise business and profit levels and avoid government intervention or public criticism;
- manage human resources more effectively through attraction and retention of talent and enhanced motivation and commitment of the workforce;
- gain acceptance of the local community and support from host country government, including favourable policy treatment.

Indeed, a number of empirical studies have provided evidence to support these claims, though sometimes they are conditional on other additional factors (e.g. Hillman and Keim, 2001; Sen and Bhattacharya, 2001; Zinkin, 2004). For example, Baron (2001: 7) argued, based on his economic modelling, that CSR not only has 'a direct effect on the costs of the firm', but also has 'a strategic effect by altering the competitive positions of firms in an industry'. Cacioppe et al.'s (2008: 681) study found that well-educated managers and professionals are likely to take into account 'the ethical and social responsibility reputations of companies when deciding whether to work for them, use their services or buy shares in their companies'. Roozen et al.'s (2001) study found that employees who work for firms that behave in an ethical way to their stakeholders are more likely to accept and be committed to ethical behaviour and suppress their self-interest for the greater good of the organisation and the community. Zinkin's (2004) study of BP's activities in China and Malaysia illustrates how an MNC can rebuild its image and maximise the 'licence to operate' in host countries through the engagement of the 'right' type of CSR activities.

Other studies have shown that socially responsible corporations may have a competitive advantage because they are more attractive to potential employees and therefore benefit from a larger talent pool of job candidates (e.g. Albinger and Freeman, 2000; Turban and Greening, 1997). They are also more likely to have a more committed workforce because employees will be proud to work for companies with favourable reputations through acting in socially and environmentally responsible ways (e.g. Brammer et al., 2007). Similarly, CSR activities are found to be positively associated with job satisfaction (Brammer et al., 2007; Valentine and Fleischman, 2008). Furthermore, CSR programmes introduced by firms may lead to 'the development of leadership skills and a high level of motivation among employees who are inspired to become involved in CSR programmes' (Cacioppe et al., 2008: 689). Involving employees in CSR initiatives enables firms to identify talent and develop new skills from their employees which may not be demonstrated in their routine work (Cacioppe et al., 2008).

It should be noted, however, that existing studies on the payoffs of improved social responsibility remain non-conclusive. For example, Sen and Bhattacharya's (2001) study found that consumers can react to companies' CSR initiatives in different ways and that CSR does not always positively influence consumers' purchasing behaviour. Similarly, Hillman and Keim's (2001) study showed that strategic stakeholder management contributes to the financial performance of the firm, whereas participation in wider social issues (i.e. an altruistic approach to CSR) does not. In addition, good corporate social performance (CSP) only has positive impact on job seekers with high levels of job choice and awareness of CSR issues, but no impact on those who have limited job choice and are unaware of or less concerned about CSR issues (Albinger and Freeman, 2000).

A number of problems have been raised by critics of CSR. Some see CSR as a distraction from the fundamental purpose of the business, as noted above (e.g. Friedman, 1962). Others question firms' motives for engaging in CSR, interpreting it as a public relations exercise and attempt to pre-empt interventions from governments and pressure groups (e.g. Rodriguez et al., 2006). Those who are concerned with companies' genuine willingness to take on CSR argue that better regulation and enforcement at national and international levels, instead of voluntary measures, are necessary to ensure that MNCs behave in an ethical and socially responsible manner (e.g. Chan and Ross, 2003).

Box 18.1 shows how the CSR activities adopted by an MNC may be a pragmatic outcome emerging from strategic business intent when faced with political pressure from the host country and the capacity of the MNC to overcome or diffuse the situation. As such, a company's CSR portfolio may not contain a coherent set of policy statements and activities.

Box 18.1   CSR of retail global giant Wal-Mart (China)

Wal-Mart opened its first store in China in 1996. After a low-key entry for the first few years, War-Mart decided in 2000 to launch a major expansion in a bid to catch up with Carrefour of France. In 2001, the State Council of China approved Wal-Mart's expansion plan of developing 60 supermarkets in 20 major cities in China, with a sales revenue target of 18 billion yuan. By March 2005, Wal-Mart had 44 stores with over 23,000 employees in China.

In November 2004, Wal-Mart China announced a US$1 million commitment to establish the China Retail Research Centre at the School of Economics and Management of Tsinghua University. This is the first academic institution in China dedicated to the research of China's fast growing retail industry. China's rapidly growing economy continues to create unprecedented opportunities for retail corporations like Wal-Mart.

(Continued)

(Continued)

The US$1 million donation for establishing the China Retail Research Centre is an example of Wal-Mart's long-term commitment to China. It is believed that Wal-Mart's support for the Centre will facilitate China's participation and cooperation in the international retail field and drive the healthy development of the country's retail sector. It is hoped that the China Retail Research Centre would develop into a world-class research institution and boost the theoretical research and management of China's retail industry.

Interestingly, Wal-Mart's enthusiasm in advancing the retail knowledge in China was not extended to the support of trade unionism. For years, Wal-Mart has been resistant to China's request to establish a trade union for its workforce, claiming that it was its global corporate HR policy to have a non-unionised workforce. Wal-Mart was publicly criticised by the All-China Federation of Trade Unions (ACFTU) in the early 2000s for its refusal to recognise the trade union. It was not until 2006 that Wal-Mart had softened its stance towards union recognition, which resulted in the establishment of its first store-level union in July 2006. Within months, more store-level unions organisations were set up amongst Wal-Mart's 50-plus stores.

However, union recognition has not brought true bargaining power or voice to the workforce. On 14 July 2008, the ACFTU concluded the first collective union contract with Wal-Mart in Shenyang City, Liaoning Province in northern China. Wal-Mart has subsequently applied this one single collective contract template to all its stores nationwide, without allowing individual store's unions to bargain. Many individual store unions were not even given the chance to sign the contract template themselves, as some store unions had been asked to sign a collective contract on behalf of other outlets in the surrounding areas. Given the significant economic disparity and labour market conditions across different regions in China, it is clear that a single nationwide collective contract is too broad to reflect local needs. But Wal-Mart held the view that there was no need to amend what had already been approved by the ACFTU. Requests from local union representatives for collective bargaining at store level were ignored by store managers. Wal-Mart's refusal to enter into genuine collective bargaining has attracted public criticism.

Sources: compiled from *China Business*, 7 August 2006; China Labor News Translations, September 2008; Cooke, 2008.

Tensions in ethical HRM and business

As noted earlier, the business case for CSR may not have a sufficient appeal for firms to adopt ethical and socially responsible employment policy. Therefore, moral and legal sanctions remain the main drivers for ethical HRM. The ethical dimension of HRM is a complex issue which has attracted considerable academic debate and is a source of tension in business decisions.

Employment ethics is a subdivision of business ethics, which according to Ackers (2006: 427) 'involves the application of general moral disciplines to the management of employees' wages and conditions'. The focus is on human relationships at inter-personal and organisational levels. At the individual level, the issue of concern is how individual employees should behave responsibly towards others including their co-workers, employer and customers. An increasing number of companies have introduced code of conducts to ensure their employees behave in a professional and ethical way, although some critics (e.g. Winstanley and Woodall, 2000) argue that this may be a disguised attempt by the company to shift at least some of its corporate responsibility on to individuals through disciplinary actions. Some companies introduce HR initiatives, such as appraisal and pay schemes, 'to encourage responsible behaviour by their staff' (Sachdev, 2006: 266). Since the behaviour of individual employees affects the image, as well as the productivity, of the firm, it is therefore in the firm's interest to ensure that all of its employees act responsibly.

At the organisational level, the issue of concern relates to the ethical dimension of the company's employment or HRM policies and practices. There are a number of potential tensions and dilemmas in socially responsible HR policies and practices and their wider business concerns (see Pinnington et al., 2007; Winstanley and Woodall, 2000 for more detailed discussions). For example:

- Should companies hire cheap labour, including children, women and agency workers who may be the least protected in the labour market, in order to reduce employment costs?
- Should companies hire the best and most able candidates to maximise productivity at the risk of excluding socially disadvantaged groups?
- Should companies invest in training and development of their employees to enhance their productivity and employability at the risk of losing them to their competitors?
- Should companies economise on their health and safety provisions in the workplace to gain a cost advantage?
- Should companies increase their organisational flexibility to gain competitive advantage by requesting their employees to work flexibly including working unsocial hours and overtime at short notice at the expense of their work-life balance?
- Should companies operating in the public sector or deprived areas adopt a performance-related pay scheme to incentivise performance that may be at odds with the public service ethos and altruistic value?
- Should companies encourage or at least tolerate freedom of association by recognising trade unions and collective bargaining, which may present challenges to management control and counter efforts to elicit employees' loyalty and identification with the firm?

These issues are particularly pertinent for western MNCs that operate in developing countries where the unemployment rate may be high and labour standards may be generally low and often are violated with little legal consequence. The difficulty in formulating and implementing corporate HR strategy for MNCs has been widely noted as a result of variations in ethical codes, moral standards, social values, laws and other institutional settings across different countries (see Chapters 1, 2 and 16 in this volume for example). Issues related to labour standards, equal opportunities and workforce diversity are even more challenging as they are often central to the debate on corporate ethical and social responsibility. In the following sections, we will discuss these issues in more detail.

3 International labour standards and decent work

The role of MNCs in disseminating good practice has been noted, albeit a process often constrained by institutional and cultural challenges (e.g. Bartlett and Ghoshal, 1989; Briscoe and Schuler, 2004; Harzing and Ruysseveldt, 2004; Rubery and Grimshaw, 2003; Schuler et al., 2003). However, it has been argued that intensifying competition at global level has exerted pressure on MNCs 'to enhance their competitiveness through on-going rounds of cost-cutting' that are centred on labour cost (Wood, 2006: 265). This is often achieved by worsening employment terms and conditions that are typically manifested in low standards of health and safety, extremely poor pay and long working hours, suppression of labour organisation, and largely the absence of workplace training, employment benefits and job security (e.g. Chan and Ross, 2003; Rodgers, 2002; Standing, 1997; Wood, 2006). Evidence from around the world has shown that the neo-classical model that relies on market forces to determine labour market outcomes is not in the interest of many, especially those from deprived regions. Global capitalism with its associated proliferation and expansion of MNCs in developing countries has so far aggravated income and spatial inequalities and reinforced dependency of the poor on the rich and of the less developed on the developed countries (Stiglitz, 2002).

The development of international labour standards is a response to the growing number of needs and challenges faced by workers and employers in the global economy. International labour standards are the norms or rules that regulate or govern working conditions and labour relations. Box 18.2 provides an indication of the scope of labour protection set by the International Labour Organisation (ILO). The ILO is one of the main actors involved in establishing international labour standards (see Rubery and Grimshaw, 2003). Founded in 1919 with an initial 42 member states, the ILO had 182 member states by May 2008. The labour standards are not imposed upon the member states as the ILO has little power to implement them. Rather, the ILO works with member states 'to promote labour standards through technical assistance and development policy' (Rubery and Grimshaw, 2003: 247).

The primary goal of the ILO is to promote opportunities for women and men to obtain decent and productive work in conditions of freedom, equity, security and human dignity. 'Decent Work' was defined in the 1999 report by the Director General of the ILO as productive work in which rights are protected, which generates an adequate income, with adequate social protection. It also means sufficient work, in the sense that all should have full access to income-earning opportunities. It marks the high road to economic and social development, a road in which employment, income and social protection can be achieved without compromising workers' rights and social standards. 'Decent Work' is the converging focus of all its four strategic objectives: the promotion of rights at work, employment, social protection, and social dialogue (ILO, 1999).

Box 18.2   International labour standards

ILO international labour standards embrace numerous aspects of labour markets, ranging from minimum wages and equal pay to health and safety regulations. These standards can be classified into six main categories:

- respect for fundamental human rights;
- protection of wages;
- employment security;
- working conditions;
- labour market and social policies;
- industrial relations.

Source: OECD, 1994: 138.

Proponents for the enforcement of labour standards in developing countries argue that such standards are necessary to provide a minimum protection to workers in these countries who otherwise are likely to be exploited by their employers due to the large size of the informal sector and the intense competition for wage employment in the formal sector (e.g. Rodgers, 2002; Standing, 1997). At the most basic level, paying a living wage by local standards is important as it is not only a human rights issue for the individuals and their families concerned; but also a mechanism to prevent developing countries from competing against each other in a race to the bottom with widening inequality and declining labour standards (Chan and Ross, 2003).

There are three key arguments for labour standards: the human rights, social justice and economic case arguments. The human rights argument sees some labour standards, such as no forced labour, as a matter of human rights universal to all societies. The social justice argument of labour standards is dependent upon the wealth and living standards of specific countries, once the human rights notion is in place. The economic case argument suggests that the provision of labour standards may create pressure on employers to enhance their labour productivity through skill upgrading and better health and safety protection (see Rubery and Grimshaw, 2003 for a more detailed discussion).

However, what constitutes a fair level of labour standards changes with time and in part is contingent upon the state of economic development of specific societies. In poor societies, relatively high labour standards may actually be detrimental to their economic development and expansion of employment opportunities and encourage the growth of an informal sector that is largely, if not entirely, unregulated (Rubery and Grimshaw, 2003). Over-regulation also reduces the competitiveness of firms and industries where the flexible deployment of labour constitutes an important part of their competitive strategy. The promotion of labour standards therefore needs to take into consideration the promotion of the twin objectives of efficiency and equity (e.g. Buchanan and Callus, 1993; Fudge and Vosko, 2001).

4 Equal opportunities

The term 'equal opportunities' is associated with employment equity legislation related to discrimination as a result of individuals' characteristics, such as gender, age, ethnicity, religion, physical ability and sexual orientation. Many governments have promulgated equal opportunity-related legislation in the last 30 years, although what the term 'equal opportunities' means and who are included in the category for protection may differ across countries. The focus and pressure for establishing EO legislation is not the same across specific nations and its introduction is often a response to the changing political, socio-economic, labour market and employment relations environment. The introduction of EO legislation has often been accompanied by the introduction of affirmative action (AA) programmes directed by the state. Some organisations have an EO policy in place partly to comply with statutory requirements and partly to portray an image that they are an EO employer. In particular, gender equality constitutes a significant part of the public debates, EO legislation and AA programmes. Unfortunately, despite the increasing provisions of anti-discrimination legislation and espoused commitment from organisations to equality, gender inequality in various stages of the employment process remains a significant feature in most countries, and is more pronounced in some than in others (e.g. Davidson and Burke, 2004; Yukongdi and Benson, 2006).

Labour law and government policy intervention
The elimination of gender inequality necessitates state intervention through legislation and affirmative action policies to provide at least the basic level of protection in

principle. However, slippage in policy implementation appears to be common across countries, albeit to varying degrees. Some national legal systems are impeded by the complexity and multiplicity of employment-related laws, directive regulations and administrative policies issued at different administrative levels. Others lack clear enforcement channels and support through which workers can seek to secure compliance with the law. In some cases, government determination to advance social equality may be compromised by its economic agenda (also see Chapter 7 in this volume for a broader discussion on governments, legislation and employment relations).

Table 18.3 provides an overview of gender equality laws and other administrative mechanisms adopted by the governments of four Asian countries – China, India, Japan and the Republic of Korea (Korea hereafter for brevity) – and their limited effects. For example, it was reported that despite the promulgation of the Equal Employment Opportunity Law (EEOL) in 1986, Japan had a much lower proportion of women managers in government organisations than it had in its corporations in the early 1990s (Steinhoff and Tanaka, 1993). The introduction of EEOL was controversial amongst the legislator, employers and the state from the outset and 'produced few gains in employment opportunities for women' (Gelb, 2000: 385). There is a widespread consensus amongst scholars in Japan that the government passed EEOL more as a response to international pressure than as an acknowledgement of changing social values in Japan (Gelb, 2000). EEOL has been criticised for its 'over-reliance on voluntary compliance' with 'little government enforcement power', although it is recognised that 'it has led to renewed efforts at litigation, increased consciousness and activism among women, and amendments to the law, passed in 1997' (Gelb, 2000: 385).

Similarly, although the Constitution of India 'allows affirmative action through reservations in education and employment' (Venkata Ratnam and Chandra, 1996: 85), the enforcement of the constitutional rights of Indian women is uneven due to 'the lack of a uniform civil code in India' (Ghosh and Roy, 1997: 904). Nevertheless, the Indian courts have been considered to be playing an important role in defending women's rights 'in a context where government, employers and unions largely remained either indifferent and unconcerned, or reluctant and ineffective in addressing the issues of gender equality' (Venkata Ratnam and Jain, 2002: 281). This is in spite of the criticism that the Indian courts suffer from a number of weaknesses including alleged corruption.

In Korea, the Gender-Equal Employment Act of 1987 'stipulates that employers can be imprisoned for up to two years if they pay different wages for work of equal value in the same business; but few, if any, employers have actually gone to jail' (van der Meulen Rodgers, 1998: 746). By condoning employers' discriminative practices, the state is actually 'perpetuating gender norms and stereotypes that disadvantage women' (Seguino, 2000: 34).

In China, state intervention as part of its socialist campaign of gender equality during its state planned economy period (1949–1978) had led to significant advances in pay and social equity for female workers. As a result, China has achieved possibly greater gender equality than industrial capitalist societies (Stockman et al., 1995). This is in spite of persisting inequalities in recruitment and promotion, particularly in government organisations (Cooke, 2006). However, the achievement of gender equality has been eroded by ensuing efforts towards marketisation and integration with the global economy, partly as a result of the loosening control of the state on business affairs.

Legislation that is intended to provide an enhanced level of equality may actually prove to be counterproductive, especially when effective enforcement remains problematic. For example, India's labour regulations are considered to be 'among the most restrictive and complex in the world' and 'have constrained the growth of the formal manufacturing sector where these laws have their widest application' (World Bank, 2006: 3). This discourages employers from creating employment with a better job quality in the formal sector and forces millions to continue to be trapped in poor quality jobs in the informal sector. Banning women from night shifts in India has also led to a reduced scope of employment for women, 'even though there is great potential for employment in information technology-related areas involving tele-work in call centres, where round-the-clock work is the norm' (Venkata Ratnam and Jain, 2002: 279). Mandatory maternity leave and the requirement of breastfeeding breaks and crèches in workplaces where the majority of workers are women are often perceived by employers as liabilities and discourage them from employing women (Venkata Ratnam and Jain, 2002).

Employer strategy and discrimination

As we can see from the above discussion, employers play an important role in influencing the level of gender (in)equality. Where firms are facing shortages of labour and talent, they may introduce a proactive HR policy to attract and retain women workers. Where the labour market is slack and business competition pressure heightened, employers often adopt a labour cost reduction strategy to keep operating costs down and women tend to be more vulnerable than men. For example, in Korea, women are 'encouraged by companies and union members to resign "voluntarily" and accept a re-employment contract as an irregular worker with lower pay and less job security when their companies are downsizing' (Chun, 2006). In Japan, new opportunities created for women by the EO laws in the late 1980s and early 1990s were then eroded when Japan's economic growth 'bubble' burst after 1992 (Gelb, 2000). It was 'the marginal nature of Japanese women's employment' used as a deliberate strategy by employers that reinforced the core employment system privileging men 'during a period of heightened international competition, reduced growth rate, a rapidly aging workforce and the inflexible hiring and firing system' (Kucera, 1998: 28). Similarly, women workers in China had been selected disproportionately and laid off or forced into early retirement during the radical downsizing that took place in the state sector during the mid-1990s and early 2000s.

Employers in Japan and Korea are reported to exert pressure, albeit now more implicitly following the introduction of EO laws in the late 1980s, persuading women

Table 18.3   Labour and EO laws in China, India, Japan and Korea

Country	Labour and equal opportunities laws	Purpose	Impact
China	Constitution (1954, latest version 2004) Labour Insurance Regulations of the People's Republic of China (1953) Announcement on Female Workers' Production Leave by the State Council (1955) Female Employees Labour Protection Regulations (1988) Regulations of Prohibited Types of Occupational Posts for Female Employees (1990) The PRC Law on Protecting Women's Rights and Interests (1992) Labour Law (1995) Employment Promotion Law (2008)	To ensure equal rights in employment between men and women To protect married women from being discriminated due to their maternity status	Ineffective enforcement, little, if any, punishment to non-compliant employers
India	Constitution (1950) The Employees State Insurance Act (1948) The Factories Act (1948) The Maternity Benefits Act (1961) Equal Remuneration Act (1976) The Sexual Harassment of Women Act (1992)	To guarantee women's equal rights	Ineffective enforcement due to lack of uniform civil code Complex and restrictive laws deter employers from creating jobs in the formal sector
Japan	Constitution (1946) Equal Employment Opportunity Law (1986, amended in 1997 to take effect in 1999)	To ensure equal rights in employment between men and women	Controversial introduction Over-reliance on voluntary compliance with little government enforcement power Limited impact on increasing women's employment but has led to increased awareness of gender inequality among women
Korea	Equal Employment Opportunity Act (1988, amended in 1989) Guidelines to Eliminate Sexual Discrimination in Employment (1991) Labour Standards Law (1998)	To guarantee equality between men and women in employment To protect women's job security on their marital status, pregnancy and childbirth To allow employers to lay off workers	Ineffective enforcement Informalisation of employment with declined employment terms and conditions

to resign when they get married and become pregnant. Age limits are also used in recruitment and selection to screen out women (Gelb, 2000). Although the 'marriage bar' is far less common in China, employers in private and foreign-funded factories are known to impose an age limit on female workers. In some ways, if the marriage bar for Japanese and Korean women aims primarily to protect men's jobs and earnings, then age discrimination in China is intended to increase labour productivity (Cooke, 2007).

The effective implementation of employment equity legislation may yield positive psychological and employment outcomes to those who were previously disadvantaged. For example, in South Africa, the Constitution of South Africa (1996) and the Employment Equity Act (1998) were introduced, through affirmative actions at workplace level, to promote the constitutional right of equality, eliminate unfair discrimination in employment and achieve a diverse workforce broadly representative of its people. These regulations are said to have led to positive outcomes for some employees. However, this positive effect may simultaneously be accompanied by a higher level of turnover or intention to quit of incumbents as a result of their improved labour market position (e.g. Wöcke and Sutherland, 2008). Therefore, where employers' efforts to build workforce relationships are undermined by labour market conditions, as is the case where employment laws are not effectively enforced, employers may have less incentive to observe regulations and adopt EO policies that develop the psychological contract with employees.

5 Diversity management

Diversity management as a SHRM initiative

Since the 1990s, a complementary, or what some would call a competing, concept to EO has emerged in the HRM literature – diversity management (DM). The concept of managing diversity has its origin in the US and emerged as an HR intervention in the mid-1980s. It is primarily a response to the demographic changes (e.g. more immigrants and women) in the workplace as well as the customer base (Agocs and Burr, 1996). It is also a response to the corporate discontent with the affirmative action approach imposed by the US government. Organisations are searching for an alternative to broaden the perceived narrow scope of affirmative action legislation that focuses primarily on recruitment. DM is seen as a way to address retention, integration and career development issues (Agocs and Burr, 1996). The growing demands from the ethnic minority, women, older, disabled, gay and lesbian groups for equal rights and the consequent human rights legislation in the 1990s and 2000s give further drive to the need for recognising, accepting and valuing individual differences at workplaces and in society more generally (Mor Barak, 2005).

The concept of diversity management began to be propagated in countries outside of North America during the late 1990s. For example, Süß and Kleiner (2007) observed a sharp increase in the use of the concept of diversity management in Germany since the late 1990s. In the UK, the concept of managing diversity has undoubtedly become more influential since the mid/late 1990s in part due to the demographic change of the workforce, but more so because DM is seen as a more comprehensive and sophisticated approach to EO management that adds value to business. The Chartered Institute of Personnel and Development (CIPD), defines diversity as 'valuing everyone as an individual – valuing people as employees, customers and clients' (CIPD, 2006: 2).

It is suggested that the objectives of DM is for organisations to increase awareness of cultural differences, develop the ability to recognise, accept and value diversity, minimise patterns of inequality experienced by those not in the mainstream, and modify organisational culture and leadership practices (Cox, 1993; Soni, 2000). DM is regarded as a better approach than EO because it adopts an inclusive approach that 'focuses on valuing people as unique individuals rather than on group-related issues covered by legislation' (CIPD, 2007: 6). More recent DM literature advocates an inclusive approach to managing diversity that goes beyond organisational and national boundaries (e.g. Mor Barak, 2005). An inclusive workplace model (Mor Barak, 2005: 8) includes the following features:

- values and utilises individual and intergroup differences within its workforce;
- cooperates with, and contributes to, its surrounding community;
- alleviates the needs of disadvantaged groups in its wider environment;
- collaborates with individuals, groups, and organisations across national and cultural boundaries.

The transition from a focus on EO to managing diversity is necessarily a move away from an emphasis on procedural justice to a Utilitarian approach that views DM as a means to an end to be managed strategically. In other words, it is a shift away from a negative perspective on disadvantaged and discriminated staff to a positive perspective of celebrating and valuing the differences among all employees and utilising them in a creative way to benefit both the organisation and individuals (Maxwell et al., 2001). Foster and Harris (2005) identified a number of key differences between managing EO and managing diversity (see Table 18.4).

However, the distinction between EO and diversity management may in practice be far less clear than the table implies (Foster and Harris, 2005). Organisations may find it awkward to promote EO policies that tend to emphasise sameness and underplay differences on the one hand, and promote diversity that aims to address individual differences on the other. Conceptual ambiguity and confused organisational practices may create indifference to EO and DM initiatives, resulting in managers and employees believing that the latter simply is the former given a different name (Foster and Harris, 2005).

According to the CIPD's (2007) survey of 285 DM managers/officers in a wide range of organisations based in the UK, only 17 per cent of survey respondents believed

Table 18.4   Key differences between managing EO and managing diversity

Equal opportunities	Managing diversity
Addresses inequality through rights	Promotes diversity for organisational benefits
Neutralises individual differences	Recognises individual differences
Treats people the same	Treats people differently
A narrow view of difference	An inclusive view of difference
A focus on HR processes	Concerns all functions of the organisation
Promote assimilation	Promote variety
An emphasis on procedures and regulation	An emphasis on organisational objectives

Source: Reprinted with permission from the publisher. 'From equal opportunities to diversity management', Foster, C. and Harris, L., in *The Strategic Management of Human Resources*, J. Leopord, L. Harris and T. Watson (2005) Pearson Education Limited.

that the business case was the most important driver stimulating their organisation to adopt DM initiatives. There was a general feeling of lack of senior management support amongst respondents and very few of the organisations participating in the survey undertook activities to mainstream diversity. Not surprisingly, there is 'little evidence of organizations mainstreaming diversity into operational practices such as marketing, product development and customer services – which is where significant gains could be made in improving business performance' (CIPD, 2007: 8). In fact, despite the active promotion by western HR consulting firms and HR associations of the moral and strategic importance of DM, legal compliance remains the top reason for organisations implementing DM initiatives (CIPD, 2007).

A large-scale survey of global Fortune 500 companies and other global organisations revealed similar attitudes – whilst all firms surveyed agreed on the importance of global diversity, 'only 50 per cent of firms surveyed reported considering global stakeholders when determining their diversity strategies, only 39 per cent provide extensive multicultural training for all employees, and only 27 per cent routinely evaluate progress towards diversity goals' (Dunavant and Heiss, 2005, cited in Nishii and Özbigin, 2007: 1883).

Diversity management and organisational performance

In ways analogous to the argument for CSR, advocates of DM believe that there are three important reasons for managing diversity (e.g. Agocs and Burr, 1996; CIPD, 2006; Cox and Blake, 1991):

- *Effective people management* – DM creates an open, inclusive workplace culture where everyone feels valued, which then helps to recruit, retain and motivate good people. Diversity can make teams more innovative and flexible which may increase their productivity and ultimately organisational performance. DM helps promote awareness of individual difference and empathy for those who are different, and encourages attitude change.

- *Market competition* – A diverse workforce can help the organisation to understand diverse customer needs, open up new market opportunities, improve market share and broaden its customer base.
- *Corporate reputation* – adopting an effective DM policy enables organisations to demonstrate their commitment to CSR through engagement with local communities.

Existing studies have provided evidence to support the assumption that strategic diversity management can lead to enhanced HR outcomes. For example, Ng and Burke's (2005) survey study of 113 MBA job seekers showed that women and ethnic minorities considered DM to be important when accepting job offers. In addition, 'high achievers and new immigrants rated organizations with diversity management as more attractive as potential employers' (Ng and Burke, 2005: 1195).

According to the CIPD (2007: 12), there is a wide range of measures that organisations may use to monitor the impact of DM. These include:

- employee attitude surveys
- number of complaints and grievances
- labour turnover
- employee performance appraisals
- absenteeism
- ability to recruit
- number of tribunal cases
- impact assessment
- level of customer satisfaction
- employee commitment surveys
- business performance
- balanced scorecard
- diversification of customer base
- improvements to problem-solving and decision-making
- psychological contract issues

It must be noted that it cannot be assumed that a positive relationship invariably holds between diversity and productivity improvement. Academic studies on diversity–performance relationships have so far yielded non-conclusive results. While some researchers argue that diversity leads to better group and ultimately organisational performance (e.g. Cox et al., 1991), others contend that diversity leads to a negative organisational performance outcome in part due to intra- and inter-group conflicts and communication deadlock derived from differences (e.g. Lau and Murnighan, 1998; Tsui et al., 1992). Moreover, there may be tensions between a collective approach to managing diverse employee groups and a more individualised approach focusing on individual needs and abilities which may actually increase, rather than decrease, inequalities (e.g. Agocs and Burr, 1996; Liff, 1996).

Other studies have revealed that the benefits of DM rhetoric can be overstated (e.g. Williams and O'Reilly, 1998; Wise and Tsehirhart, 2000), that DM initiatives may actually undermine efforts in EO programmes (e.g. Subeliani and Tsogas, 2005), and that DM may be adopted as a new disguise to mask exploitation (Taylor et al., 1997). Affirmative actions associated with DM are also found to be resented by the workforce as those recruited or promoted under AA are perceived to be less competent or qualified and thus violate the principle of merit (Ng and Burke, 2005). Studies by Kochan et al. (2003) revealed that participation in diversity education programmes does not foster a positive relationship between racial and gender diversity and performance. Richard et al. (2004) offered a reconciling 'third way' perspective which suggests that contextual factors (e.g. entrepreneurial orientation) play an important moderating role for diversity to enhance organisational performance.

Kochan et al. (2003: 17) further observed that practitioners paid little attention to analysing their organisational environment for managing diversity and that few companies 'are equipped to assess the impact of their diversity efforts on their performance'. Kochan et al. (2003) questioned whether or not the business case rhetoric of managing diversity has run its course. Nevertheless, they contended that while we may be sceptical about the positive impact of managing diversity on organisational performance, diversity is a labour market imperative as well as a societal value and expectation. Therefore, 'managers should do their best to translate diversity into positive organizational, group and individual outcomes' (Kochan et al., 2003: 18).

It is apparent that 'diversity management' is a poorly understood and controversial concept that is used 'in an all-embracing fashion to include not just the social categories of AA such as race and sex but a wide range of personal characteristics' (Ferner et al., 2005: 309). Consequently, the concept and moral soundness of DM remains a contentious issue (see Lorbiecki and Jack, 2000 for an overview of the conceptual premises and critique of DM). In addition, the utility of this US originated concept in other societal contexts has been questioned by many researchers (e.g. Agocs and Burr, 1996; Ferner et al., 2005; Healy and Oikelome, 2007; Nishii and Özbigin, 2007). In the next section, we examine the tensions and dynamics of societal patterns of diversity in different countries.

Diversity management in the global context

A number of country-specific studies have revealed unique societal contexts in which diversity issues are embedded. For example, Jones et al.'s (2000) study showed that the language used to describe diversity and the perception of diversity issues in New Zealand are markedly different from those manifested in the dominant discourse of DM embedded with US cultural assumptions. In African countries, politics assumes supreme importance in DM and ethnicity dominates 'most national debates on diversity' as the central issue (Healy and Oikelome, 2007: 1923). This is because some disadvantaged ethnic groups have been oppressed historically and there is now increasing calls for radical remedial actions to address racial grievances. By contrast, ethnic groups in Japan and Korea are relatively homogenous and as a result, gender, women's marital status, and their related employment status, may be the key source of workforce diversity (Cooke, 2007).

In the US and UK, workforce diversity may include: gender, race, ethnicity, religion, age, disability, immigration status, social class, political association, marital status, parental status, sexual orientation, ex-offenders, and so on. Many of these differences are accepted by western societies, protected by law and acknowledged in company policy. However, some of these characteristics may not be acceptable socially or legally in oriental countries like China and India (Cooke and Saini, 2007). Furthermore, significant differences may exist even within oriental countries. For example, caste, ethnicity, religion and gender are the main sources of diversity in India, whereas age, gender, disability and place of origin (e.g. rural vs. urban) are the main causes of social inequality in China. India is a newly democratised country, albeit a fragile one to some, where the talk of empowerment to the socially disadvantaged groups is emerging as a powerful weapon to connect political parties with their constituencies. By contrast, China is a socialist regime with centralised control by the communist party. Elimination of social inequality is intended to be achieved by introducing government policies and regulations through a top-down interventionist approach (Cooke and Saini, 2007). Cooke and Saini's (2007) comparative study of DM in China and India further revealed that as a SHRM concept, DM had been rarely heard of and featured even less in management discussions and presentations. In addition, management's indifferent attitude to DM may well be linked to the low level of bargaining power possessed by the disadvantaged groups in these countries.

In many developing countries, employment insecurity is relatively high and the provision of social security benefits is extended to few. Large groups of poor people are fighting for the very right to a basic living through low paid employment with long working hours and poor conditions. The fact that they are treated unfairly is much less of a concern for some and inequality in the workplace and in society generally is often accepted, internalised and unchallenged due to historically deep-rooted discrimination and the evident absence of remedial prospects.

It is perhaps not surprising at all that studies on DM in MNCs have found that attempts to roll out US domestic diversity programmes globally often fail to achieve their objectives and/or meet with strong resistance in the host country operations (e.g. Ferner et al., 2005; Nishii and Özbigin, 2007). This is mainly because the US-specific programme fails to reflect the specific demographic profile and the legal, historical, political and cultural contexts of equality in the host countries. Many US-owned MNCs studied in fact made little attempt to adapt their US-designed diversity programmes to capture local characteristics (Nishii and Özbigin, 2007). As a result, MNCs may encounter 'regulatory, normative and cognitive challenges' when designing and implementing their global DM initiative (Sippola and Smale, 2007: 1895). While the diversity philosophy may be accepted globally within the corporation, a more multi-domestic approach has been found necessary to implement the diversity initiative, as was revealed in Sippola and Smale's (2007) study.

Company-based case studies of DM in various countries further revealed the distance between reality and the inspiration projected in DM rhetoric. For instance, Dameron and Joffre's (2007: 2053) study of the integration team set up to manage the post-merger integration of France Telecom Mobile and Orange UK found that the co-existence of the French and English cultures was 'never seen as an opportunity, a differentiation and a source of creativity'. Rather, 'cultural diversity was always experienced by the members of the integration team as a difficulty to overcome' (Dameron and Joffre, 2007: 2053). Subeliani and Tsogas's (2005) study of managing diversity in a large bank in the Netherlands showed that diversity initiative was designed and implemented in large cities where a large ethnic market existed from which the bank could benefit. Employees with immigrant backgrounds are mostly recruited for lower positions, where they can be visible to customers, but promotion for them is very difficult, if not impossible. They are trapped at the lower end of the organisational hierarchy, with little freedom to express their cultural and religious views. In this case, it is clear that business motives had taken precedence over moral concerns when adopting the DM programme.

6 Sustainability through the integration of CSR and HR policy

In this chapter, we have so far discussed some of the different societal contexts for and challenges to the implementation of labour standards, EO legislation and DM initiatives. These are issues central to the HR aspect of CSR. Two objectives run through the arguments for CSR, labour standards, EO and DM – to identify and rectify discriminatory practices at workplaces and to enable organisations to gain competitive advantage through ethical and strategic HR practices. These arguments are summarised in Figure 18.3.

Adoption of CSR activities has unique implications for MNCs, particularly those operating in less developed countries where the ideas of business ethics and CSR may take on different meaning, the enforcement of legislation may be precarious and the majority of people still live in poverty. Here, HR professionals have a crucial role to play in assisting organisations to develop their CSR agendas effectively through the integration of CSR policy and HR policy.

CSR through employee involvement

There are two aspects of CSR that are linked to employees, either directly through HR practices or indirectly through the participation of employees in CSR activities.

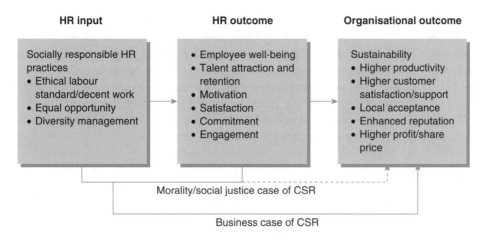

Figure 18.3 Socially responsible HR practices and business sustainability

One is the non-HRM related CSR activities that firms adopt to demonstrate their commitment to, for example, environmental protection and the development of local communities. These activities may help to attract, develop, retain and motivate employees who share similar values projected in these activities. It is believed that this positive HR outcome will lead to enhanced organisational performance. While there is now growing awareness of and commitment to CSR by MNCs, research evidence suggests that they are not engaging their employees sufficiently to get the full benefit of their investment. For example, Bhattacharya et al.'s (2008) study revealed that most companies in their study take a top-down approach to designing, implementing and managing CSR programmes. Few firms communicate systematically with their employees on the firm's CSR efforts. They rarely consider the needs and values of employees and how these can be fulfilled by developing CSR programmes to align the values of employees with the firm. Most firms do not have a clear understanding of the positive impact that CSR activities may have on employee productivity through enhanced organisational identification and commitment. It follows that better understanding of employees' needs and greater involvement of employees in CSR initiatives will help to improve the return on investment of CSR.

Indeed, tension may arise between CSR efforts and employees' perception, where the interests of the two are seen to diverge. For example, corporate donations of large sums of money to charity work may not be appreciated by employees who are low paid and work in harsh environments. This altruistic act may be seen as hypocritical and may create the impression that the firm is treating outsiders better than its own employees, therefore demotivating its staff. Kostova (1999: 313) argued that the regulatory, normative and cognitive institutions between the parent country and the host countries of an MNC may be very different ('institutional distance'). A normative institution refers to group or societal beliefs, values and norms, whereas a cognitive institution refers to people's shared knowledge and understanding. Institutional differences can make it more difficult to transfer organisational practices. Understanding local employees' attitude towards CSR will help the MNC to understand what initiatives it can or should take at the local level, which may be significantly different from what is assumed in the parent country.

Box 18.3 shows an example of how a Chinese company uses its EI scheme to help the company achieve its environmental protection target.

Box 18.3 Environment protection through employee involvement

Dongcheng Ltd is a privately owned textile dye works established in 1994 in southern China. It employs about 600 people who are mainly migrant workers from rural China. The education level is generally low among these workers and earning a reasonable wage to support the family is their main concern.

Due to the nature of the business, the cost of energy and waste (waste water and exhaust) discharge has been high each month. In recent years, environmental protection has ascended in the Chinese government's agenda. Dongcheng was increasingly being fined by the local government for its excessive waste discharge. The company had initially taken different measures in an attempt to reduce the cost. These included educating the workers and imposing energy consumption quotas on production departments. But the result had been negligible. In 2006, Mr Guan, the owner CEO of the company, decided to introduce the 'efficiency gains-sharing scheme'. Each month, a certain percentage of the company's financial gain from energy saving and reduced waste discharge is shared by its employees as a bonus. A small amount of additional funds are allocated to the subsidised staff canteen to provide extra dishes on top of the normal menu twice a month. In addition, a small amount of capital fund will also be allocated from the efficiency gain to improve the working environment in the factory.

This scheme was well received by employees and a significant saving has been made by the company through reduced cost of energy and waste treatment. Undoubtedly, financial cost, rather than a strong sense of social responsibility, was the main motive of the company in its environment protection action. Nevertheless, tangible achievement was made through an EI scheme that meets employees' needs. On this occasion, material incentive, rather than moral education, appears to be a more effective motivator for employees to help the company achieve its environment protection target.

Source: Interview with the CEO by the author in 2008.

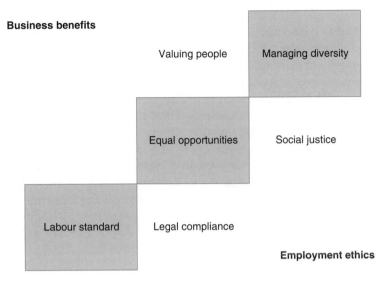

Figure 18.4   An integrated framework for socially responsible employment and HR practices

Building blocks of socially responsible HR practices

The other employee-related aspect of CSR concerns the adoption of socially responsible HR practices to fulfil a firm's social responsibility (fundamental obligation) and to attract and retain talent (competitive advantage). As we have discussed earlier, labour standards, EO and DM are three important building blocks of an ethical HR strategy (see Figure 18.4). At the minimum level, firms need to observe labour standards and EO legislation to ensure demonstrable legal compliance. Beyond that, firms have the moral obligation to look after the well-being of their employees and contribute to the economic and social development of less developed countries (Perlmutter, 1969). Legal compliance and social justice are the primary concerns of employment ethics. The business case perspective, which appears to be the dominant discourse of CSR and diversity, advances the argument further by suggesting that implementing labour standards, EO legislation and DM programmes not only fulfils firms' legal and social justice obligations, but also creates business benefits through ethical behaviour and valuing people.

Alignment of corporate CSR values and the delivery of the HR function

The significance for MNCs of maintaining a coherent corporate culture and set of values while leveraging the diversity of the global workforce has been widely noted (e.g. Brewster et al., 2005; Evans et al., 2002; Rosenzweig, 1998; Sparrow et al., 2004). The highly contextual nature of labour standards, EO and workforce diversity is likely to be even more challenging to manage due to societal differences and varying management priorities, as we have discussed in this chapter. Where certain HRM functions are outsourced to local firms in the host country, as is increasingly the practice in MNC subsidiaries, the ability of the MNC to ensure a consistent corporate approach to socially responsible HRM may be further compromised. For example, recruitment is an HR function that is most likely to be outsourced in host countries (Cooke and Budhwar, 2009). It is also an area of HRM where discrimination is most likely to take place in less developed countries (see Box 18.4 for example). Outsourcing HR functions therefore raises a question: How should MNCs collaborate with their local HR agency firms to ensure their corporate ethical standards are followed? In a way, this is a similar issue to how MNCs should ensure that their suppliers behave in a socially responsible way in an era of global sourcing and production.

Box 18.4   Outsourcing recruitment by an MNC and its impact on gender equality in China

A highly reputable pharmaceutical MNC outsourced the recruitment function of its subsidiary in China to a local recruitment agency firm. The HR Regional Director who monitored the HR function in the Asia region found out that the recruitment agency firm systematically screened out female graduate job candidates, even though their CVs were as good as, and in some cases better than, those of their male counterparts. The MNC had a global corporate policy of equal opportunities and imposed a gender ratio in its recruitment targets. As a result, the Chinese subsidiary's gender ratio statistics consistently fell below that of the corporate target. When this discriminatory practice of the recruitment agency firm was discovered, the HR director drew the attention of the staff from the agency firm to the corporate policy and requested them not to discriminate against female candidates. This request was dismissed by the Chinese recruitment staff. Instead, they tried to convince the HR director that this was a common practice in China as women employees were deemed less productive due to their family commitments. By rejecting female candidates, they argued, they were actually acting in the interest of the MNC by making sure that only the most 'productive' staff were recruited.

Source: Interview with the HR Regional Director by the author in 2007.

7 Summary and conclusions

This chapter has provided an overview of the conceptual debates concerning employment ethics, labour standards, EO and DM as central issues of CSR. Evidence of organisational practices has demonstrated the immense challenges, as well as the moral and economic imperatives, for global firms to act as socially responsible employers to sustain their business growth and the economic and social development of the host countries in which they operate. The impact of CSR is multifaceted, but the important role of ethical SHRM in CSR has been largely overlooked. Whilst national legislation and soft regulations at national and international levels, such as labour standards, may provide a minimum level of protection to workers when effectively enforced, intensive global competition may undermine incentives for firms to take on higher levels of social responsibility. Nevertheless, there is still much more firms can do to integrate their HR and CSR efforts to achieve better results for all concerned.

Discussion questions

1 'In the intensifying global competition, firms that observe international labour standards voluntarily will lose out to those that do not'. Do you agree with this statement? Provide evidence to support your answer.

2 It is argued that there is tension between implementing EO legislation that is informed by the notion of 'sameness treatment' and adopting DM programmes that focus on individual and group characteristics. How do you think this tension can be reconciled?

3 A US-owned software development MNC has been facing serious talent retention problems in its subsidiary in India. The MNC has a successful DM programme in its US operations and is intending to adopt a similar programme in its Indian operation in an attempt to improve talent recruitment and retention. Do you think this idea will work? If so, how would you design and implement the initiative in order to make it effective?

Managing diversity in a Chinese-owned multinational IT firm

Company background

Established in 1988 in Beijing, Lenovo Group Limited (formerly known as 'Legend Group Limited') is the largest IT enterprise in China. Lenovo employs some 25,000 staff in all its operations in nearly 70 countries, but with the majority of employees working in China. In 1984, with an initial capital of RMB 200,000 funded by the Chinese Academy of Sciences, a government-funded institution, 11 researchers formed the parent company of Lenovo. It was the first company to introduce the concept of home computer in China. Lenovo's main business activities are in the sale and manufacturing of desktop computers, notebook computers, mobile handsets, servers and printers. Lenovo is a stock-listed company, with the Chinese government holding over a quarter of its shares.

In April 2003, the Group adopted a new logo and the English brand name 'Lenovo', replacing the original English brand name 'Legend' in order to appeal to the international market. The English company name was also officially changed to 'Lenovo Group Limited' a year later. In December 2004, Lenovo spent US$1.25 billion to acquire IBM's PC business. This was the largest cross-border acquisition in China's IT industry (*China Business*, 13 December 2004). The acquisition process was completed in May 2005. The marriage of IBM and Lenovo created one of the world's largest PC powerhouses. IBM possessed strong competitive advantage in the higher end of the customer market in its distribution channel, high quality customer resources, which complemented that of Lenovo. The two companies have maintained a long-term cooperative strategy since the acquisition, with Lenovo having access to some of IBM's key resources, such as technology, sale force, PartnerWorld, Global Finance and IBM Credit.

The continuing expansion and globalisation of Lenovo brings a number of challenges to its HRM function, including the alignment of corporate HR strategy and DM after the acquisition of IBM's PC business. Below are some of the issues that illustrate the challenges.

Managing foreign employees in China

Lenovo's growing global presence in the IT sector has attracted an increasing number of non-Chinese citizens who wish to work in its operations in China in recent years. This is in part because they want to spend time in China to gain wider experience and a deeper understanding of the country. These foreign citizens are employed by Lenovo under the same employment conditions as those offered to the Chinese citizens. Free working meals and company subsidised accommodation are some of the company benefits that Lenovo offers to its employees. These are traditional and typical workplace welfare provisions of Chinese firms. Under the housing scheme, newly recruited single employees are provided dormitory accommodation. Since housing is expensive in Beijing, this often takes the form of one bedroom shared by a few employees of the same gender. This arrangement is normal and acceptable to the Chinese employees – Chinese students also share their dormitories in schools and universities, and in sweatshop manufacturing plants, the situation is far worse where ten or more rural migrant workers are crowded in a room with poor facilities. However, foreign employees, though only a very small number compared with the Chinese employees, find it difficult to get used to this idea because of the lack of privacy. The Company has no special policy to accommodate their needs. Different management style is another source of cultural shock to foreign employees. According to an HR manager, foreign employees all emphasise their cultural shock when they come to China. But Lenovo (China) has not developed a formal policy to manage these cultural shocks. This has led to the turnover of a few of the foreign employees and the Company has made no efforts to retain them.

Managing Chinese graduate returnees from overseas

Since the early 2000s, an increasing number of Chinese who went abroad for their higher education have been returning to China to seek employment and career development. The majority of Chinese overseas graduate returnees (known as *haigui* in China) are keen to work for, and are often the favourite candidates of, multinational firms. Lenovo is amongst the top employers of choice for which *Haiguis* want to work. These repatriated western trained graduates bring with them different life styles, perspectives and (often unrealistic) expectations that may depart from the Chinese norms. Some of them are said to be complacent and consider themselves superior to other graduate employees who have not been abroad for training. They expect high salaries up-front, fast promotion, flexibility and autonomy in their work. Turnover is common among *haiguis* when expectations are unmet or better offers are available elsewhere. How to recruit and manage overseas graduate returnees effectively is an important issue for MNCs operating in China. Companies are now reportedly more cautious in recruiting and managing these returnees because they are seen as 'demanding' employees who are difficult to retain. Lenovo shares some of these issues. Although turnover has not been a major problem, how to harmonise the relationship between *haiguis* and home-grown graduate employees is sometimes a challenge for line managers.

Gender equalities

Prior to Lenovo's acquisition of the IBM PC business unit, Lenovo had more women at the senior management level. The proportion of women in senior management has actually declined since the acquisition because it is now part of a bigger international operation.

Two main reasons are attributed to this change. One is that there is a lower proportion of women at senior management level in the acquired business unit of IBM than in the Chinese operation. Another reason is that Lenovo has been through successive rounds of senior management restructuring after the acquisition, partly to do with the post-acquisition integration and partly to do with the poaching of senior managers amongst IT firms in China. Cultural clashes triggered by the post-acquisition integration have led to the departure of a number of senior managers. When new managers are recruited, they tend to bring their own people and HR initiatives with them, which will later be displaced by their successors when the managers departed. As an HR director observed, 'It is organisational politics, rather than equal opportunities, that we consider in the recruitment of senior managers. You need to be competent as well as well-connected to get the senior management's job, and men tend to be better-connected than women in the IT sector in general.'

Developing a global diversity management strategy

According to informants from Lenovo (China), diversity is not a key issue in the workforce in China. Therefore, it is not a priority of the Company. The major task is post-acquisition integration to align the organisational cultures and become a truly international company. Nevertheless, the Company does emphasise the need for employees to respect other employees' rights and privacy. Aggressive or discriminatory behaviours are forbidden, even as jokes. These are written in the business conduct guideline for employees. However, the Company does not have any specific equal opportunities or diversity management programmes to enforce these clauses. The acquired business unit of IBM has good HR practices, for example, work-life balance and managing diversity. These have not yet been transferred to the Chinese operation due to staff shortages. There was a corporate initiative (motioned from the US side) about bringing women at international level together to have a global forum to discuss diversity issues in 2006. Unfortunately, budget constraints meant that the plan was set to one side.

The HR directors from Lenovo (US) are well aware of the challenge they face in transferring their US-developed diversity management programme to other branches across different countries and cultures. The US HR team are the people who are familiar with the concept and responsible for looking into its global diffusion, and they are approaching the task with extreme caution. This is in part, as they admitted, due to their unfamiliarity with the local environments in different parts of the world, although they are planning to visit Lenovo (China) for the first time. How to accommodate the diversity of the global workforce and leverage it to enhance the performance of the firm on the one hand, and how to develop a strong corporate culture that all employees will identify with on the other hand is their main HR concern, and a solution has yet to be found.

According to all managerial informants, the corporate priority is talent management. A new scheme called 'Mobility Plan' has been implemented at the international level. The purpose of the Plan is to give managers an opportunity to work overseas to gain international experience to be able to lead at a global level. It is not aimed at Chinese managers in principle, but in reality, has mainly involved sending Chinese managers to the US for development.

Source: Compiled by the author based on information obtained from: Lenovo company website at http://www.lenovo.com, accessed 14 December 2008; *China Business*, 13 December 2004; and interviews by the author with HR directors, senior managers and employees of Lenovo in China and US in 2007.

Case questions

1 What are the key issues of diversity management in this case study and how are they manifested?

2 How would you design a global cross-cultural management policy for Lenovo, taking into account its increasingly diverse workforce?

3 Chinese firms generally suffer from a poor image of low product quality, poor CSR and HRM. How would you help Lenovo to attract non-Chinese talent to work for the Company in its global operations, particularly outside China?

Case questions for further study and reflection

1 Imagine you are an HR manager of a European MNC in the telecommunication industry. The company already has operations in several African countries. As part of its expansion plan, you have been asked to provide an audit report on the company's CSR activities in African countries and provide suggestions on how the company can use CSR to help its expansion. How are you going to go about the task?

2 Imagine you were the HR Regional Director of the pharmaceutical MNC reported in Box 18.4. How are you going to work with the recruitment agency firm to ensure their recruitment practices are fair and conform to the company corporate values? In view of this discovery, do you think it would be necessary to review other HR outsourcing services in the Chinese subsidiary and those in other countries in the Asia region? What actions will you propose at the regional level to influence your HR outsourcing providers' business ethics?

Further reading

- Crowther, D. and Capaldi, N. (eds) (2008) *The Ashgate Research Companion to Corporate Social Responsibility*. Aldershot: Ashgate.

This edited volume contains 20 chapters authored by scholars from around the world. Each chapter focuses on a different aspect of CSR, offering a variety of theoretical lenses and a wide range of perspectives from different countries and experiences. In particular, Part II of the volume contains three chapters related to CSR and the employment relationship.

- Pinnington, A., Macklin, R. and Campbell, T. (eds) (2007) *Human Resource Management: Ethics and Employment*. Oxford: Oxford University Press.

This edited volume examines ethics and employment issues in contemporary human resource management. It contains 16 chapters on specific topics of HRM that summarise key debates and the current state of knowledge on ethics.

- Ackers, P. (2006) 'Employment ethics', in T. Redman and A. Wilkinson (eds), *Contemporary Human Resource Management: Text and Cases*. pp. 427–49. London: Financial Times Prentice Hall.

This chapter offers an overview of various theories in employment ethics as a subdivision of business ethics. It highlights the complexity of applying ethics to real-life business and employment problems through empirical examples in the British context. A case study of a chain department store is included at the end of the chapter to further illustrate the dilemma in managing the workforce in an ethical way while ensuring profitability of the business.

- Mor Barak, M. (2005) *Managing Diversity: Towards a Globally Inclusive Workplace*. Thousand Oaks: Sage.

This book demonstrates the benefits of implementing inclusive practices in the workplace. It draws examples from different countries around the world to illustrate practical solutions to managing today's diverse workforce.

- Bhattacharya, C., Sen, S. and Korschun, D. (2008) 'Using corporate social responsibility to win the war for talent', *MIT Sloan Management Review*, 49(2): 37–44.

This article derives from a study of CSR programmes in the global context to understand better when, how and why employees react to CSR. It contains a thorough diagnosis of where firms are doing badly in terms of engaging their employees in their CSR initiatives. It provides valuable insights into the challenges and opportunities facing companies that want to deploy their CSR efforts strategically in the war for talent.

- Foster, C. and Harris, L. (2005) 'From equal opportunities to diversity management', in J. Leopold, L. Harris and T. Watson (eds), *The Strategic Managing of Human Resources*. pp. 116–39. Essex: Pearson Education Ltd.

This chapter highlights tensions and issues that can arise for employers, managers and employees in the development and application of EO and DM policies. It contains several insightful mini-case studies as examples to illustrate organisational dilemmas.

- Lowry, D. (2005) 'Ethics and strategic human resourcing', in J. Leopold, L. Harris and T. Watson (eds), *The Strategic Managing of Human Resources*. pp. 88–110. Essex: Pearson Education Ltd.

This chapter provides a useful summary of different theoretical perspectives on ethics and its implications for SHRM.

- Sachdev, S. (2006) 'International corporate social responsibility and employment relations', in T. Edwards and C. Rees (eds), *International Human Resource Management: Globalization, National Systems and Multinational Companies.* pp. 262–84. Essex: Pearson Education Ltd.

This chapter contains a good list of references on issues related to CSR. It also provides a brief overview on various aspects of CSR in relation to employment relations.

- Luo, Y.D. (2006) 'Political behaviour, social responsibility, and perceived corruption: A structuration perspective', *Journal of International Business Studies*, 37(6): 747–66.

This article unites the three lenses – political behaviour, corporate social responsibility, and corruption – and evaluates the way in which MNCs manage political and social forces in a foreign emerging market. Using MNCs in China for evidence, the author argues that when perceived corruption in the business segment increases, an MNC's propensity to cooperate and be assertive with the government decreases, its focus on ethics heightens, and its philanthropic contribution diminishes.

- Sippola, A. and Smale, A. (2007) 'The global integration of diversity management: A longitudinal case study', *International Journal of Human Resource Management*, 18(11): 1895–916.

This article reports an in-depth longitudinal case study of a well-known European MNC, which has been attempting to integrate diversity management globally throughout its worldwide operations. Adopting a Finnish host-country perspective, the study identifies the challenges encountered by the MNC and highlights the demographic, cultural and institutional embeddedness of DM when transferred into a non-Anglo-Saxon host context.

- Egri, C. and Ralston, D. (2008) 'Corporate responsibility: A review of international management research from 1998 to 2007', *Journal of International Management*, 14(4): 319–39.

This article reviews corporate responsibility (CR) research in *International Management* journals during the past decade and identifies 321 articles of interest. It provides a detailed analysis of the prevalence of CR research in *International Management* journals, the prominence of the major CR themes, the degree of emphasis placed on empirical versus theoretical research, and the breath of international coverage in these articles.

- Oetzel, J. and Doh, J. (2009) 'MNEs and development: A review and reconceptualization', *Journal of World Business*, 44(2): 108–20.

This article reviews and critiques two prominent theories in the international business and international economics literatures regarding the role of MNCs in host country development: the 'spillovers' perspective on the impact of MNC investment in host countries and the liabilities of foreignness view that specifies the constraints MNCs must overcome to succeed in local, developing country markets. It proposes an alternative conceptualisation of MNC–host country relations in which MNCs and local NGOs pursue collaborative relationships that make a positive, collective contribution to host country development and to MNC and NGO strategic goals in ways that neither sector is positioned to do alone.

Internet resources

1 The International Labour Organization (ILO) (http://www.ilo.org): The tripartite United Nations agency that brings together governments, employers and workers of its member states in common action to promote decent work throughout the world. The ILO is the global body responsible for drawing up and overseeing international labour standards. Working with its Member States, the ILO seeks to ensure that labour standards are respected in practice as well as in principle.

2 Society for Human Resource Management (SHRM) (http://www.shrm.org): The world's largest professional association devoted to HRM. Its web-pages contain up-to-date research reports, case studies, professional advice and latest publications on a wide range of topics in HRM, including EO, DM and CSR.

3 European Commission (2008), the CSR website of the European Commission's Directorate-General for Enterprise and Industry (http://ec.europa.eu/enterprise/csr/index_en.htm): The website provides insight into what CSR is, why it is important, and what the European Commission is doing to promote it, with a particular interest in links between CSR and competitiveness.

4 Corporate Watch (http://www.corporatewatch.org.uk): A small independent not-for-profit research and publishing group based in the UK. It undertakes research and analysis on the social and environmental impact of large corporations, particularly multinationals, raises awareness and contributes to public debate and education.

5 The Dow Jones Sustainability Indexes (http://www.sustainability-indexes.com): Launched in 1999, the Dow Jones Sustainability Indexes track the financial performance of the leading sustainability-driven companies worldwide.

6 The World Business Council for Sustainable Development (WBCSD) (http://www.wbcsd.org): A CEO-led, global association of some 200 companies dealing exclusively with business and sustainable development. The Council provides a platform for companies to explore sustainable development, share knowledge, experiences and best practices, and to advocate business positions on these issues in a variety of forums, working with governments, non-governmental and intergovernmental organisations.

Self-assessment questions

Indicative answers to these questions can be found on the companion website at www.sagepub.co.uk/harzing3e.

1 What issues may arise if Lenovo (China) should provide single-occupancy housing arrangements for its foreign employees to accommodate their needs for privacy while continuing to provide shared dormitory for its Chinese employees?
2 Which of the issues of diversity management in Lenovo are concerned with individual diversity and which are the collective-oriented diversity issues?
3 If you are a project manager of Lenovo and have to manage two groups of graduate employees, *haiguis* and home-grown graduates, and some of the former are being demanding and causing frictions in the project team, how are you going to manage this situation?
4 Is the pattern of organisational politics displayed in the power struggle at the senior management level in Lenovo in which women are likely to be displaced or disadvantaged unique to Lenovo?
5 How would you advise the HR team of Lenovo (US) to develop a global diversity management programme for talent management?

References

Ackers, P. (2006) 'Employment ethics', in T. Redman and A. Wilkinson (eds), *Contemporary Human Resource Management: Text and Cases*. pp. 427–49. London: Financial Times/ Prentice Hall.

Agocs, C. and Burr, C. (1996) 'Employment equity, affirmative action and managing diversity: assessing the differences', *International Journal of Manpower*, 17(4/5): 30–45.

Albinger, H. and Freeman, S. (2000) 'Corporate social performance and attractiveness as an employer to different job seeking populations', *Journal of Business Ethics*, 28(3): 243–53.

Baron, D. (2001) 'Private politics, corporate social responsibility, and integrated strategy', *Journal of Economics and Management Strategy*, 10(1): 7–45.

Bartlett, C. and Ghoshal, S. (1989) *Managing Across Borders: The Transnational Solution*. Boston, MA: Harvard Business School Press.

Bhattacharya, C. and Sen, S. (2004) 'Doing better at doing good: When, why, and how consumers respond to corporate social initiatives', *California Management Review*, 47(1): 9–24.

Bhattacharya, C., Sen, S. and Korschun, D. (2008) 'Using corporate social responsibility to win the war for talent', *MIT Sloan Management Review*, 49(2): 37–44.

Brammer, S., Millington, A. and Rayton, B. (2007) 'The contribution of corporate social responsibility to organizational commitment', *International Journal of Human Resource Management*, 18(10): 1701–19.

Brewster, C., Sparrow, P. and Harris, H. (2005) 'Towards a new model of globalising HRM', *International Journal of Human Resource Management*, 16(6): 949–70.

Briscoe, D. and Schuler, R. (2004) *International Human Resource Management: Policy and Practice for the Global Enterprise*, 2nd edn. London: Routledge.

Buchanan, J. and Callus, R. (1993) 'Efficiency and equity at work: The need for labour market regulation in Australia', *Journal of Industrial Relations*, 35(5): 515–37.

Cacioppe, R., Forster, N. and Fox, M. (2008) 'A survey of managers' perceptions of corporate ethics and social responsibility and actions that may affect companies' success', *Journal of Business Ethics*, 82(3): 681–700.

Carroll, A. (1979) 'A three-dimensional conceptual model of corporate performance', *Academy of Management Review*, 4(4): 497–505.

Carroll, A. (1991) 'The pyramid of corporate social responsibility: Toward the moral management of organizational stakeholders', *Business Horizons*, 34(4): 39–48.

Carroll, A. (1999) 'Corporate social responsibility', *Business and Society*, 38(3): 268–96.

Chan, A. and Ross, R. (2003) 'Racing to the bottom: International trade without a social clause', *Third World Quarterly*, 24(6): 1011–28.

CIPD (Chartered Institute of Personnel and Development) (2006) *Diversity: An Overview*, CIPD factsheet at http://www.cipd.co.uk, accessed 20 August 2007.

CIPD (2007) *Diversity in Business: A Focus for Progress*. London: Chartered Institute of Personnel and Development.

China Labor News Translations (2008) 'Promising Wal-Mart trade union chair resigns over collective contract negotiations', at http://www.clntranslations.org, accessed on 24 September 2008.

Chun, J. (2006) The contested politics of gender and employment: Revitalising the South Korean labour movement. Draft paper by Devan Pillay, Ingemar Lindberg and Andreas Bieler (eds), *Global Working Class Project* at http://www.nottingham.ac.uk/shared/shared_gwc/documents/South_Korea.pdf, accessed 16 March 2007.

Cooke, F.L. (2007) Women's participation in economic activities in Asia: A comparison of China, India, Japan and South Korea. *Shanghai Forum*, 25–27 May, Fudan University, China.

Cooke, F.L. (2008) *Competition, Strategy and Management in China*. Basingstoke: Palgrave Macmillan.

Cooke, F.L. and Budhwar, P. (2009) 'HR offshoring and outsourcing: Research issues for IHRM', in P. Sparrow (ed.), *Handbook of International Human Resource Management*. pp. 341–61. Chichester: John Wiley.

Cooke, F.L. and Saini, D. (2007) Managing diversity in India and China: Implications for western MNCs. The *APROS 12 Conference*, Management Development Institute, Gurgaon, India, 9–12 December.

Cox, T. (1993) *Cultural Diversity in Organizations: Theory, Research and Practice*. San Francisco: Barrett-Koehler Publishers.

Cox, T. and Blake, S. (1991) 'Managing cultural diversity: Implications for organizational competitiveness', *Academy of Management Executive*, 5(3): 45–56.

Cox, T., Lobel, S. and McLeod, P. (1991) 'Effects of ethnic group cultural differences on cooperative and competitive behaviour on a group task', *Academy of Management Journal*, 34(4): 827–47.

Crowther, D. and Capaldi, N. (eds) (2008) *The Ashgate Research Companion to Corporate Social Responsibility*. Aldershot: Ashgate.

Dameron, S. and Joffre, O. (2007) 'The good and the bad: the impact of diversity management on co-operative relationships', *International Journal of Human Resource Management*, 18(11): 2037–56.

Davidson, M. and Burke, R. (eds) (2004) *Women in Management Worldwide: Progress and Prospects*. Oxford: Ashgate Publishing.

Dunavant, B.M. and Heiss, B. (2005) *Global Diversity 2005*. Washington, DC: Diversity Best Practices.

Egri, C. and Ralston, D. (2008) 'Corporate responsibility: A review of international management research from 1998 to 2007', *Journal of International Management*, 14(4): 319–39.

European Commission (2008) The Corporate Social Responsibility (CSR) website of the European Commission's Directorate-General for Enterprise and Industry at http://ec.europa.eu/enterprise/csr/index_en.htm, accessed 21 December 2008.

Evans, P., Pucik, V. and Barsoux, J. (2002) *The Global Challenge: Frameworks for International Human Resource Management*. London: McGraw-Hill.

Ferner, A., Almond, P. and Colling, T. (2005) 'Institutional theory and the cross-national transfer of employment policy: The case of "workforce diversity" in US multinationals', *Journal of International Business Studies*, 36(3): 304–21.

Foster, C. and Harris, L. (2005) 'From equal opportunities to diversity management', in J. Leopold, L. Harris and T. Watson (eds), *The Strategic Managing of Human Resources*. pp. 116–39. Essex: Pearson Education Ltd.

Freeman, E. (1984) *Strategic Management: A Stakeholder Approach*. Boston, MA: Pitman.

Friedman, M. (1962) *Capitalism and Freedom*. Chicago: The University of Chicago Press.

Fudge, J. and Vosko, L. (2001) 'By whose standards? Reregulating the Canadian labour market', *Economic and Industrial Democracy*, 22(3): 327–56.

Garriga, E. and Melé, D. (2004) 'Corporate social responsibility theories: Mapping the territory', *Journal of Business Ethics*, 53(1–2): 51–71.

Gelb, J. (2000) 'The equal employment opportunity law: A decade of change for Japanese women', *Law & Policy*, 22(3&4): 365–407.

Ghosh, R. and Roy, K. (1997) 'The changing status of women in India: Impact of urbanization and development', *International Journal of Social Economics*, 24(7/8/9): 902–17.

Harzing, A. and Ruysseveldt, J. (eds) (2004) *International Human Resource Management*. London: Sage.

Healy, G. and Oikelome, F. (2007) 'A global link between national diversity policies? The case of the migration of Nigerian physicians to the UK and USA', *International Journal of Human Resource Management*, 18(11): 1917–33.

Hillman, A. and Keim, G. (2001) 'Shareholder value, stakeholder management, and social issues: What's the bottom line?', *Strategic Management Journal*, 22(2): 125–39.

International Labour Organization (1999) International Labour Conference, 87th Session Report of the Director-General: *Decent Work*, Geneva: International Labour Organization, at http://www.ilo.org/public/english/standards/relm/ilc/ilc87/rep-i.htm, accessed 20 December 2008.

Jones, D., Pringle, J. and Shepherd, D. (2000) '"Managing diversity" meets Aotearoa/New Zealand', *Personnel Review*, 29(3): 364–80.

Kochan, T., Bezrukova, K., Ely, R., Jackson, S., Joshi, A., Jehn, K., Leonard, J., Levine, D. and Thomas, D. (2003) 'The effects of diversity on business performance: Report of the diversity research network', *Human Resource Management*, 42(1): 3–21.

Kostova, T. (1999) 'Transnational transfer of strategic organizational practices: A contextual perspective', *Academy of Management Review*, 24(2): 308–24.

Kucera, D. (1998) 'Foreign trade and men and women's employment and earnings in Germany, and Japan', *Centre for Economic Policy Analysis Working Paper 9*, at http://www.newschool.edu/cepa, accessed 16 March 2007.

Lau, D. and Murnighan, J. (1998) 'Demographic diversity and faultlines: The compositional dynamics of organizational groups', *Academy of Management Review*, 23(2): 325–40.

Liff, S. (1996) 'Two routes to managing diversity: individual differences or social group characteristics', *Employee Relations*, 19(1): 11–26.

Lorbiecki, A. and Jack, G. (2000) 'Critical turns in the evolution of diversity management', *British Journal of Management*, Special Issue, 11(3): 517–31.

Maxwell, G., Blair, S. and McDougall, M. (2001) 'Edging towards managing diversity in practice', *Employees Relations*, 23(5): 468–82.

Mor Barak, M. (2005) *Managing Diversity Towards a Globally Inclusive Workplace*. Thousand Oaks: Sage.

Ng, E. and Burke, R. (2005) 'Person-organization fit and the war for talent: Does diversity management make a difference?', *International Journal of Human Resource Management*, 16(7): 1195–210.

Nishii, L. and Özbilgin, F. (2007) 'Global diversity management: Towards a conceptual framework', *International Journal of Human Resource Management*, 18(11): 1883–94.

OECD (Organization for Economic Co-operation and Development) (1994) *Employment Outlook*, Chapter 4, Labour Standards and Economic Integration.

Perlmutter, H.V. (1969) 'The tortuous evolution of the multinational corporation', *Columbia Journal of World Business*, 4 (Jan–Feb): 9–18.

Pinnington, A., Macklin, R. and Campbell, T. (eds) (2007) *Human Resource Management: Ethics and Employment*. Oxford: Oxford University Press.

Richard O.C., Barnett, T., Dwyer, S. and Chadwick, K. (2004) 'Cultural diversity in management, firm performance, and the moderating role of entrepreneurial orientation dimensions', *Academy of Management Journal*, 47(2): 255–66.

Rodgers, J. (2002) *Decent Work and the Informal Economy*. International Labour Conference, 90th Session, Geneva: International Labour Organization.

Rodriguez, P. Siegel, D., Hillman, A. and Eden, L. (2006) 'Three lenses on the multinational enterprise: Politics, corruption, and corporate social responsibility', *Journal of International Business Studies*, 37(6): 733–46.

Roozen, I., Pelsmacker, P. and Bostyn, F. (2001) 'The ethical dimensions of decision processes of employees', *Journal of Business Ethics*, 33(2): 87–100.

Rosenzweig, P. (1998) 'Managing the new global workforce: Fostering diversity, forging consistency', *European Management Journal*, 16(6): 644–52.

Rubery, J. and Grimshaw, D. (2003) *The Organization of Employment: An International Perspective*. Basingstoke: Palgrave Macmillan.

Sachdev, S. (2006) 'International corporate social responsibility and employment relations', in T. Edwards and C. Rees (eds), *International Human Resource Management: Globalization, National Systems and Multinational Companies*. pp. 262–84. Essex: Pearson Education Ltd.

Schuler, R., Jackson, S. and Luo, Y. (2003) *Managing Human Resources in Cross-Border Alliances*. London: Routledge.

Secchi, D. (2007) 'Utilitarian, managerial and relational theories of corporate social responsibility', *International Journal of Management Reviews*, 9(4): 347–73.

Seguino, S. (2000) 'Accounting for gender in Asian economic growth', *Feminist Economics*, 6(3): 27–58.

Sen, S. and Bhattacharya, C. (2001) 'Does doing good always lead to doing better? Consumer reactions to corporate social responsibility', *Journal of Marketing Research*, 38(2): 225–43.

Sippola, A. and Smale, A. (2007) 'The global integration of diversity management: A longitudinal case study', *International Journal of Human Resource Management*, 18(11): 1895–1916.

Soni, V. (2000) 'A twenty-first-century reception for diversity in public sector: A case study', *Public Administration Review*, 60(5): 395–408.

Sparrow, P., Brewster, C. and Harris, H. (2004) *Globalizing Human Resource Management*. London: Routledge.

Standing, G. (1997) 'Globalization, labour flexibility and insecurity: The era of market regulation', *European Journal of Industrial Relations*, 3(1): 7–37.

Steinhoff, P. and Tanaka, K. (1993) 'Women managers in Japan', *International Studies of Management and Organizations*, 23(2): 25–48.

Stiglitz, J. (2002) *Globalization and Its Discontent*. London: Penguin Books.

Stockman, N., Bonney, N. and Sheng, X.W. (1995) *Women's Work in East and West: The Dual Burden of Employment and Family Life*. London: UCL Press Ltd.

Süß, S. and Kleiner, M. (2007) 'Diversity management in Germany: Dissemination and design of the concept', *International Journal of Human Resource Management*, 18(11): 1934–53.

Subeliani, D. and Tsogas, G. (2005) 'Managing diversity in the Netherlands: A case study of Rabobank', *International Journal of Human Resource Management*, 16(5): 831–85.

Taylor, P., Powell, D. and Wrench, J. (1997) *The Evaluation of Anti-Discrimination Training Activities in the United Kingdom*. Geneva: International Labour Office.

Tsui, A., Egan, T. and O'Reilly, C. (1992) 'Being different: Relational demography and organizational attachment', *Administrative Science Quarterly*, 37(4): 549–79.

Turban, D. and Greening, D. (1997) 'Corporate social performance and organizational attractiveness to prospective employees', *Academy of Management Journal*, 40(3): 658–72.

Valentine, S. and Fleischman, G. (2008) 'Ethics programs, perceived corporate social responsibility and job satisfaction', *Journal of Business Ethics*, 77(2): 159–72.

Van der Meulen Rodgers, Y. (1998) 'A reversal of fortune for Korean women: Explaining the 1983 upward turn in relative earnings', *Economic Development and Cultural Change*, 46(4): 727–48.

Venkata Ratnam, C. and Chandra, V. (1996) 'Source of diversity and the challenge before human resource management in India', *International Journal of Manpower*, 17(4/5): 76–108.

Venkata Ratnam, C. and Jain, H. (2002) 'Women in trade union in India', *International Journal of Manpower*, 23(3): 277–92.

Williams, K. and O'Reilly, C. (1998) 'Demography and diversity in organizations: A review of 40 years of research', in B.M. Staw and L.L. Cummings (eds), *Research in Organizational Behaviour*. pp. 20: 77–140. Greenwich, CT: JAI Press.

Winstanley, D. and Woodall, J. (eds) (2000) *Ethical Issues in Contemporary Human Resource Management*. London: MacMillan Business.

Wise, L.R. and Tsehirhart, M. (2000) 'Examining empirical evidence on diversity effects: How useful is diversity research for public sector managers?', *Public Administration Review,* 60(5): 386–94.

Wöcke, A. and Sutherland, M. (2008) 'The impact of employment equity regulations on psychological contracts in South Africa', *International Journal of Human Resource Management*, 19(4): 528–42.

Wood, G. (2006) 'International human resource management', in T. Redman and A. Wilkinson (eds), *Contemporary Human Resource Management: Text and Cases.* pp. 263–77. London: Financial Times Prentice Hall.

World Bank (2006) *India Country Overview 2006.* At http://worldbank.org, accessed 16 March 2007.

Yukongdi, V. and Benson, J. (eds) (2006) *Women in Asian Management.* London: Routledge.

Zinkin, J. (2004) 'Maximizing the "licence to operate": CSR from an Asian perspective', *Journal of Corporate Citizenship*, 14, Summer: 67–80.

Index

Please note that page references to Boxes, Figures and Tables will be in *italic* print